Copyright©2016 All Rights Reserved

ISBN: 978-0692663479

Publication rights Sefer Press Publishing House
Questions Comments; SeferPress@Israelmail.com

Publisher grants permission to reference short quotations (less than 400 words) in reviews, magazines, newspapers, Websites, or other publications in accordance with the citation standards at Sefer Press. Request permission to reproduce more than 400 words to SeferPress@Israelmail.com

Cover by Sefer Press 2016

Book Format by Sefer Press 2016

Hebrew:Modern Hebrew Text Form
Greek:Majority Text (Byzantine) Text Form

Commentary Editing by Al Garza PhD

For Questions Contact A.G. Ben Shlomo At
BenShlomo@Israelmail.com

Printed in the United States of America© 2016

PAUL

A RABBINIC JEWISH SOURCE COMMENTARY AND LANGUAGE STUDY BIBLE
Volume 6b

KJV-GREEK-HEBREW WITH TRANSLITERATION

Greek Majority Text And Modern Hebrew

PUBLISHED BY SEFER PRESS PUBLISHING HOUSE©2016

TABLE OF CONTENTS

Ephesians..pg.6
   Chapter 2..pg.15
   Chapter 3..pg.27
   Chapter 4..pg.35
   Chapter 5..pg.48
   Chapter 6..pg.61

Philippians..pg.72
   Chapter 1..pg.72
   Chapter 2..pg.85
   Chapter 3..pg.97
   Chapter 4..pg.108

Colossians..pg.118
   Chapter 1..pg.118
   Chapter 2..pg.130
   Chapter 3..pg.143
   Chapter 4..pg.153

1Thessalonians..pg.162
   Chapter 1..pg.162
   Chapter 2..pg.167
   Chapter 3..pg.176
   Chapter 4..pg.182
   Chapter 5..pg.193

2Thessalonians..pg.203
   Chapter 1..pg.203
   Chapter 2..pg.208
   Chapter 3..pg.217

1Timothy..pg.225
   Chapter 1..pg.225
   Chapter 2..pg.235
   Chapter 3..pg.243
   Chapter 4..pg.251
   Chapter 5..pg.257
   Chapter 6..pg.269

2Timothy..pg.279
   Chapter 1..pg.279
   Chatper 2..pg.286
   Chapter 3..pg.296
   Chapter 4..pg.303

Titus..pg.312
  Chapter 1..pg.312
  Chapter 2..pg.320
  Chapter 3..pg.326

Philemon...pg.332
  Chapter 1..pg.332

Bibliography...pg.341

TITLE: The Letters of Paul: Ephesians-Philemon

AUTHOR: Shaul/Paul of Tarsus; A Pharisee Trained By Gamaliel

DATE: 40 to 60 AD

LANGUAGE: Hebrew Then Translated Into Greek

WRITTEN TO: 1ST Century Jewish/Greek Believers

THEME: Letters To The Early Believers In Synagogues.

PaRDeS: Peshat (פְּשָׁט) — "surface" ("straight") or the literal (direct) meaning.

- Remez (רֶמֶז) — "hints" or the deep (allegoric: hidden or symbolic) meaning beyond just the literal sense.

- Derash (דְּרַשׁ) — from Hebrew darash: "inquire" ("seek") — the comparative (midrashic) meaning, as given through similar occurrences.

- Sod (סוֹד) (pronounced with a long O as in 'sore') — "secret" ("mystery") or the esoteric/mystical meaning, as given through inspiration or revelation.

THE EPISTLE OF PAUL THE APOSTLE TO THE EPHESIANS

Ephesians, Chapter 1

1. Paul, an apostle of Jesus Christ by the will of God, to the saints which are at Ephesus, and to the faithful in Christ Jesus:

Greek/Transliteration
1. Παῦλος, ἀπόστολος Ἰησοῦ χριστοῦ διὰ θελήματος θεοῦ, τοῖς ἁγίοις τοῖς οὖσιν ἐν Ἐφέσῳ καὶ πιστοῖς ἐν χριστῷ Ἰησοῦ·

1. Paulos, apostolos Yeisou christou dya theleimatos theou, tois 'agiois tois ousin en Epheso kai pistois en christo Yeisou.

Hebrew/Transliteration
א. פּוֹלוֹס שְׁלִיחַ יֵשׁוּעַ הַמָּשִׁיחַ בִּרְצוֹן אֱלֹהִים אֶל-הַקְּדוֹשִׁים בְּאֶפְסוֹס וְאֶל-אֲשֶׁר נֶאֱמָן לִבָּם לִפְנֵי יֵשׁוּעַ הַמָּשִׁיחַ:

1. Polos sh`li•ach Yeshua ha•Ma•shi•ach bir•tzon Elohim el - ha•k`do•shim be•Efsos ve•el - asher ne•e•man li•bam lif•ney Yeshua ha•Ma•shi•ach.

---

2. Grace be to you, and peace, from God our Father, and from the Lord Jesus Christ.

Greek/Transliteration
2. χάρις ὑμῖν καὶ εἰρήνη ἀπὸ θεοῦ πατρὸς ἡμῶν καὶ κυρίου Ἰησοῦ χριστοῦ.

2. charis 'umin kai eireinei apo theou patros 'eimon kai kuriou Yeisou christou.

Hebrew/Transliteration
ב. חֶסֶד וְשָׁלוֹם יִתֵּן לָכֶם אֱלֹהִים אָבִינוּ וְיֵשׁוּעַ הַמָּשִׁיחַ אֲדֹנֵינוּ:

2. Che•sed ve•sha•lom yi•ten la•chem Elohim Avi•noo ve•Yeshua ha•Ma•shi•ach Ado•ney•noo.

---

3. Blessed be the God and Father of our Lord Jesus Christ, who hath blessed us with all spiritual blessings in heavenly places in Christ:

Greek/Transliteration
3. Εὐλογητὸς ὁ θεὸς καὶ πατὴρ τοῦ κυρίου ἡμῶν Ἰησοῦ χριστοῦ, ὁ εὐλογήσας ἡμᾶς ἐν πάσῃ εὐλογίᾳ πνευματικῇ ἐν τοῖς ἐπουρανίοις ἐν χριστῷ·

3. Eulogeitos 'o theos kai pateir tou kuriou 'eimon Yeisou christou, 'o eulogeisas 'eimas en pasei eulogia pneumatikei en tois epouraniois en christo.

Hebrew/Transliteration
ג. בָּרוּךְ הוּא הָאֱלֹהִים אֲבִי אֲדֹנֵינוּ יֵשׁוּעַ הַמָּשִׁיחַ אֲשֶׁר בֵּרַךְ אֹתָנוּ מִשְּׁמֵי מְעוֹנוֹ בְּכָל-בִּרְכַּת הַנֶּפֶשׁ בַּמָּשִׁיחַ:

3. Ba•rooch hoo ha•Elohim Avi Ado•ney•noo Yeshua ha•Ma•shi•ach asher be•rach o•ta•noo mish•mey me•o•no be•chol - bir•kat ha•ne•fesh ba•Ma•shi•ach.

Rabbinic Jewish Commentary

The blessings such are blessed with are spiritual, so called to distinguish them from temporal blessings. The Jews have the like distinction of טובות זמניות, "temporal blessings", and טובות רוחניות, "spiritual blessings" (d); which latter are solid, substantial, and lasting blessings; and which concern the good of the soul or spirit of man; and are agreeable to, and desired by a spiritual man; and are applied by the Holy Spirit of God; and so the Ethiopic version renders it, "with every blessing of the Holy Spirit".

Agreeably to this way of speaking, the Targumist, Jonathan ben Uzziel, on Num_6:27 paraphrases the last clause thus, "I will bless them", במימרי, "in my word".

(d) Tzeror Hammor, fol. 79. 2.

---

4. According as he hath chosen us in him before the foundation of the world, that we should be holy and without blame before him in love:

Greek/Transliteration
4. καθὼς ἐξελέξατο ἡμᾶς ἐν αὐτῷ πρὸ καταβολῆς κόσμου, εἶναι ἡμᾶς ἁγίους καὶ ἀμώμους κατενώπιον αὐτοῦ ἐν ἀγάπῃ,

4. kathos exelexato 'eimas en auto pro kataboleis kosmou, einai 'eimas 'agious kai amomous katenopion autou en agapei,

Hebrew/Transliteration
ד. כַּאֲשֶׁר בּוֹ בְחָרָנוּ עַד לֹא נוֹסְדָה אָרֶץ לִהְיוֹת קְדֹשִׁים וּתְמִימִים לְפָנָיו:

4. Ka•a•sher bo ve•cha•ra•noo ad lo nos•da a•retz li•hee•yot k`do•shim oot•mi•mim le•fa•nav.

Rabbinic Jewish Commentary
"Yet now hear, O Jacob my servant; and Israel, whom I have chosen" Isa_44:1

A phrase somewhat like this is used by the Targumist on Ecc_11:6 where, speaking of a man's children, he says;

"It is not known unto thee which of them אתבחר למהוי טב, "is chosen to be good", this, or that, or both of them, to be alike good."

Some copies put the stop at before him; and read the phrase, "in love"; in connection with the words following, thus, "in love", or "by love hath predestinated us"; so the Syriac version.

---

5. Having predestinated us unto the adoption of children by Jesus Christ to himself, according to the good pleasure of his will,

Greek/Transliteration
5. προορίσας ἡμᾶς εἰς υἱοθεσίαν διὰ Ἰησοῦ χριστοῦ εἰς αὐτόν, κατὰ τὴν εὐδοκίαν τοῦ θελήματος αὐτοῦ,

5. proorisas 'eimas eis 'wiothesian dya Yeisou christou eis auton, kata tein eudokian tou theleimatos autou,

Hebrew/Transliteration
ה. וּבְאַהֲבָתוֹ יְעָדָנוּ מֵרֹאשׁ לִהְיוֹת לוֹ לְבָנִים עַל-יְדֵי יֵשׁוּעַ הַמָּשִׁיחַ כְּחֵפֶץ לִבּוֹ הַטּוֹב:

5. Oov•a•ha•va•to ye•a•da•noo me•rosh li•hee•yot lo le•va•nim al - ye•dey Yeshua ha•Ma•shi•ach ke•che•fetz li•bo ha•tov.

Rabbinic Jewish Commentary

"For Jacob my servant's sake, and Israel mine elect, I have even called thee by thy name: I have surnamed thee, though thou hast not known me." Isa_45:4

"Who are Israelites; to whom *pertaineth* the adoption as sons, and the glory, and the covenants, and the giving of the law, and the service *of God,* and the promises;" Rom_9:4

"To redeem them that were under the law, that we might receive the adoption of sons." Gal_4:5

This choice can only be understood of a national one, as Israel of old were chosen by YHWH. Verses 1-12 are part of an ancient Rabbinica prayer blessings for the people of God, namely Israel and her people. The Messiah was to come and fulfill the promise to Israel and all who would be grafted in to her.

---

6. To the praise of the glory of his grace, wherein he hath made us accepted in the beloved.

Greek/Transliteration
6. εἰς ἔπαινον δόξης τῆς χάριτος αὐτοῦ, ἐν ᾗ ἐχαρίτωσεν ἡμᾶς ἐν τῷ ἠγαπημένῳ·

6. eis epainon doxeis teis charitos autou, en echaritosen 'eimas en to eigapeimeno.

Hebrew/Transliteration
ו. לְתִפְאֶרֶת עֹז חַסְדּוֹ אֲשֶׁר-גָּמַל עָלֵינוּ בִּידִידוֹ:

6. Le•tif•e•ret oz chas•do asher - ga•mal aley•noo biy•di•do.

---

7. In whom we have redemption through his blood, the forgiveness of sins, according to the riches of his grace;

Greek/Transliteration
7. ἐν ᾧ ἔχομεν τὴν ἀπολύτρωσιν διὰ τοῦ αἵματος αὐτοῦ, τὴν ἄφεσιν τῶν παραπτωμάτων, κατὰ τὸν πλοῦτον τῆς χάριτος αὐτοῦ,

7. en 'o echomen tein apolutrosin dya tou 'aimatos autou, tein aphesin ton paraptomaton, kata ton plouton teis charitos autou,

Hebrew/Transliteration
ז. כִּי-בוֹ נִמְצָא פְדוּת וּסְלִיחָה לְחַטֹּאתֵינוּ בְּדָמוֹ הַשָּׁפוּךְ כַּהֲמוֹן חֲסָדָיו:

7. Ki - vo nim•tza fe•doot oos•li•cha le•cha•to•tey•noo be•da•mo ha•sha•fooch ka•ha•mon cha•sa•dav.

---

8. Wherein he hath abounded toward us in all wisdom and prudence;

Greek/Transliteration
8. ἧς ἐπερίσσευσεν εἰς ἡμᾶς ἐν πάσῃ σοφίᾳ καὶ φρονήσει,

8. 'eis eperisseusen eis 'eimas en pasei sophia kai phroneisei,

Hebrew/Transliteration
ח. אֲשֶׁר הִרְבָּה עָלֵינוּ בְּכָל־חָכְמָה וּבִינָה:

8. Asher hir•ba aley•noo be•chol - choch•ma oo•vi•na.

---

9. Having made known unto us the mystery of his will, according to his good pleasure which he hath purposed in himself:

Greek/Transliteration
9. γνωρίσας ἡμῖν τὸ μυστήριον τοῦ θελήματος αὐτοῦ, κατὰ τὴν εὐδοκίαν αὐτοῦ, ἣν προέθετο ἐν αὐτῷ

9. gnorisas 'eimin to musteirion tou theleimatos autou, kata tein eudokian autou, 'ein proetheto en auto

Hebrew/Transliteration
ט. וַיּוֹדַע לָנוּ אֶת־סוֹד רְצוֹנוֹ כַּעֲצָתוֹ הַטּוֹבָה הַיְעוּצָה בְלִבּוֹ מִקֶּדֶם:

9. Va•yo•da la•noo et - sod r`tzo•no ka•a•tza•to ha•to•va hai•oo•tza ve•li•bo mi•ke•dem.

---

10. That in the dispensation of the fullness of times he might gather together in one all things in Christ, both which are in heaven, and which are on earth; even in him:

Greek/Transliteration
10. εἰς οἰκονομίαν τοῦ πληρώματος τῶν καιρῶν, ἀνακεφαλαιώσασθαι τὰ πάντα ἐν τῷ χριστῷ, τὰ ἐπὶ τοῖς οὐρανοῖς καὶ τὰ ἐπὶ τῆς γῆς·

10. eis oikonomian tou pleiromatos ton kairon, anakephalaiosasthai ta panta en to christo, ta epi tois ouranois kai ta epi teis geis.

Hebrew/Transliteration
י. לְקַבֵּץ בַּמָּשִׁיחַ בִּמְלֹאת יְמֵי הַפְּקֻדָּה כֹּל אֲשֶׁר בַּשָּׁמַיִם וְכֹל אֲשֶׁר בָּאָרֶץ וְהָיוּ בוֹ לַאֲחָדִים:

10. Le•ka•betz ba•Ma•shi•ach bim•lot ye•mey hap•koo•da kol asher ba•sha•ma•yim ve•chol asher ba•a•retz ve•ha•yoo vo la•a•cha•dim.

11. In whom also we have obtained an inheritance, being predestinated according to the purpose of him who worketh all things after the counsel of his own will:

Greek/Transliteration
11. ἐν αὐτῷ, ἐν ᾧ καὶ ἐκληρώθημεν προορισθέντες κατὰ πρόθεσιν τοῦ τὰ πάντα ἐνεργοῦντος κατὰ τὴν βουλὴν τοῦ θελήματος αὐτοῦ,

11. en auto, en 'o kai ekleirotheimen prooristhentes kata prothesin tou ta panta energountos kata tein boulein tou theleimatos autou,

Hebrew/Transliteration
יא. וְגַם עַל-יָדוֹ נַחֲזִיק בַּמּוֹרָשָׁה כַּאֲשֶׁר נִבְחַרְנוּ לָהּ מֵאָז מִטַּעַם הָעֹשֶׂה כֹּל כַּעֲצַת חֶפְצוֹ:

11. Ve•gam al - ya•do na•cha•zik ba•mo•ra•sha ka•a•sher niv•char•noo la me•az mi•ta•am ha•o•se kol ka•a•tzat chef•tzo.

---

12. That we should be to the praise of his glory, who first trusted in Christ.

Greek/Transliteration
12. εἰς τὸ εἶναι ἡμᾶς εἰς ἔπαινον δόξης αὐτοῦ, τοὺς προηλπικότας ἐν τῷ χριστῷ·

12. eis to einai 'eimas eis epainon doxeis autou, tous proeilpikotas en to christo.

Hebrew/Transliteration
יב. לְמַעַן יֵרָאֶה עָלֵינוּ הֲדַר כְּבוֹדוֹ בִּהְיוֹת אֲנַחְנוּ הָרִאשֹׁנִים אֲשֶׁר בָּטַחְנוּ בַּמָּשִׁיחַ:

12. Le•ma•an ye•ra•eh aley•noo ha•dar k`vo•do bi•hee•yot a•nach•noo ha•ri•sho•nim asher ba•tach•noo ba•Ma•shi•ach.

---

13. In whom ye also trusted, after that ye heard the word of truth, the gospel of your salvation: in whom also after that ye believed, ye were sealed with that holy Spirit of promise,

Greek/Transliteration
13. ἐν ᾧ καὶ ὑμεῖς, ἀκούσαντες τὸν λόγον τῆς ἀληθείας, τὸ εὐαγγέλιον τῆς σωτηρίας ὑμῶν, ἐν ᾧ καὶ πιστεύσαντες ἐσφραγίσθητε τῷ πνεύματι τῆς ἐπαγγελίας τῷ ἁγίῳ,

13. en 'o kai 'umeis, akousantes ton logon teis aleitheias, to euangelion teis soteirias 'umon, en 'o kai pisteusantes esphragistheite to pneumati teis epangelias to 'agio,

Hebrew/Transliteration
יג. וּבוֹ בֹטְחִים גַּם-אַתֶּם אַחֲרֵי אֲשֶׁר שְׁמַעְתֶּם אֶת-דְּבַר הָאֱמֶת אֶת-דְּבַר הַבְּשׂרָה לִתְשׁוּעַתְכֶם וְכַאֲשֶׁר הֶאֱמַנְתֶּם בּוֹ כֵּן גַּם-נֶחְתָּמִים אַתֶּם בְּרוּחַ הַקֹּדֶשׁ כַּאֲשֶׁר דִּבֶּר:

13. Oo•vo vot•chim gam - atem a•cha•rey asher sh`ma•a•tem et - de•var ha•e•met et - de•var ha•b`so•hra lit•shoo•at•chem ve•cha•a•sher he•e•man•tem bo ken gam - nech•ta•mim atem be•Roo•ach ha•Ko•desh ka•a•sher di•ber.

Rabbinic Jewish Commentary

In whom ye also trusted,.... The Gentile believers, the Ephesians, whom the apostle now particularly addresses; and who participated of the same grace and privileges with the believing Jews.

מלה דקשוט, "the word of truth", is a phrase used by the Jews (e), for sublime and heavenly doctrine: now, by the hearing of this, faith came; and this the Gentile Ephesians heard, not only externally, but internally; so as to understand, approve, and believe it, and to put it in practice.

(e) Zohar in Numb. fol. 76. 3.

---

14. Which is the earnest of our inheritance until the redemption of the purchased possession, unto the praise of his glory.

Greek/Transliteration
14. ὅς ἐστιν ἀρραβὼν τῆς κληρονομίας ἡμῶν, εἰς ἀπολύτρωσιν τῆς περιποιήσεως, εἰς ἔπαινον τῆς δόξης αὐτοῦ.

14. 'os estin arrabon teis kleironomias 'eimon, eis apolutrosin teis peripoieiseos, eis epainon teis doxeis autou.

Hebrew/Transliteration
:יד. אֲשֶׁר עֵרָבוֹן הוּא לְמוֹרָשָׁתֵנוּ עַד אֲשֶׁר-תִּגָּאֵל וְהָיְתָה-לָנוּ לַאֲחֻזָּה לִתְהִלַּת שֵׁם כְּבוֹדוֹ

14. Asher e•ra•von hoo le•mo•ra•sha•te•noo ad asher - ti•ga•el ve•hai•ta - la•noo la•a•choo•za lit•hi•lat shem k`vo•do.

---

15. Wherefore I also, after I heard of your faith in the Lord Jesus, and love unto all the saints,

Greek/Transliteration
15. Διὰ τοῦτο κἀγώ, ἀκούσας τὴν καθ᾽ ὑμᾶς πίστιν ἐν τῷ κυρίῳ Ἰησοῦ καὶ τὴν ἀγάπην τὴν εἰς πάντας τοὺς ἁγίους,

15. Dya touto kago, akousas tein kath 'umas pistin en to kurio Yeisou kai tein agapein tein eis pantas tous 'agious,

Hebrew/Transliteration
:טו. וַאֲשֶׁר עַל-כֵּן גַּם-אָנֹכִי אַחֲרֵי שָׁמְעִי אֶת-אֱמוּנַתְכֶם בְּיֵשׁוּעַ אֲדֹנֵינוּ וְאַהֲבַתְכֶם לְכָל-הַקְּדוֹשִׁים

15. Va•a•sher al - ken gam - ano•chi a•cha•rey shom•ee et - emoo•nat•chem be•Yeshua Ado•ney•noo ve•a•ha•vat•chem le•chol - ha•k`do•shim.

---

16. Cease not to give thanks for you, making mention of you in my prayers;

Greek/Transliteration
16. οὐ παύομαι εὐχαριστῶν ὑπὲρ ὑμῶν, μνείαν ὑμῶν ποιούμενος ἐπὶ τῶν προσευχῶν μου·

16. ou pauomai euchariston 'uper 'umon, mneian 'umon poioumenos epi ton proseuchon mou.

Hebrew/Transliteration
טז. לֹא חָדַלְתִּי מֵהוֹדוֹת בַּעַדְכֶם וּלְהַזְכִּירְכֶם בִּתְפִלּוֹתַי:

16. Lo cha•dal•ti me•ho•dot ba•ad•chem ool•haz•kir•chem bit•fi•lo•tai.

---

17. That the God of our Lord Jesus Christ, the Father of glory, may give unto you the spirit of wisdom and revelation in the knowledge of him:

Greek/Transliteration
17. ἵνα ὁ θεὸς τοῦ κυρίου ἡμῶν Ἰησοῦ χριστοῦ, ὁ πατὴρ τῆς δόξης, δώῃ ὑμῖν πνεῦμα σοφίας καὶ ἀποκαλύψεως, ἐν ἐπιγνώσει αὐτοῦ·

17. 'ina 'o theos tou kuriou 'eimon Yeisou christou, 'o pateir teis doxeis, doei 'umin pneuma sophias kai apokalupseos, en epignosei autou.

Hebrew/Transliteration
יז. כִּי אֱלֹהֵי יֵשׁוּעַ הַמָּשִׁיחַ אֲדֹנֵינוּ אֲבִי הַכָּבוֹד יִתֶּן לָכֶם רוּחַ הַחָכְמָה וְהֶחָזוֹן לָדַעַת אֹתוֹ:

17. Ki Elohey Yeshua ha•Ma•shi•ach Ado•ney•noo Avi ha•ka•vod yi•ten la•chem roo•ach ha•choch•ma ve•he•cha•zon la•da•at o•to.

---

18. The eyes of your understanding being enlightened; that ye may know what is the hope of his calling, and what the riches of the glory of his inheritance in the saints,

Greek/Transliteration
18. πεφωτισμένους τοὺς ὀφθαλμοὺς τῆς καρδίας ὑμῶν, εἰς τὸ εἰδέναι ὑμᾶς τίς ἐστιν ἡ ἐλπὶς τῆς κλήσεως αὐτοῦ, καὶ τίς ὁ πλοῦτος τῆς δόξης τῆς κληρονομίας αὐτοῦ ἐν τοῖς ἁγίοις,

18. pephotismenous tous ophthalmous teis kardias 'umon, eis to eidenai 'umas tis estin 'ei elpis teis kleiseos autou, kai tis 'o ploutos teis doxeis teis kleironomias autou en tois 'agiois,

Hebrew/Transliteration
יח. וּלְהָאִיר עֵינֵי שִׂכְלְכֶם לְהַשְׂכִּיל מָה הִיא תִקְוַת קְרוּאָיו וּמָה חֹסֶן כָּבוֹד לִקְדֹשָׁיו בְּנַחֲלָתוֹ:

18. Ool•ha•eer ey•ney sich•le•chem le•has•kil ma hee tik•vat k`roo•av oo•me cho•sen ka•vod lik•do•shav be•na•cha•la•to.

Rabbinic Jewish Commentary
The phrase, עין השכל, ομμα της διανοιας, "the eye of the understanding", is Rabbinical, and often to be met with in Jewish writings (f); the Alexandrian copy, and several others,

the Complutensian edition, the Vulgate Latin, and all the Oriental versions, read, "the eyes of your heart"; and to, עיני הלבבות, "the eyes of the hearts, or minds", is a phrase used by the Jewish writers (g).

(f) Zohar in Deut. fol. 119. 3. Jetzirah, p. 22. 78. Ed. Rittangel. R. Levi ben Gersom in Gen. fol. 14. 3. & Philo de opificio Dei, p. 15. (g) Bechinat Olam, p. 260.

---

19. And what is the exceeding greatness of his power to usward who believe, according to the working of his mighty power,

Greek/Transliteration
19. καὶ τί τὸ ὑπερβάλλον μέγεθος τῆς δυνάμεως αὐτοῦ εἰς ἡμᾶς τοὺς πιστεύοντας, κατὰ τὴν ἐνέργειαν τοῦ κράτους τῆς ἰσχύος αὐτοῦ

19. kai ti to 'uperballon megethos teis dunameos autou eis 'eimas tous pisteuontas, kata tein energeyan tou kratous teis ischuos autou

Hebrew/Transliteration
:יט. וּמַה עֹצֶם גֹּדֶל גְּבוּרָתוֹ אֲשֶׁר פָּעַל בָּנוּ הַמַּאֲמִינִים בּוֹ לְפִי תֹקֶף עֻזּוֹ

19. Oo•ma o•tzem go•del ge•voo•ra•to asher pa•al ba•noo ha•ma•a•mi•nim bo le•fi to•kef oo•zo.

---

20. Which he wrought in Christ, when he raised him from the dead, and set him at his own right hand in the heavenly places,

Greek/Transliteration
20. ἣν ἐνήργησεν ἐν τῷ χριστῷ, ἐγείρας αὐτὸν ἐκ τῶν νεκρῶν, καὶ ἐκάθισεν ἐν δεξιᾷ αὐτοῦ ἐν τοῖς ἐπουρανίοις,

20. 'ein eneirgeisen en to christo, egeiras auton ek ton nekron, kai ekathisen en dexya autou en tois epouraniois,

Hebrew/Transliteration
:כ. הוּא אֲשֶׁר פָּעַל בַּמָּשִׁיחַ בַּאֲשֶׁר הֱקִימוֹ מִן-הַמֵּתִים וַיּוֹשִׁיבֵהוּ לִימִינוֹ בַּמָּרוֹם

20. Hoo asher pa•al ba•Ma•shi•ach ba•a•sher ha•ki•mo min - ha•me•tim va•yo•shi•ve•hoo li•mi•no ba•ma•rom.

---

21. Far above all principality, and power, and might, and dominion, and every name that is named, not only in this world, but also in that which is to come:

Greek/Transliteration
21. ὑπεράνω πάσης ἀρχῆς καὶ ἐξουσίας καὶ δυνάμεως καὶ κυριότητος, καὶ παντὸς ὀνόματος ὀνομαζομένου οὐ μόνον ἐν τῷ αἰῶνι τούτῳ, ἀλλὰ καὶ ἐν τῷ μέλλοντι·

21. 'uperano paseis archeis kai exousias kai dunameos kai kurioteitos, kai pantos onomatos onomazomenou ou monon en to aioni touto, alla kai en to mellonti.

Hebrew/Transliteration
כא. גָּבוֹהַּ מִכָּל-מִשְׂרָה וְשִׁלְטוֹן וּגְבוּרָה וּמֶמְשָׁלָה וּמִכָּל-אֲשֶׁר נִקְרָא בְשֵׁם גַּם-בָּעוֹלָם הַזֶּה וְגַם-בָּעוֹלָם הַבָּא:

21. Ga•vo•ha mi•kol - mis•ra ve•shil•ton oog•voo•ra oo•mem•sha•la oo•mi•kol - asher nik•ra ve•shem gam - ba•o•lam ha•ze ve•gam - ba•o•lam ha•ba.

---

22. And hath put all things under his feet, and gave him to be the head over all things to the church,

Greek/Transliteration
22. καὶ πάντα ὑπέταξεν ὑπὸ τοὺς πόδας αὐτοῦ, καὶ αὐτὸν ἔδωκεν κεφαλὴν ὑπὲρ πάντα τῇ ἐκκλησίᾳ,

22. kai panta 'upetaxen 'upo tous podas autou, kai auton edoken kephalein 'uper panta tei ekkleisia,

Hebrew/Transliteration
כב. וְכֹל שָׁת תַּחַת רַגְלָיו וַיִּתְּנֵהוּ לְרֹאשׁ לְכָל-הָעֵדָה:

22. Ve•chol shat ta•chat rag•lav va•yit•ne•hoo le•rosh le•chol - ha•e•da.

Rabbinic Jewish Commentary
The Vulgate Latin version reads, "and gave him to be the head over every church", or "all the church"; the Ethiopic version, "the whole church".

---

23. Which is his body, the fullness of him that filleth all in all.

Greek/Transliteration
23. ἥτις ἐστὶν τὸ σῶμα αὐτοῦ, τὸ πλήρωμα τοῦ τὰ πάντα ἐν πᾶσιν πληρουμένου.

23. 'eitis estin to soma autou, to pleiroma tou ta panta en pasin pleiroumenou.

Hebrew/Transliteration
כג. אֲשֶׁר הִיא גְוִיָּתוֹ וּמִלֹאוֹ כִּי מָלֵא הוּא אֶת-כֹּל בַּכֹּל:

23. Asher hee ge•vi•yato oom•lo•o ki ma•le hoo et - kol ba•kol.

Rabbinic Jewish Commentary
The fulness of the earth in Psa_24:1 is by the Jews interpreted of the souls of the righteous, and of the congregation of Israel (h).

(h) Zohar in Gen. fol. 50. 2. & in Exod. fol. 21. 2.

Ephesians, Chapter 2

1. And you hath he quickened, who were dead in trespasses and sins;

Greek/Transliteration
1. Καὶ ὑμᾶς ὄντας νεκροὺς τοῖς παραπτώμασιν καὶ ταῖς ἁμαρτίαις,

1. Kai 'umas ontas nekrous tois paraptomasin kai tais 'amartiais,

Hebrew/Transliteration
א. גַּם-אַתֶּם אֲשֶׁר מֵתִים הֱיִיתֶם בְּפִשְׁעֵיכֶם וְחַטֹּאתֵיכֶם:

1. Gam - atem asher me•tim he•yi•tem be•fish•ey•chem ve•cha•to•tey•chem.

Rabbinic Jewish Commentary
The Jews say (i),

"There is no death like that of those that transgress the words of the Torah, who are called, מתים, "dead men", and therefore the Scripture says, "turn and live"."

And again (k),

"No man is called a living man, but he who is in the way of truth in this world.----And a wicked man who does not go in the way of truth, is called, מת, "a dead man"."

And once more (l).

"Whoever is without wisdom, lo, he is כמת, "as a dead man"

The Alexandrian and Claromontane copies, and one of Stephens's, and the Vulgate Latin version, read, "dead in your trespasses and sins"; and the Syriac version, "dead in your sins and in your trespasses"; and the Ethiopic version only, "dead in your sins".

(i) Zohar in Gen, fol. 41. 3. (k) Ib. in Num. fol. 76. 1. Vid. ib;. in Exod. fol. 44. 2. (l) Caphtor, fol. 30. 2.

---

2. Wherein in time past ye walked according to the course of this world, according to the prince of the power of the air, the spirit that now worketh in the children of disobedience:

Greek/Transliteration
2. ἐν αἷς ποτὲ περιεπατήσατε κατὰ τὸν αἰῶνα τοῦ κόσμου τούτου, κατὰ τὸν ἄρχοντα τῆς ἐξουσίας τοῦ ἀέρος, τοῦ πνεύματος τοῦ νῦν ἐνεργοῦντος ἐν τοῖς υἱοῖς τῆς ἀπειθείας·

2. en 'ais pote periepateisate kata ton aiona tou kosmou toutou, kata ton archonta teis exousias tou aeros, tou pneumatos tou nun energountos en tois 'wiois teis apeitheias.

Hebrew/Transliteration
ב. כִּי-בְּאָרְחוֹתָם הֲלַכְתֶּם לְפָנִים כְּמִנְהַג בְּנֵי הָעוֹלָם הַזֶּה וְכִרְצוֹן שַׂר חֵיל הָרוּחוֹת מִתַּחַת הַשָּׁמַיִם הוּא הָרוּחַ הַמִּתְעוֹרֵר בְּלֵב בָּנִים לֹא-אָבוּ שְׁמוֹעַ:

2. Ki - ve•or•cho•tam ha•lach•tem le•fa•nim ke•min•hag b`ney ha•o•lam ha•ze
ve•chir•tzon sar cheyl ha•roo•chot mi•ta•chat ha•sha•ma•yim hoo ha•roo•ach
ha•mit•o•rer be•lev ba•nim lo - avoo sh`moa.

Rabbinic Jewish Commentary

according to the prince of the power of the air: which is not to be understood of any supposed power the devil has over the air, by divine permission, to raise winds, but of a posse, or body of devils, who have their residence in the air; for it was not only the notion of the Jews (m), that there are noxious and accusing spirits, who fly about באויר, "in the air", and that there is no space between the earth and the firmament free, and that the whole is full of a multitude of them; but also it was the opinion of the Chaldeans (n), and of Pythagoras (o), and Plato (p), that the air is full of demons: now there is a prince who is at the head of these, called Beelzebub, the prince of devils, or the lord of a fly, for the devils under him are as so many flies in the air, Mat_12:24 and by the Jews called (q), רבהון דרוחיא, "the prince of spirits"; and is here styled, the spirit that now worketh in the children of disobedience; by which spirit is meant, not the lesser devils that are under the prince, nor the spirit of the world which comes from him, and is not of God; but the adversary himself, who is a spirit, and an evil, and an unclean one; and who operates powerfully in unbelievers, for they are meant by children of disobedience, or unbelief; just as בני מהימנותא, "children of faith" (r), in the Jewish dialect, designs believers; and over these Satan has great influence, especially the reprobate part of them; whose minds he blinds, and whose hearts he fills, and puts it into them to do the worst of crimes; and indeed, he has great power over the elect themselves, while in unbelief, and leads them captive at his will; and these may be said in their unregeneracy to walk after him, when they imitate him, and do his lusts, and comply with what he suggests, dictates to them, or tempts them to.

(m) Shaare Ora, fol. 4. 1. (n) Laert. Procem. in Vit. Philos. p. 5. (o) lb. in Vit. Pythagor. p. 587. (p) Apuleius de Deo Socratis, p. 331. (q) T. Hieros. Peah, fol. 21. 2. (r) Zohar in Gen. fol. 21. 2. & 22. 4. & 27. 4. & 28. 2. & 35. 2. & 44. 1.

---

3. Among whom also we all had our conversation in times past in the lusts of our flesh, fulfilling the desires of the flesh and of the mind; and were by nature the children of wrath, even as others.

Greek/Transliteration

3. ἐν οἷς καὶ ἡμεῖς πάντες ἀνεστράφημέν ποτε ἐν ταῖς ἐπιθυμίαις τῆς σαρκὸς ἡμῶν, ποιοῦντες τὰ θελήματα τῆς σαρκὸς καὶ τῶν διανοιῶν, καὶ ἦμεν τέκνα φύσει ὀργῆς, ὡς καὶ οἱ λοιποί·

3. en 'ois kai 'eimeis pantes anestrapheimen pote en tais epithumiais teis sarkos 'eimon, poiountes ta theleimata teis sarkos kai ton dyanoion, kai eimen tekna phusei orgeis, 'os kai 'oi loipoi.

Hebrew/Transliteration

ג. וּכְמוֹהֶם גַּם-אֲנַחְנוּ רָדַפְנוּ תַאֲוֹת בְּשָׂרִים לְמַלֵּא מִשְׁאֲלוֹת הַבָּשָׂר וְהַלֵּב הָרַע עַד אֲשֶׁר-נִדְמִינוּ בְּדַרְכֵי חַיֵּינוּ לִשְׁאָר בָּנִים עוֹרְרֵי זָעַם:

3. Ooch•mo•hem gam - a•nach•noo ra•daf•noo ta•a•vot be•sa•rim le•ma•le mish•a•lot ha•ba•sar ve•ha•lev ha•ra ad asher - nid•mi•noo be•dar•chey cha•yey•noo lish•ar ba•nim o•re•rey za•am.

Rabbinic Jewish Commentary

A Jewish commentator (s) on these words, "thy first father hath sinned", Isa_43:27 has this note;

"How canst thou say thou hast not sinned? and behold thy first father hath sinned, and he is the first man, for man מוטבע בחטא, "is naturally in sin";"

(s) Kimchi in loc.

---

4. But God, who is rich in mercy, for his great love wherewith he loved us,

Greek/Transliteration
4. ὁ δὲ θεός, πλούσιος ὢν ἐν ἐλέει, διὰ τὴν πολλὴν ἀγάπην αὐτοῦ ἣν ἠγάπησεν ἡμᾶς,

4. 'o de theos, plousios on en eleei, dya tein pollein agapein autou 'ein eigapeisen 'eimas,

Hebrew/Transliteration
ד. אַךְ אֵל מְלֵא רַחֲמִים בְּרֹב אַהֲבָתוֹ אֲשֶׁר אָהַב אוֹתָנוּ:

4. Ach El ma•le ra•cha•mim be•rov aha•va•to asher ahav o•ta•noo.

Rabbinic Jewish Commentary
The divine love is often called in the Cabalistic writings of the Jews (t), אהבה רבה, "great love".

(t) Zohar in Gen. fol. 8. 4. & in Exod. fol. 102. 3. Lex. Cabal. p. 44. 45.

---

5. Even when we were dead in sins, hath quickened us together with Christ, (by grace ye are saved;)

Greek/Transliteration
5. καὶ ὄντας ἡμᾶς νεκροὺς τοῖς παραπτώμασιν συνεζωοποίησεν τῷ χριστῷ- χάριτί ἐστε σεσωσμένοι-

5. kai ontas 'eimas nekrous tois paraptomasin sunezoopoieisen to christo- chariti este sesosmenoi-

Hebrew/Transliteration
ה. הֶחֱיָנוּ עִם-הַמָּשִׁיחַ בִּהְיוֹתֵנוּ מֵתִים בַּפְּשָׁעִים וְאַךְ בְּחֶסֶד נוֹשַׁעְתֶּם:

5. He•che•ya•noo eem - ha•Ma•shi•ach bi•hi•yo•te•noo me•tim bap•sha•eem ve•ach ba•che•sed no•sha•a•tem.

Rabbinic Jewish Commentary
by grace ye are saved: the Claromontane copy and the Vulgate Latin version read, "by whose grace"; and the Arabic and Ethiopic versions, "by his grace"; either by the grace of him that quickens, or by the grace of Yeshua Messiah with whom they were quickened; the Syriac version renders it, "by his grace he hath redeemed us"; which seems to refer to the

redeeming grace of Yeshua; and so the Ethiopic version, "and hath delivered us by his grace"; and there is a change of the person into "us", which seems more agreeable to what goes before, and follows after.

---

6. And hath raised us up together, and made us sit together in heavenly places in Christ Jesus:

Greek/Transliteration
6. καὶ συνήγειρεν, καὶ συνεκάθισεν ἐν τοῖς ἐπουρανίοις ἐν χριστῷ Ἰησοῦ·

6. kai suneigeiren, kai sunekathisen en tois epouraniois en christo Yeisou.

Hebrew/Transliteration
‏ו. כִּי הֲקִימָנוּ בְּיֵשׁוּעַ הַמָּשִׁיחַ וַיִּתֶּן-לָנוּ לָשֶׁבֶת עִמּוֹ בַּמָּרוֹם:

6. Ki ha•ki•ma•noo be•Yeshua ha•Ma•shi•ach va•yi•ten - la•noo la•she•vet ee•mo ba•ma•rom.

---

7. That in the ages to come he might shew the exceeding riches of his grace in his kindness toward us through Christ Jesus.

Greek/Transliteration
7. ἵνα ἐνδείξηται ἐν τοῖς αἰῶσιν τοῖς ἐπερχομένοις τὸν ὑπερβάλλοντα πλοῦτον τῆς χάριτος αὐτοῦ ἐν χρηστότητι ἐφ᾽ ἡμᾶς ἐν χριστῷ Ἰησοῦ·

7. 'ina endeixeitai en tois aiosin tois eperchomenois ton 'uperballonta plouton teis charitos autou en chreistoteiti eph 'eimas en christo Yeisou.

Hebrew/Transliteration
‏ז. לְהַרְאוֹת בַּיָּמִים יָבֹאוּ אֶת-גֹּדֶל עֹשֶׁר חַסְדּוֹ אֲשֶׁר-גָּמַל עָלֵינוּ לְטוֹבָה בְּיֵשׁוּעַ הַמָּשִׁיחַ:

7. Le•har•ot ba•ya•mim ya•vo•oo et - go•del o•sher chas•do asher - ga•mal aley•noo le•to•va be•Yeshua ha•Ma•shi•ach.

---

8. For by grace are ye saved through faith; and that not of yourselves: it is the gift of God:

Greek/Transliteration
8. τῇ γὰρ χάριτί ἐστε σεσῳσμένοι διὰ τῆς πίστεως, καὶ τοῦτο οὐκ ἐξ ὑμῶν· θεοῦ τὸ δῶρον·

8. tei gar chariti este sesosmenoi dya teis pisteos, kai touto ouk ex 'umon. theou to doron.

Hebrew/Transliteration
‏ח. כִּי-בַחֶסֶד נוֹשַׁעְתֶּם עֵקֶב אֱמוּנַתְכֶם וְלֹא מִיֶּדְכֶם הָיְתָה זֹּאת לָכֶם כִּי-מַתַּת אֱלֹהִים הִיא:

8. Ki - va•che•sed no•sha•a•tem e•kev emoo•nat•chem ve•lo mi•ed•chem hai•ta zot la•chem ki - ma•tat Elohim hee.

Rabbinic Jewish Commentary
In the Apocrypha it says:

"And blessed is the eunuch, which with his hands hath wrought no iniquity, nor imagined wicked things against God: for unto him shall be given the "special gift of faith", and an inheritance in the temple of the Lord more acceptable to his mind." (Wisdom 3:14)

The British Messianic Jew Eric Lipson points out by writing that in Judaism, "Great stress is laid on doing good works, privately and corporately; but the prayers pleading for forgiveness (*s'lichot*) quote Isaiah's admission, 'All our righteous deeds are as filthy rags' [Isa_64:5 (Isa_64:6)]. So Israel prays, '*Avinu malkenu*, our Father, our King, be gracious unto us and answer us, for we have done no good things of any worth. Deal with us in charity and loving-kindness and save us.' " (*The Hebrew Christian*, Spring 1984, p. 17)

We must make note that the first time grace is used in the Hebrew OT TaNaKh it is used toward Noah. Noah in Hebrew is NCh, Nun, Chet. If you reverse the name Noah you will form the Hebrew word for "grace", ChN (CheN), Chet, Nun. (נח/חן). Noah, it says in the Hebrew, attained and acquired grace from YHWH. The ancient Hebrew picture for "grace" is "protection of life". YHWH proctected the life of Noah because he walked with Him. He was given the command to build the arch for him and his family. Noah is grace and grace is Noah. Grace is God's protection from death for all who walk with him. For more on this see, *Hebrew Word Pictures*; Dr.Frank T. Seekins, and the work of Ariel Cohen Alloro on *Grace*.

---

9. Not of works, lest any man should boast.

Greek/Transliteration
9. οὐκ ἐξ ἔργων, ἵνα μή τις καυχήσηται.

9. ouk ex ergon, 'ina mei tis kaucheiseitai.

Hebrew/Transliteration
ט: לֹא בִשְׂכַר מַעֲשִׂיכֶם פֶּן-יִתְהַלֵל אִישׁ

9. Lo vis•char ma•a•sey•chem pen - yit•ha•lel eesh.

---

10. For we are his workmanship, created in Christ Jesus unto good works, which God hath before ordained that we should walk in them.

Greek/Transliteration
10. Αὐτοῦ γάρ ἐσμεν ποίημα, κτισθέντες ἐν χριστῷ Ἰησοῦ ἐπὶ ἔργοις ἀγαθοῖς, οἷς προητοίμασεν ὁ θεός, ἵνα ἐν αὐτοῖς περιπατήσωμεν.

10. Autou gar esmen poieima, ktisthentes en christo Yeisou epi ergois agathois, 'ois proeitoimasen 'o theos, 'ina en autois peripateisomen.

Hebrew/Transliteration

י. כִּי אֲנַחְנוּ מַעֲשֵׂה יָדָיו נוֹצַרְנוּ בְּיֵשׁוּעַ הַמָּשִׁיחַ לְמַעֲשִׂים טוֹבִים אֲשֶׁר הֵכִין לָנוּ מִקֶּדֶם לָלֶכֶת בָּם:

10. Ki a•nach•noo ma•a•se ya•dav no•tzar•noo ve•Yeshua ha•Ma•shi•ach le•ma•a•sim to•vim asher he•chin la•noo mi•ke•dem la•le•chet bam.

---

11. Wherefore remember, that ye being in time past Gentiles in the flesh, who are called Uncircumcision by that which is called the Circumcision in the flesh made by hands;

Greek/Transliteration

11. Διὸ μνημονεύετε ὅτι ὑμεῖς ποτὲ τὰ ἔθνη ἐν σαρκί, οἱ λεγόμενοι ἀκροβυστία ὑπὸ τῆς λεγομένης περιτομῆς ἐν σαρκὶ χειροποιήτου,

11. Dio mneimoneuete 'oti 'umeis pote ta ethnei en sarki, 'oi legomenoi akrobustia 'upo teis legomeneis peritomeis en sarki cheiropoieitou,

Hebrew/Transliteration

יא. עַל-כֵּן זִכְרוּ זֹאת כִּי-גוֹיִם עַרְלֵי בָשָׂר הֱיִיתֶם לְפָנִים וְהַנִּקְרָאִים נְמוֹלֵי בָשָׂר אֲשֶׁר הוּא מַעֲשֵׂה יָדַיִם קָרְאוּ לָכֶם עֲרֵלִים:

11. Al - ken zich•roo zot ki - go•yim ar•ley va•sar he•yi•tem le•fa•nim ve•ha•nik•ra•eem Ni•mo•ley Va•sar asher hoo ma•a•se ya•da•yim kar•oo la•chem A•re•lim.

Rabbinic Jewish Commentary

who are called uncircumcision by that which is called circumcision in the flesh made by hands; that is, they were by way of reproach and contempt called uncircumcised persons; than whom none were more abominable to the Jews, and hated by them, who were called circumcised persons from that circumcision which is outward, in the flesh, in a particular part of the body; and which is done by the hands of a man, who was called מוהל, "the circumciser"; which any one might be, except a Gentile (u); an Israelite adult and skilful was preferred; yet these were not circumcised persons with that circumcision that is inward, and is of the heart, in the Spirit, and is made without the hands of men, and by the Spirit and power of God at the moment of faith.

(u) Maimon. Hilchot Milah, c. 2. sect. 1.

---

12. That at that time ye were without Christ, being aliens from the commonwealth of Israel, and strangers from the covenants of promise, having no hope, and without God in the world:

Greek/Transliteration

12. ὅτι ἦτε ἐν τῷ καιρῷ ἐκείνῳ χωρὶς χριστοῦ, ἀπηλλοτριωμένοι τῆς πολιτείας τοῦ Ἰσραήλ, καὶ ξένοι τῶν διαθηκῶν τῆς ἐπαγγελίας, ἐλπίδα μὴ ἔχοντες, καὶ ἄθεοι ἐν τῷ κόσμῳ.

12. 'oti eite en to kairo ekeino choris christou, apeillotriomenoi teis politeias tou Ysraeil, kai xenoi ton dyatheikon teis epangelias, elpida mei echontes, kai atheoi en to kosmo.

Hebrew/Transliteration
יב. וְכִי-בָעֵת הַהִיא הֱיִיתֶם בְּלֹא מָשִׁיחַ נָכְרִים לְכָל-אֶזְרָח בְּיִשְׂרָאֵל וְנָרִים לְכָל-בְּרִית וְהַבְטָחָה בְּאֶפֶס תִּקְוָה וּבְלֹא אֱלֹהִים בָּאָרֶץ:

12. Ve•chi - va•et ha•hee he•yi•tem be•lo Mashi•ach noch•rim le•chol - ez•rach be•Israel ve•za•rim le•chol - b`rit ve•hav•ta•cha be•e•fes tik•va oov•lo Elohim ba•a•retz.

Rabbinic Jewish Commentary

The Messiah is called משיחא דישראל, "the Messiah of Israel" (w), and who as he was promised, so he was sent only to the lost sheep of the house, of Israel.

The word for "commonwealth" here used, Harpocratian says (x), is commonly used by Greek writers for a "democracy" though the original constitution of the Israelites was properly a "theocracy".

Philo, the Jew (y), observes, that

"The Chaldeans call a man Enos, as if he only was truly a man that expects good things, and supports himself with good hopes; and adds, hence it is manifest that one without hope is not reckoned a man, but a beast in an human form; since he is destitute of hope, which is the property of the human soul."

Some of the Gentiles were in "theory", as they all were in practice; and they were by the Jews reckoned no other than "atheists"; it is a common saying with them (z) that

"He that dwells without the land (of Israel) is like one שאין לו אלוה, "who has no God":"

(w) Targum in Isa. xvi. 1. 5. (x) Lex. Decem Orator. p. 246. (y) De Abrahamo, p. 350, 351. (z) T. Bab. Cetubot, fol. 110. 2. Zohar in Exod. fol. 33. 1. Cosri, par. 2. sect. 22. fol. 85. 2. Tzeror Hammor, fol. 129. 4. & 135. 2. & 153. 3. & 168. 3.

---

13. But now in Christ Jesus ye who sometimes were far off are made nigh by the blood of Christ.

Greek/Transliteration
13. Νυνὶ δὲ ἐν χριστῷ Ἰησοῦ ὑμεῖς οἱ ποτὲ ὄντες μακρὰν ἐγγὺς ἐγενήθητε ἐν τῷ αἵματι τοῦ χριστοῦ.

13. Nuni de en christo Yeisou 'umeis 'oi pote ontes makran engus egeneitheite en to 'aimati tou christou.

Hebrew/Transliteration
יג. אַךְ בְּיֵשׁוּעַ הַמָּשִׁיחַ אַתֶּם הָרְחֹקִים מֵאָז נִקְרַבְתֶּם כַּיּוֹם בְּדַם הַמָּשִׁיחַ:

13. Ach be•Yeshua ha•Ma•shi•ach atem har•cho•kim me•az nik•rav•tem ka•yom be•dam ha•Ma•shi•ach.

Rabbinic Jewish Commentary
It is an observation of a Jewish writer (a) on Gen_3:9 "where art thou?" he (God) knew where he was, but he said so to show him that he was מרוחם, "afar off from" God by his sin: see Isa_59:2. (a) R. Abraham Seba, Tzeror Hammor, fol. 7. 2.

14. For he is our peace, who hath made both one, and hath broken down the middle wall of partition between us;

Greek/Transliteration
14. Αὐτὸς γάρ ἐστιν ἡ εἰρήνη ἡμῶν, ὁ ποιήσας τὰ ἀμφότερα ἕν, καὶ τὸ μεσότοιχον τοῦ φραγμοῦ λύσας,

14. Autos gar estin 'ei eireinei 'eimon, 'o poieisas ta amphotera 'en, kai to mesotoichon tou phragmou lusas,

Hebrew/Transliteration
יד. כִּי הוּא שְׁלוֹמֵנוּ אֲשֶׁר עָשָׂה שְׁנַיִם לְאֶחָד וְאֶת-הַקִּיר הַמַּבְדִּיל בֵּינֵינוּ הָרַס:

14. Ki hoo sh`lo•me•noo asher asa sh`na•yim le•e•chad ve•et - ha•kir ha•mav•dil bey•ney•noo ha•ras.

Rabbinic Jewish Commentary
This is one of the names of the Messiah with the Jews (b);

"says R. Jose the Galilean, even the name of the Messiah is called שלום, "peace"; as it is said, Isa_9:6 "the everlasting Father, the Prince of peace";"

See Mic_5:5 where it is said, "and this man shall be the peace"; which the Jewish (c) writers understand of the Messiah:

The ceremonial torah, which was made up of many hard and intolerable commands, and distinguished, and divided, and kept up a division between Jews and Gentiles: so the Jews call the Torah a wall, "if she be a wall", Son_8:9 זו תורה, "this is the Torah", say they (d): and hence we read of חומת התורה, "the wall of the Torah" (e); and sometimes the phrase, a "partition wall", is used for a division or disagreement; so R. Benjamin says (f), that between the Karaites and Rabbanites, who were the disciples of the wise men, there was מחיצה, "a middle wall of partition"; a great difference and distance; and such there was between the Jew and Gentile, by reason of the ceremonial torah; but Messiah Yeshua removed it, and made up the difference: the allusion seems to be to the wall which divided the court of Israel from the court of the Gentiles, in the temple, and which kept them at a distance in worship.

(b) Perek Shalom, fol. 20. 1. Baal Hatturim in Numb. xxv. 12. (c) Vid. Kimchi in loc. (d) T. Bab. Pesachim, fol. 87. 1. (e) Caphtor, fol. 95. 1. & 101. 1. (f) Itinerar. p. 28.

---

15. Having abolished in his flesh the enmity, even the law of commandments contained in ordinances; for to make in himself of twain one new man, so making peace;

Greek/Transliteration
15. τὴν ἔχθραν ἐν τῇ σαρκὶ αὐτοῦ, τὸν νόμον τῶν ἐντολῶν ἐν δόγμασιν, καταργήσας· ἵνα τοὺς δύο κτίσῃ ἐν ἑαυτῷ εἰς ἕνα καινὸν ἄνθρωπον, ποιῶν εἰρήνην,

15. tein echthran en tei sarki autou, ton nomon ton entolon en dogmasin, katargeisas. 'ina tous duo ktisei en 'eauto eis 'ena kainon anthropon, poion eireinein,

Hebrew/Transliteration
טו. כִּי-בִבְשָׂרוֹ מָחָה אֶת-הָאֵיבָה וְאֶת-מִצְוֹת הַחֻקִּים בַּתּוֹרָה וַיַּעַשׂ שְׁנַיִם לְאִישׁ-אֶחָד חָדָשׁ בְּנַפְשׁוֹ וּבְזֹאת עָשָׂה לָנוּ שָׁלוֹם:

15. Ki - viv•sa•ro ma•cha et - ha•ey•va ve•et - mitz•vot ha•choo•kim ba•To•rah va•ya•as sh`na•yim le•eesh - e•chad cha•dash be•naf•sho oo•va•zot asa la•noo sha•lom.

Rabbinic Jewish Commentary
even the law of commandments contained in ordinances; which consisted of many precepts, and carnal ordinances; and is so called because it was an indication of God's hatred of sin, by requiring sacrifice for it; and because it was an occasion of stirring up the enmity of the natural man, it being a burden and a weariness to the flesh, by reason of its many and troublesome rites; and because it was the cause of enmity between Jew and Gentile: the Jews say (g), that Sinai, the mount on which the Torah was given, signifies "hatred"; and that it is so called because from it descended שנאה, "hatred" or "enmity" to the nations of the world: now this Yeshua abolished, "in his flesh", or by it; not by his incarnation, but by the sacrifice of his flesh, or human nature, and that as in union with his divine nature; but not until he had fulfilled it in himself, which was one end of his coming into the world; and then he abolished it, so as that it ought not to be, and so as that it is not, and of no use and service; and that because it was faulty and deficient, weak and unprofitable, as well as intolerable; and because there was a change in the priesthood; and because it was contrary to a spirit of liberty, the great blessing of the Gospel; and that there might be a reconciliation and a coalition between Jew and Gentile.

(g) T. Bab. Sabbat, fol. 89. 1. Shemot Rabba, sect. 2. fol. 92. 4.

---

16. And that he might reconcile both unto God in one body by the cross, having slain the enmity thereby:

Greek/Transliteration
16. καὶ ἀποκαταλλάξῃ τοὺς ἀμφοτέρους ἐν ἑνὶ σώματι τῷ θεῷ διὰ τοῦ σταυροῦ, ἀποκτείνας τὴν ἔχθραν ἐν αὐτῷ·

16. kai apokatallaxei tous amphoterous en 'eni somati to theo dya tou staurou, apokteinas tein echthran en auto.

Hebrew/Transliteration
טז. כִּי עַל-הַצְּלִיב הִשְׁלִים שְׁנֵיהֶם בְּגֵו אֶחָד אֶל-הָאֱלֹהִים וַיְמַח אֶת-הָאֵיבָה בְּנַפְשׁוֹ:

16. Ki al - hatz•liv hish•lim sh`ney•hem be•gev e•chad el - ha•Elohim va•yi•mach et - ha•ey•va be•naf•sho.

---

17. And came and preached peace to you which were afar off, and to them that were nigh.

Greek/Transliteration
17. καὶ ἐλθὼν εὐηγγελίσατο εἰρήνην ὑμῖν τοῖς μακρὰν καὶ τοῖς ἐγγύς·

17. kai elthon eueingelisato eireinein 'umin tois makran kai tois engus.

Hebrew/Transliteration
יז. וַיָּבֹא וַיְבַשֵּׂר שָׁלוֹם לָרְחוֹקִים וְשָׁלוֹם לַקְּרוֹבִים:

17. Va•ya•vo vay•va•ser sha•lom lar•cho•kim ve•sha•lom lak•ro•vim.

Rabbinic Jewish Commentary
and to them that were nigh; the Alexandrian copy, some others, and the Vulgate Latin and Ethiopic versions, read "peace", in this clause, as in the former; the apostle seems to have respect to Isa_57:19 a like description and distinction of Jews and Gentiles may be observed in the writings of the Jews (h); so they say,

"The Israelites are near unto the holy King, and the rest of the nations are far from him."

(h) Zohar in Numb. fol. 89. 3.

---

18. For through him we both have access by one Spirit unto the Father.

Greek/Transliteration
18. ὅτι δι᾽ αὐτοῦ ἔχομεν τὴν προσαγωγὴν οἱ ἀμφότεροι ἐν ἑνὶ πνεύματι πρὸς τὸν πατέρα.

18. 'oti di autou echomen tein prosagogein 'oi amphoteroi en 'eni pneumati pros ton patera.

Hebrew/Transliteration
יח. כִּי-בוֹ נִפְתַּח לִשְׁנֵינוּ מָבוֹא לָגֶשֶׁת בְּרוּחַ אֶחָד אֶל-אָבִינוּ:

18. Ki - vo nif•tach lish•ney•noo ma•vo la•ge•shet be•Roo•ach e•chad el - Avi•noo.

---

19. Now therefore ye are no more strangers and foreigners, but fellowcitizens with the saints, and of the household of God;

Greek/Transliteration
19. Ἄρα οὖν οὐκέτι ἐστὲ ξένοι καὶ πάροικοι, ἀλλὰ συμπολῖται τῶν ἁγίων καὶ οἰκεῖοι τοῦ θεοῦ,

19. Ara oun ouketi este xenoi kai paroikoi, alla sumpolitai ton 'agion kai oikeioi tou theou,

Hebrew/Transliteration
יט. עַל-כֵּן אֵינְכֶם עוֹד גֵּרִים וְתוֹשָׁבִים כִּי אִם-אֶזְרְחֵי הָעִיר בְּקֶרֶב הַקְּדוֹשִׁים וּבְנֵי בֵית הָאֱלֹהִים:

19. Al - ken eyn•chem od ge•rim ve•to•sha•vim ki eem - ez•re•chey ha•eer be•ke•rev ha•k`do•shim oov•ney veit ha•Elohim.

Rabbinic Jewish Commentary
Now therefore ye are no more strangers..... Alluding to the name נכרי, "a stranger", by which the Jews called the Gentiles; meaning that they were not now strangers to God, to the grace of God, the love of God, and communion with him, nor to the throne of his grace; nor

to the Messiah, to his person, his work and office, to his righteousness, to his voice, and to believing in him; nor to the Holy Spirit, as an enlightener, a comforter, the spirit of adoption, and as a seal and earnest of future glory; nor to their own hearts, the corruption and deceitfulness of them; nor to the devices of Satan; nor to the covenant of grace, its blessings and promises.

---

20. And are built upon the foundation of the apostles and prophets, Jesus Christ himself being the chief corner stone;

Greek/Transliteration
20. ἐποικοδομηθέντες ἐπὶ τῷ θεμελίῳ τῶν ἀποστόλων καὶ προφητῶν, ὄντος ἀκρογωνιαίου αὐτοῦ Ἰησοῦ χριστοῦ,

20. epoikodomeithentes epi to themelio ton apostolon kai propheiton, ontos akrogonyaiou autou Yeisou christou,

Hebrew/Transliteration
:כ. בְּנוּיִים עַל-מוֹסְדוֹת הַשְּׁלִיחִים וְהַנְּבִיאִים שֶׁשָּׁם יֵשׁוּעַ הַמָּשִׁיחַ הָיָה לְרֹאשׁ פִּנָּה

20. Be•noo•yim al - mos•dot ha•sh`li•chim ve•ha•n`vi•eem she•sham Yeshua ha•Ma•shi•ach ha•ya le•rosh pi•na.

Rabbinic Jewish Commentary
This phrase is used by the Jews to denote excellency in a person; so a wise scholar is called אבן פינה, "a cornerstone"; (i) see Psa_118:22. It may be rendered, "the chief cornering-stone"; it being such an one that is a foundation stone, as well as a cornerstone; and reached unto, and lay at the bottom of, and supported the four corners of the building; for the foundation and corner stone in this spiritual building, is one and the same stone, Messiah Yeshua: it is said of the temple of Latona, at Buto, in Egypt, that it was made, εξ ενος λιθου, "of one stone", as Herodotus (k) an eyewitness of it, attests.

(i) Abot R. Nathan, c. 28. (k) Euterpe, c. 155.

---

21. In whom all the building fitly framed together groweth unto an holy temple in the Lord:

Greek/Transliteration
21. ἐν ᾧ πᾶσα οἰκοδομὴ συναρμολογουμένη αὔξει εἰς ναὸν ἅγιον ἐν κυρίῳ,

21. en 'o pasa oikodomei sunarmologoumenei auxei eis naon 'agion en kurio,

Hebrew/Transliteration
:כא. וּבוֹ כָּל-הַבִּנְיָן חֻבָּר וַיִּגְדַּל לְהֵיכָל קֹדֶשׁ לַיהוָה

21. Oo•vo kol - ha•bin•yan choo•bar va•yig•dal le•hey•chal ko•dosh la•Adonai.

22. In whom ye also are builded together for an habitation of God through the Spirit.

Greek/Transliteration
22. ἐν ᾧ καὶ ὑμεῖς συνοικοδομεῖσθε εἰς κατοικητήριον τοῦ θεοῦ ἐν πνεύματι.

22. en 'o kai 'umeis sunoikodomeisthe eis katoikeiterion tou theou en pneumati.

Hebrew/Transliteration
כב. ובו נבניתם גם-אתם למשכן אלהים ברוח:

22. Oo•vo niv•ney•tem gam - atem le•mish•kan Elohim ba•Roo•ach.

Ephesians, Chapter 3

1. For this cause I Paul, the prisoner of Jesus Christ for you Gentiles,

Greek/Transliteration
1. Τούτου χάριν ἐγὼ Παῦλος ὁ δέσμιος τοῦ χριστοῦ Ἰησοῦ ὑπὲρ ὑμῶν τῶν ἐθνῶν,

1. Toutou charin ego Paulos 'o desmios tou christou Yeisou 'uper 'umon ton ethnon,

Hebrew/Transliteration
א. בַּעֲבוּר זֹאת אֵפוֹא אֲנִי פוֹלוֹס הִנְנִי אֲסִיר יֵשׁוּעַ הַמָּשִׁיחַ לְמַעַנְכֶם הַגּוֹיִם:

1. Ba•a•voor zot e•fo ani Folos hi•ne•ni asir Yeshua ha•Ma•shi•ach le•ma•an•chem ha•go•yim.

---

2. If ye have heard of the dispensation of the grace of God which is given me to youward:

Greek/Transliteration
2. εἴγε ἠκούσατε τὴν οἰκονομίαν τῆς χάριτος τοῦ θεοῦ τῆς δοθείσης μοι εἰς ὑμᾶς,

2. eige eikousate tein oikonomian teis charitos tou theou teis dotheiseis moi eis 'umas,

Hebrew/Transliteration
ב. הֲלֹא שְׁמַעְתֶּם כִּי נִתְּנָה לִי פְקֻדָּתִי בְּחֶסֶד אֵל בַּעֲבוּרְכֶם:

2. Ha•lo sh`ma•a•tem ki nit•na li f`koo•da•ti be•che•sed El ba•a•voor•chem.

---

3. How that by revelation he made known unto me the mystery; (as I wrote afore in few words,

Greek/Transliteration
3. ὅτι κατὰ ἀποκάλυψιν ἐγνώρισέν μοι τὸ μυστήριον, καθὼς προέγραψα ἐν ὀλίγῳ,

3. 'oti kata apokalupsin egnorisen moi to musteirion, kathos proegrapsa en oligo,

Hebrew/Transliteration
ג. וְכִי הוֹדִיעַ לִי הַסּוֹד בַּמַּחֲזֶה כַּאֲשֶׁר כָּתַבְתִּי לְפָנִים בְּלָשׁוֹן קְצָרָה לֵאמֹר:

3. Ve•chi ho•di•a li ha•sod ba•ma•cha•ze ka•a•sher ka•tav•ti le•fa•nim be•la•shon k`tza•ra le•mor.

---

4. Whereby, when ye read, ye may understand my knowledge in the mystery of Christ)

Greek/Transliteration
4. πρὸς ὃ δύνασθε ἀναγινώσκοντες νοῆσαι τὴν σύνεσίν μου ἐν τῷ μυστηρίῳ τοῦ χριστοῦ·

4. pros 'o dunasthe anaginoskontes noeisai tein sunesin mou en to musteirio tou christou.

Hebrew/Transliteration
:ד. אִם תִּקְרְאוּ דְבָרַי תּוּכְלוּ לְהַכִּיר כִּי הַדַּעַת אִתִּי בְּסוֹד הַמָּשִׁיחַ

4. Eem tik•re•oo de•va•rai tooch•loo le•ha•kir ki ha•da•at ee•ti be•sod ha•Ma•shi•ach.

---

5. Which in other ages was not made known unto the sons of men, as it is now revealed unto his holy apostles and prophets by the Spirit;

Greek/Transliteration
5. ὃ ἑτέραις γενεαῖς οὐκ ἐγνωρίσθη τοῖς υἱοῖς τῶν ἀνθρώπων, ὡς νῦν ἀπεκαλύφθη τοῖς ἁγίοις ἀποστόλοις αὐτοῦ καὶ προφήταις ἐν πνεύματι·

5. 'o 'eterais geneais ouk egnoristhei tois 'wiois ton anthropon, 'os nun apekaluphthei tois 'agiois apostolois autou kai propheitais en pneumati.

Hebrew/Transliteration
:ה. אֲשֶׁר לֹא נוֹדַע לִבְנֵי אָדָם בְּדֹרוֹת מִקֶּדֶם כַּאֲשֶׁר נִגְלָה כַיּוֹם לִשְׁלִיחָיו הַקְּדֹשִׁים וְלִנְבִיאָיו עַל-פִּי הָרוּחַ

5. Asher lo no•da liv•ney adam be•do•rot mi•ke•dem ka•a•sher nig•la cha•yom lish•li•chav ha•k`do•shim ve•lin•vi•av al - pi ha•Roo•ach.

---

6. That the Gentiles should be fellowheirs, and of the same body, and partakers of his promise in Christ by the gospel:

Greek/Transliteration
6. εἶναι τὰ ἔθνη συγκληρονόμα καὶ σύσσωμα καὶ συμμέτοχα τῆς ἐπαγγελίας αὐτοῦ ἐν τῷ χριστῷ, διὰ τοῦ εὐαγγελίου,

6. einai ta ethnei sugkleironoma kai sussoma kai summetocha teis epangelias autou en to christo, dya tou euangeliou,

Hebrew/Transliteration
ו. כִּי יִקְחוּ הַגּוֹיִם חֵלֶק גַּם-הֵם בְּנַחֲלָתוֹ לִהְיוֹת כְּאֵבָרִים בִּגְוִיָּתוֹ וַחֲבֵרִים לִפְנֵי יֵשׁוּעַ הַמָּשִׁיחַ לְקַבֵּל הַבְטָחָתוֹ
:עַל-פִּי הַבְּשׂוֹרָה

6. Ki yik•choo ha•go•yim che•lek gam - hem be•na•cha•la•to li•hee•yot ke•e•va•rim big•vi•ya•to va•cha•ve•rim lif•ney Yeshua ha•Ma•shi•ach le•ka•bel hav•ta•cha•to al - pi ha•be•so•ra.

---

7. Whereof I was made a minister, according to the gift of the grace of God given unto me by the effectual working of his power.

Greek/Transliteration
7. οὗ ἐγενόμην διάκονος κατὰ τὴν δωρεὰν τῆς χάριτος τοῦ θεοῦ, τὴν δοθεῖσάν μοι κατὰ τὴν ἐνέργειαν τῆς δυνάμεως αὐτοῦ.

7. 'ou egenomein dyakonos kata tein dorean teis charitos tou theou, tein dotheisan moi kata tein energeyan teis dunameos autou.

Hebrew/Transliteration

ז. אֲשֶׁר הָיִיתִי לָהּ לִמְשָׁרֵת בְּמַתְּנַת חֶסֶד אֱלֹהִים אֲשֶׁר נָתַן לִי לְפִי פְּעֻלַּת גְּבוּרָתוֹ:

7. Asher ha•yi•ti la lim•sha•ret be•mat•nat che•sed Elohim asher na•tan li le•fi pe•oo•lat ge•voo•ra•to.

---

8. Unto me, who am less than the least of all saints, is this grace given, that I should preach among the Gentiles the unsearchable riches of Christ;

Greek/Transliteration

8. Ἐμοὶ τῷ ἐλαχιστοτέρῳ πάντων ἁγίων ἐδόθη ἡ χάρις αὕτη, ἐν τοῖς ἔθνεσιν εὐαγγελίσασθαι τὸν ἀνεξιχνίαστον πλοῦτον τοῦ χριστοῦ,

8. Emoi to elachistotero panton 'agion edothei 'ei charis 'autei, en tois ethnesin euangelisasthai ton anexichniaston plouton tou christou,

Hebrew/Transliteration

ח. אֲנִי הַצָּעִיר בַּצְּעִירִים בֵּין הַקְּדוֹשִׁים נָתוּן לִי הַחֶסֶד הַזֶּה לְבַשֵּׂר אֶל־הַגּוֹיִם חֹסֶן הַמָּשִׁיחַ כִּי־רַב הוּא לְאֵין חֵקֶר:

8. Ani ha•tza•eer batz•ee•rim bein ha•k`do•shim na•toon li ha•che•sed ha•ze le•va•ser el - ha•go•yim cho•sen ha•Ma•shi•ach ki - rav hoo le•ein che•ker.

Rabbinic Jewish Commentary

The phrase seems to be Jewish: there was one R. Jose "the little", who was so called, it is said, because he was קטן חסידים, "the least of saints" (l): but the apostle uses a still more diminutive word, and calls himself less than the least of them.

(l) T. Hieros. Bava Kama, fol. 3, 4. Misna Sota, c. 9. sect. 15. Juchasin, fol. 79. 2.

---

9. And to make all men see what is the fellowship of the mystery, which from the beginning of the world hath been hid in God, who created all things by Jesus Christ:

Greek/Transliteration

9. καὶ φωτίσαι πάντας τίς ἡ οἰκονομία τοῦ μυστηρίου τοῦ ἀποκεκρυμμένου ἀπὸ τῶν αἰώνων ἐν τῷ θεῷ τῷ τὰ πάντα κτίσαντι διὰ Ἰησοῦ χριστοῦ,

9. kai photisai pantas tis 'ei oikonomia tou musteiriou tou apokekrummenou apo ton aionon en to theo to ta panta ktisanti dya Yeisou christou,

Hebrew/Transliteration

ט. וּלְהָאִיר עֵינֵי־כֹל לָדַעַת עֵרֶךְ הַסּוֹד אֲשֶׁר צָפוּן הָיָה מֵעוֹלָם בֵּאלֹהִים יוֹצֵר הַכֹּל עַל־יְדֵי יֵשׁוּעַ הַמָּשִׁיחַ:

9. Ool•ha•eer ey•ney - chol la•da•at e•rech ha•sod asher tza•foon ha•ya me•o•lam be•Elohim yo•tzer ha•kol al - ye•dey Yeshua ha•Ma•shi•ach.

Rabbinic Jewish Commentary
The word παντας, rendered "all men", is left out in the Alexandrian copy.

What the apostle says of the Gospel, the Jews say of the Torah, that it was hid and treasured up two thousand years before the world was created (m); yea, they say (n), that many ages before the creation of the world it was written and left, בחיקו של הקבה, "in the bosom of God".

The phrase, "by Jesus Christ", is left out in the Alexandrian and Claromontane copies, and in the Vulgate Latin, Syriac, and Ethiopic versions.

(m) Zohar in Exod. fol. 20. 4. & in Numb. fol. 66. 3. Targ. Jon. & Jeras. in Gen. iii. 24. (n) Abot R. Nathan, c. 31. T. Bab. Sabbat, fol. 88. 2.

---

10. To the intent that now unto the principalities and powers in heavenly places might be known by the church the manifold wisdom of God,

Greek/Transliteration
10. ἵνα γνωρισθῇ νῦν ταῖς ἀρχαῖς καὶ ταῖς ἐξουσίαις ἐν τοῖς ἐπουρανίοις διὰ τῆς ἐκκλησίας ἡ πολυποίκιλος σοφία τοῦ θεοῦ,

10. 'ina gnoristhei nun tais archais kai tais exousiais en tois epouraniois dya teis ekkleisias 'ei polupoikilos sophia tou theou,

Hebrew/Transliteration
י. וּבְזֹאת יִוָּדַע עַל־פִּי הָעֵדָה לְרָאשֵׁי הַצָּבָא וּלְגִבּוֹרֵי כֹחַ בַּמָּרוֹם נִפְלָאוֹת חָכְמַת אֱלֹהִים

10. Oo•va•zot yi•va•da al - pi ha•e•da le•ra•shey ha•tza•va ool•gi•bo•rey cho•ach ba•ma•rom nif•le•ot choch•mat Elohim.

---

11. According to the eternal purpose which he purposed in Christ Jesus our Lord:

Greek/Transliteration
11. κατὰ πρόθεσιν τῶν αἰώνων ἣν ἐποίησεν ἐν χριστῷ Ἰησοῦ τῷ κυρίῳ ἡμῶν·

11. kata prothesin ton aionon 'ein epoieisen en christo Yeisou to kurio 'eimon.

Hebrew/Transliteration
יא. כָּעֵצָה אֲשֶׁר יָעַץ מִקֶּדֶם בְּיֵשׁוּעַ הַמָּשִׁיחַ אֲדֹנֵינוּ

11. Ka•e•tza asher ya•atz mi•ke•dem be•Yeshua ha•Ma•shi•ach Ado•ney•noo.

---

12. In whom we have boldness and access with confidence by the faith of him.

Greek/Transliteration
12. ἐν ᾧ ἔχομεν τὴν παρρησίαν καὶ τὴν προσαγωγὴν ἐν πεποιθήσει διὰ τῆς πίστεως αὐτοῦ.

12. en 'o echomen tein parreisian kai tein prosagogein en pepoitheisei dya teis pisteos autou.

Hebrew/Transliteration

יב. אֲשֶׁר בּוֹ נוֹסִיף אֹמֶץ לָגֶשֶׁת אֵלָיו בֶּאֱמוּנָתוֹ בְּלֵב נָכוֹן:

12. Asher bo no•sif o•metz la•ge•shet elav be•e•moo•na•to be•lev na•chon.

---

13. Wherefore I desire that ye faint not at my tribulations for you, which is your glory.

Greek/Transliteration

13. Διὸ αἰτοῦμαι μὴ ἐκκακεῖν ἐν ταῖς θλίψεσίν μου ὑπὲρ ὑμῶν, ἥτις ἐστὶν δόξα ὑμῶν.

13. Dio aitoumai mei ekkakein en tais thlipsesin mou 'uper 'umon, 'eitis estin doxa 'umon.

Hebrew/Transliteration

יג. עַל-כֵּן זֹאת אֲנִי מְבַקֵּשׁ אַל-נָא תִתְעַטְּפוּ בְּצָרוֹתַי אֲשֶׁר אֲפָפוּנִי לְמַעַנְכֶם כִּי זֹאת הִיא תִפְאַרְתְּכֶם:

13. Al - ken zot ani me•va•kesh al - na tit•at•foo ve•tza•ro•tai asher afa•foo•ni le•ma•an•chem ki zot hee tif•ar•te•chem.

---

14. For this cause I bow my knees unto the Father of our Lord Jesus Christ,

Greek/Transliteration

14. Τούτου χάριν κάμπτω τὰ γόνατά μου πρὸς τὸν πατέρα τοῦ κυρίου ἡμῶν Ἰησοῦ χριστοῦ,

14. Toutou charin kampto ta gonata mou pros ton patera tou kuriou 'eimon Yeisou christou,

Hebrew/Transliteration

יד. עַל-כֵּן אֶכְרָעָה עַל בִּרְכַּי לִפְנֵי אֲבִי אֲדוֹנֵינוּ יֵשׁוּעַ הַמָּשִׁיחַ:

14. Al - ken ech•re•ah al bir•kai lif•ney Avi Ado•ney•noo Yeshua ha•Ma•shi•ach.

---

15. Of whom the whole family in heaven and earth is named,

Greek/Transliteration

15. ἐξ οὗ πᾶσα πατριὰ ἐν οὐρανοῖς καὶ ἐπὶ γῆς ὀνομάζεται,

15. ex 'ou pasa patrya en ouranois kai epi geis onomazetai,

Hebrew/Transliteration

טו. אֲשֶׁר נִקְרָא שְׁמוֹ עַל כָּל-צִבְאוֹתָיו בַּשָּׁמַיִם וּבָאָרֶץ:

15. Asher nik•ra sh`mo al kol - tziv•o•tav ba•sha•ma•yim oo•va•a•retz.

Rabbinic Jewish Commentary
Frequent mention is made in the Jewish writings (o) of the family of the heavenly hosts, and of the family above, and the family below, to which here may be some reference. See also Heb_12:22-24

(o) Targ. in Cant. i. 15. T. Bab. Beracot, fol. 17. 1. Zohar in Exod. fol. 105. 4. Raziel, fol. 42. 1. & 45. 2. Caphtor, fol. 58. 2. Shaare Orn, fol. 14. 3.

---

16. That he would grant you, according to the riches of his glory, to be strengthened with might by his Spirit in the inner man;

Greek/Transliteration
16. ἵνα δῴη ὑμῖν, κατὰ τὸν πλοῦτον τῆς δόξης αὐτοῦ, δυνάμει κραταιωθῆναι διὰ τοῦ πνεύματος αὐτοῦ εἰς τὸν ἔσω ἄνθρωπον,

16. 'ina doei 'umin, kata ton plouton teis doxeis autou, dunamei krataiotheinai dya tou pneumatos autou eis ton eso anthropon,

Hebrew/Transliteration
:טז. וְהוּא יִתֵּן לָכֶם כְּפִי-חֹסֶן כְּבוֹדוֹ לְהִתְאַזֵּר בִּגְבוּרָה עַל-פִּי רוּחוֹ בָּאָדָם הַפְּנִימִי

16. Ve•hoo yi•ten la•chem ke•fi - cho•sen k`vo•do le•hit•a•zer big•voo•ra al - pi roo•cho ba•a•dam ha•p`ni•mi.

Rabbinic Jewish Commentary
in the inner man, is joined to the beginning of the next verse in the Arabic, Syriac, and Ethiopic versions, "in the inner man Messiah may dwell".

---

17. That Christ may dwell in your hearts by faith; that ye, being rooted and grounded in love,

Greek/Transliteration
17. κατοικῆσαι τὸν χριστὸν διὰ τῆς πίστεως ἐν ταῖς καρδίαις ὑμῶν·

17. katoikeisai ton christon dya teis pisteos en tais kardiais 'umon.

Hebrew/Transliteration
:יז. וְהַמָּשִׁיחַ יִשְׁכֹּן בְּקֶרֶב לִבְּכֶם בֶּאֱמוּנָה כִּי תַשְׁרִישׁוּ וְתִוָּסְדוּ בְּאַהֲבָה

17. Ve•ha•Ma•shi•ach yish•kon be•ke•rev lib•chem be•e•moo•na ki tash•ri•shoo ve•ti•vas•doo be•a•ha•va.

---

18. May be able to comprehend with all saints what is the breadth, and length, and depth, and height;

Greek/Transliteration
18. ἐν ἀγάπῃ ἐρριζωμένοι καὶ τεθεμελιωμένοι ἵνα ἐξισχύσητε καταλαβέσθαι σὺν πᾶσιν τοῖς ἁγίοις τί τὸ πλάτος καὶ μῆκος καὶ βάθος καὶ ὕψος,

18. en agapei errizomenoi kai tethemeliomenoi 'ina exischuseite katalabesthai sun pasin tois 'agiois ti to platos kai meikos kai bathos kai 'upsos,

Hebrew/Transliteration
יח. אָז תּוּכְלוּ לְהַשְׂכִּיל עִם כָּל-הַקְּדוֹשִׁים מַה-הוּא הָרֹחַב וְהָאֹרֶךְ וְהַגֹּבַהּ וְהָעֹמֶק:

18. Az tooch•loo le•has•kil eem kol - ha•k`do•shim ma - hoo ha•ro•chav ve•ha•o•rech ve•ha•go•va ve•ha•o•mek.

---

19. And to know the love of Christ, which passeth knowledge, that ye might be filled with all the fullness of God.

Greek/Transliteration
19. γνῶναί τε τὴν ὑπερβάλλουσαν τῆς γνώσεως ἀγάπην τοῦ χριστοῦ, ἵνα πληρωθῆτε εἰς πᾶν τὸ πλήρωμα τοῦ θεοῦ.

19. gnonai te tein 'uperballousan teis gnoseos agapein tou christou, 'ina pleirotheite eis pan to pleiroma tou theou.

Hebrew/Transliteration
יט. וּלְהִתְבּוֹנֵן בְּאַהֲבַת הַמָּשִׁיחַ אֲשֶׁר מִדַּעַת נִשְׂגָּבָה עַד-אֲשֶׁר תִּמָּלְאוּ מִכָּל-מְלֹא הָאֱלֹהִים:

19. Ool•hit•bo•nen be•a•ha•vat ha•Ma•shi•ach asher mi•da•at nis•ga•va ad - asher ti•mal•oo mi•kol - me•lo ha•Elohim.

---

20. Now unto him that is able to do exceeding abundantly above all that we ask or think, according to the power that worketh in us,

Greek/Transliteration
20. Τῷ δὲ δυναμένῳ ὑπὲρ πάντα ποιῆσαι ὑπὲρ ἐκπερισσοῦ ὧν αἰτούμεθα ἢ νοοῦμεν, κατὰ τὴν δύναμιν τὴν ἐνεργουμένην ἐν ἡμῖν,

20. To de dunameno 'uper panta poieisai 'uper ekperissou 'on aitoumetha ei nooumen, kata tein dunamin tein energoumenein en 'eimin,

Hebrew/Transliteration
כ. וְהוּא אֲשֶׁר יָדָיו רַב לוֹ לְעוֹרֵר בַּכֹּחַ לִבְּנוּ וְלַעֲשׂוֹת לָנוּ יֶתֶר עַל-כָּל-מִשְׁאֲלוֹתֵינוּ וּמַחְשְׁבוֹתֵינוּ:

20. Ve•hoo asher ya•dav rav lo le•o•rer ba•ko•ach li•be•noo ve•la•a•sot la•noo ye•ter al - kol - mish•a•lo•tey•noo oo•mach•she•vo•tey•noo.

---

21. Unto him be glory in the church by Christ Jesus throughout all ages, world without end. Amen.

Greek/Transliteration
21. αὐτῷ ἡ δόξα ἐν τῇ ἐκκλησίᾳ ἐν χριστῷ Ἰησοῦ, εἰς πάσας τὰς γενεὰς τοῦ αἰῶνος τῶν αἰώνων. Ἀμήν.

21. auto 'ei doxa en tei ekkleisia en christo Yeisou, eis pasas tas geneas tou aionos ton aionon. Amein.

Hebrew/Transliteration

כא. לוֹ הוּא הַכָּבוֹד בְּתוֹךְ הָעֵדָה וּבְיֵשׁוּעַ הַמָּשִׁיחַ מִדּוֹר לְדוֹר וּמֵהָעוֹלָם וְעַד-הָעוֹלָם אָמֵן:

21. Lo hoo ha•ka•vod be•toch ha•e•da oov•Yeshua ha•Ma•shi•ach mi•dor le•dor oo•me•ha•o•lam ve•ad - ha•o•lam Amen.

Ephesians, Chapter 4

1. I therefore, the prisoner of the Lord, beseech you that ye walk worthy of the vocation wherewith ye are called,

Greek/Transliteration
1. Παρακαλῶ οὖν ὑμᾶς ἐγώ, ὁ δέσμιος ἐν κυρίῳ, ἀξίως περιπατῆσαι τῆς κλήσεως ἧς ἐκλήθητε,

1. Parakalo oun 'umas ego, 'o desmios en kurio, axios peripateisai teis kleiseos 'eis ekleitheite,

Hebrew/Transliteration
א: וַאֲנִי אֲסִיר הָאָדוֹן אֶפְצַר בָּכֶם לָלֶכֶת כִּנְאֹוָה לַמַּצָּב הַקְּרֻאִים כָּמוֹכֶם

1. Va•a•ni asir ha•Adon ef•tzar ba•chem la•le•chet ke•na•va le•ma•tzav hak•roo•eem ka•mo•chem.

---

2. With all lowliness and meekness, with longsuffering, forbearing one another in love;

Greek/Transliteration
2. μετὰ πάσης ταπεινοφροσύνης καὶ πραότητος, μετὰ μακροθυμίας, ἀνεχόμενοι ἀλλήλων ἐν ἀγάπῃ,

2. meta paseis tapeinophrosuneis kai praoteitos, meta makrothumias, anechomenoi alleilon en agapei,

Hebrew/Transliteration
ב: בְּהַצְנֵעַ וַעֲנָוָה בְּאֹרֶךְ אַפַּיִם וְלָשֵׂאת אִישׁ אֶת־רֵעֵהוּ בְּאַהֲבָה

2. Be•hatz•ne•a va•a•na•va be•o•rech apa•yim ve•la•set eesh et - re•e•hoo be•a•ha•va.

---

3. Endeavouring to keep the unity of the Spirit in the bond of peace.

Greek/Transliteration
3. σπουδάζοντες τηρεῖν τὴν ἑνότητα τοῦ πνεύματος ἐν τῷ συνδέσμῳ τῆς εἰρήνης.

3. spoudazontes teirein tein 'enoteita tou pneumatos en to sundesmo teis eireineis.

Hebrew/Transliteration
ג: לִשְׁקֹד וְלִשְׁמֹר לְיַחַד רוּחֲכֶם בְּמַחְבֶּרֶת הַשָּׁלוֹם

3. Lish•kod ve•lish•mor le•ya•ched roo•cha•chem be•mach•be•ret ha•sha•lom.

---

4. There is one body, and one Spirit, even as ye are called in one hope of your calling;

Greek/Transliteration
4. Ἓν σῶμα καὶ ἓν πνεῦμα, καθὼς καὶ ἐκλήθητε ἐν μιᾷ ἐλπίδι τῆς κλήσεως ὑμῶν·

4. 'En soma kai 'en pneuma, kathos kai ekleitheite en mya elpidi teis kleiseos 'umon.

Hebrew/Transliteration
ד: לִהְיוֹת כְּאֲבָרִים בְּגוּף אֶחָד וּבְרוּחַ אֶחָד כַּאֲשֶׁר גַם-נִקְרָאתֶם לְמַצַּבְכֶם בְּתִקְוָה אֶחָת.

4. Li•hee•yot ke•e•va•rim be•goof e•chad oov•Roo•ach e•chad ka•a•sher gam - nik•ra•tem le•ma•tzav•chem be•tik•va e•chat.

Rabbinic Jewish Commentary
So the Jews say (p), that in the world of spirits, all, small and great, stand before YHWH; and they have a standing alike; for in the affairs of the soul, it is fit that they should be all שוים, "equal", as it is said Exo_30:15, "the rich shall not give more".

(p) Tzeror Hammor, fol. 154. 2.

---

5. One Lord, one faith, one baptism,

Greek/Transliteration
5. εἷς κύριος, μία πίστις, ἓν βάπτισμα,

5. 'eis kurios, mia pistis, 'en baptisma,

Hebrew/Transliteration
ה: אָדוֹן אֶחָד אֱמוּנָה אַחַת וּטְבִילָה אֶחָת.

5. Adon e•chad e•moo•na a•chat oot•vi•la e•chat.

---

6. One God and Father of all, who is above all, and through all, and in you all.

Greek/Transliteration
6. εἷς θεὸς καὶ πατὴρ πάντων, ὁ ἐπὶ πάντων, καὶ διὰ πάντων, καὶ ἐν πᾶσιν ἡμῖν.

6. 'eis theos kai pateir panton, 'o epi panton, kai dya panton, kai en pasin 'eimin.

Hebrew/Transliteration
ו: אֵל אֶחָד וַאֲבִי-כֹל אֲשֶׁר הוּא עַל-כֹּל וְעִם-כֹּל וּבְתוֹךְ כֻּלְּכֶם.

6. El e•chad va•Avi - chol asher hoo al - kol ve•eem - kol oov•toch kool•chem.

---

7. But unto every one of us is given grace according to the measure of the gift of Christ.

Greek/Transliteration
7. Ἑνὶ δὲ ἑκάστῳ ἡμῶν ἐδόθη ἡ χάρις κατὰ τὸ μέτρον τῆς δωρεᾶς τοῦ χριστοῦ.

7. 'Eni de 'ekasto 'eimon edothei 'ei charis kata to metron teis doreas tou christou.

Hebrew/Transliteration

:ז. אַךְ לְאִישׁ אִישׁ מִמֶּנּוּ חֻלַּק מְנָת חָסֶד כְּמִדַּת מַתְּנַת הַמָּשִׁיחַ

7. Ach le•eesh eesh mi•me•noo choo•lak m`nat cha•sed ke•mi•dat mat•nat ha•Ma•shi•ach.

---

8. Wherefore he saith, When he ascended up on high, he led captivity captive, and gave gifts unto men.

Greek/Transliteration

8. Διὸ λέγει, Ἀναβὰς εἰς ὕψος ᾐχμαλώτευσεν αἰχμαλωσίαν, καὶ ἔδωκεν δόματα τοῖς ἀνθρώποις.

8. Dio legei, Anabas eis 'upsos eichmaloteusen aichmalosian, kai edoken domata tois anthropois.

Hebrew/Transliteration

:ח. עַל־כֵּן הוּא אֹמֵר עָלָה לַמָּרוֹם שָׁבָה שֶׁבִי וַיִּתֵּן מַתָּנוֹת לָאָדָם

8. Al - ken hoo o•mer ala la•ma•rom sha•va she•vi va•yi•ten ma•ta•not la•a•dam.

Rabbinic Jewish Commentary

and gave gifts unto men; meaning the gifts of the Holy Ghost, and particularly such as qualify men for the work of the ministry; these he received באדם, "in man"; in human nature, in that nature in which he ascended to heaven; באדם הידוע למעלה, "in the man that is known above" (t), as say the Jews; and these he bestows on men, even rebellious ones, that the Lord God might dwell among them, and make them useful to others: wherefore the Jews have no reason to quarrel with the version of the apostle as they do (u); who, instead of "received gifts for" men, renders it, "gave gifts to men"; since the Messiah received in order to give, and gives in consequence of his having received them; and so Jarchi interprets the words, לתתאם, "to give them" to the children of men; and besides, as a learned man has observed (w), one and the same Hebrew word signifies to give and to receive; to which may be added that their own Targum renders it יהבתא, "and hast given gifts to the children of men"; and in like manner the Syriac and Arabic versions of Psa_68:18 render the words; very likely the apostle might use the Syriac version, which is a very ancient one: it was customary at triumphs to give gifts to the soldiers (x), to which there is an allusion here.

(t) Zohar in Numb. fol. 61. 4. (u) R. Isaac. Chizzuk Emuna, par. 2. c. 91. (w) Pocock. not. Misc. p. 24. (x) Alex. ab. Alex. ib. ut supra. (Genial. Dier. l. 6. c. 6.)

---

9. (Now that he ascended, what is it but that he also descended first into the lower parts of the earth?

Greek/Transliteration

9. Τὸ δέ, Ἀνέβη, τί ἐστιν εἰ μὴ ὅτι καὶ κατέβη πρῶτον εἰς τὰ κατώτερα μέρη τῆς γῆς;

9. To de, Anebei, ti estin ei mei 'oti kai katebei proton eis ta katotera merei teis geis?

Hebrew/Transliteration
ט. וְכִי נֹאמַר כִּי-עָלָה אֵין זֶה כִּי אִם-יָרַד בָּרִאשׁוֹנָה לְתַחְתִּיּוֹת אָרֶץ:

9. Ve•chi no•mar ki - ala eyn ze ki eem - ya•rad ba•ri•sho•na le•tach•ti•yot a•retz?

Rabbinic Jewish Commentary
The whole of his humiliation, as his descent from heaven and incarnation in the virgin's womb, where his human nature was curiously wrought in the lowest parts of the earth; and his humbling himself and becoming obedient unto death, even the death of the cross, when he was made sin and a curse for his people, and bore all the punishment due to their transgressions; and his being in Hades, in the state of the dead, in the grave, in the heart of the earth, as Jonah in the whale's belly: reference seems to be had to Psa_139:15 where "the lower parts of the earth", is interpreted by the Targum on the place of כריסא דאמא, "his mother's womb"; and so it is by Jarchi, Aben Ezra, Kimchi, and Ben Melec. The Alexandrian copy and the Ethiopic version leave out the word "first" in this clause.

---

10. He that descended is the same also that ascended up far above all heavens, that he might fill all things.)

Greek/Transliteration
10. Ὁ καταβάς, αὐτός ἐστιν καὶ ὁ ἀναβὰς ὑπεράνω πάντων τῶν οὐρανῶν, ἵνα πληρώσῃ τὰ πάντα.

10. 'O katabas, autos estin kai 'o anabas 'uperano panton ton ouranon, 'ina pleirosei ta panta.

Hebrew/Transliteration
י. הַיֹּרֵד הוּא הָעֹלֶה לְמַעְלָה מִכָּל-שְׁמֵי מָרוֹם לְמַעְלֶה אֶת-הַכֹּל:

10. Ha•yo•red hoo ha•o•le le•ma•a•la mi•kol - sh`mey ma•rom le•ma•le et - ha•kol.

---

11. And he gave some, apostles; and some, prophets; and some, evangelists; and some, pastors and teachers;

Greek/Transliteration
11. Καὶ αὐτὸς ἔδωκεν τοὺς μὲν ἀποστόλους, τοὺς δὲ προφήτας, τοὺς δὲ εὐαγγελιστάς, τοὺς δὲ ποιμένας καὶ διδασκάλους,

11. Kai autos edoken tous men apostolous, tous de propheitas, tous de euangelistas, tous de poimenas kai didaskalous,

Hebrew/Transliteration
יא. וְהוּא נָתַן אֶת-אֵלֶּה לִהְיוֹת שְׁלִיחִים וְאֶת-אֵלֶּה נְבִיאִים וְאֶת-אֵלֶּה מְבַשְּׂרִים וְאֶת-אֵלֶּה רֹעִים וּמוֹרִים:

11. Ve•hoo na•tan et - ele li•hee•yot sh`li•chim ve•et - ele n`vi•eem ve•et - ele me•vas•rim ve•et - ele ro•eem oo•mo•rim.

Rabbinic Jewish Commentary
Among the Jews there were the singular men or wise men, and the disciples of the wise men, who were their companions and assistants; and it is asked (y),

"Who is a singular man? and who is a disciple? a singular man is everyone that is fit to be appointed a pastor or governor of a congregation; and a disciple is one, that when he is questioned about any point in his doctrine, gives an answer:"

Wherefore if these two, pastors and teachers, are different, it might be thought there is some reference to this distinction, and that pastors answer to the wise men, and teachers to their disciples or assistants; and so Kimchi in Jer_3:15 interprets the pastors there of פרנסים דישראל, "the pastors of Israel", which shall be with the King Messiah, as is said in Mic_5:5 and undoubtedly Gospel ministers are meant.

---

12. For the perfecting of the saints, for the work of the ministry, for the edifying of the body of Christ:

Greek/Transliteration
12. πρὸς τὸν καταρτισμὸν τῶν ἁγίων, εἰς ἔργον διακονίας, εἰς οἰκοδομὴν τοῦ σώματος τοῦ χριστοῦ·

12. pros ton katartismon ton 'agion, eis ergon dyakonias, eis oikodomein tou somatos tou christou.

Hebrew/Transliteration
יב. לְהַשְׁלִים אֶת-הַקְּדוֹשִׁים לִמְלֶאכֶת עֲבֹדַת הַקֹּדֶשׁ לְמַעַן יִבָּנֶה גּוּף הַמָּשִׁיחַ:

12. Le•hash•lim et - ha•k`do•shim lim•le•chet avo•dat ha•ko•desh le•ma•an yi•ba•ne goof ha•Ma•shi•ach.

13. Till we all come in the unity of the faith, and of the knowledge of the Son of God, unto a perfect man, unto the measure of the stature of the fullness of Christ:

Greek/Transliteration
13. μέχρι καταντήσωμεν οἱ πάντες εἰς τὴν ἑνότητα τῆς πίστεως καὶ τῆς ἐπιγνώσεως τοῦ υἱοῦ τοῦ θεοῦ, εἰς ἄνδρα τέλειον, εἰς μέτρον ἡλικίας τοῦ πληρώματος τοῦ χριστοῦ·

13. mechri katanteisomen 'oi pantes eis tein 'enoteita teis pisteos kai teis epignoseos tou 'wiou tou theou, eis andra teleion, eis metron 'eilikias tou pleiromatos tou christou.

Hebrew/Transliteration
יג. עַד אֲשֶׁר כֻּלָּנוּ נָבוֹא לְיַחַד לְבָבֵנוּ בֶּאֱמוּנָה אַחַת וּבְדַעַת בֶּן-הָאֱלֹהִים וְהָיִינוּ לְאָדָם שָׁלֵם בַּמִּדָּה כִּמְלֹא קוֹמַת הַמָּשִׁיחַ:

13. Ad asher koo•la•noo na•vo le•ya•ched le•va•ve•noo be•e•moo•na a•chat oov•da•at Ben - ha•Elohim ve•ha•yi•noo le•a•dam sha•lem ba•mi•da kim•lo ko•mat ha•Ma•shi•ach.

Rabbinic Jewish Commentary
The phrase is taken from the Jews, who among the forms and degrees of prophecy which the prophets arrived to, and had in them the vision of God and messengers, make שעור קומה, "the measure of the stature" (z), a principal one; and is here used for the perfection of the heavenly state in the vision, and enjoyment of God and Yeshua.
(z) Maimon. in Misn. Sanhedrin, c. 11. sect. 1. Cosri, par. 4. sect. 3. p. 213. 2.

14. That we henceforth be no more children, tossed to and fro, and carried about with every wind of doctrine, by the sleight of men, and cunning craftiness, whereby they lie in wait to deceive;

Greek/Transliteration
14. ἵνα μηκέτι ὦμεν νήπιοι, κλυδωνιζόμενοι καὶ περιφερόμενοι παντὶ ἀνέμῳ τῆς διδασκαλίας, ἐν τῇ κυβείᾳ τῶν ἀνθρώπων, ἐν πανουργίᾳ πρὸς τὴν μεθοδείαν τῆς πλάνης·

14. 'ina meiketi omen neipioi, kludonizomenoi kai peripheromenoi panti anemo teis didaskalias, en tei kubeia ton anthropon, en panourgia pros tein methodeian teis planeis.

Hebrew/Transliteration
יד. לְבִלְתִּי נִהְיֶה עוֹד עוֹלָלִים נִדָּפִים וְנִגְרָשִׁים מִפְּנֵי כָל-רוּחַ בְּתוֹרַת אֲנָשִׁים וְתַרְמִיתָם אֲשֶׁר בְּנִכְלֵיהֶם יָצוּדוּ חֵרֶם:

14. Le•vil•ti ni•hee•ye od o•la•lim ni•da•fim ve•nig•ra•shim mip•ney chol - roo•ach be•to•rat a•na•shim ve•tar•mi•tam asher be•nich•ley•hem ya•tzoo•doo che•rem.

Rabbinic Jewish Commentary
by the sleight of men; either through the uncertain and changeable state of things in life; the mind of man is fickle, the life of man is uncertain, and all the affairs of human nature are subject to change, by reason of which men are easily imposed upon; or rather through the tricking arts of false teachers; the word here used is adopted by the Jews into their language, and with them **קוּבְיָא** signifies the game at dice (a); and **קוּבְיוּסְטוּס**, is a gamester at that play, and is interpreted by them, one that steals souls (b), and deceives and corrupts them; and may be filly applied to false teachers, who make use of such like artifices and juggling tricks, to deceive the hearts of the simple, as the others do to cheat men of their money.

(a) T. Bab. Erubin, fol. 82. 1. Misna Roshhashana, c. 1. sect. 8. & Sanhedrin, c. 3. sect 3. (b) T. Bab. Cholin, fol. 91. 2. & Jarchi & Tosephot in ib. & Juchasin, fol. 88. 1.

---

15. But speaking the truth in love, may grow up into him in all things, which is the head, even Christ:

Greek/Transliteratoin
15. ἀληθεύοντες δὲ ἐν ἀγάπῃ αὐξήσωμεν εἰς αὐτὸν τὰ πάντα, ὅς ἐστιν ἡ κεφαλή, ὁ χριστός,

15. aleitheuontes de en agapei auxeisomen eis auton ta panta, 'os estin 'ei kephalei, 'o christos,

Hebrew/Transliteration
טו. כִּי אִם-נַחֲזִיק בָּאֱמֶת מֵאַהֲבָה וְהָלַכְנוּ הָלוֹךְ וְגָדוֹל לִפְנֵי הַמָּשִׁיחַ אֲשֶׁר הוּא הָרֹאשׁ:

15. Ki eem - na•cha•zik ba•e•met me•a•ha•va ve•ha•lach•noo ha•loch ve•ga•dol lif•ney ha•Ma•shi•ach asher hoo ha•rosh.

16. From whom the whole body fitly joined together and compacted by that which every joint supplieth, according to the effectual working in the measure of every part, maketh increase of the body unto the edifying of itself in love.

Greek/Transliteration
16. ἐξ οὗ πᾶν τὸ σῶμα συναρμολογούμενον καὶ συμβιβαζόμενον διὰ πάσης ἁφῆς τῆς ἐπιχορηγίας, κατ᾽ ἐνέργειαν ἐν μέτρῳ ἑνὸς ἑκάστου μέρους, τὴν αὔξησιν τοῦ σώματος ποιεῖται εἰς οἰκοδομὴν ἑαυτοῦ ἐν ἀγάπῃ.

16. ex 'ou pan to soma sunarmologoumenon kai sumbibazomenon dya paseis 'apheis teis epichoreigias, kat energeyan en metro 'enos 'ekastou merous, tein auxeisin tou somatos poieitai eis oikodomein 'eautou en agapei.

Hebrew/Transliteration
טז. ובו מֻדְבָּק וּמְקֻשָּׁר כָּל־הַגּוּף עִם כָּל־פְּרָקָיו וַחֲלָקָיו אֶל־נָכוֹן אֲשֶׁר בְּאַהֲבָה יַעַבְדוּן לְהַגְדִּילוֹ וּלְהַאֲדִירוֹ כְּדֵי כֹחָם:

16. Oo•vo mood•bak oom•koo•shar kol - ha•goof eem kol - pe•ra•kav va•cha•la•kav el - na•chon asher be•a•ha•va ya•av•doon le•hag•di•lo ool•ha•a•di•ro ke•dey cho•cham.

---

17. This I say therefore, and testify in the Lord, that ye henceforth walk not as other Gentiles walk, in the vanity of their mind,

Greek/Transliteration
17. Τοῦτο οὖν λέγω καὶ μαρτύρομαι ἐν κυρίῳ, μηκέτι ὑμᾶς περιπατεῖν, καθὼς καὶ τὰ λοιπὰ ἔθνη περιπατεῖ ἐν ματαιότητι τοῦ νοὸς αὐτῶν,

17. Touto oun lego kai marturomai en kurio, meiketi 'umas peripatein, kathos kai ta loipa ethnei peripatei en mataioteiti tou no'os auton,

Hebrew/Transliteration
יז: וְעַתָּה הַעִדֹתִי בָכֶם לִפְנֵי הָאָדוֹן לֵאמֹר אַל־תֵּלְכוּ כְיֶתֶר הַגּוֹיִם אֲשֶׁר אַחֲרֵי הַבְלֵי שָׁוְא לִבָּם הֹלֵךְ:

17. Ve•a•ta ha•ee•do•ti va•chem lif•ney ha•Adon le•mor al - tel•choo ke•ye•ter ha•go•yim asher a•cha•rey hav•ley shav li•bam ho•lech.

Rabbinic Jewish Commentary
The Alexandrian copy, and some others, the Vulgate Latin and Ethiopic versions, leave out the word "other", and only read, "as the Gentiles".

---

18. Having the understanding darkened, being alienated from the life of God through the ignorance that is in them, because of the blindness of their heart:

Greek/Transliteration
18. ἐσκοτισμένοι τῇ διανοίᾳ, ὄντες ἀπηλλοτριωμένοι τῆς ζωῆς τοῦ θεοῦ διὰ τὴν ἄγνοιαν τὴν οὖσαν ἐν αὐτοῖς, διὰ τὴν πώρωσιν τῆς καρδίας αὐτῶν·

18. eskotismenoi tei dyanoia, ontes apeillotriomenoi teis zoeis tou theou dya tein agnoyan tein ousan en autois, dya tein porosin teis kardias auton.

Hebrew/Transliteration
יח. מְאוֹר דַּעְתָּם חָשַׁךְ וְחַיֵּי אֱלֹהִים מוּזָרִים לָהֶם עֵקֶב אֲשֶׁר הִקְשׁוּ רוּחָם בְּאִוַּלְתָּם.

18. Me•or da•a•tam cha•shach ve•cha•yey Elohim moo•za•rim la•hem e•kev asher hik•shoo roo•cham be•ee•val•tam.

Rabbinic Jewish Commentary
There is a judicial hardness, which God gives up men unto; and when and where this is the case, in either sense, it is no wonder men should be so ignorant of God, and so alienated from the life of him: סמיות הלב, "blindness of heart" (c), is a Rabbinical phrase.

(c) T. Bab. Cetubot, fol. 105. 1.

---

19. Who being past feeling have given themselves over unto lasciviousness, to work all uncleanness with greediness.

Greek/Transliteration
19. οἵτινες ἀπηλγηκότες ἑαυτοὺς παρέδωκαν τῇ ἀσελγείᾳ, εἰς ἐργασίαν ἀκαθαρσίας πάσης ἐν πλεονεξίᾳ.

19. 'oitines apeilgeikotes 'eautous paredokan tei aselgeia, eis ergasian akatharsias paseis en pleonexia.

Hebrew/Transliteration
יט. הֵם אֲשֶׁר טָפַשׁ לִבָּם וַיִּתְמַכְּרוּ לַעֲשׂוֹת כָּל־נְבָלָה וְתוֹעֵבָה וְלֹא יָדְעוּ שָׂבְעָה:

19. Hem asher ta•fash li•bam va•yit`mak•roo la•a•sot kol - n`va•la ve•to•e•va ve•lo yed•oo sov•ah.

---

20. But ye have not so learned Christ;

Greek/Transliteration
20. Ὑμεῖς δὲ οὐχ οὕτως ἐμάθετε τὸν χριστόν,

20. 'Umeis de ouch 'outos emathete ton christon,

Hebrew/Transliteration
כ. וְאַתֶּם לֹא כָזֹאת לְמַדְתֶּם דַּרְכֵי הַמָּשִׁיחַ:

20. Ve•a•tem lo cha•zot le•ma•de•tem dar•chey ha•Ma•shiach.

---

21. If so be that ye have heard him, and have been taught by him, as the truth is in Jesus:

Greek/Transliteration
21. εἴγε αὐτὸν ἠκούσατε καὶ ἐν αὐτῷ ἐδιδάχθητε, καθώς ἐστιν ἀλήθεια ἐν τῷ Ἰησοῦ·

21. eige auton eikousate kai en auto edidachtheite, kathos estin aleitheya en to Yeisou.

Hebrew/Transliteration
:כא. אִם רַק מַקְשִׁיבִים הֱיִיתֶם לְקוֹלוֹ וְלִמּוּדֵי דְבָרוֹ אַתֶּם כִּי הֵם אֱמֶת בִּפְנֵי יֵשׁוּעַ

21. Eem rak mak•shi•vim he•yi•tem le•ko•lo ve•li•moo•dey de•va•ro atem ki hem emet bif•ney Yeshua.

---

22. That ye put off concerning the former conversation the old man, which is corrupt according to the deceitful lusts;

Greek/Transliteration
22. ἀποθέσθαι ὑμᾶς, κατὰ τὴν προτέραν ἀναστροφήν, τὸν παλαιὸν ἄνθρωπον, τὸν φθειρόμενον κατὰ τὰς ἐπιθυμίας τῆς ἀπάτης·

22. apothesthai 'umas, kata tein proteran anastrophein, ton palaion anthropon, ton phtheiromenon kata tas epithumias teis apateis.

Hebrew/Transliteration
:כב. וְכֵן עֲזַבְתֶּם דַּרְכֵיכֶם הָרִאשֹׁנִים עַד - לְהָסִיר מֵעֲלֵיכֶם אֶת - הָאָדָם הַקַּדְמֹנִי הַנִּשְׁחָת וְהַנִּתְעֶה בְּתַאֲוָתוֹ

22. Ve•chen azav•tem dar•chey•chem ha•ri•sho•nim ad - le•ha•sir me•a•ley•chem et - ha•a•dam ha•kad•mo•ni ha•nish•chat ve•ha•nit•eh be•ta•a•va•to.

---

23. And be renewed in the spirit of your mind;

Greek/Transliteration
23. ἀνανεοῦσθαι δὲ τῷ πνεύματι τοῦ νοὸς ὑμῶν,

23. ananeousthai de to pneumati tou no'os 'umon,

Hebrew/Transliteration
:כג. לְהִתְחַדֵּשׁ בְּרוּחַ חֲדָשָׁה בְּקֶרֶב לִבְּכֶם

23. Le•hit•cha•desh be•roo•ach cha•da•sha be•ke•rev lib•chem.

Rabbinic Jewish Commentary
David did, Psa_51:10 for otherwise, this is as much the work of the Spirit of God, as renovation is at first; and he only who is sent forth, and renews the face of the earth, year by year, can renew us daily in the Spirit of our minds.

---

24. And that ye put on the new man, which after God is created in righteousness and true holiness.

Greek/Transliteration
24. καὶ ἐνδύσασθαι τὸν καινὸν ἄνθρωπον, τὸν κατὰ θεὸν κτισθέντα ἐν δικαιοσύνῃ καὶ ὁσιότητι τῆς ἀληθείας.

24. kai endusasthai ton kainon anthropon, ton kata theon ktisthenta en dikaiosunei kai 'osioteiti teis aleitheias.

Hebrew/Transliteration
כד. וְלִלְבֹּשׁ אֶת-הָאָדָם הֶחָדָשׁ הַנִּבְרָא בְצֶדֶק וּבְקֹדֶשׁ בֶּאֱמֶת כְּלֵב הָאֱלֹהִים:

24. Ve•lil•bosh et - ha•a•dam he•cha•dash ha•niv•ra ve•tze•dek oov•ko•desh be•e•met ke•lev ha•Elohim.

Rabbinic Jewish Commentary
The Jews says of a man that truly repents of sin, and does not return to it, that he is איח חדש, "a new man" (d): now to put on this new man, is not to make ourselves new creatures; for this is not by the power of man, but by the Spirit of God.

(d) Tzeror Hammor. fol. 156. 4.

---

25. Wherefore putting away lying, speak every man truth with his neighbour: for we are members one of another.

Greek/Transliteration
25. Διὸ ἀποθέμενοι τὸ ψεῦδος λαλεῖτε ἀλήθειαν ἕκαστος μετὰ τοῦ πλησίον αὐτοῦ· ὅτι ἐσμὲν ἀλλήλων μέλη.

25. Dio apothemenoi to pseudos laleite aleitheyan 'ekastos meta tou pleision autou. 'oti semen alleilon melei.

Hebrew/Transliteration
כה. עַל-כֵּן הַרְחִיקוּ שֶׁקֶר מִכֶּם וְדַבְּרוּ אֱמֶת אִישׁ אֶת-רֵעוֹ כִּי אֵבָרִים אֲנַחְנוּ אִישׁ לְאָחִיו:

25. Al - ken har•chi•koo she•ker mi•kem ve•dab•roo emet eesh et - re•o ki eva•rim a•nach•noo eesh le•a•chiv.

---

26. Be ye angry, and sin not: let not the sun go down upon your wrath:

Greek/Transliteration
26. Ὀργίζεσθε καὶ μὴ ἁμαρτάνετε· ὁ ἥλιος μὴ ἐπιδυέτω ἐπὶ τῷ παροργισμῷ ὑμῶν·

26. Orgizesthe kai mei 'amartanete. 'o 'eilios mei epidueto epi to parorgismo 'umon.

Hebrew/Transliteration
כו. רִגְזוּ וְאַל-תֶּחֱטָאוּ וְלֹא תָבוֹא הַשֶּׁמֶשׁ בְּעוֹד רֹגֶז בְּאַפְּכֶם:

26. Rig•zoo ve•al - te•che•ta•oo ve•lo ta•vo ha•she•mesh be•od ro•gez be•ap•chem.

Rabbinic Jewish Commentary
The Jews have a like distinction of anger; they say (e),

"There is an anger and an anger; there is an anger which is blessed above and below, and it is called blessed, as it is said Gen_14:19 and there is an anger which is cursed above and below, as it is said Gen_3:14"

And these two sorts are compared to "Ebal" and "Gerizzim", from the one of which proceeded blessing, and from the other cursing: anger for the most part is not only sinful, but it tends to sin, and issues in it; hence that saying of the Jews, לא תרתח ולא תחטי, "be not angry, and thou wilt not sin" (f): the spring of it is a corrupt heart, it is stirred up by the adversary, encouraged by pride, and increased by grievous words and reproachful language.

R. Jonah (g) has an expression or two like to this;

"Let not the indignation of anyone abide upon thee; and let not a night sleep with thee, and anger be against any one:"

It should be considered, that as God is slow to anger, so he does not retain it for ever; and that to retain anger, is to gratify the accuser.

(e) Zohar in Gen. fol. 104. 1. (f) T. Bab. Beracot fol. 80. 3. (g) Apud Capell. in Matt. v. 23.

---

27. Neither give place to the devil.

Greek/Transliteration
27. μηδὲ δίδοτε τόπον τῷ διαβόλῳ.

27. meide didote topon to dyabolo.

Hebrew/Transliteration
כז. פֶּן-תִּתְּנוּ מָקוֹם לַשָּׂטָן:

27. Pen - tit•noo ma•kom la•Satan.

Rabbinic Jewish Commentary

Or "to the accuser", or "slanderer"; that is, to any adversary, that takes delight in slandering and reproaching the saints; give such no room, nor reason, to calumniate the doctrine and ways of Yeshua, through an unbecoming conversation, by lying and sinful anger, or by other means; or rather the devil, the great accuser of the brethren is meant; and the Ethiopic version renders it, "do not give way to Satan"; which is done, when men indulge any lust or corruption; and when they easily fall in with his suggestions and temptations; when they are off of their watch and guard; and when they do not resist, but quietly yield unto him.

---

28. Let him that stole steal no more: but rather let him labour, working with his hands the thing which is good, that he may have to give to him that needeth.

Greek/Transliteration
28. Ὁ κλέπτων μηκέτι κλεπτέτω· μᾶλλον δὲ κοπιάτω, ἐργαζόμενος τὸ ἀγαθὸν ταῖς χερσίν, ἵνα ἔχῃ μεταδιδόναι τῷ χρείαν ἔχοντι.

28. 'O klepton meiketi klepteto. mallon de kopyato, ergazomenos to agathon tais chersin, 'ina echei metadidonai to chreian echonti.

Hebrew/Transliteration
כח. מִי שֶׁגָּנַב אַל-יֹסֶף לִגְנֹב עוֹד כִּי אִם-יַעֲמֹל לַעֲשׂוֹת טוֹב בְּיָדָיו לִהְיוֹת לוֹ לָתֵת לָאֶבְיוֹן:

28. Mee she•ga•nav al - Yosef lig•nov od ki eem - ya•a•mol la•a•sot tov be•ya•dav li•hee•yot lo la•tet la•ev•yon.

---

29. Let no corrupt communication proceed out of your mouth, but that which is good to the use of edifying, that it may minister grace unto the hearers.

Greek/Transliteration
29. Πᾶς λόγος σαπρὸς ἐκ τοῦ στόματος ὑμῶν μὴ ἐκπορευέσθω, ἀλλ᾽ εἴ τις ἀγαθὸς πρὸς οἰκοδομὴν τῆς χρείας, ἵνα δῷ χάριν τοῖς ἀκούουσιν.

29. Pas logos sapros ek tou stomatos 'umon mei ekporeuestho, all ei tis agathos pros oikodomein teis chreias, 'ina do charin tois akouousin.

Hebrew/Transliteration
:כט. כָּל־דְּבַר בְּלִיַּעַל לֹא־יֵצֵא מִפִּיכֶם כִּי אִם־דְּבָרִים טוֹבִים וּנְכֹחִים לְהָשִׁיב נֶפֶשׁ וְלָתֵת־חֵן לְשֹׁמְעֵיהֶם

29. Kol - de•var b`li•ya•al lo - ye•tze mi•pi•chem ki eem - d`va•rim to•vim oon•cho•chim le•ha•shiv ne•fesh ve•la•tet - chen le•shom•ey•hem.

Rabbinic Jewish Commentary
Agreeably to all this are some sayings of the Jews (h),

"Says R. Joshua ben Levi, for ever let not a man suffer any thing מגונה, "that is filthy", or unseemly, to proceed out of his mouth; says R. Ishmael, for ever let a man discourse בלשון נקייה, "in a pure language". Not corrupt.

(h) T. Bab. Pesachim, fol. 3. 1.

---

30. And grieve not the holy Spirit of God, whereby ye are sealed unto the day of redemption.

Greek/Transliteration
30. Καὶ μὴ λυπεῖτε τὸ πνεῦμα τὸ ἅγιον τοῦ θεοῦ, ἐν ᾧ ἐσφραγίσθητε εἰς ἡμέραν ἀπολυτρώσεως.

30. Kai mei lupeite to pneuma to 'agion tou theou, en 'o esphragistheite eis 'eimeran apolutroseos.

Hebrew/Transliteration
:ל. וְאַל־תְּעַצְּבוּ אֶת־רוּחַ הַקֹּדֶשׁ הוּא רוּחַ הָאֱלֹהִים אֲשֶׁר בּוֹ נֶחְתַּמְתֶּם אַתֶּם עַד יוֹם הַגְּאֻלָּה

30. Ve•al - te•atz•voo et - Roo•ach ha•Ko•desh hoo Roo•ach ha•Elohim asher bo nech•ta•mim atem ad yom ha•g`oo•la.

---

31. Let all bitterness, and wrath, and anger, and clamour, and evil speaking, be put away from you, with all malice:

Greek/Transliteration
31. Πᾶσα πικρία καὶ θυμὸς καὶ ὀργὴ καὶ κραυγὴ καὶ βλασφημία ἀρθήτω ἀφ᾽ ὑμῶν, σὺν πάσῃ κακίᾳ·

31. Pasa pikria kai thumos kai orgei kai kraugei kai blaspheimia artheito aph 'umon, sun pasei kakia.

Hebrew/Transliteration
לא. וְהַרְחִיקוּ מִכֶּם כָּל־מְרִירוּת לֵב וַחֲרוֹן אַף רֹגֶז וּתְלוּנָּה וּנְאָצָה עִם כָּל־דָּבָר רָע:

31. Ve•har•chi•koo mi•kem kol - me•ri•root lev va•cha•ron af ro•gez oot•loo•na oon•a•tza eem kol - da•var ra.

---

32. And be ye kind one to another, tenderhearted, forgiving one another, even as God for Christ's sake hath forgiven you.

Greek/Transliteration
32. γίνεσθε δὲ εἰς ἀλλήλους χρηστοί, εὔσπλαγχνοι, χαριζόμενοι ἑαυτοῖς, καθὼς καὶ ὁ θεὸς ἐν χριστῷ ἐχαρίσατο ἡμῖν.

32. ginesthe de eis alleilous chreistoi, eusplagchnoi, charizomenoi 'eautois, kathos kai 'o theos en christo echarisato 'eimin.

Hebrew/Transliteration
לב. אֲבָל חֹנְנִים תִּהְיוּ זֶה לָזֶה מְרַחֲמִים וְסוֹלְחִים אִישׁ לְאָחִיו כַּאֲשֶׁר גַּם־הָאֱלֹהִים סָלַח לָכֶם בַּמָּשִׁיחַ:

32. Aval cho•ne•nim ti•hi•yoo ze la•ze me•ra•cha•mim ve•sol•chim eesh le•a•chiv ka•a•sher gam - ha•Elohim sa•lach la•chem ba•Ma•shi•ach.

Ephesians, Chapter 5

1. Be ye therefore followers of God, as dear children;

Greek/Transliteration
1. Γίνεσθε οὖν μιμηταὶ τοῦ θεοῦ, ὡς τέκνα ἀγαπητά·

1. Ginesthe oun mimeitai tou theou, 'os tekna agapeita.

Hebrew/Transliteration
א. לָכֵן אַחֲרֵי אֱלֹהֵיכֶם תֵּלְכוּ כְּבָנִים אֲהוּבִים:

1. La•chen a•cha•rey Elohey•chem te•le•choo ke•va•nim ahoo•vim.

---

2. And walk in love, as Christ also hath loved us, and hath given himself for us an offering and a sacrifice to God for a sweet smelling savour.

Greek/Transliteration
2. καὶ περιπατεῖτε ἐν ἀγάπῃ, καθὼς καὶ ὁ χριστὸς ἠγάπησεν ἡμᾶς, καὶ παρέδωκεν ἑαυτὸν ὑπὲρ ἡμῶν προσφορὰν καὶ θυσίαν τῷ θεῷ εἰς ὀσμὴν εὐωδίας.

2. kai peripateite en agapei, kathos kai 'o christos eigapeisen 'eimas, kai paredoken 'eauton 'uper 'eimon prosphoran kai thusian to theo eis osmein euodias.

Hebrew/Transliteration
ב. וּבְאַהֲבָה תָכִינוּ צְעָדֵיכֶם כַּאֲשֶׁר גַּם-הַמָּשִׁיחַ אָהַב אֹתָנוּ וַיִּתֵּן אֶת-נַפְשׁוֹ תַּחַת נַפְשֵׁנוּ לְקָרְבָּן וָזֶבַח לְרֵיחַ נִיחֹחַ לֵאלֹהִים:

2. Oov•a•ha•va ta•chi•noo tze•a•dey•chem ka•a•sher gam - ha•Ma•shi•ach ahav o•ta•noo va•yi•ten et - naf•sho ta•chat naf•she•noo le•kor•ban va•ze•vach le•re•ach ni•cho•ach le•Elohim.

---

3. But fornication, and all uncleanness, or covetousness, let it not be once named among you, as becometh saints;

Greek/Transliteration
3. Πορνεία δὲ καὶ πᾶσα ἀκαθαρσία ἢ πλεονεξία μηδὲ ὀνομαζέσθω ἐν ὑμῖν, καθὼς πρέπει ἁγίοις·

3. Porneia de kai pasa akatharsia ei pleonexia meide onomazestho en 'umin, kathos prepei 'agiois.

Hebrew/Transliteration
ג. אַךְ זְנוּת וְכָל-זִמָּה וּבֶצַע לֹא יִשָּׁמַע עַל-פִּיכֶם כַּאֲשֶׁר נָכוֹן לְאַנְשֵׁי קֹדֶשׁ:

3. Ach z`noot ve•chol - zi•ma oo•ve•tza lo yi•sha•ma al - pi•chem ka•a•sher na•chon le•an•shey ko•desh.

4. Neither filthiness, nor foolish talking, nor jesting, which are not convenient: but rather giving of thanks.

Greek/Transliteration
4. καὶ αἰσχρότης, καὶ μωρολογία, ἢ εὐτραπελία, τὰ οὐκ ἀνήκοντα· ἀλλὰ μᾶλλον εὐχαριστία.

4. kai aischroteis, kai morologia, ei eutrapelia, ta ouk aneikonta. alla mallon eucharistia.

Hebrew/Transliteration
ד. וְכֵן לֹא דִבְרֵי נְבָלָה וְלֹא הוֹלֵלוֹת וְתָהֳלָה אֲשֶׁר לֹא לְתִפְאֶרֶת לָכֶם כִּי אִם-אִמְרֵי תְהִלָּה:

4. Ve•chen lo div•rey n`va•la ve•lo ho•le•lot ve•ta•ho•la asher lo le•tif•e•ret la•chem ki eem - eem•rey te•hi•la.

Rabbinic Jewish Commentary
This is what the Jews call נבול פה, "filthiness of the mouth", obscene words; which they say they do not use on feast days, as the Gentiles do (i): "foolish talking" does not so much design every imprudent thing that is said, as that which is wicked, corrupt, unsavoury, light, vain, idle, and unprofitable; and takes in all fabulous stories, and mimicking of fools in words and gestures: and "jesting", when it is with wantonness, and excites unto it, and is inconsistent with truth, and when the Scriptures are abused by it, and not our neighbour's edification, but hurt, is promoted by it, ought not to be used.

(i) Jarchi in Psal. lxxv. 3. Vid. Vajikra Rabba, sect. 24. fol. 165. 3.

---

5. For this ye know, that no whoremonger, nor unclean person, nor covetous man, who is an idolater, hath any inheritance in the kingdom of Christ and of God.

Greek/Transliteration
5. Τοῦτο γάρ ἐστε γινώσκοντες, ὅτι πᾶς πόρνος, ἢ ἀκάθαρτος, ἢ πλεονέκτης, ὅς ἐστιν εἰδωλολάτρης, οὐκ ἔχει κληρονομίαν ἐν τῇ βασιλείᾳ τοῦ χριστοῦ καὶ θεοῦ.

5. Touto gar este ginoskontes, 'oti pas pornos, ei akathartos, ei pleonekteis, 'os estin eidololatreis, ouk echei kleironomian en tei basileia tou christou kai theou.

Hebrew/Transliteration
ה. כִּי-זֹאת יָדֹעַ תֵּדְעוּ כִּי כָל-אִישׁ זֹנֶה וְטָמֵא אוֹ אֹהֵב בֶּצַע מַעֲשַׂקּוֹת אֲשֶׁר הוּא כְּעֹבֵד אֱלִילִים אֵין לָהֶם נַחֲלָה בְּמַלְכוּת מְשִׁיחֵנוּ וֵאלֹהֵינוּ:

5. Ki - zot ya•do ted•oo ki kol - eesh zo•ne ve•ta•me oh o•hev be•tza ma•a•sha•kot asher hoo ke•o•ved eli•lim eyn la•hem na•cha•la be•mal•choot me•shi•che•noo ve•Elohey•noo.

---

6. Let no man deceive you with vain words: for because of these things cometh the wrath of God upon the children of disobedience.

Greek/Transliteration
6. Μηδεὶς ὑμᾶς ἀπατάτω κενοῖς λόγοις· διὰ ταῦτα γὰρ ἔρχεται ἡ ὀργὴ τοῦ θεοῦ ἐπὶ τοὺς υἱοὺς τῆς ἀπειθείας.

6. Meideis 'umas apatato kenois logois. dya tauta gar erchetai 'ei orgei tou theou epi tous 'wious teis apeitheias.

Hebrew/Transliteration
ו. אַל-תִּתְּנוּ לִבְכֶם לִשְׁגוֹת בְּדִבְרֵי מַהְבְּלִים כִּי בִגְלַל-זֶה יְשַׁלַּח אֱלֹהִים חֲרוֹן אַפּוֹ בְּבָנִים סוֹרְרִים:

6. Al - tit•noo lib•chem lish•got be•div•rey ma•ha•bi•lim ki vig•lal - ze ye•sha•lach Elohim cha•ron apo be•va•nim so•re•rim.

---

7. Be not ye therefore partakers with them.

Greek/Transliteration
7. Μὴ οὖν γίνεσθε συμμέτοχοι αὐτῶν·

7. Mei oun ginesthe summetochoi auton.

Hebrew/Transliteration
ז. עַל-כֵּן לֹא תִהְיוּ חֲבֵרִים לָהֶם:

7. Al - ken lo ti•hi•yoo cha•ve•rim la•hem.

---

8. For ye were sometimes darkness, but now are ye light in the Lord: walk as children of light:

Greek/Transliteration
8. ἦτε γάρ ποτε σκότος, νῦν δὲ φῶς ἐν κυρίῳ· ὡς τέκνα φωτὸς περιπατεῖτε-

8. eite gar pote skotos, nun de phos en kurio. 'os tekna photos peripateite-

Hebrew/Transliteration
ח. כִּי-חֲשֵׁכָה הֱיִיתֶם לְפָנִים וְעַתָּה נֶהְפַּכְתֶּם לְאוֹרָה בַּאֲדֹנֵינוּ הִתְהַלְּכוּ-נָא כִּבְנֵי-אוֹר:

8. Ki - cha•she•cha he•yi•tem le•fa•nim ve•a•ta ne•he•pach•tem le•o•ra ba•Ado•ne•noo hit•hal•choo - na kiv•ney - or.

Rabbinic Jewish Commentary
Not only dark, but darkness itself; exceeding blind, dark, and ignorant, respecting spiritual things; so the Gentiles were wont to be called by the Jews, חושך, "darkness" (k) itself; of this darkness.

(k) Tzeror Hammor, fol. 1. 2.

9. (For the fruit of the Spirit is in all goodness and righteousness and truth;)

Greek/Transliteration
9. ὁ γὰρ καρπὸς τοῦ πνεύματος ἐν πάσῃ ἀγαθωσύνῃ καὶ δικαιοσύνῃ καὶ ἀληθείᾳ-

9. 'o gar karpos tou pneumatos en pasei agathosunei kai dikaiosunei kai aleitheia-

Hebrew/Transliteration
:ט. וְזֶה פְּרִי הָרוּחַ הוּא עֲשׂוֹת חֶסֶד לַכֹּל וְצֶדֶק וֶאֱמֶת

9. Ve•ze p`ri ha•Roo•ach hoo asot che•sed la•kol ve•tze•dek ve•e•met.

Rabbinic Jewish Commentary
The allusion is to fruits of trees: the believer is a tree of righteousness; Messiah Yeshua is his root; the Spirit is the sap, which supports and nourishes; and good works, under the influence of his grace, are the fruit: the Alexandrian copy, and some others, and the Vulgate Latin, Syriac, and Ethiopic versions, read "the fruit of light"; which agrees with the preceding words: and the genuine fruit of internal grace, or light.

---

10. Proving what is acceptable unto the Lord.

Greek/Transliteration
10. δοκιμάζοντες τί ἐστιν εὐάρεστον τῷ κυρίῳ·

10. dokimazontes ti estin euareston to kurio.

Hebrew/Transliteration
:י. וּבָחוֹן מַה-יִּיטַב בְּעֵינֵי אֲדֹנֵינוּ

10. Oo•va•chon ma - yi•tav be•ei•ney Ado•ney•noo.

---

11. And have no fellowship with the unfruitful works of darkness, but rather reprove them.

Greek/Transliteration
11. καὶ μὴ συγκοινωνεῖτε τοῖς ἔργοις τοῖς ἀκάρποις τοῦ σκότους, μᾶλλον δὲ καὶ ἐλέγχετε·

11. kai mei sugkoinoneite tois ergois tois akarpois tou skotous, mallon de kai elegchete.

Hebrew/Transliteration
:יא. וְאַל-תִּתְעָרְבוּ בְּמַעַלְלֵי רִיק וְחֹשֶׁךְ כִּי אִם-הוֹכֵחַ תּוֹכִיחוּן אֹתָם

11. Ve•al - tit•ar•voo be•ma•a•la•ley rik ve•cho•shech ki eem - ho•che•ach to•chi•choon o•tam.

Rabbinic Jewish Commentary
In Deu_22:10; agreeably to which, and to the passage here, is the sense of a Jewish commentators (l) who upon it observes, that that Torah

"Intimates that a righteous man, שלא ישתתף, "should have no fellowship" with a wicked man;"

This is to be unequally yoked, signified by the ox and the ass ploughing together:

(l) Baal Hatturira in Deut. xxii. 10.

---

12. For it is a shame even to speak of those things which are done of them in secret.

Greek/Transliteration
12. τὰ γὰρ κρυφῇ γινόμενα ὑπ᾽ αὐτῶν αἰσχρόν ἐστιν καὶ λέγειν.

12. ta gar kruphei ginomena 'up auton aischron estin kai legein.

Hebrew/Transliteration
יב. כִּי אֶת-אֲשֶׁר הֵם עֹשִׂים בַּמַּחְשָׁךְ חֶרְפָּה הִיא לְסַפֵּר:

12. Ki et - asher hem o•sim ba•mach•shach cher•pa hee le•sa•per.

---

13. But all things that are reproved are made manifest by the light: for whatsoever doth make manifest is light.

Greek/Transliteration
13. Τὰ δὲ πάντα ἐλεγχόμενα ὑπὸ τοῦ φωτὸς φανεροῦται· πᾶν γὰρ τὸ φανερούμενον φῶς ἐστίν.

13. Ta de panta elegchomena 'upo tou photos phaneroutai. pan gar to phaneroumenon phos estin.

Hebrew/Transliteration
יג. אַךְ כַּאֲשֶׁר יִוָּכְחוּ אָז יִגָּלוּ לָאוֹר מָה הֵם לָאוֹר הַמְגַלֶּה אֹתָם:

13. Ach ka•a•sher yi•va•che•choo az yi•ga•loo la•or ma hem la•or ham•ga•le o•tam.

---

14. Wherefore he saith, Awake thou that sleepest, and arise from the dead, and Christ shall give thee light.

Greek/Transliteration
14. Διὸ λέγει, Ἔγειρε ὁ καθεύδων καὶ ἀνάστα ἐκ τῶν νεκρῶν, καὶ ἐπιφαύσει σοι ὁ χριστός.

14. Dio legei, Egeire 'o katheudon kai anasta ek ton nekron, kai epiphausei soi 'o christos.

Hebrew/Transliteration
יד. וְעַל-זֶה נֶאֱמַר קוּם לְךָ נִרְדָּם הָקִיצָה מִן-הַמֵּתִים וְהַמָּשִׁיחַ יִזְרַח עָלֶיךָ:

14. Ve•al - ze ne•e•mar koom le•cha nir•dam ha•ki•tza min - ha•me•tim ve•ha•Mashi•ach yiz•rach a•le•cha.

Rabbinic Jewish Commentary
Some think the apostle refers to Isa_9:2; others to Isa_26:19; others to Isa_60:1; some are of opinion the words are cited out of an apocryphal book of Jeremy, or from some writing now lost; and some have thought them to be a saying of Yeshua, that was fresh in memory: it may not be improper to observe what Maimonides says (m), that

"The blowing of the trumpet in the beginning of the year had an intimation in it, as if was said, עורו ישינים "awake ye that sleep", from your sleep, and ye that slumber rouse up from your slumber, and search into your actions, and return by repentance, and remember your Creator;"

(m) Hilchot Heshuba, c. 3. sect 4.

---

15. See then that ye walk circumspectly, not as fools, but as wise,

Greek/Transliteration
15. Βλέπετε οὖν πῶς ἀκριβῶς περιπατεῖτε, μὴ ὡς ἄσοφοι, ἀλλ᾽ ὡς σοφοί,

15. Blepete oun pos akribos peripateite, mei 'os asophoi, all 'os sophoi,

Hebrew/Transliteration
:טו. וְעַתָּה תָּשִׂימוּ עַיִן עַל-דַּרְכֵיכֶם לְהֵיטִיב לָכֶת וְלֹא כָאֱוִילִים כִּי אִם-כַּחֲכָמִים

15. Ve•a•ta ta•si•moo a•yin al - dar•chey•chem le•hey•tiv le•chet ve•lo che•e•vi•lim ki eem - ka•cha•cha•mim.

---

16. Redeeming the time, because the days are evil.

Greek/Transliteration
16. ἐξαγοραζόμενοι τὸν καιρόν, ὅτι αἱ ἡμέραι πονηραί εἰσιν.

16. exagorazomenoi ton kairon, 'oti 'ai 'eimerai poneirai eisin.

Hebrew/Transliteration
:טז. דִּי עִדָּנָא זָבְנִין בַּעֲבוּר כִּי רָעִים הַיָּמִים

16. Di ee•da•na zav•nin ba•a•voor ki ra•eem ha•ya•mim.

Rabbinic Jewish Commentary
Or "buying time"; a like expression is used in Dan_2:8, which we render, gain time: but in the Chaldee text it is, "buy time": and so Jacchiades, a Jewish commentator on the place, renders it, העת הזאת איתאם נמכרים, "ye buy this opportunity"; and the Septuagint version uses the same phrase the apostle does here; but there it seems to signify a study to prolong time, to put off the business to another season; but here taking time for a space of time, it denotes a careful and diligent use of it, an improvement of it to the best advantage; and shows that it is valuable and precious, and is not to be trifled with, and squandered away,

and be lost, as it may be; for it can neither be recalled nor prolonged: and taking it for an opportunity of doing good to ourselves or others, it signifies that no opportunity of discharging our duty to God and man, of attending on the word and ordinances of the Gospel, and to the private and public exercises of religion, of gaining advantage to our own souls, or of gaining the souls of others, and of doing good either to the bodies or souls of men, should be neglected; but even all risks should be run, and means used to enjoy it: in the Syriac and Chaldee languages, זמנא, "time", comes from זבן, "to redeem".

---

17. Wherefore be ye not unwise, but understanding what the will of the Lord is.

Greek/Transliteration
17. Διὰ τοῦτο μὴ γίνεσθε ἄφρονες, ἀλλὰ συνιέντες τί τὸ θέλημα τοῦ κυρίου.

17. Dya touto mei ginesthe aphrones, alla sunientes ti to theleima tou kuriou.

Hebrew/Transliteration
יז. וְלֹא תִהְיוּ חַסְרֵי לֵב כִּי אִם-תַּשְׂכִּילוּ לָדַעַת מַה חֵפֶץ אֲדֹנֵינוּ:

17. Ve•lo ti•hi•yoo chas•rey lev ki eem - tash•ki•loo la•da•at ma che•fetz Ado•ney•noo.

Rabbinic Jewish Commentary
The Alexandrian copy, Syriac, Arabic, and Ethiopic versions, read the words as an exhortation, "understand ye the will of God".

---

18. And be not drunk with wine, wherein is excess; but be filled with the Spirit;

Greek/Transliteration
18. Καὶ μὴ μεθύσκεσθε οἴνῳ, ἐν ᾧ ἐστὶν ἀσωτία, ἀλλὰ πληροῦσθε ἐν πνεύματι,

18. Kai mei methuskesthe oino, en 'o estin asotia, alla pleirousthe en pneumati,

Hebrew/Transliteration
יח. וְאַל-תִּסָּבְאוּ יַיִן אֲשֶׁר רוּחַ עֲוִעִים בְּקִרְבּוֹ רַק הִמָּלְאוּ רוּחַ עֶלְיוֹן:

18. Ve•al - tis•be•oo ya•yin asher roo•ach eev•eem be•kir•bo rak hi•mal•oo Roo•ach el•yon.

Rabbinic Jewish Commentary
but be filled with the Spirit; that is, "with the Holy Spirit", as read the Vulgate Latin and Ethiopic versions.

---

19. Speaking to yourselves in psalms and hymns and spiritual songs, singing and making melody in your heart to the Lord;

Greek/Transliteration
19. λαλοῦντες ἑαυτοῖς ψαλμοῖς καὶ ὕμνοις καὶ ᾠδαῖς πνευματικαῖς, ᾄδοντες καὶ ψάλλοντες ἐν τῇ καρδίᾳ ὑμῶν τῷ κυρίῳ,

19. lalountes 'eautois psalmois kai 'umnois kai odais pneumatikais, adontes kai psallontes en tei kardia 'umon to kurio,

Hebrew/Transliteration
יט. וְאִמְרוּ בְּנַפְשְׁכֶם תְּהִלּוֹת וְשִׁירוֹת וְזִמְרוֹת יָהּ שִׁירוּ וְזַמְּרוּ בִּלְבַבְכֶם לַיהוָֹה:

19. Ve•eem•roo ve•naf•she•chem te•hi•lot ve•shi•rot ve•zim•rot Ya shi•roo ve•zam•roo vil•vav•chem la`Adonai.

Rabbinic Jewish Commentary
The psalms in general are called hymns, by Philo the Jew (n); and songs and hymns by Josephus (o); and שירות ותושבחות, "songs and praises", or "hymns", in the Talmud (p): and by "spiritual songs" are meant the same Psalms of David, Asaph and the titles of many of them are songs, and sometimes a psalm and song, and song and psalm, a song of degrees; together with all other Scriptural songs, written by inspired men; and which are called "spiritual", because they are indited by the Spirit of God, consist of spiritual matter, and are designed for spiritual edification; and are opposed to all profane, loose, and wanton songs: these three words answer to מזמורים תהלים שירים the several titles of David's Psalms.

(n) De Mutat. Nomin. p. 1062. & alibi. (o) Antiqu. l. 7. c. 12. sect. 3. (p) T. Bab. Sanhedrin, fol. 94. 1.

---

20. Giving thanks always for all things unto God and the Father in the name of our Lord Jesus Christ;

Greek/Transliteration
20. εὐχαριστοῦντες πάντοτε ὑπὲρ πάντων ἐν ὀνόματι τοῦ κυρίου ἡμῶν Ἰησοῦ χριστοῦ τῷ θεῷ καὶ πατρί,

20. eucharistountes pantote 'uper panton en onomati tou kuriou 'eimon Yeisou christou to theo kai patri,

Hebrew/Transliteration
כ. וְעַל-הַכֹּל הוֹדוּ לֵאלֹהֵינוּ אָבִינוּ תָּמִיד בְּשֵׁם יֵשׁוּעַ הַמָּשִׁיחַ אֲדֹנֵינוּ:

20. Ve•al - ha•kol ho•doo le•Elohey•noo Avi•noo ta•mid be•shem Yeshua ha•Ma•shi•ach Ado•ney•noo.

---

21. Submitting yourselves one to another in the fear of God.

Greek/Transliteration
21. ὑποτασσόμενοι ἀλλήλοις ἐν φόβῳ χριστοῦ.

21. 'upotassomenoi alleilois en phobo christou.

Hebrew/Transliteration
כא. הִכָּנְעוּ אִישׁ מִפְּנֵי אָחִיו בְּיִרְאַת אֱלֹהִים:

21. Hi•kan•oo eesh mip•ney a•chiv be•yir•at Elohim.

Rabbinic Jewish Commentary
The Ethiopic version renders it, "subject yourselves to your brethren".

---

22. Wives, submit yourselves unto your own husbands, as unto the Lord.

Greek/Transliteration
22. Αἱ γυναῖκες, τοῖς ἰδίοις ἀνδράσιν ὑποτάσσεσθε, ὡς τῷ κυρίῳ.

22. 'Ai gunaikes, tois idiois andrasin 'upotassesthe, 'os to kurio.

Hebrew/Transliteration
כב: וְהַנָּשִׁים נִכְנָעוֹת תִּהְיֶינָה מִפְּנֵי בַעֲלֵיהֶן כְּמוֹ מִפְּנֵי הָאָדוֹן

22. Ve•ha•na•shim nich•na•ot ti•hi•ye•na mip•ney va•a•ley•hen k`mo mip•ney ha•Adon.

---

23. For the husband is the head of the wife, even as Christ is the head of the church: and he is the saviour of the body.

Greek/Transliteration
23. ὅτι ἀνήρ ἐστιν κεφαλὴ τῆς γυναικός, ὡς καὶ ὁ χριστὸς κεφαλὴ τῆς ἐκκλησίας, καὶ αὐτός ἐστιν σωτὴρ τοῦ σώματος.

23. 'oti aneir estin kephalei teis gunaikos, 'os kai 'o christos kephalei teis ekkleisias, kai autos estin soteir tou somatos.

Hebrew/Transliteration
כג: כִּי הַבַּעַל הוּא-רֹאשׁ הָאִשָּׁה כְּמוֹ גַם-הַמָּשִׁיחַ רֹאשׁ הָעֵדָה וְהוּא הַמּוֹשִׁיעַ לִגְוִיָּתוֹ

23. Ki ha•ba•al hoo - rosh ha•ee•sha k`mo gam - ha•Ma•shi•ach rosh ha•e•da ve•hoo ha•mo•shia lig•vi•ya•to.

---

24. Therefore as the church is subject unto Christ, so let the wives be to their own husbands in every thing.

Greek/Transliteration
24. Ἀλλ᾽ ὥσπερ ἡ ἐκκλησία ὑποτάσσεται τῷ χριστῷ, οὕτως καὶ αἱ γυναῖκες τοῖς ἰδίοις ἀνδράσιν ἐν παντί.

24. All 'osper 'ei ekkleisia 'upotassetai to christo, 'outos kai 'ai gunaikes tois idiois andrasin en panti.

Hebrew/Transliteration
כד: אַךְ כַּאֲשֶׁר נִכְנַעַת הָעֵדָה מִלִּפְנֵי מְשִׁיחָהּ כֵּן גַּם-הַנָּשִׁים תִּכָּנַעְנָה מִלִּפְנֵי בַעֲלֵיהֶן בְּכָל-אָרְחוֹתָן

24. Ach ka•a•sher nich•na•at ha•e•da mi•lif•ney me•shi•cha ken gam - ha•na•shim ti•ka•na•a•na mi•lif•ney va•a•ley•hen be•chol - or•cho•tan.

25. Husbands, love your wives, even as Christ also loved the church, and gave himself for it;

Greek/Transliteration
25. Οἱ ἄνδρες, ἀγαπᾶτε τὰς γυναῖκας ἑαυτῶν, καθὼς καὶ ὁ χριστὸς ἠγάπησεν τὴν ἐκκλησίαν, καὶ ἑαυτὸν παρέδωκεν ὑπὲρ αὐτῆς·

25. 'Oi andres, agapate tas gunaikas 'eauton, kathos kai 'o christos eigapeisen tein ekkleisian, kai 'eauton paredoken 'uper auteis.

Hebrew/Transliteration
:כה. וְאַתֶּם אֲנָשִׁים אֱהֲבוּ אֶת-נְשֵׁיכֶם כַּאֲשֶׁר גַּם-הַמָּשִׁיחַ אֶת-עֲדָתוֹ אָהֵב וַיִּתֵּן אֶת-נַפְשׁוֹ תַּחַת נַפְשָׁהּ

25. Ve•a•tem a•na•shim e•he•voo et - n`shey•chem ka•a•sher gam - ha•Ma•shi•ach et - ada•to ahev va•yi•ten et - naf•sho ta•chat naf•sha.

---

26. That he might sanctify and cleanse it with the washing of water by the word,

Greek/Transliteration
26. ἵνα αὐτὴν ἁγιάσῃ, καθαρίσας τῷ λουτρῷ τοῦ ὕδατος ἐν ῥήματι,

26. 'ina autein 'agyasei, katharisas to loutro tou 'udatos en 'reimati,

Hebrew/Transliteration
:כו. לְמַעַן יְקַדְּשֶׁנָּה בִדְבָרוֹ אַחֲרֵי אֲשֶׁר-רָחַץ אֹתָהּ בְּמִקְוֵה מָיִם

26. Le•ma•an ye•kad•she•na vid•va•ro a•cha•rey asher - ra•chatz o•ta be•mik•ve ma•yim.

---

27. That he might present it to himself a glorious church, not having spot, or wrinkle, or any such thing; but that it should be holy and without blemish.

Greek/Transliteration
27. ἵνα παραστήσῃ αὐτὴν ἑαυτῷ ἔνδοξον τὴν ἐκκλησίαν, μὴ ἔχουσαν σπῖλον ἢ ῥυτίδα ἤ τι τῶν τοιούτων, ἀλλ᾽ ἵνα ᾖ ἁγία καὶ ἄμωμος.

27. 'ina parasteisei autein 'eauto endoxon tein ekkleisian, mei echousan spilon ei 'rutida ei ti ton toiouton, all 'ina ei 'agia kai amomos.

Hebrew/Transliteration
:כז. לְהָקִים לוֹ עֵדָה נִכְבָּדָה בָּרָה וּתְמִימָה מִבְּלִי בַהֶרֶת אוֹ פְּחֶתֶת וְכָל-מוּם אֵין בָּהּ

27. Le•ha•kim lo eda nich•ba•da ba•ra oot•mi•ma mi•b`li va•he•ret oh pe•che•tet ve•chol - moom eyn ba.

Rabbinic Jewish Commentary
The allusion seems to be to the customs and practices of the Jews, in their espousals: if a man espoused a woman on condition that she had no spots in her, and afterwards spots were found in her, she was not espoused; for spots or blemishes, as in priests, so in women,

render them unfit; as the one for service, so the other for marriage; and they reckon up eight several spots or blemishes, for which they may be rejected (q): but Messiah's people has no spots or blemishes, nor anything like them; and will never be rejected by him, but will be always pleasing in his sight.

(q) Misn. Cetubot, c. 7. sect. 7, 8. Maimon. & Bartenora in ib.

---

28. So ought men to love their wives as their own bodies. He that loveth his wife loveth himself.

Greek/Transliteration
28. Οὕτως ὀφείλουσιν οἱ ἄνδρες ἀγαπᾶν τὰς ἑαυτῶν γυναῖκας ὡς τὰ ἑαυτῶν σώματα. Ὁ ἀγαπῶν τὴν ἑαυτοῦ γυναῖκα, ἑαυτὸν ἀγαπᾷ·

28. 'Outos opheilousin 'oi andres agapan tas 'eauton gunaikas 'os ta 'eauton somata. 'O agapon tein 'eautou gunaika, 'eauton agapa.

Hebrew/Transliteration
-כח. כֵּן הַמִּצְוָה עַל - הָאֲנָשִׁים לְאַהֲבָה אֶת-נְשֵׁיהֶם כְּגוּפָם כִּי הָאֹהֵב אֶת-אִשְׁתּוֹ הוּא אֹהֵב אֶת-עַצְמוֹ וְאֶת בְּשָׂרוֹ:

28. Ken ha•mitz•va al - ha•a•na•shim le•a•ha•va et - n`shey•hem ke•goo•fam ki ha•o•hev et - eesh•to hoo o•hev et - atz•mo ve•et - be•sa•ro.

Rabbinic Jewish Commentary
It is a common saying with the Jews, that a man's wife is כגופו, "as his own body" (r); and it is one of the precepts of their wise men, that a man should honour his wife more than his body, ואהבה כגופו, and "love her as his body" (s); for as they also say, they are but one body (t); the apostle seems to speak in the language of his countrymen; however, his doctrine and theirs agree in this point.

(r) T. Bab. Beracot, fol. 24. 1. & Becorot, fol. 35. 2. Maimon. Hilchot Becorot, c. 2. sect. 17. Tzeror Hammor, fol. 18. 2. (s) T. Bab. Yebamot, fol. 62. 2. & Sanhedrin, fol. 76. 2. Derech Eretz, fol. 17. 4. Maimon Hilchot Ishot, c. 15. sect. 19. (t) Tzeror Hammor, fol. 6. 3.

---

29. For no man ever yet hated his own flesh; but nourisheth and cherisheth it, even as the Lord the church:

Greek/Transliteration
29. οὐδεὶς γάρ ποτε τὴν ἑαυτοῦ σάρκα ἐμίσησεν, ἀλλ᾽ ἐκτρέφει καὶ θάλπει αὐτήν, καθὼς καὶ ὁ κύριος τὴν ἐκκλησίαν·

29. oudeis gar pote tein 'eautou sarka emiseisen, all ektrephei kai thalpei autein, kathos kai 'o kurios tein ekkleisian.

Hebrew/Transliteration
:כט. כִּי מֵעוֹלָם לֹא-שָׂנֵא אִישׁ אֶת-בְּשָׂרוֹ רַק מְכַלְכֵּל וּמְפַנֵּק אֹתוֹ כַּאֲשֶׁר גַּם-הַמָּשִׁיחַ אֶת-עֲדָתוֹ

29. Ki me•o•lam lo - sa•ne eesh et - be•sa•ro rak me•chal•kel oom•fa•nek o•to ka•a•sher gam - ha•Ma•shi•ach et - ada•to.

Rabbinic Jewish Commentary
For no man ever yet hated his own flesh,.... This is unnatural, contrary to the first principles of nature; see Isa_58:7; which the (u) Jews understand of one that is near akin, and there is none nearer than a wife.

(u) Jarchi in loc. & R. Sol. Urbin. in Ohel Moed, fol. 85. 1.

---

30. For we are members of his body, of his flesh, and of his bones.

Greek/Transliteration
30. ὅτι μέλη ἐσμὲν τοῦ σώματος αὐτοῦ, ἐκ τῆς σαρκὸς αὐτοῦ καὶ ἐκ τῶν ὀστέων αὐτοῦ.

30. 'oti melei esmen tou somatos autou, ek teis sarkos autou kai ek ton osteon autou.

Hebrew/Transliteration
ל: כִּי-אֲבָרֵי גוּפוֹ אֲנַחְנוּ מִבְּשָׂרוֹ וּמֵעֲצָמָיו

30. Ki - eva•rey goo•fo a•nach•noo mib•sa•ro oo•me•a•tza•mav.

---

31. For this cause shall a man leave his father and mother, and shall be joined unto his wife, and they two shall be one flesh.

Greek/Transliteration
31. ἀντὶ τούτου καταλείψει ἄνθρωπος τὸν πατέρα αὐτοῦ καὶ τὴν μητέρα, καὶ προσκολληθήσεται πρὸς τὴν γυναῖκα αὐτοῦ, καὶ ἔσονται οἱ δύο εἰς σάρκα μίαν.

31. anti toutou kataleipsei anthropos ton patera autou kai tein meitera, kai proskolleitheisetai pros tein gunaika autou, kai esontai 'oi duo eis sarka mian.

Hebrew/Transliteration
לא: עַל-כֵּן יַעֲזָב-אִישׁ אֶת-אָבִיו וְאֶת-אִמּוֹ וְדָבַק בְּאִשְׁתּוֹ וְהָיוּ שְׁנֵיהֶם לְבָשָׂר אֶחָד

31. Al - ken ya•a•zov - eesh et - aviv ve•et - ee•mo ve•da•vak be•eesh•to ve•ha•yoo sh`ney•hem le•va•sar e•chad.

Rabbinic Jewish Commentary
Woman was taken from the side of man therefore at intimacy they would become one once again. "One flesh" is a reminder of how both were once one person who now share the flesh of the other but are now a unit.

---

32. This is a great mystery: but I speak concerning Christ and the church.

Greek/Transliteration
32. Τὸ μυστήριον τοῦτο μέγα ἐστίν· ἐγὼ δὲ λέγω εἰς χριστὸν καὶ εἰς τὴν ἐκκλησίαν.

32. To musteirion touto mega estin. ego de lego eis christon kai eis tein ekkleisian.

Hebrew/Transliteration
לב. גָּדוֹל הַסּוֹד הַזֶּה וַאֲנִי מְדַבֵּר עַל-הַמָּשִׁיחַ וְעַל-עֲדָתוֹ:

32. Ga•dol ha•sod ha•ze va•a•ni me•da•ber al - ha•Ma•shi•ach ve•al - ada•to.

Rabbinic Jewish Commentary
The great mystery is in the Hebrew name for man and woman, איש man and אשה woman; which contain the two letters for the name of God, the *yod* and the *hey*. When joined together they form the short version of the name Yah for YHWH. When the *yod* and the *hey* are removed from the name of man and woman it forms the word for fire, אש. Fire is the symbol for God's judgment to those who turn away from Him.

---

33. Nevertheless let every one of you in particular so love his wife even as himself; and the wife see that she reverence her husband.

Greek/Transliteration
33. Πλὴν καὶ ὑμεῖς οἱ καθ᾽ ἕνα, ἕκαστος τὴν ἑαυτοῦ γυναῖκα οὕτως ἀγαπάτω ὡς ἑαυτόν· ἡ δὲ γυνὴ ἵνα φοβῆται τὸν ἄνδρα.

33. Plein kai 'umeis 'oi kath 'ena, 'ekastos tein 'eautou gunaika 'outos agapato 'os 'eauton. 'ei de gunei 'ina phobeitai ton andra.

Hebrew/Transliteration
לג. אַךְ גַּם-אַתֶּם אִישׁ אִישׁ מִכֶּם יֶאֱהַב אֶת-אִשְׁתּוֹ כְּנַפְשׁוֹ וְהָאִשָּׁה אֶת-בַּעְלָהּ תִּירָא:

33. Ach gam - atem eesh eesh mi•kem ye•e•hav et - eesh•to ke•naf•sho ve•ha•ee•sha et - ba•a•la ti•ra.

Ephesians, Chapter 6

1. Children, obey your parents in the Lord: for this is right.

Greek/Transliteration
1. Τὰ τέκνα, ὑπακούετε τοῖς γονεῦσιν ὑμῶν ἐν κυρίῳ· τοῦτο γάρ ἐστιν δίκαιον.

1. Ta tekna, 'upakouete tois goneusin 'umon en kurio. touto gar estin dikaion.

Hebrew/Transliteration
א. שִׁמְעוּ בָנִים בְּקוֹל יֹלְדֵיכֶם בַּאֲדֹנֵינוּ כִּי דָבָר יָשָׁר הוּא:

1. Shim•oo va•nim be•kol yol•dey•chem ba•Ado•ne•noo ki da•var ya•shar hoo.

---

2. Honour thy father and mother; (which is the first commandment with promise;)

Greek/Transliteration
2. Τίμα τὸν πατέρα σου καὶ τὴν μητέρα ἥτις ἐστὶν ἐντολὴ πρώτη ἐν ἐπαγγελίᾳ,

2. Tima ton patera sou kai tein meitera 'eitis estin entolei protei en epangelia,

Hebrew/Transliteration
ב. כַּבֵּד אֶת-אָבִיךָ וְאֶת-אִמֶּךָ זֹאת הַמִּצְוָה הָרִאשׁוֹנָה אֲשֶׁר שְׂכָרָהּ בְּצִדָּהּ:

2. Ka•bed et - avi•cha ve•et - ee•me•cha zot ha•mitz•va ha•ri•sho•na asher s`cha•ra be•tzi•da.

Rabbinic Jewish Commentary
So the Jews explain כבוד, "the honour" due to parents, by, מאכיל, "giving them food, drink", and "clothing", unloosing their shoes, and leading them out and in (x).

It is the fifth commandment in the decalogue, but the first that has a promise annexed to it: it is reckoned by the Jews (y) the weightiest of the weightiest commands of the Torah; and the reward bestowed on it, is length of days, as follows.

(x) T. Hieros. Kiddushin, fol. 61. 2. T. Bab. Kiddushin, fol. 31. 1, 2. Maimon. & Bartenora in Misn. Kiddushin, c. 1. sect. 7. (y) Debarim Rabba, sect. 6. fol. 241. 3.

---

3. That it may be well with thee, and thou mayest live long on the earth.

Greek/Transliteration
3. ἵνα εὖ σοι γένηται, καὶ ἔσῃ μακροχρόνιος ἐπὶ τῆς γῆς.

3. 'ina eu soi geneitai, kai esei makrochronios epi teis geis.

Hebrew/Transliteration
ג. לְמַעַן יִיטַב לָךְ וּלְמַעַן יַאֲרִיכוּן יָמֶיךָ עַל-הָאֲדָמָה:

3. Le•ma•an yi•tav lach ool•ma•an ya•a•ri•choon ya•me•cha al - ha•a•da•ma.

Rabbinic Jewish Commentary

In this world, and that which is to come; see Deu_5:16. The Jews (z) say,

"There are four things, which if a man does, he eats the fruit of them in this world, and the capital part remains for him in the world to come; and they are these, כיבוד אב ואם; "Honouring father and mother", doing acts of beneficence, making peace between a man and his neighbour, and learning of the Torah, which answers to them all."

On those words in Deu_32:47, the Jews (a) have this paraphrase;

"Because it is your life, זה כיבוד אב ואם, "this is honouring father and mother; and through this thing ye shall prolong your days", this is beneficence."

It may be observed, that the words in this promissory part are not the same as in the decalogue, where they stand thus, "that thy days may be long upon the land which the Lord thy God giveth thee", Exo_20:12, referring to the land of Canaan; for the Torah in the form of it, in which it was delivered by Moses, only concerned the people of the Jews; wherefore to suit this Torah, and the promise of it, to others, the apostle alters the language of it.

(z) Misna Peah, c. 1. sect. 1. T. Bab. Sabbat, fol. 127. 1, & Kiddushin, fol. 40. 1. (a) T. Hieros. Peah, fol. 15. 4.

---

4. And, ye fathers, provoke not your children to wrath: but bring them up in the nurture and admonition of the Lord.

Greek/Transliteration
4. Καὶ οἱ πατέρες, μὴ παροργίζετε τὰ τέκνα ὑμῶν, ἀλλ᾽ ἐκτρέφετε αὐτὰ ἐν παιδείᾳ καὶ νουθεσίᾳ κυρίου.

4. Kai 'oi pateres, mei parorgizete ta tekna 'umon, all ektrephete auta en paideia kai nouthesia kuriou.

Hebrew/Transliteration
ד. וְהָאָבוֹת אַל-תָּעִירוּ חֲמַת בְּנֵיכֶם כִּי אִם-תְּגַדְּלוּם בְּמוּסַר אֲדֹנֵינוּ וּבְתוֹכַחְתּוֹ:

4. Ve•ha•a•vot al - ta•ee•roo cha•mat b`ney•chem ki eem - te•gad•loom be•moo•sar Ado•ney•noo oov•to•chach•to.

---

5. Servants, be obedient to them that are your masters according to the flesh, with fear and trembling, in singleness of your heart, as unto Christ;

Greek/Transliteration
5. Οἱ δοῦλοι, ὑπακούετε τοῖς κυρίοις κατὰ σάρκα, μετὰ φόβου καὶ τρόμου, ἐν ἁπλότητι τῆς καρδίας ὑμῶν, ὡς τῷ χριστῷ·

5. 'Oi douloi, 'upakouete tois kuriois kata sarka, meta phobou kai tromou, en 'aploteiti teis kardias 'umon, 'os to christo.

Hebrew/Transliteration
ה. וְאַתֶּם עֲבָדִים הַקְשִׁיבוּ לְקוֹל אֲדֹנֵיכֶם אֲדֹנֵי גְוִיַּתְכֶם בְּיִרְאָה וּרְעָדָה וּבְתָם-לֵב כְּמוֹ לַמָּשִׁיחַ:

5. Ve•a•tem a•va•dim hak•shi•voo le•kol ado•ney•chem ado•ney ge•vi•yat•chem be•yir•ah oor•a•da oov•tom - lev k`mo la•Mashi•ach.

---

6. Not with eyeservice, as menpleasers; but as the servants of Christ, doing the will of God from the heart;

Greek/Transliteration
6. μὴ κατ᾽ ὀφθαλμοδουλείαν ὡς ἀνθρωπάρεσκοι, ἀλλ᾽ ὡς δοῦλοι τοῦ χριστοῦ, ποιοῦντες τὸ θέλημα τοῦ θεοῦ ἐκ ψυχῆς,

6. mei kat ophthalmodouleian 'os anthropareskoi, all 'os douloi tou christou, poiountes to theleima tou theou ek psucheis,

Hebrew/Transliteration
ו. וְלֹא בַעֲבֹדָה לְמַרְאֵה עֵינַיִם לְהָפִיק רָצוֹן מִבְּנֵי אָדָם כִּי אִם-כְּעַבְדֵי הַמָּשִׁיחַ הָעֹשִׂים רְצוֹן אֱלֹהִים בְּכָל-נַפְשָׁם:

6. Ve•lo va•a•vo•da le•mar•eh ey•na•yim le•ha•fik ra•tzon mi•b`ney adam ki eem - ke•av•dey ha•Ma•shi•ach ha•o•sim r`tzon Elohim be•chol - naf•sham.

---

7. With good will doing service, as to the Lord, and not to men:

Greek/Transliteration
7. μετ᾽ εὐνοίας δουλεύοντες ὡς τῷ κυρίῳ καὶ οὐκ ἀνθρώποις·

7. met eunoias douleuontes 'os to kurio kai ouk anthropois.

Hebrew/Transliteration
ז. וְעֹבְדִים מִטּוּב לֵב כְּעַבְדֵי אֲדֹנֵינוּ וְלֹא כְעַבְדֵי אֲנָשִׁים:

7. Ve•ov•dim mi•toov lev ke•ov•dey Ado•ney•noo ve•lo ke•ov•dey a•na•shim.

Rabbinic Jewish Commentary
To their masters; not grudgingly, with an ill will; no otherwise, nor longer than when they are forced to it; but of a ready mind, and with a cheerful spirit, taking delight in their work, and reckoning it a pleasure to serve their masters; as an Israelite that is not sold, who does his work ברצונו, "with his good will", and according to his own mind (b).

(b) Maimon. Hilchot Abadim, c. 1. sect. 7.

---

8. Knowing that whatsoever good thing any man doeth, the same shall he receive of the Lord, whether he be bond or free.

Greek/Transliteration
8. εἰδότες ὅτι ὃ ἐάν τι ἕκαστος ποιήσῃ ἀγαθόν, τοῦτο κομιεῖται παρὰ τοῦ κυρίου, εἴτε δοῦλος, εἴτε ἐλεύθερος.

8. eidotes 'oti 'o ean ti 'ekastos poieisei agathon, touto komieitai para tou kuriou, eite doulos, eite eleutheros.

Hebrew/Transliteration
ח. הֲלֹא יְדַעְתֶּם כָּל-דָּבָר טוֹב אֲשֶׁר יַעֲשֶׂה אֹתוֹ הָאָדָם אֲדֹנֵינוּ יְשַׁלֶּם-לוֹ אִם-עֶבֶד הוּא אוֹ בֶן-חוֹרִים:

8. Ha•lo ye•da•a•tem kol - da•var tov asher ya•a•se o•to ha•a•dam Ado•ney•noo ye•sha•lem - lo eem - eved hoo oh ven - cho•rim.

---

9. And, ye masters, do the same things unto them, forbearing threatening: knowing that your Master also is in heaven; neither is there respect of persons with him.

Greek/Transliteration
9. Καὶ οἱ κύριοι, τὰ αὐτὰ ποιεῖτε πρὸς αὐτούς, ἀνιέντες τὴν ἀπειλήν· εἰδότες ὅτι καὶ ὑμῶν αὐτῶν ὁ κύριός ἐστιν ἐν οὐρανοῖς, καὶ προσωποληψία οὐκ ἔστιν παρ᾽ αὐτῷ.

9. Kai 'oi kurioi, ta auta poieite pros autous, anientes tein apeilein. eidotes 'oti kai 'umon auton 'o kurios estin en ouranois, kai prosopoleipsia ouk estin par auto.

Hebrew/Transliteration
ט. וְגַם-אַתֶּם אֲדֹנִים כֵּן תַּעֲשׂוּ לָהֶם חִדְלוּ מִגְּעָר-בָּם בַּאֲשֶׁר יְדַעְתֶּם כִּי גַם-לָהֶם וְלָכֶם אָדוֹן בַּשָּׁמַיִם אֲשֶׁר אֵין עִמּוֹ מַשּׂוֹא פָנִים:

9. Ve•gam - atem ado•nim ken ta•a•soo la•hem chid•loo mig•or - bam ba•a•sher ye•da•a•tem ki gam - la•hem ve•la•chem Adon ba•sha•ma•yim asher eyn ee•mo ma•so fa•nim.

Rabbinic Jewish Commentary
And this is a rule given by the Jews (c), that a master should not multiply clamour and anger, but should speak him (his servant) quietly, and in a still manner, and he will hear his objections, or arguments and reasons:

Jew or Gentile; whether in this, or that state and condition, or in such and such circumstances of life; whether masters or servants, bond or free, or whether Canaanitish or Hebrew servants; between which the Jews (d) made a difference, and allowed of rigour to be used to the one, but required mercy and kindness to be showed to the other; and so were respecters of persons.

(c) Maimon. Hilchot Abadim, c. 9. sect. 8. (d) Maimon. Hilchot Abadim, c. 9. sect. 8.

---

10. Finally, my brethren, be strong in the Lord, and in the power of his might.

Greek/Transliteration
10. Τὸ λοιπόν, ἀδελφοί μου, ἐνδυναμοῦσθε ἐν κυρίῳ, καὶ ἐν τῷ κράτει τῆς ἰσχύος αὐτοῦ.

10. To loipon, adelphoi mou, endunamousthe en kurio, kai en to kratei teis ischuos autou.

Hebrew/Transliteration
:י. וְיֶתֶר הַדְּבָרִים אֶחָי הִנְנִי אֹמֵר הִתְעוֹדְדוּ בַּאֲדֹנֵינוּ וּבְעֹז גְּבוּרָתוֹ

10. Ve•ye•ter ha•d`va•rim e•chai hi•ne•ni o•mer hit•o•de•doo va•Ado•ney•noo oov•oz ge•voo•ra•to.

---

11. Put on the whole armour of God, that ye may be able to stand against the wiles of the devil.

Greek/Transliteration
11. Ἐνδύσασθε τὴν πανοπλίαν τοῦ θεοῦ, πρὸς τὸ δύνασθαι ὑμᾶς στῆναι πρὸς τὰς μεθοδείας τοῦ διαβόλου.

11. Endusasthe tein panoplian tou theou, pros to dunasthai 'umas steinai pros tas methodeias tou dyabolou.

Hebrew/Transliteration
:יא. חִגְרוּ כְלִי-נֶשֶׁק אֱלֹהִים לְמַעַן תּוּכְלוּ לָקוּם לִפְנֵי נִכְלֵי הַשָּׂטָן

11. Chig•roo ch`ley - ne•shek Elohim le•ma`an tooch•loo la•koom lif•ney nich•ley ha•Satan.

---

12. For we wrestle not against flesh and blood, but against principalities, against powers, against the rulers of the darkness of this world, against spiritual wickedness in high places.

Greek/Transliteration
12. Ὅτι οὐκ ἔστιν ἡμῖν ἡ πάλη πρὸς αἷμα καὶ σάρκα, ἀλλὰ πρὸς τὰς ἀρχάς, πρὸς τὰς ἐξουσίας, πρὸς τοὺς κοσμοκράτορας τοῦ σκότους τοῦ αἰῶνος τούτου, πρὸς τὰ πνευματικὰ τῆς πονηρίας ἐν τοῖς ἐπουρανίοις.

12. 'Oti ouk estin 'eimin 'ei palei pros 'aima kai sarka, alla pros tas archas, pros tas exousias, pros tous kosmokratoras tou skotous tou aionos toutou, pros ta pneumatika teis poneirias en tois epouraniois.

Hebrew/Transliteration
יב. כִּי לֹא עִם-בָּשָׂר וָדָם מִלְחָמָה לָנוּ אַךְ עִם-אַלּוּפִים וְאֵילִים שַׁלִּיטֵי אֶרֶץ מַאְפֵּלְיָה וּמַלְאֲכֵי רָעִים אֲשֶׁר בַּמְּרוֹמִים:

12. Ki lo eem - ba•sar va•dam mil•cha•ma la•noo ach eem - aloo•fim ve•ey•lim sha•li•tey e•retz Ma•a•pelya oo•mal•a•chey ra•eem asher bam•ro•mim.

Rabbinic Jewish Commentary
The Syriac, Arabic, and Ethiopic versions, and some copies, read "you", instead of "we". For this wrestling, as Philo the Jew says (e), concerning Jacob's wrestling, is not of the body, but of the soul.

The Jews use this very word, the apostle does here, of the messenger of death; who is called darkness (f); and the devil is called by them, שר של חושך, "the prince of darkness" (g); and mention is made by them of חשוכי עלמא, "the darkness of the world" (h); from whom the apostle seems to have taken these phrases, as being in common use among the Jews; who also use it of civil governors (i), and render it, as here, "the rulers of the world", and say it signifies monarchs, such as rule from one end of the world to the other (k): some copies, and the Ethiopic version, leave out the phrase, of this world.

The Syriac and Ethiopic versions render it, "under", or "beneath heaven"; and the Arabic version, "in the air".

(e) Leg. Allegor. l. 2. p. 96, (f) Vajikra Rabba, sect. 18. fol. 160. 1. & Shirhashirim Rabba, fol. 25. 4. (g) Pesikta in Kettoreth Hassammim in Targum in Gen. fol. 9. 4. Raziel, fol. 13. 1. (h) Zohar in Lev. fol. 19. 3. (i) Bereshit Rabba, sect. 58. fol. 51. 2. (k) Tanchuma & Aruch in Guidon. Diet. Syr. Chal. p. 169.

---

13. Wherefore take unto you the whole armour of God, that ye may be able to withstand in the evil day, and having done all, to stand.

Greek/Transliteration
13. Διὰ τοῦτο ἀναλάβετε τὴν πανοπλίαν τοῦ θεοῦ, ἵνα δυνηθῆτε ἀντιστῆναι ἐν τῇ ἡμέρᾳ τῇ πονηρᾷ, καὶ ἅπαντα κατεργασάμενοι στῆναι.

13. Dya touto analabete tein panoplian tou theou, 'ina duneitheite antisteinai en tei 'eimera tei poneira, kai 'apanta katergasamenoi steinai.

Hebrew/Transliteration
יג. עַל־כֵּן קְחוּ לָכֶם כְּלִי־נֶשֶׁק אֱלֹהִים וְתוּכְלוּ לְהִתְיַצֵּב בִּפְנֵי הַקָּמִים עֲלֵיכֶם בְּיוֹם רָע וּלְהִשָּׁאֵר נִצָּבִים בִּכְלוֹת כָּל־קְרָב:

13. Al - ken ke•choo la•chem k`ley - ne•shek Elohim ve•tooch•loo le•hit•ya•tzev bif•ney ha•ka•mim aley•chem be•yom ra ool•hi•sha•er ni•tza•vim bich•lot kol - k`rav.

---

14. Stand therefore, having your loins girt about with truth, and having on the breastplate of righteousness;

Greek/Transliteration
14. Στῆτε οὖν περιζωσάμενοι τὴν ὀσφὺν ὑμῶν ἐν ἀληθείᾳ, καὶ ἐνδυσάμενοι τὸν θώρακα τῆς δικαιοσύνης,

14. Steite oun perizosamenoi tein osphun 'umon en aleitheia, kai endusamenoi ton thoraka teis dikaiosuneis,

Hebrew/Transliteration
יד. עִמְדוּ־נָא מָתְנֵיכֶם חֲגוּרֵי אֱמֶת וְשִׁרְיוֹן צֶדֶק לְבוּשְׁכֶם:

14. Eem•doo - na mot•ney•chem cha•goo•rey emet ve•shir•yon tze•dek le•voosh•chem.

Rabbinic Jewish Commentary
The girdle is a part of armour, and so considerable as sometimes to be put for the whole, Isa_5:27; and here it is mentioned in the first place.

In allusion to Isa_59:17, meaning not works of righteousness done by men, though these are a fence when rightly used against the reproaches and charges of the enemy, as they were by Samuel, 1Sa_12:3, but rather the graces of faith and love.

15. And your feet shod with the preparation of the gospel of peace;

Greek/Transliteration
15. καὶ ὑποδησάμενοι τοὺς πόδας ἐν ἑτοιμασίᾳ τοῦ εὐαγγελίου τῆς εἰρήνης·

15. kai 'upodeisamenoi tous podas en 'etoimasia tou euangeliou teis eireineis.

Hebrew/Transliteration
טו. וּפְעַמֵיכֶם יָפוֹת בַּנְעָלִים לְבַשֵּׂר בְּשׂוֹרַת הַשָׁלוֹם:

15. Oof•a•mey•chem ya•fot ban•a•lim le•va•ser b`so•rat ha•sha•lom.

Rabbinic Jewish Commentary
(l): The "preparation" of it does not design a promptitude or readiness to preach the Gospel, or to receive it, or profess it, or to give a reason of faith in it, or to endure reproach and persecution for it. The word ετοιμασια signifies a "base", or foundation; and so it is used by the Septuagint interpreters on Zec_5:11; and here it designs a firm and solid knowledge of the Gospel.

Shoes or boots, which were sometimes of iron, and sometimes of brass, are reckoned among the armour of soldiers (m).

(l) Zohar in Numb. fol. 73. 3. Tzeror Hammor, fol. 9. 3. (m) Pausan. l. 6. p. 362, 378. Julian. Orat. 2. p. 105. Alex. ab Alexandro, l. 6. c. 22.

16. Above all, taking the shield of faith, wherewith ye shall be able to quench all the fiery darts of the wicked.

Greek/Transliteration
16. ἐπὶ πᾶσιν ἀναλαβόντες τὸν θυρεὸν τῆς πίστεως, ἐν ᾧ δυνήσεσθε πάντα τὰ βέλη τοῦ πονηροῦ τὰ πεπυρωμένα σβέσαι.

16. epi pasin analabontes ton thureon teis pisteos, en 'o duneisesthe panta ta belei tou poneirou ta pepuromena sbesai.

Hebrew/Transliteration
טז. וּבְכֹל עִרְכוּ מָגֵן הָאֱמוּנָה אֲשֶׁר תּוּכְלוּ לְכַבּוֹת בּוֹ חִצִּים לֹהֲטִים מִיַּד הַצָּר:

16. Oo•va•kol eer•choo ma•gen ha•e•moo•na asher tooch•loo le•cha•bot bo chi•tzim lo•ha•tim mi•yad ha•tzar.

Rabbinic Jewish Commentary
The Jews say (n), that repentance and good works are as a shield against divine vengeance: or rather of the object of faith, that which faith makes use of as a shield; so God himself is a shield, Gen_15:1.

The disciples of the wise men are said to be (o) תריסון, "shielded men", who, as the gloss says fight in the war of the Torah.

The allusion is to βελεσι πεπυρωμενοις, "the fiery darts", cast by enemies into towns, and upon houses, in order to burn them (p). Mention is also made of גירי דאשא, "fiery darts", with the Jews (q), and of the adversary casting a dart at David (r): from these customs, and ways of speaking, the apostle borrows his phrases; and suggests, that the shield of faith is of use to quench the fiery darts of the adversary's temptations; so that they may not have the malignant influence they are designed for; which is chiefly done by faith's dealing with the blood of Yeshua. And there were ways of quenching the fiery darts alluded to; which was done by skins and hides of beasts made wet, or anointed with alum (s).

(n) Pirke Abot, c. 4. sect. 11. (o) T. Bab. Becorot, fol. 36. 1. & Gloss. in ib. (p) Apollodorus de Orig. Deorum, l. 2. p. 89. (q) Targum Jon. & Jerus. in Exod. xix. 13. (r) T. Bab. Sanhedrin, fol. 95. 1. & 107. 1. (s) Ammian. Marcellin. l. 20. c. 11.

---

17. And take the helmet of salvation, and the sword of the Spirit, which is the word of God:

Greek/Transliteration
17. Καὶ τὴν περικεφαλαίαν τοῦ σωτηρίου δέξασθαι, καὶ τὴν μάχαιραν τοῦ πνεύματος, ὅ ἐστιν ῥῆμα θεοῦ·

17. Kai tein perikephalaian tou soteiriou dexasthai, kai tein machairan tou pneumatos, 'o estin 'reima theou.

Hebrew/Transliteration
יז. וְהִתְיַצְּבוּ בְּכֹבַע הַיְשׁוּעָה וּבְחֶרֶב הָרוּחַ אֲשֶׁר הוּא דְּבַר הָאֱלֹהִים:

17. Ve•hit•yatz•voo ve•cho•va ha•y`shoo•ah oov•che•rev ha•Roo•ach asher hoo de•var ha•Elohim.

Rabbinic Jewish Commentary
So the Jews say (t), the words of the Torah are like to a sword, and speak of חרב תורה "the sword of the Torah" (u).

(t) Targum in Cant. 3. 8. (u) Bereshit Rabba, sect. 21. fol. 19. 1.

---

18. Praying always with all prayer and supplication in the Spirit, and watching thereunto with all perseverance and supplication for all saints;

Greek/Transliteration
18. διὰ πάσης προσευχῆς καὶ δεήσεως προσευχόμενοι ἐν παντὶ καιρῷ ἐν πνεύματι, καὶ εἰς αὐτὸ τοῦτο ἀγρυπνοῦντες ἐν πάσῃ προσκαρτερήσει καὶ δεήσει περὶ πάντων τῶν ἁγίων,

18. dya paseis proseucheis kai deeiseos proseuchomenoi en panti kairo en pneumati, kai eis auto touto agrupnountes en pasei proskartereisei kai deeisei peri panton ton 'agion,

Hebrew/Transliteration
יח: וְהִתְפַּלְלוּ בְּכָל-עֵת כָּל-תְּפִלָּה וּתְחִנָּה מִקֶּרֶב לֵב נָרוּחַ וְשֹׁקְדִים תִּהְיוּ לְהַעְתִּיר וּלְהִתְחַנֵּן בְּעַד כָּל-הַקְּדוֹשִׁים

18. Ve•hit•pa•le•loo ve•chol - et kol - te•fi•la oot•chi•na mi•ke•rev lev va•Roo•ach ve•shok•dim ti•hi•yoo le•ha•a•tir ool•hit•cha•nen be•ad kol - ha•k`do•shim.

---

19. And for me, that utterance may be given unto me, that I may open my mouth boldly, to make known the mystery of the gospel,

Greek/Transliteration
19. καὶ ὑπὲρ ἐμοῦ, ἵνα μοι δοθῇ λόγος ἐν ἀνοίξει τοῦ στόματός μου ἐν παρρησίᾳ γνωρίσαι τὸ μυστήριον τοῦ εὐαγγελίου,

19. kai 'uper emou, 'ina moi dothei logos en anoixei tou stomatos mou en parreisia gnorisai to musteirion tou euangeliou.

Hebrew/Transliteration
יט: וְגַם-בְּעַד נַפְשִׁי כִּי יוּשַׂם דָּבָר בְּפִי וְעֹז כִּי-אֶפְתַּח שְׂפָתַי לְהַגִּיד סוֹד הַבְּשׂוֹרָה

19. Ve•gam - be•ad naf•shi ki yoo•sam da•var be•fi ve•oz ki - ef•tach s`fa•tai le•ha•gid sod ha•b`so•hra.

Rabbinic Jewish Commentary
that I may open my mouth boldly; or "in the opening of my mouth"; the phrase is Rabbinical. The Jews (w) say, that when Moses came to write that passage, "let us make man in our image", Gen_1:26, he said before the Lord of the world, why dost thou give פתחון פה, "opening of the mouth", to heretics? i.e. an occasion to them of speaking, objecting to us, and of reproving and convincing us with respect to a plurality of persons in the Deity: and a little after they say,

"Wherever you פתחון פה, "an opening of the mouth to heretics", you will find an answer by its side, or along with it."

Now the apostle desired he might have something to say, to object to, and to reprove and convince the unbelieving Jews; that he might do this with boldness, with all faithfulness with Courage, and intrepidity, and with freedom of speech; or "openly" and "publicly", as the Syriac version renders it.

(w) Bereshit Rabba, sect. 8. fol. 7. 1. & Vajikra Rabba, sect. 21. fol. 163. 1. Megillat Esther, fol. 94. 1, 3.

---

20. For which I am an ambassador in bonds: that therein I may speak boldly, as I ought to speak.

Greek/Transliteration
20. ὑπὲρ οὗ πρεσβεύω ἐν ἁλύσει, ἵνα ἐν αὐτῷ παρρησιάσωμαι, ὡς δεῖ με λαλῆσαι.

20. 'uper 'ou presbeuo en 'alusei, 'ina en auto parreisyasomai, 'os dei me laleisai.

Hebrew/Transliteration

כ. הַבְּשׂוֹרָה אֲשֶׁר אֲנִי מַלְאָכָה אָסוּר בִּכְבָלִים וּלְהִנָּתֶן-לִי לְמַלֵּל בְּיָד רָמָה כַּאֲשֶׁר נָכוֹן לִי:

20. Ha•b`so•hra asher ani mal•a•cha a•soor bich•va•lim ool•hi•na•ten - li le•ma•lel be•yad ra•ma ka•a•sher na•chon li.

---

21. But that ye also may know my affairs, and how I do, Tychicus, a beloved brother and faithful minister in the Lord, shall make known to you all things:

Greek/Transliteration

21. Ἵνα δὲ εἰδῆτε καὶ ὑμεῖς τὰ κατ' ἐμέ, τί πράσσω, πάντα ὑμῖν γνωρίσει Τυχικὸς ὁ ἀγαπητὸς ἀδελφὸς καὶ πιστὸς διάκονος ἐν κυρίῳ·

21. 'Yna de eideite kai 'umeis ta kat eme, ti prasso, panta 'umin gnorisei Tuchikos 'o agapeitos adelphos kai pistos dyakonos en kurio.

Hebrew/Transliteration

כא. אַךְ לְבַעֲבוּר תֵּדְעוּן מַה עִמָּדִי וְכָל-אֲשֶׁר אֲנִי עֹשֶׂה הִנֵּה טוּכִיקוֹס הָאָח הָאָהוּב וְהַמְשָׁרֵת הַנֶּאֱמָן לַאֲדֹנֵינוּ יַגִּיד לָכֶם כֹּל:

21. Ach le•va•a•voor ted•oon ma ee•ma•di ve•chol - asher ani o•se hee•ne Too•chi•kos ha•ach ha•a•hoov ve•ham•sha•ret ha•ne•e•man la•Ado•ney•noo ya•gid la•chem kol.

---

22. Whom I have sent unto you for the same purpose, that ye might know our affairs, and that he might comfort your hearts.

Greek/Transliteration

22. ὃν ἔπεμψα πρὸς ὑμᾶς εἰς αὐτὸ τοῦτο, ἵνα γνῶτε τὰ περὶ ἡμῶν, καὶ παρακαλέσῃ τὰς καρδίας ὑμῶν.

22. 'on epempsa pros 'umas eis auto touto, 'ina gnote ta peri 'eimon, kai parakalesei tas kardias 'umon.

Hebrew/Transliteration

כב. כִּי לַדָּבָר הַזֶּה שְׁלַחְתִּיו אֲלֵיכֶם לְהוֹדִיעֲכֶם מַה מַּעֲשֵׂינוּ וּלְנַחֵם אֶת-לְבַבְכֶם:

22. Ki la•da•var ha•ze sh`lach•tiv aley•chem le•ho•di•a•chem ma ma•a•sey•noo ool•na•chem et - lib•chem.

---

23. Peace be to the brethren, and love with faith, from God the Father and the Lord Jesus Christ.

Greek/Transliteration

23. Εἰρήνη τοῖς ἀδελφοῖς καὶ ἀγάπη μετὰ πίστεως ἀπὸ θεοῦ πατρὸς καὶ κυρίου Ἰησοῦ χριστοῦ.

23. Eireinei tois adelphois kai agapei meta pisteos apo theou patros kai kuriou Yeisou christou.

Hebrew/Transliteration

:כג. שָׁלוֹם אַהֲבָה וֶאֱמוּנָה אֶל-הָאַחִים מֵאֵת אֱלֹהִים אָבִינוּ וּמֵאֵת יֵשׁוּעַ הַמָּשִׁיחַ אֲדֹנֵינוּ

23. Sha•lom a•ha•va ve•e•moo•na el - ha•a•chim me•et Elohim Avi•noo oo•me•et Yeshua ha•Ma•shi•ach Ado•ney•noo.

---

24. Grace be with all them that love our Lord Jesus Christ in sincerity. Amen.

Greek/Transliteration

24. Ἡ χάρις μετὰ πάντων τῶν ἀγαπώντων τὸν κύριον ἡμῶν Ἰησοῦν χριστὸν ἐν ἀφθαρσίᾳ. Ἀμήν.

24. 'Ei charis meta panton ton agaponton ton kurion 'eimon Yeisoun christon en aphtharsia. Amein.

Hebrew/Transliteration

:כד. חֶסֶד לְכָל-הָאֹהֵב אֶת-אֲדֹנֵינוּ יֵשׁוּעַ הַמָּשִׁיחַ בְּאַהֲבָה נִצַּחַת אָמֵן

24. Che•sed le•chol - ha•o•hev et - Ado•ney•noo Yeshua ha•Ma•shi•ach be•a•ha•va ni•tza•chat. Amen.

---

^end^

THE EPISTLE OF PAUL THE APOSTLE TO THE PHILIPPIANS

Philippians, Chapter 1

1. Paul and Timotheus, the servants of Jesus Christ, to all the saints in Christ Jesus which are at Philippi, with the bishops and deacons:

Greek/Transliteration
1. Παῦλος καὶ Τιμόθεος, δοῦλοι Ἰησοῦ χριστοῦ, πᾶσιν τοῖς ἁγίοις ἐν χριστῷ Ἰησοῦ τοῖς οὖσιν ἐν Φιλίπποις, σὺν ἐπισκόποις καὶ διακόνοις·

1. Paulos kai Timotheos, douloi Yeisou christou, pasin tois 'agiois en christo Yeisou tois ousin en Philippois, sun episkopois kai dyakonois.

Hebrew/Transliteration
א. פּוֹלוֹס וְטִימוֹתִיּוֹס עַבְדֵי יֵשׁוּעַ הַמָּשִׁיחַ אֶל-כָּל-הַקְּדוֹשִׁים בְּיֵשׁוּעַ הַמָּשִׁיחַ הַיּשְׁבִים בְּפִלִפִּי עִם-זִקְנֵיהֶם וּמְשָׁרְתֵיהֶם:

1. Polos ve•Timotiyos av•dey Yeshua ha•Ma•shi•ach el - kol - ha•k`do•shim be•Yeshua ha•Ma•shi•ach ha•yosh•vim be•Filipi eem - zik•ney•hem oom•shar•tey•hem.

Rabbinic Jewish Commentary
The officers of this church were "the bishops and deacons". The "bishops" were the pastors, elders, and overseers of the church, for a bishop and an elder is one and the same; see Act_20:17; where the elders of the church at Ephesus are called "overseers" or "bishops"; for the same word is used there as here; and the Syriac version here renders the word by קשישא, "elders".

---

2. Grace be unto you, and peace, from God our Father, and from the Lord Jesus Christ.

Greek/Transliteration
2. χάρις ὑμῖν καὶ εἰρήνη ἀπὸ θεοῦ πατρὸς ἡμῶν καὶ κυρίου Ἰησοῦ χριστοῦ.

2. charis 'umin kai eireinei apo theou patros 'eimon kai kuriou Yeisou christou.

Hebrew/Transliteration
ב. חֶסֶד וְשָׁלוֹם יִתֵּן לָכֶם אֱלֹהִים אָבִינוּ וְיֵשׁוּעַ הַמָּשִׁיחַ אֲדֹנֵינוּ:

2. Che•sed ve•sha•lom yi•ten la•chem Elohim Avi•noo ve•Yeshua ha•Ma•shi•ach Ado•ney•noo.

---

3. I thank my God upon every remembrance of you,

Greek/Transliteration
3. Εὐχαριστῶ τῷ θεῷ μου ἐπὶ πάσῃ τῇ μνείᾳ ὑμῶν,

3. Eucharisto to theo mou epi pasei tei mneia 'umon,

Hebrew/Transliteration
ג. אֲבָרְכָה אֶת-אֱלֹהַי בְּכָל-עֵת אֲשֶׁר אֶזְכֹּר אֶתְכֶם:

3. Avar•cha et - Elohai be•chol - et asher ez•kor et•chem.

---

4. Always in every prayer of mine for you all making request with joy,

Greek/Transliteration
4. πάντοτε ἐν πάσῃ δεήσει μου ὑπὲρ πάντων ὑμῶν μετὰ χαρᾶς τὴν δέησιν ποιούμενος,

4. pantote en pasei deeisei mou 'uper panton 'umon meta charas tein deeisin poioumenos,

Hebrew/Transliteration
ד. וְאֶעֱלֹצָה תָמִיד בְּכָל-תְּפִלּוֹתַי כַּאֲשֶׁר אֶתְפַּלֵּל בְּעַד כֻּלְּכֶם:

4. Ve•e•el•tza ta•mid be•chol - t`fi•lo•tai ka•a•sher et•pa•lel be•ad kool•chem.

---

5. For your fellowship in the gospel from the first day until now;

Greek/Transliteration
5. ἐπὶ τῇ κοινωνίᾳ ὑμῶν εἰς τὸ εὐαγγέλιον, ἀπὸ πρώτης ἡμέρας ἄχρι τοῦ νῦν·

5. epi tei koinonia 'umon eis to euangelion, apo proteis 'eimeras achri tou nun.

Hebrew/Transliteration
ה. אַתֶּם הַנִּלְוִים אֶל - הַבְּשׂוֹרָה לְמִן-הַיּוֹם הָרִאשׁוֹן וְעַד-עָתָּה:

5. Atem ha•nil•vim el - ha•be•so•ra le•min - ha•yom ha•ri•shon ve•ad - ata.

---

6. Being confident of this very thing, that he which hath begun a good work in you will perform it until the day of Jesus Christ:

Greek/Transliteration
6. πεποιθὼς αὐτὸ τοῦτο, ὅτι ὁ ἐναρξάμενος ἐν ὑμῖν ἔργον ἀγαθὸν ἐπιτελέσει ἄχρι ἡμέρας χριστοῦ Ἰησοῦ·

6. pepoithos auto touto, 'oti 'o enarxamenos en 'umin ergon agathon epitelesei achri 'eimeras christou Yeisou.

Hebrew/Transliteration
ו. וּבְזֹאת אֲנִי בֹטֵחַ כִּי הוּא אֲשֶׁר הֵחֵל לִפְעֹל דָּבָר טוֹב בָּכֶם גַּם-הוּא יְכַלֶּנּוּ עַד-יוֹם יֵשׁוּעַ הַמָּשִׁיחַ:

6. Oo•va•zot ani vo•te•ach ki hoo asher he`chel lif•ol da•var tov ba•chem gam - hoo ye•cha•le•noo ad - yom Yeshua ha•Ma•shi•ach.

7. Even as it is meet for me to think this of you all, because I have you in my heart; inasmuch as both in my bonds, and in the defence and confirmation of the gospel, ye all arepartakers of my grace.

Greek/Transliteration
7. καθώς ἐστιν δίκαιον ἐμοὶ τοῦτο φρονεῖν ὑπὲρ πάντων ὑμῶν, διὰ τὸ ἔχειν με ἐν τῇ καρδίᾳ ὑμᾶς, ἔν τε τοῖς δεσμοῖς μου καὶ ἐν τῇ ἀπολογίᾳ καὶ βεβαιώσει τοῦ εὐαγγελίου, συγκοινωνούς μου τῆς χάριτος πάντας ὑμᾶς ὄντας.

7. kathos estin dikaion emoi touto phronein 'uper panton 'umon, dya to echein me en tei kardia 'umas, en te tois desmois mou kai en tei apologia kai bebaiosei tou euangeliou, sugkoinonous mou teis charitos pantas 'umas ontas.

Hebrew/Transliteration
ז. כֵּן חָשְׁבָה נַפְשִׁי עֲלֵיכֶם בְּמֵישָׁרִים כִּי בְקֶרֶב לְבָבִי אֶשָּׂא אֶתְכֶם אִם בְּשִׁבְתִּי בְּבֵית הָאֲסוּרִים אוֹ מִדֵּי דַבְּרִי לְהַצְדִּיק אֶת-הַבְּשׂוֹרָה וּלְהַאֲדִירָהּ כִּי דְבֵקִים אַתֶּם בִּי כֻלְּכֶם בַּחֲבָלִים נָפְלוּ לִי בֶּחָסֶד:

7. Ken chash•va naf•shi aley•chem be•mey•sha•rim ki ve•ke•rev le•va•vi esa et•chem eem be•shiv•ti be•veit ha•a•soo•rim oh mee•dey dab•ri le•hatz•dik et - ha•be•so•ra oo•ha•a•di•ra ki d`ve•kim atem bi chool•chem ba•cha•va•lim naf•loo li be•cha•sed.

---

8. For God is my record, how greatly I long after you all in the bowels of Jesus Christ.

Greek/Transliteration
8. Μάρτυς γάρ μού ἐστιν ὁ θεός, ὡς ἐπιποθῶ πάντας ὑμᾶς ἐν σπλάγχνοις Ἰησοῦ χριστοῦ.

8. Martus gar mou estin 'o theos, 'os epipotho pantas 'umas en splagchnois Yeisou christou.

Hebrew/Transliteration
ח. הֵן אֱלֹהִים לִי לְעֵד כַּמָּה אֶרְחָמְכֶם בְּרַחֲמֵי יֵשׁוּעַ הַמָּשִׁיחַ:

8. Hen Elohim li le•ed ka•ma er•cham•chem be•ra•cha•mey Yeshua ha•Ma•shi•ach.

---

9. And this I pray, that your love may abound yet more and more in knowledge and in all judgment;

Greek/Transliteration
9. Καὶ τοῦτο προσεύχομαι, ἵνα ἡ ἀγάπη ὑμῶν ἔτι μᾶλλον καὶ μᾶλλον περισσεύῃ ἐν ἐπιγνώσει καὶ πάσῃ αἰσθήσει,

9. Kai touto proseuchomai, 'ina 'ei agapei 'umon eti mallon kai mallon perisseuei en epignosei kai pasei aistheisei,

Hebrew/Transliteration
ט. וְעַל-זֹאת אֶתְפַּלֵּל כִּי-תִרְבֶּה אַהֲבַתְכֶם הָלוֹךְ וְרָב בְּכָל-דַּעָה וְהַשְׂכֵּל:

9. Ve•al - zot et•pa•lel ki - tir•be aha•vat•chem ha•loch va•rav be•chol - de•ah ve•has•kel.

Rabbinic Jewish Commentary
By all "judgment", or "sense", as in the Greek text, is designed a spiritual apprehension, judgment, and sensation of things. The Syriac version renders it, "all spiritual understanding", and may intend a spiritual perception.

---

10. That ye may approve things that are excellent; that ye may be sincere and without offence till the day of Christ;

Greek/Transliteration
10. εἰς τὸ δοκιμάζειν ὑμᾶς τὰ διαφέροντα, ἵνα ἦτε εἰλικρινεῖς καὶ ἀπρόσκοποι εἰς ἡμέραν χριστοῦ,

10. eis to dokimazein 'umas ta dyapheronta, 'ina eite eilikrineis kai aproskopoi eis 'eimeran christou,

Hebrew/Transliteration
:י. לְהַכִּיר וּלְהַבְדִּיל בֵּין טוֹב לָרָע לִהְיוֹת בָּרֵי לֵב וְלֹא לְמוֹקֵשׁ עַד-יוֹם הַמָּשִׁיחַ

10. Le•ha•kir ool•hav•dil bein tov la•ra li•hee•yot ba•rey lev ve•lo le•mo•kesh ad - yom ha•Ma•shi•ach.

---

11. Being filled with the fruits of righteousness, which are by Jesus Christ, unto the glory and praise of God.

Greek/Transliteration
11. πεπληρωμένοι καρπῶν δικαιοσύνης τῶν διὰ Ἰησοῦ χριστοῦ, εἰς δόξαν καὶ ἔπαινον θεοῦ.

11. pepleiromenoi karpon dikaiosuneis ton dya Yeisou christou, eis doxan kai epainon theou.

Hebrew/Transliteration
:יא. מְלֵאִים פְּרִי צֶדֶק עַל-יְדֵי יֵשׁוּעַ הַמָּשִׁיחַ לִכְבוֹד אֱלֹהִים וְתִפְאַרְתּוֹ

11. Me•le•eem p`ri tze•dek al - ye•dey Yeshua ha•Ma•shi•ach lich•vod Elohim ve•tif•ar•to.

Rabbinic Jewish Commentary
The Alexandrian copy, the Vulgate Latin, and Ethiopic versions, read, "fruit", in the singular number, but other copies and versions, read, "fruits"; and the apostle wishes, that these saints might be "filled" with them; that is, that they might be like trees laden with fruit, which have fruit on every branch, bough, and twig; that they might abound in the performance of them, be ready to, and fruitful in every good work.

The Ethiopic version reads, "in" or "to his *Christ's* glory, and the praise of God"; and the Arabic version thus, "to the glory of God and his praise"; and so the design of the clause is to show, either that both the glory of Messiah and the praise of God are concerned in every truly good work; or that the glory of God secretly, and his praise openly, are to be sought therein.

---

12. But I would ye should understand, brethren, that the things which happened unto me have fallen out rather unto the furtherance of the gospel;

Greek/Transliteration
12. Γινώσκειν δὲ ὑμᾶς βούλομαι, ἀδελφοί, ὅτι τὰ κατ᾽ ἐμὲ μᾶλλον εἰς προκοπὴν τοῦ εὐαγγελίου ἐλήλυθεν·

12. Ginoskein de 'umas boulomai, adelphoi, 'oti ta kat eme mallon eis prokopein tou euangeliou eleiluthen.

Hebrew/Transliteration
:יב. וַאֲנִי חָפֵץ כִּי תֵדְעוּן אֶחָי זֹאת אֲשֶׁר בָּאַתְנִי בָּאָה רַק לְהוֹעִיל לַהֲלִיכוֹת הַבְּשׂוֹרָה

12. Va•a•ni cha•fetz ki ted•oon e•chai zot asher ba•at•ni ba•ah rak le•ho•eel la•ha•li•chot ha•be•so•ra.

Rabbinic Jewish Commentary
The Syriac version suggests, rendering the phrase, דסוערני דילי, "that my work makes more abundant progress in the Gospel".

---

13. So that my bonds in Christ are manifest in all the palace, and in all other places;

Greek/Transliteration
13. ὥστε τοὺς δεσμούς μου φανεροὺς ἐν χριστῷ γενέσθαι ἐν ὅλῳ τῷ πραιτωρίῳ καὶ τοῖς λοιποῖς πᾶσιν,

13. 'oste tous desmous mou phanerous en christo genesthai en 'olo to praitorio kai tois loipois pasin,

Hebrew/Transliteration
:יג. עַד אֲשֶׁר נִשְׁמַע בְּשַׁעַר הַבִּירָה וּבְכָל-שְׁאָר הַמְּקֹמוֹת כִּי אָסִיר אֲנִי לְמַעַן הַמָּשִׁיחַ

13. Ad asher nish•ma be•sha•ar ha•bi•ra oov•chol - sh`ar ha•m`ko•mot ki asir ani le•ma•an ha•Ma•shi•ach.

Rabbinic Jewish Commentary
The Arabic version reads it, "in the palace of the emperor". The word "praetorium", here used, signifies sometimes the judgment hall, or court of judicature belonging to the Roman governors, as Herod and Pilate.

---

14. And many of the brethren in the Lord, waxing confident by my bonds, are much more bold to speak the word without fear.

Greek/Transliteration
14. καὶ τοὺς πλείονας τῶν ἀδελφῶν ἐν κυρίῳ, πεποιθότας τοῖς δεσμοῖς μου, περισσοτέρως τολμᾶν ἀφόβως τὸν λόγον λαλεῖν.

14. kai tous pleionas ton adelphon en kurio, pepoithotas tois desmois mou, perissoteros tolman aphobos ton logon lalein.

Hebrew/Transliteration
יד. וְאַחִים רַבִּים הַדְּבֵקִים בַּאֲדֹנֵינוּ לָבְשׁוּ אֹמֶץ רַב לִנֹכַח מוֹסְרַי וַיַּשְׁמִיעוּ בְיֶתֶר עֹז אֶת-דְּבַר הָאֱלֹהִים בִּבְלִי-פָּחַד:

14. Ve•a•chim ra•bim ha•d`ve•kim ba•Ado•ne•noo lav•shoo o•metz rav le•no•chach moo•sa•ri va•yash•mi•oo ve•ye•ter oz et - de•var ha•Elohim biv•li - fa•chad.

Rabbinic Jewish Commentary
The word "of God", as the Vulgate Latin, Syriac, and Ethiopic versions read; and so the Alexandrian, Claromontane, and two of Stephens's copies: meaning either the essential word, the 'Lord Jesus Christ', who was the subject of their ministry; or the written word, the writings of Moses and the prophets, the books of the Old Testament, according to which they spoke.

---

15. Some indeed preach Christ even of envy and strife; and some also of good will:

Greek/Transliteration
15. Τινὲς μὲν καὶ διὰ φθόνον καὶ ἔριν, τινὲς δὲ καὶ δι᾽ εὐδοκίαν τὸν χριστὸν κηρύσσουσιν·

15. Tines men kai dya phthonon kai erin, tines de kai di eudokian ton christon keirussousin.

Hebrew/Transliteration
טו. אָמְנָם יֵשׁ מַגִּידִים עֵדוּת הַמָּשִׁיחַ מִקִּנְאָה וּמְרִיבָה וְיֵשׁ מַגִּידִים מֵרוּחַ נְדִיבָה:

15. Om•nam yesh ma•gi•dim e•doot ha•Ma•shi•ach mi•kin•ah oom•ri•va ve•yesh ma•gi•dim me•roo•ach n`di•va.

Rabbinic Jewish Commentary
That is, some of them, as the Arabic version reads; some of the brethren, that were only so in profession; wherefore these could not be the unbelieving Jews, who preached the Messiah in general, but did not believe Yeshua of Nazareth to be he, and opened the prophecies of the Old Testament relating to him, to the Gentiles; at which the apostle is by some thought to rejoice; inasmuch as this might be a means of giving light to them that were without any knowledge of the Messiah, and of leading them into an inquiry concerning him, whereby they might come to know the true Messiah, and believe in him.

and some also of good will; or "willingly" and "freely", as the Arabic version renders it.

---

16. The one preach Christ of contention, not sincerely, supposing to add affliction to my bonds:

Greek/Transliteration
16. οἱ μὲν ἐξ ἐριθείας τὸν χριστὸν καταγγέλλουσιν, οὐχ ἁγνῶς, οἰόμενοι θλῖψιν ἐπιφέρειν τοῖς δεσμοῖς μου·

16. 'oi men ex eritheias ton christon katangellousin, ouch 'agnos, oiomenoi thlipsin epipherein tois desmois mou.

Hebrew/Transliteration
טז. וְאֵלֶּה הַמַּגִּידִים עֵדוּת הַמָּשִׁיחַ מִמְּרִיבָה וְלֹא בְתָם-לֵב יַחְשְׁבוּ לְהוֹסִיף לַחַץ לְמוֹסְרָי:

16. Ve•e•le ha•ma•gi•dim e•doot ha•Ma•shi•ach mim•ri•va ve•lo be•tom - lev yach•she•voo le•ho•sif la•chatz le•moo•sa•ri.

---

17. But the other of love, knowing that I am set for the defence of the gospel.

Greek/Transliteration
17. οἱ δὲ ἐξ ἀγάπης, εἰδότες ὅτι εἰς ἀπολογίαν τοῦ εὐαγγελίου κεῖμαι.

17. 'oi de ex agapeis, eidotes 'oti eis apologian tou euangeliou keimai.

Hebrew/Transliteration
יז. אֵלֶּה הַמַּגִּידִים מֵאַהֲבָה יֹדְעִים כִּי לְהוֹצִיא צִדְקַת הַבְּשׂוֹרָה לְאוֹר אָנֹכִי עֹמֵד פֹּה:

17. Ele ha•ma•gi•dim me•a•ha•va yod•eem ki le•ho•tzi tzid•kat ha•be•so•ra le•or ano•chi o•med po.

---

18. What then? notwithstanding, every way, whether in pretence, or in truth, Christ is preached; and I therein do rejoice, yea, and will rejoice.

Greek/Transliteration
18. Τί γάρ; Πλὴν παντὶ τρόπῳ, εἴτε προφάσει εἴτε ἀληθείᾳ, χριστὸς καταγγέλλεται· καὶ ἐν τούτῳ χαίρω, ἀλλὰ καὶ χαρήσομαι.

18. Ti gar? Plein panti tropo, eite prophasei eite aleitheia, christos katangelletai. kai en touto chairo, alla kai chareisomai.

Hebrew/Transliteration
יח. אַךְ מַה אֵפוֹא עַתָּה אִם-בִּלְשׁוֹן רְמִיָּה אוֹ בִשְׂפַת אֱמֶת הֲלֹא מִכָּל-עֵבֶר הֻגַּד הַמָּשִׁיחַ עַל-פִּיהֶם וְעַל-זֶה עָלֹז אֲנִי וְגִיל תָּגִיל נַפְשִׁי:

18. Ach ma e•fo ata eem - bil•shon r`mi•ya oh bis•fat emet ha•lo mi•kol - ever hoo•gad ha•Ma•shi•ach al - pi•hem ve•al - ze a•lez ani ve•gil ta•gil naf•shi.

---

19. For I know that this shall turn to my salvation through your prayer, and the supply of the Spirit of Jesus Christ,

Greek/Transliteration

19. Οἶδα γὰρ ὅτι τοῦτό μοι ἀποβήσεται εἰς σωτηρίαν διὰ τῆς ὑμῶν δεήσεως, καὶ ἐπιχορηγίας τοῦ πνεύματος Ἰησοῦ χριστοῦ,

19. Oida gar 'oti touto moi apobeisetai eis soteirian dya teis 'umon deeiseos, kai epichoreigias tou pneumatos Yeisou christou,

Hebrew/Transliteration

יט. כִּי בִתְפִלַּתְכֶם וּבְרוּחַ יֵשׁוּעַ מְשִׁיחֵנוּ הַנָּתוּן לִי יָדַעְתִּי כִּי גַם-זֹאת תִּהְיֶה-לִי לִישׁוּעָה:

19. Ki vit•fi•lat•chem oov•Roo•ach Yeshua me•shi•che•noo ha•na•toon li ya•da•a•ti ki gam - zot ti•hi•ye - li li•shoo•ah.

---

20. According to my earnest expectation and my hope, that in nothing I shall be ashamed, but that with all boldness, as always, so now also Christ shall be magnified in my body, whether it be by life, or by death.

Greek/Transliteration

20. κατὰ τὴν ἀποκαραδοκίαν καὶ ἐλπίδα μου, ὅτι ἐν οὐδενὶ αἰσχυνθήσομαι, ἀλλ᾽ ἐν πάσῃ παρρησίᾳ, ὡς πάντοτε, καὶ νῦν μεγαλυνθήσεται χριστὸς ἐν τῷ σώματί μου, εἴτε διὰ ζωῆς εἴτε διὰ θανάτου.

20. kata tein apokaradokian kai elpida mou, 'oti en oudeni aischuntheisomai, all en pasei parreisia, 'os pantote, kai nun megaluntheisetai christos en to somati mou, eite dya zoeis eite dya thanatou.

Hebrew/Transliteration

כ. כַּאֲשֶׁר הוֹחַלְתִּי כִּי בְכָל-דְּרָכַי לֹא אֵבוֹשׁ מִשִּׁבְרִי וְכָל-מִבְטָחִי כְּאָז כֵּן עַתָּה כִּי יָרוּם הַמָּשִׁיחַ בְּמוֹ-נַפְשִׁי אִם בַּחַיִּים אִם-בַּמָּוֶת:

20. Ka•a•sher ho•chal•ti ki ve•chol - d`ra•chai lo evosh mi•shiv•ri ve•chol - miv•ta•chi ke•az ken ata ki ya•room ha•Ma•shi•ach be•mo - naf•shi eem - ba•cha•yim eem - ba•ma•vet.

---

21. For to me to live is Christ, and to die is gain.

Greek/Transliteration

21. Ἐμοὶ γὰρ τὸ ζῆν, χριστός· καὶ τὸ ἀποθανεῖν, κέρδος.

21. Emoi gar to zein, christos. kai to apothanein, kerdos.

Hebrew/Transliteration

כא. כִּי חַיָּתִי הוּא הַמָּשִׁיחַ וְהַמָּוֶת הוּא לְרִוְחָתִי:

21. Ki cha•ya•ti hoo ha•Ma•shi•ach ve•ha•ma•vet hoo le•rav•cha•ti.

Rabbinic Jewish Commentary

This is the common interpretation, and is countenanced by the Syriac, Arabic, and Ethiopic versions, which read, "to die", or "if I die, it is gain to me". His expectation is to be immediately with him; and the glory he will then enter into will lie in communion with him, in conformity to him, and in an everlasting vision of him: or thus, for me to live and to die is Messiah's gain;

---

22. But if I live in the flesh, this is the fruit of my labour: yet what I shall choose I wot not.

Greek/Transliteration
22. Εἰ δὲ τὸ ζῆν ἐν σαρκί, τοῦτό μοι καρπὸς ἔργου· καὶ τί αἱρήσομαι οὐ γνωρίζω.

22. Ei de to zein en sarki, touto moi karpos ergou. kai ti 'aireisomai ou gnorizo.

Hebrew/Transliteration
:כב. אָכֵן אִם יִנָּתְנוּ לִי חַיֵּי בְשָׂרִי לְהָבִיא עוֹד פְּרִי עֲמָלִי אָז לֹא אֵדַע מָה אֶבְחָר

22. A•chen eem yi•nat•noo li cha•yey ve•sa•ri le•ha•vee od p`ri a•ma•li az lo eda ma ev•char.

Rabbinic Jewish Commentary
For as a certain Jew (b) says,

"The righteous man desires to live to do the will of God while he lives;

But not with that view, he adds,

"To increase the reward of the soul in the world to come.

(b) Kimchi in Psal. vi. 5.

---

23. For I am in a strait betwixt two, having a desire to depart, and to be with Christ; which is far better:

Greek/Transliteration
23. Συνέχομαι δὲ ἐκ τῶν δύο, τὴν ἐπιθυμίαν ἔχων εἰς τὸ ἀναλῦσαι καὶ σὺν χριστῷ εἶναι, πολλῷ μᾶλλον κρεῖσσον·

23. Sunechomai de ek ton duo, tein epithumian echon eis to analusai kai sun christo einai, pollo mallon kreisson.

Hebrew/Transliteration
:כג. כִּי נִלְחָץ אֲנִי בֵּין שְׁתָּיִם נַפְשִׁי כָלְתָה לְהִפָּרֵד לִהְיוֹת עִם-הַמָּשִׁיחַ אֲשֶׁר הוּא טוֹב לִי מִכֹּל

23. Ki nil•chatz ani bein sh`ta•yim naf•shi chal•ta le•hi•pa•red li•hee•yot eem - ha•Ma•shi•ach asher hoo tov li mi•kol.

Rabbinic Jewish Commentary

Life and death; or between these "two counsels", as the Arabic version reads; two thoughts and desires of the mind, a desire to live for the reasons above, and a desire to die for a reason following.

having a desire to depart; to die, a way of speaking much in use with the Jews, as expressive of death; thus Abraham is represented by them speaking after this manner on account of his two sons Isaac and Ishmael, the one being righteous and the other wicked (c),

"says he, if I bless Isaac, lo, Ishmael will seek to be blessed, and he is wicked; but a servant am I, flesh and blood am I, and tomorrow אכטר מן העולם, "I shall depart out of the world", or "die"; and what pleases the holy blessed God himself in his own world, let him do: כשנפטר, "when Abraham was dismissed" or "departed", the holy blessed God appeared to Isaac and blessed him:

And again it is said (d),

"Iniquities are not atoned for, until דאתפטר מעלמא, "a man is dismissed", or "departs out of the world";

And once more (e),

"When a man נפטר מזה העולם, "departs out of this world"; according to his merit he ascends above.

Hence it appears that there is a future being and state after death: the apostle desires to depart this life, and "be", exist, be somewhere, "with Messiah"; for the only happy being after death is with him.

The Syriac version adds, לי, "to me", far better for me; and so the Arabic.

(c) Bemidbar Rabba, sect. 11. fol. 202. 3. (d) Zohar in Numb. fol. 51. 3. (e) Tzeror Hammor, fol. 2. 1.

---

24. Nevertheless to abide in the flesh is more needful for you.

Greek/Transliteration
24. τὸ δὲ ἐπιμένειν ἐν τῇ σαρκὶ ἀναγκαιότερον δι᾽ ὑμᾶς.

24. to de epimenein en tei sarki anagkaioteron di 'umas.

Hebrew/Transliteration
כד. אֶפֶס לְהַאֲרִיךְ חַיֵּי בְשָׂרִי יֹתֵר טוֹב הוּא לָכֶם:

24. E•fes le•ha•a•rich cha•yey ve•sa•ri yo•ter tov hoo la•chem.

Rabbinic Jewish Commentary
The Syriac version renders the words thus, "but business for you", or "a good will towards you compels me to abide in the body"; and the Arabic version thus, "notwithstanding I choose to remain in the flesh, and this I think very necessary for you".

25. And having this confidence, I know that I shall abide and continue with you all for your furtherance and joy of faith;

Greek/Transliteration
25. Καὶ τοῦτο πεποιθὼς οἶδα ὅτι μενῶ, καὶ συμπαραμενῶ πᾶσιν ὑμῖν εἰς τὴν ὑμῶν προκοπὴν καὶ χαρὰν τῆς πίστεως,

25. Kai touto pepoithos oida 'oti meno, kai sumparameno pasin 'umin eis tein 'umon prokopein kai charan teis pisteos,

Hebrew/Transliteration
:כה. וּבָזֹאת אֲנִי בֹטֵחַ וְיוֹדֵעַ כִּי אִוָּתֵר פֹּה וְיָשַׁבְתִּי עִם־כֻּלְּכֶם לְמַרְבֶּה הָאֱמוּנָה וְהַשִּׂמְחָה לָכֶם

25. Oo•va•zot ani vo•te•ach ve•yo•dea ki ee•va•ter po ve•ya•shav•ti eem - kool•chem le•mar•be ha•e•moo•na ve•ha•sim•cha la•chem.

Rabbinic Jewish Commentary
The phrase is Jewish; mention is made in the writings of the Jews (f) of חדוה דמהימנותא, "The joy of faith",

(f) Zohar in Gen. fol. 113. 4. & in Exod. fol. 36. 4.

---

26. That your rejoicing may be more abundant in Jesus Christ for me by my coming to you again.

Greek/Transliteration
26. ἵνα τὸ καύχημα ὑμῶν περισσεύῃ ἐν χριστῷ Ἰησοῦ ἐν ἐμοί, διὰ τῆς ἐμῆς παρουσίας πάλιν πρὸς ὑμᾶς.

26. 'ina to kaucheima 'umon perisseuei en christo Yeisou en emoi, dya teis emeis parousias palin pros 'umas.

Hebrew/Transliteration
:כו. וְתִתְפָּאַרְתְּכֶם לִפְנֵי יֵשׁוּעַ הַמָּשִׁיחַ תִּגְדַּל בִּי כַּאֲשֶׁר אָשׁוּבָה אֲלֵיכֶם

26. Ve•tif•ar•te•chem lif•ney Yeshua ha•Ma•shi•ach tig•dal bi ka•a•sher ashoo•va aley•chem.

---

27. Only let your conversation be as it becometh the gospel of Christ: that whether I come and see you, or else be absent, I may hear of your affairs, that ye stand fast in one spirit, with one mind striving together for the faith of the gospel;

Greek/Transliteration
27. Μόνον ἀξίως τοῦ εὐαγγελίου τοῦ χριστοῦ πολιτεύεσθε, ἵνα εἴτε ἐλθὼν καὶ ἰδὼν ὑμᾶς, εἴτε ἀπών, ἀκούσω τὰ περὶ ὑμῶν, ὅτι στήκετε ἐν ἑνὶ πνεύματι, μιᾷ ψυχῇ συναθλοῦντες τῇ πίστει τοῦ εὐαγγελίου,

27. Monon axios tou euangeliou tou christou politeuesthe, 'ina eite elthon kai idon 'umas, eite apon, akouso ta peri 'umon, 'oti steikete en 'eni pneumati, mya psuchei sunathlountes tei pistei tou euangeliou,

Hebrew/Transliteration

כז. רַק שִׂימוּ דַרְכְּכֶם כַּאֲשֶׁר יָאֲתָה לִבְשׂוֹרַת הַמָּשִׁיחַ וְכִי אָבוֹא לִרְאֹתְכֶם אוֹ לִשְׁמֹעַ אֹזֶן מֵרָחוֹק אָז אֶמְצָא כִּי רוּחַ אֶחָד בָּכֶם וְנֶפֶשׁ אַחַת לְהִלָּחֵם יַחְדָּו מִלְחֲמוֹת אֱמוּנַת הַבְּשׂרָה:

27. Rak si•moo dar•ke•chem ka•a•sher ya•a•ta liv•so•rat ha•Ma•shi•ach ve•chi avo lir•ot•chem oh le•she•ma o•zen me•ra•chok az em•tza ki roo•ach e•chad ba•chem ve•ne•fesh a•chat le•hi•la•chem yach•dav mil•cha•mot emoo•nat ha•be•so•ra.

Rabbinic Jewish Commentary

The allusion is to cities which have their peculiar laws and rules, to which the citizens are to conform; and such as behave according to them act up to the character of good citizens, and becoming, and worthy of the charter by which they hold their privileges and immunities. A church of Messiah is as a city, and is often so called; the members of it are citizens, fellow citizens, one with another, and of the household of God, and have laws and rules according to which they are to conduct themselves.

---

28. And in nothing terrified by your adversaries: which is to them an evident token of perdition, but to you of salvation, and that of God.

Greek/Transliteration

28. καὶ μὴ πτυρόμενοι ἐν μηδενὶ ὑπὸ τῶν ἀντικειμένων· ἥτις αὐτοῖς μέν ἐστιν ἔνδειξις ἀπωλείας, ὑμῖν δὲ σωτηρίας, καὶ τοῦτο ἀπὸ θεοῦ·

28. kai mei pturomenoi en meideni 'upo ton antikeimenon. 'eitis autois men estin endeixis apoleias, 'umin de soteirias, kai touto apo theou.

Hebrew/Transliteration

כח. וְאַל-תִּירְאוּ וְאַל-תַּעַרְצוּ מִפְּנֵי הַקָּמִים עֲלֵיכֶם זֶה הוּא לָהֶם לְאוֹת כִּלָּיוֹן וְלָכֶם לִתְשׁוּעָה וְגַם-זֹאת יָצְאָה מֵעִם הָאֱלֹהִים:

28. Ve•al - ti•ra•oo ve•al - ta•ar•tzoo mip•ney ha•ka•mim aley•chem ze hoo la•hem le•ot ki•la•yon ve•la•chem lit•shoo•ah ve•gam - zot yatz•ah me•eem ha•Elohim.

---

29. For unto you it is given in the behalf of Christ, not only to believe on him, but also to suffer for his sake;

Greek/Transliteration

29. ὅτι ὑμῖν ἐχαρίσθη τὸ ὑπὲρ χριστοῦ, οὐ μόνον τὸ εἰς αὐτὸν πιστεύειν, ἀλλὰ καὶ τὸ ὑπὲρ αὐτοῦ πάσχειν·

29. 'oti 'umin echaristhei to 'uper christou, ou monon to eis auton pisteuein, alla kai to 'uper autou paschein.

Hebrew/Transliteration

כט. אֲשֶׁר נָתַן לָכֶם גַּם-לְהַאֲמִין בַּמָּשִׁיחַ וְגַם-לְהִתְעַנּוֹת בִּגְלָלוֹ:

29. Asher na•tan la•chem gam - le•ha•a•min ba•Ma•shi•ach ve•gam - le•hit•a•not big•la•lo.

Rabbinic Jewish Commentary
The Alexandrian copy reads, "to us it is given"

30. Having the same conflict which ye saw in me, and now hear to be in me.

Greek/Transliteration
30. τὸν αὐτὸν ἀγῶνα ἔχοντες οἷον εἴδετε ἐν ἐμοί, καὶ νῦν ἀκούετε ἐν ἐμοί.
30. ton auton agona echontes 'oion eidete en emoi, kai nun akouete en emoi.

Hebrew/Translation
ל׃ וְנַפְתּוּלֵי אֱלֹהִים נִפְתַּלְתֶּם כָּמֹנִי כַּאֲשֶׁר רְאִיתֶם אֹתִי וְכַאֲשֶׁר הִנְּכֶם שֹׁמְעִים עָלַי כַּיּוֹם הַזֶּה

30. Ve•naf•too•ley Elohim nif•tal•tem ka•mo•ni ka•a•sher r`ee•tem o•ti ve•cha•a•sher hin•chem shom•eem a•lai ka•yom ha•ze.

Philippians, Chapter 2

1. If there be therefore any consolation in Christ, if any comfort of love, if any fellowship of the Spirit, if any bowels and mercies,

Greek/Transliteration
1. Εἴ τις οὖν παράκλησις ἐν χριστῷ, εἴ τι παραμύθιον ἀγάπης, εἴ τις κοινωνία πνεύματος, εἴ τις σπλάγχνα καὶ οἰκτιρμοί,

1. Ei tis oun parakleisis en christo, ei ti paramuthion agapeis, ei tis koinonia pneumatos, ei tis splagchna kai oiktirmoi,

Hebrew/Transliteration
:א. לָכֵן אִם-יֵשׁ נֹחַם מָה בַּמָּשִׁיחַ אִם-יֵשׁ אַהֲבָה מְשִׁיבַת נָפֶשׁ אִם-יֵשׁ חִבּוּר הָרוּחַ אִם-יֵשׁ רַחֲמִים וַחֲסָדִים

1. La•chen eem - yesh no•cham ma ba•Ma•shi•ach eem - yesh a•ha•va me•shi•vat na•fesh eem - yesh chi•boor ha•Roo•ach eem - yesh ra•cha•mim va•cha•sa•dim.

---

2. Fulfill ye my joy, that ye be likeminded, having the same love, being of one accord, of one mind.

Greek/Transliteration
2. πληρώσατέ μου τὴν χαράν, ἵνα τὸ αὐτὸ φρονῆτε, τὴν αὐτὴν ἀγάπην ἔχοντες, σύμψυχοι, τὸ ἓν φρονοῦντες·

2. pleirosate mou tein charan, 'ina to auto phroneite, tein autein agapein echontes, sumpsuchoi, to 'en phronountes.

Hebrew/Transliteration
:ב. הַשְׁלִימוּ-נָא שְׂשׂוֹן לְבָבִי וְהִתְאַחֲדוּ בְדֵעָה אַחַת אַהֲבָה אַחַת נֶפֶשׁ אַחַת וְלֵב אֶחָד

2. Hash•li•moo - na s`son le•va•vi ve•hit•a•cha•doo ve•de•ah a•chat a•ha•va a•chat ne•fesh a•chat ve•lev e•chad.

---

3. Let nothing be done through strife or vainglory; but in lowliness of mind let each esteem other better than themselves.

Greek/Transliteration
3. μηδὲν κατὰ ἐριθείαν ἢ κενοδοξίαν, ἀλλὰ τῇ ταπεινοφροσύνῃ ἀλλήλους ἡγούμενοι ὑπερέχοντας ἑαυτῶν·

3. meiden kata eritheian ei kenodoxian, alla tei tapeinophrosunei alleilous 'eigoumenoi 'uperechontas 'eauton.

Hebrew/Transliteration
:ג. אַל-תַּעֲשׂוּ דָבָר בִּמְרִיבָה אוֹ בִכְבוֹד שָׁוְא כִּי אִם-בְּעַנְוַתְכֶם תַּחְשְׁבוּ אִישׁ אֶת-אָחִיו לְגָדוֹל מִמֶּנּוּ

3. Al - ta•a•soo da•var bim•ri•va oh bich•vod shav ki eem - be•an•vat•chem tach•she•voo eesh et - a•chiv le•ga•dol mi•me•noo.

4. Look not every man on his own things, but every man also on the things of others.

Greek/Transliteration
4. μὴ τὰ ἑαυτῶν ἕκαστος σκοπεῖτε, ἀλλὰ καὶ τὰ ἑτέρων ἕκαστος.

4. mei ta 'eauton 'ekastos skopeite, alla kai ta 'eteron 'ekastos.

Hebrew/Transliteration
ד. אַל-יָחוּשׁ אִישׁ לְטוֹבַת נַפְשׁוֹ לְבַדּוֹ כִּי אִם-גַּם לְטוֹבַת רֵעֵהוּ:

4. Al - ya•choosh eesh le•to•vat naf•sho le•va•do ki eem - gam le•to•vat re•e•hoo.

---

5. Let this mind be in you, which was also in Christ Jesus:

Greek/Transliteration
5. Τοῦτο γὰρ φρονείσθω ἐν ὑμῖν ὃ καὶ ἐν χριστῷ Ἰησοῦ·

5. Touto gar phroneistho en 'umin 'o kai en christo Yeisou.

Hebrew/Transliteration
ה. וִיהִי כֵן לִבְכֶם כִּלְבַב יֵשׁוּעַ הַמָּשִׁיחַ:

5. Vi•y`hi chen lib•chem kil•vav Yeshua ha•Ma•shi•ach.

Rabbinic Jewish Commentary
The Arabic version renders it, "let that humility be perceived in you".

The Syriac version, "think ye the same thing as Jesus Christ"; let the same condescending spirit and humble deportment appear in you as in him.

---

6. Who, being in the form of God, thought it not robbery to be equal with God:

Greek/Transliteration
6. ὃς ἐν μορφῇ θεοῦ ὑπάρχων, οὐχ ἁρπαγμὸν ἡγήσατο τὸ εἶναι ἴσα θεῷ,

6. 'os en morphei theou 'uparchon, ouch 'arpagmon 'eigeisato to einai isa theo,

Hebrew/Transliteration
ו. הוּא אֲשֶׁר בְּמוֹצָאוֹתָיו נִמְצָא בִדְמוּת אֱלֹהִים וּבְכָל-זֹאת לֹא חָשַׁב הֱיוֹתוֹ שָׁוֶה לֵאלֹהִים כְּשָׁלָל לוֹ:

6. Hoo asher be•mo•tza•o•tav nim•tza vid•moot Elohim oov•chol - zot lo cha•shav he•yo•to sha•ve le•Elohim ke•sha•lal lo.

Rabbinic Jewish Commentary
The Heathens themselves (g) say cannot be comprehended nor seen, and so not to be inquired after; and they use the same word the apostle does here (h): and now Messiah being in this glorious form, or having the same divine nature with the Father, with all the infinite and unspeakable glories of it.

To be "in the form of God", and to be "equal with God", signify the same thing, the one is explanative of the other: and this divine form and equality, or true and proper deity, he did not obtain by force and rapine, by robbery and usurpation and as Adam by his instigation also affected; and so the mind of a wicked man, as Philo the Jew says (i), being a lover of itself and impious, οιομενος ισος ειναι θεω, "thinks itself to be equal with God", a like phrase with this here used.

The apostle is speaking not of what Yeshua was, or did in his incarnate state, but of what he was and thought himself to be, before he became man; wherefore the above sense is to be preferred as the genuine one.

(g) Socraticus, Xenophon, & Aristo Chius, apud Minuc. Felic. Octav. p. 20. & Hostanes apud Caecil. Cyprian. de Idol. van. p. 46. (h) Laertii proem. ad Vit. Philosoph. p. 7. (i) Leg. Alleg. l. 1. p. 48, 49.

---

7. But made himself of no reputation, and took upon him the form of a servant, and was made in the likeness of men:

Greek/Transliteration
7. ἀλλ᾽ ἑαυτὸν ἐκένωσεν, μορφὴν δούλου λαβών, ἐν ὁμοιώματι ἀνθρώπων γενόμενος·

7. all 'eauton ekenosen, morphein doulou labon, en 'omoiomati anthropon genomenos.

Hebrew/Transliteration
ז: כִּי אִם-הִתְנַצֵּל אֶת-כְּבוֹדוֹ וַיִּלְבַּשׁ דְּמוּת עָבֶד וַיְהִי כְתַבְנִית אַחַד הָאָדָם

7. Ki eem - hit•na•tzel et - k`vo•do va•yil•bash d`moot a•ved vay•hi ke•tav•nit achad ha•a•dam.

Rabbinic Jewish Commentary
So he was often prophesied of as a servant, in Isa_42:1, in which several places he is called in the Targum, עבדי משיחא, "my servant the Messiah": put these two together, "the form of God", and "the form of a servant", and admire the amazing stoop!

---

8. And being found in fashion as a man, he humbled himself, and became obedient unto death, even the death of the cross.

Greek/Transliteration
8. καὶ σχήματι εὑρεθεὶς ὡς ἄνθρωπος, ἐταπείνωσεν ἑαυτόν, γενόμενος ὑπήκοος μέχρι θανάτου, θανάτου δὲ σταυροῦ.

8. kai scheimati 'euretheis 'os anthropos, etapeinosen 'eauton, genomenos 'upeikoos mechri thanatou, thanatou de staurou.

Hebrew/Transliteration
ח: וְאַחֲרֵי אֲשֶׁר נִמְצָא כְאָדָם לַתֹּאַר הִשְׁפִּיל נַפְשׁוֹ וַיִּכָּנַע עַד-מָוֶת עַד-מוֹת עַל-הָעֵץ

8. Ve•a•cha•rey asher nim•tza che•a•dam la•to•ar hish•pil naf•sho va•yi•ka•na ad - ma•vet ad - moot al - ha•etz.

Rabbinic Jewish Commentary

And being found in fashion as a man,.... Not that he had only the show and appearance of a man, but he was really a man; for "as" here, denotes not merely the likeness of a thing, but the thing itself, as in Mat_14:5, ως here, answers to the Hebrew which is sometimes by the Jews (k) said to be כף הדמיון, and signifies likeness, and sometimes כף האמתות, and designs truth and reality; which is the sense in which the particle is to be taken here.

even the death of the cross; which was both painful and shameful; it was an accursed one, and showed that he bore the curse of the Torah, and was made a curse for us: this was a punishment usually inflicted on servants, and is called a servile punishment (l); and such was the form which he took, when he was found in fashion as a man: this is now the great instance of humility the apostle gives, as a pattern of it to the saints, and it is a matchless and unparalleled one.

(k) Vid. Kimchi in Josh. iii. 4. (l) Lipsins de Cruce, l. 1. c. 12.

---

9. Wherefore God also hath highly exalted him, and given him a name which is above every name:

Greek/Transliteration
9. Διὸ καὶ ὁ θεὸς αὐτὸν ὑπερύψωσεν, καὶ ἐχαρίσατο αὐτῷ ὄνομα τὸ ὑπὲρ πᾶν ὄνομα·

9. Dio kai 'o theos auton 'uperupsosen, kai echarisato auto onoma to 'uper pan onoma.

Hebrew/Transliteration
ט. עַל-כֵּן גַּם-הָאֱלֹהִים הֱרִימוֹ עַל וַיִּתֶּן-לוֹ שֵׁם נַעֲלֶה מִכָּל-שֵׁם:

9. Al - ken gam - ha•Elohim he•ri•mo al va•yi•ten - lo shem na•a•le mi•kol - shem.

Rabbinic Jewish Commentary

The Syriac version renders it, "which is more excellent than every name"; and the Arabic version translates it, "which is more eminent than every name"; and the Ethiopic version thus, "which is greater than every name".

It is a more clear point, that he is God over all blessed for evermore; and it will still be more manifest at his glorious appearing, that he is the great God, as well as our Saviour: to which may be added, that the name YHWH in the plate of gold on the high priest's forehead, was set above the other word; so says Maimonides (m),

"The plate of gold was two fingers broad, and it reached from ear to ear; and there was written upon it two lines, "holiness YHWH"; קדש, "holiness", was written below, and ליהוה מלמעלה, "to YHWH above."

Yinnon is the name that represents the preexisting Messiah aroused the curiosity of Maharsha (Rabbi Shmuel Eliezar Halevi Idels) In his important commentary to the Talmud, he notes that if the two *nuns* are replaced with *hes*, "Yinnon" (y-n-v-n) becomes "LORD" (y-h-v-h). His conclusion is that such "defective" spelling serves as a hint that in the days of Messiah, he will be called LORD: [YHWH]... "In the days of Messiah the name y-h-v-h... will be the ordinary name...so that even Messiah is called by this name, as it says in chapter 'The Boat' (b.Bava Batra 75b), Messiah will be called by the name of the LORD, as it says, 'This is his name by which He will be called: the LORD Our Righteousness' (Jer.23:6)

But 'before the sun,' meaning before the creation of the world, the name of Messiah was not fully called by the name y-h-v-h but by y-n-v-n to hint at the name LORD" (Chiddushei Aggadot, Nedarim 39.b) As quoted from, *The Concealed Light; Names of Messiah in Jewish Sources*, by Tsvi Sadan.

---

10. That at the name of Jesus every knee should bow, of things in heaven, and things in earth, and things under the earth;

Greek/Transliteration
10. ἵνα ἐν τῷ ὀνόματι Ἰησοῦ πᾶν γόνυ κάμψῃ ἐπουρανίων καὶ ἐπιγείων καὶ καταχθονίων,

10. 'ina en to onomati Yeisou pan gonu kampsei epouranion kai epigeion kai katachthonion,

Hebrew/Transliteration
י. כִּי לְשֵׁם יֵשׁוּעַ תִּכְרַע כָּל-בֶּרֶךְ אֲשֶׁר בַּשָּׁמַיִם וַאֲשֶׁר בָּאָרֶץ וַאֲשֶׁר מִתַּחַת לָאָרֶץ:

10. Ki le•shem Yeshua tich•ra kol - be•rech asher ba•sha•ma•yim va•a•sher ba•a•retz va•a•sher mi•ta•chat la•a•retz.

Rabbinic Jewish Commentary
The Jews indeed, upon hearing the name YHWH pronounced by the high priest, in the holy of holies, used to bow: they say (n),

"That the priests, and the people, that stand in the court, when they hear Shemhamphorash (i.e. the name "YHWH") pronounced by the high priest, היו כורעים, "bowed", and worshipped, and fell upon their faces, and said, "blessed be the name of the glory of his kingdom, for ever and ever."

(n) T. Bab. Yoma, fol. 66. 1. Maimon. Yom Haccippurim, c. 2. sect. 7.

---

11. And that every tongue should confess that Jesus Christ is Lord, to the glory of God the Father.

Greek/Transliteration
11. καὶ πᾶσα γλῶσσα ἐξομολογήσηται ὅτι κύριος Ἰησοῦς χριστός, εἰς δόξαν θεοῦ πατρός.

11. kai pasa glossa exomologeiseitai 'oti kurios Yeisous christos, eis doxan theou patros.

Hebrew/Transliteration
יא. וְכָל-לָשׁוֹן תִּשָּׁבַע כִּי יֵשׁוּעַ הַמָּשִׁיחַ הוּא הָאָדוֹן לִכְבוֹד אֱלֹהִים הָאָב:

11. Ve•chol - la•shon ti•sha•va ki Yeshua ha•Ma•shi•ach hoo ha•Adon lich•vod Elohim ha•Av.

12. Wherefore, my beloved, as ye have always obeyed, not as in my presence only, but now much more in my absence, work out your own salvation with fear and trembling.

Greek/Transliteration
12. Ὥστε, ἀγαπητοί μου, καθὼς πάντοτε ὑπηκούσατε, μὴ ὡς ἐν τῇ παρουσίᾳ μου μόνον, ἀλλὰ νῦν πολλῷ μᾶλλον ἐν τῇ ἀπουσίᾳ μου, μετὰ φόβου καὶ τρόμου τὴν ἑαυτῶν σωτηρίαν κατεργάζεσθε·

12. 'Oste, agapeitoi mou, kathos pantote 'upeikousate, mei 'os en tei parousia mou monon, alla nun pollo mallon en tei apousia mou, meta phobou kai tromou tein 'eauton soteirian katergazesthe.

Hebrew/Transliteration
יב. עַל־כֵּן אֲהוּבֵי נַפְשִׁי כַּאֲשֶׁר שְׁמַעְתֶּם אֵלַי תָּמִיד בִּהְיוֹתִי לִפְנֵיכֶם וְגַם־עוֹד יֶתֶר הַרְבֵּה כַּיּוֹם בִּהְיוֹתִי מֵרָחוֹק עִבְדוּ בְיִרְאָה וּבִרְעָדָה לְיֵשַׁע נַפְשְׁכֶם:

12. Al - ken a•hoo•vey naf•shi ka•a•sher sh`ma•a•tem e•lai ta•mid bi•hi•yo•ti lif•ney•chem ve•gam - od ye•ter har•be ka•yom bi•hi•yo•ti me•ra•chok eev•doo ve•yir•ah oo•vir•a•da le•ye•sha naf•she•chem.

Rabbinic Jewish Commentary
The Syriac version renders the words, פלוחו פולחנא דחייכון, "do the work", or "business of your lives"; the work you are to do in your generation, which God has prescribed and directed you to, which the grace of God teaches, and the love of Christ constrains to. Do all that "with fear and trembling".

---

13. For it is God which worketh in you both to will and to do of his good pleasure.

Greek/Transliteration
13. ὁ θεὸς γάρ ἐστιν ὁ ἐνεργῶν ἐν ὑμῖν καὶ τὸ θέλειν καὶ τὸ ἐνεργεῖν ὑπὲρ τῆς εὐδοκίας.

13. 'o theos gar estin 'o energon en 'umin kai to thelein kai to energein 'uper teis eudokias.

Hebrew/Transliteration
יג. כִּי אֱלֹהִים הוּא הַנֹּתֵן לָכֶם כֹּחַ לַחְפֹּץ וְגַם־לַעֲשׂוֹת כְּחֶפְצוֹ:

13. Ki Elohim hoo ha•no•ten la•chem ko•ach lach•potz ve•gam - la•a•sot ke•chef•tzo.

Rabbinic Jewish Commentary
The word here used signifies an inward, powerful, and efficacious operation; and the "king's manuscript", mentioned by Grotius and Hammond, adds another word to it, which makes the sense still stronger, reading it thus, "which worketh in you", δυναμει, "by power"; not by moral persuasion, but by his own power, the power of his efficacious grace. The Alexandrian copy reads, δυναμεις, "powers", or "mighty works".

the Syriac version renders it, "both to will and to do that", דצבין אנתון, "which ye will", or according to your good will.

14. Do all things without murmurings and disputings:

Greek/Transliteration

14. Πάντα ποιεῖτε χωρὶς γογγυσμῶν καὶ διαλογισμῶν,

14. Panta poieite choris gongusmon kai dyalogismon,

Hebrew/Transliteration

יד. וְכֹל אֲשֶׁר תַּעֲשׂוּ עֲשׂוּ בִּבְלִי תְלוּנָה וּבִבְלִי מָדוֹן:

14. Ve•chol asher ta•a•soo a•soo biv•li t`loo•na oo•viv•li ma•don.

---

15. That ye may be blameless and harmless, the sons of God, without rebuke, in the midst of a crooked and perverse nation, among whom ye shine as lights in the world;

Greek/Transliteration

15. ἵνα γένησθε ἄμεμπτοι καὶ ἀκέραιοι, τέκνα θεοῦ ἀμώμητα ἐν μέσῳ γενεᾶς σκολιᾶς καὶ διεστραμμένης, ἐν οἷς φαίνεσθε ὡς φωστῆρες ἐν κόσμῳ,

15. 'ina geneisthe amemptoi kai akeraioi, tekna theou amomeita en meso geneas skolyas kai diestrammeneis, en 'ois phainesthe 'os phosteires en kosmo,

Hebrew/Transliteration

טו. לְבַעֲבוּר תִּהְיוּ זַכִּים וּתְמִימִים כִּבְנֵי אֱלֹהִים בִּבְלִי-מוּם בְּתוֹךְ דּוֹר עִקֵּשׁ וּפְתַלְתֹּל אֲשֶׁר-תָּאִירוּ בֵינֵיהֶם כִּמְאֹרֹת עֲלֵי-הָאָרֶץ:

15. Le•va•a•voor ti•hi•yoo za•kim oot•mi•mim kiv•ney Elohim biv•li - moom be•toch dor ee•kesh oof•tal•tol asher - ta•ee•roo vey•ne•hem kim•o•rot aley - ha•a•retz.

---

16. Holding forth the word of life; that I may rejoice in the day of Christ, that I have not run in vain, neither laboured in vain.

Greek/Transliteration

16. λόγον ζωῆς ἐπέχοντες, εἰς καύχημα ἐμοὶ εἰς ἡμέραν χριστοῦ, ὅτι οὐκ εἰς κενὸν ἔδραμον, οὐδὲ εἰς κενὸν ἐκοπίασα.

16. logon zoeis epechontes, eis kaucheima emoi eis 'eimeran christou, 'oti ouk eis kenon edramon, oude eis kenon ekopiasa.

Hebrew/Transliteration

טז. כִּי תֹאחֲזוּן בִּדְבַר הַחַיִּים לִהְיוֹת לִי לְתִפְאֶרֶת בְּיוֹם הַמָּשִׁיחַ כִּי לֹא חַשְׁתִּי לָרִיק וְלֹא יָגַעְתִּי לַתֹּהוּ:

16. Ki to•cha•zoon bid•var ha•cha•yim li•hee•yot li le•tif•e•ret be•yom ha•Ma•shi•ach ki lo chash•ti la•rik ve•lo ya•ga•a•ti la•to•hoo.

---

17. Yea, and if I be offered upon the sacrifice and service of your faith, I joy, and rejoice with you all.

Greek/Transliteration

17. Ἀλλ' εἰ καὶ σπένδομαι ἐπὶ τῇ θυσίᾳ καὶ λειτουργίᾳ τῆς πίστεως ὑμῶν, χαίρω καὶ συγχαίρω πᾶσιν ὑμῖν·

17. All ei kai spendomai epi tei thusia kai leitourgia teis pisteos 'umon, chairo kai sugchairo pasin 'umin.

Hebrew/Transliteration

יז. וְגַם לוּ יֻשְׁפַּךְ דָּמִי עֲלֵי-זֶבַח וַעֲבֹדָה לֶאֱמוּנַתְכֶם אָשִׂישׂ עַל-כֻּלְּכֶם וְאָגִילָה:

17. Ve•gam loo yi•sha•fech da•mi aley - ze•vach va•a•vo•da le•e•moo•nat•chem asis al - kool•chem ve•a•gi•la.

---

18. For the same cause also do ye joy, and rejoice with me.

Greek/Transliteration

18. τὸ δ' αὐτὸ καὶ ὑμεῖς χαίρετε καὶ συγχαίρετέ μοι.

18. to d auto kai 'umeis chairete kai sugchairete moi.

Hebrew/Transliteration

יח. וְכֵן שִׂישׂוּ גַם-אַתֶּם וְגִילוּ עִמָּדִי:

18. Ve•chen si•soo gam - atem ve•gi•loo ee•ma•di.

---

19. But I trust in the Lord Jesus to send Timotheus shortly unto you, that I also may be of good comfort, when I know your state.

Greek/Transliteration

19. Ἐλπίζω δὲ ἐν κυρίῳ Ἰησοῦ, Τιμόθεον ταχέως πέμψαι ὑμῖν, ἵνα κἀγὼ εὐψυχῶ, γνοὺς τὰ περὶ ὑμῶν.

19. Elpizo de en kurio Yeisou, Timotheon tacheos pempsai 'umin, 'ina kago eupsucho, gnous ta peri 'umon.

Hebrew/Transliteration

יט. וַאֲנִי תוֹחַלְתִּי בְּיֵשׁוּעַ אֲדֹנֵינוּ לִשְׁלֹחַ לָכֶם מְהֵרָה אֶת-טִימוֹתִיּוֹס לְהָשִׁיב נַפְשִׁי גַּם-אֲנִי כַּאֲשֶׁר אֵדַע מָה עִמָּכֶם:

19. Va•a•ni to•chal•ti ve•Yeshua Ado•ney•noo lish•lo•ach la•chem me•he•ra et - Ti•mo•ti•yos le•ha•shiv naf•shi gam - ani ka•a•sher eda ma ee•ma•chem.

---

20. For I have no man likeminded, who will naturally care for your state.

Greek/Transliteration

20. Οὐδένα γὰρ ἔχω ἰσόψυχον, ὅστις γνησίως τὰ περὶ ὑμῶν μεριμνήσει.

20. Oudena gar echo isopsuchon, 'ostis gneisios ta peri 'umon merimneisei.

Hebrew/Transliteration

:כ. כִּי זוּלָתוֹ אֵין-אִתִּי אִישׁ כִּלְבָבִי הַדֹּאֵג לָכֶם מִמְּקוֹר נַפְשׁוֹ

20. Ki zoo•la•to eyn - ee•ti eesh kil•va•vi ha•do•eg la•chem mim•kor naf•sho.

---

21. For all seek their own, not the things which are Jesus Christ's.

Greek/Transliteration

21. Οἱ πάντες γὰρ τὰ ἑαυτῶν ζητοῦσιν, οὐ τὰ χριστοῦ Ἰησοῦ.

21. 'Oi pantes gar ta 'eauton zeitousin, ou ta christou Yeisou.

Hebrew/Transliteration

:כא. כִּי כֻלָּם חֶפְצֵי נַפְשָׁם יִדְרֹשׁוּן וְלֹא חֶפְצֵי יֵשׁוּעַ הַמָּשִׁיחַ

21. Ki choo•lam chef•tzey naf•sham yid•ro•shoon ve•lo chef•tzey Yeshua ha•Ma•shi•ach.

---

22. But ye know the proof of him, that, as a son with the father, he hath served with me in the gospel.

Greek/Transliteration

22. Τὴν δὲ δοκιμὴν αὐτοῦ γινώσκετε, ὅτι ὡς πατρὶ τέκνον, σὺν ἐμοὶ ἐδούλευσεν εἰς τὸ εὐαγγέλιον.

22. Tein de dokimein autou ginoskete, 'oti 'os patri teknon, sun emoi edouleusen eis to euangelion.

Hebrew/Transliteration

:כב. וְרַק אֹתוֹ יְדַעְתֶּם כִּי צָרוּף הוּא בַּעֲלִיל וּכְבֵן לִפְנֵי אָבִיו עָבַד עִמִּי בִּמְלֶאכֶת הַבְּשׂרָה

22. Ve•rak o•to ye•da•a•tem ki tza•roof hoo ba•a•lil ooch•ven lif•ney aviv avad ee•mi be•mal•a•choot ha•be•so•ra.

---

23. Him therefore I hope to send presently, so soon as I shall see how it will go with me.

Greek/Transliteration

23. Τοῦτον μὲν οὖν ἐλπίζω πέμψαι, ὡς ἂν ἀπίδω τὰ περὶ ἐμέ, ἐξαυτῆς·

23. Touton men oun elpizo pempsai, 'os an apido ta peri eme, exauteis.

Hebrew/Transliteration

:כג. אֲקַוֶּה כִּי אֶשְׁלָחֶנּוּ לָכֶם בְּקֶרֶב הַיָּמִים אַחֲרֵי אֲשֶׁר אֶרְאֶה מַה-יַּעֲשֶׂה בִּי

23. A•ka•ve ki esh•la•che•noo la•chem be•ke•rev ha•ya•mim a•cha•rey asher er•eh ma - ye•a•se bi.

---

24. But I trust in the Lord that I also myself shall come shortly.

Greek/Transliteration
24. πέποιθα δὲ ἐν κυρίῳ, ὅτι καὶ αὐτὸς ταχέως ἐλεύσομαι.

24. pepoitha de en kurio, 'oti kai autos tacheos eleusomai.

Hebrew/Transliteration
כד. אַךְ בַּאֲדֹנֵינוּ בָטַחְתִּי כִּי גַם-אָנֹכִי אָבוֹא אֲלֵיכֶם מְהֵרָה:

24. Ach ba•Ado•ne•noo va•tach•ti ki gam - ano•chi avo aley•chem me•he•ra.

---

25. Yet I supposed it necessary to send to you Epaphroditus, my brother, and companion in labour, and fellowsoldier, but your messenger, and he that ministered to my wants.

Greek/Transliteration
25. Ἀναγκαῖον δὲ ἡγησάμην Ἐπαφρόδιτον τὸν ἀδελφὸν καὶ συνεργὸν καὶ συστρατιώτην μου, ὑμῶν δὲ ἀπόστολον, καὶ λειτουργὸν τῆς χρείας μου, πέμψαι πρὸς ὑμᾶς·

25. Anagkaion de 'eigeisamein Epaphroditon ton adelphon kai sunergon kai sustratiotein mou, 'umon de apostolon, kai leitourgon teis chreias mou, pempsai pros 'umas.

Hebrew/Transliteration
כה. וְרָאִיתִי כִּי נָכוֹן הַדָּבָר לִשְׁלֹחַ לָכֶם אֶת-אֶפַּפְרוֹדִיטוֹס אָחִי סוֹמֵךְ יָדִי בַּעֲבֹדָתִי וְגֶבֶר עֲמִיתִי בְּמִלְחַמְתִּי הֲלֹא הוּא הַשָּׁלוּחַ מִכֶּם וְהַנֹּתֵן לִי מַחְסֹרָי:

25. Ve•ra•ee•ti ki na•chon ha•da•var lish•lo•ach la•chem et - Epaf•ro•ditos achi so•mech ya•di ba•a•vo•da•ti ve•ge•ver ami•ti be•mil•cham•ti ha•lo hoo ha•sha•loo•ach mi•kem ve•ha•no•ten li mach•so•rai.

Rabbinic Jewish Commentary
One of this name lived at Rome about this time, and was one of Nero's freemen (o), but not the same person here intended. This person has a very high character.

(o) Artinn. Epictet. l. 1. c. 1, 19, 26. & Aurel. Victor. Epitome Rom. Imp. in Nerone.

---

26. For he longed after you all, and was full of heaviness, because that ye had heard that he had been sick.

Greek/Transliteration
26. ἐπειδὴ ἐπιποθῶν ἦν πάντας ὑμᾶς, καὶ ἀδημονῶν, διότι ἠκούσατε ὅτι ἠσθένησεν·

26. epeidei epipothon ein pantas 'umas, kai adeimonon, dioti eikousate 'oti eistheneisen.

Hebrew/Transliteration

:כו. כִּי נִכְסְפָה נַפְשׁוֹ לְכֻלְּכֶם וְיִתְעַצֵּב אֶל - לִבּוֹ בַּעֲבוּר אֲשֶׁר שְׁמַעְתֶּם כִּי חָלָה

26. Ki nich•se•fa naf•sho le•chool•chem ve•yit•a•tzev el - li•bo ba•a•voor asher sh`ma•a•tem ki cha•la.

---

27. For indeed he was sick nigh unto death: but God had mercy on him; and not on him only, but on me also, lest I should have sorrow upon sorrow.

Greek/Transliteration

27. καὶ γὰρ ἠσθένησεν παραπλήσιον θανάτῳ, ἀλλὰ ὁ θεὸς αὐτὸν ἠλέησεν, οὐκ αὐτὸν δὲ μόνον, ἀλλὰ καὶ ἐμέ, ἵνα μὴ λύπην ἐπὶ λύπην σχῶ.

27. kai gar eistheneisen parapleision thanato, alla 'o theos auton eileeisen, ouk auton de monon, alla kai eme, 'ina mei lupein epi lupein scho.

Hebrew/Transliteration

כז. כִּי אָמֵן חָלֹה חָלָה וְנָטָה לָמוּת אַךְ הָאֱלֹהִים הִטָּה אֵלָיו חָסֶד וְלֹא אֵלָיו לְבַדּוֹ כִּי אִם-גַּם אֵלַי לְבִלְתִּי הוֹסִיף :לִי יָגוֹן עַל-יָגוֹן

27. Ki amen cha•lo cha•la ve•na•ta la•moot ach ha•Elohim hita elav cha•sed ve•lo elav le•va•do ki eem - gam e•lai le•vil•ti ho•sif li ya•gon al - ya•gon.

---

28. I sent him therefore the more carefully, that, when ye see him again, ye may rejoice, and that I may be the less sorrowful.

Greek/Transliteration

28. Σπουδαιοτέρως οὖν ἔπεμψα αὐτόν, ἵνα, ἰδόντες αὐτὸν πάλιν, χαρῆτε, κἀγὼ ἀλυπότερος ὦ.

28. Spoudaioteros oun epempsa auton, 'ina, idontes auton palin, chareite, kago alupoteros o.

Hebrew/Transliteration

:כח. עַל-כֵּן חַשְׁתִּי לְשַׁלְּחוֹ לְמַעַן תִּרְאֻהוּ וְתָשִׂישׂוּ בוֹ וְנִגְרַע יָגוֹן מִמֶּנִּי

28. Al - ken chash•ti le•shal•cho le•ma•an tir•oo•hoo ve•ta•si•soo vo ve•nig•ra ya•gon mi•me•ni.

---

29. Receive him therefore in the Lord with all gladness; and hold such in reputation:

Greek/Transliteration

29. Προσδέχεσθε οὖν αὐτὸν ἐν κυρίῳ μετὰ πάσης χαρᾶς, καὶ τοὺς τοιούτους ἐντίμους ἔχετε·

29. Prosdechesthe oun auton en kurio meta paseis charas, kai tous toioutous entimous echete.

Hebrew/Transliteration
כט. אֲשֶׁר לְזֹאת קַדְּמוּ פָנָיו בַּאֲדֹנֵינוּ בְּשָׂשׂוֹן רָב וְהָבוּ כָבוֹד לַאֲנָשִׁים כָּמֹהוּ:

29. Asher la•zot kad•moo fa•nav ba•Ado•ne•noo be•sa•son rav ve•ha•voo cha•vod la•a•na•shim ka•mo•hoo.

---

30. Because for the work of Christ he was nigh unto death, not regarding his life, to supply your lack of service toward me.

Greek/Transliteration
30. ὅτι διὰ τὸ ἔργον τοῦ χριστοῦ μέχρι θανάτου ἤγγισεν, παραβουλευσάμενος τῇ ψυχῇ, ἵνα ἀναπληρώσῃ τὸ ὑμῶν ὑστέρημα τῆς πρός με λειτουργίας.

30. 'oti dya to ergon tou christou mechri thanatou eingisen, parabouleusamenos tei psuchei, 'ina anapleirosei to 'umon 'ustereima teis pros me leitourgias.

Hebrew/Transliteration
ל. כִּי הִגִּיעַ עַד-שַׁעֲרֵי מָוֶת בַּעֲבוּר עֲבֹדַת הַמָּשִׁיחַ וַיַּשְׁלֵךְ נַפְשׁוֹ מִנֶּגֶד לְמַעַן הִמָּנוֹת הַחֶסְרוֹן אֲשֶׁר קָצְרָה יֶדְכֶם לְסָמְכֵנִי:

30. Ki hi•gi•a ad - sha•a•rey ma•vet ba•a•voor avo•dat ha•Ma•shi•ach va•yash•lech naf•sho mi•ne•ged le•ma•an hi•ma•not ha•ches•ron asher katz•ra yed•chem le•som•che•ni.

Philippians, Chapter 3

1\. Finally, my brethren, rejoice in the Lord. To write the same things to you, to me indeed is not grievous, but for you it is safe.

Greek/Transliteration
1. Τὸ λοιπόν, ἀδελφοί μου, χαίρετε ἐν κυρίῳ. Τὰ αὐτὰ γράφειν ὑμῖν, ἐμοὶ μὲν οὐκ ὀκνηρόν, ὑμῖν δὲ ἀσφαλές.

1\. To loipon, adelphoi mou, chairete en kurio. Ta auta graphein 'umin, emoi men ouk okneiron, 'umin de asphales.

Hebrew/Transliteration
א. וְיֶתֶר הַדְּבָרִים אַחַי הִנְנִי אֹמֵר שִׂמְחוּ בַּאֲדֹנֵינוּ הֵן לִכְתֹּב אֲלֵיכֶם מִשְׁנֵה דָבָר לֹא לְטֹרַח עָלַי וְטוֹב לָכֶם כִּי אֲשַׁנֵּן דְּבָרָי:

1\. Ve•ye•ter ha•d`va•rim a•chai hi•ne•ni o•mer sim•choo va•Ado•ney•noo hen lich•tov aley•chem mish•ne da•var lo le•to•rach a•lai ve•tov la•chem ki asha•nen de•va•rai.

2\. Beware of dogs, beware of evil workers, beware of the concision.

Greek/Transliteration
2. Βλέπετε τοὺς κύνας, βλέπετε τοὺς κακοὺς ἐργάτας, βλέπετε τὴν κατατομήν·

2\. Blepete tous kunas, blepete tous kakous ergatas, blepete tein katatomein.

Hebrew/Transliteration
ב. הִשָּׁמְרוּ מִפְּנֵי הַכְּלָבִים הִשָּׁמְרוּ מִפְּנֵי פֹעֲלֵי אָוֶן הִשָּׁמְרוּ מִפְּנֵי קְצוּצֵי עָרְלָה:

2\. Hi•sham•roo mip•ney ha•k`la•vim hi•sham•roo mip•ney fo•a•ley aven hi•sham•roo mip•ney ke•tzoo•tzey or•la.

Rabbinic Jewish Commentary
By whom are meant the "judaizing" teachers, who were for imposing the works and ceremonies of the Torah upon the Gentiles, as necessary to salvation; and they have the name retorted on them they used to give to the Gentiles; see Mat_15:26; nor should they think it too severe, since the Jews themselves say (p),

"The face of that generation (in which the Messiah shall come) shall he, כפני הכלב, "as the face of a dog".

(p) Misn. Sota, c. 9. sect. 15.

3\. For we are the circumcision, which worship God in the spirit, and rejoice in Christ Jesus, and have no confidence in the flesh.

Greek/Transliteration
3. ἡμεῖς γάρ ἐσμεν ἡ περιτομή, οἱ πνεύματι θεοῦ λατρεύοντες, καὶ καυχώμενοι ἐν χριστῷ Ἰησοῦ, καὶ οὐκ ἐν σαρκὶ πεποιθότες·

3. 'eimeis gar esmen 'ei peritomei, 'oi pneumati theou latreuontes, kai kauchomenoi en Christo Yeisou, kai ouk en sarki pepoithotes.

Hebrew/Transliteration
ג. כִּי אֲנַחְנוּ בְּנֵי בְרִית הַמּוּלוֹת אֲנַחְנוּ אֲשֶׁר נַעֲבֹד אֶת-אֱלֹהִים בָּרוּחַ וַאֲשֶׁר בְּיֵשׁוּעַ הַמָּשִׁיחַ נִתְהַלָּל וְלֹא נָשִׂים בְּבָשָׂר מִבְטַחֵנוּ:

3. Ki a•nach•noo b`ney ve•rit ha•moo•lot a•nach•noo asher na•a•vod et - Elohim ba•roo•ach va•a•sher be•Yeshua ha•Ma•shi•ach nit•ha•lel ve•lo na•sim be•va•sar miv•ta•che•noo.

---

4. Though I might also have confidence in the flesh. If any other man thinketh that he hath whereof he might trust in the flesh, I more:

Greek/Transliteration
4. καίπερ ἐγὼ ἔχων πεποίθησιν καὶ ἐν σαρκί· εἴ τις δοκεῖ ἄλλος πεποιθέναι ἐν σαρκί, ἐγὼ μᾶλλον·

4. kaiper ego echon pepoitheisin kai en sarki. ei tis dokei allos pepoithenai en sarki, ego mallon.

Hebrew/Transliteration
ד. אַף כִּי יֶשׁ-לִי לִבְטֹחַ גַּם-בְּבָשָׂר וְאִם-יָשִׂים אִישׁ בַּבָּשָׂר מִבְטָחוֹ הֲלֹא רַב לִי מִמֶּנּוּ:

4. Af ki yesh - li liv•to•ach gam - be•va•sar ve•eem - ya•sim eesh ba•ba•sar miv•ta•cho ha•lo rav li mi•me•noo.

---

5. Circumcised the eighth day, of the stock of Israel, of the tribe of Benjamin, an Hebrew of the Hebrews; as touching the law, a Pharisee;

Greek/Transliteration
5. περιτομῇ ὀκταήμερος, ἐκ γένους Ἰσραήλ, φυλῆς Βενιαμίν, Ἑβραῖος ἐξ Ἑβραίων, κατὰ νόμον Φαρισαῖος,

5. peritomei oktaeimeros, ek genous Ysraeil, phuleis Benyamin, 'Ebraios ex 'Ebraion, kata nomon Pharisaios,

Hebrew/Transliteration
ה. נִמּוֹל בֶּן-שְׁמֹנַת יָמִים מִגֶּזַע יִשְׂרָאֵל מִשֵּׁבֶט בִּנְיָמִין עִבְרִי בֶן-עִבְרִי וּבְדַת הַתּוֹרָה פָּרוּשׁ:

5. Ni•mol ben - sh`mo•nat ya•mim mi•ge•za Israel mi•she•vet Bin•yamin Eev•ri ben - Eev•ri oov•dat ha•Torah Pa•roosh.

Rabbinic Jewish Commentary
The Jews valued themselves much upon it, and treated the Gentiles with contempt for the want of it; and would neither converse with them in a civil or religious way, because they were uncircumcised: but the apostle was no Gentile, or an uncircumcised person; he had this mark in his flesh to glory in as well as others, if it had been lawful to trust in it; he was the subject of this ordinance while it was a standing one, and before it was abolished by

Yeshua; and it was performed on him at the precise time fixed in the original institution of it, which was not always observed; for not to take notice of Jewish proselytes; who were circumcised at any age, when they became such, whether in youth, manhood, or old age; and which by the way shows, that the apostle was no proselyte, but a natural Jew; Gershom, the son of Moses, was not circumcised till some years after his birth; and all the while the children of Israel were in the wilderness this ordinance was neglected, till Joshua had led them into Canaan's land, and then he circumcised all that generation that was born in the wilderness, some of whom must be near forty years of age; and in after times it was usual with the Jews, for one reason or another, to put off circumcision to a longer time. Take the following story as an illustration of this (q):

"It is a tradition of R. Nathan; once, says he, I went to the cities of the sea, and a woman came to me who had circumcised her first son, and he died; the second, and he died; the third she brought to me; I saw him that he was red, I said unto her, my daughter, "wait a while" for him till his blood is swallowed up in him; she waited for him a while, and circumcised him, and he lived; and they called him Nathan the Babylonian, after my name. And again another time I went to the province of Cappadocia (the Jerusalem Talmud (r) has it Caesarea of Cappadocia), a certain woman came to me, who had circumcised her first son, and he died; the second, and he died; the third, (the above Talmud adds, and he died, the fourth,) she brought to me, I saw that he was green, I inspected him, and the blood of the covenant was not in him, I said unto her, my daughter, המתינו, "tarry a while" for him; (the Jerusalem Talmud has it, הניחוהו לאחר זמן, "let him alone to another time";) till his blood fall in him, she waited for him, and circumcised him, and he lived; and they called him Nathan the Babylonian, after my name.

The Jewish canon, with regard to the time of circumcision, runs thus (s):

"An infant may be circumcised at eight days, or at nine, or at ten, or at eleven, or at twelve, neither less nor more (not less than eight, nor more than twelve), how? according to its course at eight. If it is born between the two evenings, it is circumcised on the ninth day; if between the two evenings of the sabbath eve, it is circumcised on the tenth day; if on a feast day after the sabbath, it is circumcised on the eleventh; if on the two days of the beginning of the year, it is circumcised on the twelfth. An infant that is sick, they do not circumcise him until he is recovered."

And in the last case, they reckon seven days from the time of the recovery of the child, as Maimonides (t) observes; with whom may be read other cases, in which circumcision was not always performed on the eighth day, but sometimes was deferred, and sometimes it was done the same day the child was born. But circumcision on the eighth day was reckoned most valid and authentic, and according to rule; and therefore it is not without reason, that the apostle mentions the time of his circumcision, and puts an emphasis upon it.

He was an Hebrew by the father and mother's side both; he was a genuine Hebrew. The Arabians have the same way of speaking; and with them a genuine Arab is called an Arab of the Arabs (u) as here. Some there were whose mothers were Hebrews, and their fathers Gentiles; such an one was Timothy, Act_16:1; and there were others whose fathers were Hebrews, and their mothers Gentiles; and these are thought by some to be the same the Talmudists (w) call, חללים, "profane": they not being reckoned so holy as such whose fathers and mothers were both Hebrews.

As touching the law, a Pharisee: with respect to the interpretation and observance of the law, which was according to the traditions of the elders, and not the literal and genuine sense of it, he followed; and was of the sect of the Pharisees, which was strictest sect among the Jews, and in the greatest esteem among the people: and though they had put many false glosses on the Scripture, and held many erroneous principles, and were very tenacious of human traditions, yet they were preferable to the Sadducees, who denied the resurrection of the dead, and other things; and were more zealous in their devotion and religion, and more strict in their morals, and external holiness of life and conversation.

(q) T. Bab. Cholin, fol. 47. 2. (r) T. Hieros. Yebamot, fol. 7. 4. (s) Misn. Sabbat, c. 19. sect. 5. Vid. Maimon. & Bartenora in ib. & Misn. Eracin, c. 2. sect. 2. & Bartenora in ib. (t) Hilch. Mila, c. 1. 16. (u) Pocock. Specim. A. ab. Hist. p. 3, 9. (w) T. Bab. Kiddushin, fol. 69. 1.

---

6. Concerning zeal, persecuting the church; touching the righteousness which is in the law, blameless.

Greek/Transliteration
6. κατὰ ζῆλον διώκων τὴν ἐκκλησίαν, κατὰ δικαιοσύνην τὴν ἐν νόμῳ γενόμενος ἄμεμπτος.

6. kata zeilon diokon tein ekkleisian, kata dikaiosunein tein en nomo genomenos amemptos.

Hebrew/Transliteration
:ו. מִצַד הַקִנְאָה רָדַפְתִּי אֶת-עֲדַת הַמָשִׁיחַ וּמִצַד צִדְקַת הַתּוֹרָה לֹא נִמְצָא בִי שֶׁמֶץ דָּבָר

6. Mi•tzad ha•kin•ah ra•daf•ti et - adat ha•Ma•shi•ach oo•mi•tzad tzid•kat ha•Torah lo nim•tza vi she•metz da•var.

---

7. But what things were gain to me, those I counted loss for Christ.

Greek/Transliteration
7. Ἀλλ' ἅτινα ἦν μοι κέρδη, ταῦτα ἥγημαι διὰ τὸν χριστὸν ζημίαν.

7. All 'atina ein moi kerdei, tauta 'eigeimai dya ton christon zeimian.

Hebrew/Transliteration
:ז. אַךְ-מוֹתַר כָּל-אֵלֶּה חָשַׁבְתִּי לִי לְמַחְסוֹר בַּעֲבוּר הַמָשִׁיחַ

7. Ach - mo•tar kol - ele cha•shav•ti li le•mach•sor ba•a•voor ha•Ma•shi•ach.

Rabbinic Jewish Commentary
Hence, what before he pleased himself much with, and promised himself much from, he could not now reflect upon with any pleasure and satisfaction of mind; which is the sense of this phrase with Jewish writers (x): so it is observed of a drunken man, when he comes to himself; and it is told him what he did when in liquor, he grieves at it, ויחשב הכל הפסד ולא ריוח, "and counts all loss and not gain"; i.e. can take no pleasure in a reflection on it,

(x) Sepher Cosri, p. 3, sect. 16. fol. 152. 1.

8. Yea doubtless, and I count all things but loss for the excellency of the knowledge of Christ Jesus my Lord: for whom I have suffered the loss of all things, and do count them but dung, that I may win Christ,

Greek/Transliteration
8. Ἀλλὰ μὲν οὖν καὶ ἡγοῦμαι πάντα ζημίαν εἶναι διὰ τὸ ὑπερέχον τῆς γνώσεως χριστοῦ Ἰησοῦ τοῦ κυρίου μου· δι' ὃν τὰ πάντα ἐζημιώθην, καὶ ἡγοῦμαι σκύβαλα εἶναι, ἵνα χριστὸν κερδήσω,

8. Alla men oun kai 'eigoumai panta zeimian einai dya to 'uperechon teis gnoseos christou Yeisou tou kuriou mou. di 'on ta panta ezeimiothein, kai 'eigoumai skubala einai, 'ina christen kerdeiso,

Hebrew/Transliteration
ח. כִּי אָמֵן הֲלֹא אֶת־כֹּל אֲחַשְׁבָה לְחֶסְרוֹן מִפְּנֵי יִתְרוֹן דַּעַת יֵשׁוּעַ הַמָּשִׁיחַ אֲדֹנִי אֲשֶׁר הִתְנַצַּלְתִּי בַעֲבוּרוֹ אֶת־כֹּל אֲשֶׁר לִי וּלְדֹמֶן חֲשַׁבְתִּים לְמַעַן יִהְיֶה לִּי הַמָּשִׁיחַ שְׂכָרִי:

8. Ki amen ha•lo et - kol a•chash•va le•ches•ron mip•ney yit•ron da•at Yeshua ha•Ma•shi•ach Adoni asher hit•na•tzal•tee va•a•voo•ro et - kol asher li ool•do•men cha•shav•tim le•ma•an yi•hee•ye li ha•Ma•shi•ach s`cha•ri.

---

9. And be found in him, not having mine own righteousness, which is of the law, but that which is through the faith of Christ, the righteousness which is of God by faith:

Greek/Transliteration
9. καὶ εὑρεθῶ ἐν αὐτῷ, μὴ ἔχων ἐμὴν δικαιοσύνην τὴν ἐκ νόμου, ἀλλὰ τὴν διὰ πίστεως χριστοῦ, τὴν ἐκ θεοῦ δικαιοσύνην ἐπὶ τῇ πίστει·

9. kai 'euretho en auto, mei echon emein dikaiosunein tein ek nomou, alla tein dya pisteos christou, tein ek theou dikaiosunein epi tei pistei.

Hebrew/Transliteration
ט. לְהִמָּצֵא דָבֵק בּוֹ אָנֹכִי אֲשֶׁר צִדְקָתִי אֵינֶנָּה מִן־הַתּוֹרָה כִּי אִם־מִמְּקוֹר אֱמוּנַת הַמָּשִׁיחַ הִיא הַצְּדָקָה מִמְּקוֹר אֱלֹהִים בָּאֱמוּנָה:

9. Le•hi•ma•tze da•vek bo ano•chi asher tzid•ka•ti ey•ne•na min - ha•Torah ki eem - mim•kor emoo•nat ha•Ma•shi•ach hee ha•tz`da•ka mim•kor Elohim ba•e•moo•na.

Rabbinic Jewish Commentary
This last clause, "by faith", is omitted in the Syriac and Ethiopic versions, and seems to be read by them as belonging to the beginning of Phi_3:10.

---

10. That I may know him, and the power of his resurrection, and the fellowship of his sufferings, being made conformable unto his death;

Greek/Transliteration
10. τοῦ γνῶναι αὐτὸν καὶ τὴν δύναμιν τῆς ἀναστάσεως αὐτοῦ, καὶ τὴν κοινωνίαν τῶν παθημάτων αὐτοῦ, συμμορφούμενος τῷ θανάτῳ αὐτοῦ,

10. tou gnonai auton kai tein dunamin teis anastaseos autou, kai tein koinonian ton patheimaton autou, summorphoumenos to thanato autou,

Hebrew/Transliteration
י. כִּי אֹתוֹ אֲבַקֵּשׁ לָדַעַת עִם-עֹז תְּקוּמָתוֹ לָקַחַת חֵלֶק בְּמַכְאֹבָיו וְלִהְיוֹת כְּמַתְכֻּנְתּוֹ בְּמוֹתוֹ:

10. Ki o•to ava•kesh la•da•at eem - oz te•koo•ma•to la•ka•chat che•lek be•mach•o•vav ve•li•hi•yot ke•mat•koon•to be•mo•to.

Rabbinic Jewish Commentary
That I may know him,.... The Ethiopic version reads "by faith"; and to the same sense the Syriac.

What the Jews deprecated, the apostle was desirous of; namely, sharing in the sorrows and sufferings of the Messiah, and which they reckon the greatest happiness to be delivered from,

"The disciples of R. Eleazar (y) asked him, what a man should do that he may be delivered מחבלו של משיח, "from the sorrows of the Messiah?" he must study in the Torah, and in beneficence.

And elsewhere they say (z),

"He that keeps the three meals on the sabbath day shall be delivered from three punishments, מחבלו של משיח, "from the sorrows of the Messiah", and from the damnation of gehenna, and from the war of Gog and Magog.

(y) T. Bab. Sanhedrin, fol. 98. 2. (z) T. Bab. Sabbat, fol. 118. 1. See Cetubot, fol. 111. 1.

---

11. If by any means I might attain unto the resurrection of the dead.

Greek/Transliteration
11. εἴ πως καταντήσω εἰς τὴν ἐξανάστασιν τῶν νεκρῶν.

11. ei pos katanteiso eis tein exanastasin ton nekron.

Hebrew/Transliteration
יא. אוּלַי אוּכַל לַעֲמֹד לְגוֹרָלִי לִתְקוּמָה מִן-הַמֵּתִים:

11. Oo•lai oo•chal la•a•mod le•go•ra•li lit•koo•ma min - ha•me•tim.

---

12. Not as though I had already attained, either were already perfect: but I follow after, if that I may apprehend that for which also I am apprehended of Christ Jesus.

Greek/Transliteration
12. Οὐχ ὅτι ἤδη ἔλαβον, ἢ ἤδη τετελείωμαι· διώκω δέ, εἰ καὶ καταλάβω ἐφ᾽ ᾧ καὶ κατελήφθην ὑπὸ τοῦ χριστοῦ Ἰησοῦ.

12. Ouch 'oti eidei elabon, ei eidei teteleiomai. dioko de, ei kai katalabo eph 'o kai kateleiphthein 'upo tou christou Yeisou.

Hebrew/Transliteration
יב. לֹא כְמוֹ אִם-כְּבָר הִשַּׂגְתִּי חֶפְצִי אוֹ הִגַּעְתִּי עַד-תַּכְלִית אֲבָל אָרוּץ אַחֲרָיו אוּלַי אַשִּׂיגֶנּוּ כַּאֲשֶׁר בַּעֲבוּר זֶה נֶאֱחַזְתִּי בְּיַד יֵשׁוּעַ הַמָּשִׁיחַ גַּם-אָנִי:

12. Lo che•mo eem - k`var hi•sag•ti chef•tzi oh hi•ga•a•ti ad - tach•lit aval aroo•tz a•cha•rav oo•lai asi•ge•noo ka•a•sher ba•a•voor ze ne•e•chaz•ti ve•yad Yeshua ha•Ma•shi•ach gam - ani.

Rabbinic Jewish Commentary
The metaphor is taken from runners in a race, who pursue it with eagerness, press forward with all might and main, to get up to the mark, in order to receive the prize; accordingly the Syriac version renders it, רהט אנא, "I run", and so the Arabic: the apostle's sense is, that though he had not yet reached the mark, he pressed forward towards it, he had it in view, he stretched and exerted himself, and followed up very closely to it, in hope of enjoying the prize.

---

13. Brethren, I count not myself to have apprehended: but this one thing I do, forgetting those things which are behind, and reaching forth unto those things which are before,

Greek/Transliteration
13. Ἀδελφοί, ἐγὼ ἐμαυτὸν οὐ λογίζομαι κατειληφέναι· ἓν δέ, τὰ μὲν ὀπίσω ἐπιλανθανόμενος, τοῖς δὲ ἔμπροσθεν ἐπεκτεινόμενος,

13. Adelphoi, ego emauton ou logizomai kateileiphenai. 'en de, ta men opiso epilanthanomenos, tois de emprosthen epekteinomenos,

Hebrew/Transliteration
יג. אַחַי לֹא אָמַרְתִּי בְלִבִּי כִּי הִשַּׂגְתִּי חֶפְצִי אַךְ-אַחַת אָמַרְתִּי לִשְׁכֹּחַ אֶת-אֲשֶׁר מֵאַחֲרַי וְלִנְטוֹת בְּכָל-מְאֹדִי אֶל-אֲשֶׁר לְפָנָי:

13. A•chai lo amar•ti ve•li•bi ki hi•sag•ti chef•tzi ach - a•chat amar•ti lish•ko•ach et - asher me•a•cha•rai ve•lin•tot be•chol - me•o•di el - asher le•fa•nai.

---

14. I press toward the mark for the prize of the high calling of God in Christ Jesus.

Greek/Transliteration
14. κατὰ σκοπὸν διώκω ἐπὶ τὸ βραβεῖον τῆς ἄνω κλήσεως τοῦ θεοῦ ἐν χριστῷ Ἰησοῦ.

14. kata skopon dioko epi to brabeion teis ano kleiseos tou theou en christo Yeisou.

Hebrew/Transliteration
יד. וְרָץ אֲנִי אֶל-הַמַּטָּרָה אֶל-שְׂכַר הַמְּרוּצָה כַּאֲשֶׁר קְרָאַנִי אֱלֹהִים וַיְרוֹמְמֵנִי בְּיֵשׁוּעַ הַמָּשִׁיחַ:

14. Ve•ratz ani el - ha•ma•ta•ra el - s`char ha•me•roo•tza ka•a•sher ke•ra•a•ni Elohim vay•ro•me•me•nee be•Yeshua ha•Ma•shi•ach.

Rabbinic Jewish Commentary

The allusion is to the white line, or mark, which the runners in the Olympic games made up to, and to which he that came first received the prize; and by which the apostle intends the Lord Yeshua Messsiah, who is **σκοπος**, "the scope", or "mark", of all the thoughts, purposes, and counsels of God, to which they all aim, and in which they all centre.

---

15. Let us therefore, as many as be perfect, be thus minded: and if in any thing ye be otherwise minded, God shall reveal even this unto you.

Greek/Transliteration
15. Ὅσοι οὖν τέλειοι, τοῦτο φρονῶμεν· καὶ εἴ τι ἑτέρως φρονεῖτε, καὶ τοῦτο ὁ θεὸς ὑμῖν ἀποκαλύψει·

15. 'Osoi oun teleioi, touto phronomen. kai ei ti 'eteros phroneite, kai touto 'o theos 'umin apokalupsei.

Hebrew/Transliteration
טו. וְעַתָּה כָּל-הַשְּׁלֵמִים מֵאִתָּנוּ כְּמוֹ כֵן יַחְשֹׁבוּ וְאִם-יֵשׁ בֵּינֵיכֶם הַחֹשְׁבִים לֹא-כֵן גַּם-זֹאת יְגַלֶּה לָכֶם אֱלֹהִים:

15. Ve•a•ta kol - hash•le•mim me•ee•ta•noo k`mo chen yach•sho•voo ve•eem - yesh bey•ney•chem ha•chosh•vim lo - chen gam - zot ye•ga•le la•chem Elohim.

---

16. Nevertheless, whereto we have already attained, let us walk by the same rule, let us mind the same thing.

Greek/Transliteration
16. πλὴν εἰς ὃ ἐφθάσαμεν, τῷ αὐτῷ στοιχεῖν κανόνι, τὸ αὐτὸ φρονεῖν.

16. plein eis 'o ephthasamen, to auto stoichein kanoni, to auto phronein.

Hebrew/Transliteration
טז. רַק אֶל-אֲשֶׁר הִגַּעְנוּ בַּמְּסִלָּה הַזֹּאת נִתְהַלְּכָה בְּמַעְגָּל אֶחָד וּבְלֵב אֶחָד:

16. Rak el - asher hi•ga•a•noo bam•si•la ha•zot nit•ha•le•cha be•ma•a•gal e•chad oov•lev e•chad.

---

17. Brethren, be followers together of me, and mark them which walk so as ye have us for an ensample.

Greek/Transliteration
17. Συμμιμηταί μου γίνεσθε, ἀδελφοί, καὶ σκοπεῖτε τοὺς οὕτως περιπατοῦντας, καθὼς ἔχετε τύπον ἡμᾶς.

17. Summimeitai mou ginesthe, adelphoi, kai skopeite tous 'outos peripatountas, kathos echete tupon 'eimas.

Hebrew/Transliteration

יז. לְכוּ אַחַי בְּעִקְּבוֹתַי וְהִתְבּוֹנְנוּ אֶל-הַהֹלְכִים כֵּן כַּאֲשֶׁר הָיִינוּ לָכֶם לְמוֹפֵת:

17. Le•choo a•chai be•eek•vo•tai ve•hit•bo•ne•noo el - ha•hol•chim ken ka•a•sher ha•yi•noo la•chem le•mo•fet.

---

18. (For many walk, of whom I have told you often, and now tell you even weeping, that they are the enemies of the cross of Christ:

Greek/Transliteration
18. Πολλοὶ γὰρ περιπατοῦσιν, οὓς πολλάκις ἔλεγον ὑμῖν, νῦν δὲ καὶ κλαίων λέγω, τοὺς ἐχθροὺς τοῦ σταυροῦ τοῦ χριστοῦ·

18. Polloi gar peripatousin, 'ous pollakis elegon 'umin, nun de kai klaion lego, tous echthrous tou staurou tou christou.

Hebrew/Transliteration

יח. כִּי רַבִּים הֵם הַהֹלְכִים אֲשֶׁר אָמַרְתִּי לָכֶם עַל-אֹדוֹתָם וְעַתָּה גַם-בִּבְכִי אֲנִי אֹמֵר כִּי-אֹיְבֵי צְלִיב הַמָּשִׁיחַ הֵם:

18. Ki ra•bim hem ha•hol•chim asher amar•ti la•chem al - o•do•tam ve•at gam - biv•chi ani o•mer ki - or•vey tze•liv ha•Ma•shi•ach hem.

---

19. Whose end is destruction, whose God is their belly, and whose glory is in their shame who mind earthly things.)

Greek/Transliteration
19. ὧν τὸ τέλος ἀπώλεια, ὧν ὁ θεὸς ἡ κοιλία, καὶ ἡ δόξα ἐν τῇ αἰσχύνῃ αὐτῶν, οἱ τὰ ἐπίγεια φρονοῦντες.

19. 'on to telos apoleya, 'on 'o theos 'ei koilia, kai 'ei doxa en tei aischunei auton, 'oi ta epigeya phronountes.

Hebrew/Transliteration

יט. אֲשֶׁר אַחֲרִיתָם אֲבַדּוֹן וֵאלֹהֵיהֶם הוּא הַבֶּטֶן וּכְבוֹדָם בְּבָשְׁתָּם וְאַף-הֶגְיוֹנָם הַבְלֵי חָלֶד:

19. Asher a•cha•ri•tam ava•don ve•Elohey•hem hoo ha•be•ten ooch•vo•dam be•vosh•tam ve•af - heg•yo•nam hav•ley cha•led.

Rabbinic Jewish Commentary

The belly was the god of the Cyclops, they sacrificed to none but to themselves, and to the greatest of the gods, their own belly (a); as money is the covetous man's god, whom he loves, adores, and puts his confidence in, so the belly is the god of the sensualist, the epicure, and voluptuous person.

The idol Baal Peor, and which is no other than the Priapus of the Heathens, is called by this name, Hos_9:10; so the prophets of Baal are in the Septuagint on 1Ki_18:19 called the prophets, της αισχυνης, "of that shame"; it may be the apostle may have a regard to the secret debaucheries of these persons; or because they made their belly their god, he calls it their shame in which they gloried, and which was the name given to the idols of the Gentiles.

The Arabic version renders it, "who entertain earthly opinions"; and some by, "earthly things" understand the ceremonies of the Torah, called the elements and rudiments of the world, which these false teachers were fond of, and were very diligent to inculcate and urge the observance of.

(a) Euripides.

---

20. For our conversation is in heaven; from whence also we look for the Saviour, the Lord Jesus Christ:

Greek/Transliteration
20. Ἡμῶν γὰρ τὸ πολίτευμα ἐν οὐρανοῖς ὑπάρχει, ἐξ οὗ καὶ σωτῆρα ἀπεκδεχόμεθα, κύριον Ἰησοῦν χριστόν·

20. 'Eimon gar to politeuma en ouranois 'uparchei, ex 'ou kai soteira apekdechometha, kurion Yeisoun christon.

Hebrew/Transliteration
:כ. כִּי הֶגְיוֹנֵנוּ הֶגְיוֹן אֶזְרָחִים בַּשָּׁמַיִם אֲשֶׁר מִשָּׁם נְחַכֶּה לְמוֹשִׁיעֵנוּ הוּא יֵשׁוּעַ הַמָּשִׁיחַ אֲדֹנֵינוּ

20. Ki heg•yo•ne•noo heg•yon ez•ra•chim ba•sha•ma•yim asher mi•sham n`cha•ke le•Mo•shi•e•noo hoo Yeshua ha•Ma•shi•ach Ado•ney•noo.

Rabbinic Jewish Commentary
The Ethiopic version renders it, "we have our city in heaven"; and the words may be truly rendered, "our citizenship is in heaven"; that is, the city whereof we are freemen is heaven, and we behave ourselves here below, as citizens of that city above: heaven is the saints' city.

---

21. Who shall change our vile body, that it may be fashioned like unto his glorious body, according to the working whereby he is able even to subdue all things unto himself.

Greek/Transliteration
21. ὃς μετασχηματίσει τὸ σῶμα τῆς ταπεινώσεως ἡμῶν, εἰς τὸ γενέσθαι αὐτὸ σύμμορφον τῷ σώματι τῆς δόξης αὐτοῦ, κατὰ τὴν ἐνέργειαν τοῦ δύνασθαι αὐτὸν καὶ ὑποτάξαι ἑαυτῷ τὰ πάντα.

21. 'os metascheimatisei to soma teis tapeinoseos 'eimon, eis to genesthai auto summorphon to somati teis doxeis autou, kata tein energeyan tou dunasthai auton kai 'upotaxai 'eauto ta panta.

Hebrew/Transliteration
:כא. אֲשֶׁר יְשַׁנֶּה אֶת-גוּפֵנוּ הַשָּׁפֵל וִישַׁוֵּהוּ בְתֹאַר גּוּף כְּבוֹדוֹ כְּפִי-פְעֻלַּת כֹּחוֹ אֲשֶׁר בְּיָדוֹ לָשִׁית כֹּל תַּחַת-רַגְלָיו

21. Asher ye•sha•ne et - goo•fe•noo ha•sha•fel viy•sha•ve•hoo ve•to•ar goof k`vo•do ke•fi - fe•oo•lat ko•cho asher be•ya•do la•sheet kol ta•chat - rag•lav.

Rabbinic Jewish Commentary

So the Jews say (b), that "the evil imagination, or corruption of nature, goes along with man in the hour of death, but does not return with him when the dead arise.

The Jews (c) have a notion, that "the holy blessed God will beautify the bodies of the righteous in future time, like the beauty of the first Adam:

But their beauty and glory will be greater than that, it will be like the glory of the second Adam, the Lord from heaven, whose image they shall then bear: and whereas this requires almighty power, of which Yeshua Messiah is possessed, it will be done.

according to the working, the energy of his power and might; or as the Syriac version renders it, "according to his great power"; which was put forth in raising himself from the dead, and whereby he was declared to be the Son of God.

(b) Midrash Tillim apud Galatin. de Arcan. Cathol. ver. l. 12. c. 2. (c) Midrash Hanneelam in Zohar in Gen. fol. 69. 1.

Philippians, Chapter 4

1. Therefore, my brethren dearly beloved and longed for, my joy and crown, so stand fast in the Lord, my dearly beloved.

Greek/Transliteration
1. Ὥστε, ἀδελφοί μου ἀγαπητοὶ καὶ ἐπιπόθητοι, χαρὰ καὶ στέφανός μου, οὕτως στήκετε ἐν κυρίῳ, ἀγαπητοί.

1. 'Oste, adelphoi mou agapeitoi kai epipotheitoi, chara kai stephanos mou, 'outos steikete en kurio, agapeitoi.

Hebrew/Transliteration
א: עַל-כֵּן אַחִים אֲהוּבִים מַחֲמַדֵּי נַפְשִׁי מְשׂוֹשׂ לִבִּי וַעֲטֶרֶת רֹאשִׁי עִמְדוּ הָכֵן לִפְנֵי אֲדֹנֵינוּ יְדִידִים

1. Al - ken a•chim ahoo•vim ma•cha•ma•dey naf•shi me•sos li•bi va•a•te•ret ro•shi eem•doo ha•chen lif•ney Ado•ney•noo ye•di•dim.

Rabbinic Jewish Commentary
These epithets are joined with the word "brethren", in the Vulgate Latin, Syriac, and Arabic versions, and read thus, "my dearly beloved, and longed for brethren"; and in the Ethiopic version, "our beloved brethren".

---

2. I beseech Euodias, and beseech Syntyche, that they be of the same mind in the Lord.

Greek/Transliteration
2. Εὐοδίαν παρακαλῶ, καὶ Συντύχην παρακαλῶ, τὸ αὐτὸ φρονεῖν ἐν κυρίῳ.

2. Euodian parakalo, kai Suntuchein parakalo, to auto phronein en kurio.

Hebrew/Transliteration
ב: הִנְנִי דֹרֵשׁ מִן-אַבְהוֹדִיָּה וְגַם כֵּן מִן-סוּנְטִיכִי לְהִתְהַלֵּךְ בְּלֵב אֶחָד לִפְנֵי אֲדֹנֵינוּ

2. Hi•ne•ni do•resh min - Av•ho•di•ya ve•gam ken min - Soon•ti•chi le•hit•ha•lech be•lev e•chad lif•ney Ado•ney•noo.

Rabbinic Jewish Commentary
The Arabic version renders it, "that ye entertain one and the same opinion concerning the faith of the Lord".

---

3. And I intreat thee also, true yokefellow, help those women which laboured with me in the gospel, with Clement also, and with other my fellowlabourers, whose names are in the book of life.

Greek/Transliteration
3. Ναί, ἐρωτῶ καί σε, σύζυγε γνήσιε, συλλαμβάνου αὐταῖς, αἵτινες ἐν τῷ εὐαγγελίῳ συνήθλησάν μοι, μετὰ καὶ Κλήμεντος, καὶ τῶν λοιπῶν συνεργῶν μου, ὧν τὰ ὀνόματα ἐν βίβλῳ ζωῆς.

3. Nai, eroto kai se, suzuge gneisie, sullambanou autais, 'aitines en to euangelio suneithleisan moi, meta kai Kleimentos, kai ton loipon sunergon mou, 'on ta onomata en biblo zoeis.

Hebrew/Transliteration
ג-. וְאַלֶיךָ חָבֵר נֶאֱמָן הַנִּצְמָד-לִי בַּעֲבֹדָה אֶקְרָא-נָא לַעֲזֹר לָהֶן אֲשֶׁר עָבְדוּ עִמִּי יַחְדָּו בִּמְלֶאכֶת הַבְּשׂוֹרָה עִם קְלִימִיס וְעִם-יֶתֶר סֹמְכֵי יָדַי אֲשֶׁר שְׁמוֹתָם בְּסֵפֶר הַחַיִּים:

3. Ve•e•le•cha cha•ver ne•e•man ha•nitz•mad - li ba•a•vo•da ek•ra - na la•a•zor la•hen asher av•doo ee•mi yach•dav be•mal•a•choot ha•be•so•ra eem - K•li•mis ve•eem - ye•ter som•chey ya•di asher sh`mo•tam be•se•fer ha•cha•yim.

Rabbinic Jewish Commentary
And I entreat thee also, true yoke fellow,.... Not his wife, as some think (d), for he had none, as appears from 1Co_7:7, at the writing of which epistle he was at Ephesus, where he stayed some little time, and then went to Jerusalem. The word used is of the masculine gender, and designs a man and not a woman: some think it is the proper name of a man, who was called "Syzygus", and so the Arabic interpreter seems to understand it; and by the apostle, true "Syzygus", signifying that as was his name, so was he, really and in truth, a companion and fellow labourer, that drew in the same yoke with him; the Syriac version renders it, "the son of my yoke", and the Ethiopic version, "my brother and my companion".

The word may very well be thought to answer to the Hebrew word חבר, often used in Jewish writings, for an associate, a colleague, and a disciple of the wise men, to which the apostle may allude.

(d) Vid. Euseb. Eccl. Hist. l. 3. c. 30.

---

4. Rejoice in the Lord always: and again I say, Rejoice.

Greek/Transliteration
4. Χαίρετε ἐν κυρίῳ πάντοτε· πάλιν ἐρῶ, χαίρετε.

4. Chairete en kurio pantote. palin ero, chairete.

Hebrew/Transliteration
ד. שִׂישׂוּ בַאֲדֹנֵינוּ תָּמִיד וְעוֹד אֶשְׁנֶה לֵאמֹר שִׂישׂוּ בוֹ מָשׂוֹשׂ:

4. Si•soo va•Ado•ney•noo ta•mid ve•od esh•ne le•mor si•soo vo ma•sos.

---

5. Let your moderation be known unto all men. The Lord is at hand.

Greek/Transliteration
5. Τὸ ἐπιεικὲς ὑμῶν γνωσθήτω πᾶσιν ἀνθρώποις. Ὁ κύριος ἐγγύς.

5. To epieikes 'umon gnostheito pasin anthropois. 'O kurios engus.

Hebrew/Transliteration
ה. עַנְוַת רוּחֲכֶם תִּוָּדַע לְכָל-בְּנֵי אָדָם קָרוֹב הוּא אֲדֹנֵינוּ:

5. An•vat roo•cha•chem ti•va•da le•chol - b`ney adam ka•rov hoo Ado•ney•noo.

Rabbinic Jewish Commentary
The Vulgate Latin reads, "your modesty". The Syriac and Arabic versions, "your meekness", or "humility"; graces which accompany moderation, and are very necessary to it, but not that itself. The Ethiopic version renders it, "your authority", which by no means agrees; for moderation lies not in exerting authority and power to the uttermost, at least with rigour, but in showing clemency and lenity.

The Syriac version reads, "our Lord": and the Ethiopic version, "God is at hand".

---

6. Be careful for nothing; but in every thing by prayer and supplication with thanksgiving let your requests be made known unto God.

Greek/Transliteration
6. Μηδὲν μεριμνᾶτε, ἀλλ᾽ ἐν παντὶ τῇ προσευχῇ καὶ τῇ δεήσει μετὰ εὐχαριστίας τὰ αἰτήματα ὑμῶν γνωριζέσθω πρὸς τὸν θεόν.

6. Meiden merimnate, all en panti tei proseuchei kai tei deeisei meta eucharistias ta aiteimata 'umon gnorizestho pros ton theon.

Hebrew/Transliteration
:ו. הַרְחִיקוּ כָל-דְּאָגָה מִכֶּם אַךְ הוֹדִיעוּ כָל-מִשְׁאֲלוֹתֵיכֶם בִּתְפִלָּה בִּתְחִנָּה וּבְתוֹדָה לֵאלֹהֵינוּ

6. Har•chi•koo chol - de•a•ga mi•kem ach ho•di•oo chol - mish•alo•tey•chem bit•fi•la bit•chi•na oov•to•da le•Elohey•noo.

Rabbinic Jewish Commentary
but in everything. The Syriac and Ethiopic versions render it, "in every time": always, constantly, every day, as often as there is opportunity, and need requires. The Vulgate Latin and Arabic versions join it with the following clause, "in every prayer and supplication"; but the grammatical construction of the words will not admit of such a version; it is best to understand it of every thing, or case, which should be brought to God.

---

7. And the peace of God, which passeth all understanding, shall keep your hearts and minds through Christ Jesus.

Greek/Transliteration
7. Καὶ ἡ εἰρήνη τοῦ θεοῦ ἡ ὑπερέχουσα πάντα νοῦν, φρουρήσει τὰς καρδίας ὑμῶν καὶ τὰ νοήματα ὑμῶν ἐν χριστῷ Ἰησοῦ.

7. Kai 'ei eireinei tou theou 'ei 'uperechousa panta noun, phroureisei tas kardias 'umon kai ta noeimata 'umon en christo Yeisou.

Hebrew/Transliteration
:ז. וְהָאֱלֹהִים יְצַו אֶת-שְׁלוֹמוֹ אֲשֶׁר לֹא יְכִילֶנּוּ כָל-שֵׂכֶל לִנְצֹר אֶת-לִבְּכֶם וְאֶת-הֶגְיוֹן רוּחֲכֶם בְּיֵשׁוּעַ הַמָּשִׁיחַ

7. Ve•ha•Elohim ye•tzav et - Sh`lo•mo asher lo ye•chi•le•noo chol - se•chel lin•tzor et - lib•chem ve•et - heg•yon roo•cha•chem be•Yeshua ha•Ma•shi•ach.

Rabbinic Jewish Commentary

That peace of conscience, which arises from a view of peace made by Christ; of justification by his righteousness, and atonement by his sacrifice; and which may be called "the peace of Christ", as the Alexandrian copy reads.

shall keep your hearts and minds through Jesus Christ, or "in Christ Jesus": some read these words prayer wise, or as a wish, "let it", or "may it keep", so the Vulgate Latin.

---

8. Finally, brethren, whatsoever things are true, whatsoever things are honest, whatsoever things are just, whatsoever things are pure, whatsoever things are lovely, whatsoever things are of good report; if there be any virtue, and if there be any praise, think on these things.

Greek/Transliteration

8. Τὸ λοιπόν, ἀδελφοί, ὅσα ἐστὶν ἀληθῆ, ὅσα σεμνά, ὅσα δίκαια, ὅσα ἁγνά, ὅσα προσφιλῆ, ὅσα εὔφημα, εἴ τις ἀρετὴ καὶ εἴ τις ἔπαινος, ταῦτα λογίζεσθε.

8. To loipon, adelphoi, 'osa estin aleithei, 'osa semna, 'osa dikaya, 'osa 'agna, 'osa prosphilei, 'osa eupheima, ei tis aretei kai ei tis epainos, tauta logizesthe.

Hebrew/Transliteration

ח. סוֹף דָּבָר אַחַי שִׂימוּ לִבְּכֶם אֵיזֶה דָּבָר אֱמֶת הוּא אֵיזֶה נִכְבָּדוֹת בּוֹ וְאֵיזֶה מְכוֹבוֹ יֹשֶׁר אֵיזֶה הוּא זָךְ אֵיזֶה הוּא נֶחְמָד וְאֵיזֶה לוֹ שֵׁם טוֹב אִם-יֵשׁ מַעֲשֵׂה צְדָקָה אוֹ דָּבָר לוֹ נָאוָה תְּהִלָּה שִׂימוּ לִבְּכֶם לְכָל-אֵלֶּה:

8. Sof da•var a•chai si•moo lib•chem ey•ze da•var emet hoo ey•ze nich•ba•dot bo ve•ey•ze me•cho•no yo•sher ey•ze hoo zach ey•ze hoo nech•mad ve•ey•ze lo shem tov eem - yesh ma•a•se tze•da•ka oh da•var lo na•va te•hi•la si•moo lib•chem le•chol - ele.

Rabbinic Jewish Commentary

whatsoever things are pure; or "chaste", in words and deeds, in opposition to all filthiness and foolish talking, to obscene words and actions. The Vulgate Latin and Arabic versions render it, "whatsoever things are holy".

and if there be any praise; that is praiseworthy among men, and deserves commendation, even though in an unjust steward, Luk_16:8, it should be regarded. The Vulgate Latin adds, "of discipline", without any authority from any copy. The Claromontane manuscript reads, "if any praise of knowledge".

---

9. Those things, which ye have both learned, and received, and heard, and seen in me, do: and the God of peace shall be with you.

Greek/Transliteration

9. Ἃ καὶ ἐμάθετε καὶ παρελάβετε καὶ ἠκούσατε καὶ εἴδετε ἐν ἐμοί, ταῦτα πράσσετε· καὶ ὁ θεὸς τῆς εἰρήνης ἔσται μεθ' ὑμῶν.

9. 'A kai emathete kai parelabete kai eikousate kai eidete en emoi, tauta prassete. kai 'o theos teis eireineis estai meth 'umon.

Hebrew/Transliteration
ט. וְכֹל אֲשֶׁר לְמַדְתֶּם וְקִבַּלְתֶּם וּכְמַעֲשַׂי אֲשֶׁר שְׁמַעְתֶּם אוֹ רְאִיתֶם כֵּן תַּעֲשׂוּ גַּם-אַתֶּם וֵאלֹהֵי הַשָּׁלוֹם יְהִי עִמָּכֶם:

9. Ve•chol asher le•ma•de•tem ve•ki•bal•tem ooch•ma•a•sai asher sh`ma•a•tem oh r`ee•tem ken ta•a•soo gam - atem ve•Elohey ha•sha•lom ye•hee ee•ma•chem.

---

10. But I rejoiced in the Lord greatly, that now at the last your care of me hath flourished again; wherein ye were also careful, but ye lacked opportunity.

Greek/Transliteration
10. Ἐχάρην δὲ ἐν κυρίῳ μεγάλως, ὅτι ἤδη ποτὲ ἀνεθάλετε τὸ ὑπὲρ ἐμοῦ φρονεῖν· ἐφ' ᾧ καὶ ἐφρονεῖτε, ἠκαιρεῖσθε δέ.

10. Echarein de en kurio megalos, 'oti eidei pote anethalete to 'uper emou phronein. eph 'o kai ephroneite, eikaireisthe de.

Hebrew/Transliteration
י. וַאֲנִי שָׂמַחְתִּי בַּאֲדֹנֵינוּ עַד-מְאֹד כִּי עוֹד יָנוּב חֵילְכֶם וְתָשִׂימוּ עַיִן לָחוּשׁ לִי אַף כִּי-עֵינֵיכֶם שַׂמְתֶּם לָחוּשׁ לִי תָּמִיד אֲבָל לֹא הָיוּ לָכֶם יָדַיִם:

10. Va•a•ni sa•mach•ti va•Ado•ney•noo ad - me•od ki od ya•noov cheyl•chem ve•ta•si•moo a•yin la•choosh li af ki - ey•ne•chem sam•tem la•choosh li ta•mid aval lo ha•yoo la•chem ya•da•yim.

Rabbinic Jewish Commentary
The allusion is to trees, which in the summer season bear much fruit, in autumn cast their leaves, and in the winter are entirely bare, and in the spring of the year revive again, and put forth leaves and fruit: and just so it is with the saints, they are compared to trees, and are called trees of righteousness, Isa_61:3, and are fruitful ones, Jer_23:3; but they have their winter seasons, when they are barren and unfruitful, and look as if they were dead.

The Vulgate Latin version renders it, "but ye were busied", or taken up and employed in business; or it was for want of ability; for the words will bear to be rendered, "but ye lacked ability"; and to this sense does the Syriac version render it, אלא לא ספקין הויתון, "but ye were not sufficient"; or had not a sufficiency, were not able to do it, and therefore to be easily excused.

---

11. Not that I speak in respect of want: for I have learned, in whatsoever state I am, therewith to be content.

Greek/Transliteration
11. Οὐχ ὅτι καθ' ὑστέρησιν λέγω· ἐγὼ γὰρ ἔμαθον, ἐν οἷς εἰμί, αὐτάρκης εἶναι.

11. Ouch 'oti kath 'ustereisin lego. ego gar emathon, en 'ois eimi, autarkeis einai.

Hebrew/Transliteration
יא. וְלֹא בַעֲבוּר מַחְסֹרִי אֲנִי דֹבֵר כֵּן כִּי לָמַדְתִּי לִהְיוֹת שָׂמֵחַ בְּחֶלְקִי:

11. Ve•lo va•a•voor mach•so•rai ani do•ver ken ki la•ma•de•ti li•hee•yot sa•me•ach be•chel•ki.

Rabbinic Jewish Commentary
He was not only content with food and raiment, and such things as he had, but even when he had nothing at all; when he had neither bread to eat nor clothes to wear; when he was in hunger and thirst, in cold and nakedness, as was sometimes his case; and therefore he does not say here, that he had learnt to be content with such things as he had, but εν οις ειμι, "in what I am": and this he had not by nature, but by grace.

---

12. I know both how to be abased, and I know how to abound: every where and in all things I am instructed both to be full and to be hungry, both to abound and to suffer need.

Greek/Transliteration
12. Οἶδα καὶ ταπεινοῦσθαι, οἶδα καὶ περισσεύειν· ἐν παντὶ καὶ ἐν πᾶσιν μεμύημαι καὶ χορτάζεσθαι καὶ πεινᾶν, καὶ περισσεύειν καὶ ὑστερεῖσθαι.

12. Oida kai tapeinousthai, oida kai perisseuein. en panti kai en pasin memueimai kai chortazesthai kai peinan, kai perisseuein kai 'ustereisthai.

Hebrew/Transliteration
יב. יֹדֵעַ אֲנִי לַעֲמֹד בִּשְׁפַל הַמַּדְרֵגָה וְלַעֲמֹד בְּהִיוֹת לִי דַּי וְהוֹתֵר בְּכָל-מָקוֹם וּבְכָל-עֵת הִסְכַּנְתִּי לִשְׂבֹּעַ וְגַם-לִרְעֹב לִחְיוֹת בְּמוֹתָר וְגַם-בְּמַחְסוֹר:

12. Yo•de•a ani la•a•mod bish•fal ha•mad•re•ga ve•la•a•mod bi•hee•yot li dai ve•ho•ter be•chol - ma•kom oov•chol - et his•kan•ti lis•bo•a ve•gam - lir•ov lich•yot be•mo•tar ve•gam - be•mach•sor.

---

13. I can do all things through Christ which strengtheneth me.

Greek/Transliteration
13. Πάντα ἰσχύω ἐν τῷ ἐνδυναμοῦντί με χριστῷ.

13. Panta ischuo en to endunamounti me christo.

Hebrew/Transliteration
יג. אֶת-כֹּל אוּכַל בְּיַד הַמָּשִׁיחַ הַמְאַזְּרֵנִי חָיִל:

13. Et - kol oo•chal be•yad ha•Ma•shi•ach ham•az•re•ni cha•yil.

Rabbinic Jewish Commentary
The Vulgate Latin and Ethiopic versions leave out the word "Christ", and only read "him"; and so the Alexandrian copy and others; but intend Christ as those that express it: strength to perform duty and to bear sufferings is in Christ, and which he communicates to his people; he strengthens them with strength in their souls, internally, as the word here used signifies; by virtue of which they can do whatever he enjoins them or calls them to, though without him they can do nothing.

14. Notwithstanding ye have well done, that ye did communicate with my affliction.

Greek/Transliteration
14. Πλὴν καλῶς ἐποιήσατε συγκοινωνήσαντές μου τῇ θλίψει.

14. Plein kalos epoieisate sugkoinoneisantes mou tei thlipsei.

Hebrew/Transliteration
יד. אֲבָל אַתֶּם הֵיטַבְתֶּם עָשׂוֹ כִּי הִתְחַבַּרְתֶּם עִמִּי בְּצָרָתִי:

14. Aval atem hey•tav•tem a•so ki hit•cha•bar•tem ee•mi be•tza•ra•ti.

---

15. Now ye Philippians know also, that in the beginning of the gospel, when I departed from Macedonia, no church communicated with me as concerning giving and receiving, but ye only.

Greek/Transliteration
15. Οἴδατε δὲ καὶ ὑμεῖς, Φιλιππήσιοι, ὅτι ἐν ἀρχῇ τοῦ εὐαγγελίου, ὅτε ἐξῆλθον ἀπὸ Μακεδονίας, οὐδεμία μοι ἐκκλησία ἐκοινώνησεν εἰς λόγον δόσεως καὶ λήψεως, εἰ μὴ ὑμεῖς μόνοι·

15. Oidate de kai 'umeis, Philippeisioi, 'oti en archei tou euangeliou, 'ote exeilthon apo Makedonias, oudemia moi ekkleisia ekoinoneisen eis logon doseos kai leipseos, ei mei 'umeis monoi.

Hebrew/Transliteration
טו. גַּם-דְּעוּ-נָא בְּנֵי פִילִפִּי כְּצֵאתִי מִן-מַקְדּוֹנְיָא בִּתְחִלַּת הַבְּשׂוֹרָה לֹא הָיְתָה עֵדָה אֲשֶׁר-בָּאָה בְדִבְרֵי מַשָּׂא וּמַתָּן עִמָּדִי זוּלָתִי אַתֶּם לְבַדְּכֶם:

15. Gam - de•oo - na b`ney Fi•li•pi ke•tze•ti min - Mak•don•ya bit•chi•lat ha•be•so•ra lo hai•ta eda asher - ba•ah ve•div•rey ma•sa oo•ma•tan ee•ma•di zoo•la•tee atem le•vad•chem.

Rabbinic Jewish Commentary
The Ethiopic version reads, "when ye went from Macedonia with me": but is not supported by any copy or other version.

The phrase, "giving and receiving", which is often used by the Jews for trading and commerce (e); and the allusion is to the keeping of accounts by men in business, by debtor and creditor, in a book, putting down in one column what is delivered out, and in the other what is received, whereby accounts are kept clear: the apostle's meaning is, that whereas he and his fellow ministers had delivered out spiritual things to this church, they had in return communicated their carnal things; so that there was a proper account kept, which was not observed by other churches, and which was greatly to the commendation of this.

(e) Vid. Kimchi in Psal. xv. 3. & Targum in Isa. ix. 4.

16. For even in Thessalonica ye sent once and again unto my necessity.

Greek/Transliteration
16. ὅτι καὶ ἐν Θεσσαλονίκῃ καὶ ἅπαξ καὶ δὶς εἰς τὴν χρείαν μοι ἐπέμψατε.

16. 'oti kai en Thessalonikei kai 'apax kai dis eis tein chreian moi epempsate.

Hebrew/Transliteration
טז. כִּי גַם-לְתַסְלוֹנִיקִי שְׁלַחְתֶּם לִי פַעַם וּשְׁתַיִם דֵּי מַחְסֹרָי:

16. Ki gam - le•Tas•loniki sh`lach•tem li pa•am oosh•ta•yim dey mach•so•rai.

---

17. Not because I desire a gift: but I desire fruit that may abound to your account.
Greek/Transliteration
17. Οὐχ ὅτι ἐπιζητῶ τὸ δόμα, ἀλλ᾽ ἐπιζητῶ τὸν καρπὸν τὸν πλεονάζοντα εἰς λόγον ὑμῶν.

17. Ouch 'oti epizeito to doma, all epizeito ton karpon ton pleonazonta eis logon 'umon.

Hebrew/Transliteration
יז. וְלֹא מַתָּן אֲנִי מְבַקֵּשׁ כִּי אִם-פֶּרְיְכֶם מְבַקֵּשׁ אֲנִי כִּי יִשְׂגֶּה לָכֶם לָרֹב:

17. Ve•lo ma•tan ani me•va•kesh ki eem - per•ye•chem me•va•kesh ani ki yis•ge la•chem la•rov.

---

18. But I have all, and abound: I am full, having received of Epaphroditus the things which were sent from you, an odour of a sweet smell, a sacrifice acceptable, wellpleasing to God.

Greek/Transliteration
18. Ἀπέχω δὲ πάντα καὶ περισσεύω· πεπλήρωμαι, δεξάμενος παρὰ Ἐπαφροδίτου τὰ παρ᾽ ὑμῶν, ὀσμὴν εὐωδίας, θυσίαν δεκτήν, εὐάρεστον τῷ θεῷ.

18. Apecho de panta kai perisseuo. pepleiromai, dexamenos para Epaphroditou ta par 'umon, osmein euodias, thusian dektein, euareston to theo.

Hebrew/Transliteration
יח. אַךְ עַתָּה יֶשׁ-לִי כֹל דַּי דֵּי וְהוֹתֵר וַאֲנִי מָלֵאתִי כִּי לָקַחְתִּי מִיַּד אֶפַפְרוֹדִיטוֹס אֶת-אֲשֶׁר שְׁלַחְתֶּם לִי לְרֵיחַ נִיחֹחַ מִנְחָה עֲרֵבָה לְרָצוֹן לֵאלֹהִים:

18. Ach ata yesh - li chol dai ve•ho•ter va•a•ni ma•le•ti ki la•kach•ti mi•yad Epaf•ro•ditos et - asher sh`lach•tem li le•re•ach ni•cho•ach min•cha a•re•va le•ra•tzon le•Elohim.

Rabbinic Jewish Commentary
Or "I have received all things", as the Syriac version renders it; all that they had sent by Epaphroditus; and for which he now gives a receipt; and by virtue of which he now abounded; and which abundance of his was not so much owing to the largeness of their

presents, as to the peace of his mind; looking upon this gift of theirs, though it might be but small in itself, a fulness to him.

---

19. But my God shall supply all your need according to his riches in glory by Christ Jesus.

Greek/Transliteration
19. Ὁ δὲ θεός μου πληρώσει πᾶσαν χρείαν ὑμῶν κατὰ τὸν πλοῦτον αὐτοῦ ἐν δόξῃ, ἐν χριστῷ Ἰησοῦ.

19. 'O de theos mou pleirosei pasan chreian 'umon kata ton plouton autou en doxei, en Christo Yeisou.

Hebrew/Transliteration
יט. ואלהי ימלא כל-מחסרכם בעשרו ובכבודו בישוע המשיח:

19. Velohai ye•ma•le chol - mach•sor•chem be•osh•ro oo•vich•vo•do be•Yeshua ha•Ma•shi•ach.

Rabbinic Jewish Commentary
But my God shall supply all your need,.... Or "fulfil all your need": the Jews, when they would comfort any, under the loss of any worldly enjoyment, used to say, המקום ימלא לך חסרונך, "God fulfil", or "will fulfil thy need" (f). The Vulgate Latin, Syriac, and Arabic versions, read these words as a wish or prayer, "but may my God supply" or "fulfil all your need".

(f) T. Bab. Betacot, fol. 16. 2. Debarim Rabba, sect. 4. fol. 239. 4.

---

20. Now unto God and our Father be glory for ever and ever. Amen.

Greek/Transliteration
20. Τῷ δὲ θεῷ καὶ πατρὶ ἡμῶν ἡ δόξα εἰς τοὺς αἰῶνας τῶν αἰώνων. Ἀμήν.

20. To de theo kai patri 'eimon 'ei doxa eis tous aionas ton aionon. Amein.

Hebrew/Transliteration
כ. ולאלהינו אבינו הכבוד לעולם ועד אמן:

20. Ve•le•Elohey•noo Avi•noo ha•ka•vod le•o•lam va•ed Amen.

---

21. Salute every saint in Christ Jesus. The brethren which are with me greet you.

Greek/Transliteration
21. Ἀσπάσασθε πάντα ἅγιον ἐν χριστῷ Ἰησοῦ. Ἀσπάζονται ὑμᾶς οἱ σὺν ἐμοὶ ἀδελφοί.

21. Aspasasthe panta 'agion en christo Yeisou. Aspazontai 'umas 'oi sun emoi adelphoi.

Hebrew/Transliteration
כא. שַׁאֲלוּ לְשָׁלוֹם כָּל-הַקְּדוֹשִׁים בְּיֵשׁוּעַ הַמָּשִׁיחַ הָאַחִים אֲשֶׁר עִמָּדִי שֹׁאֲלִים לִשְׁלוֹמְכֶם:

21. Sha•a•loo lish•lom kol - ha•k`do•shim be•Yeshua ha•Ma•shi•ach ha•a•chim asher ee•ma•di sho•a•lim lish•lom•chem.

---

22. All the saints salute you, chiefly they that are of Caesar's household.

Greek/Transliteration
22. Ἀσπάζονται ὑμᾶς πάντες οἱ ἅγιοι, μάλιστα δὲ οἱ ἐκ τῆς Καίσαρος οἰκίας.

22. Aspazontai 'umas pantes 'oi 'agioi, malista de 'oi ek teis Kaisaros oikias.

Hebrew/Transliteration
כב. כָּל-הַקְּדוֹשִׁים שֹׁאֲלִים לִשְׁלוֹמְכֶם וּבְרֹאשָׁם אֵלֶּה אֲשֶׁר מִבֵּית קֵיסָר:

22. Kol - ha•k`do•shim sho•a•lim lish•lom•chem oov•ro•sham ele asher mi•beit Key•sar.

Rabbinic Jewish Commentary
chiefly they that are of Caesar's household; for by means of the apostle's bonds, which were made manifest in the emperor's palace, Yeshua Messiah was made known to some there likewise; though Nero, the then reigning emperor, was a very wicked prince, and his court a very debauched one, yet the grace of God reached some there: who these were cannot be said; as for the conjecture that Seneca the philosopher, Nero's master, was one of them, it is without foundation; the eight letters of his to the Apostle Paul, and the six letters of the apostle to him, are spurious, though of ancient date, being made mention of by Austin and Jerom (g): a like groundless conjecture is that, that Lucan the poet, Seneca's brother's son, was another; for there is nothing in his writings, or in any account of him, any more than in the former, that shows him to be a Christian. Torpes, a man in great favour and dignity in Nero's court, and Evellius his counsellor, who both suffered martyrdom under him, according to the Roman martyrology, are also mentioned.

(g) Vid. Fabricii Bibliothec. Latin, p. 69.

---

23. The grace of our Lord Jesus Christ be with you all. Amen.

Greek/Transliteration
23. Ἡ χάρις τοῦ κυρίου Ἰησοῦ χριστοῦ μετὰ πάντων ὑμῶν. Ἀμήν.

23. 'Ei charis tou kuriou Yeisou christou meta panton 'umon. Amein.

Hebrew/Transliteration
כג. חֶסֶד יֵשׁוּעַ הַמָּשִׁיחַ אֲדֹנֵינוּ עִם-כֻּלְּכֶם אָמֵן:

23. Che•sed Yeshua ha•Ma•shi•ach Ado•ney•noo eem - kool•chem Amen.

Rabbinic Jewish Commentary
The Vulgate Latin and Ethiopic versions read, "with your spirit", as in Gal_6:18; and so the Alexandrian copy and some others read.

^end^

THE EPISTLE OF PAUL THE APOSTLE TO THE COLOSSIANS

Colossians, Chapter 1

1. Paul, an apostle of Jesus Christ by the will of God, and Timotheus our brother,

Greek/Transliteration
1. Παῦλος ἀπόστολος Ἰησοῦ χριστοῦ διὰ θελήματος θεοῦ, καὶ Τιμόθεος ὁ ἀδελφός,

1. Paulos apostolos Yeisou christou dya theleimatos theou, kai Timotheos 'o adelphos,

Hebrew/Transliteration
א. פּוֹלוֹס שְׁלִיחַ יֵשׁוּעַ הַמָּשִׁיחַ בִּרְצוֹן הָאֱלֹהִים אֲנִי וְטִימוֹתִיּוֹס אָחִינוּ:

1. Polos sh`li•ach Yeshua ha•Ma•shi•ach bir•tzon ha•Elohim ani ve•Timotiyos achi•noo.

---

2. To the saints and faithful brethren in Christ which are at Colosse: Grace be unto you, and peace, from God our Father and the Lord Jesus Christ.

Greek/Trasnliteration
2. τοῖς ἐν Κολασσαῖς ἁγίοις καὶ πιστοῖς ἀδελφοῖς ἐν χριστῷ· χάρις ὑμῖν καὶ εἰρήνη ἀπὸ θεοῦ πατρὸς ἡμῶν καὶ κυρίου Ἰησοῦ χριστοῦ.

2. tois en Kolassais 'agiois kai pistois adelphois en christo. charis 'umin kai eireinei apo theou patros 'eimon kai kuriou Yeisou christou.

Hebrew/Transliteration
ב. אֶל־הַקְּדוֹשִׁים וְהָאַחִים הַנֶּאֱמָנִים בַּמָּשִׁיחַ יֹשְׁבֵי קוֹלָסָא חֶסֶד וְשָׁלוֹם יִתֵּן לָכֶם אֱלֹהִים אָבִינוּ וַאֲדוֹנֵינוּ יֵשׁוּעַ הַמָּשִׁיחַ:

2. El - ha•k`do•shim ve•ha•a•chim ha•ne•e•ma•nim ba•Ma•shi•ach yosh•vey Ko•lasa che•sed ve•sha•lom yi•ten la•chem Elohim Avi•noo va•Ado•ney•noo Yeshua ha•Ma•shi•ach.

---

3. We give thanks to God and the Father of our Lord Jesus Christ, praying always for you,

Greek/Transliteration
3. Εὐχαριστοῦμεν τῷ θεῷ καὶ πατρὶ τοῦ κυρίου ἡμῶν Ἰησοῦ χριστοῦ, πάντοτε περὶ ὑμῶν προσευχόμενοι,

3. Eucharistoumen to theo kai patri tou kuriou 'eimon Yeisou christou, pantote peri 'umon proseuchomenoi,

Hebrew/Transliteration
ג. הִנֵּה אֲנַחְנוּ מוֹדִים לֵאלֹהִים אֲבִי יֵשׁוּעַ הַמָּשִׁיחַ אֲדֹנֵינוּ וּמִתְפַּלְלִים בַּעַדְכֶם תָּמִיד:

3. Hee•ne a•nach•noo mo•dim le•Elohim Avi Yeshua ha•Ma•shi•ach Ado•ney•noo oo•mit•pa•le•lim ba•ad•chem ta•mid.

---

4. Since we heard of your faith in Christ Jesus, and of the love which ye have to all the saints,

Greek/Transliteration
4. ἀκούσαντες τὴν πίστιν ὑμῶν ἐν χριστῷ Ἰησοῦ, καὶ τὴν ἀγάπην τὴν εἰς πάντας τοὺς ἁγίους,

4. akousantes tein pistin 'umon en christo Yeisou, kai tein agapein tein eis pantas tous 'agious,

Hebrew/Transliteration
ד: אַחֲרֵי אֲשֶׁר שָׁמַעְנוּ אֱמוּנַתְכֶם בְּיֵשׁוּעַ הַמָּשִׁיחַ וְאַהֲבַתְכֶם לְכָל-הַקְּדוֹשִׁים

4. A•cha•rey asher sha•ma•a•noo emoo•nat•chem be•Yeshua ha•Ma•shi•ach ve•a•ha•vat•chem le•chol - ha•k`do•shim.

---

5. For the hope which is laid up for you in heaven, whereof ye heard before in the word of the truth of the gospel;

Greek/Transliteration
5. διὰ τὴν ἐλπίδα τὴν ἀποκειμένην ὑμῖν ἐν τοῖς οὐρανοῖς, ἣν προηκούσατε ἐν τῷ λόγῳ τῆς ἀληθείας τοῦ εὐαγγελίου,

5. dya tein elpida tein apokeimenein 'umin en tois ouranois, 'ein proeikousate en to logo teis aleitheias tou euangeliou,

Hebrew/Transliteration
ה: בַּעֲבוּר הַתִּקְוָה הַצְּפוּנָה לָכֶם בַּשָּׁמַיִם אֲשֶׁר שְׁמַעְתֶּם מֵאָז מִפִּי אִמְרֵי אֱמֶת בַּבְּשׂוֹרָה

5. Ba•a•voor ha•tik•va hatz•foo•na la•chem ba•sha•ma•yim asher sh`ma•a•tem me•az mi•pi eem•rey emet bab•so•ra.

---

6. Which is come unto you, as it is in all the world; and bringeth forth fruit, as it doth also in you, since the day ye heard of it, and knew the grace of God in truth:

Greek/Transliteration
6. τοῦ παρόντος εἰς ὑμᾶς, καθὼς καὶ ἐν παντὶ τῷ κόσμῳ, καὶ ἔστιν καρποφορούμενον, καὶ αὐξανόμενον καθὼς καὶ ἐν ὑμῖν ἀφ᾽ ἧς ἡμέρας ἠκούσατε καὶ ἐπέγνωτε τὴν χάριν τοῦ θεοῦ ἐν ἀληθείᾳ·

6. tou parontos eis 'umas, kathos kai en panti to kosmo, kai estin karpophoroumenon, kai auxanomenon kathos kai en 'umin aph 'eis 'eimeras eikousate kai epegnote tein charin tou theou en aleitheia.

Hebrew/Transliteration
ו. אֲשֶׁר הוּבְאָה אֲלֵיכֶם כְּמוֹ גַם בְּכָל-הָאָרֶץ וּפֹרִיָּה וַעֲנֵפָה בַּאֲשֶׁר הִיא שָׁם כְּמוֹ גַם-בְּתוֹכְכֶם לְמִן-הַיּוֹם אֲשֶׁר שְׁמַעְתֶּם וְיָדֹעַ יְדַעְתֶּם חֶסֶד אֱלֹהִים בֶּאֱמֶת:

6. Asher hoov•ah aley•chem k`mo gam be•chol - ha•a•retz oo•fo•ri•ya va•a•ne•fa ba•a•sher hee sham k`mo gam - be•to•cha•chem le•min - ha•yom asher sh`ma•a•tem ve•ya•doa ye•da•a•tem che•sed Elohim be•e•met.

Rabbinic Jewish Commentary
That is, the Gospel, which came to them from God, from heaven, from Yeshua, out of Jerusalem, from whence the word of YHWH was to come, by the ministers of the Gospel, who being sent, came to Colosse, and there preached it; and so the Syriac version renders the words הי דאתכרזת, "which is preached unto you".

It was come, εις υμας, "into you", as the phrase may be rendered, into their very hearts, and wrought effectually there, enlightening, convincing, comforting, and instructing them; where it had a place, and remained; for the words may be read, as they are by the Arabic version, "which is present with you".

and bringeth forth fruit: The Vulgate Latin adds, "and increaseth"; the Syriac version has the same; and it is so read in some Greek copies, as in the Alexandrian copy, two of Stephens's, and in the Complutensian edition; and may intend the spread of the Gospel among others, besides those who first received it, and the growing fruitfulness of the professors of it under its influence.

---

7. As ye also learned of Epaphras our dear fellowservant, who is for you a faithful minister of Christ;

Greek/Transliteration
7. καθὼς καὶ ἐμάθετε ἀπὸ Ἐπαφρᾶ τοῦ ἀγαπητοῦ συνδούλου ἡμῶν, ὅς ἐστιν πιστὸς ὑπὲρ ὑμῶν διάκονος τοῦ χριστοῦ,

7. kathos kai emathete apo Epaphra tou agapeitou sundoulou 'eimon, 'os estin pistos 'uper 'umon dyakonos tou christou,

Hebrew/Transliteration
ז. וְכַאֲשֶׁר גַּם-כֵּן לְמַדְתֶּם מִפִּי אֶפַפְרָס יְדִידֵנוּ הָעֹבֵד עִמָּנוּ יַחְדָּו הוּא מְשָׁרֵת הַמָּשִׁיחַ נֶאֱמָן לִפְנֵיכֶם:

7. Ve•cha•a•sher gam - ken le•ma•de•tem mi•pi Epaf•ras ye•di•de•noo ha•o•ved ee•ma•noo yach•dav hoo me•sha•ret ha•Ma•shi•ach ne•e•man lif•ney•chem.

---

8. Who also declared unto us your love in the Spirit.

Greek/Transliteration
8. ὁ καὶ δηλώσας ἡμῖν τὴν ὑμῶν ἀγάπην ἐν πνεύματι.

8. 'o kai deilosas 'eimin tein 'umon agapein en pneumati.

Hebrew/Transliteration
ח. וְהוּא הִגִּיד לָנוּ אֶת-אַהֲבַתְכֶם לְפִי הָרוּחַ:

8. Ve•hoo hi•gid la•noo et - aha•vat•chem le•fi ha•Roo•ach.

---

9. For this cause we also, since the day we heard it, do not cease to pray for you, and to desire that ye might be filled with the knowledge of his will in all wisdom and spiritual understanding;

Greek/Transliteration
9. Διὰ τοῦτο καὶ ἡμεῖς, ἀφ᾽ ἧς ἡμέρας ἠκούσαμεν, οὐ παυόμεθα ὑπὲρ ὑμῶν προσευχόμενοι, καὶ αἰτούμενοι ἵνα πληρωθῆτε τὴν ἐπίγνωσιν τοῦ θελήματος αὐτοῦ ἐν πάσῃ σοφίᾳ καὶ συνέσει πνευματικῇ,

9. Dya touto kai 'eimeis, aph 'eis 'eimeras eikousamen, ou pauometha 'uper 'umon proseuchomenoi, kai aitoumenoi 'ina pleirotheite tein epignosin tou theleimatos autou en pasei sophia kai sunesei pneumatikei,

Hebrew/Transliteration
ט. בַּעֲבוּר זֹאת גַּם-אֲנַחְנוּ מִן-הַיּוֹם אֲשֶׁר שְׁמַעֲנוּ כָזֹאת לֹא חָדַלְנוּ מֵהִתְפַּלֵּל וּמֵהִתְחַנֵּן בַּעַדְכֶם כִּי תִמָּלְאוּ דַעַת רְצוֹן אֵל בְּכָל-חָכְמָה וּתְבוּנָה הָעֶלְיוֹנָה:

9. Ba•a•voor zot gam - a•nach•noo min - ha•yom asher sha•ma•a•noo cha•zot lo cha•dal•noo me•hit•pa•lel oo•me•hit•cha•nen ba•ad•chem ki ti•mal•oo da•at r`tzon El be•chol - choch•ma oot•voo•na ha•el•yo•na.

---

10. That ye might walk worthy of the Lord unto all pleasing, being fruitful in every good work, and increasing in the knowledge of God;

Greek/Transliteration
10. περιπατῆσαι ὑμᾶς ἀξίως τοῦ κυρίου εἰς πᾶσαν ἀρέσκειαν, ἐν παντὶ ἔργῳ ἀγαθῷ καρποφοροῦντες καὶ αὐξανόμενοι εἰς τὴν ἐπίγνωσιν τοῦ θεοῦ·

10. peripateisai 'umas axios tou kuriou eis pasan areskeyan, en panti ergo agatho karpophorountes kai auxanomenoi eis tein epignosin tou theou.

Hebrew/Transliteration
י. לְהִתְהַלֵּךְ כַּטּוֹב בְּעֵינֵי הָאָדוֹן לְכָל-חֵפֶץ לִבּוֹ לַעֲשׂוֹת פְּרִי בְּכָל-מַעֲשֶׂה טוֹב וּלְהוֹסִיף דַּעַת אֱלֹהִים:

10. Le•hit•ha•lech ka•tov be•ei•ney ha•Adon le•chol - che•fetz li•bo la•a•sot p`ri be•chol - ma•a•se tov ool•ho•sif da•at Elohim.

Rabbinic Jewish Commentary
That ye might walk worthy of the Lord,.... The Vulgate Latin version reads, "of God"; to which the Ethiopic version agrees.

unto all pleasing. The Syriac reads it, "that ye may please God in all good works".

11. Strengthened with all might, according to his glorious power, unto all patience and longsuffering with joyfulness;

Greek/Transliteration
11. ἐν πάσῃ δυνάμει δυναμούμενοι κατὰ τὸ κράτος τῆς δόξης αὐτοῦ, εἰς πᾶσαν ὑπομονὴν καὶ μακροθυμίαν μετὰ χαρᾶς·

11. en pasei dunamei dunamoumenoi kata to kratos teis doxeis autou, eis pasan 'upomonein kai makrothumian meta charas.

Hebrew/Transliteration
יא. לְהִתְאַזֵּר בְּכָל-עֹז כְּעֹז כְּבוֹדוֹ לְכָל-תּוֹחֶלֶת וְאֹרֶךְ רוּחַ בְּלֵב שָׂמֵחַ:

11. Le•hit•a•zer be•chol - oz ke•oz k`vo•do le•chol - to•che•let ve•o•rech roo•ach be•lev sa•me•ach.

---

12. Giving thanks unto the Father, which hath made us meet to be partakers of the inheritance of the saints in light:

Greek/Transliteration
12. εὐχαριστοῦντες τῷ πατρὶ τῷ ἱκανώσαντι ἡμᾶς εἰς τὴν μερίδα τοῦ κλήρου τῶν ἁγίων ἐν τῷ φωτί,

12. eucharistountes to patri to 'ikanosanti 'eimas eis tein merida tou kleirou ton 'agion en to photi,

Hebrew/Transliteration
יב. וּלְהוֹדוֹת לְאָבִינוּ אֲשֶׁר הֱכִינָנוּ לָקַחַת חֵלֶק בְּנַחֲלַת קְדֹשָׁיו בְּמוֹ-אוֹר:

12. Ool•ho•dot le•Avi•noo asher he•chi•na•noo la•ka•chat che•lek be•na•cha•lat ke•do•shav be•mo - or.

Rabbinic Jewish Commentary
Giving thanks unto the Father,..... To God the Father, as the Vulgate Latin and the Syriac versions read the clause; and the Complutensian edition, and some copies, "God and the Father"; who is both the Father of Christ by nature, and of all his people by adoption. The Ethiopic version renders it, as an exhortation or advice, "give ye thanks to the Father"; and so the Syriac version: but the words rather seem to be spoken in the first, than in the second person, and are to be considered in connection with Col_1:9. So when the apostle had made an end of his petitions, he enters upon thanksgiving to God.

This may be said in reference to a notion of the Jews, that the "light" which God created on the first day is that goodness which he has laid up for them that fear him, and is what he has treasured up for the righteous in the world to come (d).

One copy, as Beza observes, reads it, "which hath called us to be partakers" and so does the Ethiopic version.

(d) Zohar in Gen. fol. 6. 3. & in Exod. fol. 32. 3. & in Lev. xiv. 4. & xxxvii. 4. Bereshit Rabba, fol. 3. 2.

13. Who hath delivered us from the power of darkness, and hath translated us into the kingdom of his dear Son:

Greek/Transliteration
13. ὃς ἐρρύσατο ἡμᾶς ἐκ τῆς ἐξουσίας τοῦ σκότους, καὶ μετέστησεν εἰς τὴν βασιλείαν τοῦ υἱοῦ τῆς ἀγάπης αὐτοῦ,

13. 'os errusato 'eimas ek teis exousias tou skotous, kai metesteisen eis tein basileian tou 'wiou teis agapeis autou,

Hebrew/Transliteration
יג. וַאֲשֶׁר הִצִּיל אֶת-נַפְשֵׁנוּ מִמֶּמְשֶׁלֶת הַחֹשֶׁךְ וַיִּתֶּן-לָנוּ מָקוֹם בְּמַמְלֶכֶת בְּנוֹ אֲשֶׁר אָהֵב:

13. Va•a•sher hi•tzil et - naf•she•noo mi•mem•she•let ha•cho•shech va•yi•ten - la•noo ma•kom be•mam•le•chet B`no asher ahev.

Rabbinic Jewish Commentary
With the Jews, one of the names of the adversary is חשך, "darkness" (e). Moreover, the darkness of sin, ignorance, and unbelief.

(e) Shirhashirim Rabba, fol. 25. 4.

---

14. In whom we have redemption through his blood, even the forgiveness of sins:

Greek/Transliteration
14. ἐν ᾧ ἔχομεν τὴν ἀπολύτρωσιν, τὴν ἄφεσιν τῶν ἁμαρτιῶν·

14. en 'o echomen tein apolutrosin, tein aphesin ton 'amartion.

Hebrew/Transliteration
יד. וּבוֹ נִמְצָא פְדוּת בְּדָמוֹ וּסְלִיחָה לְחַטֹּאתֵינוּ:

14. Oo•vo nim•tza fe•doot be•da•mo oos•li•cha le•cha•to•tey•noo.

Rabbinic Jewish Commentary
through his blood. This phrase is left out indeed in the Syriac and Ethiopic versions, and in the Complutensian edition, and in some copies.

---

15. Who is the image of the invisible God, the firstborn of every creature:

Greek/Transliteration
15. ὅς ἐστιν εἰκὼν τοῦ θεοῦ τοῦ ἀοράτου, πρωτότοκος πάσης κτίσεως·

15. 'os estin eikon tou theou tou aoratou, prototokos paseis ktiseos.

Hebrew/Transliteration
טו. וְהוּא צֶלֶם אֱלֹהִים אֲשֶׁר פָּנָיו לֹא יֵרָאוּ וּבְכוֹר כָּל-נִבְרָא:

15. Ve•hoo tze•lem Elohim asher pa•nav lo ye•ra•oo oov•chor kol - niv•ra.

Rabbinic Jewish Commentary

Philo, the Jew (f), often speaks of the λογος, or Word of God, as the image of God. Also, this may be understood of him as Mediator, in whom, as such, is a most glorious display of the love, grace, and mercy of God, of his holiness and righteousness, of his truth and faithfulness, and of his power and wisdom.

He is the "first Parent", or bringer forth of every creature into being, as the word will bear to be rendered, if instead of **πρωτοτοκος**, we read **πρωτοτοκος**; which is no more than changing the place of the accent, and may be very easily ventured upon, as is done by an ancient writer (g), who observes, that the word is used in this sense by Homer, and is the same as **πρωτογονος**, "first Parent", and **πρωτοκτιστης**, "first Creator". Yeshua is also the "firstborn" from the dead, verse 18.

The Messiah is higher than the kings of the earth, or the hosts in heaven, the highest rank of creatures, being the Creator and upholder of all, as the following words show; so the Jews make the word "firstborn" to be synonymous with the word "king", and explain it by גדול ושר, "a great one", and "a prince" (h); see Psa_89:27.

(f) De Mund. Opific. p. 6. de Plant. Noe, p. 216, 217. de Coufus. Ling. p. 341. de Somniis, p. 600. de Monarch. p. 823. (g) Isidior. Pelusiot. l. 3. Ep. 31. (h) R. Sol. Urbin. Ohel Moed, fol. 50. 1.

---

16. For by him were all things created, that are in heaven, and that are in earth, visible and invisible, whether they be thrones, or dominions, or principalities, or powers: all things were created by him, and for him:

Greek/Transliteration

16. ὅτι ἐν αὐτῷ ἐκτίσθη τὰ πάντα, τὰ ἐν τοῖς οὐρανοῖς καὶ τὰ ἐπὶ τῆς γῆς, τὰ ὁρατὰ καὶ τὰ ἀόρατα, εἴτε θρόνοι, εἴτε κυριότητες, εἴτε ἀρχαί, εἴτε ἐξουσίαι· τὰ πάντα δι᾽ αὐτοῦ καὶ εἰς αὐτὸν ἔκτισται·

16. 'oti en auto ektisthei ta panta, ta en tois ouranois kai ta epi teis geis, ta 'orata kai ta aorata, eite thronoi, eite kurioteites, eite archai, eite exousiai. ta panta di autou kai eis auton ektistai.

Hebrew/Transliteration

טז. כִּי-בוֹ נִבְרְאוּ כֹל אֲשֶׁר בַּשָּׁמַיִם וַאֲשֶׁר בָּאָרֶץ הַנִּגְלוֹת וְהַנִּסְתָּרוֹת אִם כִּסְאוֹת וּמֶמְשָׁלוֹת אוֹ כָל-מִשְׂרָה וְשִׁלְטוֹן כֻּלָּם בּוֹ וּלְמַעֲנוֹ נִבְרָאוּ:

16. Ki - vo niv•re•oo kol asher ba•sha•ma•yim va•a•sher ba•a•retz ha•nig•lot ve•ha•nis•ta•rot eem kis•ot oo•mem•sha•lot oh chol - mis•ra ve•shil•ton koo•lam bo ool•ma•a•no niv•ra•oo.

Rabbinic Jewish Commentary

The things in the airy heavens, the fowls thereof, were on the fifth day created by him; and the things in the starry heaven, the sun, moon, and stars, were on the fourth day ordained by him; and the inhabitants of the third heaven, the hosts, were made by him, Heb_1:7; and, as the Jewish writers (i) say, on the second day of the creation, though some say on the fifth.

Thus, in a book of theirs, which they esteem very ancient, and ascribe to the patriarch Abraham, it is said (k),

"There is no messenger/angel in which the name YHWH is not found, which is everywhere, as the soul is in every member; wherefore men ought to allow YHWH to reign in all the members, ובכל כרסין, "and in all the thrones", and in all the angels, and in every member of men.

And elsewhere, speaking of the garments of God,

"By these (say they (l)) ברא קבה כרסיין, "the holy blessed God created the thrones", and the hosts of heaven, and the living creatures, and the "seraphim", and the heavens, and the earth, and all that he created.

And the thrones in Dan_7:9; are interpreted (m), of

"The superior princes, למלאכים רוחניים, "the spiritual messengers", who sit first in the kingdom; and they are called in the words of the Rabbis, "the throne of glory"; for so is the way of kings, that their princes sit before them, everyone on his throne, according to their dignity.

(i) Targum Jon. in Gen. i. 26. Bereshit Rabba, fol. 1. 1. & 3. 3. Menass. ben Israel, Conciliator in Gen. Qu. 12. (k) Sepher Jetzira, p. 17, Ed. Rittangel. (l) Tikkune Zohar in ib. p. 127, 128. & Zohar in Exod. fol. 18. 2. & in Lev. fol. 39. 1. & 47. 2. (m) Abarbinel in Dan. fol. 45. 4. & 46. 4.

---

17. And he is before all things, and by him all things consist.

Greek/Transliteration
17. καὶ αὐτός ἐστιν πρὸ πάντων, καὶ τὰ πάντα ἐν αὐτῷ συνέστηκεν.

17. kai autos estin pro panton, kai ta panta en auto sunesteiken.

Hebrew/Transliteration
:יז. וְהוּא קַדְמוֹן לְכָל-דָּבָר וְעַל-פִּיו הֵם עֹמְדִים כֻּלָּם

17. Ve•hoo kad•mon le•chol - da•var ve•al - piv hem om•dim koo•lam.

---

18. And he is the head of the body, the church: who is the beginning, the firstborn from the dead; that in all things he might have the preeminence.

Greek/Transliteration
18. Καὶ αὐτός ἐστιν ἡ κεφαλὴ τοῦ σώματος, τῆς ἐκκλησίας· ὅς ἐστιν ἀρχή, πρωτότοκος ἐκ τῶν νεκρῶν, ἵνα γένηται ἐν πᾶσιν αὐτὸς πρωτεύων·

18. Kai autos estin 'ei kephalei tou somatos, teis ekkleisias. 'os estin archei, prototokos ek ton nekron, 'ina geneitai en pasin autos proteuon.

Hebrew/Transliteration
:יח. הוּא רֹאשׁ הָעֵדָה אֲשֶׁר הִיא גְוִיָּתוֹ וְגַם-רֹאשׁ וּבְכוֹר שָׁקָם מִן-הַמֵּתִים לִהְיוֹתוֹ רִאשׁוֹן לַכֹּל

18. Hoo rosh ha•e•da asher hee ge•vi•yato ve•gam - rosh oov•chor she•kam min - ha•me•tim li•hi•yo•to ri•shon la•kol.

---

19. For it pleased the Father that in him should all fullness dwell;

Greek/Transliteration
19. ὅτι ἐν αὐτῷ εὐδόκησεν πᾶν τὸ πλήρωμα κατοικῆσαι,

19. 'oti en auto eudokeisen pan to pleiroma katoikeisai,

Hebrew/Transliteration
יט. כִּי-כֵן רָצָה אֱלֹהִים אֲשֶׁר בּוֹ יִשְׁכֹּן מְלֹא הַכֹּל:

19. Ki - chen ra•tza Elohim asher bo yish•kon me•lo ha•kol.

---

20. And, having made peace through the blood of his cross, by him to reconcile all things unto himself; by him, I say, whether they be things in earth, or things in heaven.

Greek/Transliteration
20. καὶ δι᾽ αὐτοῦ ἀποκαταλλάξαι τὰ πάντα εἰς αὐτόν, εἰρηνοποιήσας διὰ τοῦ αἵματος τοῦ σταυροῦ αὐτοῦ, δι᾽ αὐτοῦ, εἴτε τὰ ἐπὶ τῆς γῆς, εἴτε τὰ ἐπὶ τοῖς οὐρανοῖς.

20. kai di autou apokatallaxai ta panta eis auton, eireinopoieisas dya tou 'aimatos tou staurou autou, di autou, eite ta epi teis geis, eite ta epi tois ouranois.

Hebrew/Transliteration
כ. וְכֵן עַל-יָדוֹ יַהֲפֹךְ לֵב כֻּלָּם לְהִתְרַצּוֹת אֵלָיו אַחֲרֵי אֲשֶׁר עַל-יָדוֹ בְּדַם הַצְּלָב עָשָׂה שָׁלוֹם לְכֻלָּם לְכָל-אֲשֶׁר בָּאָרֶץ וּלְכָל-אֲשֶׁר בַּשָּׁמָיִם:

20. Ve•chen al - ya•do ya•ha•foch lev koo•lam le•hit•ra•tzot elav a•cha•rey asher al - ya•do be•dam hatz•lav asa sha•lom le•choo•lam le•chol - asher ba•a•retz ool•chol – asher ba•sha•ma•yim.

---

21. And you, that were sometime alienated and enemies in your mind by wicked works, yet now hath he reconciled

Greek/Transliteration
21. Καὶ ὑμᾶς ποτὲ ὄντας ἀπηλλοτριωμένους καὶ ἐχθροὺς τῇ διανοίᾳ ἐν τοῖς ἔργοις τοῖς πονηροῖς, νυνὶ δὲ ἀποκατήλλαξεν

21. Kai 'umas pote ontas apeillotriomenous kai echthrous tei dyanoia en tois ergois tois poneirois, nuni de apokateillaxen

Hebrew/Transliteration
כא. וְגַם-אַתֶּם אֲשֶׁר מוּזָרִים הֱיִיתֶם לְפָנִים וְאֹיְבִים מִמְּקוֹר הַלֵּב עֵקֶב מַעֲשֵׂיכֶם הָרָעִים:

21. Ve•gam - atem asher moo•za•rim he•yi•tem le•fa•nim ve•oy•vim mim•kor ha•lev e•kev ma•a•sey•chem ha•ra•eem.

---

22. In the body of his flesh through death, to present you holy and unblameable and unreproveable in his sight:

Greek/Transliteration

22. ἐν τῷ σώματι τῆς σαρκὸς αὐτοῦ διὰ τοῦ θανάτου, παραστῆσαι ὑμᾶς ἁγίους καὶ ἀμώμους καὶ ἀνεγκλήτους κατενώπιον αὐτοῦ·

22. en to somati teis sarkos autou dya tou thanatou, parasteisai 'umas 'agious kai amomous kai anegkleitous katenopion autou.

Hebrew/Transliteration

כב. הָפַךְ עַתָּה אֶת-לִבְּכֶם לְהִתְרַצּוֹת אֵלָיו בְּעַצְמוֹ וּבִבְשָׂרוֹ בְּמוֹתוֹ לַהֲקִימְכֶם קְדשִׁים לְפָנָיו זַכִּים מֵעָוֹן וּנְקִיִּים מִכָּל-שֶׁמֶץ דָּבָר:

22. Ha•fach ata et - lib•chem le•hit•ra•tzot elav be•atz•mo oo•viv•sa•ro be•mo•to la•ha•kim•chem k`do•shim le•fa•nav za•kim me•avon oon•ki•yim mi•kol - she•metz da•var.

---

23. If ye continue in the faith grounded and settled, and be not moved away from the hope of the gospel, which ye have heard, and which was preached to every creature which is under heaven; whereof I Paul am made a minister;

Greek/Transliteration

23. εἴγε ἐπιμένετε τῇ πίστει τεθεμελιωμένοι καὶ ἑδραῖοι, καὶ μὴ μετακινούμενοι ἀπὸ τῆς ἐλπίδος τοῦ εὐαγγελίου οὗ ἠκούσατε, τοῦ κηρυχθέντος ἐν πάσῃ τῇ κτίσει τῇ ὑπὸ τὸν οὐρανόν, οὗ ἐγενόμην ἐγὼ Παῦλος διάκονος.

23. eige epimenete tei pistei tethemeliomenoi kai 'edraioi, kai mei metakinoumenoi apo teis elpidos tou euangeliou 'ou eikousate, tou keiruchthentos en pasei tei ktisei tei 'upo ton ouranon, 'ou egenomein ego Paulos dyakonos.

Hebrew/Transliteration

כג. רַק אִם-תַּעַמְדוּ מְיֻסָּדִים וְהָכֵן בָּאֱמוּנָה וְלֹא תַרְפּוּ מִתּוֹחֶלֶת הַבְּשׂרָה אֲשֶׁר שְׁמַעְתֶּם בְּאָזְנֵיכֶם וַאֲשֶׁר שׂוּמָה בְּאָזְנֵי כָל-יְצוּר תַּחַת הַשָּׁמַיִם וַאֲנִי פוֹלוֹס הָיִיתִי לָהּ לִמְשָׁרֵת:

23. Rak eem - ta•am•doo me•yoo•sa•dim ve•ha•chen ba•e•moo•na ve•lo tar•poo mi•to•che•let ha•be•so•ra asher sh`ma•a•tem be•oz•ney•chem va•a•sher soo•ma ve•oz•ney chol - ye•tzoor ta•chat ha•sha•ma•yim va•a•ni Folos ha•yi•ti la lim•sha•ret.

---

24. Who now rejoice in my sufferings for you, and fill up that which is behind of the afflictions of Christ in my flesh for his body's sake, which is the church:

Greek/Transliteration

24. Νῦν χαίρω ἐν τοῖς παθήμασιν ὑπὲρ ὑμῶν, καὶ ἀνταναπληρῶ τὰ ὑστερήματα τῶν θλίψεων τοῦ χριστοῦ ἐν τῇ σαρκί μου ὑπὲρ τοῦ σώματος αὐτοῦ, ὅ ἐστιν ἡ ἐκκλησία·

24. Nun chairo en tois patheimasin 'uper 'umon, kai antanapleiro ta 'ustereimata ton thlipseon tou christou en tei sarki mou 'uper tou somatos autou, 'o estin 'ei ekkleisia.

Hebrew/Transliteration

כד. וְעַתָּה הִנְנִי שָׂמֵחַ בְּעִנְיֵי כִּי אֶתְעַנֶּה בִּגְלַלְכֶם וְחֵלֶק הַנֶּעְדָּר מִן-חֶבְלֵי הַמָּשִׁיחַ אַשְׁלִים אֲנִי בִּבְשָׂרִי בְּעַד גְּוִיָּתוֹ הֲלֹא הִיא עֲדָתוֹ:

24. Ve•a•ta hi•ne•ni sa•me•ach be•on•yi ki et•a•ne big•lal•chem ve•che•lek ha•ne•e•dar min - chev•ley ha•Ma•shi•ach ash•lim ani biv•sa•ri be•ad ge•vi•yato ha•lo hee ada•to.

---

25. Whereof I am made a minister, according to the dispensation of God which is given to me for you, to fulfill the word of God;

Greek/Transliteration

25. ἧς ἐγενόμην ἐγὼ διάκονος, κατὰ τὴν οἰκονομίαν τοῦ θεοῦ τὴν δοθεῖσάν μοι εἰς ὑμᾶς, πληρῶσαι τὸν λόγον τοῦ θεοῦ,

25. 'eis egenomein ego dyakonos, kata tein oikonomian tou theou tein dotheisan moi eis 'umas, pleirosai ton logon tou theou,

Hebrew/Transliteration

כה. אֲשֶׁר הָיִיתִי לָהּ לִמְשָׁרֵת כְּפִי-פְקֻדַּת אֱלֹהִים הַנְּתוּנָה לִי בַּעֲבוּרְכֶם לְמַלֹּאת אֶת-דְּבַר אֱלֹהִים:

25. Asher ha•yi•ti la lim•sha•ret ke•fi - f koo•dat Elohim ha•ne•too•na li ba•a•voor•chem le•ma•lot et - de•var Elohim.

---

26. Even the mystery which hath been hid from ages and from generations, but now is made manifest to his saints:

Greek/Transliteration

26. τὸ μυστήριον τὸ ἀποκεκρυμμένον ἀπὸ τῶν αἰώνων καὶ ἀπὸ τῶν γενεῶν· νυνὶ δὲ ἐφανερώθη τοῖς ἁγίοις αὐτοῦ,

26. to musteirion to apokekrummenon apo ton aionon kai apo ton geneon. nuni de ephanerothei tois 'agiois autou,

Hebrew/Transliteration

כו. הוּא הַסּוֹד אֲשֶׁר צָפוּן הָיָה מֵעוֹלָם וּמִדּוֹר דּוֹר וְעַתָּה נִגְלָה לִקְדֹשָׁיו:

26. Hoo ha•sod asher tza•foon ha•ya me•o•lam oo•mi•dor dor ve•a•ta nig•la lik•do•shav.

---

27. To whom God would make known what is the riches of the glory of this mystery among the Gentiles; which is Christ in you, the hope of glory:

Greek/Transliteration

27. οἷς ἠθέλησεν ὁ θεὸς γνωρίσαι τί τὸ πλοῦτος τῆς δόξης τοῦ μυστηρίου τούτου ἐν τοῖς ἔθνεσιν, ὅς ἐστιν χριστὸς ἐν ὑμῖν, ἡ ἐλπὶς τῆς δόξης·

27. 'ois eitheleisen 'o theos gnorisai ti to ploutos teis doxeis tou musteiriou toutou en tois ethnesin, 'os estin christos en 'umin, 'ei elpis teis doxeis.

Hebrew/Transliteration
כז. כִּי-חָפֵץ אֱלֹהִים לְהוֹדִיעָם מַה רַב עֹשֶׁר וְכָבוֹד בְּסוֹד הַזֶּה לַגּוֹיִם הֲלֹא הוּא הַמָּשִׁיחַ בְּתוֹכֲכֶם צְבִי כָל-חֶמְדָּה:

27. Ki - cha•fetz Elohim le•ho•di•am ma rav o•sher ve•cha•vod ba•sod ha•ze la•go•yim ha•lo hoo ha•Ma•shi•ach be•to•cha•chem tze•vi chol - chem•da.

---

28. Whom we preach, warning every man, and teaching every man in all wisdom; that we may present every man perfect in Christ Jesus:

Greek/Transliteration
28. ὃν ἡμεῖς καταγγέλλομεν, νουθετοῦντες πάντα ἄνθρωπον, καὶ διδάσκοντες πάντα ἄνθρωπον ἐν πάσῃ σοφίᾳ, ἵνα παραστήσωμεν πάντα ἄνθρωπον τέλειον ἐν χριστῷ Ἰησοῦ·

28. 'on 'eimeis katangellomen, nouthetountes panta anthropon, kai didaskontes panta anthropon en pasei sophia, 'ina parasteisomen panta anthropon teleion en christo Yeisou.

Hebrew/Transliteration
כח. אֲשֶׁר בְּשׂרָתוֹ אֲנַחְנוּ מְבַשְּׂרִים לְהַזְהִיר אֶת-כָּל-אִישׁ וּלְלַמְּדוֹ בְּלֵבָב חָכְמָה עַד-אֲשֶׁר נַצִּיגֶנּוּ כְּאָדָם שָׁלֵם בַּמָּשִׁיחַ יֵשׁוּעַ:

28. Asher be•so•ra•to a•nach•noo me•vas•rim le•haz•hir et - kol - eesh oo•le•lam•do bil•vav choch•ma ad - asher na•tzi•ge•noo ke•a•dam sha•lem ba•Ma•shi•ach Yeshua.

---

29. Whereunto I also labour, striving according to his working, which worketh in me mightily.

Greek/Transliteration
29. εἰς ὃ καὶ κοπιῶ, ἀγωνιζόμενος κατὰ τὴν ἐνέργειαν αὐτοῦ, τὴν ἐνεργουμένην ἐν ἐμοὶ ἐν δυνάμει.

29. eis 'o kai kopio, agonizomenos kata tein energeyan autou, tein energoumenein en emoi en dunamei.

Hebrew/Transliteration
כט. זֶה הוּא אֲשֶׁר בּוֹ אֲנִי עָמֵל וְעֹדֵר בְּלֹא לֵב וָלֵב כְּכֹחַ יָדוֹ הַחֲזָקָה עָלָי:

29. Ze hoo asher bo ani amel ve•o•der be•lo lev ve•lev ke•cho•ach ya•do ha•cha•za•ka a•lai.

Rabbinic Jewish Commentary
The Syriac version, which renders it, ומתכף, "and make supplication"; that is, with that effectual fervent prayer, which was powerfully wrought in him.

Colossians, Chapter 2

1. For I would that ye knew what great conflict I have for you, and for them at Laodicea, and for as many as have not seen my face in the flesh;

Greek/Transliteration
1. Θέλω γὰρ ὑμᾶς εἰδέναι ἡλίκον ἀγῶνα ἔχω περὶ ὑμῶν καὶ τῶν ἐν Λαοδικείᾳ, καὶ ὅσοι οὐχ ἑωράκασιν τὸ πρόσωπόν μου ἐν σαρκί,

1. Thelo gar 'umas eidenai 'eilikon agona echo peri 'umon kai ton en Laodikeia, kai 'osoi ouch 'eorakasin to prosopon mou en sarki,

Hebrew/Transliteration
א. וַאֲנִי חָפַצְתִּי כִּי תֵדְעוּן מָה-רַבּוּ הַקְּרָבוֹת אֲשֶׁר עָרַכְתִּי בַּעַדְכֶם וּבְעַד-אַנְשֵׁי לוֹדְקְיָא וּבְעַד-כֹּל אֲשֶׁר לֹא-רָאוּ אֹתִי פָּנִים בְּפָנִים:

1. Va•a•ni cha•fatz•ti ki ted•oon ma - ra•boo hak•ra•vot asher a•rach•ti ba•ad•chem oov•ad - an•shey Lood•ke•ya oov•ad - kol asher lo - ra•oo o•ti pa•nim be•fa•nim.

Rabbinic Jewish Commentary
and for them at Laodicea; the saints of that place, the assembly of Messiah which was there; and is the rather mentioned, because near to Colosse: it was a famous city by the river Lycus, first called Diospolis, and then Rhoas (p), and afterwards Laodicea; it was the metropolis of Phrygia, in which Colosse stood.

---

2. That their hearts might be comforted, being knit together in love, and unto all riches of the full assurance of understanding, to the acknowledgement of the mystery of God, and of the Father, and of Christ;

Greek/Transliteration
2. ἵνα παρακληθῶσιν αἱ καρδίαι αὐτῶν, συμβιβασθέντων ἐν ἀγάπῃ, καὶ εἰς πάντα πλοῦτον τῆς πληροφορίας τῆς συνέσεως, εἰς ἐπίγνωσιν τοῦ μυστηρίου τοῦ θεοῦ καὶ πατρὸς καὶ τοῦ χριστοῦ,

2. 'ina parakleithosin 'ai kardiai auton, sumbibasthenton en agapei, kai eis panta plouton teis pleirophorias teis suneseos, eis epignosin tou musteiriou tou theou kai patros kai tou christou,

Hebrew/Transliteration
ב. לְמַעַן יִמְצְאוּ נֹחַם בְּלִבָּם לִהְיוֹת קְשׁוּרִים בְּאַהֲבָתָם וּבְכָל-חֹסֶן אוֹר שִׂכְלָם יַשְׂכִּילוּ אֶל-נָכוֹן סוֹד הָאֱלֹהִים אָבִינוּ וְסוֹד הַמָּשִׁיחַ:

2. Le•ma•an yim•tze•oo no•cham be•li•bam li•hee•yot ke•shoo•rim be•a•ha•va•tam oov•chol - cho•sen or sich•lam yas•ki•loo el - na•chon sod ha•Elohim Avi•noo ve•sod ha•Ma•shi•ach.

Rabbinic Jewish Commentary
The copulative "and" before "the Father", is left out in the Vulgate Latin, Syriac, and Arabic versions, which read "the mystery of God the Father"; and with it, it may be rendered, as it sometimes is, God, "even the Father": though the word "God" may be considered essentially, and as after distinguished into two of the persons of the Godhead.

3. In whom are hid all the treasures of wisdom and knowledge.

Greek/Transliteration
3. ἐν ᾧ εἰσιν πάντες οἱ θησαυροὶ τῆς σοφίας καὶ τῆς γνώσεως ἀπόκρυφοι.

3. en 'o eisin pantes 'oi theisauroi teis sophias kai teis gnoseos apokruphoi.

Hebrew/Transliteration
ג. אֲשֶׁר בּוֹ צְפוּנִים כָּל-אֹצְרוֹת הַחָכְמָה וְהַדָּעַת:

3. Asher bo tz`foo•nim kol - otz•rot ha•choch•ma ve•ha•da•at.

Rabbinic Jewish Commentary
Being said to be "hid" in him, shows the excellency of the wisdom and knowledge that is in him only valuable things being hid, or compared to hid treasure; that this cannot be had without knowing him; that it is imperfect in the present state, and is not yet fully and clearly revealed; and therefore should be inquired after, and searched for, and Messiah Yeshua should be applied unto for it: גנזי חכמתא, "treasures of wisdom", is a phrase used by the Targumist (q),

(q) Jonathan ben Uzziel in Exod. xl. 4.

---

4. And this I say, lest any man should beguile you with enticing words.

Greek/Transliteration
4. Τοῦτο δὲ λέγω, ἵνα μή τις ὑμᾶς παραλογίζηται ἐν πιθανολογίᾳ.

4. Touto de lego, 'ina mei tis 'umas paralogizeitai en pithanologia.

Hebrew/Transliteration
ד. וְכָזֹאת אֲנִי אֹמֵר פֶּן-יַדִּיחַ אֶתְכֶם אִישׁ בְּשִׂפְתֵי חֲלָקוֹת:

4. Ve•cha•zot ani o•mer pen - ya•di•ach et•chem eesh be•sif•tey cha•la•kot.

---

5. For though I be absent in the flesh, yet am I with you in the spirit, joying and beholding your order, and the stedfastness of your faith in Christ.

Greek/Transliteration
5. Εἰ γὰρ καὶ τῇ σαρκὶ ἄπειμι, ἀλλὰ τῷ πνεύματι σὺν ὑμῖν εἰμί, χαίρων καὶ βλέπων ὑμῶν τὴν τάξιν, καὶ τὸ στερέωμα τῆς εἰς χριστὸν πίστεως ὑμῶν.

5. Ei gar kai tei sarki apeimi, alla to pneumati sun 'umin eimi, chairon kai blepon 'umon tein taxin, kai to stereoma teis eis christon pisteos 'umon.

Hebrew/Transliteration
ה. כִּי אַף-אִם בִּבְשָׂרִי רָחוֹק אֲנִי מִכֶּם בְּכָל-זֹאת בְּרוּחִי הִנְנִי אֶצְלְכֶם וְנַפְשִׁי שְׂמֵחָה לִרְאוֹת סֵדֶר הֲלִיכוֹתֵיכֶם וְתֹקֶף אֱמוּנַתְכֶם בַּמָּשִׁיחַ:

5. Ki af - eem biv•sa•ri ra•chok ani mi•kem be•chol - zot be•roo•chi hi•ne•ni etz•le•chem ve•naf•shi s`me•cha lir•ot se•der ha•li•cho•tey•chem ve•to•kef emoo•nat•chem ba•Ma•shi•ach.

---

6. As ye have therefore received Christ Jesus the Lord, so walk ye in him:

Greek/Transliteration

6. Ὡς οὖν παρελάβετε τὸν χριστὸν Ἰησοῦν τὸν κύριον, ἐν αὐτῷ περιπατεῖτε,

6. 'Os oun parelabete ton christon Yeisoun ton kurion, en auto peripateite,

Hebrew/Transliteration

ו. עַל־כֵּן כַּאֲשֶׁר קִבַּלְתֶּם אֶת הַמָּשִׁיחַ אֶת־יֵשׁוּעַ אֲדֹנֵינוּ כֵּן־גַּם־תִּתְהַלְכוּ לְפָנָיו:

6. Al - ken ka•a•sher ki•bal•tem et ha•Ma•shi•ach et - Yeshua Ado•ney•noo ken - gam - tit•hal•choo le•fa•nav.

---

7. Rooted and built up in him, and stablished in the faith, as ye have been taught, abounding therein with thanksgiving.

Greek/Transliteration

7. ἐρριζωμένοι καὶ ἐποικοδομούμενοι ἐν αὐτῷ, καὶ βεβαιούμενοι ἐν τῇ πίστει, καθὼς ἐδιδάχθητε, περισσεύοντες ἐν αὐτῇ ἐν εὐχαριστίᾳ.

7. errizomenoi kai epoikodomoumenoi en auto, kai bebaioumenoi en tei pistei, kathos edidachtheite, perisseuontes en autei en eucharistia.

Hebrew/Transliteration

ז. מַשְׁרִישִׁים וּבְנוּיִם בּוֹ לַעֲמֹד הָכֵן בָּאֱמוּנָה כַּאֲשֶׁר לֻמַּדְתֶּם וְלַעֲשׂוֹת חַיִל בְּאִמְרֵי תוֹדָה:

7. Mash•ri•shim oov•noo•yim bo la•a•mod ha•chen ba•e•moo•na ka•a•sher loo•ma•de•tem ve•la•a•sot cha•yil be•eem•rey to•da.

---

8. Beware lest any man spoil you through philosophy and vain deceit, after the tradition of men, after the rudiments of the world, and not after Christ.

Greek/Transliteration

8. Βλέπετε μή τις ὑμᾶς ἔσται ὁ συλαγωγῶν διὰ τῆς φιλοσοφίας καὶ κενῆς ἀπάτης, κατὰ τὴν παράδοσιν τῶν ἀνθρώπων, κατὰ τὰ στοιχεῖα τοῦ κόσμου, καὶ οὐ κατὰ χριστόν·

8. Blepete mei tis 'umas estai 'o sulagogon dya teis philosophias kai keneis apateis, kata tein paradosin ton anthropon, kata ta stoicheia tou kosmou, kai ou kata christon.

Hebrew/Transliteration

ח. הִשָּׁמְרוּ לָכֶם פֶּן־תִּהְיוּ לְשָׁלָל לְמַחְקְרֵי אִישׁ בְּמַשְׂאוֹת שָׁוְא לְפִי מִצְוַת אֲנָשִׁים מְלֻמָּדָה כְּדֶרֶךְ הָעוֹלָם וְלֹא כְּדֶרֶךְ הַמָּשִׁיחַ:

8. Hi•sham•roo la•chem pen - ti•hi•yoo le•sha•lal le•mech•ke•rey eesh be•mas•ot shav le•fi mitz•vat a•na•shim me•loo•ma•da ke•de•rech ha•o•lam ve•lo che•de•rech ha•Ma•shi•ach.

Rabbinic Jewish Commentary
In a word, the apostle here condemns the philosophy of the Jews, and of the Greek Gnostics; the former had introduced natural philosophy into the worship and service of God, and the things appertaining to their religion; and had made the tabernacle and temple, and the most holy place, and the things belonging thereunto, emblems and hieroglyphics of natural things; as of the sun, moon, and stars, and their influences, and of the four elements, and of moral virtue as appears from the writings of Josephus (r), and Philo (s).

(r) Antiqu. l. 3. c. 6. sect. 4. 7. (s) De Congressu quaerend. Erud. p. 440. 441. de Vita Mosis, l. 3. p. 665, &c. quod deterius pot. p. 184.

---

9. For in him dwelleth all the fullness of the Godhead bodily.

Greek/Transliteration
9. ὅτι ἐν αὐτῷ κατοικεῖ πᾶν τὸ πλήρωμα τῆς θεότητος σωματικῶς,

9. 'oti en auto katoikei pan to pleroma teis theoteitos somatikos,

Hebrew/Transliteration
ט. כִּי כָל-מְלֹא אֱלֹהִים שָׁכֵן בְּתוֹכוֹ כְּמוֹ בְּתוֹךְ גְּוִיָּה:

9. Ki chol - me•lo Elohim sha•chen be•to•cho k`mo be•toch ge•vi•ya.

Rabbinic Jewish Commentary
That is to deity what the human body is to an human soul, it is the house in which it dwells: so Philo the Jew (t) calls the "Logos" the house of God, who is the soul of the universe; and elsewhere says (u), that God himself has filled the divine Logos wholly with incorporeal powers. The Godhead dwells in Messiah Yeshua as in a tabernacle, in allusion to the tabernacle of Moses, which looked mean without side, but glorious within; where God granted his presence, and accepted the sacrifices of his people; the human nature of Yeshua is the true antitypical tabernacle, which God pitched, and not man; and sometimes is called a temple, in allusion to Solomon's; and which is filled with the train of the divine perfections, signified by fulness here.

(t) De migr. Abraham, p. 389. (u) De Sommiis, p. 574.

---

10. And ye are complete in him, which is the head of all principality and power:

Greek/Transliteration
10. καί ἐστε ἐν αὐτῷ πεπληρωμένοι, ὅς ἐστιν ἡ κεφαλὴ πάσης ἀρχῆς καὶ ἐξουσίας·

10. kai este en auto pepleiromenoi, 'os estin 'ei kephalei paseis archeis kai exousias.

Hebrew/Transliteration
י. וְאַתֶּם מְמֻלָּאִים בּוֹ אֲשֶׁר הוּא הָרֹאשׁ לְכָל-מִשְׂרָה וְשִׁלְטוֹן:

10. Ve•a•tem me•moo•la•eem bo asher hoo ha•rosh le•chol - mis•ra ve•shil•ton.

Rabbinic Jewish Commentary
With the Jews, "Metatron", which with them is the name of the messenger in Exo_23:20 and seems to be a corruption of the word "mediator", and to design the Messiah, is said (w) to be King over all the messengers.

(w) Zohar in Deut. fol. 120. 8.

---

11. In whom also ye are circumcised with the circumcision made without hands, in putting off the body of the sins of the flesh by the circumcision of Christ:

Greek/Transliteration
11. ἐν ᾧ καὶ περιετμήθητε περιτομῇ ἀχειροποιήτῳ, ἐν τῇ ἀπεκδύσει τοῦ σώματος τῶν ἁμαρτιῶν τῆς σαρκός, ἐν τῇ περιτομῇ τοῦ χριστοῦ,

11. en 'o kai perietmeitheite peritomei acheiropoieito, en tei apekdusei tou somatos ton 'amartion teis sarkos, en tei peritomei tou christou,

Hebrew/Transliteration
יא. וְגַם-בּוֹ נְמַלְתֶּם לֹא בְמִילַת מְלֶאכֶת יָד כִּי אִם-בְּהָסִירְכֶם אֶת-גְּוִיַּת הַבָּשָׂר הַחוֹטֵא הֲלֹא הִיא בְּרִית הַמּוּלוֹת לַמָּשִׁיחַ:

11. Ve•gam - bo n'mool•tem lo ve•moo•lat me•le•chet yad ki eem - ba•ha•sir•chem et - ge•vi•yat ha•ba•sar ha•cho•te ha•lo hee ve•rit ha•moo•lot la•Mashi•ach.

Rabbinic Jewish Commentary
This is said to prevent an objection that might be made to the perfection of these Gentile believers, because they were not circumcised; for the Jews thought that perfection lay in circumcision, at least that there could be no perfection without it:

"Great is circumcision (say they (x)), for notwithstanding all the commands which Abraham our father did, he was not called perfect until he was circumcised; as it is written, Gen_17:1; "walk before me, and be thou perfect:".

in putting off the body of the sins of the flesh. The Vulgate Latin version leaves out the word "sins", and so the Alexandrian copy and some others; and the Syriac version the word "body": by "the flesh" is meant corrupt nature, which is born of the flesh, and propagated in a carnal way, and is the source and spring of all sin.

(x) Misn. Nedarim, c. 3. sect. 11.

---

12. Buried with him in baptism, wherein also ye are risen with him through the faith of the operation of God, who hath raised him from the dead.

Greek/Transliteration
12. συνταφέντες αὐτῷ ἐν τῷ βαπτίσματι, ἐν ᾧ καὶ συνηγέρθητε διὰ τῆς πίστεως τῆς ἐνεργείας τοῦ θεοῦ, τοῦ ἐγείραντος αὐτὸν ἐκ τῶν νεκρῶν.

12. suntaphentes auto en to baptismati, en 'o kai suneigertheite dya teis pisteos teis energeias tou theou, tou egeirantos auton ek ton nekron.

Hebrew/Transliteration
יב. אֲשֶׁר נִקְבַּרְתֶּם עִמּוֹ בַּטְבִילָה וְכֵן גַּם-עִמּוֹ קַמְתֶּם עַל-יְדֵי אֱמוּנַתְכֶם בִּגְבוּרַת אֱלֹהִים אֲשֶׁר הֲקִימוֹ מִן-הַמֵּתִים:

12. Asher nik•bar•tem ee•mo vat•vi•la ve•chen gam - ee•mo kam•tem al - ye•dey emoo•nat•chem big•voo•rat Elohim asher ha•ki•mo min - ha•me•tim.

---

13. And you, being dead in your sins and the uncircumcision of your flesh, hath he quickened together with him, having forgiven you all trespasses;

Greek/Transliteration
13. Καὶ ὑμᾶς, νεκροὺς ὄντας ἐν τοῖς παραπτώμασιν καὶ τῇ ἀκροβυστίᾳ τῆς σαρκὸς ὑμῶν, συνεζωοποίησεν ὑμᾶς σὺν αὐτῷ, χαρισάμενος ἡμῖν πάντα τὰ παραπτώματα,

13. Kai 'umas, nekrous ontas en tois paraptomasin kai tei akrobustia teis sarkos 'umon, sunezoopoieisen 'umas sun auto, charisamenos 'eimin panta ta paraptomata,

Hebrew/Transliteration
יג. וְאַתֶּם אֲשֶׁר מֵתִים הֱיִיתֶם בְּפִשְׁעֵיכֶם וּבְעָרְלַת בָּשָׂר הֶחֱיָה גַם-אֶתְכֶם עִמּוֹ כִּי סָלַח לְכֹל פְּשָׁעֵינוּ:

13. Ve•a•tem asher me•tim he•yi•tem be•fish•ey•chem oov•or•lat ba•sar he•che•ya gam - et•chem ee•mo ki sa•lach le•chol pe•sha•ey•noo.

Rabbinic Jewish Commentary
and the uncircumcision of your flesh; which is to be taken not literally, for the prepuce, or foreskin of their flesh, which was a sign and token of the corruption of nature, but figuratively that itself; it being usual with the Jews to call the vitiosity of nature ערל, "uncircumcision"; which, they say (y), is one of the seven names of יצר רע, "the evil imagination", or corrupt nature, denoting the pollution, loathsomeness, and abominableness of it.

(y) Zohar in Exod. fol. 106. 1. Caphtor, fol. 52. 2.

---

14. Blotting out the handwriting of ordinances that was against us, which was contrary to us, and took it out of the way, nailing it to his cross;

Greek/Transliteration
14. ἐξαλείψας τὸ καθ᾽ ἡμῶν χειρόγραφον τοῖς δόγμασιν, ὃ ἦν ὑπεναντίον ἡμῖν· καὶ αὐτὸ ἦρκεν ἐκ τοῦ μέσου, προσηλώσας αὐτὸ τῷ σταυρῷ·

14. exaleipsas to kath 'eimon cheirographon tois dogmasin, 'o ein 'upenantion 'eimin. kai auto eirken ek tou mesou, proseilosas auto to stauro.

Hebrew/Transliteration
יד. וְאֶת-סֵפֶר חֹבֵנוּ הוּא סֵפֶר הַחֻקִּים אֲשֶׁר עָנָה בָנוּ מָחָה וְהָגוֹ מִן-הַמְסִלָּה וַיִּתְקָעֵהוּ בַּצְּלָב:

14. Ve•et - se•fer cho•ve•noo hoo se•fer ha•choo•kim asher ana va•noo ma•cha ve•ha•go min - ha•me•si•la va•yit•ka•e•hoo batz•lav.

Rabbinic Jewish Commentary

The Jews (z) call שטר חוב, "the writing of the debt", and is the very phrase the Syriac version uses here: now this was as a debt book, which showed and testified the debts of men; that is, their sins, how many they are guilty of, and what punishment is due unto them.

It is thought to be an allusion to a custom in some countries, to cancel bonds, or antiquate edicts and decrees, by driving a nail through them, so that they could not be legible any more: or it may be to the writing of Pilate, which contained the charge and accusation against Yeshua; and which was placed over his head upon the cross, and fastened to it with nails (a); every nail in the cross made a scissure in this handwriting, or the curses of the Torah, that lay against us, whereby it was so rent and torn, as to be of no force: thus the Holy Spirit makes use of various expressions, to show that there is no curse in the Torah standing against the saints; it is blotted out, and cannot be read; it is took away, and cannot be seen; it is nailed to the cross of Yeshua, and is torn to pieces thereby, that nothing can ever be produced from it to their hurt and condemnation, only the blessings of the Torah remain.

(z) Tzeror Hammor, fol. 87. 1, 3. (a) Nonnus in Joh. xix. 19. Vid. Niccqueti Titulus S. Crucis, l. 1. c. 18. p. 128.

---

15. And having spoiled principalities and powers, he made a shew of them openly, triumphing over them in it.

Greek/Transliteration
15. ἀπεκδυσάμενος τὰς ἀρχὰς καὶ τὰς ἐξουσίας, ἐδειγμάτισεν ἐν παρρησίᾳ, θριαμβεύσας αὐτοὺς ἐν αὐτῷ.

15. apekdusamenos tas archas kai tas exousias, edeigmatisen en parreisia, thryambeusas autous en auto.

Hebrew/Transliteration
טו. וַיַּפְשֵׁט שָׂרֵי צְבָאוֹת וְשַׁלִּיטֵי תֵבֵל וְנֶגֶד הַשֶּׁמֶשׁ נְתָנָם לְרַאֲוָה בָּם וְשָׁם גָּאֹה גָּאָה עֲלֵיהֶם:

15. Va•yaf•shet sa•rey tze•va•ot ve•sha•li•tey te•vel ve•ne•ged ha•she•mesh n`ta•nam le•ra•a•va bam ve•sham ga•oh ga•ah aley•hem.

Rabbinic Jewish Commentary

Some render the word απεκδυσαμενος, "having put off", or "unclothed": and which some of the ancient writers apply to the flesh of Yeshua, and understand it of his putting off the flesh by death, whereby he gave the death blow to the adversary and his powers, Heb_2:14, to which sense agrees the Syriac version, which renders the words, ובשלח פגרה, "and by the putting off of his body, he exposed to shame principalities and powers".

---

16. Let no man therefore judge you in meat, or in drink, or in respect of an holyday, or of the new moon, or of the Sabbath days:

Greek/Transliteration
16. Μὴ οὖν τις ὑμᾶς κρινέτω ἐν βρώσει ἢ ἐν πόσει, ἢ ἐν μέρει ἑορτῆς ἢ νουμηνίας ἢ σαββάτων·

16. Mei oun tis 'umas krineto en brosei ei en posei, ei en merei 'eorteis ei noumeinias ei sabbaton.

Hebrew/Transliteration
‏טז. עַל-כֵּן אֵין לְאִישׁ לְהַרְשִׁיעַ אֶתְכֶם עוֹד עַל-דְּבַר מַאֲכָל וּמִשְׁקֶה אוֹ עַל-דְּבַר מוֹעֵד רֹאשׁ חֹדֶשׁ אוֹ שַׁבָּת:

16. Al - ken eyn le•eesh le•har•shi•a et•chem od al - de•var ma•a•chal oo•mash•ke oh al - de•var mo•ed rosh cho•desh oh Sha•bat.

Rabbinic Jewish Commmentary

The Syriac version renders it, בדודכון, "let no man trouble you", or make you uneasy, by imposing ceremonies on you: the sense is, that the apostle would not have them submit to the yoke they would lay upon them, nor be terrified by their anathemas against them, for the non-observance of the things that follow.

There was no distinction of meats and drinks before the Torah, but all sorts of herbs and animals, without limitation, were given to be food for men; by the ceremonial Torah a difference was made between them, some were allowed, and others were forbidden.

Some (c) think the apostle respects the Mishna, or oral torah of the Jews, in which are several treatises concerning a good day, or an holyday, the beginning of the new year, and the sabbath, which treatises are divided into sections or chapters; and that it is one of these sections or chapters, containing rules about these things, that is here regarded; and then the sense is, let no man judge you or condemn you, for your non-observance of feast days, new moons, and sabbaths, by any part, chapter, or section, of יום טוב, or by anything out of the treatise "concerning a feast day"; or by any part, chapter, or section, of ראש השנה, the treatise "concerning the beginning of the year"; or by any part, chapter, or section, of שבת, the treatise "concerning the sabbath"; and if these treatises are referred to, it proves the antiquity of the Mishna. The Syriac version renders it, בפולגא דעאדא, "in the divisions of the feast": frequent mention is made of פרוס החג, "the division", or "half of the feast", in the Jewish writings: thus for instance it is said (d),

"Three times in a year they clear the chamber (where the half-shekels were put), בפרוס, "in the half", or middle of the passover, in the middle of Pentecost, and in the middle of the feast.

Again (e).

"There are three times for tithing of beasts, in the middle of the passover, in the middle of Pentecost, and the middle of the feast;

That is, of tabernacles: and this, the Jewish commentators say (f), was fifteen days before each of these festivals: now whether it was to this, פרוס, "middle", or "half space", before each and any of these feasts the apostle refers to, may be considered:

or of the new moon; which the Jews were obliged to observe, by attending religious worship, and offering sacrifices; see Num_28:11 2Ki_4:23.

It is the sense of the Jews themselves, that the Gentiles are not obliged to keep their sabbath; no, not the proselyte of the gate, or he that dwelt in any of their cities; for they say (g), that "it is lawful for a proselyte of the gate to do work on the sabbath day for himself, as for an Israelite on a common feast day; R. Akiba says, as for all Israelite on a feast day; R. Jose says, it is lawful for a proselyte of the gate to do work on the sabbath day for himself, as for an Israelite on a common or week day:

And this last is the received sense of the nation; nay, they assert that a Gentile that keeps a sabbath is guilty of death (h); see <u>Mar 2:27</u>. Yea, they say (i), that "if a Gentile sabbatizes, or keeps a sabbath, though on any of the days of the week, if he makes or appoints it as a sabbath for himself, he is guilty of the same.

It is the general sense of that people, that the sabbath was peculiarly given to the children of Israel; and that the Gentiles, strangers, or others, were not punishable for the neglect and breach of it (k); that it is a special and an additional precept, which, with some others, were given them at Marah, over and above the seven commands, which the sons of Noah were only obliged to regard (l); and that the blessing and sanctifying of it were by the manna provided for that day; and that the passage in Gen_2:3; refers not to the then present time, but על העתיד, "to time to come", to the time of the manna (m).

(c) Vid. Casaubon. Epist. ep. 24. (d) Misn. Shekalim, c. 3. sect. 1. (e) Misn. Becorot, c. 9. sect. 5. (f) Maimon. & Bartenora in ib. (g) T. Bab. Ceritot, fol. 9. 1. Piske Tosaphot Yebamot. art. 84. Maimon. Hilch. Sabbat, c. 20. sect. 14. (h) T. Bab. Sanhedrin, fol. 58. 2. (i) Maimon. Hilch. Melachim, c. 10. sect. 9. (k) T. Bab. Betza, fol. 16. 1. Seder Tephillot, fol. 76. 1. Ed. Amtst. (l) T. Bab. Sanhedrin, fol. 56. 2. Seder Olam Rabba, p. 17. & Zuta, p. 101. Ed. Meyer. (m) Jarchi & Baal Hatturim in Gen. ii. 3. Pirke Eliezer, c. 18.

---

17. Which are a shadow of things to come; but the body is of Christ.

Greek/Transliteration
17. ἅ ἐστιν σκιὰ τῶν μελλόντων, τὸ δὲ σῶμα χριστοῦ.

17. 'a estin skya ton mellonton, to de soma christou.

Hebrew/Transliteration
יז. כִּי-הֵם רַק-צְלָלִים לַדְּבָרִים אֲשֶׁר הִתְעַתְּדוּ לָבוֹא וּמְקוֹרָם הוּא בַּמָּשִׁיחַ:

17. Ki - hem rak - tze•la•lim la•d`va•rim asher hit•a•te•doo la•vo oom•ko•ram hoo ba•Ma•shi•ach.

Rabbinic Jewish Commentary
The allusion seems to be to a way of speaking among the Jews, who were wont to call the root, foundation, substance, and essence of a thing, גופא, "the body of it" (n): so they say (o),

"The constitutions concerning the sanctification of the offerings and the tithes, are, both the one and the other, גופי תורה, "the bodies", or substantial parts of the Torah:

And again (p), that "the constitutions or rules about the sabbath, the festivals and prevarications, they are as mountains that hang by an hair; for the Scripture is small, and the constitutions are many; the judgments and the services, the purifications and uncleannesses, and the incests, they have, upon which they can support themselves, and these, and these, are גופי תורה, "the bodies of the Torah":

They say (q) of a small section, or paragraph, that all the bodies of the Torah depend upon it: once more (r),

"The sabbaths, and the good days (the feasts or holy days) are גופן, "the bodies" of the sign;

Which the phylacteries or frontlets were for; but our apostle says, that Messiah is the body and substance of all these shadows, in opposition to these sayings and notions of the Jews: some connect this last clause with the former part of the following verse, rendering it as the Arabic version thus, "because of the communion of the body of Christ, let no man condemn you"; and the Ethiopic version thus, "and let no man account you fools, because of the body of Christ", but there is nothing in the text to support these versions.

(n) Vid. Misn. Abot, c. 3. sect. 18. & Bartenora in ib. & Halicot Olam, par. 2. c. 1. p. 48. (o) T. Bab. Sabbat, fol. 32. 1. (p) Misn. Chagiga, c. 1. sect. 8. T. Bab. Chagiga, fol. 11. 2. (q) T. Bab. Beracot, fol. 63. 1. (r) T. Bab. Menachot, fol. 36. 2. Vid. T. Bab. Ceritot, fol. 5. 1.

---

18. Let no man beguile you of your reward in a voluntary humility and worshipping of angels, intruding into those things which he hath not seen, vainly puffed up by his fleshly mind,

Greek/Transliteration
18. Μηδεὶς ὑμᾶς καταβραβευέτω θέλων ἐν ταπεινοφροσύνῃ καὶ θρησκείᾳ τῶν ἀγγέλων, ἃ μὴ ἑώρακεν ἐμβατεύων, εἰκῇ φυσιούμενος ὑπὸ τοῦ νοὸς τῆς σαρκὸς αὐτοῦ,

18. Meideis 'umas katabrabeueto thelon en tapeinophrosunei kai threiskeia ton angelon, 'a mei 'eoraken embateuon, eikei phusioumenos 'upo tou no'os teis sarkos autou,

Hebrew/Transliteration
יח. אַל-יָעֹז אִישׁ לְהַחֲלִיף אֶת-מַשְׂכֻּרְתְּכֶם כִּי יִתְאַמֵּר בְּשִׁפְלוּת רוּחַ וְנָתוֹן כָּבוֹד לַמַּלְאָכִים וְעֹמֵד בִּדְבָרִים אֲשֶׁר לֹא רָאוּ עֵינָיו וּמִתְנַשֵּׂא לַשָּׁוְא בְּעֶשְׁתֹּנוֹת בָּשָׂר:

18. Al - ya•oz eesh le•ha•cha•lif et - mas•koor•te•chem ki yit•a•mer be•shif•loot roo•ach ve•na•ton ka•vod la•mal•a•chim ve•o•med bid•va•rim asher lo ra•oo ey•nav oo•mit•na•se la•shav be•esh•to•not ba•sar.

Rabbinic Jewish Commentary

"worshipping of angels/messengers" was a practice which very early prevailed among some that were called Christians, and for a long time continued in Phrygia and Pisidia; some make Simon Magus, and others Cerinthus, the author of this idolatry; but was not only a branch of the Platonic philosophy, and so a part of that philosophy and vain deceit before mentioned, Col_2:8, which these men might have borrowed from the Gentiles, but was a notion and practice of the Jews: before the Babylonish captivity, the names of angels/messengers, other than "the Messneger of YHWH", were not known, nor are they ever mentioned by name in Scripture; hence they say (s), that "the names of angels/messengers came up with them, or by their means from Babylon. After this they began to talk much of them, and to have too high a veneration for them, and ascribe too much to them; and observing that the Torah was ordained, spoken, and given by them, and

139

that the administration of things under the former dispensation was greatly by their means, they fell to worshipping of them (t).

That the Jews did, and do worship angels/messengers, and make use of them as mediators and intercessors, is clear from their liturgy, or prayer books, where they say (u).

"מלאכי רחמים‎", "O ye messengers of mercies", or ye merciful messengers, ministers of the most High, entreat now the face of God for good.

And elsewhere (w),

"They say three times, let Juhach keep us, let Juhach deliver us, and let Juhach help us:

Now Juhach was the name of a messenger, who they supposed had the care of men, and is taken from the final letters of those words in Psa_91:11, "for he shall give his messengers charge over thee": so they speak of a messenger whom they call Sandalphon, who they say is appointed over the prayers of the righteous (x): with this notion the judaizing and false teachers seem to have been tinctured, and against which the apostle here cautions the saints, lest, under a show of humility, they should be drawn into it.

(s) T. Hieros. Roshhashanah, fol. 56. 4. (t) Vid. Clement. Alex Stromat. l. 6. p. 635. (u) Seder Tephillot, Ed. Basil fol. 222. 2. (w) Ib. fol. 335. 1. (x) Zohar in Gen. fol. 97. 2. & in Exod. fol. 24. 3.

---

19. And not holding the Head, from which all the body by joints and bands having nourishment ministered, and knit together, increaseth with the increase of God.

Greek/Transliteration
19. καὶ οὐ κρατῶν τὴν κεφαλήν, ἐξ οὗ πᾶν τὸ σῶμα, διὰ τῶν ἁφῶν καὶ συνδέσμων ἐπιχορηγούμενον καὶ συμβιβαζόμενον, αὔξει τὴν αὔξησιν τοῦ θεοῦ.

19. kai ou kraton tein kephalein, ex 'ou pan to soma, dya ton 'aphon kai sundesmon epichoreigoumenon kai sumbibazomenon, auxei tein auxeisin tou theou.

Hebrew/Transliteration
יט. וְאֵינֶנּוּ מַחֲזִיק בָּרֹאשׁ אֲשֶׁר מְקֻשָּׁר בּוֹ כָּל-הַגּוּף בִּפְרָקָיו וּמֵיתָרָיו וּמִמֶּנּוּ יִמְצָא אוֹן-לוֹ וְיִגְדַּל כַּאֲשֶׁר יְגַדְּלֶנּוּ אֱלֹהִים:

19. Ve•ey•ne•noo ma•cha•zik ba•rosh asher me•koo•shar bo kol - ha•goof bif•ra•kav oo•mey•ta•rav oo•mi•me•noo yim•tza on - lo ve•yig•dal ka•a•sher ye•gad•le•noo Elohim.

---

20. Wherefore if ye be dead with Christ from the rudiments of the world, why, as though living in the world, are ye subject to ordinances,

Greek/Transliteration
20. Εἰ ἀπεθάνετε σὺν χριστῷ, ἀπὸ τῶν στοιχείων τοῦ κόσμου, τί ὡς ζῶντες ἐν κόσμῳ δογματίζεσθε,

20. Ei apethanete sun christo, apo ton stoicheion tou kosmou, ti 'os zontes en kosmo dogmatizesthe,

Hebrew/Transliteration
כ. לָכֵן אִם-מַתֶּם עִם-הַמָּשִׁיחַ בַּעֲזָבְכֶם יְסוֹדוֹת הָעוֹלָם לָמָּה-זֶּה בְּעוֹדְכֶם חַיִּים בָּעוֹלָם תּוֹאִילוּ לָכֶת אַחֲרֵי-צַו לֵאמֹר:

20. La•chen eem - ma•tem eem - ha•Ma•shi•ach ba•a•zov•chem ye•so•dot ha•o•lam la•ma - ze be•od•chem cha•yim ba•o•lam to•ee•loo le•chet a•cha•rey - tzav le•mor.

Rabbinic Jewish Commentary
of the world: the ordinances of a worldly sanctuary, the rites and ceremonies of the world, or state of the Jews, in opposition to, and distinction from, the Gospel dispensation, or times of the Messiah, called, and that by them, עולם הבא, "the world to come": these were like letters to a language, or like the grammar, which contains the rudiments of it; these were the first principles of the oracles of God, which led to Messiah, and had their accomplishment and end in him; and so believers were dead unto them, and delivered from them, as they were also to the world and were entered into the world to come.

are ye subject to ordinances?: The ordinances and appointments of the Jewish fathers, the traditions of the elders, their constitutions and decrees, which are collected together, and make up their Mishna, or oral torah, see verse 22.

---

21. (Touch not; taste not; handle not;

Greek/Transliteration
21. Μὴ ἅψῃ, μηδὲ γεύσῃ, μηδὲ θίγῃς-

21. Mei 'apsei, meide geusei, meide thigeis-

Hebrew/Transliteration
כא. לֹא תִקְרַב הָלֹם לֹא תִטְעַם לֹא תִגָּע:

21. Lo tik•rav ha•lom lo tit•am lo ti•ga.

Rabbinic Jewish Commentary
There is a treatise in their Mishna, called Oholot, which gives many rules, and is full of decrees about things מטמאים במגע, "that defile by touching". And so they likewise said, "taste not", neither the fat, nor the blood of any creature which might be eaten itself, nor swine's flesh, nor the flesh of any creature that chewed the cud, or divided the hoof; nor might the Nazarites taste wine, or strong drink, or vinegar made of either, or moist grapes, or even the kernels and husks; and if a man ate but the quantity of an olive of any of the above things, he was, according to the Jewish canons, to be cut off, or beaten (x): and they also said, "handle not"; or, as the Syriac and Arabic read, "do not come near", or "draw not nigh", to a Gentile, to one of another nation, or any unclean person, to whom they forbid any near approach or conversation; or "handle not" any of the above things. Some think that these several rules have respect only to meats; as "touch not", that is, do not eat of things forbidden ever so little; nay, "taste not", do not let anything of them come within your lips; yea, "handle not", do not so much as touch them with your fingers. Others think that touch not regards abstinence from women; see 1Co_7:1; and respects the prohibition of marriage by some in those times; and "taste not", the forbearance of certain meats, at certain times,

which God had not restrained any from; and "handle not", that is, make no use of, or enjoy your own goods, and so designs that voluntary poverty which some entered into under the direction of false teachers.

(x) Maimon. Maacolot Asurot, c. 7. sect. 1. & c. 14. sect. 2. & Nezirut, c. 5. sect. 3.

---

22. Which all are to perish with the using;) after the commandments and doctrines of men?

Greek/Transliteration
22. ἅ ἐστιν πάντα εἰς φθορὰν τῇ ἀποχρήσει- κατὰ τὰ ἐντάλματα καὶ διδασκαλίας τῶν ἀνθρώπων;

22. 'a estin panta eis phthoran tei apochreisei- kata ta entalmata kai didaskalias ton anthropon?

Hebrew/Transliteration
כב. וְהֵם כֻּלָּם חֻקִּים עֹשֵׂיהֶם לֹא יִחְיוּ בָהֶם כְּמִצְוַת וְחֻקֵּיהֶם:

22. Ve•hem koo•lam choo•kim o•sey•hem lo yich•yoo va•hem ke•mitz•vat ve•choo•key•hem.

---

23. Which things have indeed a shew of wisdom in will worship, and humility, and neglecting of the body; not in any honour to the satisfying of the flesh.

Greek/Transliteration
23. ῞Ατινά ἐστιν λόγον μὲν ἔχοντα σοφίας ἐν ἐθελοθρησκείᾳ καὶ ταπεινοφροσύνῃ καὶ ἀφειδίᾳ σώματος, οὐκ ἐν τιμῇ τινὶ πρὸς πλησμονὴν τῆς σαρκός.

23. 'Atina estin logon men echonta sophias en ethelothreiskeia kai tapeinophrosunei kai apheidia somatos, ouk en timei tini pros pleismonein teis sarkos.

Hebrew/Transliteration
כג. אֲשֶׁר לָהֶם מַרְאֵה פְּנֵי הַחָכְמָה מִחוּץ בְּיִרְאַת אֱלֹהִים וּבְשִׁפְלוּת רוּחַ וּלְעַנּוֹת אֶת-גּוּפָם כַּאֲשֶׁר בָּדוּ מִלִּבָּם וְכָל-אַלֶּה לֹא לְכָבוֹד לָהֶם כִּי אִם-בִּשְׂרָם יִמְצָא חֵפֶץ בָּמוֹ:

23. Asher la•hem mar•eh f ney ha•choch•ma mi•choo•tz be•yir•at Elohim oov•shif•loot roo•ach ool•a•not et - goo•fam ka•a•sher ba•doo mi•li•bam ve•chol - ele lo le•cha•vod la•hem ki eem - be•sa•ram yim•tza che•fetz ba•mo.

Rabbinic Jewish Commentary
The authors of them set up for men of wisdom, and were esteemed such, and are often styled חכמים, "wise men"; and their scholars that received their traditions, and explained and enforced them on others, תלמידי החכמים, "the disciples of the wise men": and they pretended, that these constitutions of theirs were "a hedge for the Torah", and for the honour of it, and to preserve it, and keep men from transgressing it; and this carried in it some appearance of wisdom.

Colossians, Chapter 3

1\. If ye then be risen with Christ, seek those things which are above, where Christ sitteth on the right hand of God.

Greek/Transliteration
1\. Εἰ οὖν συνηγέρθητε τῷ χριστῷ, τὰ ἄνω ζητεῖτε, οὗ ὁ χριστός ἐστιν ἐν δεξιᾷ τοῦ θεοῦ καθήμενος.

1\. Ei oun suneigertheite to christo, ta ano zeiteite, 'ou 'o christos estin en dexya tou theou katheimenos.

Hebrew/Transliteration
א: וְעַתָּה אִם-קַמְתֶּם עִם-הַמָּשִׁיחַ בַּקְשׁוּ אֵת אֲשֶׁר לְמַעְלָה אֲשֶׁר שָׁם הַמָּשִׁיחַ יֹשֵׁב לִימִין אֱלֹהִים.

1\. Ve•a•ta eem - kam•tem eem - ha•Ma•shi•ach bak•shoo et asher le•ma•a•la asher sham ha•Ma•shi•ach yo•shev li•y`min Elohim.

2\. Set your affection on things above, not on things on the earth.

Greek/Transliteration
2\. Τὰ ἄνω φρονεῖτε, μὴ τὰ ἐπὶ τῆς γῆς.

2\. Ta ano phroneite, mei ta epi teis geis.

Hebrew/Transliteration
ב: שִׂימוּ לִבְכֶם לַאֲשֶׁר מֵעָל וְלֹא לַאֲשֶׁר בָּאָרֶץ.

2\. Si•moo lib•chem la•a•sher me•al ve•lo la•a•sher ba•a•retz.

3\. For ye are dead, and your life is hid with Christ in God.

Greek/Transliteration
3\. Ἀπεθάνετε γάρ, καὶ ἡ ζωὴ ὑμῶν κέκρυπται σὺν τῷ χριστῷ ἐν τῷ θεῷ.

3\. Apethanete gar, kai 'ei zoei 'umon kekruptai sun to christo en to theo.

Hebrew/Transliteration
ג: כִּי-מֵתִים אַתֶּם וְחַיֵּיכֶם צְפוּנִים עִם-הַמָּשִׁיחַ בֵּאלֹהִים.

3\. Ki - me•tim atem ve•cha•yey•chem tz`foo•nim eem - ha•Ma•shi•ach be•Elohim.

4\. When Christ, who is our life, shall appear, then shall ye also appear with him in glory.

Greek/Transliteration
4\. Ὅταν ὁ χριστὸς φανερωθῇ, ἡ ζωὴ ἡμῶν, τότε καὶ ὑμεῖς σὺν αὐτῷ φανερωθήσεσθε ἐν δόξῃ.

4. 'Otan 'o christos phanerothei, 'ei zoei 'eimon, tote kai 'umeis sun auto phanerotheisesthe en doxei.

Hebrew/Transliteration
ד. וְכַאֲשֶׁר יוֹפִיעַ הַמָּשִׁיחַ אֲשֶׁר הוּא חַיֵּינוּ אָז גַּם-אַתֶּם תּוֹפִיעוּ עִמּוֹ בִּכְבוֹדוֹ:

4. Ve•cha•a•sher yo•fi•a ha•Ma•shi•ach asher hoo cha•yey•noo az gam - atem to•fi•oo ee•mo bich•vo•do.

Rabbinic Jewish Commentary

The Vulgate Latin version, and some copies, read, "your life". The Jews have a saying (y),

"That lives depend upon the son of Jesse," meaning, upon Messiah.

(y) Zohar in Gen. fol. 2. 3.

---

5. Mortify therefore your members which are upon the earth; fornication, uncleanness, inordinate affection, evil concupiscence, and covetousness, which is idolatry:

Greek/Transliteration
5. Νεκρώσατε οὖν τὰ μέλη ὑμῶν τὰ ἐπὶ τῆς γῆς, πορνείαν, ἀκαθαρσίαν, πάθος, ἐπιθυμίαν κακήν, καὶ τὴν πλεονεξίαν, ἥτις ἐστὶν εἰδωλολατρεία,

5. Nekrosate oun ta melei 'umon ta epi teis geis, porneian, akatharsian, pathos, epithumian kakein, kai tein pleonexian, 'eitis estin eidololatreia,

Hebrew/Transliteration
ה. עַל-כֵּן הַכְחִידוּ כְּלֵי תַאֲוַתְכֶם בָּאָרֶץ זְנוּנִים שִׁקּוּצִים וּתְשׁוּקוֹת זָרוֹת יֵצֶר רָע וְאַהֲבַת בֶּצַע אֲשֶׁר דָּמְתָה לַעֲבֹדַת אֱלִילִים:

5. Al - ken hach•chi•doo k`ley ta•a•vat•chem ba•a•retz ze•noo•nim shi•koo•tzim oot•shoo•kot za•rot ye•tzer ra ve•a•ha•vat be•tza asher dam•ta la•a•vo•dat eli•lim.

Rabbinic Jewish Commentary

It is the same with יצר הרע, "the evil imagination", or corruption of nature so much spoken of by the Jews. This here is what is forbidden by that Torah, "thou shalt not covet", Exo_20:17; and includes every fleshly lust and inordinate desire, or every desire after that which is not lawful, or does not belong to a man; as what is another's property, his wife, or goods, or anything that is his.

Some think, that by this πλεονεξια rendered "covetousness", is meant, that greedy desire after the commission of all uncleanness, and impure actions, which were perpetrated by the followers of Simon Magus in their religious assemblies, and under the notion of worship, and as acceptable to God, and therefore called idolatry.

---

6. For which things' sake the wrath of God cometh on the children of disobedience:

Greek/Transliteration
6. δι᾽ ἃ ἔρχεται ἡ ὀργὴ τοῦ θεοῦ ἐπὶ τοὺς υἱοὺς τῆς ἀπειθείας·

6. di 'a erchetai 'ei orgei tou theou epi tous 'wious teis apeitheias.

Hebrew/Transliteration
:ו. כִּי בִגְלַל אֵלֶּה שְׁפוּכָה חֲמַת אֱלֹהִים עַל־בְּנֵי הַמֶּרִי

6. Ki vig•lal ele sh`foo•cha cha•mat Elohim al - b`ney ha•me•ri.

---

7. In the which ye also walked some time, when ye lived in them.

Greek/Transliteration
7. Ἐν οἷς καὶ ὑμεῖς περιεπατήσατέ ποτε, ὅτε ἐζῆτε ἐν αὐτοῖς.

7. En 'ois kai 'umeis periepateisate pote, 'ote ezeite en autois.

Hebrew/Transliteration
:ז. וְגַם־אַתֶּם לְפָנִים כַּאֲשֶׁר יְשַׁבְתֶּם בְּתוֹכָם כֵּן הֲלַכְתֶּם בְּדַרְכֵיהֶם

7. Ve•gam - atem le•fa•nim ka•a•sher ye•shav•tem be•to•cham ken ha•lach•tem be•dar•chey•hem.

---

8. But now ye also put off all these; anger, wrath, malice, blasphemy, filthy communication out of your mouth.

Greek/Transliteration
8. Νυνὶ δὲ ἀπόθεσθε καὶ ὑμεῖς τὰ πάντα, ὀργήν, θυμόν, κακίαν, βλασφημίαν, αἰσχρολογίαν ἐκ τοῦ στόματος ὑμῶν·

8. Nuni de apothesthe kai 'umeis ta panta, orgein, thumon, kakian, blaspheimian, aischrologian ek tou stomatos 'umon.

Hebrew/Transliteration
:ח. אַךְ־עַתָּה הָסִירוּ כָל־אֵלֶּה מֵעֲלֵיכֶם גַּם־אַתֶּם זַעַף וְעֶבְרָה וְרִשְׁעָה וַחֲרָפוֹת וְדִבְרֵי נְבָלָה מִפִּיכֶם

8. Ach - ata ha•si•roo chol - ele me•a•ley•chem gam - atem za•af ve•ev•ra ve•rish•ah va•cha•ra•fot ve•div•rey n`va•la mi•pi•chem.

---

9. Lie not one to another, seeing that ye have put off the old man with his deeds;

Greek/Transliteration
9. μὴ ψεύδεσθε εἰς ἀλλήλους, ἀπεκδυσάμενοι τὸν παλαιὸν ἄνθρωπον σὺν ταῖς πράξεσιν αὐτοῦ,

9. mei pseudesthe eis alleilous, apekdusamenoi ton palaion anthropon sun tais praxesin autou,

Hebrew/Transliteration
:ט. אַל־תְּשַׁקְּרוּ אִישׁ בַּעֲמִיתוֹ אַחֲרֵי אֲשֶׁר פְּשַׁטְתֶּם אֶת־הָאָדָם הַקַּדְמֹנִי עִם־פְּעָלָיו

9. Al - te•shak•roo eesh ba•a•mi•to a•cha•rey asher pe•sha•te•tem et - ha•a•dam ha•kad•mo•ni eem - pe•a•lav.

---

10. And have put on the new man, which is renewed in knowledge after the image of him that created him:

Greek/Transliteration
10. καὶ ἐνδυσάμενοι τὸν νέον, τὸν ἀνακαινούμενον εἰς ἐπίγνωσιν κατ᾽ εἰκόνα τοῦ κτίσαντος αὐτόν·

10. kai endusamenoi ton neon, ton anakainoumenon eis epignosin kat eikona tou ktisantos auton.

Hebrew/Transliteration
י. וּלְבַשְׁתֶּם אֶת-הָאָדָם הֶחָדָשׁ הוּא אֲשֶׁר הִתְחַדֵּשׁ בְּדַעַת כְּצֶלֶם יֹצְרוֹ:

10. Ool•vash•tem et - ha•a•dam he•cha•dash hoo asher hit•cha•desh be•da•at ke•tze•lem yotz•ro.

---

11. Where there is neither Greek nor Jew, circumcision nor uncircumcision, Barbarian, Scythian, bond nor free: but Christ is all, and in all.

Greek/Transliteration
11. ὅπου οὐκ ἔνι Ἕλλην καὶ Ἰουδαῖος, περιτομὴ καὶ ἀκροβυστία, βάρβαρος, Σκύθης, δοῦλος, ἐλεύθερος· ἀλλὰ τὰ πάντα καὶ ἐν πᾶσιν χριστός.

11. 'opou ouk eni 'Ellein kai Youdaios, peritomei kai akrobustia, barbaros, Skutheis, doulos, eleutheros. alla ta panta kai en pasin christos.

Hebrew/Transliteration
יא. אֲשֶׁר אֵין-בּוֹ יְוָנִי אוֹ יְהוּדִי נִמּוֹל אוֹ עָרֵל נִלְעַג לָשׁוֹן פֶּרֶא אָדָם עֶבֶד אוֹ בֶן-חוֹרִים כִּי הַכֹּל וּבַכֹּל הוּא הַמָּשִׁיחַ:

11. Asher eyn - bo Ye•va•ni oh Ye•hoo•di ni•mol oh arel nil•ag la•shon pe•re adam eved oh ven - cho•rim ki ha•kol oo•va•kol hoo ha•Ma•shi•ach.

Rabbinic Jewish Commentary
Barbarian, Scythian; all such were Barbarians to the Romans, that did not speak their language; and as were such also to the Greeks, who were not of their nation, and therefore Greeks and Barbarians are opposed to each other, see Rom_1:14 and so they are here in the Syriac version, which reads "Greek" and "Barbarian". The Arabic version, instead of "Barbarian", reads "Persian", because it may be, a Persian is so accounted by the Arabians; and because the Scythians were, of all people, the most barbarous and unpolished (z), and were had in great disdain by others, therefore the apostle mentions them, as being within the reach of the powerful and efficacious grace of God; nor were the fierceness of their dispositions, and the impoliteness of their manners, any bar unto it. Remarkable is the saying of Anacharsis the Scythian, who being reproached by a Grecian, because he was a Scythian, replied (a),

"My country is a reproach to me, but thou art a reproach to thy country."

but Christ is all, and in all; he is "all" efficiently; So, with the Jews, the Shekinah is called כל, "all" (b): and this likewise, with the Cabalists (c), is one of the names of the living God, and well agrees with Messiah, who has all things in him; and is the reason they give for this divine appellation: and Messiah is "in all"; in all places, being infinite, immense, and incomprehensible, as God, and so is everywhere by his power, upholding all things by it; and in all his churches, by his gracious presence, and in the hearts of all his regenerate ones, of whatsoever nation, state, and condition they be: he is revealed in them, formed within them, and dwells in their hearts by faith; and is all in all to them, exceeding precious, altogether lovely, the chiefest among ten thousands, and whom they esteem above all creatures and things. The Arabic version reads, "Christ is above all, and in all".

(z) Vid. Justin. l. 2. c. 1, 2, 3. Plin. l. 4. c. 12. & 6. 17. Herodot. l. 4. c. 46. (a) Laertius in Vita Anacharsis. (b) Tzeror Hammot, fol. 28. 2. (c) Shaare Ora, fol. 6. 1. & 22. 2. & 25. 3.

---

12. Put on therefore, as the elect of God, holy and beloved, bowels of mercies, kindness, humbleness of mind, meekness, longsuffering;

Greek/Transliteration
12. Ἐνδύσασθε οὖν, ὡς ἐκλεκτοὶ τοῦ θεοῦ, ἅγιοι καὶ ἠγαπημένοι, σπλάγχνα οἰκτιρμοῦ, χρηστότητα, ταπεινοφροσύνην, πραότητα, μακροθυμίαν·

12. Endusasthe oun, 'os eklektoi tou theou, 'agioi kai eigapeimenoi, splagchna oiktirmou, chreistoteita, tapeinophrosunein, praoteita, makrothumian.

Hebrew/Transliteration
יב. וְאַתֶּם כִּבְחִירֵי הָאֱלֹהִים קְדֹשָׁיו וִידִידָיו לִבְשׁוּ רַחֲמִים וַחֲסָדִים מִמְּקוֹר לִבְכֶם רוּחַ שְׁפָלָה עֲנָוָה וְאֶרֶךְ אַפָּיִם:

12. Ve•a•tem kiv•chi•rey ha•Elohim ki•k`do•shav viy•di•dav liv•shoo ra•cha•mim va•cha•sa•dim mim•kor lib•chem roo•ach sh`fa•la ana•va ve•o•rech apa•yim.

Rabbinic Jewish Commentary
להתלבשא ברוח קדושה, "to be clothed with the Holy Spirit", is a phrase used by the Cabalistic scholars (d); and is indeed a Scripture phrase, "the Spirit of the Lord came upon", לבשה, clothed Zechariah, 2Ch_24:20 and so Esther is said, by the Jewish writers (e), to be "clothed with the Holy Spirit" Here the metaphor is taken from the putting off of clothes; and what is here directed to, is like Joseph's coat, a coat of many colours.

(d) Sepher Jetzirah, Nethib, 17. p. 136, (e) T. Megilla, fol. 14. 2. & 15. 1. Zohar in Numb. fol. 70. 3. & 76. 2. & Raya Mehimna in Zohar in Lev. fol. 38. 3.

---

13. Forbearing one another, and forgiving one another, if any man have a quarrel against any: even as Christ forgave you, so also do ye.

Greek/Transliteration
13. ἀνεχόμενοι ἀλλήλων, καὶ χαριζόμενοι ἑαυτοῖς, ἐάν τις πρός τινα ἔχῃ μομφήν· καθὼς καὶ ὁ χριστὸς ἐχαρίσατο ὑμῖν, οὕτως καὶ ὑμεῖς·

13. anechomenoi alleilon, kai charizomenoi 'eautois, ean tis pros tina echei momphein. Kathos kai 'o christos echarisato 'umin, 'outos kai 'umeis.

Hebrew/Transliteration
יג. לְשֵׂאת אִישׁ אֶת-פְּנֵי רֵעֵהוּ וְלִסְלֹחַ לוֹ לִדְבַר רִיב כִּי-יִמָּצֵא בֵינֵיכֶם וּכְמוֹ אֲדֹנֵינוּ סָלַח לָכֶם כֵּן תִּסְלְחוּ גַּם אַתֶּם:

13. La•set eesh et - p`ney re•e•hoo ve•lis•lo•ach lo lid•var riv ki - yi•ma•tze vey•ne•chem ooch•mo Ado•ney•noo sa•lach la•chem ken tis•le•choo gam - atem.

---

14. And above all these things put on charity, which is the bond of perfectness.

Greek/Transliteration
14. ἐπὶ πᾶσιν δὲ τούτοις τὴν ἀγάπην, ἥτις ἐστὶν σύνδεσμος τῆς τελειότητος.

14. epi pasin de toutois tein agapein, 'eitis estin sundesmos teis teleioteitos.

Hebrew/Transliteration
יד. וְעַל-כָּל-אֵלֶּה לִבְשׁוּ אַהֲבָה אֲשֶׁר הִיא אֲגֻדַּת הַתְּמִימִים:

14. Ve•al - kol - ele liv•shoo a•ha•va asher hee agoo•dat hat•mi•mim.

---

15. And let the peace of God rule in your hearts, to the which also ye are called in one body; and be ye thankful.

Greek/Transliteration
15. Καὶ ἡ εἰρήνη τοῦ θεοῦ βραβευέτω ἐν ταῖς καρδίαις ὑμῶν, εἰς ἣν καὶ ἐκλήθητε ἐν ἑνὶ σώματι· καὶ εὐχάριστοι γίνεσθε.

15. Kai 'ei eireinei tou theou brabeueto en tais kardiais 'umon, eis 'ein kai ekleitheite en 'eni somati. kai eucharistoi ginesthe.

Hebrew/Transliteration
טו. וּשְׁלוֹם הָאֱלֹהִים אֲשֶׁר - נִבְחַרְתֶּם לוֹ בְּגוּף אֶחָד יִמְשֹׁל בְּקֶרֶב לִבְּכֶם וְאֶת-טוּבוֹ תַּכִּירוּ:

15. Oosh•lom ha•Elohim asher - niv•char•tem lo be•goof e•chad yim•shol be•ke•rev lib•chem ve•et - too•vo ta•ki•roo.

Rabbinic Jewish Commentary
The Vulgate Latin, Syriac, and, Ethiopic versions, read, "the peace of Christ"; and so the Alexandrian copy, and some others.

---

16. Let the word of Christ dwell in you richly in all wisdom; teaching and admonishing one another in psalms and hymns and spiritual songs, singing with grace in your hearts to the Lord.

Greek/Transliteration
16. Ὁ λόγος τοῦ χριστοῦ ἐνοικείτω ἐν ὑμῖν πλουσίως ἐν πάσῃ σοφίᾳ· διδάσκοντες καὶ νουθετοῦντες ἑαυτούς, ψαλμοῖς, καὶ ὕμνοις, καὶ ᾠδαῖς πνευματικαῖς, ἐν χάριτι ᾄδοντες ἐν τῇ καρδίᾳ ὑμῶν τῷ κυρίῳ.

16. 'O logos tou christou enoikeito en 'umin plousios en pasei sophia. didaskontes kai nouthetountes 'eautous, psalmois, kai 'umnois, kai odais pneumatikais, en chariti adontes en tei kardia 'umon to kurio.

Hebrew/Transliteration
-טז. וְתוֹרַת הַמָּשִׁיחַ תִּהְיֶה בְפִיכֶם תָּמִיד בְּכָל-חָכְמָה לְלַמֵּד וּלְעוֹרֵר אִישׁ אֶת-אָחִיהוּ בִּתְהִלּוֹת וְשִׁירוֹת וְזִמְרוֹת יָהּ וּמִקֶּרֶב לִבְּכֶם תָּשִׁירוּ לֵאלֹהִים בְּתוֹדָה:

16. Ve•to•rat ha•Ma•shi•ach ti•hi•ye ve•fi•chem ta•mid be•chol - choch•ma le•la•med ool•o•rer eesh et - a•chi•hoo bit•hi•lot ve•shi•rot ve•zim•rot - Ya oo•mi•ke•rev lib•chem ta•shi•roo le•Elohim be•to•da.

Rabbinic Jewish Commentary
Let the word of Christ dwell in you,.... The Alexandrian copy and Arabic version read, "the word of God"; by which may be meant the whole Scripture, all the writings of the Old and New Testament, which are by inspiration of God, were endited by the spirit of Christ, speak and testify of him, and were written for his sake, and on his account, and therefore may be called his word.

richly; that is, largely, plentifully, in an abundant manner, as this word signifies; see 1Ti_6:17 and so the Vulgate Latin version renders it here, "abundantly"; and to the same sense the Arabic version.

in all wisdom; or, "unto all wisdom"; in order to attain to all wisdom.

Teaching and admonishing one another. The Syriac version renders it, "teach and instruct yourselves".

in psalms, and hymns, and spiritual songs; referring very probably to the title of several of David's psalms, מַשְׂכִּיל; "Maschil", which signifies giving instruction, or causing to understand; these psalms, and the singing of them, being appointed as an ordinance, of God to teach, instruct, admonish, and edify the believers.

The object here, as there, is "to the Lord"; the Lord Yeshua Messiah, to the glory, of his person and grace: the Alexandrian copy, and the Vulgate Latin, Syriac, and Ethiopic versions read, "to God": and indeed God, in the three divine Persons, and in all his perfections and works, is the object of praise, and his glory is the end of singing praise.

---

17. And whatsoever ye do in word or deed, do all in the name of the Lord Jesus, giving thanks to God and the Father by him.

Greek/Transliteration
17. Καὶ πᾶν ὅ τι ἂν ποιῆτε, ἐν λόγῳ ἢ ἐν ἔργῳ, πάντα ἐν ὀνόματι κυρίου Ἰησοῦ, εὐχαριστοῦντες τῷ θεῷ καὶ πατρὶ δι' αὐτοῦ.

17. Kai pan 'o ti an poieite, en logo ei en ergo, panta en onomati kuriou Yeisou, eucharistountes to theo kai patri di autou.

Hebrew/Transliteration
יז. וְכֹל אֲשֶׁר-תַּעֲשׂוּ גַּם-בְּדָבָר שְׂפָתַיִם גַּם-בְּמַעֲשֵׂה יָדַיִם עָשׂוּ כֹל בְּשֵׁם יֵשׁוּעַ אֲדֹנֵינוּ וּלְהֹדוֹת עַל-יָדוֹ לֵאלֹהִים אָבִינוּ:

17. Ve•chol asher - ta•a•soo gam - bid•var s`fa•ta•yim gam - be•ma•a•se ya•da•yim a•soo chol be•shem Yeshua Ado•ney•noo ool•ho•dot al - ya•do le•Elohim Avi•noo.

---

18. Wives, submit yourselves unto your own husbands, as it is fit in the Lord.

Greek/Transliteration
18. Αἱ γυναῖκες, ὑποτάσσεσθε τοῖς ἰδίοις ἀνδράσιν, ὡς ἀνῆκεν ἐν κυρίῳ.

18. 'Ai gunaikes, 'upotassesthe tois idiois andrasin, 'os aneiken en kurio.

Hebrew/Transliteration
יח. וְאַתֵּנָה נָשִׁים הִכָּנַעְנָה לְבַעֲלֵיכֶן כַּמִּשְׁפָּט לִפְנֵי אֲדֹנֵינוּ:

18. Ve•a•te•na na•shim hi•ka•na•a•na le•va•a•ley•chen ka•mish•pat lif•ney Ado•ney•noo.

---

19. Husbands, love your wives, and be not bitter against them.

Greek/Transliteration
19. Οἱ ἄνδρες, ἀγαπᾶτε τὰς γυναῖκας, καὶ μὴ πικραίνεσθε πρὸς αὐτάς.

19. 'Oi andres, agapate tas gunaikas, kai mei pikrainesthe pros autas.

Hebrew/Transliteration
יט. בַּעֲלֵי אִשָּׁה אֶהֱבוּ אֶת-נְשֵׁיכֶם וְלֹא תִהְיוּ לָהֶן לְמֹרַת רוּחַ:

19. Ba•a•ley ee•sha e•he•voo et - n`shey•chem ve•lo ti•hi•yoo la•hen le•mo•rat roo•ach.

---

20. Children, obey your parents in all things: for this is well pleasing unto the Lord.

Greek/Transliteration
20. Τὰ τέκνα, ὑπακούετε τοῖς γονεῦσιν κατὰ πάντα· τοῦτο γάρ ἐστιν εὐάρεστον ἐν κυρίῳ.

20. Ta tekna, 'upakouete tois goneusin kata panta. touto gar estin euareston en kurio.

Hebrew/Transliteration
כ. שִׁמְעוּ בָנִים אֶל-יַלְדֵיכֶם לְכֹל אֲשֶׁר יֹאמְרוּן כִּי לְרָצוֹן הוּא לַאֲדֹנֵנוּ:

20. Shim•oo va•nim el - yol•dey•chem le•chol asher yo•me•roon ki le•ra•tzon hoo la•Ado•ne•noo.

---

21. Fathers, provoke not your children to anger, lest they be discouraged.

Greek/Transliteration
21. Οἱ πατέρες, μὴ ἐρεθίζετε τὰ τέκνα ὑμῶν, ἵνα μὴ ἀθυμῶσιν.

21. 'Oi pateres, mei erethizete ta tekna 'umon, 'ina mei athumosin.

Hebrew/Transliteration
כא. אָבוֹת אַל-תַּכְעִיסוּ אֶת-בְּנֵיכֶם פֶּן-יֹאמְרוּ נוֹאָשׁ:

21. Avot al - tach•ee•soo et - b`ney•chem pen - yom•roo no•ash.

---

22. Servants, obey in all things your masters according to the flesh; not with eyeservice, as menpleasers; but in singleness of heart, fearing God:

Greek/Transliteration
22. Οἱ δοῦλοι, ὑπακούετε κατὰ πάντα τοῖς κατὰ σάρκα κυρίοις, μὴ ἐν ὀφθαλμοδουλείαις ὡς ἀνθρωπάρεσκοι, ἀλλ᾽ ἐν ἁπλότητι καρδίας, φοβούμενοι τὸν θεόν·

22. 'Oi douloi, 'upakouete kata panta tois kata sarka kuriois, mei en ophthalmodouleiais 'os anthropareskoi, all en 'aploteiti kardias, phoboumenoi ton theon.

Hebrew/Transliteration
כב. וְאַתֶּם עֲבָדִים שִׁמְעוּ אֶל-אֲדֹנֵיכֶם אֲדֹנֵי הַבָּשָׂר לְכֹל אֲשֶׁר יֹאמְרוּן וְלֹא בַעֲבֹדָה לְמַרְאֵה עֵינַיִם לְהָפִיק רָצוֹן מִבְּנֵי אָדָם כִּי אִם-בְּתָם-לֵב כְּיִרְאֵי יְהוָֹה:

22. Ve•a•tem a•va•dim shim•oo el - ado•ney•chem ado•ney ha•ba•sar le•chol asher yo•me•roon ve•lo va•a•vo•da le•mar•eh ey•na•yim le•ha•fik ra•tzon mi•b`ney adam ki eem - be•tom - lev ke•yir•ey Adonai.

---

23. And whatsoever ye do, do it heartily, as to the Lord, and not unto men;

Greek/Transliteration
23. καὶ πᾶν ὅ τι ἐὰν ποιῆτε, ἐκ ψυχῆς ἐργάζεσθε, ὡς τῷ κυρίῳ καὶ οὐκ ἀνθρώποις·

23. kai pan 'o ti ean poieite, ek psucheis ergazesthe, 'os to kurio kai ouk anthropois.

Hebrew/Transliteration
כג. וְכֹל אֲשֶׁר תַּעֲשׂוּ עֲשׂוּ בְכָל-נַפְשְׁכֶם כְּמוֹ לַיהוָֹה וְלֹא לִבְנֵי-אָדָם:

23. Ve•chol asher ta•a•soo a•soo ve•chol - naf•she•chem k`mo la`Adonai ve•lo liv•ney - adam.

24. Knowing that of the Lord ye shall receive the reward of the inheritance: for ye serve the Lord Christ.

Greek/Transliteration
24. εἰδότες ὅτι ἀπὸ κυρίου λήψεσθε τὴν ἀνταπόδοσιν τῆς κληρονομίας· τῷ γὰρ κυρίῳ χριστῷ δουλεύετε.

24. eidotes 'oti apo kuriou leipsesthe tein antapodosin teis kleironomias. to gar kurio Christo douleuete.

Hebrew/Transliteration
:כד. הֵן יְדַעְתֶּם כִּי מֵאֵת יְהוָה תִּקְחוּ שְׂכַרְכֶם וְנַחֲלַתְכֶם כִּי אֶת-אֲדֹנֵינוּ הַמָּשִׁיחַ אַתֶּם עֹבְדִים

24. Hen ye•da•a•tem ki me•et Adonai tik•choo s`char•chem ve•na•cha•lat•chem ki et - Ado•ney•noo ha•Ma•shi•ach atem ov•dim.

---

25. But he that doeth wrong shall receive for the wrong which he hath done: and there is no respect of persons.

Greek/Transliteration
25. Ὁ δὲ ἀδικῶν κομιεῖται ὃ ἠδίκησεν· καὶ οὐκ ἔστιν προσωποληψία.

25. 'O de adikon komieitai 'o eidikeisen. kai ouk estin prosopoleipsia.

Hebrew/Transliteration
:כה. כִּי הַמְעַוֵּל יִקְצֹר-עָוֶל כַּאֲשֶׁר עָשָׂה וְאֵין מַשּׂוֹא פָנִים

25. Ki ha•me•a•vel yik•tzor - avel ka•a•sher asa ve•eyn ma•so fa•nim.

Rabbinic Jewish Commentary
and there is no respect of persons. The Vulgate Latin and Arabic Versions add, "with God"; which undoubtedly is the sense; he regards not the rich more than the poor; he makes no difference between bond and free, the servant and the master; he will not take the part of the one, because he is a master, nor neglect, the other, because he is a servant, but will do that which is just and right with regard to them both.

Colossians, Chapter 4

1. Masters, give unto your servants that which is just and equal; knowing that ye also have a Master in heaven.

Greek/Transliteration
1. Οἱ κύριοι, τὸ δίκαιον καὶ τὴν ἰσότητα τοῖς δούλοις παρέχεσθε, εἰδότες ὅτι καὶ ὑμεῖς ἔχετε κύριον ἐν οὐρανοῖς.

1. 'Oi kurioi, to dikaion kai tein isoteita tois doulois parechesthe, eidotes 'oti kai 'umeis echete kurion en ouranois.

Hebrew/Transliteration
א. וְגַם-אַתֶּם אֲדֹנִים בְּצֶדֶק וּבְמִשְׁפָּט תַּעֲבִידוּן אֶת-עַבְדֵיכֶם הֲלֹא יְדַעְתֶּם כִּי גַם-לָכֶם אָדוֹן בַּשָּׁמָיִם:

1. Ve•gam - atem ado•nim be•tze•dek oov•mish•pat ta•a•vi•doon et - av•dey•chem ha•lo ye•da•a•tem ki gam - la•chem Adon ba•sha•ma•yim.

---

2. Continue in prayer, and watch in the same with thanksgiving;

Greek/Transliteration
2. Τῇ προσευχῇ προσκαρτερεῖτε, γρηγοροῦντες ἐν αὐτῇ ἐν εὐχαριστίᾳ·

2. Tei proseuchei proskartereite, greigorountes en autei en eucharistia.

Hebrew/Transliteration
ב. הִתְעוֹרְרוּ לְהִתְפַּלֵּל תָּמִיד וְשִׁקְדוּ לְהַעְתִּיר בְּתוֹדָה:

2. Hit•o•re•roo li•hit•pa•lel ta•mid ve•shik•doo le•ha•a•tir be•to•da.

Rabbinic Jewish Commentary
This is what the Jews call עיון תפלה, "the attention of prayer" (f), and כונת הלב, "the intention of the heart"; and which, they say (g), is the root of prayer, the main and principal thing in it; and that every prayer which is not with intention, is no prayer (h); and which, they observe, lies in this, that a man turns his heart from all (other) thoughts, and seems to himself as if he stood before the divine Majesty.

(f) T. Bab. Bava Bathra, fol. 164. 2. & Sabbat, fol. 127. 1. (g) R. Aben Ezra in Psal. lxxviii. 37. (h) Maimon. Hilch. Tephilla, c. 4. sect. 15, 16.

---

3. Withal praying also for us, that God would open unto us a door of utterance, to speak the mystery of Christ, for which I am also in bonds:

Greek/Transliteration
3. προσευχόμενοι ἅμα καὶ περὶ ἡμῶν, ἵνα ὁ θεὸς ἀνοίξῃ ἡμῖν θύραν τοῦ λόγου, λαλῆσαι τὸ μυστήριον τοῦ χριστοῦ, δι᾽ ὃ καὶ δέδεμαι·

3. proseuchomenoi 'ama kai peri 'eimon, 'ina 'o theos anoixei 'eimin thuran tou logou, laleisai to musteirion tou christou, di 'o kai dedemai.

Hebrew/Transliteration
ג. וְחַלּוּ אֶת-פְּנֵי הָאֱלֹהִים גַּם-בַּעֲדֵנוּ לִפְתֹחַ לָנוּ שַׁעַר לָרִיב שְׂפָתֵינוּ לְגַלּוֹת סוֹד הַמָּשִׁיחַ אֲשֶׁר בִּגְלָלוֹ אָסוּר אָנִי:

3. Ve•cha•loo et - p`ney ha•Elohim gam - ba•a•de•noo lif•to•ach la•noo sha•ar le•niv s`fa•tey•noo le•ga•lot sod ha•Ma•shi•ach asher big•la•lo a•soor ani.

Rabbinic Jewish Commentary
that God would open to us a door of utterance; or "of the word"; so the Vulgate Latin, Syriac, Arabic; and Ethiopic versions. The Alexandrian copy adds, "with boldness", or "boldly".

---

4. That I may make it manifest, as I ought to speak.

Greek/Transliteration
4. ἵνα φανερώσω αὐτό, ὡς δεῖ με λαλῆσαι.

4. 'ina phaneroso auto, 'os dei me laleisai.

Hebrew/Transliteration
ד. לְמַעַן יִוָּדַע לַכֹּל כַּאֲשֶׁר אַבִּיעַ כַּמִּשְׁפָּט:

4. Le•ma•an yi•va•da la•kol ka•a•sher abi•a ka•mish•pat.

---

5. Walk in wisdom toward them that are without, redeeming the time.

Greek/Transliteration
5. Ἐν σοφίᾳ περιπατεῖτε πρὸς τοὺς ἔξω, τὸν καιρὸν ἐξαγοραζόμενοι.

5. En sophia peripateite pros tous exo, ton kairon exagorazomenoi.

Hebrew/Transliteration
ה. הִתְהַלְּכוּ בִתְבוּנָה בְּקֶרֶב אֵלֶּה אֲשֶׁר מִחוּץ לַעֲדָתֵנוּ וְהוֹקִירוּ אֶת-הָעֵת:

5. Hit•hal•choo vit•voo•na be•ke•rev ele asher mi•choo•tz la•a•da•te•noo ve•ho•ki•roo et -ha•et.

---

6. Let your speech be always with grace, seasoned with salt, that ye may know how ye ought to answer every man.

Greek/Transliteration
6. Ὁ λόγος ὑμῶν πάντοτε ἐν χάριτι, ἅλατι ἠρτυμένος, εἰδέναι πῶς δεῖ ὑμᾶς ἑνὶ ἑκάστῳ ἀποκρίνεσθαι.

6. 'O logos 'umon pantote en chariti, 'alati eirtumenos, eidenai pos dei 'umas 'eni 'ekasto apokrinesthai.

Hebrew/Transliteration
:ו. יְהִי דְבַרְכֶם מָהוּל בְּחֵן כְּמוֹ מְמֻלָּח בַּמֶּלַח וְתֵדְעוּ לְהָשִׁיב נְכֹחוֹת לְכָל-אִישׁ וָאִישׁ

6. Ye•hee d`var•chem ma•hool be•chen k`mo me•moo•lach ba•me•lach ve•ted•oo le•ha•shiv n`cho•chot le•chol - eesh va•eesh.

---

7. All my state shall Tychicus declare unto you, who is a beloved brother, and a faithful minister and fellowservant in the Lord:

Greek/Transliteration
7. Τὰ κατ᾽ ἐμὲ πάντα γνωρίσει ὑμῖν Τυχικός, ὁ ἀγαπητὸς ἀδελφὸς καὶ πιστὸς διάκονος καὶ σύνδουλος ἐν κυρίῳ·

7. Ta kat eme panta gnorisei 'umin Tuchikos, 'o agapeitos adelphos kai pistos dyakonos kai sundoulos en kurio.

Hebrew/Transliteration
:ז. עַל-דְּבַר מַעֲמָדִי הֲלֹא טוּכִיקוֹס יַגִּיד לָכֶם הַכֹּל הוּא אָח אָהוּב וּמְשָׁרֵת נֶאֱמָן גֶּבֶר עֲמִיתִי וְעֶבֶד לַאֲדֹנֵינוּ

7. Al - de•var ma•a•ma•di ha•lo Too•chi•kos ya•gid la•chem ha•kol hoo ach a•hoov oom•sha•ret ne•e•man gever ami•ti ve•e•ved la•Ado•ney•noo.

---

8. Whom I have sent unto you for the same purpose, that he might know your estate, and comfort your hearts;

Greek/Transliteration
8. ὃν ἔπεμψα πρὸς ὑμᾶς εἰς αὐτὸ τοῦτο, ἵνα γνῷ τὰ περὶ ὑμῶν καὶ παρακαλέσῃ τὰς καρδίας ὑμῶν·

8. 'on epempsa pros 'umas eis auto touto, 'ina gno ta peri 'umon kai parakalesei tas kardias 'umon.

Hebrew/Transliteration
:ח. כִּי לַדָּבָר הַזֶּה שְׁלַחְתִּיו אֲלֵיכֶם לָדַעַת אֶת-שְׁלוֹמֵנוּ וּלְדַבֵּר נִחֻמִים עַל-לִבְּכֶם

8. Ki la•da•var ha•ze sh`lach•tiv aley•chem la•da•at et - sh`lo•me•noo ool•da•ber ni•choo•mim al - lib•chem.

Rabbinic Jewish Commentary
that he might know your estate. The Arabic version renders it, "that I may know your estate" by him when he returned again.

---

9. With Onesimus, a faithful and beloved brother, who is one of you. They shall make known unto you all things which are done here.

Greek/Transliteration
9. σὺν Ὀνησίμῳ τῷ πιστῷ καὶ ἀγαπητῷ ἀδελφῷ, ὅς ἐστιν ἐξ ὑμῶν. Πάντα ὑμῖν γνωριοῦσιν τὰ ὧδε.

9. sun Oneisimo to pisto kai agapeito adelpho, 'os estin ex 'umon. Panta 'umin gnoriousin ta 'ode.

Hebrew/Transliteration

ט: וְעִמּוֹ גַם-אוֹנִיסִימוֹס בֶּן-אַרְצְכֶם אָח נֶאֱמָן וְיַקִּיר לִי הֵמָּה יוֹדִיעוּ אֶתְכֶם כָּל-אֲשֶׁר נַעֲשָׂה פֹּה

9. Ve•ee•mo gam - Oni•si•mos ben - ar•tze•chem ach ne•e•man ve•ya•kir li he•ma yo•di•oo et•chem kol - asher na•a•sa po.

Rabbinic Jewish Commentary

With Onesimus,..... Who had been Philemon's servant, ran away from him, and was met with and converted by the Apostle Paul, of whom he says many things in his epistle to his master. According to the Apostolic Constitutions, he was afterwards bishop of Beyrhoea; and some say he suffered martyrdom under Domitian; a servant of this name is mentioned by Suetonius (i), Ignatius (k) speaks of one Onesimus as bishop of Ephesus.

(i) In Vit. Galbae, c. 13. (k) Ep. ad Ephes. p. 17. & ad Antioch. ascript. p. 89.

---

10. Aristarchus my fellowprisoner saluteth you, and Marcus, sister's son to Barnabas, (touching whom ye received commandments: if he come unto you, receive him;)

Greek/Transliteration

10. Ἀσπάζεται ὑμᾶς Ἀρίσταρχος ὁ συναιχμάλωτός μου, καὶ Μᾶρκος ὁ ἀνεψιὸς Βαρνάβα, περὶ οὗ ἐλάβετε ἐντολάς- ἐὰν ἔλθῃ πρὸς ὑμᾶς, δέξασθε αὐτόν·

10. Aspazetai 'umas Aristarchos 'o sunaichmalotos mou, kai Markos 'o anepsios Barnaba, peri 'ou elabete entolas- ean elthei pros 'umas, dexasthe auton.

Hebrew/Transliteration

י. אֲרִיסְטַרְכוֹס אֲשֶׁר הוּא עָצוּר עִמָּדִי שֹׁאֵל לִשְׁלוֹמְכֶם גַּם-מַרְקוֹס בֶּן-אֲחוֹת בַּר-נַבָּא אֲשֶׁר נִדְרַשְׁתֶּם לְקַבֵּל פָּנָיו בְּבוֹאוֹ:

10. Aris•tar•chos asher hoo atzoor ee•ma•di sho•el lish•lom•chem gam - Markos ben - a•chot Bar - Naba asher nid•rash•tem le•ka•bel pa•nav be•vo•o.

Rabbinic Jewish Commentary

Aristarchus my fellow prisoner saluteth you,..... This man was a man of Macedonia, and a Thessalonian; Act_19:29 which hinders not but that he might be of the circumcision, or a Jew, as is suggested in the following verse; for he might be born at Thessalonica, and yet be of Jewish parents; nor is his Greek name any objection to it, for the Jews themselves say, that the greatest part of the Israelites that were out of the land, their names are as the names of strangers (l): he was a constant companion of the apostle, and one of his fellow labourers, as in Phm_1:24 and now a prisoner with him at Rome; and who having some knowledge of the members of the church at Colosse, takes this opportunity of sending his Christian salutation to them.

and Marcus, sister's son to Barnabas; The Arabic version calls him here, the "brother's son of Barnabas": and the Syriac version, בר דדה, "his uncle's son": however, Barnabas being so great a man as he was, and so well known, it added some credit to Mark, that he was a relation of his.

(l) T. Bab. Gittin, fol. 11. 2.

11. And Jesus, which is called Justus, who are of the circumcision. These only are my fellowworkers unto the kingdom of God, which have been a comfort unto me.

Greek/Transliteration
11. καὶ Ἰησοῦς ὁ λεγόμενος Ἰοῦστος, οἱ ὄντες ἐκ περιτομῆς· οὗτοι μόνοι συνεργοὶ εἰς τὴν βασιλείαν τοῦ θεοῦ, οἵτινες ἐγενήθησάν μοι παρηγορία.

11. kai Yeisous 'o legomenos Youstos, 'oi ontes ek peritomeis. 'outoi monoi sunergoi eis tein basileian tou theou, 'oitines egeneitheisan moi pareigoria.

Hebrew/Transliteration
יא. וְגַם-יֵשׁוּעַ הַנִּקְרָא בְשֵׁם יוֹסְטוֹס אֲשֶׁר הֵם מִן-הַגְּמוֹלִים הֵם לְבַדָּם תָּמְכוּ בְיָדִי בְּמַלְכוּת הָאֱלֹהִים וַיְשִׁיבוּ אֶת-נַפְשִׁי:

11. Ve•gam - Yeshua ha•nik•ra ve•shem Yoostos asher hem min - ha•ni•mo•lim hem le•va•dam tam•choo ve•ya•di be•mal•choot ha•Elohim va•ya•shi•voo et - naf•shi.

Rabbinic Jewish Commentary
And Jesus, which is called Justus,.... The former of these names is the same with Joshua, and was very frequent with the Jews, and the later a surname that was sometimes given to men remarkable for holiness and righteousness: so Joseph, called Barsabas, is surnamed Justus, Act_1:23 and James, the brother of our Lord, was called by the Jews James the Just (m).

(m) Euseb. Eccl. Hist. l. 2. c. 1.

---

12. Epaphras, who is one of you, a servant of Christ, saluteth you, always labouring fervently for you in prayers, that ye may stand perfect and complete in all the will of God.

Greek/Transliteration
12. Ἀσπάζεται ὑμᾶς Ἐπαφρᾶς ὁ ἐξ ὑμῶν, δοῦλος χριστοῦ, πάντοτε ἀγωνιζόμενος ὑπὲρ ὑμῶν ἐν ταῖς προσευχαῖς, ἵνα στῆτε τέλειοι καὶ πεπληρωμένοι ἐν παντὶ θελήματι τοῦ θεοῦ.

12. Aspazetai 'umas Epaphras 'o ex 'umon, doulos christou, pantote agonizomenos 'uper 'umon en tais proseuchais, 'ina steite teleioi kai pepleiromenoi en panti theleimati tou theou.

Hebrew/Transliteration
יב. אֶפַּפְרָס בֶּן-אַרְצְכֶם וְעֶבֶד יֵשׁוּעַ הַמָּשִׁיחַ שֹׁאֵל לִשְׁלוֹמְכֶם הוּא אֲשֶׁר גָּבַר בִּתְפִלּוֹתָיו בְּכָל-עֵת לְהַעֲמִידְכֶם לִפְנֵי הָאֱלֹהִים שְׁלֵמִים וּמְמֻלָּאִים בִּמְלֹא חֶפְצוֹ:

12. Epaf•ras ben - ar•tze•chem ve•e•ved Yeshua ha•Ma•shi•ach sho•el lish•lom•chem hoo asher ga•var bit•fi•lo•tav be•chol - et le•ha•a•mid•chem lif•ney ha•Elohim sh`le•mim oo•me•moo•la•eem bim•lo chef•tzo.

13. For I bear him record, that he hath a great zeal for you, and them that are in Laodicea, and them in Hierapolis.

Greek/Transliteration
13. Μαρτυρῶ γὰρ αὐτῷ ὅτι ἔχει ζῆλον πολὺν ὑπὲρ ὑμῶν καὶ τῶν ἐν Λαοδικείᾳ καὶ τῶν ἐν Ἱεραπόλει.

13. Marturo gar auto 'oti echei zeilon polun 'uper 'umon kai ton en Laodikeia kai ton en 'Yerapolei.

Hebrew/Transliteration
יג. כִּי עֵד אֲנִי לוֹ אֲשֶׁר קִנְאָתוֹ גָדְלָה לָכֶם וּלְיֹשְׁבֵי לוּדְקְיָא וּלְיֹשְׁבֵי הִירָפּוֹלִיס:

13. Ki ed ani lo asher kin•a•to gad•la la•chem ool•yosh•vey Lood•ke•ya ool•yosh•vey Hira•polis.

---

14. Luke, the beloved physician, and Demas, greet you.

Greek/Transliteration
14. Ἀσπάζεται ὑμᾶς Λουκᾶς ὁ ἰατρὸς ὁ ἀγαπητός, καὶ Δημᾶς.

14. Aspazetai 'umas Loukas 'o iatros 'o agapeitos, kai Deimas.

Hebrew/Transliteration
יד. יְדִידֵנוּ לוּקָס הָרֹפֵא וְדִימָס שֹׁאֲלִים לִשְׁלוֹמְכֶם:

14. Ye•di•de•noo Loo•kas ha•ro•fe ve•Di•mas sho•a•lim lish•lom•chem.

Rabbinic Jewish Commentary
Jerom (n) calls the Evangelist Luke, the physician of Antioch, for from thence he was; and being converted by the Apostle Paul, as is very probable, though some make him to be one of the seventy disciples, he became a physician of bodies, a physician of souls: some say (o) he was a scholar of Galen, the famous physician, and others that he was his sister's son; who having heard of Yehsua's miracles, set out with his master Galen for Judea, to know the truth of them, of which they doubted; Galen died by the way, Luke came to Yeshua, and being taught by him, became one of the seventy disciples. The apostle calls him "beloved", not on account of his profession, in which he might be useful to many, but as he was a brother in Yeshua, a minister of the Gospel, and a fellow labourer of his. This is the same person as Lucas, mentioned along with Demas, and others, as here, in Phm_1:24. The name perhaps is Roman, but was, however, well known among the Jews; for they say (p), the

"Witnesses that sign a divorce, and their names are as the names of strangers, what is to be done with it? there is none comes into our hands (is received) but לוקוס "Lukus" and "Lus", and we allow it to be right:"

Upon which the gloss says, because these were famous names.

The Jews make frequent mention of R. דימי, "Dimi", or "Demi", in their writings (q), which perhaps is the same name with this.

(n) Catalog. Script. Eccles. p. 91. Vid. Nicephor. Hist. l. 2. c. 43. (o) Vid. Castell. Lex. Polyglott. col. 1894. (p) T. Bab. Gittin, fol. 11. 2. (q) T. Bab. Gittin, fol. 19. 2. Nazir, fol. 36. 1. Sota, fol. 43. 2. Bava Kama, fol. 43.

---

15. Salute the brethren which are in Laodicea, and Nymphas, and the church which is in his house.

Greek/Transliteration
15. Ἀσπάσασθε τοὺς ἐν Λαοδικείᾳ ἀδελφούς, καὶ Νυμφᾶν, καὶ τὴν κατ᾽ οἶκον αὐτοῦ ἐκκλησίαν.

15. Aspasasthe tous en Laodikeia adelphous, kai Numphan, kai tein kat oikon autou ekkleisian.

Hebrew/Transliteration
טו. שַׁאֲלוּ לִשְׁלוֹם אַחֵינוּ אֲשֶׁר בְּלוּדְקְיָא וְלִשְׁלוֹם נוּמְפָס וְהַקָּהָל אֲשֶׁר בְּבֵיתָם:

15. Sha•a•loo lish•lom achey•noo asher be•Lood•ke•ya ve•lish•lom Noom•fas ve•ha•ka•hal asher be•vey•tam.

---

16. And when this epistle is read among you, cause that it be read also in the church of the Laodiceans; and that ye likewise read the epistle from Laodicea.

Greek/Transliteration
16. Καὶ ὅταν ἀναγνωσθῇ παρ᾽ ὑμῖν ἡ ἐπιστολή, ποιήσατε ἵνα καὶ ἐν τῇ Λαοδικαίων ἐκκλησίᾳ ἀναγνωσθῇ, καὶ τὴν ἐκ Λαοδικείας ἵνα καὶ ὑμεῖς ἀναγνῶτε.

16. Kai 'otan anagnosthei par 'umin 'ei epistolei, poieisate 'ina kai en tei Laodikaion ekkleisia anagnosthei, kai tein ek Laodikeias 'ina kai 'umeis anagnote.

Hebrew/Transliteration
טז. אַחֲרֵי קְרִיאַת הָאִגֶּרֶת הַזֹּאת בְּאָזְנֵיכֶם תְּנוּהָ לְהִקָּרֵא גַּם-בְּאָזְנֵי קְהַל לוּדְקְיָא וְהָאִגֶּרֶת אֲשֶׁר לְלוּדְקְיָא תִּקְרְאוּ בָהּ גַּם-אַתֶּם:

16. A•cha•rey k`ri•at ha•ee•ge•ret ha•zot be•oz•ney•chem te•noo•ha le•hi•ka•re gam - be•oz•ney k`hal Lood•ke•ya ve•ha•ee•ge•ret asher le•Lood•ke•ya tik•re•oo va gam - atem.

Rabbinic Jewish Commentary
and that ye likewise read the epistle from Laodicea; which was not an epistle of the apostle to the Laodiceans, as some have thought, but one that was "written from" thence, as the Syriac version renders it. Marcion, the heretic, called the epistle to the Ephesians, the epistle to the Laodiceans, but without any reason; and others have forged an epistle which bears this name, and appears to be a collection out of others, and chiefly from the epistle to the Philippians; and which being short, and may gratify the curious who cannot otherwise come at it, I shall transcribe it, and is as follows (r).

"Paul an Apostle, not of men, neither by man, but by Jesus Christ; to the brethren which are of Laodicea, grace be unto you, and peace from God our Father and the Lord Jesus Christ. I give thanks to Christ in every prayer of mine, that ye continue and persevere in good works, expecting the promise in the day of judgment: neither let the vain speeches of some that pretend to truth disturb you, so as to turn you from the truth of the Gospel which is preached by me; and now the Lord cause that those who belong to me may be serviceable for the furtherance of the truth of the Gospel, and doing kind actions, which are of salvation unto eternal life: and now my bonds are manifest which I suffer in Christ, in which I am glad and rejoice; and this is to my perpetual salvation which is done by your prayers, the Holy Ghost supplying, whether by life or by death; for me to live is life in Christ, and to die is joy; and he will do his own mercy in you, that ye may have the same love, and be unanimous: therefore, most beloved, as ye have heard of the presence of the Lord, so think ye, and do in fear, and you shall have life for ever; for it is God that worketh in you; and whatsoever ye do, do without sin; and what is best, most beloved, rejoice in the Lord Jesus Christ, and take heed of all filth in all gain; let your petitions be openly with God, be ye steadfast in the sense of Christ: and whatsoever things are sound and true, and chaste and just, and lovely, do; and what ye have heard and received retain in the heart, and peace shall be with you. Salute all the brethren with an holy kiss; all the saints salute you; the grace of our Lord Jesus Christ be with your spirit. Amen. Cause this to be read to the Colossians, and that which is of the Colossians to you."

Every one on reading it will easily see that it is a spurious piece, a collection out of other epistles, and very ill put together: however, the apostle here does not speak of any epistle written to the church of Laodicea, but of one that was written from thence; which some think was written by himself, and that he means his first epistle to Timothy, which is said to be written from Laodicea; and the rather, because in that the qualifications of the ministers of the Gospel are given; and also suitable instructions for the discharge of their work, and so very proper to be read in the presence of Archippus; who, from the following verse, seems to have been remiss and negligent, and needed stirring up to the performance of his office: but from Col_2:1 it appears, that the apostle had not been at Laodices when he wrote this, and had not so much as seen any of the faces of the brethren there in the flesh; it therefore seems rather to be an epistle which was sent from Laodicea to him, or to the Colossians; which having something in it very instructive and useful, the apostle desires it might be publicly read.

(r) Jachasin, fol. 87. 2. & 117. 1.

---

17. And say to Archippus, Take heed to the ministry which thou hast received in the Lord, that thou fulfill it.

Greek/Transliteration
17. Καὶ εἴπατε Ἀρχίππῳ, Βλέπε τὴν διακονίαν ἣν παρέλαβες ἐν κυρίῳ, ἵνα αὐτὴν πληροῖς.

17. Kai eipate Archippo, Blepe tein dyakonian 'ein parelabes en kurio, 'ina autein pleirois.

Hebrew/Transliteration
יז. וְאִמְרוּ אֶל-אַרְכִּפּוֹס זָכוֹר אֶת-מִשְׁמֶרֶת הַכְּהֻנָּה אֲשֶׁר לָקַחְתָּ מִלִּפְנֵי הָאָדוֹן לְמַלֹּאתָהּ:

17. Ve•eem•roo el - Ar•chipos za•chor et - mish•me•ret ha•k`hoo•na asher la•kach•ta mi•lif•ney ha•Adon le•ma•lo•ta.

160

18. The salutation by the hand of me Paul. Remember my bonds. Grace be with you. Amen.

Greek/Transliteration
18. Ὁ ἀσπασμὸς τῇ ἐμῇ χειρὶ Παύλου. Μνημονεύετέ μου τῶν δεσμῶν. Ἡ χάρις μεθ' ὑμῶν. Ἀμήν.

18. 'O aspasmos tei emei cheiri Paulou. Mneimoneuete mou ton desmon. 'Ei charis meth 'umon. Amein.

Hebrew/Transliteration
יח. זֹאת שְׁאֵלַת שָׁלוֹם בִּכְתָב יָדִי אֲנִי פוֹלוֹס זִכְרוּ לְמוֹסְרָי וְחֶסֶד אֵל עִמָּכֶם אָמֵן:

18. Zot sh`e•lat sha•lom bich•tav ya•di ani Folos zich•roo le•mo•se•rai ve•che•sed El ee•ma•chem Amen.

^end^

THE FIRST EPISTLE OF PAUL THE APOSTLE TO THE THESSALONIANS

1 Thessalonians, Chapter 1

1. Paul, and Silvanus, and Timotheus, unto the church of the Thessalonians which is in God the Father and in the Lord Jesus Christ: Grace be unto you, and peace, from God our Father, and the Lord Jesus Christ.

Greek/Transliteration

1. Παῦλος καὶ Σιλουανὸς καὶ Τιμόθεος, τῇ ἐκκλησίᾳ Θεσσαλονικέων ἐν θεῷ πατρί, καὶ κυρίῳ Ἰησοῦ χριστῷ· χάρις ὑμῖν καὶ εἰρήνη ἀπὸ θεοῦ πατρὸς ἡμῶν καὶ κυρίου Ἰησοῦ χριστοῦ.

1. Paulos kai Silouanos kai Timotheos, tei ekkleisia Thessalonikeon en theo patri, kai kurio Yeisou christo. charis 'umin kai eireinei apo theou patros 'eimon kai kuriou Yeisou christou.

Hebrew/Transliteration

א. פּוֹלוֹס וְסִלְוָנוֹס וְטִימוֹתִיּוֹס אֶל-עֲדַת הַתַּסְלוֹנִיקִים הַדְּבֵקִים בֵּאלֹהִים אָבִינוּ וּבְיֵשׁוּעַ הַמָּשִׁיחַ אֲדֹנֵינוּ חֶסֶד לָכֶם וְשָׁלוֹם מֵאֵת אֱלֹהִים אָבִינוּ וַאֲדוֹנֵינוּ יֵשׁוּעַ הַמָּשִׁיחַ:

1. Polos ve•Silvanos ve•Timotiyos el - adat ha•Tas•lo•ni•kim ha•d`ve•kim be•Elohim Avi•noo oov•Yeshua ha•Ma•shi•ach Ado•ney•noo che•sed la•chem ve•sha•lom me•et Elohim Avi•noo va•Ado•ney•noo Yeshua ha•Ma•shi•ach.

---

2. We give thanks to God always for you all, making mention of you in our prayers;

Greek/Transliteration

2. Εὐχαριστοῦμεν τῷ θεῷ πάντοτε περὶ πάντων ὑμῶν, μνείαν ὑμῶν ποιούμενοι ἐπὶ τῶν προσευχῶν ἡμῶν,

2. Eucharistoumen to theo pantote peri panton 'umon, mneian 'umon poioumenoi epi ton proseuchon 'eimon,

Hebrew/Transliteration

ב. הִנֵּה אֲנַחְנוּ מְבָרְכִים אֶת-הָאֱלֹהִים בְּכָל-עֵת עַל-כֻּלְּכֶם וְלֹא נֶחְדַּל מֵהַזְכִּיר אֶתְכֶם בִּתְפִלּוֹתֵינוּ:

2. Hee•ne a•nach•noo me•var•chim et - ha•Elohim be•chol - et al - kool•chem ve•lo nech•dal me•haz•kir et•chem bit•fi•lo•tey•noo.

---

3. Remembering without ceasing your work of faith, and labour of love, and patience of hope in our Lord Jesus Christ, in the sight of God and our Father;

Greek/Transliteration

3. ἀδιαλείπτως μνημονεύοντες ὑμῶν τοῦ ἔργου τῆς πίστεως, καὶ τοῦ κόπου τῆς ἀγάπης, καὶ τῆς ὑπομονῆς τῆς ἐλπίδος τοῦ κυρίου ἡμῶν Ἰησοῦ χριστοῦ, ἔμπροσθεν τοῦ θεοῦ καὶ πατρὸς ἡμῶν·

3. adyaleiptos mneimoneuontes 'umon tou ergou teis pisteos, kai tou kopou teis agapeis, kai teis 'upomoneis teis elpidos tou kuriou 'eimon Yeisou christou, emprosthen tou theou kai patros 'eimon.

Hebrew/Transliteration

ג. בְּזָכְרֵנוּ תָמִיד לִפְנֵי אֱלֹהֵינוּ אָבִינוּ אֶת-מַעֲשֵׂיכֶם בֶּאֱמוּנָה אֶת-עֲבֹדַתְכֶם בְּאַהֲבָה וְאֶת-מִבְטַח עֻזְּכֶם בְּתִקְוָה בַּאֲדֹנֵינוּ יֵשׁוּעַ הַמָּשִׁיחַ:

3. Be•zoch•re•noo ta•mid lif•ney Elohey•noo Avi•noo et - ma•a•sey•chem be•e•moo•na et - avo•dat•chem be•a•ha•va ve•et - miv•tach ooz•chem be•tik•va ba•Ado•ne•noo Yeshua ha•Ma•shi•ach.

Rabbinic Jewish Commentary

The phrase "without ceasing", is, by the Vulgate Latin, Syriac, and Ethiopic versions, joined to the last clause of the preceding verse.

The Vulgate Latin, Arabic, and Ethiopic versions render it, "the work of your faith"; and so some copies, and the Syriac version, "the works of your faith". The Targumist in Hab_1:12 represents God as holy בעובדי הימנותא, "in works of faith".

---

4. Knowing, brethren beloved, your election of God.

Greek/Transliteration
4. εἰδότες, ἀδελφοὶ ἠγαπημένοι ὑπὸ θεοῦ, τὴν ἐκλογὴν ὑμῶν·

4. eidotes, adelphoi eigapeimenoi 'upo theou, tein eklogein 'umon.

Hebrew/Transliteration
ד. כִּי יָדַעְנוּ אַחִים כִּי בְחִירֵי הָאֱלֹהִים אַתֶּם וִידִידָיו:

4. Ki ya•da•a•noo a•chim ki be•chi•rey ha•Elohim atem viy•di•dav.

---

5. For our gospel came not unto you in word only, but also in power, and in the Holy Ghost, and in much assurance; as ye know what manner of men we were among you for your sake.

Greek/Transliteration
5. ὅτι τὸ εὐαγγέλιον ἡμῶν οὐκ ἐγενήθη εἰς ὑμᾶς ἐν λόγῳ μόνον, ἀλλὰ καὶ ἐν δυνάμει, καὶ ἐν πνεύματι ἁγίῳ, καὶ ἐν πληροφορίᾳ πολλῇ, καθὼς οἴδατε οἷοι ἐγενήθημεν ἐν ὑμῖν δι᾽ ὑμᾶς.

5. 'oti to euangelion 'eimon ouk egeneithei eis 'umas en logo monon, alla kai en dunamei, kai en pneumati 'agio, kai en pleirophoria pollei, kathos oidate 'oioi egeneitheimen en 'umin di 'umas.

Hebrew/Transliteration
ה. בַּאֲשֶׁר גַּם-בְּשׂרָתֵנוּ לֹא הִשְׁמַעְנוּ אֶתְכֶם בְּקוֹל דְּבָרִים לְבָד כִּי אִם-גַּם-בִּגְבוּרָה וּבְרוּחַ הַקֹּדֶשׁ וּבְבִטְחָה עֲצֻמָה כַּאֲשֶׁר רְאִיתֶם אֵיךְ הָלַכְנוּ בְתוֹכְכֶם לְטוֹב לָכֶם:

5. Ba•a•sher gam - be•sora•te•noo lo hish•ma•a•noo et•chem be•kol d`va•rim le•vad ki eem - gam - big•voo•ra oov•Roo•ach ha•Ko•desh oo•ve•vit•cha a•tzoo•ma ka•a•sher r`ee•tem eych ha•lach•noo ve•to•cha•chem le•tov la•chem.

Rabbinic Jewish Commentary
That not only externally, which to have is a great blessing, but internally, εις υμας, "into you"; it came not barely into their ears vocally, and into their heads notionally; but into their hearts, and worked effectually there; it was mixed with faith, and was profitable; it became the ingrafted word, and dwelt richly in them.

---

6. And ye became followers of us, and of the Lord, having received the word in much affliction, with joy of the Holy Ghost:

Greek/Transliteration
6. Καὶ ὑμεῖς μιμηταὶ ἡμῶν ἐγενήθητε καὶ τοῦ κυρίου, δεξάμενοι τὸν λόγον ἐν θλίψει πολλῇ μετὰ χαρᾶς πνεύματος ἁγίου,

6. Kai 'umeis mimeitai 'eimon egeneitheite kai tou kuriou, dexamenoi ton logon en thlipsei pollei meta charas pneumatos 'agiou,

Hebrew/Transliteration
ו. וְאַתֶּם הֲלַכְתֶּם בְּעִקְּבוֹתֵינוּ וּבְעִקְּבוֹת אֲדֹנֵינוּ וַתְּקַבְּלוּ אֶת-דְּבָרֵינוּ וְלִבְּכֶם עָלֵץ בְּרוּחַ הַקֹּדֶשׁ אַף כִּי-צָרָה גְדוֹלָה מְצָאַתְכֶם:

6. Ve•a•tem ha•lach•tem be•eek•vo•tey•noo oov•eek•vot Ado•ney•noo vat•kab•loo et - de•va•rey•noo ve•lib•chem alatz be•Roo•ach ha•Ko•desh af ki - tza•ra ge•do•la me•tza•at•chem.

---

7. So that ye were ensamples to all that believe in Macedonia and Achaia.

Greek/Transliteration
7. ὥστε γενέσθαι ὑμᾶς τύπους πᾶσιν τοῖς πιστεύουσιν ἐν τῇ Μακεδονίᾳ καὶ τῇ Ἀχαΐᾳ.

7. 'oste genesthai 'umas tupous pasin tois pisteuousin en tei Makedonia kai tei Achaia.

Hebrew/Transliteration
ז. עַד אֲשֶׁר הֱיִיתֶם לְמוֹפֵת לְכָל-אַנְשֵׁי אֱמוּנָה בְּמַקְדּוֹנְיָא וּבַאֲכַיָא:

7. Ad asher he•yi•tem le•mo•fet le•chol - an•shey e•moo•na be•Mak•don•ya oo•va•A•cha•ya.

---

8. For from you sounded out the word of the Lord not only in Macedonia and Achaia, but also in every place your faith to God-ward is spread abroad; so that we need not to speak any thing.

Greek/Transliteration
8. Ἀφ᾽ ὑμῶν γὰρ ἐξήχηται ὁ λόγος τοῦ κυρίου οὐ μόνον ἐν τῇ Μακεδονίᾳ καὶ ἐν τῇ Ἀχαΐᾳ, ἀλλὰ καὶ ἐν παντὶ τόπῳ ἡ πίστις ὑμῶν ἡ πρὸς τὸν θεὸν ἐξελήλυθεν, ὥστε μὴ χρείαν ἡμᾶς ἔχειν λαλεῖν τι.

8. Aph 'umon gar exeicheitai 'o logos tou kuriou ou monon en tei Makedonia kai en tei Achaia, alla kai en panti topo 'ei pistis 'umon 'ei pros ton theon exeleiluthen, 'oste mei chreian 'eimas echein lalein ti.

Hebrew/Transliteration
ח. כִּי מִכֶּם יָצָא קוֹל דְּבַר יְהֹוָה לֹא לְבַד בְּמַקְדּוֹנְיָא וּבַאֲכַיָא כִּי אִם-גַּם בְּכָל-מָקוֹם יָצָא שֵׁמַע אֱמוּנַתְכֶם בֵּאלֹהִים עַד אֲשֶׁר לֹא נוֹתַר לָנוּ לְדַבֵּר-עוֹד דָּבָר:

8. Ki mi•kem ya•tza kol de•var Adonai lo le•vad be•Mak•don•ya oo•va•A•cha•ya ki eem - gam be•chol - ma•kom ya•tza she•ma emoo•nat•chem be•Elohim ad asher lo no•tar la•noo le•da•ber - od da•var.

---

9. For they themselves shew of us what manner of entering in we had unto you, and how ye turned to God from idols to serve the living and true God;

Greek/Transliteration
9. αὐτοὶ γὰρ περὶ ἡμῶν ἀπαγγέλλουσιν ὁποίαν εἴσοδον ἔσχομεν πρὸς ὑμᾶς, καὶ πῶς ἐπεστρέψατε πρὸς τὸν θεὸν ἀπὸ τῶν εἰδώλων, δουλεύειν θεῷ ζῶντι καὶ ἀληθινῷ,

9. autoi gar peri 'eimon apangellousin 'opoian eisodon eschomen pros 'umas, kai pos epestrepsate pros ton theon apo ton eidolon, douleuein theo zonti kai aleithino,

Hebrew/Transliteration
ט. כִּי הַשֹּׁמְעִים הִגִּידוּ בְּפִיהֶם אֵיךְ בָּאנוּ אֲלֵיכֶם וְאֵיךְ עֲזַבְתֶּם אֶת-הָאֱלִילִים וַתָּשׁוּבוּ אֶל-הָאֱלֹהִים לַעֲבֹד אֱלֹהִים חַיִּים אֱלֹהֵי אֱמֶת:

9. Ki ha•shom•eem hi•gi•doo ve•fi•hem eych ba•noo aley•chem ve•eych azav•tem et - ha•e•li•lim va•ta•shoo•voo el - ha•Elohim la•a•vod Elohim cha•yim Elohey emet.

Rabbinic Jewish Commentary
The Thessalonians before the Gospel came among them were idolaters; here the "Dii Cabiri", the great and chief gods of the Gentiles, were worshipped; as Jupiter and Bacchus, Ceres and Proserpina, Pluto and Mercury, Castor and Pollux, and Esculapius; these the Macedonians, and particularly the Thessalonians, worshipped with great devotion and reverence (d).

(d) Gutherlothus de mysteriis Deor. Cabirorum, c. 15. p. 94, 95. Jul. Firmicus. de errore prof. relig. p. 18.

---

10. And to wait for his Son from heaven, whom he raised from the dead, even Jesus, which delivered us from the wrath to come.

Greek/Transliteration
10. καὶ ἀναμένειν τὸν υἱὸν αὐτοῦ ἐκ τῶν οὐρανῶν, ὃν ἤγειρεν ἐκ τῶν νεκρῶν, Ἰησοῦν, τὸν ῥυόμενον ἡμᾶς ἀπὸ τῆς ὀργῆς τῆς ἐρχομένης.

10. kai anamenein ton 'wion autou ek ton ouranon, 'on eigeiren ek ton nekron,
Yeisoun, ton 'ruomenon 'eimas apo teis orgeis teis erchomeneis.

Hebrew/Transliteration

י. וּלְחַכּוֹת לִבְנוֹ מִן-הַשָּׁמַיִם לְיֵשׁוּעַ אֲשֶׁר הֱקִימוֹ מִן-הַמֵּתִים וַאֲשֶׁר הוּא מַצִּילֵנוּ לֶעָתִיד לָבוֹא מֵחֲרוֹן אָף:

10. Ool•cha•kot liv•no min - ha•sha•ma•yim le•Yeshua asher ha•ki•mo min - ha•me•tim va•a•sher hoo ma•tzi•le•noo le•a•tid la•vo me•cha•ron af.

1 Thessalonians, Chapter 2

1. For yourselves, brethren, know our entrance in unto you, that it was not in vain:

Greek/Transliteration
1. Αὐτοὶ γὰρ οἴδατε, ἀδελφοί, τὴν εἴσοδον ἡμῶν τὴν πρὸς ὑμᾶς, ὅτι οὐ κενὴ γέγονεν·

1. Autoi gar oidate, adelphoi, tein eisodon 'eimon tein pros 'umas, 'oti ou kenei gegonen.

Hebrew/Transliteration
א. הֵן נַפְשְׁכֶם אַחַי יֹדְעַת כִּי בֹאֵנוּ אֲלֵיכֶם לֹא-הָיָה לָרִיק:

1. Hen naf•she•chem a•chai yo•da•at ki vo•e•noo aley•chem lo - ha•ya la•rik.

---

2. But even after that we had suffered before, and were shamefully entreated, as ye know, at Philippi, we were bold in our God to speak unto you the gospel of God with much contention.

Greek/Transliteration
2. ἀλλὰ προπαθόντες καὶ ὑβρισθέντες, καθὼς οἴδατε, ἐν Φιλίπποις, ἐπαρρησιασάμεθα ἐν τῷ θεῷ ἡμῶν λαλῆσαι πρὸς ὑμᾶς τὸ εὐαγγέλιον τοῦ θεοῦ ἐν πολλῷ ἀγῶνι.

2. alla propathontes kai 'ubristhentes, kathos oidate, en Philippois, eparreisyasametha en to theo 'eimon laleisai pros 'umas to euangelion tou theou en pollo agoni.

Hebrew/Transliteration
ב. כִּי אַחֲרֵי הַתְּלָאָה אֲשֶׁר מְצָאַתְנוּ וְאַחֲרֵי אֲשֶׁר הִתְעַלְלוּ בָנוּ בְּפִילִפִּי הֲלֹא יְדַעְתֶּם כִּי אָז מָצָאנוּ עֹז בֵּאלֹהֵינוּ לְהַגִּיד לָכֶם בְּשׂרַת הָאֱלֹהִים נֶגֶד צֹרְרִים רַבִּים:

2. Ki a•cha•rey hat•la•ah asher me•tza•at•noo ve•a•cha•rey asher hit•a•le•loo va•noo be•Filipi ha•lo ye•da•a•tem ki az ma•tza•noo oz be•Elohey•noo le•ha•gid la•chem b`so•rat ha•Elohim ne•ged tzo•re•rim ra•bim.

---

3. For our exhortation was not of deceit, nor of uncleanness, nor in guile:

Greek/Transliteration
3. Ἡ γὰρ παράκλησις ἡμῶν οὐκ ἐκ πλάνης, οὐδὲ ἐξ ἀκαθαρσίας, οὔτε ἐν δόλῳ·

3. 'Ei gar parakleisis 'eimon ouk ek planeis, oude ex akatharsias, oute en dolo.

Hebrew/Transliteration
ג. כִּי לֹא מִפִּי מַשְׁגֶּה יָצְאָה עֵדוּתֵנוּ וְלֹא מִקֶּרֶב טָמֵא שְׂפָתַיִם וְלֹא מִלָּשׁוֹן רְמִיָּה:

3. Ki lo mi•pi mash•ge yatz•ah e•doo•te•noo ve•lo mi•ke•rev t`me s`fa•ta•yim ve•lo mi•la•shon r`mi•ya.

4. But as we were allowed of God to be put in trust with the gospel, even so we speak; not as pleasing men, but God, which trieth our hearts.

Greek/Transliteration
4. ἀλλὰ καθὼς δεδοκιμάσμεθα ὑπὸ τοῦ θεοῦ πιστευθῆναι τὸ εὐαγγέλιον, οὕτως λαλοῦμεν, οὐχ ὡς ἀνθρώποις ἀρέσκοντες, ἀλλὰ τῷ θεῷ τῷ δοκιμάζοντι τὰς καρδίας ἡμῶν.

4. alla kathos dedokimasmetha 'upo tou theou pisteutheinai to euangelion, 'outos laloumen, ouch 'os anthropois areskontes, alla to theo to dokimazonti tas kardias 'eimon.

Hebrew/Transliteration
ד. כִּי כַּאֲשֶׁר מָצָא אֱלֹהִים לִבֵּנוּ נָכוֹן לְפָנָיו וַיַּפְקֵד בְּיָדֵינוּ אֶת-הַבְּשׂוֹרָה כֵּן נְדַבֵּרָה לֹא לְהָפִיק רָצוֹן מִבְּנֵי-אָדָם כִּי אִם-מֵאֱלֹהִים הַבֹּחֵן לֵבָב:

4. Ki cha•a•sher ma•tza Elohim li•be•noo na•chon le•fa•nav va•yaf•ked be•ya•dey•noo et - ha•be•so•ra ken n`da•be•ra lo le•ha•fik ra•tzon mi•b`ney - adam ki eem - me•Elohim ha•bo•chen le•vav.

---

5. For neither at any time used we flattering words, as ye know, nor a cloke of covetousness; God is witness:

Greek/Transliteration
5. Οὔτε γάρ ποτε ἐν λόγῳ κολακείας ἐγενήθημεν, καθὼς οἴδατε, οὔτε ἐν προφάσει πλεονεξίας· θεὸς μάρτυς·

5. Oute gar pote en logo kolakeias egeneitheimen, kathos oidate, oute en prophasei pleonexias. theos martus.

Hebrew/Transliteration
ה. הֵן יְדַעְתֶּם כִּי מֵעוֹדֵנוּ לֹא בָאנוּ בִשְׂפַת חֲלָקוֹת וְלֹא בְנִכְלֵי בֹצְעֵי בָצַע אֱלֹהִים לָנוּ לְעֵד:

5. Hen ye•da•a•tem ki me•o•de•noo lo va•noo vis•fat cha•la•kot ve•lo ve•nich•ley votz•ey va•tza Elohim la•noo le•ed.

---

6. Nor of men sought we glory, neither of you, nor yet of others, when we might have been burdensome, as the apostles of Christ.

Greek/Transliteration
6. οὔτε ζητοῦντες ἐξ ἀνθρώπων δόξαν, οὔτε ἀφ᾽ ὑμῶν οὔτε ἀπὸ ἄλλων, δυνάμενοι ἐν βάρει εἶναι, ὡς χριστοῦ ἀπόστολοι,

6. oute zeitountes ex anthropon doxan, oute aph 'umon oute apo allon, dunamenoi en barei einai, 'os christou apostoloi,

Hebrew/Transliteration
ו. גַּם לֹא-בִקַּשְׁנוּ כְבוֹד אֲנָשִׁים לֹא מִיֶּדְכֶם וְלֹא מִידֵי אֲחֵרִים אַף כִּי-הָיְתָה לָּנוּ צְדָקָה לְהַעֲמִיס עֲלֵיכֶם לְכַלְכְּלֵנוּ כִּשְׁלִיחֵי הַמָּשִׁיחַ:

6. Gam lo - vi•kash•noo che•vod a•na•shim lo mi•ed•chem ve•lo mi•dey a•che•rim af ki - hai•ta la•noo tze•da•ka le•ha•a•mis aley•chem le•chal•ke•le•noo kish•li•chey ha•Ma•shi•ach.

---

7. But we were gentle among you, even as a nurse cherisheth her children:

Greek/Transliteration
7. ἀλλ᾽ ἐγενήθημεν ἤπιοι ἐν μέσῳ ὑμῶν ὡς ἂν τροφὸς θάλπῃ τὰ ἑαυτῆς τέκνα·

7. all egeneitheimen eipioi en meso 'umon 'os an trophos thalpei ta 'eauteis tekna.

Hebrew/Transliteration
ז. אַךְ בִּנְעִמוֹת הָלַכְנוּ עִמָּכֶם בְּאֹמֶנֶת אֲשֶׁר תִּשָּׂא אֶת-בְּנָהּ בְּחֵיקָהּ:

7. Ach bin•ee•mot ha•lach•noo ee•ma•chem be•o•me•net asher ti•sa et - b`na be•chey•ka.

Rabbinic Jewish Commentary
The Vulgate Latin and Ethiopic versions, instead of "gentle", read, "little children"; as the word signifies, by adding a letter to it, and expresses much the same as the other, that they were harmless and modest, and disinterested; and sought not themselves neither honour nor wealth, but the real good of others, and were kind and tender, and affectionate to them.

A like simile is used by the Jews (e), who say,

"He that rises in the night to study in the Torah, the Torah makes known to him his offences; and not in a way of judgment, but כאמא, as a mother makes known to her son, with gentle words".

But the ministration of the Gospel is much more gentle.

(e) Zohar in Lev. fol. 10. 2.

---

8. So being affectionately desirous of you, we were willing to have imparted unto you, not the gospel of God only, but also our own souls, because ye were dear unto us.

Greek/Transliteration
8. οὕτως, ὁμειρόμενοι ὑμῶν, εὐδοκοῦμεν μεταδοῦναι ὑμῖν οὐ μόνον τὸ εὐαγγέλιον τοῦ θεοῦ, ἀλλὰ καὶ τὰς ἑαυτῶν ψυχάς, διότι ἀγαπητοὶ ἡμῖν γεγένησθε.

8. 'outos, 'omeiromenoi 'umon, eudokoumen metadounai 'umin ou monon to euangelion tou theou, alla kai tas 'eauton psuchas, dioti agapeitoi 'eimin gegeneisthe.

Hebrew/Transliteration
ח. וְכֵן זֶה כַמָּה נִכְסֹף נִכְסַפְנוּ לָכֶם עַד אֲשֶׁר-אָמַרְנוּ לָתֵת לָכֶם גַּם-בְּשׂוֹרַת הָאֱלֹהִים וְגַם-נַפְשֵׁנוּ בַּעַדְכֶם כִּי-יְקַרְתֶּם בְּעֵינֵינוּ עַד-מְאֹד:

8. Ve•chen ze cha•ma nich•sof nich•saf•noo la•chem ad asher - amar•noo la•tet la•chem gam - b`so•rat ha•Elohim ve•gam - naf•she•noo ba•ad•chem ki - ye•kar•tem be•ey•ney•noo ad - me•od.

9. For ye remember, brethren, our labour and travail: for labouring night and day, because we would not be chargeable unto any of you, we preached unto you the gospel of God.

Greek/Transliteration
9. Μνημονεύετε γάρ, ἀδελφοί, τὸν κόπον ἡμῶν καὶ τὸν μόχθον· νυκτὸς γὰρ καὶ ἡμέρας ἐργαζόμενοι, πρὸς τὸ μὴ ἐπιβαρῆσαί τινα ὑμῶν, ἐκηρύξαμεν εἰς ὑμᾶς τὸ εὐαγγέλιον τοῦ θεοῦ.

9. Mneimoneuete gar, adelphoi, ton kopon 'eimon kai ton mochthon. nuktos gar kai 'eimeras ergazomenoi, pros to mei epibareisai tina 'umon, ekeiruxamen eis 'umas to euangelion tou theou.

Hebrew/Transliteration
ט. הֲלֹא תִזְכְּרוּ אַחַי אֶת-הֶעָמָל וְאֶת-הַיְגִיעָה אֵיךְ עָבַדְנוּ לַיְלָה וְיוֹמָם לְבִלְתִּי הֱיוֹת לְמַשָּׂא עַל-אִישׁ מִכֶּם כַּאֲשֶׁר הִגַּדְנוּ לָכֶם בְּשׂוֹרַת הָאֱלֹהִים:

9. Ha•lo tiz•ke•roo a•chai et - he•a•mal ve•et - hai•gi•ah eych avad•noo lai•la ve•yo•mam le•vil•ti he•yot le•ma•sa al - eesh mi•kem ka•a•sher hi•gad•noo la•chem b`so•rat ha•Elohim.

Rabbinic Jewish Commentary
For ye remember brethren, our labour and travail,..... The great pains they took, even to weariness. The Vulgate Latin version renders the last word, "weariness"; and the Arabic version, "anxiety"; and the Ethiopic version, "affliction".

for labouring night and day; at our handicraft, or "at the work of our hands", as the Syriac version renders it; which they continually attended to, even night and day, when they were not preaching the Gospel, or disputing with the Jews, or praying and conversing with those that believed, or refreshing themselves with food and rest.

---

10. Ye are witnesses, and God also, how holily and justly and unblameably we behaved ourselves among you that believe:

Greek/Transliteration
10. Ὑμεῖς μάρτυρες καὶ ὁ θεός, ὡς ὁσίως καὶ δικαίως καὶ ἀμέμπτως ὑμῖν τοῖς πιστεύουσιν ἐγενήθημεν·

10. 'Umeis martures kai 'o theos, 'os 'osios kai dikaios kai amemptos 'umin tois pisteuousin egeneitheimen.

Hebrew/Transliteration
י. עֵדִים אַתֶּם וְעֵד אֱלֹהִים כִּי בְקֹדֶשׁ בְּצֶדֶק וּבְתָמִים הָלַכְנוּ לִפְנֵיכֶם שֹׁמְרֵי אֱמוּנִים:

10. E•dim atem ve•ed Elohim ki ve•ko•desh be•tze•dek oov•ta•mim ha•lach•noo lif•ney•chem shom•rey e•moo•nim.

Rabbinic Jewish Commentary
The Syriac version joins the last clause of the preceding verse with this, and reads the whole thus, "ye are witnesses, and God also, how purely and justly we preached unto you the Gospel of God, and how unblamable we were among all that believed".

11. As ye know how we exhorted and comforted and charged every one of you, as a father doth his children,

Greek/Transliteration
11. καθάπερ οἴδατε ὡς ἕνα ἕκαστον ὑμῶν, ὡς πατὴρ τέκνα ἑαυτοῦ, παρακαλοῦντες ὑμᾶς καὶ παραμυθούμενοι

11. kathaper oidate 'os 'ena 'ekaston 'umon, 'os pateir tekna 'eautou, parakalountes 'umas kai paramuthoumenoi

Hebrew/Transliteration
יא. כַּאֲשֶׁר אַתֶּם יֹדְעִים כִּי-כְאָב אֶל-בָּנָיו כֵּן דִּבַּרְנוּ דִבְרֵי מוּסָר וְתַנְחוּמִים עַל-לֵב כָּל-אִישׁ מִכֶּם:

11. Ka•a•sher atem yod•eem ki - che•av el - ba•nav ken di•bar•noo div•rey moo•sar ve•tan•choo•mim al - lev kol - eesh mi•kem.

---

12. That ye would walk worthy of God, who hath called you unto his kingdom and glory.

Greek/Transliteration
12. καὶ μαρτυρόμενοι, εἰς τὸ περιπατῆσαι ὑμᾶς ἀξίως τοῦ θεοῦ τοῦ καλοῦντος ὑμᾶς εἰς τὴν ἑαυτοῦ βασιλείαν καὶ δόξαν.

12. kai marturomenoi, eis to peripateisai 'umas axios tou theou tou kalountos 'umas eis tein 'eautou basileian kai doxan.

Hebrew/Transliteration
יב. וַנָּעִיד בָּכֶם לָלֶכֶת בְּדֶרֶךְ יְשָׁרָה לִפְנֵי אֱלֹהִים אֲשֶׁר קָרָא אֶתְכֶם לִכְבוֹד מַלְכוּתוֹ:

12. Va•na•eed ba•chem la•le•chet be•de•rech ye•sha•ra lif•ney Elohim asher ka•ra et•chem lich•vod mal•choo•to.

---

13. For this cause also thank we God without ceasing, because, when ye received the word of God which ye heard of us, ye received it not as the word of men, but as it is in truth, the word of God, which effectually worketh also in you that believe.

Greek/Transliteration
13. Διὰ τοῦτο καὶ ἡμεῖς εὐχαριστοῦμεν τῷ θεῷ ἀδιαλείπτως, ὅτι παραλαβόντες λόγον ἀκοῆς παρ' ἡμῶν τοῦ θεοῦ, ἐδέξασθε οὐ λόγον ἀνθρώπων, ἀλλὰ καθώς ἐστιν ἀληθῶς, λόγον θεοῦ, ὃς καὶ ἐνεργεῖται ἐν ὑμῖν τοῖς πιστεύουσιν.

13. Dya touto kai 'eimeis eucharistoumen to theo adyaleiptos, 'oti paralabontes logon akoeis par 'eimon tou theou, edexasthe ou logon anthropon, alla kathos estin aleithos, logon theou, 'os kai energeitai en 'umin tois pisteuousin.

Hebrew/Transliteration
יג. וּבַעֲבוּר זֹאת גַּם-אֲנַחְנוּ לֹא נֶחְדַּל מֵהוֹדוֹת אֶת-אֱלֹהֵינוּ כִּי הֶאֱזַנְתֶּם לִדְבַר הָאֱלֹהִים אֲשֶׁר הִשְׁמַעֲנוּ בְּאָזְנֵיכֶם לֹא כִדְבַר אֲנָשִׁים כִּי אִם-קִבַּלְתֶּם אֹתוֹ כִדְבַר הָאֱלֹהִים לַאֲמִתּוֹ אֲשֶׁר רַב כֹּחוֹ לְמַאֲמִינִים:

13. Oo•va•a•voor zot gam - a•nach•noo lo nech•dal me•ho•dot et - Elohey•noo ki he•e•zan•tem lid•var ha•Elohim asher hish•ma•a•noo ve•oz•ney•chem lo chid•var a•na•shim ki eem - ki•bal•tem o•to ki•d`var ha•Elohim la•a•mi•to asher rav ko•cho le•ma•a•mi•nim.

Rabbinic Jewish Commentary
because, when ye received the word of God which ye heard of us; or "the word of hearing of God", as the Vulgate Latin version from the Greek text literally renders it.

---

14. For ye, brethren, became followers of the churches of God which in Judaea are in Christ Jesus: for ye also have suffered like things of your own countrymen, even as they have of the Jews:

Greek/Transliteration
14. Ὑμεῖς γὰρ μιμηταὶ ἐγενήθητε, ἀδελφοί, τῶν ἐκκλησιῶν τοῦ θεοῦ τῶν οὐσῶν ἐν τῇ Ἰουδαίᾳ ἐν χριστῷ Ἰησοῦ· ὅτι τὰ αὐτὰ ἐπάθετε καὶ ὑμεῖς ὑπὸ τῶν ἰδίων συμφυλετῶν, καθὼς καὶ αὐτοὶ ὑπὸ τῶν Ἰουδαίων,

14. 'Umeis gar mimeitai egeneitheite, adelphoi, ton ekkleision tou theou ton ouson en tei Youdaia en christo Yeisou. 'oti ta auta epathete kai 'umeis 'upo ton idion sumphuleton, kathos kai autoi 'upo ton Youdaion,

Hebrew/Transliteration
יד. כִּי נִמְשַׁלְתֶּם אַחֲרֵי לִקְהִלּוֹת הָאֱלֹהִים בְּיֵשׁוּעַ הַמָּשִׁיחַ אֲשֶׁר־בְּאֶרֶץ יְהוּדָה כִּי עַם הָאָרֶץ הֵצִיקוּ לָכֶם כַּאֲשֶׁר הַיְּהוּדִים הֵצִיקוּ לָהֶן:

14. Ki nim•shal•tem a•chai lik•hi•lot ha•Elohim be•Yeshua ha•Ma•shi•ach asher - be•e•retz Yehooda ki am ha•a•retz he•tzi•koo la•chem ka•a•sher ha•Ye•hoo•dim he•tzi•koo la•hen.

---

15. Who both killed the Lord Jesus, and their own prophets, and have persecuted us; and they please not God, and are contrary to all men:

Greek/Transliteration
15. τῶν καὶ τὸν κύριον ἀποκτεινάντων Ἰησοῦν καὶ τοὺς ἰδίους προφήτας, καὶ ἡμᾶς ἐκδιωξάντων, καὶ θεῷ μὴ ἀρεσκόντων, καὶ πᾶσιν ἀνθρώποις ἐναντίων,

15. ton kai ton kurion apokteinanton Yeisoun kai tous idious propheitas, kai 'eimas ekdioxanton, kai theo mei areskonton, kai pasin anthropois enantion,

Hebrew/Transliteration
טו. הֲלֹא הֵם אֲשֶׁר הֵמִיתוּ אֶת־יֵשׁוּעַ אֲדֹנֵינוּ וְאֶת־הַנְּבִיאִים וְגַם־אֹתָנוּ גֵּרְשׁוּ מִגֵּו וְהֵם לֹא טוֹבִים בְּעֵינֵי אֱלֹהִים וּנְלוֹזִים לִפְנֵי כָּל־אָדָם:

15. Ha•lo hem asher he•mi•too et - Yeshua Ado•ney•noo ve•et - ha•n`vi•eem ve•gam - o•ta•noo ger•shoo mi•gev ve•hem lo to•vim be•ei•ney Elohim oon•lo•zim lif•ney chol - adam.

16. Forbidding us to speak to the Gentiles that they might be saved, to fill up their sins alway: for the wrath is come upon them to the uttermost.

Greek/Transliteration
16. κωλυόντων ἡμᾶς τοῖς ἔθνεσιν λαλῆσαι ἵνα σωθῶσιν, εἰς τὸ ἀναπληρῶσαι αὐτῶν τὰς ἁμαρτίας πάντοτε· ἔφθασεν δὲ ἐπ᾽ αὐτοὺς ἡ ὀργὴ εἰς τέλος.

16. koluonton 'eimas tois ethnesin laleisai 'ina sothosin, eis to anapleirosai auton tas 'amartias pantote. ephthasen de ep autous 'ei orgei eis telos.

Hebrew/Transliteration
טז. אֲשֶׁר סָגְרוּ עָלֵינוּ מִקְרֹא אֶל-הַגּוֹיִם לִתְשׁוּעָה וּבְזֹאת מָלְאָה סְאַת עֲוֹנָם כְּדַרְכָּם תָּמִיד וַחֲרוֹן אַף הִשִּׂיגָם עַד-לְכָלָה:

16. Asher sag•roo aley•noo mik•ro el - ha•go•yim lit•shoo•ah oo•va•zot mal•ah se•at a•vo•nam ke•dar•kam ta•mid va•cha•ron af hi•si•gam ad - le•cha•le.

Rabbinic Jewish Commentary
The believing Jews, through ignorance, did at first disapprove of the ministry of the word to the Gentiles, Act_11:1, such was the aversion of that nation to all others, and which perfectly agrees with their general sentiments, which forbid the explanation of the Torah to the Gentiles; and therefore it need not be wondered at, that they should do all that in them lay to hinder the entrance and spread of the Gospel among them, of which take the following proof (f):

"Whoever has not the holy name sealed and bound in his flesh (i.e. is not circumcised) אסיר לאודעא ליה מלה דאוריתא "it is forbidden to make known to him a word of the Torah", and much less to study in it--and whoever is not circumcised, and they give to him את זציר דאוריתא, "the least thing in the Torah", it is as if he destroyed the world, and dealt falsely with the name of God--Hillell and Shammai did not make known to Onkelos a word of the Torah, until he was circumcised--and the traditions are, that even though a man is circumcised, yet if he does not do the commands of the Torah, lo, he is as a Gentile in all things, and "it is forbidden to teach him the words of the Torah".

Nay, it is a rule with the Jews (g), that

"If a Gentile studies in the Torah, he is guilty of death:"

for the wrath is come upon them to the uttermost: as temporal ruin and destruction, which was now near at hand, and hung over their heads; and therefore is said to be come to them, and which in a little time fell upon their nation and city, and temple, even to the uttermost, to the last degree; and was, as the Arabic version renders it, "wrath consuming"; or "the consummation, and that determined poured upon the desolate", spoken of in Dan_9:27 and which, as it is come upon them, will remain "unto the end".

(f) Zohar in Lev. fol. 30. 2, 3. (g) T. Bab. Sanhedrin, fol. 59. 1. Maimon. Hilchot Melachim, c. 10. sect. 9.

---

17. But we, brethren, being taken from you for a short time in presence, not in heart, endeavoured the more abundantly to see your face with great desire.

Greek/Transliteration
17. Ἡμεῖς δέ, ἀδελφοί, ἀπορφανισθέντες ἀφ᾽ ὑμῶν πρὸς καιρὸν ὥρας, προσώπῳ οὐ καρδίᾳ, περισσοτέρως ἐσπουδάσαμεν τὸ πρόσωπον ὑμῶν ἰδεῖν ἐν πολλῇ ἐπιθυμίᾳ·

17. 'Eimeis de, adelphoi, aporphanisthentes aph 'umon pros kairon 'oras, prosopo ou kardia, perissoteros espoudasamen to prosopon 'umon idein en pollei epithumia.

Hebrew/Transliteration
יז- וַאֲנַחְנוּ אַחַי אַחֲרֵי אֲשֶׁר-רָחַקְנוּ מִכֶּם זֶה מְעַט כְּמַסְתִּירֵי פָנִים וְלֹא כְמַרְחִיקֵי לֵב בִּקַּשְׁנוּ מְאֹד לִרְאוֹת אֶת-פְּנֵיכֶם בְּחֵשֶׁק-רָב:

17. Va•a•nach•noo a•chai a•cha•rey asher - ra•chak•noo mi•kem ze me•at ke•mas•ti•rey fa•nim ve•lo che•mar•chi•key lev bi•kash•noo me•od lir•ot et - p`ney•chem be•che•shek - rav.

---

18. Wherefore we would have come unto you, even I Paul, once and again; but Satan hindered us.

Greek/Transliteration
18. διὸ ἠθελήσαμεν ἐλθεῖν πρὸς ὑμᾶς, ἐγὼ μὲν Παῦλος καὶ ἅπαξ καὶ δίς, καὶ ἐνέκοψεν ἡμᾶς ὁ Σατανᾶς.

18. dio eitheleisamen elthein pros 'umas, ego men Paulos kai 'apax kai dis, kai enekopsen 'eimas 'o Satanas.

Hebrew/Transliteration
יח: עַל-כֵּן הוֹאַלְנוּ לָבוֹא אֲלֵיכֶם אֲנִי פוֹלוֹס גַּם-פַּעַם גַּם-פַּעֲמַיִם וְהַשָּׂטָן עֲצָרָנוּ:

18. Al - ken ho•al•noo la•vo aley•chem ani Folos gam - pa•am gam - pa•a•ma•yim ve•ha•Sa•tan a•tza•ra•noo.

Rabbinic Jewish Commentary
once and again: or "once and twice" so the Jews used (h) to speak פעם ראשונה ושנייה, "one time and a second"; that is, several times.

but Satan hindered us. The Syriac and Ethiopic versions read, "hindered me"; by moving the mob which rose at Thessalonica, to go to Berea, and disturb the apostle there; which obliged him, contrary to his will, to go to Athens instead of returning to Thessalonica, as he intended.

(h) Maimon. in Hilch. Chobel, c. 5. sect. 10.

---

19. For what is our hope, or joy, or crown of rejoicing? Are not even ye in the presence of our Lord Jesus Christ at his coming?

Greek/Transliteration
19. Τίς γὰρ ἡμῶν ἐλπὶς ἢ χαρὰ ἢ στέφανος καυχήσεως; Ἢ οὐχὶ καὶ ὑμεῖς, ἔμπροσθεν τοῦ κυρίου ἡμῶν Ἰησοῦ ἐν τῇ αὐτοῦ παρουσίᾳ;

19. Tis gar 'eimon elpis ei chara ei stephanos kaucheiseos? Ei ouchi kai 'umeis, emprosthen tou kuriou 'eimon Yeisou en tei autou parousia?

Hebrew/Transliteration
:יט. כִּי מַה תִּקְוָתֵנוּ מַה שִׂמְחָתֵנוּ וּמַה עֲטֶרֶת תִּפְאַרְתֵּנוּ הֲלֹא אַתֶּם הִנְּכֶם לִפְנֵי יֵשׁוּעַ הַמָּשִׁיחַ אֲדֹנֵינוּ בְּבֹאוֹ

19. Ki ma tik•va•te•noo ma sim•cha•te•noo oo•ma ate•ret tif•ar•te•noo ha•lo atem hin•chem lif•ney Yeshua ha•Ma•shi•ach Ado•ney•noo be•vo•o?

Rabbinic Jewish Commentary
crown of rejoicing: which is but a stronger phrase, to press the joy they had in their conversion and perseverance, in allusion to crowns wore at times of rejoicing, as at marriage feasts, and the like: hence we read (i) of the crowns of the bridegrooms, and of the brides, which were forbidden the use of in the war of Vespasian; the latter were made of gold, in the form of the city of Jerusalem, and from thence called golden cities (k); and the former, some say, were made of salt and sulphur, to put them in mind of the destruction of the Sodomites, for their unnatural lusts (l); others of a salt stone as clear as crystal, or of the stone Bdellium, painted in the colour of sulphur (m); and some were made of myrtles and roses, but in the war of Vespasian only those made of reeds were used (n); these crowns at weddings seem to be the "beautiful crowns" in Eze_23:42 where the Septuagint use the same phrase as here, στεφανον καυχησεως, "a crown of rejoicing", or "glorying": the Hebrew phrase עֲטֶרֶת תִּפְאָרֶת, may be rendered "a crown of glory", as the phrase here is by the Vulgate Latin and Arabic versions.

(i) Misna Sota. c. 9. sect. 14. (k) Maimon. in Misna Sota, & in Sabbat, c. 6. sect. 1. (l) Ez Hechaim M. S. apud Wagenseil in Sota ib. (m) Bartenora in Misna Sota, c. 9. sect. 14. (n) T. Bab. Sota, fol. 49. 2.

---

20. For ye are our glory and joy.

Greek/Transliteration
20. Ὑμεῖς γάρ ἐστε ἡ δόξα ἡμῶν καὶ ἡ χαρά.

20. 'Umeis gar este 'ei doxa 'eimon kai 'ei chara.

Hebrew/Transliteration
:כ. כִּי הֵן אַתֶּם כְּבוֹדֵנוּ וְשִׂמְחָתֵנוּ

20. Ki hen atem k`vo•de•noo ve•sim•cha•te•noo.

Rabbinic Jewish Commentary
For ye are our glory and joy. Or "our joy", as the Syriac, Arabic, and Ethiopic versions read.

1 Thessalonians, Chapter 3

1. Wherefore when we could no longer forbear, we thought it good to be left at Athens alone;

Greek/Transliteration
1. Διὸ μηκέτι στέγοντες, εὐδοκήσαμεν καταλειφθῆναι ἐν Ἀθήναις μόνοι,

1. Dio meiketi stegontes, eudokeisamen kataleiphtheinai en Atheinais monoi,

Hebrew/Transliteration
‏א. עַל־כֵּן כַּלְכֵּל לֹא יָכֹלְנוּ עוֹד וַנֵּאוֹת לְהִוָּתֵר בְּאַתִינַס לְבַדֵּנוּ:

1. Al - ken kal•kel lo ya•chol•noo od va•ne•ot le•hi•va•ter Be•Ati•nas le•va•de•noo.

Rabbinic Jewish Commentary
Wherefore when we could no longer forbear,.... Or "bear", as the word properly signifies; or "bear that", as the Ethiopic version reads; that is, "that desire", as the Arabic version renders it; that ardent and longing desire of seeing them again, expressed in the latter part of the preceding chapter; which was as fire in their bones, and was retained with great pain and uneasiness; but now they could hold it no longer, and like Jeremiah, Jer_20:9 were weary with forbearing, and could not stay; or it was like a burden, which they stood up under as long as they could, even Paul, Silas, and Timothy, but now it became insupportable.

---

2. And sent Timotheus, our brother, and minister of God, and our fellowlabourer in the gospel of Christ, to establish you, and to comfort you concerning your faith:

Greek/Transliteration
2. καὶ ἐπέμψαμεν Τιμόθεον τὸν ἀδελφὸν ἡμῶν καὶ διάκονον τοῦ θεοῦ καὶ συνεργὸν ἡμῶν ἐν τῷ εὐαγγελίῳ τοῦ χριστοῦ, εἰς τὸ στηρίξαι ὑμᾶς καὶ παρακαλέσαι ὑμᾶς περὶ τῆς πίστεως ὑμῶν,

2. kai epempsamen Timotheon ton adelphon 'eimon kai dyakonon tou theou kai sunergon 'eimon en to euangelio tou christou, eis to steirixai 'umas kai parakalesai 'umas peri teis pisteos 'umon,

Hebrew/Transliteration
‏ב. וְאֶת־אָחִינוּ טִימוֹתִיּוֹס מְשָׁרֵת־אֵל בִּבְשׂוֹרַת הַמָּשִׁיחַ שְׁלַחְנוּ לְחַזֵּק אֶת־לִבְּכֶם וּלְהַזְהִיר אֶתְכֶם בֶּאֱמוּנַתְכֶם:

2. Ve•et - achi•noo Ti•mo•ti•yos me•sha•ret - El biv•so•rat ha•Ma•shi•ach sha•lach•noo le•cha•zek et - lib•chem ool•haz•hir et•chem be•e•moo•nat•chem.

---

3. That no man should be moved by these afflictions: for yourselves know that we are appointed thereunto.

Greek/Transliteration
3. τὸ μηδένα σαίνεσθαι ἐν ταῖς θλίψεσιν ταύταις· αὐτοὶ γὰρ οἴδατε ὅτι εἰς τοῦτο κείμεθα.

3. to meidena sainesthai en tais thlipsesin tautais. autoi gar oidate 'oti eis touto keimetha.

Hebrew/Transliteration

ג: לְבִלְתִּי יָנוֹעַ לֵב-אִישׁ מִפְּנֵי הַצָּרוֹת הָאֵלֶּה הֲלֹא בְנַפְשְׁכֶם יְדַעְתָּם כִּי לְזֹאת יָעַדְנוּ

3. Le•vil•ti yi•noa lev - eesh mip•ney ha•tza•rot ha•e•le ha•lo ve•naf•she•chem ye•da•a•tem ki la•zot yoo•ad•noo.

---

4. For verily, when we were with you, we told you before that we should suffer tribulation; even as it came to pass, and ye know.

Greek/Transliteration

4. Καὶ γὰρ ὅτε πρὸς ὑμᾶς ἦμεν, προελέγομεν ὑμῖν ὅτι μέλλομεν θλίβεσθαι, καθὼς καὶ ἐγένετο καὶ οἴδατε.

4. Kai gar 'ote pros 'umas eimen, proelegomen 'umin 'oti mellomen thlibesthai, kathos kai egeneto kai oidate.

Hebrew/Transliteration

ד: כִּי גַם-הִגַּדְנוּ לָכֶם מֵאָז בִּהְיוֹתֵנוּ אֶצְלְכֶם כִּי-צָרָה תָבוֹא עָלֵינוּ וְכֵן גַּם-בָּאָה כַּאֲשֶׁר יְדַעְתֶּם

4. Ki gam - hi•gad•noo la•chem me•az bi•hi•yo•te•noo etz•le•chem ki - tza•ra ta•vo aley•noo ve•chen gam - ba•ah ka•a•sher ye•da•a•tem.

---

5. For this cause, when I could no longer forbear, I sent to know your faith, lest by some means the tempter have tempted you, and our labour be in vain.

Greek/Transliteration

5. Διὰ τοῦτο κἀγώ, μηκέτι στέγων, ἔπεμψα εἰς τὸ γνῶναι τὴν πίστιν ὑμῶν, μήπως ἐπείρασεν ὑμᾶς ὁ πειράζων, καὶ εἰς κενὸν γένηται ὁ κόπος ἡμῶν.

5. Dya touto kago, meiketi stegon, epempsa eis to gnonai tein pistin 'umon, meipos epeirasen 'umas 'o peirazon, kai eis kenon geneitai 'o kopos 'eimon.

Hebrew/Transliteration

ה- וְעַל-כֵּן גַּם אֲנִי נִלְאֵיתִי כַלְכֵּל וָאֶשְׁלַח לָדַעַת עַל-דְּבַר אֱמוּנַתְכֶם אִם לֹא נִסָּה הַמְנַסֶּה אֶתְכֶם לָתֵת אֶת-עֲמָלֵנוּ לָרִיק

5. Ve•al - ken gam ani nil•ey•ti kal•kel va•esh•lach la•da•at al - de•var emoo•nat•chem eem lo ni•sa ham•na•se et•chem la•tet et - ama•le•noo la•rik.

---

6. But now when Timotheus came from you unto us, and brought us good tidings of your faith and charity, and that ye have good remembrance of us always, desiring greatly to see us, as we also to see you:

Greek/Transliteration
6. Ἄρτι δὲ ἐλθόντος Τιμοθέου πρὸς ἡμᾶς ἀφ᾽ ὑμῶν, καὶ εὐαγγελισαμένου ἡμῖν τὴν πίστιν καὶ τὴν ἀγάπην ὑμῶν, καὶ ὅτι ἔχετε μνείαν ἡμῶν ἀγαθὴν πάντοτε, ἐπιποθοῦντες ἡμᾶς ἰδεῖν, καθάπερ καὶ ἡμεῖς ὑμᾶς·

6. Arti de elthontos Timotheou pros 'eimas aph 'umon, kai euangelisamenou 'eimin tein pistin kai tein agapein 'umon, kai 'oti echete mneian 'eimon agathein pantote, epipothountes 'eimas idein, kathaper kai 'eimeis 'umas.

Hebrew/Transliteration
ו. וְעַתָּה כַּאֲשֶׁר שָׁב אֵלֵינוּ טִימוֹתִיּוֹס מִכֶּם וַיְבַשְּׂרֵנוּ עַל-דְּבַר אֱמוּנַתְכֶם וְאַהֲבַתְכֶם כִּי זְכַרְתֶּם אֹתָנוּ לְטוֹבָה בְּכָל-עֵת וְכִי תִתְאַוּוּ לִרְאוֹת אֶת-פָּנֵינוּ כַּאֲשֶׁר גַּם-אֲנַחְנוּ מִתְאַוִּים לִרְאוֹת אֶת-פְּנֵיכֶם:

6. Ve•a•ta ka•a•sher shav e•ley•noo Ti•mo•ti•yos mi•kem vay•vas•re•noo al - de•var emoo•nat•chem ve•a•ha•vat•chem ki ze•char•tem o•ta•noo le•to•va be•chol - et ve•chi tit•a•voo lir•ot et - pa•ney•noo ka•a•sher gam - a•nach•noo mit•a•vim lir•ot et - p`ney•chem.

---

7. Therefore, brethren, we were comforted over you in all our affliction and distress by your faith:

Greek/Transliteration
7. διὰ τοῦτο παρεκλήθημεν, ἀδελφοί, ἐφ᾽ ὑμῖν ἐπὶ πάσῃ τῇ θλίψει καὶ ἀνάγκῃ ἡμῶν διὰ τῆς ὑμῶν πίστεως·

7. dya touto parekleitheimen, adelphoi, eph 'umin epi pasei tei thlipsei kai anagkei 'eimon dya teis 'umon pisteos.

Hebrew/Transliteration
ז. לָזֹאת אֵפוֹא אַחַי בְּכָל-צָרוֹת וְרָעוֹת מָצָאנוּ תַנְחוּמִים בָּכֶם בִּגְלַל אֱמוּנַתְכֶם:

7. Le•zot e•fo e•chai be•chol - tza•rot ve•ra•ot ma•tza•noo tan•choo•mim ba•chem big•lal emoo•nat•chem.

Rabbinic Jewish Commentary
Therefore, brethren, we were comforted over, you,..... Or "in you", as the Vulgate Latin version; or "from you", as the Arabic; or "by you", as the Syriac; or "for you", as the Ethiopic; that is, on account of them, either by what they had heard was in them, or had heard from them.

by your faith: by the report of it, that it grew exceedingly, and that they walked in the truth; 1Jo_5:4. The Alexandrian copy reads, "in all your distress and affliction, and by your faith.".

---

8. For now we live, if ye stand fast in the Lord.

Greek/Transliteration
8. ὅτι νῦν ζῶμεν, ἐὰν ὑμεῖς στήκετε ἐν κυρίῳ.

8. 'oti nun zomen, ean 'umeis steikete en kurio.

Hebrew/Transliteration
ח. כִּי חַיִּים אֲנַחְנוּ הַיּוֹם אִם רַק עֹמְדִים אַתֶּם הָכֵן לִפְנֵי אֲדֹנֵינוּ:

8. Ki cha•yim a•nach•noo ha•yom eem rak om•dim atem ha•chen lif•ney Ado•ney•noo.

Rabbinic Jewish Commentary
if ye stand fast in the Lord: or "our Lord", as the Syriac and Ethiopic versions read; that is, "in the faith of the Lord", as the Arabic version renders it.

---

9. For what thanks can we render to God again for you, for all the joy wherewith we joy for your sakes before our God;

Greek/Transliteration
9. Τίνα γὰρ εὐχαριστίαν δυνάμεθα τῷ θεῷ ἀνταποδοῦναι περὶ ὑμῶν, ἐπὶ πάσῃ τῇ χαρᾷ ᾗ χαίρομεν δι᾽ ὑμᾶς ἔμπροσθεν τοῦ θεοῦ ἡμῶν,

9. Tina gar eucharistian dunametha to theo antapodounai peri 'umon, epi pasei tei chara chairomen di 'umas emprosthen tou theou 'eimon,

Hebrew/Transliteration
ט. כִּי בַמֶּה-בּוֹדָה מַה-נָּשִׁיב לֵאלֹהִים בַּעֲבוּרְכֶם עַל כָּל-הַשִּׂמְחָה אֲשֶׁר שָׂמַחְנוּ עֲלֵיכֶם לִפְנֵי אֱלֹהֵינוּ:

9. Ki va•me - no•de ma - na•shiv le•Elohim ba•a•voor•chem al kol - ha•sim•cha asher sa•mach•noo aley•chem lif•ney Elohey•noo.

---

10. Night and day praying exceedingly that we might see your face, and might perfect that which is lacking in your faith?

Greek/Transliteration
10. νυκτὸς καὶ ἡμέρας ὑπὲρ ἐκπερισσοῦ δεόμενοι εἰς τὸ ἰδεῖν ὑμῶν τὸ πρόσωπον, καὶ καταρτίσαι τὰ ὑστερήματα τῆς πίστεως ὑμῶν;

10. nuktos kai 'eimeras 'uper ekperissou deomenoi eis to idein 'umon to prosopon, kai katartisai ta 'ustereimata teis pisteos 'umon?

Hebrew/Transliteration
י. לַיְלָה וְיוֹמָם נַעְתִּיר וְנִתְפַּלֵּל כִּי יִנָּתֶן לָנוּ לִרְאוֹת אֶת-פְּנֵיכֶם וּלְהַשְׁלִים אֵת אֲשֶׁר-לָכֶם בֶּאֱמוּנַתְכֶם:

10. Lai•la ve•yo•mam na•a•tir ve•nit•pa•lel ki yi•na•ten la•noo lir•ot et - p`ney•chem ool•hash•lim et asher - la•chem be•e•moo•nat•chem?

Rabbinic Jewish Commentary
Though these saints had deficiencies in their faith, yet they were not what the Jews call (o) מחוסרי אמנה, "such as are deficient in faith", or want faith entirely, a phrase somewhat like this which is here used.

(o) Maimon. Hilch. Mechira, c. 7. sect. 8, 9.

11. Now God himself and our Father, and our Lord Jesus Christ, direct our way unto you.

Greek/Transliteration
11. Αὐτὸς δὲ ὁ θεὸς καὶ πατὴρ ἡμῶν, καὶ ὁ κύριος ἡμῶν Ἰησοῦς χριστός, κατευθύναι τὴν ὁδὸν ἡμῶν πρὸς ὑμᾶς·

11. Autos de 'o theos kai pateir 'eimon, kai 'o kurios 'eimon Yeisous christos, kateuthunai tein 'odon 'eimon pros 'umas.

Hebrew/Transliteration
יא. וֵאלֹהֵינוּ אָבִינוּ וְיֵשׁוּעַ הַמָּשִׁיחַ אֲדֹנֵינוּ יְיַשֵּׁר אֶת-דַּרְכֵּנוּ אֲלֵיכֶם:

11. Ve•Elohey•noo Avi•noo ve•Yeshua ha•Ma•shi•ach Ado•ney•noo ye•ya•sher et - dar•ke•noo aley•chem.

---

12. And the Lord make you to increase and abound in love one toward another, and toward all men, even as we do toward you:

Greek/Transliteration
12. ὑμᾶς δὲ ὁ κύριος πλεονάσαι καὶ περισσεύσαι τῇ ἀγάπῃ εἰς ἀλλήλους καὶ εἰς πάντας, καθάπερ καὶ ἡμεῖς εἰς ὑμᾶς,

12. 'umas de 'o kurios pleonasai kai perisseusai tei agapei eis alleilous kai eis pantas, kathaper kai 'eimeis eis 'umas,

Hebrew/Transliteration
יב. וְאֶתְכֶם יַרְבֶּה וְכֵן יִתֵּן לָכֶם אֲדֹנֵינוּ לְהוֹסִיף בְּאַהֲבַת אִישׁ לְרֵעֵהוּ וּבְאַהֲבַת כָּל-אָדָם כַּאֲשֶׁר גַּם-אֲנַחְנוּ נוֹסִיף לְאַהֲבָה אֶתְכֶם:

12. Ve•et•chem yar•be ve•chen yi•ten la•chem Ado•ney•noo le•ho•sif be•a•ha•vat eesh le•re•e•hoo oov•a•ha•vat kol - adam ka•a•sher gam - a•nach•noo no•sif le•a•ha•va et•chem.

---

13. To the end he may stablish your hearts unblameable in holiness before God, even our Father, at the coming of our Lord Jesus Christ with all his saints.

Greek/Transliteration
13. εἰς τὸ στηρίξαι ὑμῶν τὰς καρδίας ἀμέμπτους ἐν ἁγιωσύνῃ, ἔμπροσθεν τοῦ θεοῦ καὶ πατρὸς ἡμῶν, ἐν τῇ παρουσίᾳ τοῦ κυρίου ἡμῶν Ἰησοῦ χριστοῦ μετὰ πάντων τῶν ἁγίων αὐτοῦ.

13. eis to steirixai 'umon tas kardias amemptous en 'agiosunei, emprosthen tou theou kai patros 'eimon, en tei parousia tou kuriou 'eimon Yeisou christou meta panton ton 'agion autou.

Hebrew/Transliteration
יג. וְכֵן יְכוֹנֵן אֶת-לִבְּכֶם בַּקֹּדֶשׁ וְלֹא יִמָּצֵא בָכֶם שֶׁמֶץ דָּבָר לִפְנֵי אֱלֹהֵינוּ אָבִינוּ בְּיוֹם בּוֹא יֵשׁוּעַ הַמָּשִׁיחַ אֲדֹנֵינוּ עִם-כָּל-קְדֹשָׁיו:

13. Ve•chen ye•cho•nen et - lib•chem ba•ko•desh ve•lo yi•ma•tze va•chem she•metz da•var lif•ney Elohey•noo Avi•noo be•yom bo Yeshua ha•Ma•shi•ach Ado•ney•noo eem - kol - ke•do•shav.

Rabbinic Jewish Commentary
The apostle prays, that they might be "unblamable in holiness", the Alexandrian copy reads, "in righteousness" so one of Stephens's.

with all his saints; The Vulgate Latin, Arabic, and Ethiopic versions add, "Amen"; and so does Beza's ancient copy, and the Alexandrian manuscript.

1 Thessalonians, Chapter 4

1. Furthermore then we beseech you, brethren, and exhort you by the Lord Jesus, that as ye have received of us how ye ought to walk and to please God, so ye would abound more and more.

Greek/Transliteration
1. Λοιπὸν οὖν, ἀδελφοί, ἐρωτῶμεν ὑμᾶς καὶ παρακαλοῦμεν ἐν κυρίῳ Ἰησοῦ καθὼς παρελάβετε παρ᾽ ἡμῶν τὸ πῶς δεῖ ὑμᾶς περιπατεῖν καὶ ἀρέσκειν θεῷ, ἵνα περισσεύητε μᾶλλον.

1. Loipon oun, adelphoi, erotomen 'umas kai parakaloumen en kurio Yeisou kathos parelabete par 'eimon to pos dei 'umas peripatein kai areskein theo, 'ina perisseueite mallon.

Hebrew/Transliteration
א. סוֹף דָּבָר אַחַי נִדְרֹשׁ מִכֶּם וְנַזְהִיר אֶתְכֶם בְּשֵׁם יֵשׁוּעַ אֲדֹנֵינוּ כַּאֲשֶׁר קִבַּלְתֶּם מִפִּינוּ לְהִתְהַלֵּךְ בְּמֵישָׁרִים וְלִמְצֹא חֵן בְּעֵינֵי אֱלֹהִים וְכַאֲשֶׁר גַּם-אַתֶּם הֹלְכִים כֵּן תַּעֲשׂוּ וְכֵן תּוֹסִיפוּ:

1. Sof da•var a•chai nid•rosh mi•kem ve•naz•hir et•chem be•shem Yeshua Ado•ney•noo ka•a•sher ki•bal•tem mi•pi•noo le•hit•ha•lech be•mey•sha•rim ve•lim•tzo chen be•ei•ney Elohim ve•cha•a•sher gam - atem hol•chim ken ta•a•soo ve•chen to•si•foo.

Rabbinic Jewish Commentary
so ye would abound more and more: Beza's ancient copy, and another manuscript, as also the Alexandrian copy, and some others, add between the preceding, and this last clause, "as ye also walk"; and so the Vulgate Latin and Ethiopic versions seem to have read; commending them for their present and past walk and conversation, in order to persuade and encourage them to go forward.

---

2. For ye know what commandments we gave you by the Lord Jesus.

Greek/Transliteration
2. Οἴδατε γὰρ τίνας παραγγελίας ἐδώκαμεν ὑμῖν διὰ τοῦ κυρίου Ἰησοῦ.

2. Oidate gar tinas parangelias edokamen 'umin dya tou kuriou Yeisou.

Hebrew/Transliteration
ב. כִּי יְדַעְתֶּם אֶת-הַמִּצְוֹת אֲשֶׁר נָתַנּוּ לָכֶם בְּשֵׁם יֵשׁוּעַ אֲדֹנֵינוּ:

2. Ki ye•da•a•tem et - ha•mitz•vot asher na•ta•noo la•chem be•shem Yeshua Ado•ney•noo.

---

3. For this is the will of God, even your sanctification, that ye should abstain from fornication:

Greek/Transliteration
3. Τοῦτο γάρ ἐστιν θέλημα τοῦ θεοῦ, ὁ ἁγιασμὸς ὑμῶν, ἀπέχεσθαι ὑμᾶς ἀπὸ τῆς πορνείας·

3. Touto gar estin theleima tou theou, 'o 'agyasmos 'umon, apechesthai 'umas apo teis porneias.

Hebrew/Transliteration
:ג. כִּי זֶה רְצוֹן אֱלֹהִים כִּי קְדֹשִׁים תִּהְיוּ וְתִנָּזְרוּ מִן-הַזְּנוּת

3. Ki ze r`tzon Elohim ki k`do•shim ti•hi•yoo ve•ti•naz•roo min - haz•noot.

Rabbinic Jewish Commentary
The Syriac version renders it, "from all fornication"; on this subject the apostle enlarges in some following verses.

---

4. That every one of you should know how to possess his vessel in sanctification and honour;

Greek/Transliteration
4. εἰδέναι ἕκαστον ὑμῶν τὸ ἑαυτοῦ σκεῦος κτᾶσθαι ἐν ἁγιασμῷ καὶ τιμῇ,

4. eidenai 'ekaston 'umon to 'eautou skeuos ktasthai en 'agyasmo kai timei,

Hebrew/Transliteration
:ד. וְכָל-אִישׁ מִכֶּם יָבִין לִשְׁמֹר כֵּלָיו בְּקֹדֶשׁ וּבְכָבוֹד

4. Ve•chol - eesh mi•kem ya•vin lish•mor kil•yo be•ko•desh oov•cha•vod.

Rabbinic Jewish Commentary
By which may be meant, either a man's wife, or his body, and it is not very easy to determine which, for the Jews call both by this name. Sometimes they call (p) a woman גולם, which the gloss says is a "vessel" unfinished. It is reported (q), that when R. Eleazar died, Rabbenu Hakkadosh would have married his widow, and she would not, because she was כלי של קדושה, "a vessel of holiness", greater than he. Moreover, it is said (r), that

"He that forces (a young woman) must drink בעציצו, "in his own vessel" how drink in his own vessel? though she be lame, though she be blind, and though she is stricken with ulcers."

The commentators (s) on the passage add,

"In the vessel which he has chosen; that is to say, whether he will or not, he must marry her;"

See Pro_5:15. And again, they sometimes call a man's wife his tent: hence that saying (t),

"There is no tent but his wife", as it is said, Deu_5:30, go, say to them, get you into your tents again."

The Jews, in agreement with the apostle, called (u), מקדש עצמו, "a man's sanctifying himself", and is chaste, and honourable. And it may be observed, that the Jews use the same phrase concerning conjugal embraces as the apostle does here. One of their canons runs thus (w):

"Though a man's wife is free for him at all times, it is fit and proper for a disciple of a wise man to use himself בקדושה, "in", or "to sanctification".

The body is indeed called a "vessel"; see 2Co_4:7, because in it the soul is contained, and the soul makes use of it, and its members, as instruments, for the performance of various actions; and, with Jewish writers, we read of כלי גופו, "the vessel of his body" (x); so then, for a man to possess his vessel in sanctification and honour, is to keep under his body and bring it into subjection, and preserve it in purity and chastity.

(p) T. Bab. Sanhedrin, fol 22. 2. (q) Juchasin, fol. 48. 2. Shalsheleth Hakkabala, fol. 23. 1. (r) Misna Cetubot, c. 3. sect. 4, 5. (s) Jarchi & Bartenora in ib. (t) T. Bab. Moed Katon, fol. 7. 2. & 15. 2. (u) Maimon. in Misn. Sanhedrin, c. 7. sect. 4. (w) Maimon. Hilch Deyot, c. 5. sect. 4. (x) Caphtor, fol. 57. 2.

---

5. Not in the lust of concupiscence, even as the Gentiles which know not God:

Greek/Transliteration
5. μὴ ἐν πάθει ἐπιθυμίας, καθάπερ καὶ τὰ ἔθνη τὰ μὴ εἰδότα τὸν θεόν·

5. mei en pathei epithumias, kathaper kai ta ethnei ta mei eidota ton theon.

Hebrew/Transliteration
ה. לֹא-בְתַאֲוָה וַעֲגָבִים כְּדֶרֶךְ הַגּוֹיִם אֲשֶׁר לֹא יָדְעוּ אֶת-הָאֱלֹהִים:

5. Lo - ve•ta•a•va va•a•ga•vim ke•de•rech ha•go•yim asher lo yad•oo et - ha•Elohim.

---

6. That no man go beyond and defraud his brother in any matter: because that the Lord is the avenger of all such, as we also have forewarned you and testified.

Greek/Transliteration
6. τὸ μὴ ὑπερβαίνειν καὶ πλεονεκτεῖν ἐν τῷ πράγματι τὸν ἀδελφὸν αὐτοῦ· διότι ἔκδικος ὁ κύριος περὶ πάντων τούτων, καθὼς καὶ προείπομεν ὑμῖν καὶ διεμαρτυράμεθα.

6. to mei 'uperbainein kai pleonektein en to pragmati ton adelphon autou. dioti ekdikos 'o kurios peri panton touton, kathos kai proeipomen 'umin kai diemarturametha.

Hebrew/Transliteration
ו. וְלֹא-יַפְרִיץ אִישׁ אֶת-אָחִיו וְלֹא יוֹנֶנּוּ בַּדָּבָר הַזֶּה כִּי נֹקֵם יְהֹוָה עַל-כָּל-אֵלֶּה כַּאֲשֶׁר הִגַּדְנוּ וְהַעִידֹנוּ בָכֶם מֵאָז:

6. Ve•lo - yif•rotz eesh et - a•chiv ve•lo yo•ne•noo ba•da•var ha•ze ki no•kem Adonai al - kol - ele ka•a•sher hi•gad•noo ve•ha•ee•do•noo va•chem me•az.

Rabbinic Jewish Commentary
The matter, or business referred to, is not trade, but the subject of chastity or uncleanness the apostle is speaking of, both before and after; and the phrases used either design the act of adultery, coveting a brother's wife, and lying with her, and so a defrauding and wronging of him by defiling his bed; or rather sodomitical practices, an unnatural lust and desire in men after men, and copulation with them; for υπερβαινειν, rendered, "go beyond", answers

to בא על, "to go upon", or "lie with", so often used in Jewish writings for lying with women, men, and beasts, in an unlawful way. Thus, for instance (y),

"These are to be burned, הבא על אשה, "he that lies with a woman", and her daughter."

And again (z),

"These are to be beaten, הבא על, "he that lies with" his sister, or his father's sister."

And the word πλεονεκτειν, translated "defraud", signifies a greedy, insatiable, and unnatural lust and desire after a man, a brother, or the committing of sodomitical practices with greediness.

because that the Lord is the avenger of all such; or "with respect to all these things", as the Vulgate Latin and Syriac versions render it; or "for all these things", as the Arabic and Ethiopic versions; as fornication, adultery, lasciviousness, and all sorts of abominable uncleanness.

(y) Misna Sanhedrim, c. 9. sect. 1. (z) Misna Maccot, c. 3. sect. 1.

---

7. For God hath not called us unto uncleanness, but unto holiness.

Greek/Transliteration
7. Οὐ γὰρ ἐκάλεσεν ἡμᾶς ὁ θεὸς ἐπὶ ἀκαθαρσίᾳ, ἀλλ᾽ ἐν ἁγιασμῷ.

7. Ou gar ekalesen 'eimas 'o theos epi akatharsia, all en 'agyasmo.

Hebrew/Transliteration
ז: כִּי לֹא-לְתוֹעֵבָה קָרָא אֹתָנוּ אֱלֹהֵינוּ כִּי אִם-לְדֶרֶךְ הַקֹּדֶשׁ.

7. Ki lo - le•to•e•va ka•ra o•ta•noo Elohey•noo ki eem - le•de•rech ha•ko•desh.

Rabbinic Jewish Commentary
For God hath not called us,.... The Syriac version reads "you".

---

8. He therefore that despiseth, despiseth not man, but God, who hath also given unto us his holy Spirit.

Greek/Transliteration
8. Τοιγαροῦν ὁ ἀθετῶν οὐκ ἄνθρωπον ἀθετεῖ, ἀλλὰ τὸν θεὸν τὸν καὶ δόντα τὸ πνεῦμα αὐτοῦ τὸ ἅγιον εἰς ὑμᾶς.

8. Toigaroun 'o atheton ouk anthropon athetei, alla ton theon ton kai donta to pneuma autou to 'agion eis 'umas.

Hebrew/Transliteration
ח: וְעַל-כֵּן הַבֹּזֶה לֹא אֶת-אָדָם הוּא בֹזֶה כִּי אִם-אֶת-אֱלֹהִים אֲשֶׁר נָתַן לָכֶם רוּחַ קָדְשׁוֹ.

8. Ve•al - ken ha•bo•ze lo et - adam hoo vo•ze ki eem - et - Elohim asher na•tan la•chem Roo•ach Kod•sho.

Rabbinic Jewish Commentary
The Syriac and Arabic versions read, "who hath given unto you his Holy Spirit"; and so all Stephens's copies; which furnishes out a fresh reason or argument, dissuading from uncleanness, since God had given them his "Spirit" to convince them of sin, of righteousness, and of judgment, so that they were not ignorant of the things warned against; and he had given them his Spirit as an "holy" Spirit, as a Spirit of sanctification.

---

9. But as touching brotherly love ye need not that I write unto you: for ye yourselves are taught of God to love one another.

Greek/Transliteration
9. Περὶ δὲ τῆς φιλαδελφίας οὐ χρείαν ἔχετε γράφειν ὑμῖν· αὐτοὶ γὰρ ὑμεῖς θεοδίδακτοί ἐστε εἰς τὸ ἀγαπᾶν ἀλλήλους·

9. Peri de teis philadelphias ou chreian echete graphein 'umin. autoi gar 'umeis theodidaktoi este eis to agapan alleilous.

Hebrew/Transliteration
ט. וְעַל־דְּבַר אַהֲבַת אַחִים אֵין־לָנוּ לִכְתֹּב דָּבָר אֲלֵיכֶם כִּי הֵלָּא אַתֶּם לִמּוּדֵי אֱלֹהִים לְאַהֲבָה אִישׁ אֶת־אָחִיו:

9. Ve•al - de•var a•ha•vat a•chim eyn - la•noo lich•tov da•var aley•chem ki ha•lo atem li•moo•dey Elohim le•a•ha•va eesh et - a•chiv.

Rabbinic Jewish Commentary
ye need not that I write unto you. The Vulgate Latin version reads, "we have no need to write unto you"; and so some copies.

---

10. And indeed ye do it toward all the brethren which are in all Macedonia: but we beseech you, brethren, that ye increase more and more;

Greek/Transliteration
10. καὶ γὰρ ποιεῖτε αὐτὸ εἰς πάντας τοὺς ἀδελφοὺς τοὺς ἐν ὅλῃ τῇ Μακεδονίᾳ. Παρακαλοῦμεν δὲ ὑμᾶς, ἀδελφοί, περισσεύειν μᾶλλον,

10. kai gar poieite auto eis pantas tous adelphous tous en 'olei tei Makedonia. Parakaloumen de 'umas, adelphoi, perisseuein mallon,

Hebrew/Transliteration
י. וְכֵן גַּם־עֲשִׂיתֶם לְכָל־אֲחֵיכֶם אֲשֶׁר בְּמַקְדּוֹנְיָא כֻּלָּהּ רַק־נִתְחַנֵּן אֲלֵיכֶם אַחַי כִּי כֵן תַּעֲשׂוּ וְכֵן תּוֹסִיפוּ:

10. Ve•chen gam - asi•tem le•chol - a•chey•chem asher be•Mak•don•ya choo•la rak - nit•cha•nen aley•chem a•chai ki chen ta•a•soo ve•chen to•si•foo.

Rabbinic Jewish Commentary
but we beseech you, brethren. The Alexandrian copy reads, "beloved brethren"; and the Syriac version, "I beseech you, my brethren: that ye increase more and more"; in showing love to the brethren.

11. And that ye study to be quiet, and to do your own business, and to work with your own hands, as we commanded you;

Greek/Transliteration
11. καὶ φιλοτιμεῖσθαι ἡσυχάζειν, καὶ πράσσειν τὰ ἴδια, καὶ ἐργάζεσθαι ταῖς ἰδίαις χερσὶν ὑμῶν, καθὼς ὑμῖν παρηγγείλαμεν·

11. kai philotimeisthai 'eisuchazein, kai prassein ta idya, kai ergazesthai tais idiais chersin 'umon, kathos 'umin pareingeilamen.

Hebrew/Transliteration
:יא. וְתִתְאַמְּצוּ לָשֶׁבֶת בְּהַשְׁקֵט לַעֲשׂוֹת אִישׁ אֶת-מְלַאכְתּוֹ וְלִחְיוֹת עַל-יְגִיעַ כַּפָּיו כַּאֲשֶׁר צִוִּינוּ אֶתְכֶם

11. Ve•tit•am•tzoo la•she•vet be•hash•ket la•a•sot eesh et - me•lach•to ve•lich•yot al - ye•gi•a ka•pav ka•a•sher tzi•vi•noo et•chem.

Rabbinic Jewish Commentary
The Jews call ארץ דרך, "the way of the earth", or the business of life:

"There are four things, (they say (a)) in which a man should employ himself continually, with all his might, and these are they, the Torah, and good works, and prayer, and the business of life;"

Upon which the gloss has this note by way of explanation,

"If a man is an artificer (let him attend) to his art; if a merchant to his merchandise, and if he is a soldier to war;"

And which may serve to illustrate the apostle's sense

(a) T. Bab. Beracot, fol. 32. 2.

---

12. That ye may walk honestly toward them that are without, and that ye may have lack of nothing.

Greek/Transliteration
12. ἵνα περιπατῆτε εὐσχημόνως πρὸς τοὺς ἔξω, καὶ μηδενὸς χρείαν ἔχητε.

12. 'ina peripateite euscheimonos pros tous exo, kai meidenos chreian echeite.

Hebrew/Transliteration
:יב. וּבְכֵן תִּתְהַלְּכוּ בְמִישׁוֹר אֶת-אֵלֶּה אֲשֶׁר מִחוּץ לַעֲדָתֵנוּ וְלֹא יֶחְסַר לָכֶם כָּל-דָּבָר

12. Oov•chen tit•hal•choo ve•mi•shor et - ele asher mi•choo•tz la•a•da•te•noo ve•lo yech•sar la•chem kol - da•var.

---

13. But I would not have you to be ignorant, brethren, concerning them which are asleep, that ye sorrow not, even as others which have no hope.

Greek/Transliteration
13. Οὐ θέλομεν δὲ ὑμᾶς ἀγνοεῖν, ἀδελφοί, περὶ τῶν κεκοιμημένων, ἵνα μὴ λυπῆσθε, καθὼς καὶ οἱ λοιποὶ οἱ μὴ ἔχοντες ἐλπίδα.

13. Ou thelomen de 'umas agnoein, adelphoi, peri ton kekoimeimenon, 'ina mei lupeisthe, kathos kai 'oi loipoi 'oi mei echontes elpida.

Hebrew/Transliteration
יג׃ וְעַל־דְּבַר יְשֵׁנֵי עָפָר חֲפַצְנוּ כִּי תֵדְעוּן כִּי לֹא לָכֶם לְהִתְאַבֵּל כָּאֲנָשִׁים אֲשֶׁר אֵין־לָהֶם תִּקְוָה

13. Ve•al - de•var ye•she•ney afar cha•fatz•noo ki ted•oon ki lo la•chem le•hit•a•bel ka•a•na•shim asher eyn - la•hem tik•va.

Rabbinic Jewish Commentary
The Alexandrian copy and others, the Complutensian edition, the Vulgate Latin, Arabic, and Ethiopic versions read, "we would not have you to be ignorant"

This way of speaking is used frequently both in the Old and the New Testament; see 1Ki_2:10 1Co_15:20 and very often with the Targumists; so the Targum on Ecc_3:4 "a time to weep", paraphrases it,

"A time to weep על שכיבא, "over them that are asleep":"

and in Ecc_4:2.

"I praised ית שכיבא, "those that are asleep".

It is observed by the Jews (b) on those words in Gen_23:2 and "Abraham came to mourn for Sarah" that

"It is not said to weep for Sarah, but to mourn for her; "for such a woman as this, it is not fit to weep", after her soul is joined in the bundle of life, but to mourn for her, and do her great honour at her funeral; though because it is not possible that a man should not weep for his dead, it is said at the end, "and to weep for her":"

But here the words are to be understood of the other Gentiles that were in a state of nature and unregeneracy, who had no knowledge of the resurrection of the dead, or and hope of a future state, and of enjoying their friends in it: they are called οι λοιποι, "the rest"; and the Syriac version renders it, "other men".

(b) Tzeror Hamnaor, fol. 23. 4.

---

14. For if we believe that Jesus died and rose again, even so them also which sleep in Jesus will God bring with him.

Greek/Transliteration
14. Εἰ γὰρ πιστεύομεν ὅτι Ἰησοῦς ἀπέθανεν καὶ ἀνέστη, οὕτως καὶ ὁ θεὸς τοὺς κοιμηθέντας διὰ τοῦ Ἰησοῦ ἄξει σὺν αὐτῷ.

14. Ei gar pisteuomen 'oti Yeisous apethanen kai anestei, 'outos kai 'o theos tous koimeithentas dya tou Yeisou axei sun auto.

Hebrew/Transliteration
יד. כִּי כַאֲשֶׁר נַאֲמִין כִּי יֵשׁוּעַ מֵת וַיְחִי כֵן גַּם-אֶת-הַיְשֵׁנִים עַל-יְדֵי יֵשׁוּעַ יָקִים אֱלֹהִים לְפָנָיו:

14. Ki cha•a•sher na•a•min ki Yeshua met va•ye•chi ken gam - et - hay•she•nim al - ye•dey Yeshua ya•kim Elohim le•fa•nav.

Rabbinic Jewish Commentary
The saints that are dead are not only represented as asleep, as before, but as "asleep in Yeshua"; to distinguish them from the other dead, the wicked; for the phrase of sleeping in death is promiscuously used of good and bad, though most commonly applied to good men: and so say the Jews (c),

"We used to speak of just men, not as dead, but as sleeping; saying, afterwards such an one fell asleep, signifying that the death of the righteous is nothing else than a sleep."

(c) Shebet Juda, p. 294. Ed. Gent.

---

15. For this we say unto you by the word of the Lord, that we which are alive and remain unto the coming of the Lord shall not prevent them which are asleep.

Greek/Transliteration
15. Τοῦτο γὰρ ὑμῖν λέγομεν ἐν λόγῳ κυρίου, ὅτι ἡμεῖς οἱ ζῶντες οἱ περιλειπόμενοι εἰς τὴν παρουσίαν τοῦ κυρίου, οὐ μὴ φθάσωμεν τοὺς κοιμηθέντας.

15. Touto gar 'umin legomen en logo kuriou, 'oti 'eimeis 'oi zontes 'oi perileipomenoi eis tein parousian tou kuriou, ou mei phthasomen tous koimeithentas.

Hebrew/Transliteration
טו. כִּי כָזֹאת אָנוּ אֹמְרִים לָכֶם בִּדְבַר יְהֹוָה כִּי אֲנַחְנוּ הַנִּשְׁאָרִים פֹּה בַחַיִּים לְמוֹעֵד בּוֹא אֲדֹנֵינוּ לֹא נְקַדֵּם אֶת-הַיְשֵׁנִים:

15. Ki cha•zot a•noo om•rim la•chem bid•var Adonai ki a•nach•noo ha•nish•a•rim po va•cha•yim le•mo•ed bo Ado•ney•noo lo n`ka•dem et - hay•she•nim.

---

16. For the Lord himself shall descend from heaven with a shout, with the voice of the archangel, and with the trump of God: and the dead in Christ shall rise first:

Greek/Transliteration
16. Ὅτι αὐτὸς ὁ κύριος ἐν κελεύσματι, ἐν φωνῇ ἀρχαγγέλου, καὶ ἐν σάλπιγγι θεοῦ, καταβήσεται ἀπ᾽ οὐρανοῦ, καὶ οἱ νεκροὶ ἐν χριστῷ ἀναστήσονται πρῶτον·

16. 'Oti autos 'o kurios en keleusmati, en phonei archangelou, kai en salpingi theou, katabeisetai ap ouranou, kai 'oi nekroi en christo anasteisontai proton.

Hebrew/Transliteration
טז. כִּי בִתְרוּעָה יֵרֵד אֲדֹנֵינוּ מִן-הַשָּׁמַיִם בְּקוֹל שׁוֹפָר אֱלֹהִים מִפִּי שַׂר-צְבָא הַמָּרוֹם וְהַמֵּתִים בַּמָּשִׁיחַ יָקוּמוּ אָז רִאשׁוֹנָה:

16. Ki vit•roo•ah ye•red Ado•ney•noo min - ha•sha•ma•yim be•kol sho•far Elohim mi•pi sar - tz`va ha•ma•rom ve•ha•me•tim ba•Ma•shi•ach ya•koo•moo az ri•sho•na.

Rabbinic Jewish Commentary

with a shout; The Vulgate Latin, Syriac, and Ethiopic versions render it, "in", or "with command"; and the Arabic version, "with his own government", or "authority"; that is, he shall descend, either by the command of his Father, as man and Mediator, having authority from him, as the son of man, to execute judgment; or with his commanding power and authority over the mighty messengers, that shall descend with him.

with the voice of the archangel; The Syriac version renders it, "the head", or "prince of messengers"; and which whether, it will be an articulate voice, such as was expressed at the grave of Lazarus; or a violent clap of thunder, which is the voice of God; or the exertion of the power of Messiah Yeshua, is not certain.

and with the trump of God; This is said in allusion to the trumpet which was heard on Mount Sinai at the giving of the Torah, and of which the Jews say (d), that it מאחא מיתיא, "quickened the dead"; for they have a notion, that, when the Israelites first heard the voice of the YHWH, they died; but upon hearing it the second time, they returned to life (e): and they suppose also in the time, to come, at the resurrection of the dead, a trumpet will be blown, which will quicken the dead (f), and the day of judgment (g); and this is reckoned by them as one of the signs of the Messiah's coming (h).

"Michael shall shout with a great shout, and the graves of the dead shall be opened at Jerusalem, and the holy blessed God will restore the dead to life, and Messiah the son of David shall come,".

And the dead in Christ shall rise first; this agrees with the notions of the Jews, who thought that some will rise before others;

"Wheresoever thou findest the dead, take them and bury them, and I will give thee the first place in my resurrection." (2 Esdras 2:23)

Having mentioned those words in Psa_116:9 "I will walk before the Lord in the land of the living", it is asked (i),

"Is there no land of the living but Tyre and its neighbours, and Caesarea, and its neighbours, where is cheapness and fulness? says R. Simeon ben Lekish, in the name of Bar Kaphra, the land in which the dead live, תחילה, "first", in the days of the Messiah:"

And on the same place elsewhere (k) they observe, that

"Our Rabbis say two things, or give two reasons, why the fathers loved to be buried in the land of Israel, because the dead in the land of Israel חיים תחילה, "live", or "rise first", in the days of the Messiah, and shall enjoy the years of the Messiah:"

And in another place (l) they take notice of what is written in Isa_26:19 "and the earth shall cast out the dead": says R. Jochanan,

"The dead which are in the land (i.e. of Israel), they shall "live first"; as it is said, "thy dead men shall live, together with my dead body shall they arise": these are they that are without the land; "awake and sing ye that dwell in the dust", these are they that die in the wilderness:"

And again (m), "as it is said,

Isa 40:26 "that bringeth out their host by numbers", come see, it is said, all that die in the land of Israel יקומון בקדמיתא, "shall rise first", because the holy blessed God shall awake them, and raise them, according to Isa_26:19."

Once more they say (n),

"They that study in the law as they ought, these are they that shall "rise first" to everlasting life, as it is said Dan_12:2, "and many of them that sleep in the dust of the earth shall awake, some to everlasting life" and these are for everlasting life, because they study in everlasting life, which is the law:"

To which may be added the following passage (o),

"They that are worthy to be buried in the land of Israel, shall "be raised first"--and they shall be raised and quickened before the rest of the children of the world, who draw the waters of the law; and they draw, because they study to draw out of the waters of the law; and they are strengthened by the tree of life, and they shall go out "first", because the tree of life is the cause why they shall "rise first":"

They sometimes endeavour to fix the time, how long they will rise before the rest (p);

"Many of those that sleep" these are the righteous that shall "go before" others in life, and how many years shall they go before them? R. Judah says, two hundred and ten years; R. Isaac says, two hundred and fourteen; according to others, the righteous shall go (or be raised) a year before the rest of men; says R. Nachman, it will be according to the computation (of time) that the carcass has been in the dust; R. Jose replies, if so, there will be many resurrections."

These instances may suffice to show, that the Jews had a notion of some persons rising before others, to which the apostle may have some reference; though his sense is not only this, but also that the dead in Messiah Yeshua shall rise before the living saints are changed, and taken up to be with Yeshua, and so shall not go before to him; which illustrates and proves what he had before asserted.

(d) Targum Jon. in Exod. xx. 18. (e) Kettoreth Hassamamim in ib. (f) Mechilta in ib. & Abarbinel, Mashmia Jeshua, fol. 11. 4. (g) Zohar in Lev. fol. 42. 2. 4. (h) Abkath Rocel, p. 138. Ed. Huls. (i) T. Hieros. Kilaim, fol. 32. 3. & Cetubot, fol. 35. 2. Bereshit Rabba, sect. 74. fol. 65. 1. (k) Bereshit Rabba, sect. 96. fol. 83. 4. & 84. 1. & Shemot Rabba, sect. 32. fol. 135. 2. (l) Zohar in Gen. fol. 68. 4. (m) Zohar in Gen. fol. 79. 3. (n) Ib. fol. 100. 3. (o) Ib. fol. 103. 1. (p) Ib. fol. 83. 1.

---

17. Then we which are alive and remain shall be caught up together with them in the clouds, to meet the Lord in the air: and so shall we ever be with the Lord.

Greek/Transliteration
17. ἔπειτα ἡμεῖς οἱ ζῶντες, οἱ περιλειπόμενοι, ἅμα σὺν αὐτοῖς ἁρπαγησόμεθα ἐν νεφέλαις εἰς ἀπάντησιν τοῦ κυρίου εἰς ἀέρα· καὶ οὕτως πάντοτε σὺν κυρίῳ ἐσόμεθα.

17. epeita 'eimeis 'oi zontes, 'oi perileipomenoi, 'ama sun autois 'arpageisometha en nephelais eis apanteisin tou kuriou eis aera. kai 'outos pantote sun kurio esometha.

Hebrew/Transliteration
יז. וְאַחֲרֵי-כֵן אֲנַחְנוּ הַנִּשְׁאָרִים בַּחַיִּים נִלָּקַח וְנַעֲלֶה עִמָּהֶם יַחְדָּו בַּעֲנָנִים לִקְרַאת הָאָדוֹן בִּרְקִיעַ הַשָּׁמָיִם וְכֵן נִהְיֶה עִם-הָאָדוֹן לָנֶצַח:

17. Ve•a•cha•rey - chen a•nach•noo ha•nish•a•rim ba•cha•yim ni•la•kach ve•na•a•le ee•ma•hem yach•dav ba•a•na•nim lik•rat ha•Adon bir•kia ha•sha•ma•yim ve•chen ni•hee•ye eem - ha•Adon la•ne•tzach.

Rabbinic Jewish Commentary
The resurrection by the Mahometans is called לקא אללה (q), "a meeting of God", or a going to meet God:

(q) Alkoran, Surat. 6. v. 31. p. 113. Ed. Hinckelman.

---

18. Wherefore comfort one another with these words.

Greek/Transliteration
18. Ὥστε παρακαλεῖτε ἀλλήλους ἐν τοῖς λόγοις τούτοις.

18. 'Oste parakaleite alleilous en tois logois toutois.

Hebrew/Transliteration
יח. לָכֵן אֵפוֹא נַחֲמוּ אִישׁ אֶת-רֵעֵהוּ בִּדְבָרִים כָּאֵלֶּה:

18. La•chen e•fo na•cha•moo eesh et - re•e•hoo bid•va•rim ka•e•le.

Rabbinic Jewish Commentary
Some copies read, "with these words of the spirit"; and so the Arabic version, "with these spiritual words": for such they are, being the word of God.

1 Thessalonians, Chapter 5

1. But of the times and the seasons, brethren, ye have no need that I write unto you.

Greek/Transliteration
1. Περὶ δὲ τῶν χρόνων καὶ τῶν καιρῶν, ἀδελφοί, οὐ χρείαν ἔχετε ὑμῖν γράφεσθαι.

1. Peri de ton chronon kai ton kairon, adelphoi, ou chreian echete 'umin graphesthai.

Hebrew/Transliteration
א. וְעַל-דְּבַר הָעִתִּים וְהַזְּמַנִּים אֵין-דָּבָר אַחַי לְהִכָּתֵב לָכֶם:

1. Ve•al - de•var ha•ee•tim ve•haz•ma•nim eyn - da•var a•chai le•hi•ka•tev la•chem.

Rabbinic Jewish Commentary
But of the times and the seasons, brethren,..... Of the coming of Christ, his "appointed time" and "his day", as the Ethiopic version renders it.

The Vulgate Latin and Arabic versions read, "ye have no need that we write unto you".

---

2. For yourselves know perfectly that the day of the Lord so cometh as a thief in the night.

Greek/Transliteration
2. Αὐτοὶ γὰρ ἀκριβῶς οἴδατε ὅτι ἡ ἡμέρα κυρίου ὡς κλέπτης ἐν νυκτὶ οὕτως ἔρχεται·

2. Autoi gar akribos oidate 'oti 'ei 'eimera kuriou 'os klepteis en nukti 'outos erchetai.

Hebrew/Transliteration
ב. הֲלֹא יְדַעְתֶּם הֵיטֵב כִּי יוֹם-יְהוָה כְּגַנָּב בַּלַּיְלָה יָבוֹא:

2. Ha•lo ye•da•a•tem hei•tev ki yom - Adonai ke•ga•nav ba•lai•la ya•vo.

---

3. For when they shall say, Peace and safety; then sudden destruction cometh upon them, as travail upon a woman with child; and they shall not escape.

Greek/Transliteration
3. ὅταν γὰρ λέγωσιν, Εἰρήνη καὶ ἀσφάλεια, τότε αἰφνίδιος αὐτοῖς ἐφίσταται ὄλεθρος, ὥσπερ ἡ ὠδὶν τῇ ἐν γαστρὶ ἐχούσῃ, καὶ οὐ μὴ ἐκφύγωσιν.

3. 'otan gar legosin, Eireinei kai asphaleya, tote aiphnidios autois ephistatai olethros, 'osper 'ei odin tei en gastri echousei, kai ou mei ekphugosin.

Hebrew/Transliteration
ג. כַּאֲשֶׁר יֹאמְרוּ שָׁלוֹם וְשַׁלְוָה אָז פִּתְאֹם יָבוֹא עֲלֵיהֶם אֵידָם כְּחֶבְלֵי יוֹלֵדָה וְלֹא יִמָּלֵט לָהֶם פָּלִיט:

3. Ka•a•sher yom•roo sha•lom ve•shal•va az pit•om ya•vo aley•hem ey•dam ke•chev•ley yo•le•da ve•lo yi•ma•let la•hem pa•lit.

4. But ye, brethren, are not in darkness, that that day should overtake you as a thief.

Greek/Transliteration
4. Ὑμεῖς δέ, ἀδελφοί, οὐκ ἐστὲ ἐν σκότει, ἵνα ἡ ἡμέρα ὑμᾶς ὡς κλέπτης καταλάβῃ·

4. 'Umeis de, adelphoi, ouk este en skotei, 'ina 'ei 'eimera 'umas 'os klepteis katalabei.

Hebrew/Transliteration
ד. אֲבָל אַתֶּם אַחַי אֵינְכֶם בַּחֹשֶׁךְ אֲשֶׁר יָבוֹא עֲלֵיכֶם הַיּוֹם כְּגַנָּב :

4. Aval atem a•chai eyn•chem ba•cho•shech asher ya•vo aley•chem ha•yom ke•ga•nav.

---

5. Ye are all the children of light, and the children of the day: we are not of the night, nor of darkness.

Greek/Transliteration
5. πάντες ὑμεῖς υἱοὶ φωτός ἐστε καὶ υἱοὶ ἡμέρας· οὐκ ἐσμὲν νυκτὸς οὐδὲ σκότους·

5. pantes 'umeis 'wioi photos este kai 'wioi 'eimeras. ouk esmen nuktos oude skotous.

Hebrew/Transliteration
ה. כִּי כֻלְּכֶם בְּנֵי אוֹר וּבְנֵי יוֹם אַתֶּם לֹא בְנֵי לַיְלָה וְלֹא בְנֵי חֹשֶׁךְ אֲנָחְנוּ :

5. Ki chool•chem b`ney or oov•ney yom atem lo v`ney lai•la ve•lo v`ney cho•shech a•nach•noo.

Rabbinic Jewish Commentary
The Syriac and Arabic versions read; and the former changes the person, and reads, "ye are not the children of the night".

---

6. Therefore let us not sleep, as do others; but let us watch and be sober.

Greek/Transliteration
6. ἄρα οὖν μὴ καθεύδωμεν ὡς καὶ οἱ λοιποί, ἀλλὰ γρηγορῶμεν καὶ νήφωμεν.

6. ara oun mei katheudomen 'os kai 'oi loipoi, alla greigoromen kai neiphomen.

Hebrew/Transliteration
ו. עַל־כֵּן אֵין לָנוּ לִישׁוֹן כִּשְׁאָר הָאֲנָשִׁים כִּי אִם־נִשְׁקֹד וְנִשְׁתַּמֵּר מִשִּׁכָּרוֹן :

6. Al - ken eyn la•noo li•shon kish•ar ha•a•na•shim ki eem - nish•kod ve•nish•ta•mer mi•shi•ka•ron.

Rabbinic Jewish Commentary
The Arabic version renders it, "let us repent"; and the Ethiopic version, "let us understand";

7. For they that sleep sleep in the night; and they that be drunken are drunken in the night.

Greek/Transliteration
7. Οἱ γὰρ καθεύδοντες νυκτὸς καθεύδουσιν· καὶ οἱ μεθυσκόμενοι, νυκτὸς μεθύουσιν.

7. 'Oi gar katheudontes nuktos katheudousin. kai 'oi methuskomenoi, nuktos methuousin.

Hebrew/Transliteration
ז. כִּי הַיְשֵׁנִים יִישְׁנוּ בַלָּיְלָה וְהַשִּׁכֹּרִים יִשְׁכְּרוּן בַּלָּיְלָה:

7. Ki hay•she•nim yish•noo va•lai•la ve•ha•shi•ko•rim yish•ke•roon ba•lai•la.

---

8. But let us, who are of the day, be sober, putting on the breastplate of faith and love; and for an helmet, the hope of salvation.

Greek/Transliteration
8. Ἡμεῖς δέ, ἡμέρας ὄντες, νήφωμεν, ἐνδυσάμενοι θώρακα πίστεως καὶ ἀγάπης, καὶ περικεφαλαίαν, ἐλπίδα σωτηρίας.

8. 'Eimeis de, 'eimeras ontes, neiphomen, endusamenoi thoraka pisteos kai agapeis, kai perikephalaian, elpida soteirias.

Hebrew/Transliteration
ח. וַאֲנַחְנוּ בְּנֵי יוֹם נִשְׁתַּמֵּר וְנִלְבַּשׁ מִשִּׁכָּרוֹן שִׁרְיוֹן אֱמוּנָה וְאַהֲבָה וּלְכוֹבַע לָנוּ תִּקְוַת הַיְשׁוּעָה:

8. Va•a•nach•noo v`ney yom nish•ta•mer mi•shi•ka•ron ve•nil•bash shir•yon e•moo•na ve•a•ha•va ool•cho•va la•noo tik•vat ha•y`shoo•ah.

Rabbinic Jewish Commentary
putting on the breastplate of faith and love; this is the coat of mail, 1Sa_17:5 which was made of iron or brass; and the Ethiopic version here calls it, "the iron coat." The allusion seems to be to the high priest's breastplate of judgment, in which were put the Thummim and Urim, which signify perfections and lights; faith may answer to the former, and love to the latter.

---

9. For God hath not appointed us to wrath, but to obtain salvation by our Lord Jesus Christ,

Greek/Transliteration
9. Ὅτι οὐκ ἔθετο ἡμᾶς ὁ θεὸς εἰς ὀργήν, ἀλλ᾽ εἰς περιποίησιν σωτηρίας διὰ τοῦ κυρίου ἡμῶν Ἰησοῦ χριστοῦ,

9. 'Oti ouk etheto 'eimas 'o theos eis orgein, all eis peripoieisin soteirias dya tou kuriou 'eimon Yeisou christou,

Hebrew/Transliteration
ט. כִּי לֹא-יָצַר אוֹתָנוּ אֱלֹהִים לְכַלֹּתֵנוּ בְאַפּוֹ כִּי אִם-לְהָבִיא לָנוּ יְשׁוּעָה בְּיַד-יֵשׁוּעַ הַמָּשִׁיחַ אֲדֹנֵינוּ:

9. Ki lo - ya•tzar o•ta•noo Elohim le•cha•lo•te•noo ve•a•po ki eem - le•ha•vee la•noo ye•shoo•ah be•yad - Yeshua ha•Ma•shi•ach Ado•ney•noo.

---

10. Who died for us, that, whether we wake or sleep, we should live together with him.

Greek/Transliteration
10. τοῦ ἀποθανόντος ὑπὲρ ἡμῶν, ἵνα, εἴτε γρηγορῶμεν εἴτε καθεύδωμεν, ἅμα σὺν αὐτῷ ζήσωμεν.

10. tou apothanontos 'uper 'eimon, 'ina, eite greigoromen eite katheudomen, 'ama sun auto zeisomen.

Hebrew/Transliteration
י. הוּא אֲשֶׁר מֵת בַּעֲדֵנוּ וְאִם־נָקִיץ אוֹ־נִישַׁן עִמּוֹ נִחְיֶה יַחְדָּו:

10. Hoo asher met ba•a•de•noo ve•eem - na•kitz oh - ni•shan ee•mo nich•ye yach•dav.

---

11. Wherefore comfort yourselves together, and edify one another, even as also ye do.

Greek/Transliteration
11. Διὸ παρακαλεῖτε ἀλλήλους, καὶ οἰκοδομεῖτε εἰς τὸν ἕνα, καθὼς καὶ ποιεῖτε.

11. Dio parakaleite alleilous, kai oikodomeite 'eis ton 'ena, kathos kai poieite.

Hebrew/Transliteration
יא. עַל־כֵּן הַזְהִירוּ אִישׁ אֶת־רֵעֵהוּ וְהָשִׁיבוּ אִישׁ אֶת־נֶפֶשׁ אָחִיו כַּאֲשֶׁר עֲשִׂיתֶם עַד־כֹּה:

11. Al - ken haz•hi•roo eesh et - re•e•hoo ve•ha•shi•voo eesh et - ne•fesh a•chiv ka•a•sher asi•tem ad - ko.

---

12. And we beseech you, brethren, to know them which labour among you, and are over you in the Lord, and admonish you;

Greek/Transliteration
12. Ἐρωτῶμεν δὲ ὑμᾶς, ἀδελφοί, εἰδέναι τοὺς κοπιῶντας ἐν ὑμῖν, καὶ προϊσταμένους ὑμῶν ἐν κυρίῳ, καὶ νουθετοῦντας ὑμᾶς,

12. Erotomen de 'umas, adelphoi, eidenai tous kopiontas en 'umin, kai proistamenous 'umon en kurio, kai nouthetountas 'umas,

Hebrew/Transliteration
יב. וַאֲנַחְנוּ נִפְצַר בָּכֶם אַחִים לָדַעַת בְּשׂוּם לֵב אֶת־הָעֲמֵלִים בָּכֶם וְאֶת־הַנִּצָּבִים עֲלֵיכֶם בְּשֵׁם הָאָדוֹן וְאֶת־הַמּוֹכִיחִים אֶתְכֶם:

12. Va•a•nach•noo nif•tzar ba•chem a•chim la•da•at be•soom lev et - ha•a•me•lim ba•chem ve•et - ha•ni•tza•vim aley•chem be•shem ha•Adon ve•et - ha•mo•chi•chim et•chem.

Rabbinic Jewish Commentary
The Arabic version renders it, in the love of the Lord; the phrase, "in the Lord", is omitted in the Syriac version.

---

13. And to esteem them very highly in love for their work's sake. And be at peace among yourselves.

Greek/Transliteration
13. καὶ ἡγεῖσθαι αὐτοὺς ὑπὲρ ἐκπερισσοῦ ἐν ἀγάπῃ διὰ τὸ ἔργον αὐτῶν. Εἰρηνεύετε ἐν ἑαυτοῖς.

13. kai 'eigeisthai autous 'uper ekperissou en agapei dya to ergon auton. Eireineuete en 'eautois.

Hebrew/Transliteration
יג. וּלְהַכִּיר יְקַר עֶרְכָּם הַגָּדוֹל לְאַהֲבָה אֹתָם לְמַעַן פָּעֳלָם וְהַחֲזִיקוּ שָׁלוֹם בֵּינֵיכֶם:

13. Ool•ha•kir ye•kar er•kam ha•ga•dol le•a•ha•va o•tam le•ma•an pa•o•lam ve•ha•cha•zi•koo sha•lom bey•ney•chem.

Rabbinic Jewish Commentary
And to esteem them very highly,.... Or, as the Ethiopic version renders it, "honour them abundantly"; for such are worthy of double honour, and to be had in reputation

in love; not in fear, nor in hypocrisy and dissimulation; not in word and in tongue only, but from the heart and real affection: the Syriac version renders it, "that they be esteemed by you with more abundant love".

And be at peace among yourselves. The Vulgate Latin version reads, "with them"; and so the Syriac version, connecting the former clause with this, "for their works' sake have peace with them"; that is, with the ministers of the word.

---

14. Now we exhort you, brethren, warn them that are unruly, comfort the feebleminded, support the weak, be patient toward all men.

Greek/Transliteration
14. Παρακαλοῦμεν δὲ ὑμᾶς, ἀδελφοί, νουθετεῖτε τοὺς ἀτάκτους, παραμυθεῖσθε τοὺς ὀλιγοψύχους, ἀντέχεσθε τῶν ἀσθενῶν, μακροθυμεῖτε πρὸς πάντας.

14. Parakaloumen de 'umas, adelphoi, noutheteite tous ataktous, paramutheisthe tous oligopsuchous, antechesthe ton asthenon, makrothumeite pros pantas.

Hebrew/Transliteration
יד. וְאַתֶּם אַחַינוּ נַזְהִיר אֶתְכֶם הוֹכִיחוּ אֶת-הַמַּמְרִים אִמְּצוּ אֶת-רַכֵּי הַלֵּבָב סַעֲדוּ אֶת-הַחוֹלִים וְהַאֲרִיכוּ אַף לְכָל-אָדָם:

14. Ve•a•tem achey•noo naz•hir et•chem ho•chi•choo et - ha•mam•rim am•tzoo et - ra•key ha•le•vav sa•a•doo et - ha•cho•lim ve•ha•a•ri•choo af le•chol - adam.

Rabbinic Jewish Commentary

Support the weak; who are weak in faith and knowledge, strengthen them, hold them up; or as the Syriac version renders it, "take the burden of the weak" and carry it, bear their infirmities, as directed in Rom_15:1.

---

15. See that none render evil for evil unto any man; but ever follow that which is good, both among yourselves, and to all men.

Greek/Transliteration
15. Ὁρᾶτε μή τις κακὸν ἀντὶ κακοῦ τινι ἀποδῷ· ἀλλὰ πάντοτε τὸ ἀγαθὸν διώκετε καὶ εἰς ἀλλήλους καὶ εἰς πάντας.

15. 'Orate mei tis kakon anti kakou tini apodo. alla pantote to agathon diokete kai eis alleilous kai eis pantas.

Hebrew/Transliteration
טו. הִשָּׁמְרוּ פֶּן-יִגְמֹל אִישׁ לְאִישׁ רָעָה תַּחַת רָעָה כִּי אִם-רִדְפוּ לְהֵיטִיב תָּמִיד לְאִישׁ אִישׁ מִכֶּם וְגַם לְכָל-אָדָם:

15. Hi•sham•roo pen - yig•mol eesh le•eesh ra•ah ta•chat ra•ah ki eem - rid•foo le•hey•tiv ta•mid le•eesh eesh mi•kem ve•gam le•chol - adam.

---

16. Rejoice evermore.

Greek/Transliteration
16. Πάντοτε χαίρετε·

16. Pantote chairete.

Hebrew/Transliteration
טז. וְאַךְ שְׂמֵחִים תִּהְיוּ כָּל-הַיָּמִים:

16. Ve•ach s`me•chim ti•hi•yoo kol - ha•ya•mim.

---

17. Pray without ceasing.

Greek/Transliteration
17. ἀδιαλείπτως προσεύχεσθε·

17. adyaleiptos proseuchesthe.

Hebrew/Transliteration
יז. וְלֹא תַחְדְּלוּ מֵהִתְפַּלֵּל תָּמִיד:

17. Ve•lo tach•de•loo me•hit•pa•lel ta•mid.

Rabbinic Jewish Commentary
The Ethiopic version renders the words, "pray frequently".

18. In every thing give thanks: for this is the will of God in Christ Jesus concerning you.

Greek/Transliteration
18. ἐν παντὶ εὐχαριστεῖτε· τοῦτο γὰρ θέλημα θεοῦ ἐν χριστῷ Ἰησοῦ εἰς ὑμᾶς.

18. en panti eucharisteite. touto gar theleima theou en christo Yeisou eis 'umas.

Hebrew/Transliteration
יח. הוֹדוּ עַל־כָּל־דָּבָר כִּי־זֶה לָכֶם חֵפֶץ אֱלֹהִים בְּיֵשׁוּעַ הַמָּשִׁיחַ:

18. Ho•doo al - kol - da•var ki - ze la•chem che•fetz Elohim be•Yeshua ha•Ma•shi•ach.

Rabbinic Jewish Commentary
in Christ Jesus concerning you; either declared in and by him, who has made known the whole of the will of God, and so the Arabic version, "which he wills of you by Jesus Christ"; or which is exemplified in Yeshua, who for, and in all things, gave thanks to God, and had his will resigned to his in every circumstance of life; or, which being done, is acceptable to God through Messiah Yeshua. The Alexandrian copy reads, "for this is the will of God towards you in Christ Jesus"

---

19. Quench not the Spirit.

Greek/Transliteration
19. Τὸ πνεῦμα μὴ σβέννυτε·

19. To pneuma mei sbennute.

Hebrew/Transliteration
יט. לֹא תְכַבּוּ אֶת־הָרוּחַ:

19. Lo te•cha•boo et - ha•Roo•ach.

---

20. Despise not prophesyings.

Greek/Transliteration
20. προφητείας μὴ ἐξουθενεῖτε·

20. propheiteias mei exoutheneite.

Hebrew/Transliteration
כ. וְאֶת־הַנְּבוּאוֹת לֹא תִפְרָעוּ:

20. Ve•et - han•voo•ot lo tif•ra•oo.

Rabbinic Jewish Commentary
Just as in our days, if persons have not had a liberal education, and do not understand Latin, Greek, and Hebrew, though they have ministerial gifts, and are capable of explaining the word to edification and comfort, yet are set at nought and rejected, which should not be.

21. Prove all things; hold fast that which is good.

Greek/Transliteration
21. πάντα δὲ δοκιμάζετε· τὸ καλὸν κατέχετε·

21. panta de dokimazete. to kalon katechete.

Hebrew/Transliteration
כא. בַּחֲנוּ כָּל-דָּבָר וְהַחֲזִיקוּ בַּטוֹב:

21. Ba•cha•noo kol - da•var ve•ha•cha•zi•koo ba•tov.

---

22. Abstain from all appearance of evil.

Greek/Transliteration
22. ἀπὸ παντὸς εἴδους πονηροῦ ἀπέχεσθε.

22. apo pantos eidous poneirou apechesthe.

Hebrew/Transliteration
כב. וּמִכָּל-שֶׁמֶץ דָּבָר רָע אַף לְמַרְאֵה עַיִן הַרְחִיקוּ רַגְלֵיכֶם:

22. Oo•mi•kol - she•metz da•var ra af le•mar•eh a•yin har•chi•koo rag•ley•chem.

Rabbinic Jewish Commentary
The (w) Jews have a saying,

"Take care of a light as of a heavy commandment,"

That is, take care of committing a lesser, as a greater sin, and from the first motions of sin; but from every occasion of it, and what leads unto it, and has the appearance of it, or may be suspected of others to be sin, and so give offence, and be a matter of scandal. The Jews have a saying very agreeable to this (x),

"Remove thyself afar off (or abstain) from filthiness, and from everything, הדומה לו, "that is like unto it"."

(w) Pirke Abot, c. 2. sect. 1. (x) Apud Drusium in loc.

---

23. And the very God of peace sanctify you wholly; and I pray God your whole spirit and soul and body be preserved blameless unto the coming of our Lord Jesus Christ.

Greek/Transliteration
23. Αὐτὸς δὲ ὁ θεὸς τῆς εἰρήνης ἁγιάσαι ὑμᾶς ὁλοτελεῖς· καὶ ὁλόκληρον ὑμῶν τὸ πνεῦμα καὶ ἡ ψυχὴ καὶ τὸ σῶμα ἀμέμπτως ἐν τῇ παρουσίᾳ τοῦ κυρίου ἡμῶν Ἰησοῦ χριστοῦ τηρηθείη.

23. Autos de 'o theos teis eireineis 'agyasai 'umas 'oloteleis. kai 'olokleiron 'umon to pneuma kai 'ei psuchei kai to soma amemptos en tei parousia tou kuriou 'eimon Yeisou christou teireitheiei.

Hebrew/Transliteration

כג. וֵאלֹהֵי הַשָּׁלוֹם הוּא יְקַדֵּשׁ אֶתְכֶם מֵהָחֵל וְעַד-כָּלָה וְיִשְׁמָרְכֶם מִכָּל-רָע בְּרוּחַ נֶפֶשׁ וּגְוִיָּה לְמוֹעֵד בּוֹא אֲדֹנֵינוּ יֵשׁוּעַ הַמָּשִׁיחַ:

23. Ve•Elohey ha•sha•lom hoo ye•ka•desh et•chem me•ha•chel ve•ad - ka•le ve•yish•mor•chem mi•kol - ra be•roo•ach ne•fesh oog•vi•ya le•mo•ed bo Ado•ney•noo Yeshua ha•Ma•shi•ach.

Rabbinic Jewish Commentary

A like division of man is made by the Jews: says one of their writers (y).

"A man cannot know God, unless he knows נפשו ונשמתו וגופו, "his soul, his breath, or his spirit, and his body"."

Says (z) R. Isaac,

"Worthy are the righteous in this world, and in the world to come, for lo, they are all holy; their body is holy, their soul is holy, their spirit, and their breath is holy".

(y) Aben Ezra in Exod. xxxi. 18. (z) Zohar in Lev. fol. 29. 2.

---

24. Faithful is he that calleth you, who also will do it.

Greek/Transliteration
24. Πιστὸς ὁ καλῶν ὑμᾶς, ὃς καὶ ποιήσει.

24. Pistos 'o kalon 'umas, 'os kai poieisei.

Hebrew/Transliteration
:כד. נֶאֱמָן הוּא הַקֹּרֵא אֶתְכֶם וְהוּא גַּם-יַעֲשֶׂה

24. Ne•e•man hoo ha•ko•re et•chem ve•hoo gam - ya•a•se.

Rabbinic Jewish Commentary

The Arabic version renders this last clause, "and will execute his promise": and the effectual calling is a sure pledge of glorification; whom God calls he justifies and glorifies; as sure as he gives grace, he will give glory; and whom he calls to his eternal glory, he will make perfect, stablish, strengthen, and settle. The Complutensian edition reads, "who also will make your hope firm"; that is, with respect to the above things.

---

25. Brethren, pray for us.

Greek/Transliteration
25. Ἀδελφοί, προσεύχεσθε περὶ ἡμῶν.

25. Adelphoi, proseuchesthe peri 'eimon.

Hebrew/Transliteration
:כה. אָנָּא אַחַי הִתְפַּלְלוּ-נָא בַּעֲדֵנוּ

25. Ana e•chai hit•pa•le•loo - na ba•a•de•noo.

---

26. Greet all the brethren with an holy kiss.

Greek/Transliteration
26. Ἀσπάσασθε τοὺς ἀδελφοὺς πάντας ἐν φιλήματι ἁγίῳ.

26. Aspasasthe tous adelphous pantas en phileimati 'agio.

Hebrew/Transliteration
:כו. שַׁאֲלוּ לְשָׁלוֹם כָּל־הָאַחִים בִּנְשִׁיקַת הַקֹּדֶשׁ

26. Sha•a•loo lish•lom kol - ha•a•chim bin•shi•kat ha•ko•desh.

---

27. I charge you by the Lord that this epistle be read unto all the holy brethren.

Greek/Transliteration
27. Ὁρκίζω ὑμᾶς τὸν κύριον, ἀναγνωσθῆναι τὴν ἐπιστολὴν πᾶσιν τοῖς ἁγίοις ἀδελφοῖς.

27. 'Orkizo 'umas ton kurion, anagnostheinai tein epistolein pasin tois 'agiois adelphois.

Hebrew/Transliteration
:כז. הִנְנִי מַשְׁבִּיעֲכֶם בַּאדֹנֵינוּ לָתֵת הָאִגֶּרֶת הַזֹּאת לְהִקָּרֵא בְאָזְנֵי כָל־הָאַחִים הַקְּדוֹשִׁים

27. Hi•ne•ni mash•bi•a•chem ba•Ado•ne•noo la•tet ha•ee•ge•ret ha•zot le•hi•ka•re ve•oz•ney chol - ha•a•chim ha•k`do•shim.

---

28. The grace of our Lord Jesus Christ be with you. Amen.

Greek/Transliteration
28. Ἡ χάρις τοῦ κυρίου ἡμῶν Ἰησοῦ χριστοῦ μεθ᾽ ὑμῶν. Ἀμήν.

28. 'Ei charis tou kuriou 'eimon Yeisou christou meth 'umon. Amein.

Hebrew/Transliteration
:כח. חֶסֶד יֵשׁוּעַ הַמָּשִׁיחַ אֲדֹנֵינוּ עִמָּכֶם אָמֵן

28. Che•sed Yeshua ha•Ma•shi•ach Ado•ney•noo ee•ma•chem Amen.

---

^end^

THE SECOND EPISTLE OF PAUL THE APOSTLE TO THE THESSALONIANS

2 Thessalonians, Chapter 1

1. Paul, and Silvanus, and Timotheus, unto the church of the Thessalonians in God our Father and the Lord Jesus Christ:

Greek/Transliteration

1. Παῦλος καὶ Σιλουανὸς καὶ Τιμόθεος τῇ ἐκκλησίᾳ Θεσσαλονικέων ἐν θεῷ πατρὶ ἡμῶν καὶ κυρίῳ Ἰησοῦ χριστῷ·

1. Paulos kai Silouanos kai Timotheos tei ekkleisia Thessalonikeon en theo patri 'eimon kai kurio Yeisou christo.

Hebrew/Transliteration

א. פּוֹלוֹס וְסִלְוָנוֹס וְטִימוֹתִיּוֹס אֶל-עֲדַת הַתַּסְלוֹנִיקִים הַדְּבֵקִים בֵּאלֹהִים אָבִינוּ וּבְיֵשׁוּעַ הַמָּשִׁיחַ אֲדֹנֵינוּ:

1. Polos ve•Silvanos ve•Timotiyos el - adat ha•Tas•lo•ni•kim ha•d`ve•kim be•Elohim Avi•noo oov•Yeshua ha•Ma•shi•ach Ado•ney•noo.

---

2. Grace unto you, and peace, from God our Father and the Lord Jesus Christ.

Greek/Transliteration

2. χάρις ὑμῖν καὶ εἰρήνη ἀπὸ θεοῦ πατρὸς ἡμῶν καὶ κυρίου Ἰησοῦ χριστοῦ.

2. charis 'umin kai eireinei apo theou patros 'eimon kai kuriou Yeisou christou.

Hebrew/Transliteration

ב. חֶסֶד וְשָׁלוֹם יִתֵּן לָכֶם אֱלֹהִים אָבִינוּ וְיֵשׁוּעַ הַמָּשִׁיחַ אֲדֹנֵינוּ:

2. Che•sed ve•sha•lom yi•ten la•chem Elohim Avi•noo ve•Yeshua ha•Ma•shi•ach Ado•ney•noo.

---

3. We are bound to thank God always for you, brethren, as it is meet, because that your faith groweth exceedingly, and the charity of every one of you all toward each other aboundeth;

Greek/Transliteration

3. Εὐχαριστεῖν ὀφείλομεν τῷ θεῷ πάντοτε περὶ ὑμῶν, ἀδελφοί, καθὼς ἄξιόν ἐστιν, ὅτι ὑπεραυξάνει ἡ πίστις ὑμῶν, καὶ πλεονάζει ἡ ἀγάπη ἑνὸς ἑκάστου πάντων ὑμῶν εἰς ἀλλήλους·

3. Eucharistein opheilomen to theo pantote peri 'umon, adelphoi, kathos axion estin, 'oti 'uperauxanei 'ei pistis 'umon, kai pleonazei 'ei agapei 'enos 'ekastou panton 'umon eis alleilous.

Hebrew/Transliteration

ג. כַּמָּה עָלֵינוּ לְהוֹדוֹת לֵאלֹהִים תָּמִיד בַּעֲבוּרְכֶם אַחַי כַּאֲשֶׁר נָכוֹן לָנוּ כִּי אֱמוּנַתְכֶם הֹלֶכֶת הָלוֹךְ וְגָדֹל וְאַהֲבַת רֵעִים הֹלוֹךְ וְרָב בֵּין כֻּלְּכֶם:

3. Ka•ma aley•noo le•ho•dot le•Elohim ta•mid ba•a•voor•chem a•chai ka•a•sher na•chon la•noo ki emoo•nat•chem ho•le•chet ha•loch ve•ga•dol ve•a•ha•vat re•eem ha•loch va•rav bein kool•chem.

---

4. So that we ourselves glory in you in the churches of God for your patience and faith in all your persecutions and tribulations that ye endure:

Greek/Transliteration
4. ὥστε ἡμᾶς αὐτοὺς ἐν ὑμῖν καυχᾶσθαι ἐν ταῖς ἐκκλησίαις τοῦ θεοῦ ὑπὲρ τῆς ὑπομονῆς ὑμῶν καὶ πίστεως ἐν πᾶσιν τοῖς διωγμοῖς ὑμῶν καὶ ταῖς θλίψεσιν αἷς ἀνέχεσθε·

4. 'oste 'eimas autous en 'umin kauchasthai en tais ekkleisiais tou theou 'uper teis 'upomoneis 'umon kai pisteos en pasin tois diogmois 'umon kai tais thlipsesin 'ais anechesthe.

Hebrew/Transliteration
ד. עַד אֲשֶׁר גַּם-אֲנַחְנוּ נִתְפָּאֵר בָּכֶם לִפְנֵי קְהִלּוֹת הָאֱלֹהִים עַל-סַבְלְכֶם וֶאֱמוּנַתְכֶם בְּכָל-הָעֹשֶׁק וְהַמְּרוּצָה אֲשֶׁר פָּגְעוּ בָכֶם:

4. Ad asher gam - a•nach•noo nit•pa•er ba•chem lif•ney ke•hi•lot ha•Elohim al - soo•bal•chem ve•e•moo•nat•chem be•chol - ha•o•shek ve•ham•roo•tza asher pag•oo va•chem.

---

5. Which is a manifest token of the righteous judgment of God, that ye may be counted worthy of the kingdom of God, for which ye also suffer:

Greek/Transliteration
5. ἔνδειγμα τῆς δικαίας κρίσεως τοῦ θεοῦ, εἰς τὸ καταξιωθῆναι ὑμᾶς τῆς βασιλείας τοῦ θεοῦ, ὑπὲρ ἧς καὶ πάσχετε·

5. endeigma teis dikaias kriseos tou theou, eis to kataxiotheinai 'umas teis basileias tou theou, 'uper 'eis kai paschete.

Hebrew/Transliteration
ה. עֵדוּת לֵאלֹהִים כִּי יָשָׁר מִשְׁפָּטוֹ לֵאמֹר כִּי נְבוֹנִים אַתֶּם לְמַלְכוּתוֹ אֲשֶׁר עָלֶיהָ נְתַתֶּם שִׁכְמְכֶם לִסְבֹּל:

5. E•doot le•Elohim ki ya•shar mish•pe•to le•mor ki n`cho•nim atem le•mal•choo•to asher a•le•ha n`ta•tem shich•me•chem lis•bol.

---

6. Seeing it is a righteous thing with God to recompense tribulation to them that trouble you;

Greek/Transliteration
6. εἴπερ δίκαιον παρὰ θεῷ ἀνταποδοῦναι τοῖς θλίβουσιν ὑμᾶς θλῖψιν,

6. eiper dikaion para theo antapodounai tois thlibousin 'umas thlipsin,

Hebrew/Transliteration

ו׃ כַּאֲשֶׁר גַּם-צַדִּיק הוּא אֱלֹהִים לְהָשִׁיב צָרָה לְצֹרְרֵיכֶם׃

6. Ka•a•sher gam - tza•dik hoo Elohim le•ha•shiv tza•ra le•tzo•re•rey•chem.

---

7. And to you who are troubled rest with us, when the Lord Jesus shall be revealed from heaven with his mighty angels,

Greek/Transliteration

7. καὶ ὑμῖν τοῖς θλιβομένοις ἄνεσιν μεθ᾽ ἡμῶν, ἐν τῇ ἀποκαλύψει τοῦ κυρίου Ἰησοῦ ἀπ᾽ οὐρανοῦ μετ᾽ ἀγγέλων δυνάμεως αὐτοῦ,

7. kai 'umin tois thlibomenois anesin meth 'eimon, en tei apokalupsei tou kuriou Yeisou ap ouranou met angelon dunameos autou,

Hebrew/Transliteration

ז׃ וְלָכֶם הָעֲשׁוּקִים יִתֵּן רְוָחָה אִתָּנוּ לְעֵת הִגָּלוֹת נִגְלוֹת יֵשׁוּעַ אֲדֹנֵינוּ מִן-הַשָּׁמַיִם עִם-מַלְאָכָיו גִּבֹּרֵי כֹחַ

7. Ve•la•chem ha•a•shoo•kim yi•ten r`va•cha ee•ta•noo le•et hi•ga•lot nig•lot Yeshua Ado•ney•noo min - ha•sha•ma•yim eem - mal•a•chav gi•bo•rey cho•ach.

Rabbinic Jewish Commentary

The words from the original text may be rendered, "with the angels/messengers of his power"; as they are by the Vulgate Latin, Arabic, and Ethiopic versions.

---

8. In flaming fire taking vengeance on them that know not God, and that obey not the gospel of our Lord Jesus Christ:

Greek/Transliteration

8. ἐν πυρὶ φλογός, διδόντος ἐκδίκησιν τοῖς μὴ εἰδόσιν θεόν, καὶ τοῖς μὴ ὑπακούουσιν τῷ εὐαγγελίῳ τοῦ κυρίου ἡμῶν Ἰησοῦ·

8. en puri phlogos, didontos ekdikeisin tois mei eidosin theon, kai tois mei 'upakouousin to euangelio tou kuriou 'eimon Yeisou.

Hebrew/Transliteration

ח׃ לִנְקֹם נָקָם בְּלַהֲבַת אֵשׁ מֵאֵת אֵלֶּה אֲשֶׁר לֹא-יָדְעוּ אֶת-הָאֱלֹהִים וְלֹא שָׁמְעוּ אֶת-בְּשׂוֹרַת יֵשׁוּעַ הַמָּשִׁיחַ אֲדֹנֵינוּ׃

8. Lin•kom na•kam be•la•ha•vat esh me•et ele asher lo - yad•oo et - ha•Elohim ve•lo sham•oo et - b`so•rat Yeshua ha•Ma•shi•ach Ado•ney•noo.

Rabbinic Jewish Commentary

It is a tradition of the Jews (z), that the angel Gabriel descended בשלהובא דאשא, "in a flame of fire", to burn Moses, as he was in the inn, when upon his journey from Midian to Egypt: or this clause may be read in construction with the following, as it is in the Vulgate Latin and Syriac versions, "in flaming fire taking vengeance"; and so expresses the manner in which vengeance will be taken on the wicked nation, Israel.

(z) Zohar in Gen. fol. 63. 2.

9. Who shall be punished with everlasting destruction from the presence of the Lord, and from the glory of his power;

Greek/Transliteration
9. οἵτινες δίκην τίσουσιν, ὄλεθρον αἰώνιον ἀπὸ προσώπου τοῦ κυρίου καὶ ἀπὸ τῆς δόξης τῆς ἰσχύος αὐτοῦ,

9. 'oitines dikein tisousin, olethron aionion apo prosopou tou kuriou kai apo teis doxeis teis ischuos autou,

Hebrew/Transliteration
:ט. אֲשֶׁר יֵעָנְשׁוּ לְהִשָּׁמְדָם עֲדֵי-עַד מִלִּפְנֵי הָאָדוֹן וּמֵהֲדַר גְּאוֹנוֹ

9. Asher ye•an•shoo le•hi•sham•dam adey - ad mi•lif•ney ha•Adon oo•me•ha•dar ge•o•no.

---

10. When he shall come to be glorified in his saints, and to be admired in all them that believe (because our testimony among you was believed) in that day.

Greek/Transliteration
10. ὅταν ἔλθῃ ἐνδοξασθῆναι ἐν τοῖς ἁγίοις αὐτοῦ, καὶ θαυμασθῆναι ἐν πᾶσιν τοῖς πιστεύσασιν ὅτι ἐπιστεύθη τὸ μαρτύριον ἡμῶν ἐφ᾽ ὑμᾶς ἐν τῇ ἡμέρᾳ ἐκείνῃ.

10. 'otan elthei endoxastheinai en tois 'agiois autou, kai thaumastheinai en pasin tois pisteusasin 'oti episteuthei to marturion 'eimon eph 'umas en tei 'eimera ekeinei.

Hebrew/Transliteration
:י. בַּיּוֹם הַהוּא כַּאֲשֶׁר יָבוֹא לְהִכָּבֵד בִּקְדֹשָׁיו וְלִהְיוֹת לְפֶלֶא בְּכָל-מַאֲמִינָיו כִּי עֵדוּתֵנוּ אֲשֶׁר שְׁמַעְתֶּם מִפִּינוּ אֱמֶת

10. Ba•yom ha•hoo ka•a•sher ya•vo le•hi•ka•ved bik•do•shav ve•li•hi•yot le•fe•le be•chol - ma•a•mi•nav ki e•doo•te•noo asher sh`ma•a•tem mi•pi•noo emet.

Rabbinic Jewish Commentary
The Arabic version renders it, "for our testimony will be true in that day"; that is, it will appear to be so, everything we have said will be accomplished then. The Syriac version is very remote, "that our testimony concerning you may be believed in that day".

---

11. Wherefore also we pray always for you, that our God would count you worthy of this calling, and fulfil all the good pleasure of his goodness, and the work of faith with power:

Greek/Transliteration
11. Εἰς ὃ καὶ προσευχόμεθα πάντοτε περὶ ὑμῶν, ἵνα ὑμᾶς ἀξιώσῃ τῆς κλήσεως ὁ θεὸς ἡμῶν, καὶ πληρώσῃ πᾶσαν εὐδοκίαν ἀγαθωσύνης καὶ ἔργον πίστεως ἐν δυνάμει·

11. Eis 'o kai proseuchometha pantote peri 'umon, 'ina 'umas axiosei teis kleiseos 'o theos 'eimon, kai pleirosei pasan eudokian agathosuneis kai ergon pisteos en dunamei.

Hebrew/Transliteration

יא. אֲשֶׁר לָזֹאת נִתְפַּלֵּל תָּמִיד לֵאלֹהֵינוּ לְהָכִין אֶת-לִבְּכֶם אֵלָיו כַּאֲשֶׁר קָרָא אֶתְכֶם וּלְהַשְׁלִים חֶפְצוֹ הַטּוֹב בָּכֶם וְכָל-מַעֲשֵׂה הָאֱמוּנָה בִּגְבוּרָתוֹ:

11. Asher la•zot nit•pa•lel ta•mid le•Elohey•noo le•ha•chin et - lib•chem elav ka•a•sher ka•ra et•chem ool•hash•lim chef•tzo ha•tov ba•chem ve•chol - ma•a•se ha•e•moo•na big•voo•ra•to.

Rabbinic Jewish Commentary

The Syriac version reads, "your calling", as in 1Co_1:26. The Vulgate Latin reads, "his own calling", meaning their effectual calling.

The Arabic version reads, "the work of faith on him"; The Arabic and Ethiopic versions read, "by his own power": which is greatly displayed in the production of faith at first.

---

12. That the name of our Lord Jesus Christ may be glorified in you, and ye in him, according to the grace of our God and the Lord Jesus Christ.

Greek/Transliteration

12. ὅπως ἐνδοξασθῇ τὸ ὄνομα τοῦ κυρίου ἡμῶν Ἰησοῦ ἐν ὑμῖν, καὶ ὑμεῖς ἐν αὐτῷ, κατὰ τὴν χάριν τοῦ θεοῦ ἡμῶν καὶ κυρίου Ἰησοῦ χριστοῦ.

12. 'opos endoxasthei to onoma tou kuriou 'eimon Yeisou en 'umin, kai 'umeis en auto, kata tein charin tou theou 'eimon kai kuriou Yeisou christou.

Hebrew/Transliteration

יב. לְמַעַן יִכָּבֵד בָּכֶם שֵׁם יֵשׁוּעַ הַמָּשִׁיחַ אֲדֹנֵינוּ וְאַתֶּם תִּכָּבְדוּ בוֹ כְּחַסְדֵי אֱלֹהֵינוּ וְיֵשׁוּעַ הַמָּשִׁיחַ אֲדֹנֵינוּ:

12. Le•ma•an yi•ka•ved ba•chem shem Yeshua ha•Ma•shi•ach Ado•ney•noo ve•a•tem ti•kav•doo vo ke•chas•dey Elohey•noo ve•Yeshua ha•Ma•shi•ach Ado•ney•noo.

2 Thessalonians, Chapter 2

1. Now we beseech you, brethren, by the coming of our Lord Jesus Christ, and by our gathering together unto him,

Greek/Transliteration

1. Ἐρωτῶμεν δὲ ὑμᾶς, ἀδελφοί, ὑπὲρ τῆς παρουσίας τοῦ κυρίου ἡμῶν Ἰησοῦ χριστοῦ, καὶ ἡμῶν ἐπισυναγωγῆς ἐπ᾽ αὐτόν,

1. Erotomen de 'umas, adelphoi, 'uper teis parousias tou kuriou 'eimon Yeisou christou, kai 'eimon episunagogeis ep auton,

Hebrew/Transliteration

א: וְעַל-דְּבַר יֵשׁוּעַ הַמָּשִׁיחַ אֲדֹנֵינוּ אֲשֶׁר יָבוֹא וַאֲשֶׁר יְקַבְּצֵנוּ אֵלָיו זֹאת בַּקָּשָׁתֵנוּ מִכֶּם אֶחָי

1. Ve•al - de•var Yeshua ha•Ma•shi•ach Ado•ney•noo asher ya•vo va•a•sher ye•kab•tze•noo elav zot ba•ka•sha•te•noo mi•kem e•chai.

Rabbinic Jewish Commentary

In the Ethiopic version, as they may, "concerning the coming of our Lord Jesus Christ"; this will be the gathering together of all the belivers of God; and so the Arabic version reads, "the gathering of us all".

---

2. That ye be not soon shaken in mind, or be troubled, neither by spirit, nor by word, nor by letter as from us, as that the day of Christ is at hand.

Greek/Transliteration

2. εἰς τὸ μὴ ταχέως σαλευθῆναι ὑμᾶς ἀπὸ τοῦ νοός, μήτε θροεῖσθαι, μήτε διὰ πνεύματος, μήτε διὰ λόγου, μήτε δι᾽ ἐπιστολῆς ὡς δι᾽ ἡμῶν, ὡς ὅτι ἐνέστηκεν ἡ ἡμέρα τοῦ χριστοῦ·

2. eis to mei tacheos saleutheinai 'umas apo tou no'os, meite throeisthai, meite dya pneumatos, meite dya logou, meite di epistoleis 'os di 'eimon, 'os 'oti enesteiken 'ei 'eimera tou christou.

Hebrew/Transliteration

ב. אַל-נָא יֵתַר לִבְכֶם פִּתְאֹם וְאַל-תָּחִילוּ לֹא מִפְּנֵי-רוּחַ וְלֹא מִפְּנֵי שְׁמוּעָה וְלֹא מִפְּנֵי אִגֶּרֶת אֲשֶׁר יֹאמְרוּן כִּי יָצְאָה מִיָּדֵינוּ לֵאמֹר יוֹם הַמָּשִׁיחַ הִנֵּה בָא:

2. Al - na yi•tar lib•chem pit•om ve•al - ta•chi•loo lo mip•ney - roo•ach ve•lo mip•ney sh`moo•ah ve•lo mip•ney ee•ge•ret asher yom•roon ki yatz•ah mi•ya•dey•noo le•mor yom ha•Ma•shi•ach hee•ne va.

Rabbinic Jewish Commentary

The Alexandrian copy, and some others, read, "the day of the Lord"; and so the Vulgate Latin version; and accordingly the Syriac and Ethiopic versions, "the day of our Lord".

3. Let no man deceive you by any means: for that day shall not come, except there come a falling away first, and that man of sin be revealed, the son of perdition;

Greek/Transliteration
3. μή τις ὑμᾶς ἐξαπατήσῃ κατὰ μηδένα τρόπον· ὅτι ἐὰν μὴ ἔλθῃ ἡ ἀποστασία πρῶτον, καὶ ἀποκαλυφθῇ ὁ ἄνθρωπος τῆς ἁμαρτίας, ὁ υἱὸς τῆς ἀπωλείας,

3. mei tis 'umas exapateisei kata meidena tropon. 'oti ean mei elthei 'ei apostasia proton, kai apokaluphthei 'o anthropos teis 'amartias, 'o 'wios teis apoleias,

Hebrew/Transliteration
ג. אַל-יוֹלִיךְ אֶתְכֶם אִישׁ לְתֹהוּ וְלֹא תָבֹאוּ לוֹ כִּי לֹא-יָבוֹא אִם-לֹא בָרִאשׁוֹנָה יִהְיֶה הַמַּעַל וְנִגְלָה אִישׁ הַחַטָּאָה בֶּן-הָאֲבַדּוֹן:

3. Al - yo•lich et•chem eesh le•to•hoo ve•lo to•voo lo ki lo - ya•vo eem - lo va•ri•sho•na yi•hee•ye ha•ma•al ve•nig•la eesh ha•cha•ta•ah ben - ha•a•va•don.

---

4. Who opposeth and exalteth himself above all that is called God, or that is worshipped; so that he as God sitteth in the temple of God, shewing himself that he is God.

Greek/Transliteration
4. ὁ ἀντικείμενος καὶ ὑπεραιρόμενος ἐπὶ πάντα λεγόμενον θεὸν ἢ σέβασμα, ὥστε αὐτὸν εἰς τὸν ναὸν τοῦ θεοῦ ὡς θεὸν καθίσαι, ἀποδεικνύντα ἑαυτὸν ὅτι ἐστὶν θεός.

4. 'o antikeimenos kai 'uperairomenos epi panta legomenon theon ei sebasma, 'oste auton eis ton naon tou theou 'os theon kathisai, apodeiknunta 'eauton 'oti estin theos.

Hebrew/Transliteration
ד. אֲשֶׁר יִתְקוֹמֵם וְיִתְגַּדֵּל עַל-כָּל-אֵל וַעֲבֹדַת הַשֵּׁם עַד-כִּי גַם-יֵשֵׁב בְּהֵיכַל אֱלֹהִים כֵּאלֹהִים לֵאמֹר הוּא הָאֱלֹהִים:

4. Asher yit•ko•mem ve•yit•ga•del al - kol - el va•a•vo•dat ha•Shem ad - ki gam - ye•shev be•hey•chal Elohim ke•Elohim le•mor hoo ha•Elohim.

Rabbinic Jewish Commentary
The Syriac version renders the last clause, ודחלא, "and religion"; and the Greek word does signify religion, worship, or devotion, as it is translated, in Act_17:23 but here the act of worship is put for the object, and is rightly rendered, "or that which is worshipped"; as it is in the Vulgate Latin version, and in the Arabic version, "or that which is to be worshipped"; and it was usual with the Jews to call God the object of worship, by the name of worship itself, and by which they used to swear: it is said (c) of R. Benjamin the just, that he was appointed over the alms chest; one time a woman came to him and said, Rabbi, relieve me; he replied to her, העבודה, "by the worship" (that is, by God who is worshipped) there is nothing in the alms chest: and elsewhere (d) it is said by one, concerning two that were fatherless, for whom the collectors of alms gathered, העבוד, "by the worship", they go before my daughter: and a little after, העבודה, "by the worship", these things are holy to thee; where the gloss says, it is an oath: and so here the word is to be understood of Deity itself.

Rome is by the Jewish (e) writers called "Magdiel", which signifies "magnifying itself"; the reason is, שיתגדל, "because it magnifies itself" above all these (f); that is, above all kingdoms and states.

The Ethiopic version renders it, "in the house of God"; the sense is, that he governed the world by his word, and was deservedly believed to be God on earth; and their canon law (g) says,

"It is clearly enough shown, that the Roman Emperor cannot be loosed or bound by any secular power; since it is evident that he is called God and it is manifest that God cannot be judged by men:"

And the Ceasars is expressly called (h) "our Lord God": the Ethiopic version reads, "he shall say to all, I am the Lord God"; Eze_28:2, the Alexandrian copy, and some others, and the Vulgate Latin version, leave out the phrase, "as God", but the Syriac retains it.

(c) T. Bab. Bava Bathra, fol. 11. 1. (d) T. Bab. Taanith, fol. 24. 1. (e) Jarchi in Gen. xxxvi. 43. (f) Abarbinel in Dan. fol. 42. 3. (g) Gratian. Decret. dist. 96. can. "satis". (h) Extrarag. "cum inter".

---

5. Remember ye not, that, when I was yet with you, I told you these things?

Greek/Transliteration
5. Οὐ μνημονεύετε ὅτι ἔτι ὢν πρὸς ὑμᾶς, ταῦτα ἔλεγον ὑμῖν;

5. Ou mneimoneuete 'oti eti on pros 'umas, tauta elegon 'umin?

Hebrew/Transliteration
ה. הֲלֹא תִזְכְּרוּ כִּי דִבַּרְתִּי אֲלֵיכֶם כַּדְּבָרִים הָאֵלֶּה בְּעוֹד הָיִיתִי עִמָּכֶם:

5. Ha•lo tiz•ke•roo ki di•bar•ti aley•chem ka•d`va•rim ha•e•le be•od ha•yi•ti ee•ma•chem?

---

6. And now ye know what withholdeth that he might be revealed in his time.

Greek/Transliteration
6. Καὶ νῦν τὸ κατέχον οἴδατε, εἰς τὸ ἀποκαλυφθῆναι αὐτὸν ἐν τῷ ἑαυτοῦ καιρῷ.

6. Kai nun to katechon oidate, eis to apokaluphtheinai auton en to 'eautou kairo.

Hebrew/Transliteration
ו. וְכֵן יְדַעְתֶּם אֶת-אֲשֶׁר יַעַצְרֶנּוּ עַתָּה לְמַעַן יִגָּלֶה בְּעִתּוֹ:

6. Ve•chen ye•da•a•tem et - asher ya•atz•re•noo ata le•ma•an yi•ga•le be•ee•to.

Rabbinic Jewish Commentary

The Roman empire and emperors; these stood in his way, and while this empire lasted, and the emperors wore the imperial crown, and sat on the throne, and held the government in their hands. The whore of Babylon, Israel, takes her seat, and sits upon the seven hills of Rome.

The Ethiopic version renders it, "until his time appointed came": wherefore till the time that God had fixed for the appearance of this monster of iniquity, Vespasian, his son of perdition, Titus, the Roman empire must continue, and Roman emperors must keep their place and dignity to prevent his appearance sooner.

The word here used, which is rendered "withholdeth", or "letteth", as in the next verse, signifies a ruler or governor, and answers to the Hebrew word עצר, "to keep back, or restrain"; and which is used of kings, who by their laws and government restrain and withhold people from doing what they would; see 1Sa_9:17 to which the apostle, who well understood the Hebrew language, doubtless had reference; so יורש עצר, is rendered, "a magistrate", in Jdg_18:7.

---

7. For the mystery of iniquity doth already work: only he who now letteth will let, until he be taken out of the way.

Greek/Transliteration
7. Τὸ γὰρ μυστήριον ἤδη ἐνεργεῖται τῆς ἀνομίας· μόνον ὁ κατέχων ἄρτι, ἕως ἐκ μέσου γένηται,

7. To gar musteirion eidei energeitai teis anomias. monon 'o katechon arti, 'eos ek mesou geneitai,

Hebrew/Transliteration
ז. כִּי סוֹד הַפֶּשַׁע כְּבָר הֵחֵל לְהוֹצִיא פָעֳלָתוֹ אָפֵס הָעֹצֵר יַעְצְרֶנּוּ עַד אֲשֶׁר יוּסַר מִתּוֹךְ הַמְסִלָּה:

7. Ki sod ha•pe•sha k`var he`chel le•ho•tzi fe•oo•la•to e•fes ha•o•tzer ya•atz•re•noo ad asher yoo•sar mi•toch ha•me•si•la.

---

8. And then shall that Wicked be revealed, whom the Lord shall consume with the spirit of his mouth, and shall destroy with the brightness of his coming:

Greek/Transliteration
8. καὶ τότε ἀποκαλυφθήσεται ὁ ἄνομος, ὃν ὁ κύριος ἀναλώσει τῷ πνεύματι τοῦ στόματος αὐτοῦ, καὶ καταργήσει τῇ ἐπιφανείᾳ τῆς παρουσίας αὐτοῦ·

8. kai tote apokaluphtheisetai 'o anomos, 'on 'o kurios analosei to pneumati tou stomatos autou, kai katargeisei tei epiphaneia teis parousias autou.

Hebrew/Transliteration
ח. וְאָז יִגָּלֶה הַפֶּשַׁע אֲשֶׁר יְמִיתֶנּוּ הָאָדוֹן יֵשׁוּעַ בְּרוּחַ שְׂפָתָיו וּבִבְרַק פָּנָיו יַכְחִידֶנּוּ:

8. Ve•az yi•ga•le ha•po•shea asher ye•mi•te•noo ha•Adon Yeshua be•roo•ach s`fa•tav oo•viv•rak pa•nav yach•chi•de•noo.

Rabbinic Jewish Commentary
whom the Lord shall consume with the spirit of his mouth: that is, the "Lord Jesus", as the Alexandrian copy, and Vulgate Latin version read; and the Syriac version, "our Lord Jesus": who is Lord of lords, and God over all; and so able to do what he is here said he shall do.

The Ethiopic version, "whom the Spirit of our Lord Jesus shall cast out".

In this passage there is a manifest reference to Isa_11:4, "with the breath of his mouth shall he slay the wicked": which the Targumist paraphrases,

"With the words of his lips he shall slay ארמילוס רשיעא, "Armillus the wicked":"

And which the Jews say will be done by the Messiah at his coming;

"For so (i) (say they) that phrase in Deu_22:8 "if a man fall from thence", has respect to Armillus the wicked, who at the coming of our Messiah will be slain, as it is said in Isa_11:4'

This Armillus, the Jews say (k), is the head of all idolatry, the tenth king who shall reign at Rome, the city of Satan, the adversary; that he shall rise up after Gog and Magog, and shall go up to Jerusalem, and slay Messiah ben Joseph, and shall himself be slain by Messiah the son of David; yea, they say expressly (l), it is the same whom the Gentiles call antichrist: it is the same with Romulus the first king of the Romans, and designs a Roman, the Roman antichrist; and it may be observed, that the Targumist interprets "the breath of his mouth", by his word; and so says another of their writers (m),

"The meaning is by the word of his lips, for the word goes out of the mouth with the vapour and breath:"

Such an expression as this is said (n) to be used by Moses, when he was bid by God to answer the angels/messengers who objected to his having the Torah given him;

"I am afraid (says he) they will slay (or burn me), בהבל שבפיהם, "with the breath of their mouth":"

Much more may this be feared from the breath of Messiah's mouth.

(i) Tzeror Hammor, fol. 148. 2. (k) Apud Buxtorf. Lex. Talmud. col. 221, 222, 223. (l) Abkath Rochel, par. 1. sign. 7. p. 52. (m) In Ohel Moed. fol. 19. 1. (n) T. Bab. Sabbat, fol. 88. 2.

---

9. Even him, whose coming is after the working of Satan with all power and signs and lying wonders,

Greek/Transliteration
9. οὗ ἐστιν ἡ παρουσία κατ᾽ ἐνέργειαν τοῦ Σατανᾶ ἐν πάσῃ δυνάμει καὶ σημείοις καὶ τέρασιν ψεύδους,

9. 'ou estin 'ei parousia kat energeyan tou Satana en pasei dunamei kai seimeiois kai terasin pseudous,

Hebrew/Transliteration
ט: זֶה הוּא אֲשֶׁר יָבוֹא כְּשָׂטָן בַּעֲלִילוֹתָיו בְּרָב־כֹּחַ בְּאֹתֹת וּבְמוֹפְתִים מִמְּקוֹר אַכְזָב

9. Ze hoo asher ya•vo che•Satan ba•a•li•lo•tav be•rov - ko•ach be•o•tot oov•mof•tim mi•ma•kor ach•zav.

10. And with all deceivableness of unrighteousness in them that perish; because they received not the love of the truth, that they might be saved.

Greek/Transliteration
10. καὶ ἐν πάσῃ ἀπάτῃ τῆς ἀδικίας ἐν τοῖς ἀπολλυμένοις, ἀνθ᾽ ὧν τὴν ἀγάπην τῆς ἀληθείας οὐκ ἐδέξαντο εἰς τὸ σωθῆναι αὐτούς.

10. kai en pasei apatei teis adikias en tois apollumenois, anth 'on tein agapein teis aleitheias ouk edexanto eis to sotheinai autous.

Hebrew/Transliteration
:י. וּבְכָל-אָוֶן וּרְמִיָּה בֵּין הָאֹבְדִים הֲלֹא הֵם אֲשֶׁר לֹא רָצוּ לְהִוָּשֵׁע בְּאַהֲבַת הָאֱמֶת

10. Oov•chol - aven oor•mi•ya bein ha•ov•dim ha•lo hem asher lo ra•tzoo le•hi•va•sha be•a•ha•vat ha•e•met.

---

11. And for this cause God shall send them strong delusion, that they should believe a lie:

Greek/Transliteration
11. Καὶ διὰ τοῦτο πέμψει αὐτοῖς ὁ θεὸς ἐνέργειαν πλάνης, εἰς τὸ πιστεῦσαι αὐτοὺς τῷ ψεύδει·

11. Kai dya touto pempsei autois 'o theos energeyan planeis, eis to pisteusai autous to pseudei.

Hebrew/Transliteration
:יא. וּבַעֲבוּר זֹאת יְשַׁלַּח בָּם אֱלֹהִים מַשְׁאוֹת שָׁוְא וּמַדּוּחִים לְמַעַן יַאֲמִינוּ בַּשָּׁקֶר

11. Oo•va•a•voor zot ye•sha•lach bam Elohim mas•ot shav oo•ma•doo•chim le•ma•an ya•a•mi•noo ba•sha•ker.

Rabbinic Jewish Commentary
Or "efficacy of error", which God may be said to send; and the Alexandrian copy reads, "does send"; because it is not a bare permission but a voluntary one.

---

12. That they all might be damned who believed not the truth, but had pleasure in unrighteousness.

Greek/Transliteration
12. ἵνα κριθῶσιν πάντες οἱ μὴ πιστεύσαντες τῇ ἀληθείᾳ, ἀλλ᾽ εὐδοκήσαντες ἐν τῇ ἀδικίᾳ.

12. 'ina krithosin pantes 'oi mei pisteusantes tei aleitheia, all eudokeisantes en tei adikia.

Hebrew/Transliteration
:יב. וְיֵאָשְׁמוּ כָל-אֵלֶּה אֲשֶׁר לֹא שָׁעוּ אֶל-דִּבְרֵי אֱמֶת וְאַחֲרֵי אָוֶן לִבָּם הֹלֵךְ

12. Ve•ye•esh•moo kol - ele asher lo sha•oo el - div•rey emet ve•a•cha•rey aven li•bam ho•lech.

---

13. But we are bound to give thanks alway to God for you, brethren beloved of the Lord, because God hath from the beginning chosen you to salvation through sanctification of the Spirit and belief of the truth:

Greek/Transliteration
13. Ἡμεῖς δὲ ὀφείλομεν εὐχαριστεῖν τῷ θεῷ πάντοτε περὶ ὑμῶν, ἀδελφοὶ ἠγαπημένοι ὑπὸ κυρίου, ὅτι εἵλετο ὑμᾶς ὁ θεὸς ἀπ᾽ ἀρχῆς εἰς σωτηρίαν ἐν ἁγιασμῷ πνεύματος, καὶ πίστει ἀληθείας·

13. 'Eimeis de opheilomen eucharistein to theo pantote peri 'umon, adelphoi eigapeimenoi 'upo kuriou, 'oti 'eileto 'umas 'o theos ap archeis eis soteirian en 'agyasmo pneumatos, kai pistei aleitheias.

Hebrew/Transliteration
יג. וַאֲנַחְנוּ אַחִים נְכוֹן לִבֵּנוּ לְהוֹדוֹת לֵאלֹהִים תָּמִיד עֲלֵיכֶם בְּחִירֵי אֲדֹנֵינוּ כִּי מֵרֵאשִׁית בָּחַר בָּכֶם אֱלֹהִים וַיְהִי לָכֶם לִישׁוּעָה אַחֲרֵי אֲשֶׁר הִתְקַדַּשְׁתֶּם בָּרוּחַ וֶאֱמוּנַתְכֶם אֱמֶת:

13. Va•a•nach•noo a•chim na•chon li•be•noo le•ho•dot le•Elohim ta•mid aley•chem be•chi•rey Ado•ney•noo ki me•re•sheet ba•char ba•chem Elohim vay•hi la•chem li•shoo•ah a•cha•rey asher hit•ka•dish•tem ba•Roo•ach ve•e•moo•nat•chem emet.

Rabbinic Jewish Commentary
The "belief" or "faith" of this intends, not an historical faith, or a mere assent to truth; but a cordial embracing of it, a receiving of the love of the truth, a feeling of the power of it unto salvation, and a believing in Yeshua Messiah, the substance of it.

---

14. Whereunto he called you by our gospel, to the obtaining of the glory of our Lord Jesus Christ.

Greek/Transliteration
14. εἰς ὃ ἐκάλεσεν ὑμᾶς διὰ τοῦ εὐαγγελίου ἡμῶν, εἰς περιποίησιν δόξης τοῦ κυρίου ἡμῶν Ἰησοῦ χριστοῦ.

14. eis 'o ekalesen 'umas dya tou euangeliou 'eimon, eis peripoieisin doxeis tou kuriou 'eimon Yeisou christou.

Hebrew/Transliteration
יד. וְהוּא קָרָא אֶתְכֶם לְכָל-אֵלֶּה עַל-פִּי בְשׂוֹרָתֵנוּ לָתֵת לָכֶם חֵלֶק בִּכְבוֹד יֵשׁוּעַ הַמָּשִׁיחַ אֲדֹנֵינוּ:

14. Ve•hoo ka•ra et•chem le•chol - ele al - pi be•sora•te•noo la•tet la•chem che•lek bich•vod Yeshua ha•Ma•shi•ach Ado•ney•noo.

Rabbinic Jewish Commentary
The Syriac version renders it, "that ye may be a glory to our Lord Jesus Christ": as the saints will be at the last day, and to all eternity, when they shall be raised again, and have the glory of God upon them, and be forever with the Lord.

15. Therefore, brethren, stand fast, and hold the traditions which ye have been taught, whether by word, or our epistle.

Greek/Transliteration
15. Ἄρα οὖν, ἀδελφοί, στήκετε, καὶ κρατεῖτε τὰς παραδόσεις ἃς ἐδιδάχθητε, εἴτε διὰ λόγου, εἴτε δι᾽ ἐπιστολῆς ἡμῶν.

15. Ara oun, adelphoi, steikete, kai krateite tas paradoseis 'as edidachtheite, eite dya logou, eite di epistoleis 'eimon.

Hebrew/Transliteration
טו: וְעַתָּה אַחַי עִמְדוּ הָכֵן וְהַחֲזִיקוּ בַלֶּקַח הַנָּתוּן לָכֶם עַל-דִּבְרֵי פִינוּ אוֹ עַל-פִּי אִגַּרְתֵּנוּ.

15. Ve•a•ta a•chai eem•doo ha•chen ve•ha•cha•zi•koo va•le•kach ha•na•toon la•chem al - div•rey fi•noo oh al - pi ee•gar•te•noo.

Rabbinic Jewish Commentary
whether by word, or our epistle, that is, by "our" word, as well as by our epistle, and so the Arabic version reads.

---

16. Now our Lord Jesus Christ himself, and God, even our Father, which hath loved us, and hath given us everlasting consolation and good hope through grace,

Greek/Transliteration
16. Αὐτὸς δὲ ὁ κύριος ἡμῶν Ἰησοῦς χριστός, καὶ ὁ θεὸς καὶ πατὴρ ἡμῶν ὁ ἀγαπήσας ἡμᾶς, καὶ δοὺς παράκλησιν αἰωνίαν καὶ ἐλπίδα ἀγαθὴν ἐν χάριτι,

16. Autos de 'o kurios 'eimon Yeisous christos, kai 'o theos kai pateir 'eimon 'o agapeisas 'eimas, kai dous parakleisin aionian kai elpida agathein en chariti,

Hebrew/Transliteration
טז: וְיֵשׁוּעַ הַמָּשִׁיחַ אֲדֹנֵינוּ וְאָבִינוּ אֱלֹהֵינוּ אֲשֶׁר אָהַב אֹתָנוּ וּבְחַסְדּוֹ נָתַן לָנוּ נֹחַם עֲדֵי-עַד וְתִקְוָה טוֹבָה.

16. Ve•Yeshua ha•Ma•shi•ach Ado•ney•noo ve•Avi•noo Elohey•noo asher ahav o•ta•noo oov•chas•do na•tan la•noo no•cham adey - ad ve•tik•va to•va.

Rabbinic Jewish Commentary
The Arabic version reads, "our Lord Jesus Christ, our Father"; and the Ethiopic version also, "our Lord Jesus Christ, God our Father"

The Syriac version reads, "in his grace"; and the Ethiopic version, "a good hope; and his grace".

---

17. Comfort your hearts, and stablish you in every good word and work.

Greek/Transliteration
17. παρακαλέσαι ὑμῶν τὰς καρδίας, καὶ στηρίξαι ὑμᾶς ἐν παντὶ λόγῳ καὶ ἔργῳ ἀγαθῷ.

17. parakalesai 'umon tas kardias, kai steirixai 'umas en panti logo kai ergo agatho.

Hebrew/Transliteration
יז. הוּא יְנַחֵם אֶת-לִבְכֶם וִיכוֹנֵן אֹתָם בְּכָל-מַעֲשֶׂה טוֹב וּבְכָל-דָּבָר:

17. Hoo ye•na•chem et - lib•chem vi•cho•nen o•tam be•chol - ma•a•se tov oov•chol - da•var.

Rabbinic Jewish Commentary
The Arabic version reads, "comfort your hearts by his grace", joining the last clause of the preceding verse to this.

2 Thessalonians, Chapter 3

1. Finally, brethren, pray for us, that the word of the Lord may have free course, and be glorified, even as it is with you:

Greek/Transliteration
1. Τὸ λοιπόν, προσεύχεσθε, ἀδελφοί, περὶ ἡμῶν, ἵνα ὁ λόγος τοῦ κυρίου τρέχῃ καὶ δοξάζηται, καθὼς καὶ πρὸς ὑμᾶς,

1. To loipon, proseuchesthe, adelphoi, peri 'eimon, 'ina 'o logos tou kuriou trechei kai doxazeitai, kathos kai pros 'umas,

Hebrew/Transliteration
א. סוֹף דָּבָר אַחַי הִתְפַּלְלוּ עָלֵינוּ וּדְבַר יְהֹוָה יָרוּץ וְנֶאְדָּר כַּאֲשֶׁר נֶאְדָּר הוּא בָּכֶם:

1. Sof da•var a•chai hit•pa•le•loo aley•noo oo•d`var Adonai ya•rootz ve•ne•e•dar ka•a•sher ne•e•dar hoo ba•chem.

Rabbinic Jewish Commentary
that the word of the Lord may have free course. By "the word of the Lord", or "of God", as the Vulgate Latin and Ethiopic versions read, is meant the Gospel.

---

2. And that we may be delivered from unreasonable and wicked men: for all men have not faith.

Greek/Transliteration
2. καὶ ἵνα ῥυσθῶμεν ἀπὸ τῶν ἀτόπων καὶ πονηρῶν ἀνθρώπων· οὐ γὰρ πάντων ἡ πίστις.

2. kai 'ina 'rusthomen apo ton atopon kai poneiron anthropon. ou gar panton 'ei pistis.

Hebrew/Transliteration
ב. וְלָנוּ תִהְיֶה פְלֵיטָה מִמְּתֵי אָוֶן וְאַנְשֵׁי רֶשַׁע כִּי לֹא כָל-אֲנָשִׁים אֱמוּנָה בָם:

2. Ve•la•noo ti•hi•ye fe•ley•ta mim•tey aven ve•an•shey re•sha ki lo chol - a•na•shim e•moo•na vam.

Rabbinic Jewish Commentary
The Jews say (o), that

"He that studies not in the torah, לאו ביה מהימנותא, "there is no faith in him"--and it is forbidden to come near him, or to trade with him, or to walk with him, "because there is no faith in him"."

The apostle seems to allude to this custom.

(o) Zohar in Lev. fol. 33. 2.

3. But the Lord is faithful, who shall stablish you, and keep you from evil.

Greek/Transliteration
3. Πιστὸς δέ ἐστιν ὁ κύριος, ὃς στηρίξει ὑμᾶς καὶ φυλάξει ἀπὸ τοῦ πονηροῦ.

3. Pistos de estin 'o kurios, 'os steirixei 'umas kai phulaxei apo tou poneirou.

Hebrew/Transliteration
:ג. אַךְ אֲדֹנֵינוּ נֶאֱמָן הוּא אֲשֶׁר יְעוֹדֵד אֶתְכֶם וְיִשְׁמָרְכֶם מִן-הָרָע

3. Ach Ado•ney•noo ne•e•man hoo asher ye•o•ded et•chem ve•yish•mar•chem min - ha•ra.

Rabbinic Jewish Commentary
But the Lord is faithful,.... Or "God" as the Vulgate Latin and Ethiopic versions read, as do also the Alexandrian and Claromontane copies.

---

4. And we have confidence in the Lord touching you, that ye both do and will do the things which we command you.

Greek/Transliteration
4. Πεποίθαμεν δὲ ἐν κυρίῳ ἐφ᾽ ὑμᾶς, ὅτι ἃ παραγγέλλομεν ὑμῖν, καὶ ποιεῖτε καὶ ποιήσετε.

4. Pepoithamen de en kurio eph 'umas, 'oti 'a parangellomen 'umin, kai poieite kai poieisete.

Hebrew/Transliteration
:ד. וַאֲנַחְנוּ בְּטוּחִים עֲלֵיכֶם בַּאדֹנֵינוּ כִּי-עֹשִׂים אַתֶּם כְּמִצְוָתֵנוּ וְכֵן תַּעֲשׂוּ בַּיָּמִים הַבָּאִים

4. Va•a•nach•noo be•too•chim aley•chem ba•Ado•ne•noo ki - o•sim atem ke•mitz•va•te•noo ve•chen ta•a•soo ba•ya•mim ha•ba•eem.

---

5. And the Lord direct your hearts into the love of God, and into the patient waiting for Christ.

Greek/Transliteration
5. Ὁ δὲ κύριος κατευθύναι ὑμῶν τὰς καρδίας εἰς τὴν ἀγάπην τοῦ θεοῦ, καὶ εἰς τὴν ὑπομονὴν τοῦ χριστοῦ.

5. 'O de kurios kateuthunai 'umon tas kardias eis tein agapein tou theou, kai eis tein 'upomonein tou christou.

Hebrew/Transliteration
:ה. וַאֲדֹנֵינוּ יַטֶּה אֶת-לְבַבְכֶם לְאַהֲבָה אֶת-אֱלֹהֵיכֶם וּלְהוֹחִיל לִמְשִׁיחֲכֶם

5. Va•Ado•ney•noo ya•te et - lib•chem le•a•ha•va et - Elohe•chem ool•ho•chil li•Me•shi•cha•chem.

6. Now we command you, brethren, in the name of our Lord Jesus Christ, that ye withdraw yourselves from every brother that walketh disorderly, and not after the tradition which he received of us.

Greek/Transliteration
6. Παραγγέλλομεν δὲ ὑμῖν, ἀδελφοί, ἐν ὀνόματι τοῦ κυρίου ἡμῶν Ἰησοῦ χριστοῦ, στέλλεσθαι ὑμᾶς ἀπὸ παντὸς ἀδελφοῦ ἀτάκτως περιπατοῦντος, καὶ μὴ κατὰ τὴν παράδοσιν ἣν παρέλαβον παρ᾽ ἡμῶν.

6. Parangellomen de 'umin, adelphoi, en onomati tou kuriou 'eimon Yeisou christou, stellesthai 'umas apo pantos adelphou ataktos peripatountos, kai mei kata tein paradosin 'ein parelabon par 'eimon.

Hebrew/Transliteration
ו. וַאֲנַחְנוּ מְצַוִּים אֶתְכֶם אַחֵינוּ בְּשֵׁם יֵשׁוּעַ הַמָּשִׁיחַ אֲדֹנֵינוּ לְהִבָּדֵל מִכָּל־אָח הַהֹלֵךְ בְּדֶרֶךְ עִקֵּשׁ וְלֹא לְפִי הַקַּבָּלָה אֲשֶׁר קִבֵּל מִמֶּנּוּ:

6. Va•a•nach•noo me•tza•vim et•chem achey•noo be•shem Yeshua ha•Ma•shi•ach Ado•ney•noo le•hi•ba•del mi•kol - ach ha•ho•lech be•de•rech ee•kesh ve•lo le•fi ha•ka•ba•la asher ki•bel mi•me•noo.

Rabbinic Jewish Commentary
And so the Ethiopic version here renders it, "that ye remove every brother". From this passage we learn who they are that are to be excommunicated or removed from the communion of gatherings, all disorderly walkers; what the act of excommunication is, it is a withdrawing from them, a separating them from the assembly, and its communion; and who they are that have the power to do it, the whole fraternity or body of the church; and also the authority for it, an apostolical command, in the name of Yeshua.

---

7. For yourselves know how ye ought to follow us: for we behaved not ourselves disorderly among you;

Greek/Transliteration
7. Αὐτοὶ γὰρ οἴδατε πῶς δεῖ μιμεῖσθαι ἡμᾶς· ὅτι οὐκ ἠτακτήσαμεν ἐν ὑμῖν,

7. Autoi gar oidate pos dei mimeisthai 'eimas. 'oti ouk eitakteisamen en 'umin,

Hebrew/Transliteration
ז. הֲלֹא יְדַעְתֶּם אֵת אֲשֶׁר עֲלֵיכֶם לָלֶכֶת בְּעִקְּבוֹתֵינוּ כִּי לֹא כִנְלוֹזִים בְּמַעְגְּלוֹתָם הָלַכְנוּ לִפְנֵיכֶם:

7. Ha•lo ye•da•a•tem et asher aley•chem la•le•chet be•eek•vo•tey•noo ki lo chin•lo•zim be•ma•ag•lo•tam ha•lach•noo lif•ney•chem.

---

8. Neither did we eat any man's bread for nought; but wrought with labour and travail night and day, that we might not be chargeable to any of you:

Greek/Transliteration
8. οὐδὲ δωρεὰν ἄρτον ἐφάγομεν παρά τινος, ἀλλ᾽ ἐν κόπῳ καὶ μόχθῳ, νύκτα καὶ ἡμέραν ἐργαζόμενοι, πρὸς τὸ μὴ ἐπιβαρῆσαί τινα ὑμῶν·

8. oude dorean arton ephagomen para tinos, all en kopo kai mochtho, nukta kai 'eimeran ergazomenoi, pros to mei epibareisai tina 'umon.

Hebrew/Transliteration

ח: וְלֶחֶם אִישׁ לֹא אָכַלְנוּ חִנָּם כִּי אִם-בְּעָמָל וּבִתְלָאָה לַיְלָה וְיוֹמָם לְבִלְתִּי נְהְיֵה עַל-אִישׁ מִכֶּם לְטֹרַח

8. Ve•le•chem eesh lo a•chal•noo chi•nam ki eem - be•a•mal oo•vit•la•ah lai•la ve•yo•mam le•vil•ti ni•hee•ye al - eesh mi•kem la•to•rach.

Rabbinic Jewish Commentary

And so Maimonides says the ancient Jewish Rabbis behaved, and with a like view: wherefore, says he (p),

"If a man is a wise man, and an honourable man, and poor, let him employ himself in some handicraft business, even though a mean one, and not distress men (or be burdensome to them); it is better to strip the skins of beasts that have been torn, than to say to the people, I am a considerable wise (or learned) man, I am a priest, take care of me, and maintain me; and so the wise men have ordered: and some of the greatest doctors have been hewers of wood, and carriers of timber, and drawers of water for the gardens, and have wrought in iron and coals, and have not required anything of the congregation; nor would they take anything of them, when they would have given to them."

(p) Hilchot Mattanot Anayim, c. 10. sect. 18.

---

9. Not because we have not power, but to make ourselves an ensample unto you to follow us.

Greek/Transliteration

9. οὐχ ὅτι οὐκ ἔχομεν ἐξουσίαν, ἀλλ᾽ ἵνα ἑαυτοὺς τύπον δῶμεν ὑμῖν εἰς τὸ μιμεῖσθαι ἡμᾶς.

9. ouch 'oti ouk echomen exousian, all 'ina 'eautous tupon domen 'umin eis to mimeisthai 'eimas.

Hebrew/Transliteration

ט: לֹא מֵאֲשֶׁר אֵין-צְדָקָה לָנוּ כִּי אִם-לִהְיוֹת לְמוֹפֵת לָכֶם בְּנַפְשֵׁנוּ אֲשֶׁר תֵּלְכוּ בְּעִקְבוֹתֵינוּ

9. Lo me•a•sher eyn - tze•da•ka la•noo ki eem - li•hee•yot le•mo•fet la•chem be•naf•she•noo asher tel•choo be•eek•vo•tey•noo.

---

10. For even when we were with you, this we commanded you, that if any would not work, neither should he eat.

Greek/Transliteration

10. Καὶ γὰρ ὅτε ἦμεν πρὸς ὑμᾶς, τοῦτο παρηγγέλλομεν ὑμῖν ὅτι εἴ τις οὐ θέλει ἐργάζεσθαι, μηδὲ ἐσθιέτω.

10. Kai gar 'ote eimen pros 'umas, touto pareingellomen 'umin 'oti ei tis ou thelei ergazesthai, meide esthieto.

Hebrew/Transliteration
י. כִּי גַם-בִּהְיוֹתֵנוּ עִמָּכֶם צִוִּינוּ אֶתְכֶם לֵאמֹר אִם מָאֵן יְמָאֵן אִישׁ לַעֲשׂוֹת בִּמְלָאכָה גַם-אָכוֹל לֹא יֹאכַל:

10. Ki gam - bi•hi•yo•te•noo ee•ma•chem tzi•vi•noo et•chem le•mor eem ma•en ye•ma•en eesh la•a•sot bim•la•cha gam - a•chol lo yo•chel.

Rabbinic Jewish Commentary

we commanded you, that if any would not work, neither should he eat; The Ethiopic version reads in the singular number, "when I was with you, I commanded you"; using the above words, which were a sort of a proverb with the Jews, and is frequently used by them, דאי לא אכיל, or לעי לא נגיס, "that if a man would not work, he should not eat" (q). And again (r),

"He that labours on the evening of the sabbath (or on weekdays), he shall eat on the sabbath day; and he who does not labour on the evening of the sabbath, from whence shall he eat (or what right and authority has he to eat) on the sabbath day?"

Not he that could not work through weakness, bodily diseases, or old age, the necessities of such are to be distributed to, and they are to be taken care of, and provided with the necessaries of life by the officers of the church; but those that can work, and will not, ought to starve, for any assistance that should be given them by the members of the church, or the officers of it.

(q) Bereshit Rabba, sect. 14. fol. 13. 1. Echa Rabbati, fol. 48. 4. & Midrash Koholet, fol. 65. 4. (r) T. Bab. Avoda Zara, fol. 3. 1.

---

11. For we hear that there are some which walk among you disorderly, working not at all, but are busybodies.

Greek/Transliteration
11. Ἀκούομεν γάρ τινας περιπατοῦντας ἐν ὑμῖν ἀτάκτως, μηδὲν ἐργαζομένους, ἀλλὰ περιεργαζομένους.

11. Akouomen gar tinas peripatountas en 'umin ataktos, meiden ergazomenous, alla periergazomenous.

Hebrew/Transliteration
יא. כִּי שָׁמַעְנוּ כִּי-יֵשׁ בָּכֶם אֲנָשִׁים מְעַקְּשֵׁי דָרֶךְ אֲשֶׁר לֹא יִגְּעוּ בְדֵי מְלָאכָה כִּי אִם-יִגְּעוּ בְדֵי רִיק:

11. Ki sha•ma•a•noo ki - yesh ba•chem a•na•shim me•ak•shey de•rech asher lo yig•oo ve•dey me•la•cha ki eem - yig•oo ve•dey rik.

---

12. Now them that are such we command and exhort by our Lord Jesus Christ, that with quietness they work, and eat their own bread.

Greek/Transliteration
12. Τοῖς δὲ τοιούτοις παραγγέλλομεν καὶ παρακαλοῦμεν διὰ τοῦ κυρίου ἡμῶν Ἰησοῦ χριστοῦ, ἵνα μετὰ ἡσυχίας ἐργαζόμενοι τὸν ἑαυτῶν ἄρτον ἐσθίωσιν.

12. Tois de toioutois parangellomen kai parakaloumen dya tou kuriou 'eimon Yeisou christou, 'ina meta 'eisuchias ergazomenoi ton 'eauton arton esthiosin.

Hebrew/Transliteration
יב. וְאֶת-אֲנָשִׁים כָּאֵלֶּה אֲנַחְנוּ מְצַוִּים וּמְבַקְשִׁים מֵהֶם לִפְנֵי יֵשׁוּעַ הַמָּשִׁיחַ אֲדֹנֵינוּ לַעֲשׂוֹת בְּנַחַת מְלַאכְתָּם וְלֶאֱכֹל אֶת-לַחְמָם מִיגִיעַ כַּפֵּיהֶם:

12. Ve•et - a•na•shim ka•e•le a•nach•noo me•tza•vim oom•vak•shim me•hem lif•ney Yeshua ha•Ma•shi•ach Ado•ney•noo la•a•sot be•na•chat me•lach•tam ve•le•e•chol et - lach•mam miy•gi•a ka•pey•hem.

---

13. But ye, brethren, be not weary in well doing.

Greek/Transliteration
13. Ὑμεῖς δέ, ἀδελφοί, μὴ ἐκκακήσητε καλοποιοῦντες.

13. 'Umeis de, adelphoi, mei ekkakeiseite kalopoiountes.

Hebrew/Transliteration
יג. וְאַתֶּם אֶחָי אַל-תִּהְיוּ עֲיֵפִים בַּעֲשׂוֹתְכֶם טוֹב:

13. Ve•a•tem e•chai al - ti•hi•yoo a•ye•fim ba•a•sot•chem tov.

---

14. And if any man obey not our word by this epistle, note that man, and have no company with him, that he may be ashamed.

Greek/Transliteration
14. Εἰ δέ τις οὐχ ὑπακούει τῷ λόγῳ ἡμῶν διὰ τῆς ἐπιστολῆς, τοῦτον σημειοῦσθε, καὶ μὴ συναναμίγνυσθε αὐτῷ, ἵνα ἐντραπῇ,

14. Ei de tis ouch 'upakouei to logo 'eimon dya teis epistoleis, touton seimeiousthe, kai mei sunanamignusthe auto, 'ina entrapei,

Hebrew/Transliteration
יד. וְאִישׁ אֲשֶׁר לֹא-יִשְׁמַע אֶת-דְּבָרֵנוּ בָּאִגֶּרֶת הַזֹּאת הַתְווּ אֹתוֹ לְבַד וְלֹא תִתְעָרְבוּ בְחֶבְרָתוֹ לְמַעַן יֵבוֹשׁ:

14. Ve•eesh asher lo - yish•ma et - d`va•re•noo ba•ee•ge•ret ha•zot hat•voo o•to le•vad ve•lo tit•ar•voo ve•chev•ra•to le•ma•an ye•vosh.

Rabbinic Jewish Commentary
note that man; some read this clause in connection with the preceding phrase, "by this epistle", or by an epistle; and so the Ethiopic version, "show", or "signify him by an epistle"; that is, give us notice of it by an epistle, that we may take him under our cognizance, and severely chastise him, according to the power and authority given us by Yeshua; but that phrase rather belongs to the preceding words: and the clause here respects the notice the church should take of such a person; not in a private way, or merely by way of admonition and reproof, such as is given before rejection from communion; but by the black mark of excommunication; lay him under censure, exclude him from your communion, put a brand upon him as a scabbed sheep, and separate him from the flock; and so the Syriac version renders it, יתפרש, "let him be separated from you".

The Jews say (s),

"In matters of heaven (of God or religion), if a man does not return privately, מכלימין, they "put him to shame" publicly; and publish his sin, and reproach him to his face, and despise and set him at nought until he returns to do well."

(s) Maimon, Hilch. Deyot, c. 6. sect. 8.

---

15. Yet count him not as an enemy, but admonish him as a brother.

Greek/Transliteration
15. καὶ μὴ ὡς ἐχθρὸν ἡγεῖσθε, ἀλλὰ νουθετεῖτε ὡς ἀδελφόν.

15. kai mei 'os echthron 'eigeisthe, alla noutheteite 'os adelphon.

Hebrew/Transliteration
טו. וְאַל-תַּחְשְׁבֻהוּ לְאֹיֵב כִּי אִם-הוֹכֵחַ תּוֹכִיחוּן אֹתוֹ כְּאָח:

15. Ve•al - tach•she•voo•hoo le•o•yev ki eem - ho•che•ach to•chi•choon o•to ke•ach.

Rabbinic Jewish Commentary
This seems to be levelled against the Jews, who allowed of hatred to incorrigible persons: they say (t),

"An hater that is spoken of in the Torah, is not of the nations of the world, but of Israel; but how shall an Israelite hate an Israelite? does not the Scripture say, "thou shall not hate thy brother in thine heart?" the wise men say, when a man sees him alone, who has committed a transgression, and he admonishes him, and he does not return, lo, it is מצוה לשונאו, "a commandment to hate him" until he repents and turns from his wickedness."

(t) Maimon. Hilchot Rotzeach, c. 13. sect. 14.

---

16. Now the Lord of peace himself give you peace always by all means. The Lord be with you all.

Greek/Transliteration
16. Αὐτὸς δὲ ὁ κύριος τῆς εἰρήνης δῴη ὑμῖν τὴν εἰρήνην διὰ παντὸς ἐν παντὶ τρόπῳ. Ὁ κύριος μετὰ πάντων ὑμῶν.

16. Autos de 'o kurios teis eireineis doei 'umin tein eireinein dya pantos en panti tropo. 'O kurios meta panton 'umon.

Hebrew/Transliteration
טז. וַאֲדוֹן הַשָּׁלוֹם הוּא יִתֵּן לָכֶם שָׁלוֹם בְּכֹל אֲשֶׁר תִּפְנוּ כָּל-הַיָּמִים וַאֲדֹנֵינוּ יְהִי עִם-כֻּלְּכֶם:

16. Va•Adon ha•sha•lom hoo yi•ten la•chem sha•lom be•chol asher tif•noo kol - ha•ya•mim va•Ado•ney•noo ye•hee eem - kool•chem.

17. The salutation of Paul with mine own hand, which is the token in every epistle: so I write.

Greek/Transliteration
17. Ὁ ἀσπασμὸς τῇ ἐμῇ χειρὶ Παύλου, ὅ ἐστιν σημεῖον ἐν πάσῃ ἐπιστολῇ· οὕτως γράφω.

17. 'O aspasmos tei emei cheiri Paulou, 'o estin seimeion en pasei epistolei. 'outos grapho.

Hebrew/Transliteration
יז. זֹאת שְׁאֵלַת שָׁלוֹם בִּכְתָב יָדִי אֲנִי פוֹלוֹס אֲשֶׁר הוּא לְאוֹת בְּכָל-אִגְּרוֹתַי כָּזֶה אֲנִי כֹתֵב:

17. Zot sh`e•lat sha•lom bich•tav ya•di ani Folos asher hoo le•ot be•chol - eeg•ro•tai ka•ze ani cho•tev.

---

18. The grace of our Lord Jesus Christ be with you all. Amen.

Greek/Transliteration
18. Ἡ χάρις τοῦ κυρίου ἡμῶν Ἰησοῦ χριστοῦ μετὰ πάντων ὑμῶν. Ἀμήν.

18. 'Ei charis tou kuriou 'eimon Yeisou christou meta panton 'umon. Amein.

Hebrew/Transliteration
יח. חֶסֶד יֵשׁוּעַ הַמָּשִׁיחַ אֲדֹנֵינוּ עִם-כֻּלְּכֶם אָמֵן:

18. Che•sed Yeshua ha•Ma•shi•ach Ado•ney•noo eem - kool•chem Amen.

---

^end^

THE FIRST EPISTLE OF PAUL THE APOSTLE TO TIMOTHY

1 Timothy, Chapter 1

1. Paul, an apostle of Jesus Christ by the commandment of God our Saviour, and Lord Jesus Christ, which is our hope;

Greek/Transliteration

1. Παῦλος ἀπόστολος Ἰησοῦ χριστοῦ κατ᾽ ἐπιταγὴν θεοῦ σωτῆρος ἡμῶν, καὶ κυρίου Ἰησοῦ χριστοῦ τῆς ἐλπίδος ἡμῶν,

1. Paulos apostolos Yeisou christou kat epitagein theou soteiros 'eimon, kai kuriou Yeisou christou teis elpidos 'eimon,

Hebrew/Transliteration

א. פּוֹלוֹס שְׁלִיחַ יֵשׁוּעַ הַמָּשִׁיחַ עַל-פִּי דְבַר הָאֱלֹהִים מוֹשִׁיעֵנוּ וְעַל-פִּי הָאָדוֹן יֵשׁוּעַ הַמָּשִׁיחַ תִּקְוָתֵנוּ:

1. Polos sh`li•ach Yeshua ha•Ma•shi•ach al - pi de•var ha•Elohim Mo•shi•e•noo ve•al – pi ha•Adon Yeshua ha•Ma•shi•ach tik•va•te•noo.

---

2. Unto Timothy, my own son in the faith: Grace, mercy, and peace, from God our Father and Jesus Christ our Lord.

Greek/Transliteration

2. Τιμοθέῳ γνησίῳ τέκνῳ ἐν πίστει· χάρις, ἔλεος, εἰρήνη ἀπὸ θεοῦ πατρὸς ἡμῶν καὶ χριστοῦ Ἰησοῦ τοῦ κυρίου ἡμῶν.

2. Timotheo gneisio tekno en pistei. charis, eleos, eireinei apo theou patros 'eimon kai christou Yeisou tou kuriou 'eimon.

Hebrew/Transliteration

ב. אֶל-טִימוֹתִיּוֹס בְּנִי כְּבֶן מַחֲלָצַי מִמְּקוֹר אֱמוּנָה חֶסֶד רַחֲמִים וְשָׁלוֹם לְךָ מֵאֵת אֱלֹהִים אָבִינוּ וּמֵאֵת יֵשׁוּעַ הַמָּשִׁיחַ אֲדֹנֵינוּ:

2. El - Ti•mo•ti•yos b`ni ke•ven me•cha•la•tzai mim•kor e•moo•na che•sed ra•cha•mim ve•sha•lom le•cha me•et Elohim Avi•noo oo•me•et Yeshua ha•Ma•shi•ach Ado•ney•noo.

---

3. As I besought thee to abide still at Ephesus, when I went into Macedonia, that thou mightest charge some that they teach no other doctrine,

Greek/Transliteration

3. Καθὼς παρεκάλεσά σε προσμεῖναι ἐν Ἐφέσῳ, πορευόμενος εἰς Μακεδονίαν, ἵνα παραγγείλῃς τισὶν μὴ ἑτεροδιδασκαλεῖν,

3. Kathos parekalesa se prosmeinai en Epheso, poreuomenos eis Makedonian, 'ina parangeileis tisin mei 'eterodidaskalein,

Hebrew/Transliteration
:ג. בְּלֶכְתִּי לְמַקְדּוֹנְיָא בִקַשְׁתִּיךָ לָשֶׁבֶת בְּאֶפְסוֹס לְצַוֹּת עַל-אֲנָשִׁים אֲחָדִים לְבִלְתִּי יוֹרוּ תּוֹרָה נָכְרִיָּה

3. Be•lech•ti le•Mak•donya bi•kash•ti•cha la•she•vet be•Efsos le•tza•vot al - a•na•shim a•cha•dim le•vil•ti yo•roo to•rah noch•ri•ya.

---

4. Neither give heed to fables and endless genealogies, which minister questions, rather than godly edifying which is in faith: so do.

Greek/Transliteration
4. μηδὲ προσέχειν μύθοις καὶ γενεαλογίαις ἀπεράντοις, αἵτινες ζητήσεις παρέχουσιν μᾶλλον ἢ οἰκονομίαν θεοῦ τὴν ἐν πίστει.

4. meide prosechein muthois kai genealogiais aperantois, 'aitines zeiteiseis parechousin mallon ei oikonomian theou tein en pistei.

Hebrew/Transliteration
ד. וְלֹא יִתְעַסְּקוּ בְדִבְרֵי אַגָּדָה וּבְתוֹלְדוֹת הַדֹּרוֹת חֶשְׁבּוֹנוֹת לְאֵין-קֵץ הַנֹּתְנִים יָדַיִם לְהִתְוַכֵּחַ וְלֹא לְחַזֵּק בֵּית-אֱלֹהִים בָּאֱמוּנָה:

4. Ve•lo yit•as•koo ve•div•rey aga•da oov•tol•dot ha•do•rot chish•vo•not le•ein - ketz ha•not•nim ya•da•yim le•hit•va•ke•ach ve•lo le•cha•zek beit - Elohim ba•e•moo•na.

Rabbinic Jewish Commentary

Some care Ezra took of this matter, when the Jews returned from the Babylonish captivity. It is said (a), that עשרה יוחסין,

"Ten genealogies (or ten sorts of persons genealogized) came out of Babylon; priests, Levites, Israelites, profane (or unfit for the priesthood, though they sprung from priests) proselytes, freemen (servants made free), bastards, Nethinim or Gibeonites, such whose father was not known, and those that were took up in the streets.

These Ezra brought up to Jerusalem thus distinguished, that they might be taken care of by the sanhedrim, and kept distinct; but these would often intermix and cause disputes; and sometimes these mixtures were connived at through partiality or fear (b).

"Says R. Jochanan, by the temple, it is in our hands, (the gloss adds, to discover the illegitimate families of the land of Israel,) but what shall I do? for lo, the great men of this age are hid (or impure): in which he agreed with R. Isaac, who said, the family that is hid, let it be hid. Abai also saith, we have learned this by tradition, there was a family of the house of Tzeriphah, beyond Jordan, and a son of Zion, (a famous man, a man of authority,) set it at a distance, (proclaimed it illegitimate,) by his authority. And again, there was another, and he made it near (or pronounced it right) by his power. Again, there was another family, and the wise men would not discover it.

By which we may see what management there was in these things, and what a foundation was laid for questions and debates. Of these public and private genealogies; Mat_1:16, to which may be added what R. Benjamin says (c) of some Jews in his time, who were the Rechabites, and were very numerous, and had a prince over them of the house of David; and, adds he, they have a genealogical book, ומשגרות שאלות, "and extracts of questions", which I should be tempted to render "clusters of questions", which are with the head of the captivity; and this comes very near to what our apostle here says. And when it is observed, that Herod, that he might hide the meanness of his descent and birth, burnt all the genealogical writings in the public archives (d), it must be still more difficult to fix the true account of things; and for the loss of the genealogical book, the public one, the Jews express a very great concern: for they say (e), that "from the time the book of genealogies was hid, the strength of the wise men was weakened, and the light of their eyes grew dim. Says Mar Zutra, between Azel and Azel, (that is, between 1Ch_8:38 and 1Ch_9:44) there is need of four hundred camel loads of commentaries.

So intricate an affair, and such an endless business was this. And this affair of genealogies might be now the more the subject of inquiry among judaizing Christians, since there was, and still is, an expectation among the Jews, that in the times of the Messiah these things will be set aright. Says Maimonides (f),

"in the days of the King Messiah, when his kingdom shall be settled, and all Israel shall be gathered to him, יתייחסו כולם, "they shall all of them be genealogized", according to his word, by the Holy Ghost, as it is said, Mal_3:3 he shall purify the sons of Levi, and say, this is a genealogized priest, and this is a genealogized Levite; and shall drive them away who are not genealogized (or related) to Israel, as it is said, Ezr_2:63. Hence you learn, that by the Holy Spirit they shall be genealogized, those that arrogate and proclaim their genealogy; and he shall not genealogize Israel but by their tribes, for he shall make known that this is of such a tribe, and this is of such a tribe; but he shall not say concerning such an one he is a bastard, and this is a servant; for so shall it be, that the family that is obscure shall be obscure.

Or else the genealogical account of their traditions may be meant, which they trace from Moses to Joshua, from Joshua to the elders, from the elders to the prophets, from the prophets to the men of the great synagogue, and from one doctor to another (g), which to pursue is endless, tedious, and tiresome.

(a) Misn. Kiddnshin, c. 4. sect. 1. (b) T. Bab. Kiddushin, fol. 71. 1. & Hieros. Kiddushin, fol. 65. 3. (c) Massaot, p. 83. (d) Euseb. Eccl. Hist. l. 1. c. 7. (e) T. Bab. Pesachim, fol. 62. 2. (f) Hilchot Melacim, c. 12. sect. 3. (g) Pirke Abot, c. 1. sect. 1, &c.

---

5. Now the end of the commandment is charity out of a pure heart, and of a good conscience, and of faith unfeigned:

Greek/Transliteration
5. Τὸ δὲ τέλος τῆς παραγγελίας ἐστὶν ἀγάπη ἐκ καθαρᾶς καρδίας καὶ συνειδήσεως ἀγαθῆς καὶ πίστεως ἀνυποκρίτου·

5. To de telos teis parangelias estin agapei ek katharas kardias kai suneideiseos agatheis kai pisteos anupokritou.

Hebrew/Transliteration
:ה. כִּי-תַכְלִית מִצְוַת הַתּוֹרָה הִיא אַהֲבָה בְּלֵב טָהוֹר בְּרוּחַ נָכוֹן וּבֶאֱמוּנָה נְקִיָּה מִכָּל-סִיג

5. Ki - tach•lit mitz•vat ha•Torah hee a•ha•va be•lev ta•hor be•roo•ach na•chon oo•ve•e•moo•na n`ki•ya mi•kol - sig.

6. From which some having swerved have turned aside unto vain jangling;

Greek/Transliteration
6. ὧν τινες ἀστοχήσαντες ἐξετράπησαν εἰς ματαιολογίαν,

6. 'on tines astocheisantes exetrapeisan eis mataiologian,

Hebrew/Transliteration
‏ו. אַךְ יֵשׁ אֲשֶׁר נָטוּ מִנִּי-אֹרַח וַיֵּלְכוּ אַחֲרֵי הֶהָבֶל:

6. Ach yesh asher na•too mi•ni - o•rach va•yel•choo a•cha•rey he•ha•vel.

---

7. Desiring to be teachers of the law; understanding neither what they say, nor whereof they affirm.

Greek/Transliteration
7. θέλοντες εἶναι νομοδιδάσκαλοι, μὴ νοοῦντες μήτε ἃ λέγουσιν, μήτε περὶ τίνων διαβεβαιοῦνται.

7. thelontes einai nomodidaskaloi, mei noountes meite 'a legousin, meite peri tinon dyabebaiountai.

Hebrew/Transliteration
‏ז. יִתְאַמְּרוּ לִהְיוֹת מוֹרִים בַּתּוֹרָה וְלֹא-יָבִינוּ אֵת אֲשֶׁר יְדַבֵּרוּן וְלֹא אֶת-הַדָּבָר אֲשֶׁר עָלָיו יַחֲלֹטוּן:

7. Yit•am•roo li•hee•yot mo•rim ba•To•rah ve•lo - ya•vi•noo et asher ye•da•be•roon ve•lo et - ha•da•var asher alav yach•lo•toon.

---

8. But we know that the law is good, if a man use it lawfully;

Greek/Transliteration
8. Οἴδαμεν δὲ ὅτι καλὸς ὁ νόμος, ἐάν τις αὐτῷ νομίμως χρῆται,

8. Oidamen de 'oti kalos 'o nomos, ean tis auto nomimos chreitai,

Hebrew/Transliteration
‏ח. הֵן הַתּוֹרָה יָדַעְנוּ כִּי טוֹבָה הִיא אִם-יֵלֵךְ הָאָדָם בִּנְתִיבוֹתֶיהָ כַּמִּשְׁפָּט:

8. Hen ha•Torah ya•da•a•noo ki to•va hee eem - ye•lech ha•a•dam bin•ti•vo•te•ha ka•mish•pat.

---

9. Knowing this, that the law is not made for a righteous man, but for the lawless and disobedient, for the ungodly and for sinners, for unholy and profane, for murderers of fathers and murderers of mothers, for manslayers,

Greek/Transliteration
9. εἰδὼς τοῦτο, ὅτι δικαίῳ νόμος οὐ κεῖται, ἀνόμοις δὲ καὶ ἀνυποτάκτοις, ἀσεβέσιν καὶ ἁμαρτωλοῖς, ἀνοσίοις καὶ βεβήλοις, πατρολῴαις καὶ μητρολῴαις, ἀνδροφόνοις,

9. eidos touto, 'oti dikaio nomos ou keitai, anomois de kai anupotaktois, asebesin kai 'amartolois, anosiois kai bebeilois, patroloais kai meitroloais, androphonois,

Hebrew/Transliteration

ט. וְהוּא יָבִין כִּי תוֹרָה נְתוּנָה לֹא לְאַנְשֵׁי צֶדֶק כִּי אִם-לִבְנֵי בְלִיַּעַל מֹרְדִים פֹּשְׁעִים וְחַטָּאִים עֹשֵׂי תוֹעֵבָה וּנְבָלָה מַכֵּי אָב וְאֵם אוֹ מְרַצְּחִים:

9. Ve•hoo ya•vin ki To•rah n`too•na lo le•an•shey tze•dek ki eem - liv•ney ve•li•ya•al mor•dim psh•eem ve•cha•ta•eem o•sey to•e•va oon•va•la ma•key av ve•em oh me•ratz•chim.

Rabbinic Jewish Commentary

The words δικαιω νομος ου κειται, may be rendered, "the law does not lie upon a righteous man", or against him.

But for the lawless and disobedient; by the "lawless" are meant, not the Gentiles, which were without the written Torah, but such who have it, and despise and reject it, and live not according to it, but transgress it: and "the disobedient" design such who are not subject to it: who are sons of Belial, children without the yoke; who cast the Torah of YHWH behind their backs; who are not, nor can they be subject to it, without the powerful and efficacious grace of God.

The Syriac and Arabic versions render them, and against this there was an express law, Exo_21:15. According to the Pompeian law, one guilty of parricide was to be sewed up in a sack with a dog, a cock, a viper, and an ape, and cast into the sea, or into a river (h).

(h) Pompon. Laetus de Leg. Rom. p. 156.

---

10. For whoremongers, for them that defile themselves with mankind, for menstealers, for liars, for perjured persons, and if there be any other thing that is contrary to sound doctrine;

Greek/Transliteration

10. πόρνοις, ἀρσενοκοίταις, ἀνδραποδισταῖς, ψεύσταις, ἐπιόρκοις, καὶ εἴ τι ἕτερον τῇ ὑγιαινούσῃ διδασκαλίᾳ ἀντίκειται,

10. pornois, arsenokoitais, andrapodistais, pseustais, epiorkois, kai ei ti 'eteron tei 'ugyainousei didaskalia antikeitai,

Hebrew/Transliteration

י. נֹאֲפִים וְשֹׁכְבִים אֶת-זָכָר גֹּנְבֵי נֶפֶשׁ בָּנִים כֶּחָשִׁים וְנִשְׁבָּעִים לַשֶּׁקֶר וְעוֹד אֲחֵרִים כְּמוֹהֶם מַמְרִים בְּתוֹרַת חַיִּים

10. No•a•fim ve•shoch•vim et - za•char gon•vey ne•fesh ba•nim ke•cha•shim ve•nish•ba•eem la•sha•ker ve•od a•che•rim ke•mo•hem mam•rim be•to•rat cha•yim.

Rabbinic Jewish Commentary

for men stealers; who decoyed servants or free men, and stole them away, and sold them for slaves; this practice was condemned by the Flavian law among the Romans (i), and was not allowed of among the Grecians (k); the death with which such were punished was strangling, according to the Jews (l).

(i) Pompon. Laetus de Leg. Rom. p. 154. (k) Philostrat. Vit. Apollon. l. 8. c. 3. (l) Mishna Sanhedria, c. 10. sect. 1. & Maimon. Hilch. Geniba, c. 9. sect. 1.

---

11. According to the glorious gospel of the blessed God, which was committed to my trust.

Greek/Transliteration
11. κατὰ τὸ εὐαγγέλιον τῆς δόξης τοῦ μακαρίου θεοῦ, ὃ ἐπιστεύθην ἐγώ.

11. kata to euangelion teis doxeis tou makariou theou, 'o episteuthein ego.

Hebrew/Transliteration
יא. כְּפִי בְשׂוֹרַת כְּבוֹד הָאֱלֹהִים בָּרוּךְ הוּא אֲשֶׁר הִפְקִיד בְּיָדִי:

11. Ke•fi be•so•rat k`vod ha•Elohim ba•rooch hoo asher hif•kid be•ya•di.

---

12. And I thank Christ Jesus our Lord, who hath enabled me, for that he counted me faithful, putting me into the ministry;

Greek/Transliteration
12. Καὶ χάριν ἔχω τῷ ἐνδυναμώσαντί με χριστῷ Ἰησοῦ τῷ κυρίῳ ἡμῶν, ὅτι πιστόν με ἡγήσατο, θέμενος εἰς διακονίαν,

12. Kai charin echo to endunamosanti me christo Yeisou to kurio 'eimon, 'oti piston me 'eigeisato, themenos eis dyakonian,

Hebrew/Transliteration
יב. וּלְיֵשׁוּעַ הַמָּשִׁיחַ אֲדֹנֵינוּ הַמְאַזְּרֵנִי חַיִל אֶתֵּן תְּהִלָּה כִּי מָצָא אֶת-לְבָבִי נֶאֱמָן לְפָנָיו וַיַּקְרֵב אֹתִי לְשָׁרְתוֹ:

12. Ool•Yeshua ha•Ma•shi•ach Ado•ney•noo ham•az•re•ni cha•yil e•ten te•hi•la ki ma•tza et - le•va•vi ne•e•man le•fa•nav va•yak•rev o•ti le•shar•to.

---

13. Who was before a blasphemer, and a persecutor, and injurious: but I obtained mercy, because I did it ignorantly in unbelief.

Greek/Transliteration
13. τὸν πρότερον ὄντα βλάσφημον καὶ διώκτην καὶ ὑβριστήν· ἀλλὰ ἠλεήθην, ὅτι ἀγνοῶν ἐποίησα ἐν ἀπιστίᾳ·

13. ton proteron onta blaspheimon kai dioktein kai 'ubristein. alla eileeithein, 'oti agnoon epoieisa en apistia.

Hebrew/Transliteration
יג. אָנֹכִי אֲשֶׁר מְגַדֵּף הָיִיתִי לְפָנִים מְרַדֵּף וּמְחַבֵּל אַךְ רֻחַמְתִּי כִּי עָשִׂיתִי בִשְׁגָגָה בִּבְלִי-אֱמוּנָה:

13. Ano•chi asher me•ga•def ha•yi•ti le•fa•nim me•ra•def oom•cha•bel ach roo•cham•ti ki a•si•ti vish•ga•ga biv•li - e•moo•na.

14. And the grace of our Lord was exceeding abundant with faith and love which is in Christ Jesus.

Greek/Transliteration
14. ὑπερεπλεόνασεν δὲ ἡ χάρις τοῦ κυρίου ἡμῶν μετὰ πίστεως καὶ ἀγάπης τῆς ἐν χριστῷ Ἰησοῦ.

14. 'uperepleonasen de 'ei charis tou kuriou 'eimon meta pisteos kai agapeis teis en christo Yeisou.

Hebrew/Transliteration
יד. וַיִּגְדַּל חֶסֶד אֲדֹנֵינוּ עָלַי עַד-מְאֹד וֶאֱמוּנָה וְאַהֲבָה בְּיֵשׁוּעַ מְשִׁיחֵנוּ:

14. Va•yig•dal che•sed Ado•ney•noo a•lai ad - me•od ve•e•moo•na ve•a•ha•va be•Yeshua Me•shi•che•noo.

---

15. This is a faithful saying, and worthy of all acceptation, that Christ Jesus came into the world to save sinners; of whom I am chief.

Greek/Transliteration
15. Πιστὸς ὁ λόγος καὶ πάσης ἀποδοχῆς ἄξιος, ὅτι χριστὸς Ἰησοῦς ἦλθεν εἰς τὸν κόσμον ἁμαρτωλοὺς σῶσαι, ὧν πρῶτός εἰμι ἐγώ·

15. Pistos 'o logos kai paseis apodocheis axios, 'oti christos Yeisous eilthen eis ton kosmon 'amartolous sosai, 'on protos eimi ego.

Hebrew/Transliteration
טו. אֱמֶת הַדָּבָר וְרָאֲתָה לְכָל-אָדָם לְקַבְּלוֹ כִּי יֵשׁוּעַ הַמָּשִׁיחַ בָּא אֶל-הָאָרֶץ לְהוֹשִׁיעַ אֶת-הַחַטָּאִים וְאָנֹכִי הָרֹאשׁ לָהֶם:

15. Emet ha•da•var ve•ya•a•ta le•chol - adam le•kab•lo ki Yeshua ha•Ma•shi•ach ba el - ha•a•retz le•ho•shi•a et - ha•cha•ta•eem ve•a•no•chi ha•rosh la•hem.

Rabbinic Jewish Commentary
This is a faithful saying, and worthy of all acceptation; Indeed, sometimes the words of the prophets are so called by them; so that passage in Joe_2:13 is called קבלה, "Cabala" (n), some thing delivered and received; upon which one of their commentators (o) has these words,

"Whatever a prophet commands the Israelites, makes known unto them, or exhorts them to, is a Cabala."

(m) Pirke Abot, c. 1. sect. 1. (n) Mishn. Taanith, c. 2. sect. 1. (o) Jarchi Mishn. Taanith, c. 2. sect. 1.

---

16. Howbeit for this cause I obtained mercy, that in me first Jesus Christ might shew forth all longsuffering, for a pattern to them which should hereafter believe on him to life everlasting.

Greek/Transliteration
16. ἀλλὰ διὰ τοῦτο ἠλεήθην, ἵνα ἐν ἐμοὶ πρώτῳ ἐνδείξηται Ἰησοῦς χριστὸς τὴν πᾶσαν μακροθυμίαν, πρὸς ὑποτύπωσιν τῶν μελλόντων πιστεύειν ἐπ᾽ αὐτῷ εἰς ζωὴν αἰώνιον.

16. alla dya touto eileeithein, 'ina en emoi proto endeixeitai Yeisous christos tein pasan makrothumian, pros 'upotuposin ton mellonton pisteuein ep auto eis zoein aionion.

Hebrew/Transliteration
טז. וּבַעֲבוּר זֹאת רֻחַמְתִּי לְמַעַן יְגַלֶּה בִּי יֵשׁוּעַ הַמָּשִׁיחַ רִאשׁנָה אֶת-כָּל-אֹרֶךְ רוּחוֹ לִהְיוֹת לְמוֹפֵת לַבָּאִים אַחֲרַי אֲשֶׁר יַאֲמִינוּ בוֹ לְחַיֵּי עוֹלָם:

16. Oo•va•a•voor zot roo•cham•ti le•ma•an ye•ga•le bi Yeshua ha•Ma•shi•ach ri•sho•na et - kol - o•rech roo•cho li•hee•yot le•mo•fet la•ba•eem a•cha•rai asher ya•a•mi•noo vo le•cha•yey o•lam.

---

17. Now unto the King eternal, immortal, invisible, the only wise God, be honour and glory for ever and ever. Amen.

Greek/Transliteration
17. Τῷ δὲ βασιλεῖ τῶν αἰώνων, ἀφθάρτῳ, ἀοράτῳ, μόνῳ σοφῷ θεῷ, τιμὴ καὶ δόξα εἰς τοὺς αἰῶνας τῶν αἰώνων. Ἀμήν.

17. To de basilei ton aionon, aphtharto, aorato, mono sopho theo, timei kai doxa eis tous aionas ton aionon. Amein.

Hebrew/Transliteration
יז. וּלְמֶלֶךְ עוֹלָם שֹׁכֵן עַד אֲשֶׁר עַיִן לֹא תְשׁוּרֶנּוּ הוּא אֱלֹהִים אֶחָד וְהֶחָכָם לְבַדּוֹ לוֹ הַגְּדֻלָּה וְהַתִּפְאֶרֶת מֵהָעוֹלָם וְעַד-הָעוֹלָם אָמֵן:

17. Ool•Me•lech o•lam sho•chen ad asher a•yin lo te•shoo•re•noo hoo Elohim e•chad ve•he•cha•cham le•va•do lo ha•g`doo•la ve•ha•tif•eret me•ha•o•lam ve•ad - ha•o•lam Amen.

Rabbinic Jewish Commentary
Messiah is the eternal King, whose is the kingdom of nature, providence, and grace; his throne is for ever and ever, and of his kingdom and government there is no end; he is the "King of ages", as the phrase may be rendered, and so his kingdom is called מלכות כל עולמים, "the kingdom of all ages", Psa_145:13 and which endures throughout all generations; and this distinguishes him from all other kings. Scarce any king ever reigned an age, but Yeshua does reign, Heb_2:8, and will reign throughout all ages. No regard is here had, as some have thought, to the Aeones of the Gnostics and Valentinians; but rather the apostle adopts a phrase into his doxology, frequently used by the Jews in their prayers, many of which begin after this manner,

"blessed art thou, O Lord our God, מלך העולם "the king of the age, or world".

And רבון כל העולמים, "Lord of all ages, or worlds", &c. (p). Other attributes and epithets follow.

(p) Seder Tephillot, fol. 2. 2. & 3. 2. & 37. 1, 2. Ed. Basil. fol. 2. 1, 2. & 3. 1. & 4. 1. & 5. 2. & passim, Ed. Amsterdam.

18. This charge I commit unto thee, son Timothy, according to the prophecies which went before on thee, that thou by them mightest wage a good warfare;

Greek/Transliteration
18. Ταύτην τὴν παραγγελίαν παρατίθεμαί σοι, τέκνον Τιμόθεε, κατὰ τὰς προαγούσας ἐπὶ σὲ προφητείας, ἵνα στρατεύῃ ἐν αὐταῖς τὴν καλὴν στρατείαν,

18. Tautein tein parangelian paratithemai soi, teknon Timothee, kata tas proagousas epi se propheiteias, 'ina strateuei en autais tein kalein strateian,

Hebrew/Transliteration
יח. אֶת־הַמִּצְוָה הַזֹּאת אֲנִי מְצַוְּךָ הַיּוֹם טִימוֹתִיּוֹס בְּנִי כַּאֲשֶׁר דִּבְּרוּ עָלֶיךָ הַנְּבוּאוֹת מֵאָז אֲשֶׁר עַל־פִּיהֶן תִּלָּחֵם מִלְחֶמֶת צֶדֶק:

18. Et - ha•mitz•va ha•zot ani me•tzav•cha ha•yom Ti•mo•ti•yos b`ni ka•a•sher dib•roo a•le•cha han•voo•ot me•az asher al - pi•hen ti•la•chem mil•che•met tze•dek.

---

19. Holding faith, and a good conscience; which some having put away concerning faith have made shipwreck:

Greek/Transliteration
19. ἔχων πίστιν καὶ ἀγαθὴν συνείδησιν, ἥν τινες ἀπωσάμενοι περὶ τὴν πίστιν ἐναυάγησαν·

19. echon pistin kai agathein suneideisin, 'ein tines aposamenoi peri tein pistin enauageisan.

Hebrew/Transliteration
יט. כִּי תַחֲזִיק בֶּאֱמוּנָה וּבְרוּחַ נָכוֹן וְלֹא כָאֲנָשִׁים אֲשֶׁר הָיְתָה רוּחַ אַחֶרֶת אִתָּם וָאֳנִיַּת אֱמוּנָתָם נִשְׁבְּרָה:

19. Ki ta•cha•zik be•e•moo•na oov•roo•ach na•chon ve•lo cha•a•na•shim asher hai•ta roo•ach a•che•ret ee•tam va•o•ni•at emoo•na•tam nish•be•ra.

---

20. Of whom is Hymenaeus and Alexander; whom I have delivered unto Satan, that they may learn not to blaspheme.

Greek/Transliteration
20. ὧν ἐστιν Ὑμέναιος καὶ Ἀλέξανδρος, οὓς παρέδωκα τῷ Σατανᾷ, ἵνα παιδευθῶσιν μὴ βλασφημεῖν.

20. 'on estin 'Umenaios kai Alexandros, 'ous paredoka to Satana, 'ina paideuthosin mei blaspheimein.

Hebrew/Transliteration
כ. וּמֵהֶם הוּמְנִיּוֹס וְאַלְכְּסַנְדְּרוֹס אֲשֶׁר הִסְגַּרְתִּים בְּיַד הַשָּׂטָן לְמַעַן יִוָּסְרוּ וְלֹא יְגַדְּפוּ עוֹד:

20. Oo•me•hem Hoom•niyos va•Alex•san•dros asher his•gar•tim be•yad ha•Satan le•ma•an yi•vas•roo ve•lo ye•gad•foo od.

Rabbinic Jewish Commentary

It seems by their names that they were both Greeks; Alexander is a known name among the Greeks, since the times of Alexander the great, and even became common among the Jews; Act_4:6, and Hymenaeus was a name among the Grecians, from Hymen, the Heathen god of marriage: one of this name is mentioned among those said to be raised from the dead by Aesculapius (q); there was also a bishop of Jerusalem of this name (r).

(q) Apollodorus de Orig. Deor. l. 3. p. 172. (r) Euseb. Eccl. Hist. l. 7. c. 14. 30.

1 Timothy, Chapter 2

1. I exhort therefore, that, first of all, supplications, prayers, intercessions, and giving of thanks, be made for all men;

Greek/Transliteration
1. Παρακαλῶ οὖν πρῶτον πάντων ποιεῖσθαι δεήσεις, προσευχάς, ἐντεύξεις, εὐχαριστίας, ὑπὲρ πάντων ἀνθρώπων·

1. Parakalo oun proton panton poieisthai deeiseis, proseuchas, enteuxeis, eucharistias, 'uper panton anthropon.

Hebrew/Transliteration
א. וְזֹאת אֲנִי דֹרֵשׁ מִמְּךָ לִפְנֵי כָל-דָּבָר לְהַעְתִּיר רִנָּה וּתְפִלָּה תְּחִנָּה וְתוֹדָה בְּעַד כָּל-בְּנֵי-אָדָם:

1. Ve•zot ani do•resh mim•cha lif•ney chol - da•var le•ha•a•tir rina oot•fi•la te•chi•na ve•to•da be•ad kol - b`ney - adam.

---

2. For kings, and for all that are in authority; that we may lead a quiet and peaceable life in all godliness and honesty.

Greek/Transliteration
2. ὑπὲρ βασιλέων καὶ πάντων τῶν ἐν ὑπεροχῇ ὄντων, ἵνα ἤρεμον καὶ ἡσύχιον βίον διάγωμεν ἐν πάσῃ εὐσεβείᾳ καὶ σεμνότητι.

2. 'uper basileon kai panton ton en 'uperochei onton, 'ina eiremon kai 'eisuchion bion dyagomen en pasei eusebeia kai semnoteiti.

Hebrew/Transliteration
ב. בְּעַד מַלְכֵי אֶרֶץ וְכָל-אֲשֶׁר מִשְׂרָה עַל-שִׁכְמָם לְמַעַן נִחְיֶה חַיֵּי מְנוּחָה וְשַׁלְוָה בְּיִרְאַת אֱלֹהִים וּבְיִשְׁרַת לֵבָב:

2. Be•ad mal•chey e•retz ve•chol - asher mis•ra al - shich•mam le•ma•an nich•ye cha•yey me•noo•cha ve•shal•va be•yir•at Elohim oov•yish•rat le•vav.

Rabbinic Jewish Commentary
The Arabic version renders it, "that they may be preserved": that is, kings, and all in authority. It is a saying of R. Hananiah, or Ananias, the sagan of the priests (s),

"Pray for the peace or safety of the kingdom (one of their commentators on it adds (t), even of the nations of the world, which is remarkable, and agrees with the exhortation of the apostle); for if there was no fear of that, men would devour one another alive."

(s) Pirke Abot, c. 3. sect. 2. (t) Bartenora in Pirke Abot, c. 3. sect. 2.

---

3. For this is good and acceptable in the sight of God our Saviour;

Greek/Transliteration
3. τοῦτο γὰρ καλὸν καὶ ἀπόδεκτον ἐνώπιον τοῦ σωτῆρος ἡμῶν θεοῦ,

3. touto gar kalon kai apodekton enopion tou soteiros 'eimon theou,

Hebrew/Transliteration
:ג. טוֹב הַדָּבָר הַזֶּה וּלְרָצוֹן בְּעֵינֵי אֱלֹהִים מוֹשִׁיעֵנוּ

3. Tov ha•da•var ha•ze ool•ra•tzon be•ei•ney Elohim Mo•shi•e•noo.

---

4. Who will have all men to be saved, and to come unto the knowledge of the truth.

Greek/Transliteration
4. ὃς πάντας ἀνθρώπους θέλει σωθῆναι καὶ εἰς ἐπίγνωσιν ἀληθείας ἐλθεῖν.

4. 'os pantas anthropous thelei sotheinai kai eis epignosin aleitheias elthein.

Hebrew/Transliteration
:ד. אֲשֶׁר חָפֵץ יַחְפֹּץ כִּי יִוָּשְׁעוּ כָל-בְּנֵי-אָדָם וְיִלְמְדוּ לָדַעַת אֶת-אֲמִתּוֹ

4. Asher cha•fotz yach•potz ki yi•vash•oo chol - b`ney - adam ve•yil•me•doo la•da•at et - ami•to.

---

5. For there is one God, and one mediator between God and men, the man Christ Jesus;

Greek/Transliteration
5. Εἷς γὰρ θεός, εἷς καὶ μεσίτης θεοῦ καὶ ἀνθρώπων, ἄνθρωπος χριστὸς Ἰησοῦς,

5. 'Eis gar theos, 'eis kai mesiteis theou kai anthropon, anthropos christos Yeisous,

Hebrew/Transliteration
:ה. כִּי אֱלֹהִים אֶחָד הוּא וּמֵלִיץ אֶחָד בֵּין אֱלֹהִים וּבֵין אֲנָשִׁים הוּא הָאִישׁ יֵשׁוּעַ הַמָּשִׁיחַ

5. Ki Elohim e•chad hoo oo•me•litz e•chad bein Elohim oo•vein a•na•shim hoo ha•eesh Yeshua ha•Ma•shi•ach.

Rabbinic Jewish Commentary
So the Jews say of the Messiah (u), that he is אל אמצעי, "a Mediator, God", a middle person between God and men. And they call him עמודא דאמצעיתא, "the Pillar of mediation" (w) or the middle Pillar; that is, the Mediator or Reconciler. And Philo (x) the Jew speaks of the word, as μεσος, a "middle" person, and standing in the middle between the dead and the living, and between God and men. The Ethiopic version here renders it, "there is one elect of God"; which is one of the characters of the Messiah, Isa_42:1.

(u) R. Albo, Sepher Ikkarim, orat 2. c. 28. (w) Sepher Jetzira, p. 126. (x) Quis rerum divin. Hares, p. 508, 509, 510.

6. Who gave himself a ransom for all, to be testified in due time.

Greek/Transliteration
6. ὁ δοὺς ἑαυτὸν ἀντίλυτρον ὑπὲρ πάντων, τὸ μαρτύριον καιροῖς ἰδίοις,

6. 'o dous 'eauton antilutron 'uper panton, to marturion kairois idiois,

Hebrew/Transliteration
:ו. אֲשֶׁר נָתַן אֶת-נַפְשׁוֹ כֹּפֶר בְּעַד כָּל-בְּנֵי אָדָם וְעֵדוּת זוּ עָלֵינוּ לְהַשְׁמִיעַ לְעֵת מֹצְאָ

6. Asher na•tan et - naf•sho ko•fer be•ad kol - b`ney adam ve•e•doot zoo aley•noo le•hash•mi•a le•et me•tzo.

Rabbinic Jewish Commentary
What the Mediator gave as a ransom for men is "himself", his body and his soul, which were both made an offering for sin; and his life, which is the result of union between soul and body; his whole human nature as in union with his divine person, and so might be truly said to be himself: this he gave into the hands of men, of justice and of death; and that voluntarily, which shows his great love to his people; and also as a "ransom", or a ransom price for them, αντιλυτρον, in their room and stead; to ransom them from the slavery of sin, and damnation by it, from the captivity of the Satan, and the bondage of the Torah, and from the grave, death, ruin, and destruction: and this ransom was given for "all".

The Hebrew word כל, all, to which this answers, signifies sometimes many, a multitude, and sometimes only a part of a multitude, as Kimchi observes (y).

We (z) read, that when the people of Israel comforted the high priest upon the death of his wife, or any relation, they used to say to him, אנו כפרתך, "we are thy atonement", expiation, or ransom; that is, as the commentators (a) explain it, by us thou shalt be atoned, for we will be in thy room and stead, with respect to all things that shall come upon thee; but here the High priest and Mediator is the atonement and ransom for the people.

(y) Sepher Shorash. rad. כלל (z) Misna Sanhedrin, c. 2. sect. 1. (a) Jarchi & Bartenona in ib.

---

7. Whereunto I am ordained a preacher, and an apostle, (I speak the truth in Christ, and lie not;) a teacher of the Gentiles in faith and verity.

Greek/Transliteration
7. εἰς ὃ ἐτέθην ἐγὼ κῆρυξ καὶ ἀπόστολος· ἀλήθειαν λέγω ἐν χριστῷ, οὐ ψεύδομαι· διδάσκαλος ἐθνῶν ἐν πίστει καὶ ἀληθείᾳ.

7. eis 'o etethein ego keirux kai apostolos. aleitheyan lego en christo, ou pseudomai. Didaskalos ethnon en pistei kai aleitheia.

Hebrew/Transliteration
:ז. וַאֲנִי נִקְרֵאתִי לִהְיוֹת-לָהּ לְמַגִּיד וְשָׁלִיחַ וּמוֹרֶה אֱמֶת וֶאֱמוּנָה לַגּוֹיִם הֵן אֱמֶת אֲדַבֵּרָה בַּמָּשִׁיחַ וְלֹא שֶׁקֶר מִלָּי

7. Va•a•ni nik•re•ti li•hee•yot - la le•ma•gid ve•sha•li•ach oo•mo•re emet ve•e•moo•na la•go•yim hen emet ada•be•ra ba•Ma•shi•ach ve•lo she•ker mi•lai.

8. I will therefore that men pray every where, lifting up holy hands, without wrath and doubting.

Greek/Transliteration
8. Βούλομαι οὖν προσεύχεσθαι τοὺς ἄνδρας ἐν παντὶ τόπῳ, ἐπαίροντας ὁσίους χεῖρας, χωρὶς ὀργῆς καὶ διαλογισμοῦ.

8. Boulomai oun proseuchesthai tous andras en panti topo, epairontas 'osious cheiras, choris orgeis kai dyalogismou.

Hebrew/Transliteration
ח. וְלָכֵן הִנְנִי מְבַקֵּשׁ כִּי הָאֲנָשִׁים יִתְפַּלְלוּ בְכָל-מָקוֹם וְיִשְׂאוּ יְדֵיהֶם קֹדֶשׁ בִּבְלִי-כַעַשׂ וּמָדוֹן:

8. Ve•la•chen hi•ne•ni me•va•kesh ki ha•a•na•shim yit•pa•le•loo ve•chol - ma•kom ve•yis•oo ye•dey•hem ko•desh biv•li - cha•as oo•ma•don.

Rabbinic Jewish Commentary
This seems to be said in opposition to a Jewish notion, that the temple at Jerusalem was the only place for prayer, and that prayer made elsewhere ought to be directed towards that. The Jews say (b), that

"There is no way for the prayer of the nations of the world to ascend, seeing the gates of heaven are only opened in the land of Israel.--And again, that the prayers without the land have no way to go up before the Lord, but the Israelites send them without the land opposite Jerusalem; and when they come to Jerusalem, from thence they remove and ascend above.-- No prayer ascends above from that place in which it is made, till it come to the land of Israel, and from thence to Jerusalem, and from thence to the sanctuary, and then it ascends above."

They have also many rules concerning places of private prayer, as that care should be taken that it be not in a place where there is any filth; or any bad scent (c).

Lifting up holy hands; lifting up of hands was a prayer gesture among the Heathens (d), and so it was among the Jews (e). R. Simeon lift up his hands in prayer to the blessed God, and prayed his prayer. Yea, they (f) say,

"It is forbidden a man to lift up his hands above, except in prayer, and in blessings to his Lord, and supplications, as it is said, Gen_14:22 which is interpreted of lifting up of hands in prayer."

And this was an emblem of the elevation of the heart in prayer to God, without which the former would be of little avail. It is an observation of the Jews (g), we have found prayer without lifting up of hands, but we never found lifting up of hands without prayer. And these hands must be holy and pure; there must be purity of heart, and cleanness of hands, or a freedom from any governing sin, which renders prayer unacceptable unto God; see Isa_1:15. The apostle alludes to a custom of the Jews, who always used to wash their hands before prayer;

"Then Holofernes commanded his guard that they should not stay her: thus she abode in the camp three days, and went out in the night into the valley of Bethulia, and washed herself in a fountain of water by the camp. And when she came out, she besought the Lord God of Israel to direct her way to the raising up of the children of her people." (Judith 12:7,8)

So it is said (h) of the Septuagint interpreters, that after the Jewish manner they washed their hands and prayed. The account Maimonides gives (i), is this:

"Cleanness of hands, how is it done? a man must wash his hands up to the elbow, and after that pray; if a man is on a journey, and the time of prayer is come, and he has no water, if there is between him and water four miles, which are eight thousand cubits, he may go to the place of water, and wash, and after that pray. If there is between him more than that, he may rub his hands, and pray. But if the place of water is behind him, he is not obliged to go back but a mile; but if he has passed from the water more than that, he is not obliged to return, but he rubs his hands and prays; they do not make clean for prayer but the hands only, in the rest of prayers, except the morning prayer; but before the morning prayer a man washes his face, his hands and feet, and after that prays."

But, alas! what does all this washing signify? Unless, as Philo the Jew (k), expresses it, a man lifts up pure, and, as one may say, virgin hands, to heaven, and so prays.

Maimonides (l) says,

"Men may not stand praying, either with laughter, or with levity, nor with confabulation, "nor with contention, nor with anger", but with the words of the Torah."

And it is a saying of R. Chanina,

"In a day of "wrath", a man may not pray (m)."

(b) Shaare Ors, fol. 24. 2, 3. (c) Maimon. Hilchot Tephilla, c. 4. sect. 8, 9. (d) Apuleius de Mundo, p. 276. (e) Zohar in Exod. fol 4. 2. (f) lb. in Numb. fol. 79. 1. (g) T. Hieros. Taaniot, fol. 67. 2. (h) Arist. Hist. 70. p. 98. (i) Hilch. Tephilla, c. 4. sect. 2, 3. (k) De Charitate, p. 698. Vid. ib. de Victim. Offerent. p. 848. (l) Hilch. Tephilla, c. 4. sect. 18. (m) T. Bab. Erubin, fol. 65. 1.

---

9. In like manner also, that women adorn themselves in modest apparel, with shamefacedness and sobriety; not with broided hair, or gold, or pearls, or costly array;

Greek/Transliteration
9. Ὡσαύτως καὶ τὰς γυναῖκας ἐν καταστολῇ κοσμίῳ, μετὰ αἰδοῦς καὶ σωφροσύνης, κοσμεῖν ἑαυτάς, μὴ ἐν πλέγμασιν, ἢ χρυσῷ, ἢ μαργαρίταις, ἢ ἱματισμῷ πολυτελεῖ,

9. 'Osautos kai tas gunaikas en katastolei kosmio, meta aidous kai sophrosuneis, kosmein 'eautas, mei en plegmasin, ei chruso, ei margaritais, ei 'imatismo polutelei,

Hebrew/Transliteration
ט. וּכְמוֹ כֵן גַּם-הַנָּשִׁים תִּלְבַּשְׁנָה שִׂמְלוֹת-חֵן הָרְאוּיוֹת לָהֶן בְּבֹשֶׁת פָּנִים וּבְטוּב טַעַם לֹא בְחַחְלְפוֹת רֹאשָׁן וְלֹא בְזָהָב וּפְנִינִים וְלֹא בְמַחְלָצוֹת יְקָרוֹת:

9. Ooch•mo chen gam - ha•na•shim til•bash•na sim•lot - chen har•oo•yot la•hen be•vo•shet pa•nim oov•toov ta•am lo ve•chach•le•fot ro•shan ve•lo ve•za•hav oof•ni•nim ve•lo ve•mach•la•tzot ye•ka•rot.

Rabbinic Jewish Commentary
The Ethiopic version renders it, "so let the women be clothed in prayer".

The Jews always appeared in their best clothes on the sabbath day; this is one of their rules: (n).

"For the honour of the sabbath, every man must be clothed, כסות נקייה, "with clean or neat apparel" and clothing on the weekday must not be as clothing on the sabbath day; and if a man can make no change, he must let down his talith (or upper garment, his cloak); so that his clothing may not be as the clothing of the weekdays, when that was girt up about him."

It was also a complaint of Chrysostom's many hundreds of years ago, that some who came to public worship, appeared in such a dress, as if they came rather to dance than to pray; such apparel should be avoided: it is said of Pythagoras (o), that he taught the inhabitants of Crotona, the men literature, and the women chastity and modesty; and by his disputations so far prevailed upon the latter, as to lay aside their garments of gold and other ornaments of their dignity, as instruments of luxury; all which they brought into the temple of Juno, and dedicated them to that goddess; declaring, that shamefacedness or chastity, and not garments, are the true ornaments of matrons.

(n) Maimon. Hilch. Subbat. c. 30. sect. 3. (o) Justin. ex Trogo. l. 20. c. 4.

---

10. But (which becometh women professing godliness) with good works.

Greek/Transliteration
10. ἀλλ᾽ ὃ πρέπει γυναιξὶν ἐπαγγελλομέναις θεοσέβειαν, δι᾽ ἔργων ἀγαθῶν.

10. all 'o prepei gunaixin epangellomenais theosebeyan, di ergon agathon.

Hebrew/Transliteration
י׃ כִּי אִם-בְּמַעֲשִׂים טוֹבִים כַּאֲשֶׁר נָכוֹן לַנָּשִׁים אֲשֶׁר בְּיִרְאַת אֱלֹהִים חֶפְצָן.

10. Ki eem - be•ma•a•sim to•vim ka•a•sher na•chon la•na•shim asher be•yir•at Elohim chef•tzan.

---

11. Let the woman learn in silence with all subjection.

Greek/Transliteration
11. Γυνὴ ἐν ἡσυχίᾳ μανθανέτω ἐν πάσῃ ὑποταγῇ.

11. Gunei en 'eisuchia manthaneto en pasei 'upotagei.

Hebrew/Transliteration
יא׃ הָאִשָּׁה תִּלְמַד בְּהַשְׁקֵט וְנַפְשָׁהּ כָּלִיל תִּכָּנֵעַ

11. Ha•ee•sha til•mad be•hash•ket ve•naf•sha ka•lil ti•ka•ne•a.

12. But I suffer not a woman to teach, nor to usurp authority over the man, but to be in silence.

Greek/Transliteration
12. Γυναικὶ δὲ διδάσκειν οὐκ ἐπιτρέπω, οὐδὲ αὐθεντεῖν ἀνδρός, ἀλλ᾽ εἶναι ἐν ἡσυχίᾳ.

12. Gunaiki de didaskein ouk epitrepo, oude authentein andros, all einai en 'eisuchia.

Hebrew/Transliteration
יב: וְאֵינֶנִּי נֹתֵן לָאִשָּׁה לְלַמֵּד וְלֹא לְהִשְׂתָּרֵר עַל-הָאִישׁ כִּי אִם-הַחֲרֵשׁ תַּחֲרִישׁ

12. Ve•ey•ne•ni no•ten la•ee•sha le•la•med ve•lo le•his•ta•rer al - ha•eesh ki eem - ha•cha•resh ta•cha•rish.

---

13. For Adam was first formed, then Eve.

Greek/Transliteration
13. Ἀδὰμ γὰρ πρῶτος ἐπλάσθη, εἶτα Εὕα·

13. Adam gar protos eplasthei, eita Eua.

Hebrew/Transliteration
יג: כִּי אָדָם נוֹצַר רִאשֹׁנָה וְאַחֲרֵי-כֵן חַוָּה

13. Ki adam no•tzar ri•sho•na ve•a•cha•rey - chen Chava.

---

14. And Adam was not deceived, but the woman being deceived was in the transgression.

Greek/Transliteration
14. καὶ Ἀδὰμ οὐκ ἠπατήθη, ἡ δὲ γυνὴ ἀπατηθεῖσα ἐν παραβάσει γέγονεν·

14. kai Adam ouk eipateithei, 'ei de gunei apateitheisa en parabasei gegonen.

Hebrew/Transliteration
יד. וְאָדָם לֹא נִפְתָּה כִּי אִם-הָאִשָּׁה כַּאֲשֶׁר שָׁמְעָה דִּבְרֵי הַמְפַתֶּה עָבְרָה בְּרִית

14. Ve•a•dam lo nif•ta ki eem - ha•ee•sha ka•a•sher sham•ah div•rey ham•fa•te av•ra b`rit.

Rabbinic Jewish Commentary
And therefore she is called by the Jews (p) אם העון, "the mother of iniquity and sin"; to which they refer, Psa_51:5. And they say, (q) she was the cause of death to Adam, and to all the world. And they observe (r) the order of the punishment of the serpent, Eve, and Adam, as of their sin; the serpent was first accursed, then Eve, and last of all Adam. They say

"(s) Samael (the serpent) could not subvert Adam, till the serpent came and turned the heart of Eve, and Eve turned his heart, and they both sinned; wherefore it is said, "the woman which thou gavest me"; Samael had no power to turn him, till Eve came, and she was the cause of his eating."

The Ethiopic version renders the text, "Adam hath not deceived, the woman hath deceived and prevaricated".

(p) Tzeror Hammor, fol. 141. 3. (q) T. Hieros. Sabbat, fol. 5. 2. Zohar in Gen. fol. 27. 3. Caphtor, fol. 37. 2. (r) T. Bab. Erubin, fol. 18. 1. & Taanith, fol. 15. 2. Bereshit Rabba, sect. 20. fol. 17. 1. (s) Midrash Ruth in Zohar in Gen. fol. 27. 3.

---

15. Notwithstanding she shall be saved in childbearing, if they continue in faith and charity and holiness with sobriety.

Greek/Transliteration
15. σωθήσεται δὲ διὰ τῆς τεκνογονίας, ἐὰν μείνωσιν ἐν πίστει καὶ ἀγάπῃ καὶ ἁγιασμῷ μετὰ σωφροσύνης.

15. sotheisetai de dya teis teknogonias, ean meinosin en pistei kai agapei kai 'agyasmo meta sophrosuneis.

Hebrew/Transliteration
טו. אַךְ יֶשׁ-לָהּ תְּשׁוּעָה בַּבָּנִים אֲשֶׁר תֵּלֵד אִם צְנוּעָה הִיא וּבְמַעְגְּלֵי אֱמוּנָה וְאַהֲבָה וּבְדֶרֶךְ הַקֹּדֶשׁ תֵּיטִיב לָכֶת

15. Ach yesh - la te•shoo•ah va•ba•nim asher te•led eem tze•noo•ah hee oov•ma•ag•ley e•moo•na ve•a•ha•va oov•de•rech ha•ko•desh tey•tiv la•chet.

Rabbinic Jewish Commentary
The Jews say (t), for three transgressions women die in childbearing; because they do not take care of their menstrues, and of the cake of the firstfruits, and of lighting the lamp (when the sabbath approaches).

The Vulgate Latin version reads in the singular, "if she continues".

(t) Misn. Sabbat, c. 2. sect. 6.

1 Timothy, Chapter 3

1. This is a true saying, If a man desire the office of a bishop, he desireth a good work.

Greek/Transliteration
1. Πιστὸς ὁ λόγος· εἴ τις ἐπισκοπῆς ὀρέγεται, καλοῦ ἔργου ἐπιθυμεῖ.

1. Pistos 'o logos. ei tis episkopeis oregetai, kalou ergou epithumei.

Hebrew/Transliteration
א. הֵן דְּבַר אֱמֶת הוּא אִישׁ כִּי-יְבַקֵּשׁ מִשְׁמֶרֶת רֹאשׁ הָעֵדָה מְבַקֵּשׁ טוֹב:

1. Hen de•var emet hoo eesh ki - ye•va•kesh mish•me•ret rosh ha•e•da me•va•kesh tov.

Rabbinic Jewish Commentary
The Syriac version renders it, "if a man desires presbytery, or eldership"; and it lies in preaching the word, administering the ordinances of the Gospel, and taking care of the discipline of the church, and in the visiting, inspection, and oversight of it; as the word επισκοπη, "episcopacy", here used, signifies; and this work and office may be lawfully and laudably desired, with a view to the glory of God.

---

2. A bishop then must be blameless, the husband of one wife, vigilant, sober, of good behaviour, given to hospitality, apt to teach;

Greek/Tranliteration
2. Δεῖ οὖν τὸν ἐπίσκοπον ἀνεπίληπτον εἶναι, μιᾶς γυναικὸς ἄνδρα, νηφάλεον, σώφρονα, κόσμιον, φιλόξενον, διδακτικόν·

2. Dei oun ton episkopon anepileipton einai, myas gunaikos andra, neiphaleon, sophrona, kosmion, philoxenon, didaktikon.

Hebrew/Transliteration
ב. אַךְ רֹאשׁ הָעֵדָה תָּמִים יִהְיֶה בְּלֹא שֶׁמֶץ דָּבָר בַּעַל-אִשָּׁה אַחַת שָׂם דַּרְךְּ נְבוֹן דָּבָר וְרָצוּי לִבְנֵי אָדָם דְּלָתָיו לְאֹרַח יִפְתַּח וְאִישׁ מַשְׂכִּיל לְלַמֵּד:

2. Ach rosh ha•e•da ta•mim yi•hee•ye be•lo she•metz da•var ba•al - ee•sha a•chat sam de•rech n`von da•var ve•ra•tzooy liv•ney adam de•la•tav le•o•re•ach yif•tach ve•eesh mas•kil le•la•med.

Rabbinic Jewish Commentary
Now polygamy and divorces had very much obtained among the Jews; nor could the believing Jews be easily and at once brought off of them. And though they were not lawful nor to be allowed of in any; yet they were especially unbecoming and scandalous in officers of churches. So the high priest among the Jews, even when polygamy was in use, might not marry, or have two wives, at once; if he did, he could not minister in his office until he divorced one of them (u). For it is written, Lev_21:13, "he shall take a wife", אחת ולא שתים, "one, and not two" (w). And the same that is said of the high priest, is said of all other priests; see Eze_44:22, likewise the Egyptian priests might not marry more wives than one, though others might have as many as they pleased (x): and so the Flamines among the Romans (y).

(u) Maimon. Issurc Bia, c. 7. sect. 13. & Cele Hamikdash. c. 5. sect. 10. (w) T. Bab. Yebamot, fol. 59. 1. (x) Diodor. Sicul. l. 1. p. 51. vide Tertull. de monogamia, c. 17. & Exhort. castitat. c. 13. (y) Alex. ab. Alex. Genial Dier. l. 6. c. 12.

---

3. Not given to wine, no striker, not greedy of filthy lucre; but patient, not a brawler, not covetous;

Greek/Transliteration
3. μὴ πάροινον, μὴ πλήκτην, μὴ αἰσχροκερδῆ, ἀλλ᾽ ἐπιεικῆ, ἄμαχον, ἀφιλάργυρον·

3. mei paroinon, mei pleiktein, mei aischrokerdei, all epieikei, amachon, aphilarguron.

Hebrew/Transliteration
ג: לֹא שֹׁתֶה שִׁכּוֹר וְלֹא בַעַל מַהֲלָמוֹת כִּי אִם-עֹשֵׂה רְצוֹן זוּלָתוֹ רֹדֵף שָׁלוֹם וּמֹאֵס בְּבֶצַע כָּסֶף

3. Lo sho•te shi•kor ve•lo va•al ma•ha•loo•mot ki eem - o•se r`tzon zoo•la•to ro•def sha•lom oo•mo•es be•ve•tza ka•sef.

Rabbinic Jewish Commentary
The Syriac version renders it, "who does not transgress over wine", or go beyond due bounds in the use of it, who is not immoderate in it; the Arabic version renders it, "not insolent through wine", as one that is heated with it is fierce and furious, and wrangling and quarrelsome, and often very mischievous and injurious; and this sense is followed by some.

Not greedy of filthy lucre; not covetous of getting money, of amassing wealth and riches together; or desirous of popular applause and glory from men. This clause is not in the Alexandrian copy, nor in five of Beza's manuscripts and other copies, nor is it in the Vulgate Latin version, nor in any of the Oriental versions.

---

4. One that ruleth well his own house, having his children in subjection with all gravity;

Greek/Transliteration
4. τοῦ ἰδίου οἴκου καλῶς προϊστάμενον, τέκνα ἔχοντα ἐν ὑποταγῇ μετὰ πάσης σεμνότητος.

4. tou idiou oikou kalos proistamenon, tekna echonta en 'upotagei meta paseis semnoteitos.

Hebrew/Transliteration
ד: וְגַם הוּא שֹׁרֵר בְּבֵיתוֹ וּבָנָיו נִכְנָעִים לְפָנָיו וּמוֹרָאוֹ עֲלֵיהֶם

4. Ve•gam hoo sho•rer be•vey•to oo•va•nav nich•na•eem le•fa•nav oo•mo•ra•o aley•hem.

5. (For if a man know not how to rule his own house, how shall he take care of the church of God?)

Greek/Transliteration
5. Εἰ δέ τις τοῦ ἰδίου οἴκου προστῆναι οὐκ οἶδεν, πῶς ἐκκλησίας θεοῦ ἐπιμελήσεται;

5. Ei de tis tou idiou oikou prosteinai ouk oiden, pos ekkleisias theou epimeleisetai?

Hebrew/Transliteration
:ה. כִּי אִם־לֹא יֵדַע אִישׁ לִהְיוֹת שֹׁרֵר בְּבֵיתוֹ אֵיכָה יְכַלְכֵּל אֶת־עֲדַת אֱלֹהִים

5. Ki eem - lo ye•da eesh li•hee•yot sho•rer be•vey•to ey•cha ye•chal•kel et - adat Elohim?

---

6. Not a novice, lest being lifted up with pride he fall into the condemnation of the devil.

Greek/Transliteration
6. Μὴ νεόφυτον, ἵνα μὴ τυφωθεὶς εἰς κρίμα ἐμπέσῃ τοῦ διαβόλου.

6. Mei neophuton, 'ina mei tuphotheis eis krima empesei tou dyabolou.

Hebrew/Transliteration
:ו. אַף לֹא תַלְמִיד חָדָשׁ פֶּן־יָרוּם לְבָבוֹ וְהַמַּשְׂטִין יַרְשִׁיעֶנּוּ בַּדִּין

6. Af lo tal•mid cha•dash pen - ya•room le•va•vo ve•ha•mas•tin yar•shi•e•noo ba•din.

Rabbinic Jewish Commentary
Not a novice,..... Or one newly planted, the Arabic version adds, "in the faith". the Hebrew word נטע, "a plant", is by the Septuagint in Job_14:9 rendered by this very word.

---

7. Moreover he must have a good report of them which are without; lest he fall into reproach and the snare of the devil.

Greek/Transliteration
7. Δεῖ δὲ αὐτὸν καὶ μαρτυρίαν καλὴν ἔχειν ἀπὸ τῶν ἔξωθεν, ἵνα μὴ εἰς ὀνειδισμὸν ἐμπέσῃ καὶ παγίδα τοῦ διαβόλου.

7. Dei de auton kai marturian kalein echein apo ton exothen, 'ina mei eis oneidismon empesei kai pagida tou dyabolou.

Hebrew/Transliteration
:ז. וְגַם־שֵׁם טוֹב נָחוּץ לוֹ מִפִּי הָעֹמְדִים מִחוּץ לְבִלְתִּי יְהִי לָבוּז וּלְבִלְתִּי יִפֹּל בְּפַח הַמַּשְׂטִין

7. Ve•gam - shem tov na•chootz lo mi•pi ha•om•dim mi•choo•tz le•vil•ti ye•hee la•vooz ool•vil•ti yi•pol be•fach ha•mas•tin.

Rabbinic Jewish Commentary

The Jews have a regard to the wisdom, prudence, gravity, and manners, of a man they appoint as a minister of a congregation. Their rule is this (z):

"They do not appoint a messenger or minister of a congregation, but he who is the greatest in the congregation for wisdom and works; and if he is an elderly man, it is the better; and they take care that the messenger or minister of the congregation be a man whose voice is pleasant, and he is used to read: but he whose beard is not full grown, though he is a very considerable man, he may not be a minister of the congregation, because of the honour of the congregation."

(z) Maimon. Hilchot Tephilla, c. 8. sect. 11.

---

8. Likewise must the deacons be grave, not doubletongued, not given to much wine, not greedy of filthy lucre;

Greek/Transliteration
8. Διακόνους ὡσαύτως σεμνούς, μὴ διλόγους, μὴ οἴνῳ πολλῷ προσέχοντας, μὴ αἰσχροκερδεῖς,

8. Dyakonous 'osautos semnous, mei dilogous, mei oino pollo prosechontas, mei aischrokerdeis,

Hebrew/Transliteration
ח. וְכֵן הַמְשָׁרְתִים מְכֻבָּדִים יִהְיוּ לֹא דְבָרִים בְּלֵב וָלֵב לֹא סֹבְאֵי יַיִן וְלֹא נֹטִים אַחֲרֵי הַבָּצַע:

8. Ve•chen ha•me•shar•tim me•choo•ba•dim yi•hee•yoo lo dov•rim be•lev va•lev lo sov•ey ya•yin ve•lo no•tim a•cha•rey ha•ba•tza.

---

9. Holding the mystery of the faith in a pure conscience.

Greek/Transliteration
9. ἔχοντας τὸ μυστήριον τῆς πίστεως ἐν καθαρᾷ συνειδήσει.

9. echontas to musteirion teis pisteos en kathara suneideisei.

Hebrew/Transliteration
ט. נֹצְרִים סוֹד הָאֱמוּנָה בְּלֵב טָהוֹר:

9. Notz•rim sod ha•e•moo•na be•lev ta•hor.

Rabbinic Jewish Commentary

The doctrine of the Gospel, called the "faith", because it contains things to be believed; proposes Yeshua the object of faith; is the means by which faith comes, and is unprofitable without it: it is called "the mystery", because it is of divine revelation, and could have never been discovered by human reason; and now it is revealed, the modus of many things contained in it remains a mystery; several of the doctrines of it are mysterious ones, particularly the doctrine of the Trinity; and which the ancient Jews call by this very name, (a) רזא דמהימנותא, "the mystery of faith"; the incarnation of the Son of God, the union of the saints to Messiah Yeshua, and their communion with him, and the resurrection of the dead, with others. Now this mysterious doctrine of faith is to be held by deacons.

(a) Zohar in Gen. fol. 12. 4. & 13. 1, 2. & in Exod. fol. 66. 3.

---

10. And let these also first be proved; then let them use the office of a deacon, being found blameless.

Greek/Transliteration
10. Καὶ οὗτοι δὲ δοκιμαζέσθωσαν πρῶτον, εἶτα διακονείτωσαν, ἀνέγκλητοι ὄντες.

10. Kai 'outoi de dokimazesthosan proton, eita dyakoneitosan, anegkleitoi ontes.

Hebrew/Transliteration
י: וְגַם-הֵם יִבָּחֲנוּ בָרִאשֹׁנָה וְאִם שֶׁמֶץ דָּבָר לֹא נִמְצָא בָם יִקְרְבוּ לְשָׁרֵת

10. Ve•gam - hem yi•ba•cha•noo va•ri•sho•na ve•eem she•metz da•var lo nim•tza vam yik•re•voo le•sha•ret.

---

11. Even so must their wives be grave, not slanderers, sober, faithful in all things.

Greek/Transliteration
11. Γυναῖκας ὡσαύτως σεμνάς, μὴ διαβόλους, νηφαλέους, πιστὰς ἐν πᾶσιν.

11. Gunaikas 'osautos semnas, mei dyabolous, neiphaleous, pistas en pasin.

Hebrew/Transliteration
יא: וּכְמוֹ כֵן גַּם-הַנָּשִׁים כְּבוּדוֹת תִּהְיֶינָה צוֹפִיּוֹת הֲלִיכוֹתֵיהֶן וְנֶאֱמָנוֹת בַּכֹּל וְלֹא שֹׂטְנוֹת בִּלְשׁוֹנָן

11. Ooch•mo chen gam - ha•na•shim k`voo•dot ti•hi•ye•na tzo•fi•yot ha•li•cho•tey•hen ve•ne•e•ma•not ba•kol ve•lo sot•not bil•sho•nan.

---

12. Let the deacons be the husbands of one wife, ruling their children and their own houses well.

Greek/Transliteration
12. Διάκονοι ἔστωσαν μιᾶς γυναικὸς ἄνδρες, τέκνων καλῶς προϊστάμενοι καὶ τῶν ἰδίων οἴκων.

12. Dyakonoi estosan myas gunaikos andres, teknon kalos proistamenoi kai ton idion oikon.

Hebrew/Transliteration
יב: וְהַמְשָׁרְתִים בַּעֲלֵי אִשָּׁה אַחַת יִהְיוּ הַמְכַלְכְּלִים בְּנֵיהֶם וּבָתֵּיהֶם כַּמִּשְׁפָּט

12. Ve•ham•shar•tim ba•a•ley ee•sha a•chat yi•hee•yoo ha•m`chal•ke•lim b`ney•hem oo•va•tey•hem ka•mish•pat.

13. For they that have used the office of a deacon well purchase to themselves a good degree, and great boldness in the faith which is in Christ Jesus.

Greek/Transliteration
13. Οἱ γὰρ καλῶς διακονήσαντες βαθμὸν ἑαυτοῖς καλὸν περιποιοῦνται, καὶ πολλὴν παρρησίαν ἐν πίστει τῇ ἐν χριστῷ Ἰησοῦ.

13. 'Oi gar kalos dyakoneisantes bathmon 'eautois kalon peripoiountai, kai pollein parreisian en pistei tei en christo Yeisou.

Hebrew/Transliteration
יג. כִּי אֵלֶּה אֲשֶׁר יְשָׁרְתוּן כַּמִּשְׁפָּט יִקְנוּ לָהֶם מַעֲלָה רָמָה וְיֶתֶר-עֹז בֶּאֱמוּנָה בְּיַשׁוּעַ הַמָּשִׁיחַ:

13. Ki ele asher ye•shar•toon ka•mish•pat yik•noo la•hem ma•a•la ra•ma ve•ye•ter - az be•e•moo•na be•Yeshua ha•Ma•shi•ach.

Rabbinic Jewish Commentary
purchase to themselves a good degree; not an higher office, as that of presbytery or episcopacy, which is a sense calculated to serve a hierarchy; nor a degree in glory and happiness hereafter; but rather an increase of gifts and grace; or a degree of respect and honour in the church: or the sense is, they possess and enjoy, which is the meaning of the word rendered "purchase", a very honourable office in the church; and which is so to them, they using it well, and discharging it in an honourable manner; unless the apostle should design what the Jews called דרגא דמהימנותא, "a degree of faith" (b).

(b) Zohar in Exod. fol. 36. 3.

---

14. These things write I unto thee, hoping to come unto thee shortly:

Greek/Transliteration
14. Ταῦτά σοι γράφω, ἐλπίζων ἐλθεῖν πρὸς σὲ τάχιον·

14. Tauta soi grapho, elpizon elthein pros se tachion.

Hebrew/Transliteration
יד. כָּזֹאת כָּתַבְתִּי לְךָ בְּתוֹחַלְתִּי כִּי אָחִישׁ לָבֹא אֵלֶיךָ:

14. Ka•zot ka•tav•ti le•cha be•to•chal•ti ki a•chish la•vo e•le•cha.

---

15. But if I tarry long, that thou mayest know how thou oughtest to behave thyself in the house of God, which is the church of the living God, the pillar and ground of the truth.

Greek/Transliteration
15. ἐὰν δὲ βραδύνω, ἵνα εἰδῇς πῶς δεῖ ἐν οἴκῳ θεοῦ ἀναστρέφεσθαι, ἥτις ἐστὶν ἐκκλησία θεοῦ ζῶντος, στύλος καὶ ἑδραίωμα τῆς ἀληθείας.

15. ean de braduno, 'ina eideis pos dei en oiko theou anastrephesthai, 'eitis estin ekkleisia theou zontos, stulos kai 'edraioma teis aleitheias.

Hebrew/Transliteration
טו. וְאִם-אַחַר מָבוֹא תֵּדַע בָּזֹאת אֵיךְ לְהִתְהַלֵּךְ בְּבֵית אֱלֹהִים הֲלֹא הִיא עֲדַת אֵל חַי עַמּוּד הָאֱמֶת וִיסוֹדָהּ:

15. Ve•eem - e•char mi•bo te•da ba•zot eych le•hit•ha•lech be•veit Elohim ha•lo hee adat El chai a•mood ha•e•met viy•so•da.

Rabbinic Jewish Commentary

And this way of speaking is used by the Jews, both of persons and things; so Zebulun is said (c) to be עמוד התורה, "the pillar of the Torah"; and it is said (d) of

"The great sanhedrim in Jerusalem, they are the root of the oral Torah; and they are עמודי ההוראה, "the pillars of doctrine"; and from them go forth the statutes and judgments unto Israel;"

And the same is said of things as of persons. Maimonides says (e),

"The foundation of foundations and the pillar of wisdom, is to know that there is a first Being, that gives being to all beings;"

And R. Sangari, another of their writers, says, (f).

"There are two things which are עמודי התורה, "the pillars of the Torah"; the one is, that the Torah is from God; the other is, that it is received with a faithful (or sincere) heart, from the congregation:"

To which may be added, that it is said (g) that

"The mystery of faith is "the root and ground" of the world";"

All which may serve to illustrate this passage.

(c) Tzeror Hammor, fol. 152. 1. (d) Maimon. Hilchot Memarim, c. 1. sect. 1. (e) Hilchot Yesode Hattora, c. 1. sect. 1. (f) Cosri, par. 3. sect. 23. fol. 159. 2. (g) Zohar in Gen. fol. 124. 1.

---

16. And without controversy great is the mystery of godliness: God was manifest in the flesh, justified in the Spirit, seen of angels, preached unto the Gentiles, believed on in the world, received up into glory.

Greek/Transliteration
16. Καὶ ὁμολογουμένως μέγα ἐστὶν τὸ τῆς εὐσεβείας μυστήριον· θεὸς ἐφανερώθη ἐν σαρκί, ἐδικαιώθη ἐν πνεύματι, ὤφθη ἀγγέλοις, ἐκηρύχθη ἐν ἔθνεσιν, ἐπιστεύθη ἐν κόσμῳ, ἀνελήφθη ἐν δόξῃ.

16. Kai 'omologoumenos mega estin to teis eusebeias musteirion. theos ephanerothei en sarki, edikaiothei en pneumati, ophthei angelois, ekeiruchthei en ethnesin, episteuthei en kosmo, aneleiphthei en doxei.

Hebrew/Transliteration
טז. אָמְנָם גָּדוֹל סוֹד הַחֲסִידוּת אֱלֹהִים נִגְלָה בַבָּשָׂר וְצִדְקָתוֹ נִגְלָתָה בָרוּחַ מַלְאָכִים רָאוּ פָנָיו וְגוֹיִם הִתְבַּשְּׂרוּ יְשׁוּעָתוֹ אֱמוּנָתוֹ מָלְאָה תֵבֵל וַיַּעַל לַמָּרוֹם בְּכָבוֹד:

16. Om•nam ga•dol sod ha•cha•si•doot Elohim nig•la va•ba•sar ve•tzid•ka•to nig•le•ta va•Roo•ach mal•a•chim ra•oo fa•nav ve•go•yim hit•bas•roo ye•shoo•a•to emoo•na•to mal•ah te•vel va•ya•al la•ma•rom be•cha•vod.

1 Timothy, Chapter 4

1. Now the Spirit speaketh expressly, that in the latter times some shall depart from the faith, giving heed to seducing spirits, and doctrines of devils;

Greek/Transliteration
1. Τὸ δὲ πνεῦμα ῥητῶς λέγει, ὅτι ἐν ὑστέροις καιροῖς ἀποστήσονταί τινες τῆς πίστεως, προσέχοντες πνεύμασιν πλάνοις καὶ διδασκαλίαις δαιμονίων,

1. To de pneuma 'reitos legei, 'oti en 'usterois kairois aposteisontai tines teis pisteos, prosechontes pneumasin planois kai didaskaliais daimonion,

Hebrew/Transliteration
א. וְהָרוּחַ יַגִּיד דַּי־בָּאֵר כִּי בְּאַחֲרִית הַיָּמִים יִתְעוּ אֲנָשִׁים מֵאָרְחוֹת אֱמוּנָה וְיִזְנוּ אַחֲרֵי רוּחוֹת מַתְעָתְעִים וְתוֹרֹת הַשֵּׁדִים:

1. Ve•ha•Roo•ach ya•gid dey - va•er ki ve•a•cha•rit ha•ya•mim yit•oo a•na•shim me•or•chot e•moo•na ve•yiz•noo a•cha•rey roo•chot me•ta•at•eem ve•to•rot ha•she•dim.

---

2. Speaking lies in hypocrisy; having their conscience seared with a hot iron;

Greek/Transliteration
2. ἐν ὑποκρίσει ψευδολόγων, κεκαυτηριασμένων τὴν ἰδίαν συνείδησιν,

2. en 'upokrisei pseudologon, kekauteiryasmenon tein idian suneideisin,

Hebrew/Transliteration
ב. עַל־יְדֵי מַטִּיפֵי כָזָב וְשִׂפְתֵי חֲנֵפִים אֲשֶׁר לִבָּם קָשֶׁה כְּנִכְוֶה בְּבַרְזֶל לֹהֵט:

2. Al - ye•dey ma•ti•fey cha•zav ve•sif•tey cha•ne•fim asher li•bam ka•she ke•nich•ve be•var•zel lo•het.

---

3. Forbidding to marry, and commanding to abstain from meats, which God hath created to be received with thanksgiving of them which believe and know the truth.

Greek/Transliteration
3. κωλυόντων γαμεῖν, ἀπέχεσθαι βρωμάτων, ἃ ὁ θεὸς ἔκτισεν εἰς μετάληψιν μετὰ εὐχαριστίας τοῖς πιστοῖς καὶ ἐπεγνωκόσιν τὴν ἀλήθειαν.

3. koluonton gamein, apechesthai bromaton, 'a 'o theos ektisen eis metaleipsin meta eucharistias tois pistois kai epegnokosin tein aleitheyan.

Hebrew/Transliteration
ג. אֵלֶּה הֵם אֲשֶׁר לֹא יִתְּנוּ לָקַחַת אִשָּׁה וּמַאַכְלֵי שׁוֹנִים יַרְחִיקוּן אֲשֶׁר נָתַן אֱלֹהִים לֶאֱכֹל בְּתוֹדָה לְאַנְשֵׁי אֱמוּנָה וְיֹדְעֵי אֱמֶת:

3. Ele hem asher lo yit•noo la•ka•chat ee•sha oo•ma•a•chali sho•nim yar•chi•koon asher na•tan Elohim le•e•chol be•to•da le•an•shey e•moo•na ve•yod•ey emet.

4. For every creature of God is good, and nothing to be refused, if it be received with thanksgiving:

Greek/Transliteration
4. Ὅτι πᾶν κτίσμα θεοῦ καλόν, καὶ οὐδὲν ἀπόβλητον, μετὰ εὐχαριστίας λαμβανόμενον·

4. 'Oti pan ktisma theou kalon, kai ouden apobleiton, meta eucharistias lambanomenon.

Hebrew/Transliteration
ד. כִּי כֹל אֲשֶׁר עָשָׂה אֱלֹהִים טוֹב הוּא וְאֵין פִּגּוּל מְאוּמָה אִם-בְּתוֹדָה יֵאָכֵל:

4. Ki chol asher asa Elohim tov hoo ve•eyn pi•gool me•oo•ma eem - be•to•da ye•a•chel.

---

5. For it is sanctified by the word of God and prayer.

Greek/Transliteration
5. ἁγιάζεται γὰρ διὰ λόγου θεοῦ καὶ ἐντεύξεως.

5. 'agyazetai gar dya logou theou kai enteuxeos.

Hebrew/Transliteration
ה. כִּי יִתְקַדַּשׁ בְּאִמְרֵי-אֵל וּבְרָכָתוֹ:

5. Ki yit•ka•desh be•eem•rey - El oo•vir•cha•to.

Rabbinic Jewish Commentary
So the Israelites, when they had eaten, and were full, were to bless YHWH, Deu_8:10. And thus our Lord Yeshua, at meals, used to take the food, and bless it or ask a blessing on it, Mat_14:19. And so did the Essenes among the Jews (h), and the Christians in Tertullian's (i) time; and the practice is highly necessary and commendable, nor ought it to be disused.

(h) Porphyr. de Abstinentia, l. 4. sect. 12. (i) Apolog. c. 39.

---

6. If thou put the brethren in remembrance of these things, thou shalt be a good minister of Jesus Christ, nourished up in the words of faith and of good doctrine, whereunto thou hast attained.

Greek/Transliteration
6. Ταῦτα ὑποτιθέμενος τοῖς ἀδελφοῖς καλὸς ἔσῃ διάκονος Ἰησοῦ χριστοῦ, ἐντρεφόμενος τοῖς λόγοις τῆς πίστεως, καὶ τῆς καλῆς διδασκαλίας ᾗ παρηκολούθηκας.

6. Tauta 'upotithemenos tois adelphois kalos esei dyakonos Yeisou christou, entrephomenos tois logois teis pisteos, kai teis kaleis didaskalias pareikoloutheikas.

Hebrew/Transliteration
ו. אִם-תָּשִׂים כַּדְּבָרִים הָאֵלֶּה לִפְנֵי הָאַחִים מְשָׁרֵת טוֹב תִּהְיֶה לְיֵשׁוּעַ מְשִׁיחֵנוּ וְאָמוֹן עֲלֵי-אָרְחוֹת אֱמוּנָה וְתוֹרָה יְשָׁרָה אֲשֶׁר דָּבְקָה נַפְשְׁךָ אַחֲרֶיהָ:

6. Eem - ta•sim ka•d`va•rim ha•e•le lif•ney ha•a•chim me•sha•ret tov ti•hi•ye le•Yeshua me•shi•che•noo ve•a•moon aley - or•chot e•moo•na ve•to•rah ye•sha•ra asher dav•ka naf•she•cha acha•re•ha.

Rabbinic Jewish Commentary
So Philo the Jew (k) speaks of the soul, being "nourished with sciences", and not with food and drink, which the body needs; and a little after he says, you see the food of the soul what it is, it is the continual word of God.

(k) Allegor. l. 2. p. 90, 92.

---

7. But refuse profane and old wives' fables, and exercise thyself rather unto godliness.

Greek/Transliteration
7. Τοὺς δὲ βεβήλους καὶ γραώδεις μύθους παραιτοῦ. Γύμναζε δὲ σεαυτὸν πρὸς εὐσέβειαν·

7. Tous de bebeilous kai graodeis muthous paraitou. Gumnaze de seauton pros eusebeyan.

Hebrew/Transliteration
ז. אַךְ הַרְחֵק מֵאַגָּדוֹת סָרוֹת טַעַם כְּשִׂיחוֹת נָשִׁים זְקֵנוֹת וַחֲנֹךְ לְנַפְשְׁךָ בִּפְעֻלּוֹת יִרְאַת אֱלֹהִים:

7. Ach har•chek me•a•ga•dot sa•rot ta•am ke•si•chot na•shim z`ke•not va•cha•noch le•naf•she•cha bif•oo•lot yir•at Elohim.

---

8. For bodily exercise profiteth little: but godliness is profitable unto all things, having promise of the life that now is, and of that which is to come.

Greek/Transliteration
8. ἡ γὰρ σωματικὴ γυμνασία πρὸς ὀλίγον ἐστὶν ὠφέλιμος· ἡ δὲ εὐσέβεια πρὸς πάντα ὠφέλιμός ἐστιν, ἐπαγγελίαν ἔχουσα ζωῆς τῆς νῦν καὶ τῆς μελλούσης.

8. 'ei gar somatikei gumnasia pros oligon estin ophelimos. 'ei de eusebeya pros panta ophelimos estin, epangelian echousa zoeis teis nun kai teis mellouseis.

Hebrew/Transliteration
ח. כִּי בִּפְעֻלּוֹת הַגּוּף תִּשְׁתַּכֵּר מְעַט מִזְעָר וְיִרְאַת אֱלֹהִים לְהוֹעִיל לְךָ בְּכָל-אֲשֶׁר תִּפְנֶה וּשְׂכָרָהּ אִתָּהּ חַיֵּי הָעוֹלָם הַזֶּה וְחַיֵּי הָעוֹלָם הַבָּא:

8. Ki bif•oo•lot ha•goof tis•ta•ker me•at miz•ar ve•yir•at Elohim le•ho•eel le•cha be•chol - asher tif•ne oos•cha•ra ee•ta cha•yey ha•o•lam ha•ze ve•cha•yey ha•o•lam ha•ba.

Rabbinic Jewish Commentary
Syriac and Arabic versions read; and the latter renders the phrase "bodily recreation"

9. This is a faithful saying and worthy of all acceptation.

Greek/Transliteration
9. Πιστὸς ὁ λόγος καὶ πάσης ἀποδοχῆς ἄξιος.

9. Pistos 'o logos kai paseis apodocheis axios.

Hebrew/Transliteration
ט. וְהַדָּבָר הַזֶּה אֱמֶת הוּא וְיָאֲתָה לְכָל-אָדָם לְקַבְּלוֹ:

9. Ve•ha•da•var ha•ze emet hoo ve•ya•a•ta le•chol - adam le•kab•lo.

---

10. For therefore we both labour and suffer reproach, because we trust in the living God, who is the Saviour of all men, specially of those that believe.

Greek/Transliteration
10. Εἰς τοῦτο γὰρ καὶ κοπιῶμεν καὶ ὀνειδιζόμεθα, ὅτι ἠλπίκαμεν ἐπὶ θεῷ ζῶντι, ὅς ἐστιν σωτὴρ πάντων ἀνθρώπων, μάλιστα πιστῶν.

10. Eis touto gar kai kopiomen kai oneidizometha, 'oti eilpikamen epi theo zonti, 'os estin soteir panton anthropon, malista piston.

Hebrew/Transliteration
י. וּבַעֲבוּר הַדָּבָר הַזֶּה עָמַלְנוּ וְיָגַעְנוּ יַעַן כִּי-שָׂמְנוּ בָאֵל-חַי מַחְסֵנוּ הַמּוֹשִׁיעַ לְכָל-אָדָם וְעַל-יֶתֶר לַמַּאֲמִינִים בּוֹ:

10. Oo•va•a•voor ha•da•var ha•ze amal•noo ve•ya•ga•a•noo ya•an ki - sam•noo ve•el - chai mach•se•noo ha•Mo•shia le•chol - adam ve•al - ye•ter la•ma•a•mi•nim bo.

Rabbinic Jewish Commentary
This epithet of God seems to be taken out of Psa_17:7 where he is called מושיע חוסים, "the Saviour of them that trust", or believe.

---

11. These things command and teach.

Greek/Transliteration
11. Παράγγελλε ταῦτα καὶ δίδασκε.

11. Parangelle tauta kai didaske.

Hebrew/Transliteration
יא. וְאַתָּה תְּצַוֶּה כַּדְּבָרִים הָאֵלֶּה וּתְלַמֵּד אֹתָם:

11. Ve•a•ta te•tza•ve ka•d`va•rim ha•e•le oot•la•med o•tam.

12. Let no man despise thy youth; but be thou an example of the believers, in word, in conversation, in charity, in spirit, in faith, in purity.

Greek/Transliteration
12. Μηδείς σου τῆς νεότητος καταφρονείτω, ἀλλὰ τύπος γίνου τῶν πιστῶν ἐν λόγῳ, ἐν ἀναστροφῇ, ἐν ἀγάπῃ, ἐν πνεύματι, ἐν πίστει, ἐν ἁγνείᾳ.

12. Meideis sou teis neoteitos kataphroneito, alla tupos ginou ton piston en logo, en anastrophei, en agapei, en pneumati, en pistei, en 'agneia.

Hebrew/Transliteration
יב. אַל־יָבוּז לְךָ אִישׁ לֵאמֹר עוֹדְךָ נַעַר רַק הֱיֵה לַמַּאֲמִינִים לְמוֹפֵת בִּדְבָרֶיךָ בְּמַעֲשֶׂיךָ בְּאַהֲבָתְךָ בְּרוּחַ בֶּאֱמוּנָתְךָ וּבְבֹר לְבָבֶךָ:

12. Al - ya•vooz le•cha eesh le•mor od•cha na•ar rak he•ye la•ma•a•mi•nim le•mo•fet bid•va•re•cha be•ma•a•se•cha be•a•ha•vat•cha be•roo•ach be•e•moo•na•te•cha oo•ve•vor le•va•ve•cha.

---

13. Till I come, give attendance to reading, to exhortation, to doctrine.

Greek/Transliteration
13. Ἕως ἔρχομαι, πρόσεχε τῇ ἀναγνώσει, τῇ παρακλήσει, τῇ διδασκαλίᾳ.

13. 'Eos erchomai, proseche tei anagnosei, tei parakleisei, tei didaskalia.

Hebrew/Transliteration
יג. וְשָׁמַרְתָּ לַהֲגוֹת בִּסְפָרִים תָּמִיד לְהַשְׁמִיעַ מוּסָרְךָ וְלִקְחֲךָ עַד-בֹּאִי אֵלֶיךָ:

13. Ve•sha•mar•ta la•ha•got bis•fa•rim ta•mid le•hash•mi•a moo•sar•cha ve•lik•cha•cha ad - bo•ee e•le•cha.

Rabbinic Jewish Commentary
Give attendance to reading; that is, of the Scriptures, which the Jews call מקרא, "reading".

"Says R. Tanchum Bar Chanilai, for ever let a man divide his years or life into three parts; one third (let him spend) in the Mikra, (the Scriptures, and the reading of them,) another third in the Mishna, and the other third in the Talmud." (l)

(l) T. Bab. Avoda Zara, fol. 19. 2.

---

14. Neglect not the gift that is in thee, which was given thee by prophecy, with the laying on of the hands of the presbytery.

Greek/Transliteration
14. Μὴ ἀμέλει τοῦ ἐν σοὶ χαρίσματος, ὃ ἐδόθη σοι διὰ προφητείας μετὰ ἐπιθέσεως τῶν χειρῶν τοῦ πρεσβυτερίου.

14. Mei amelei tou en soi charismatos, 'o edothei soi dya propheiteias meta epitheseos ton cheiron tou presbuteriou.

Hebrew/Transliteration
:יד. אַל-תֶּרֶף יָדֶיךָ מִמַּתַּת שָׁמַיִם אֲשֶׁר נִתְּנָה לְךָ בִּדְבַר נְבוּאָה כַּאֲשֶׁר סָמְכוּ הַזְּקֵנִים אֶת-יְדֵיהֶם עָלֶיךָ

14. Al - te•ref ya•de•cha mi•ma•tat sha•ma•yim asher nit•na le•cha bid•var n`voo•ah ka•a•sher sam•choo haz`ke•nim et - ye•dey•hem a•le•cha.

Rabbinic Jewish Commentary

The apostle in calling those that joined with him, in putting hands on Timothy, the "presbytery or eldership", may have some reference to זקני העדה, "the elders of the congregation", which laid hands on the bullock for a sin offering, Lev_4:15 by whom some understand the great sanhedrim (m); others (n), not all the elders, but some particular persons, in number three; and so the ordination of a Rabbi was by three (o); hence we read of סמיכה בזקינים, "imposition of hands by the elders" (p).

(m) Bartenora in Misn. Menachot, c. 9. sect. 3. (n) Siphri in Maimon. in Misn. ib. c. 9. sect. 7. (o) Misn. Sanhedrin, c. 1. sect. 3. & Maimon. & Bartenora in ib. (p) T. Hieros. Horayot, fol. 46. 2.

---

15. Meditate upon these things; give thyself wholly to them; that thy profiting may appear to all.

Greek/Transliteration
15. Ταῦτα μελέτα, ἐν τούτοις ἴσθι, ἵνα σου ἡ προκοπὴ φανερὰ ᾖ ἐν πᾶσιν.

15. Tauta meleta, en toutois isthi, 'ina sou 'ei prokopei phanera ei en pasin.

Hebrew/Transliteration
:טו. שִׁיתָה כָל-הֶגְיוֹנְךָ וּמַעֲנֶיךָ בַּדְּבָרִים הָאֵלֶּה וְכָל-אָדָם יֶחֱזֶה בְּךָ כַּאֲשֶׁר תַּעֲלֶה מַעֲלָה מָּעְלָה

15. Shi•ta kol - heg•yon•cha oo•ma•a•ya•ne•cha bad•va•rim ha•e•le ve•chol - adam ye•che•ze be•cha ka•a•sher ta•a•le ma•a•la ma•a•la.

---

16. Take heed unto thyself, and unto the doctrine; continue in them: for in doing this thou shalt both save thyself, and them that hear thee.

Greek/Transliteration
16. Ἔπεχε σεαυτῷ καὶ τῇ διδασκαλίᾳ. Ἐπίμενε αὐτοῖς· τοῦτο γὰρ ποιῶν καὶ σεαυτὸν σώσεις καὶ τοὺς ἀκούοντάς σου.

16. Epeche seauto kai tei didaskalia. Epimene autois. touto gar poion kai seauton soseis kai tous akouontas sou.

Hebrew/Transliteration
טז. שָׁמוֹר אֶת-נַפְשְׁךָ וְאֶת-דִּבְרֵי הַתּוֹרֹת וְשִׁוִּיתָ אֹתָם לְנֶגְדְּךָ תָּמִיד וְאִם כֵּן תַּעֲשֶׂה גַּם-אֶת-נַפְשְׁךָ וְגַם אֶת-נֶפֶשׁ שֹׁמְעֶיךָ תּוֹשִׁיעַ:

16. Sh`mor et - naf•she•cha ve•et - div•rey ha•to•rot ve•shi•vita o•tam le•neg•de•cha ta•mid ve•eem ken ta•a•se gam - et - naf•she•cha ve•gam et - ne•fesh shom•e•cha to•shi•a.

1 Timothy, Chapter 5

1. Rebuke not an elder, but intreat him as a father; and the younger men as brethren;

Greek/Transliteration
1. Πρεσβυτέρῳ μὴ ἐπιπλήξῃς, ἀλλὰ παρακάλει ὡς πατέρα· νεωτέρους, ὡς ἀδελφούς·

1. Presbutero mei epipleixeis, alla parakalei 'os patera. neoterous, 'os adelphous.

Hebrew/Transliteration
א. אַל-תִּגְעַר בְּזָקֵן כִּי אִם-כְּאָב תַּזְהִירֵנּוּ וְאֶת-הַצְּעִירִים כְּאַחִים:

1. Al - tig•ar be•za•ken ki eem - ke•av taz•hi•re•noo ve•et - hatz•ee•rim ke•a•chim.

---

2. The elder women as mothers; the younger as sisters, with all purity.

Greek/Transliteration
2. πρεσβυτέρας, ὡς μητέρας· νεωτέρας, ὡς ἀδελφάς, ἐν πάσῃ ἁγνείᾳ.

2. presbuteras, 'os meiteras. neoteras, 'os adelphas, en pasei 'agneia.

Hebrew/Transliteration
ב. אֶת-הַזְּקֵנוֹת כְּאִמּוֹת וְאֶת-הַצְּעִירוֹת כַּאֲחָיוֹת בְּמַחֲשָׁבָה כֻלָּהּ זַכָּה:

2. Et - haz•ke•not ke•ee•mot ve•et - hatz•ee•rot ka•a•cha•yot be•ma•cha•sha•va koo•la za•ka.

---

3. Honour widows that are widows indeed.

Greek/Transliteration
3. Χήρας τίμα τὰς ὄντως χήρας.

3. Cheiras tima tas ontos cheiras.

Hebrew/Transliteration
ג. כַּבֵּד אֶת-הָאַלְמָנוֹת אֲשֶׁר הֵנָּה אַלְמָנוֹת נְכֹחוֹת:

3. Ka•bed et - ha•al•ma•not asher he•na al•ma•not n`cho•chot.

Rabbinic Jewish Commentary
So, with the Jews, giving gifts to persons, and making presents to them, is called honour. When Manoah asked the Messenger's name, that he might do him honour, when his saying came to pass, Jdg_13:17 the sense, according to them, is (q),

"That I may inquire in what place I may find thee, when thy prophecy is fulfilled, and give thee דורון, "a gift"; for there is no honour but what signifies a gift, as it is said, Num_22:17, "honouring I will honour thee"."

So giving gifts to the poor, or providing for their maintenance, is doing them honour; and that this is the sense here, appears by what follows in the context.

(q) Bemidbar Rabba, sect. 10. fol. 199. 4.

---

4. But if any widow have children or nephews, let them learn first to shew piety at home, and to requite their parents: for that is good and acceptable before God.

Greek/Transliteration
4. Εἰ δέ τις χήρα τέκνα ἢ ἔκγονα ἔχει, μανθανέτωσαν πρῶτον τὸν ἴδιον οἶκον εὐσεβεῖν, καὶ ἀμοιβὰς ἀποδιδόναι τοῖς προγόνοις· τοῦτο γάρ ἐστιν ἀπόδεκτον ἐνώπιον τοῦ θεοῦ.

4. Ei de tis cheira tekna ei ekgona echei, manthanetosan proton ton idion oikon eusebein, kai amoibas apodidonai tois progonois. touto gar estin apodekton enopion tou theou.

Hebrew/Transliteration
ד. וְכִי-יִהְיוּ בָנִים לְאַלְמָנָה אוֹ-בְּנֵי בָנִים רִאשֹׁנִים הֵם לִלְמֹד לַעֲשׂוֹת חֶסֶד עִם-בֵּית מוֹלַדְתָּם וּלְהָשִׁיב גְּמוּל לְיוֹלְדֵיהֶם כִּי הַדָּבָר הַזֶּה טוֹב הוּא וְרָצוּי לִפְנֵי אֱלֹהֵינוּ:

4. Ve•chi - yi•hee•yoo va•nim le•al•ma•na oh - v`ney va•nim ri•sho•nim hem lil•mod la•a•sot che•sed eem - beit mo•la•de•tam ool•ha•shiv g`mool le•yol•dey•hem ki ha•da•var ha•ze tov hoo ve•ra•tzooy lif•ney Elohey•noo.

Rabbinic Jewish Commentary
The Ethiopic version expresses it, "let the children first learn to do well to their own house", or family. It is the duty of children to take care of their parents in old age, and provide for them, when they cannot for themselves.

---

5. Now she that is a widow indeed, and desolate, trusteth in God, and continueth in supplications and prayers night and day.

Greek/Transliteration
5. Ἡ δὲ ὄντως χήρα καὶ μεμονωμένη ἤλπικεν ἐπὶ τὸν θεόν, καὶ προσμένει ταῖς δεήσεσιν καὶ ταῖς προσευχαῖς νυκτὸς καὶ ἡμέρας.

5. 'Ei de ontos cheira kai memonomenei eilpiken epi ton theon, kai prosmenei tais deeisesin kai tais proseuchais nuktos kai 'eimeras.

Hebrew/Transliteration
ה. אָכֵן אַלְמָנָה גַלְמוּדָה נְכֹחָה הֲלֹא הִיא אֲשֶׁר תָּשִׂים בֵּאלֹהִים מִבְטַחָהּ וְתִתְפַּלֵּל תָּמִיד תְּפִלּוֹת וְתַחֲנוּנִים לַיְלָה וָיוֹם:

5. A•chen al•ma•na gal•moo•da n`cho•cha ha•lo hee asher ta•sim be•Elohim miv•ta•cha ve•tit•pa•lel ta•mid te•fi•lot ve•ta•cha•noo•nim lai•la va•yom.

Rabbinic Jewish Commentary
A real widow, whom the Jews (r) call גמורה, "a perfect one", in opposition to one that is divorced, or a brother's widow, that has had the shoe plucked off for her.

(r) Jarchi in Exek. xliv. 22.

6. But she that liveth in pleasure is dead while she liveth.

Greek/Transliteration
6. Ἡ δὲ σπαταλῶσα, ζῶσα τέθνηκεν.

6. 'Ei de spatalosa, zosa tethneiken.

Hebrew/Transliteration
:ו. אַךְ הָרֹדֶפֶת חַיֵּי בְשָׂרִים מֵתָה הִיא בְּחַיֶּיהָ

6. Ach ha•ro•de•fet cha•yey ve•sa•rim me•ta hee be•cha•ye•ha.

Rabbinic Jewish Commentary
It is a common, saying to be met with in Jewish writers, רשעים בחייהן קרויין מתים, "the wicked while alive are said to be dead" (s). And they say (t) also, that men are called מתים, "dead", from the time they sin; and that he that sins is accounted כמת, "as a dead man" (u).

(s) T. Bab. Beracot, fol. 18. 2. & Hieros. Beracot, fol. 4. 4. Midrash Kohelet, fol. 78. 2. Tzeror Hammor, fol. 58. 3. Caphtor, fol. 79. 1, 2. & 84. 1. Jarchi in Gen. xi. 32. & Baal Hatturim in Deut. xvii. 6. (t) Tzeror Hammer, fol. 5. 9. (u) Ib. fol. 6. 2. & 127. 2.

---

7. And these things give in charge, that they may be blameless.

Greek/Transliteration
7. Καὶ ταῦτα παράγγελλε, ἵνα ἀνεπίληπτοι ὦσιν.

7. Kai tauta parangelle, 'ina anepileiptoi osin.

Hebrew/Transliteration
:ז. וְאַתָּה תְּצַוֶּה כָאֵלֶּה לְבִלְתִּי יִמָּצֵא בָהֶן שֶׁמֶץ דָּבָר

7. Ve•a•ta te•tza•ve cha•e•le le•vil•ti yi•ma•tze va•hen she•metz da•var.

---

8. But if any provide not for his own, and specially for those of his own house, he hath denied the faith, and is worse than an infidel.

Greek/Transliteration
8. Εἰ δέ τις τῶν ἰδίων καὶ μάλιστα τῶν οἰκείων οὐ προνοεῖ, τὴν πίστιν ἤρνηται, καὶ ἔστιν ἀπίστου χείρων.

8. Ei de tis ton idion kai malista ton oikeion ou pronoei, tein pistin eirneitai, kai estin apistou cheiron.

Hebrew/Transliteration
:ח. וּמִי הוּא אֲשֶׁר לֹא יְכַלְכֵּל קְרֹבָיו וְגַם מִבְּנֵי בֵיתוֹ יִתְעַלָּם הוּא בֹגֵד בָּאֱמוּנָה וְרַע מִמְּכַחֵשׁ בַּיהוָֹה

8. Oo•mi hoo asher lo ye•chal•kel k`ro•vav ve•gam mi•b`ney vey•to yit•a•lam hoo vo•ged ba•e•moo•na ve•ra mim•cha•chesh ba•Adonai.

Rabbinic Jewish Commentary

The Jews (w) have a rule or canon, which obliged men to take care of their families, which runs thus:

"As a man is bound to provide for his wife, so he is bound to provide for his sons and daughters, the little ones, until they are six years old; and from thenceforward he gives them food till they are grown up, according to the order of the wise men; if he will not, they reprove him, and make him ashamed, and oblige him; yea, if he will not, they publish him in the congregation, and say such an one is cruel, and will not provide for his children; and lo, he is worse than an unclean fowl, which feeds her young."

(w) Maimon. Hilchot Ishot, c. 12. sect. 14.

---

9. Let not a widow be taken into the number under threescore years old, having been the wife of one man,

Greek/Transliteration
9. Χήρα καταλεγέσθω μὴ ἔλαττον ἐτῶν ἑξήκοντα, γεγονυῖα ἑνὸς ἀνδρὸς γυνή,

9. Cheira katalegestho mei elatton eton 'exeikonta, gegonuia 'enos andros gunei,

Hebrew/Transliteration
ט. לֹא תָבוֹא אַלְמָנָה עַל-סֵפֶר הַקָּהָל בִּלְתִּי מִבַּת-שִׁשִּׁים שָׁנָה וָמַעְלָה אֲשֶׁר הָיְתָה אֵשֶׁת אִישׁ אֶחָד

9. Lo ta•vo al•ma•na al - se•fer ha•ka•hal bil•tee mi•bat - shi•shim sha•na va•ma•ala asher hai•ta eshet eesh e•chad.

Rabbinic Jewish Commentary

The age of sixty years was by the Jews (x) reckoned זקנה, "old age", but not under.

(x) Pirke Abot, c. 5. sect. 21.

---

10. Well reported of for good works; if she have brought up children, if she have lodged strangers, if she have washed the saints' feet, if she have relieved the afflicted, if she have diligently followed every good work.

Greek/Transliteration
10. ἐν ἔργοις καλοῖς μαρτυρουμένη, εἰ ἐτεκνοτρόφησεν, εἰ ἐξενοδόχησεν, εἰ ἁγίων πόδας ἔνιψεν, εἰ θλιβομένοις ἐπήρκεσεν, εἰ παντὶ ἔργῳ ἀγαθῷ ἐπηκολούθησεν.

10. en ergois kalois marturoumenei, ei eteknotropheisen, ei exenodocheisen, ei 'agion podas enipsen, ei thlibomenois epeirkesen, ei panti ergo agatho epeikoloutheisen.

Hebrew/Transliteration
י. וְיֶשׁ-לָהּ עֵדוּת עַל-מַעֲשֶׂיהָ הַטּוֹבִים כִּי גִדְּלָה בָנִים וְאֹרְחִים הֵבִיאָה בָּיִת כִּי רָחֲצָה רַגְלֵי הַקְּדוֹשִׁים וְהוֹצִיאָה נֶפֶשׁ נַעֲנָה מִמְּצוּקוֹתֶיהָ וְכִי רָדְפָה כָּל-מַעֲשֶׂה טוֹב:

10. Ve•yesh - la e•doot al - ma•a•se•ha ha•to•vim ki gid•la va•nim ve•or•chim he•vi•ah ba•yit ki ra•cha•tza rag•ley ha•k`do•shim ve•ho•tzi•ah ne•fesh na•a•na mim•tzoo•ko•te•ha ve•chi rad•fa kol - ma•a•se tov.

Rabbinic Jewish Commentary
The (y) Jews say many things בכבוד אכסניא, "in honour of hospitality" or entertaining of strangers, especially of receiving into their houses the disciples of the wise men, and giving them food and drink, and the use of their goods; this was what gave persons a very great character with them, and highly recommended them.

(y) T. Bab. Beracot, fol. 63. 2.

---

11. But the younger widows refuse: for when they have begun to wax wanton against Christ, they will marry;

Greek/Transliteration
11. Νεωτέρας δὲ χήρας παραιτοῦ· ὅταν γὰρ καταστρηνιάσωσιν τοῦ χριστοῦ, γαμεῖν θέλουσιν,

11. Neoteras de cheiras paraitou. 'otan gar katastreinyasosin tou christou, gamein thelousin,

Hebrew/Transliteration
יא. אַךְ אַלְמָנוֹת צְעִירוֹת אַל-תְּקַבֵּל כִּי כַּאֲשֶׁר טָפַשׁ לִבָּן וּפָרְקוּ עֹל הַמָּשִׁיחַ מֵעַל צַוָּארָן כֵּן תֶּחֱשַׁק נַפְשָׁן לְהִבָּעֵל:

11. Ach al•ma•not tze•ee•rot al - te•ka•bel ki ka•a•sher ta•fash li•ban oo•far•koo ol ha•Ma•shi•ach me•al tza•va•ran ken te•che•shak naf•shan le•hi•ba•el.

---

12. Having damnation, because they have cast off their first faith.

Greek/Transliteration
12. ἔχουσαι κρίμα, ὅτι τὴν πρώτην πίστιν ἠθέτησαν.

12. echousai krima, 'oti tein protein pistin eitheteisan.

Hebrew/Transliteration
יב. וְהִנֵּה עֲוֺנָן עֲלֵיהֶן כִּי הֵפֵרוּ מִבְטָא שְׂפָתֵיהֶן מֵרֹאשׁ:

12. Ve•he•na a•vo•nan aley•hen ki he•fe•roo miv•ta s`fa•tey•hen me•rosh.

---

13. And withal they learn to be idle, wandering about from house to house; and not only idle, but tattlers also and busybodies, speaking things which they ought not.

Greek/Transliteration
13. Ἅμα δὲ καὶ ἀργαὶ μανθάνουσιν, περιερχόμεναι τὰς οἰκίας, οὐ μόνον δὲ ἀργαὶ ἀλλὰ καὶ φλύαροι καὶ περίεργοι, λαλοῦσαι τὰ μὴ δέοντα.

13. 'Ama de kai argai manthanousin, perierchomenai tas oikias, ou monon de argai alla kai phluaroi kai periergoi, lalousai ta mei deonta.

Hebrew/Transliteration
יג. וְהֵן הֵנָּה בַּעֲצַלְתַּיִם תִּלְמֹדְנָה לָסֹב מִבַּיִת לָבָיִת וְלֹא־לְבַד בַּעֲצַלְתַּיִם כִּי אִם־גַּם־לְבַטֵּא הֶבֶל וּלְהוֹצִיא דִבָּה וְשִׂיחַ אֲשֶׁר לֹא טוֹב:

13. Ve•hen he•na ba•a•tzal•ta•yim til•mod•na la•sov mi•ba•yit la•va•yit ve•lo - le•vad ba•a•tzal•ta•yim ki eem - gam - le•va•te he•vel ool•ho•tzee di•ba ve•si•ach asher lo tov.

Rabbinic Jewish Commentary

The Jews (z) call אלמנה שובבית, "the gadding widow"; who, as the gloss says,

"Goes about and visits her neighbours continually; and these are they that corrupt the world."

Of this sort of women must the Jews be understood, when they say (a), it is one of the properties of them to be יוצאניות "going out", or gadding abroad, as Dinah did; and that it is another to be דבריות, "talkative".

(z) T. Bab. Sota, fol. 22. 1. (a) Bereshit Rabba, sect. 45. fol. 40. 3.

---

14. I will therefore that the younger women marry, bear children, guide the house, give none occasion to the adversary to speak reproachfully.

Greek/Transliteration
14. Βούλομαι οὖν νεωτέρας γαμεῖν, τεκνογονεῖν, οἰκοδεσποτεῖν, μηδεμίαν ἀφορμὴν διδόναι τῷ ἀντικειμένῳ λοιδορίας χάριν.

14. Boulomai oun neoteras gamein, teknogonein, oikodespotein, meidemian aphormein didonai to antikeimeno loidorias charin.

Hebrew/Transliteration
יד. וְעַל־כֵּן רְצוֹנִי כִּי תְבַקֵּשְׁנָה הַצְּעִירוֹת לְהִנָּשֵׂא לָלֶדֶת בָּנִים וְלָשׂוּם עַיִן עַל־הֲלִיכוֹת הַבַּיִת וְלֹא לָתֵת תֹּאֲנָה לְשׂוֹטֵן לְדַבֵּר שִׂטְנָה עָלֵינוּ:

14. Ve•al - ken r`tzo•ni ki te•va•kesh•na hatz•ee•rot le•hi•na•se la•le•det ba•nim ve•la•soom a•yin al - ha•li•chot ha•ba•yit ve•lo la•tet to•a•na le•so•ten le•da•ber sit•na aley•noo.

---

15. For some are already turned aside after Satan.

Greek/Transliteration
15. Ἤδη γάρ τινες ἐξετράπησαν ὀπίσω τοῦ Σατανᾶ.

15. Eidei gar tines exetrapeisan opiso tou Satana.

Hebrew/Transliteration
טו. כִּי אֲחָדוֹת כְּבָר סָרוּ אַחֲרֵי הַשָּׂטָן:

15. Ki a•cha•dot k`var sa•roo a•cha•rey ha•Satan.

16. If any man or woman that believeth have widows, let them relieve them, and let not the church be charged; that it may relieve them that are widows indeed.

Greek/Transliteration
16. Εἴ τις πιστὸς ἢ πιστὴ ἔχει χήρας, ἐπαρκείτω αὐταῖς, καὶ μὴ βαρείσθω ἡ ἐκκλησία, ἵνα ταῖς ὄντως χήραις ἐπαρκέσῃ.

16. Ei tis pistos ei pistei echei cheiras, eparkeito autais, kai mei bareistho 'ei ekkleisia, 'ina tais ontos cheirais eparkesei.

Hebrew/Transliteration
טז. כִּי-תִהְיֶינָה אַלְמָנוֹת בְּבֵית בֶּן-אֱמוּנָה אוֹ בַת-אֱמוּנָה תְּכַלְכֵּל אֶתְהֶן וְלֹא תִהְיֶיןָ לְמַשָּׂא עַל-עֲדַת אֱלֹהִים לְמַעַן תַּשִּׂיג יָדָם לְכַלְכֵּל אַלְמְנוֹתֵיהֶם הַנְּכֹחוֹת:

16. Ki - ti•hi•ye•na al•ma•not be•veit ben - e•moo•na oh vat - e•moo•na te•chal•kel et•hen ve•lo ti•hi•ye•na le•ma•sa al - adat Elohim le•ma•an ta•sig ya•dam le•chal•kel al•me•no•tey•hem ha•ne•cho•chot.

---

17. Let the elders that rule well be counted worthy of double honour, especially they who labour in the word and doctrine.

Greek/Transliteration
17. Οἱ καλῶς προεστῶτες πρεσβύτεροι διπλῆς τιμῆς ἀξιούσθωσαν, μάλιστα οἱ κοπιῶντες ἐν λόγῳ καὶ διδασκαλίᾳ.

17. 'Oi kalos proestotes presbuteroi dipleis timeis axiousthosan, malista 'oi kopiontes en logo kai didaskalia.

Hebrew/Transliteration
יז. הַזְּקֵנִים הַשֹּׁמְרִים מִשְׁמַרְתָּם הֵיטֵב יְכֻבְּדוּ בְכָבוֹד מִשְׁנֶה וְיוֹתֵר מֵהֶם אֲשֶׁר עֲבֹדָתָם בִּדְבַר אֱלֹהִים וּבְלִקְחוֹ:

17. Haz`ke•nim ha•shom•rim mish•mar•tam hei•tev ye•choob•doo be•cha•vod mish•ne ve•yo•ter me•hem asher avo•da•tam bid•var Elohim oov•lik•cho.

Rabbinic Jewish Commentary
The phrase seems to be Jewish, a like one is often to be met with in Jewish writings: Rabbenu was sitting לעי באורייתא,

"And labouring in the words" before the congregation of the Babylonians at Tzippore (b);"

And again (c),

"R. Jonah gave tithes to R. Acha bar Alia, not because he was a priest, but because he לעי באוריתא, "laboured in the words".

And they say (d),

"There is no greater reward for a man in the world, as for him דלעי באוריתא, "who labours in the words".

Hence we read (e) of עמל תורה, "the labour of the Torah", which they say the mouth is made for, and of labourers in the Torah (f); and such persons they judged worthy of the greatest respect, and to be preferred to others. For, they say (g),

"If a congregation is obliged to give a salary to a doctor (or ruler of the synagogue), and to a minister of the congregation, and it is not in their power to give to both; if the ruler is a famous man, and great in the Torah, and expert in doctrine, he is to be preferred, but if not the minister of the congregation is to be preferred."

(b) Bereshit Rabba, sect. 33. fol. 28. 3. (c) T. Hieros. Masser, Sheni, fol. 56. 2. (d) Zohar in Gen. fol. 60. 4. & pasira. (e) T. Bab. Sanhedrin, fol. 99. 2. (f) Derech Eretz, fol. 17. 4. (g) Jore Des, Tit. 251. sect. 13.

---

18. For the scripture saith, Thou shalt not muzzle the ox that treadeth out the corn. And, The labourer is worthy of his reward.

Greek/Transliteration
18. Λέγει γὰρ ἡ γραφή, Βοῦν ἀλοῶντα οὐ φιμώσεις· καί, Ἄξιος ὁ ἐργάτης τοῦ μισθοῦ αὐτοῦ.

18. Legei gar 'ei graphei, Boun aloonta ou phimoseis. kai, Axios 'o ergateis tou misthou autou.

Hebrew/Transliteration
יח. כִּי-הַכָּתוּב אֹמֵר לֹא-תַחְסֹם שׁוֹר בְּדִישׁוֹ וְעוֹד נֶאֱמַר הַפּוֹעֵל יֵשׁ שָׂכָר לִפְעֻלָּתוֹ:

18. Ki - ha•ka•toov o•mer lo - tach•som shor be•di•sho ve•od ne•e•mar ha•po•el yesh sa•char lif•oo•la•to.

---

19. Against an elder receive not an accusation, but before two or three witnesses.

Greek/Transliteration
19. Κατὰ πρεσβυτέρου κατηγορίαν μὴ παραδέχου, ἐκτὸς εἰ μὴ ἐπὶ δύο ἢ τριῶν μαρτύρων.

19. Kata presbuterou kateigorian mei paradechou, ektos ei mei epi duo ei trion marturon.

Hebrew/Transliteration
יט. עַל-זָקֵן לֹא תְקַבֵּל שִׂטְנָה בִּלְתִּי אִם-עַל-פִּי שְׁנַיִם אוֹ-שְׁלֹשָׁה עֵדִים:

19. Al - za•ken lo te•ka•bel sit•na bil•tee eem - al - pi sh`na•yim oh - sh`lo•sha e•dim.

---

20. Them that sin rebuke before all, that others also may fear.

Greek/Transliteration
20. Τοὺς ἁμαρτάνοντας ἐνώπιον πάντων ἔλεγχε, ἵνα καὶ οἱ λοιποὶ φόβον ἔχωσιν.

20. Tous 'amartanontas enopion panton elegche, 'ina kai 'oi loipoi phobon echosin.

Hebrew/Transliteration
כ. וְאֵלֶּה אֲשֶׁר חָטְאוּ הוֹכֵחַ תּוֹכִיחַ אֹתָם בִּפְנֵי כֹל לְמַעַן יִשְׁמְעוּן גַּם-הֵם וְיִירָאוּן:

20. Ve•e•le asher chat•oo ho•che•ach to•chi•ach o•tam bif•ney chol le•ma•an yish•me•oon gam - hem ve•yi•ra•oon.

Rabbinic Jewish Commentary
Some read the words, "them that sin before all, rebuke"; not only admonish once and again, but degrade them from their office, and withdraw from them, as from other disorderly persons, and cut them off, and cast them out of the church, and that in a public manner; and so the Arabic version renders it, "before the congregation": which was done only in case of notorious offences: and which rule is observed by the Jews, and runs thus (h);

"A wise man, an elder in wisdom, and so a prince, or the father of the sanhedrim, that sins, they do not excommunicate him (with Niddui) always בפרהסיא, "publicly", unless he does as Jeroboam the son of Nebat and his companions; but when he sins other sins, they chastise him privately."

The Syriac version reads, "other men"; and the Arabic version, "the rest of the people". The phrase seems to be taken out of Deu_13:11.

(h) Maimon. Talmud Tora, c. 7. sect. 1.

---

21. I charge thee before God, and the Lord Jesus Christ, and the elect angels, that thou observe these things without preferring one before another, doing nothing by partiality.

Greek/Transliteration
21. Διαμαρτύρομαι ἐνώπιον τοῦ θεοῦ καὶ κυρίου Ἰησοῦ χριστοῦ καὶ τῶν ἐκλεκτῶν ἀγγέλων, ἵνα ταῦτα φυλάξῃς χωρὶς προκρίματος, μηδὲν ποιῶν κατὰ πρόσκλησιν.

21. Dyamarturomai enopion tou theou kai kuriou Yeisou christou kai ton eklekton angelon, 'ina tauta phulaxeis choris prokrimatos, meiden poion kata proskleisin.

Hebrew/Transliteration
כא. הַעִדֹתִי בְךָ הַיּוֹם נֶגֶד הָאֱלֹהִים וְיֵשׁוּעַ הַמָּשִׁיחַ וְנֶגֶד הַמַּלְאָכִים בְּחִירֵי-יָהּ לִשְׁמֹר אֶת-הַדְּבָרִים הָאֵלֶּה וְלֹא לְהַטּוֹת מִשְׁפָּט וּבְכָל-אֲשֶׁר תַּעֲשֶׂה לֹא-תִשָּׂא פְנֵי גָבֶר:

21. Ha•ee•do•ti ve•cha ha•yom ne•ged ha•Elohim ve•Yeshua ha•Ma•shi•ach ve•ne•ged ha•mal•a•chim be•chi•rey - Ya lish•mor et - ha•d`va•rim ha•e•le ve•lo le•ha•tot mish•pat oov•chol - asher ta•a•se lo - ti•sa f`ney ga•ver.

Rabbinic Jewish Commentary
And the elect angels; by whom are meant not some of the angels/messengers, the more choice, excellent, and principal among them; as the seven angels/messengers in the Apocryha:

"I am Raphael, one of the seven holy angels/messengers, which present the prayers of the saints, and which go in and out before the glory of the Holy One." (Tobit 12:15)

But this is a spurious account, and not to be credited; nor was it an ancient tradition of the Jews, that there were seven principal angels.

So Agrippa (i), in his speech to the Jews, exhorting them to fidelity to the Romans, beseeches them by their holy things, και τους ιερους αγγελους του υεου, "and the holy angels of God", and their common country, that is, the good of it, that they would remain steadfast.

The Arabic version renders it, "without haste", or precipitancy; to which agrees the advice of the men of the great congregation, or Ezra's congregation, who were in his time, and succeeded him; הוו מתונים בדין, "be slow in judgment" (k), or long at it.

(i) Joseph. de Bello Jud. l. 2. c. 16. sect. 4. (k) Pirke Abot, c. 1. sect. 1. Vid. Maimon in ib.

---

22. Lay hands suddenly on no man, neither be partaker of other men's sins: keep thyself pure.

Greek/Transliteration
22. Χεῖρας ταχέως μηδενὶ ἐπιτίθει, μηδὲ κοινώνει ἁμαρτίαις ἀλλοτρίαις· σεαυτὸν ἁγνὸν τήρει.

22. Cheiras tacheos meideni epitithei, meide koinonei 'amartiais allotriais. seauton 'agnon teirei.

Hebrew/Transliteration
כב. אַל־תִּסְמֹךְ יָדֶיךָ עַל־אִישׁ בְּחִפָּזוֹן וְלֹא תִתְעָרֵב בַּעֲוֹנוֹת אֲחֵרִים וְאֶת־טָהֳרַת נַפְשְׁךָ תִּשְׁמֹר:

22. Al - tis•moch ya•de•cha al - eesh be•chi•pa•zon ve•lo tit•a•rev ba•a•vo•not a•che•rim ve•et - ta•ho•rat naf•she•cha tish•mor.

Rabbinic Jewish Commentary
The Jews, an ordination of one of their Rabbis is called סמיכה, "imposition of hands", though they performed it by words, and not by laying on of hands; which now by them is not judged necessary (l).

(l) Misn. Sanhedrin, c. 1. sect. 3. & Maimon. & Bartenora in ib. Juthasin, fol. 60. 1. & Maimon. Hilchot Sanhedrin, c. 4. sect. 1, 2.

---

23. Drink no longer water, but use a little wine for thy stomach's sake and thine often infirmities.

Greek/Transliteration
23. Μηκέτι ὑδροπότει, ἀλλ᾽ οἴνῳ ὀλίγῳ χρῶ, διὰ τὸν στόμαχόν σου καὶ τὰς πυκνάς σου ἀσθενείας.

23. Meiketi 'udropotei, all oino oligo chro, dya ton stomachon sou kai tas puknas sou astheneias.

Hebrew/Transliteration
כג. אַל־תִּשְׁתֶּה עוֹד מַיִם כִּי אִם־קַח לְךָ מְעַט־יַיִן שְׁקוּי לְבִטְנֶךָ כִּי חַלָּשׁ אַתָּה לָרֹב:

23. Al - tish•te od ma•yim ki eem - kach le•cha me•at - ya•yin shi•kooy le•vit•ne•cha ki cha•lash ata la•rov.

Rabbinic Jewish Commentary
but use a little wine; some, by "a little wine", understand not the quantity, but the quality of the wine; a thin, small, weak wine, or wine mixed with water; and so the Ethiopic version renders the words, "drink no more simple water", (or water only,) "but mix a little wine"; though rather the quantity is intended, and which is mentioned.

for thy stomach's sake; to help digestion, and to remove the disorders which might attend it: the Ethiopic version renders it, "for the pain of the liver", and "for thy perpetual disease"; which last might be a pain in his head, arising from the disorder of his stomach.

---

24. Some men's sins are open beforehand, going before to judgment; and some men they follow after.

Greek/Transliteration
24. Τινῶν ἀνθρώπων αἱ ἁμαρτίαι πρόδηλοί εἰσιν, προάγουσαι εἰς κρίσιν· τισὶν δὲ καὶ ἐπακολουθοῦσιν.

24. Tinon anthropon 'ai 'amartiai prodeiloi eisin, proagousai eis krisin. tisin de kai epakolouthousin.

Hebrew/Transliteration
כד. יֵשׁ בְּנֵי אָדָם אֲשֶׁר עֲוֹנוֹתָם גְּלוּיִם וּמַקְדִּימִים לָבוֹא לִפְנֵיהֶם לְמִשְׁפָּט וְיֵשׁ אֲשֶׁר עֲוֹנוֹתָם מְאַחֲרִים לָבוֹא אַחֲרֵיהֶם:

24. Yesh b`ney adam asher avo•no•tam g`loo•yim oo•mak•di•mim la•vo lif•ney•hem le•mish•pat ve•yesh asher avo•no•tam me•a•cha•rim la•vo a•cha•rey•hem.

Rabbinic Jewish Commentary
Much such a way of speaking is used by the Jews; who say (m),

"Whoever committeth one transgression, (a notorious one,) in this world, it joins to him, "and goes before him" ליום הדין "to the day of judgment".

(m) T. Bab. Sota, fol. 3. 2. Vid. Avoda Zara, fol. 5. 1.

---

25. Likewise also the good works of some are manifest beforehand; and they that are otherwise cannot be hid.

Greek/Transliteration
25. Ὡσαύτως καὶ τὰ καλὰ ἔργα πρόδηλά ἐστιν· καὶ τὰ ἄλλως ἔχοντα κρυβῆναι οὐ δύνανται.

25. 'Osautos kai ta kala erga prodeila estin. kai ta allos echonta krubeinai ou dunantai.

Hebrew/Transliteration

כה. וּכְמוֹ כֵן גַּם-הַמַּעֲשִׂים הַטּוֹבִים נוֹדָעִים הֵם וְאֵלֶּה אֲשֶׁר לֹא-כֵן לֹא יוּכְלוּ לְהִסָּתֵר:

25. Ooch•mo chen gam - ha•ma•a•sim ha•to•vim no•da•eem hem ve•e•le asher lo - chen lo yooch•loo le•hi•sa•ter.

1 Timothy, Chapter 6

1. Let as many servants as are under the yoke count their own masters worthy of all honour, that the name of God and his doctrine be not blasphemed.

Greek/Transliteration

1. Ὅσοι εἰσὶν ὑπὸ ζυγὸν δοῦλοι, τοὺς ἰδίους δεσπότας πάσης τιμῆς ἀξίους ἡγείσθωσαν, ἵνα μὴ τὸ ὄνομα τοῦ θεοῦ καὶ ἡ διδασκαλία βλασφημῆται.

1. 'Osoi eisin 'upo zugon douloi, tous idious despotas paseis timeis axious 'eigeisthosan, 'ina mei to onoma tou theou kai 'ei didaskalia blaspheimeitai.

Hebrew/Transliteration

א. הָעֲבָדִים הַנֹּשְׂאִים עֹל יִתְּנוּ כָבוֹד לַאֲדֹנֵיהֶם כְּכָל-אֲשֶׁר יָאֲתָה לָהֶם וְלֹא-יְחֻלַּל שֵׁם אֱלֹהִים וְתוֹרָתוֹ:

1. Ha•a•va•dim ha•nos•eem oo•lam yit•noo cha•vod la•a•do•ney•hem ke•chol - asher ya•a•ta la•hem ve•lo - ye•choo•lal shem Elohim ve•to•ra•to.

---

2. And they that have believing masters, let them not despise them, because they are brethren; but rather do them service, because they are faithful and beloved, partakers of the benefit. These things teach and exhort.

Greek/Transliteration

2. Οἱ δὲ πιστοὺς ἔχοντες δεσπότας μὴ καταφρονείτωσαν, ὅτι ἀδελφοί εἰσιν· ἀλλὰ μᾶλλον δουλευέτωσαν, ὅτι πιστοί εἰσιν καὶ ἀγαπητοὶ οἱ τῆς εὐεργεσίας ἀντιλαμβανόμενοι. Ταῦτα δίδασκε καὶ παρακάλει.

2. 'Oi de pistous echontes despotas mei kataphroneitosan, 'oti adelphoi eisin. alla mallon douleuetosan, 'oti pistoi eisin kai agapeitoi 'oi teis euergesias antilambanomenoi. Tauta didaske kai parakalei.

Hebrew/Transliteration

ב. וְאֵלֶּה אֲשֶׁר גַּם-אֲדֹנֵיהֶם אַנְשֵׁי אֱמוּנָה אַל-יְחַשְּׁבוּם לְנִקְלִים בַּעֲבוּר כִּי-אַחִים הֵם כִּי אִם-בְּחֵפֶץ יֶתֶר יַעֲבְדוּן אֶת-הַחֹלְקִים טוּב עֲבֹדָתָם בִּגְלַל אֱמוּנָתָם וְאַהֲבָתָם וְלִמַּדְתָּ אֶת-הַדְּבָרִים הָאֵלֶּה וְגַם-תְּצַוֶּה עֲלֵיהֶם:

2. Ve•e•le asher gam - ado•ney•hem an•shey e•moo•na al - ye•chash•voom le•nik•lim ba•a•voor ki - a•chim hem ki eem - be•che•fetz ye•ter ya•av•doon et - ha•chol•kim toov avo•da•tam big•lal emoo•na•tam ve•a•ha•va•tam ve•li•ma•de•ta et - ha•d`va•rim ha•e•le ve•gam - te•tza•ve aley•hem.

---

3. If any man teach otherwise, and consent not to wholesome words, even the words of our Lord Jesus Christ, and to the doctrine which is according to godliness;

Greek/Transliteration

3. Εἴ τις ἑτεροδιδασκαλεῖ, καὶ μὴ προσέρχεται ὑγιαίνουσιν λόγοις, τοῖς τοῦ κυρίου ἡμῶν Ἰησοῦ χριστοῦ, καὶ τῇ κατ᾽ εὐσέβειαν διδασκαλίᾳ,

3. Ei tis 'eterodidaskalei, kai mei proserchetai 'ugyainousin logois, tois tou kuriou 'eimon Yeisou christou, kai tei kat eusebeyan didaskalia,

Hebrew/Transliteration
ג. אִישׁ כִּי-יוֹרֶה דֶרֶךְ אַחֶרֶת וְלֹא יָשִׁית לִבּוֹ לַדְּבָרִים הַנֶּאֱמָנִים לְיֵשׁוּעַ הַמָּשִׁיחַ אֲדֹנֵינוּ וּלְדִבְרֵי מוּסָר בְּיִרְאַת אֱלֹהִים:

3. Eesh ki - yo•re de•rech a•che•ret ve•lo ya•sheet li•bo la•d`va•rim ha•ne•e•ma•nim le•Yeshua ha•Ma•shi•ach Ado•ney•noo ool•div•rey moo•sar be•yir•at Elohim.

---

4. He is proud, knowing nothing, but doting about questions and strifes of words, whereof cometh envy, strife, railings, evil surmisings,

Greek/Transliteration
4. τετύφωται, μηδὲν ἐπιστάμενος, ἀλλὰ νοσῶν περὶ ζητήσεις καὶ λογομαχίας, ἐξ ὧν γίνεται φθόνος, ἔρις, βλασφημίαι, ὑπόνοιαι πονηραί,

4. tetuphotai, meiden epistamenos, alla noson peri zeiteiseis kai logomachias, ex 'on ginetai phthonos, eris, blaspheimiai, 'uponoyai poneirai,

Hebrew/Transliteration
ד. אִישׁ יָהִיר הוּא וְאֵין תְּבוּנָה בּוֹ כִּי נָגוּעַ הוּא בְּדִבְרֵי רִיבוֹת לְהוֹכֵחַ מִלִּים וּמִמְּקוֹרָם תֵּצֵא קִנְאָה תִגְרָה נְאָצָה וְלֵב חֹרֵשׁ רָעָה:

4. Eesh ya•hir hoo ve•eyn te•voo•na vo ki na•goo•a hoo be•div•rey ri•vot le•ho•chach mi`lim oo•mim•ko•ram te•tze kin•ah tig•ra n`a•tza ve•lev cho•resh ra•ah.

---

5. Perverse disputings of men of corrupt minds, and destitute of the truth, supposing that gain is godliness: from such withdraw thyself.

Greek/Transliteration
5. διαπαρατριβαὶ διεφθαρμένων ἀνθρώπων τὸν νοῦν, καὶ ἀπεστερημένων τῆς ἀληθείας, νομιζόντων πορισμὸν εἶναι τὴν εὐσέβειαν. Ἀφίστασο ἀπὸ τῶν τοιούτων.

5. dyaparatribai diephtharmenon anthropon ton noun, kai apestereimenon teis aleitheias, nomizonton porismon einai tein eusebeyan. Aphistaso apo ton toiouton.

Hebrew/Transliteration
ה. מִלְחֲמוֹת הֲבָלִים בֵּין תֹּעֵי רוּחַ אֲשֶׁר הָאֱמֶת בְּתוֹכָם נֶעְדֶּרֶת וְיִרְאַת שָׁמַיִם בְּיָדָם לַעֲשׂוֹת מִקְנֶה וְקִנְיָן סוּר מֵאֲנָשִׁים כָּאֵלֶּה:

5. Mil•cha•mot ha•va•lim bein to•ey roo•ach asher ha•e•met be•to•cham ne•e•de•ret ve•yir•at sha•ma•yim be•ya•dam la•a•sot mik•ne ve•kin•yan soor me•a•na•shim ka•e•le.

---

6. But godliness with contentment is great gain.

Greek/Transliteration
6. Ἔστιν δὲ πορισμὸς μέγας ἡ εὐσέβεια μετὰ αὐταρκείας·

6. Estin de porismos megas 'ei eusebeya meta autarkeias.

Hebrew/Transliteration
:ו. אָמְנָם יִרְאַת אֱלֹהִים וְלֵב שָׂמֵחַ בְּחֶלְקוֹ קִנְיָן גָּדוֹל הוּא

6. Om•nam yir•at Elohim ve•lev sa•me•ach be•chel•ko kin•yan ga•dol hoo.

Rabbinic Jewish Commentary
The Jews have a saying (n), that

"He is a rich man whose spirit rests in, or is contented with his riches;"

that is, as the gloss explains it.

"Who rejoices in his portion, be it little or much: thus, though godliness is not gain, nor gain godliness, in the sense of the false teachers, yet is it true gain in a spiritual sense."

(n) T. Bab. Sabbat, fol. 25. 2.

---

7. For we brought nothing into this world, and it is certain we can carry nothing out.

Greek/Transliteration
7. οὐδὲν γὰρ εἰσηνέγκαμεν εἰς τὸν κόσμον, δῆλον ὅτι οὐδὲ ἐξενεγκεῖν τι δυνάμεθα·

7. ouden gar eiseinegkamen eis ton kosmon, deilon 'oti oude exenegkein ti dunametha.

Hebrew/Transliteration
:ז. כִּי לֹא-הֵבֵאנוּ מְאוּמָה לְתֵבֵל אַרְצֵנוּ וְיָדַעְנוּ כִּי לֹא נוֹצִיא מִמֶּנָּה מְאוּמָה

7. Ki lo - he•ve•noo me•oo•ma le•te•vel ar•tze•noo ve•ya•da•a•noo ki lo no•tzi mi•me•na me•oo•ma.

Rabbinic Jewish Commentary
The Jews have a saying like this (o), that

"As a man comes (into the world), בחליטין, "simply" or "nakedly", so he goes out in like manner."

(o) Bereshit Rabba, sect. 42. fol. 36. 3.

---

8. And having food and raiment let us be therewith content.

Greek/Transliteration
8. ἔχοντες δὲ διατροφὰς καὶ σκεπάσματα τούτοις ἀρκεσθησόμεθα.

8. echontes de dyatrophas kai skepasmata toutois arkestheisometha.

Hebrew/Transliteration
:ח. עַל-כֵּן בִּהְיוֹת לָנוּ לֶחֶם לֶאֱכֹל וּבֶגֶד לִלְבֹּשׁ נִשְׂמְחָה בְחֶלְקֵנוּ

8. Al - ken bi•hee•yot la•noo le•chem le•e•chol oo•ve•ged lil•bosh nis•me•cha be•chel•ke•noo.

---

9. But they that will be rich fall into temptation and a snare, and into many foolish and hurtful lusts, which drown men in destruction and perdition.

Greek/Transliteration
9. Οἱ δὲ βουλόμενοι πλουτεῖν ἐμπίπτουσιν εἰς πειρασμὸν καὶ παγίδα καὶ ἐπιθυμίας πολλὰς ἀνοήτους καὶ βλαβεράς, αἵτινες βυθίζουσιν τοὺς ἀνθρώπους εἰς ὄλεθρον καὶ ἀπώλειαν.

9. 'Oi de boulomenoi ploutein empiptousin eis peirasmon kai pagida kai epithumias pollas anoeitous kai blaberas, 'aitines buthizousin tous anthropous eis olethron kai apoleyan.

Hebrew/Transliteration
ט. וְהַמְבַקְשִׁים לְהַעֲשִׁיר יִלָכְדוּ בְמַסוֹת וּבְמוֹקְשִׁים וּבְרֹב תַּאֲוַת כֶּסֶל וּמַשְׁחָת וּבְאַחֲרִיתָם יֵרְדוּ לִבְאֵר שַׁחַת וַאֲבַדּוֹן:

9. Ve•ham•vak•shim le•ha•a•shir yi•lach•doo ve•ma•sot oov•mok•shim oov•rov ta•a•vat ke•sel oo•mosh•chat oov•a•cha•ri•tam yer•doo liv•er sha•chat va•a•va•don.

Rabbinic Jewish Commentary
So the phrase יצריהון טפשא, "their foolish lust", is used by the Targumist in Eze_20:25 and the corruption of nature in general is by the Jews called the old and foolish king, in Ecc_4:13. They ask (p),

"Why is he called a king? because all obey him; why is he called old? because he is joined to him (a man) from his birth to his old age; and why is he called כסיל, "foolish?" because he teaches him an evil way, which he knows not how to warn him of again."

(p) Midrash Kohelet, fol. 70. 2.

---

10. For the love of money is the root of all evil: which while some coveted after, they have erred from the faith, and pierced themselves through with many sorrows.

Greek/Transliteration
10. Ῥίζα γὰρ πάντων τῶν κακῶν ἐστιν ἡ φιλαργυρία· ἧς τινες ὀρεγόμενοι ἀπεπλανήθησαν ἀπὸ τῆς πίστεως, καὶ ἑαυτοὺς περιέπειραν ὀδύναις πολλαῖς.

10. 'Riza gar panton ton kakon estin 'ei philarguria. 'eis tines oregomenoi apeplaneitheisan apo teis pisteos, kai 'eautous periepeiran odunais pollais.

Hebrew/Transliteration
י. כִּי שֹׁרֶשׁ כָּל-רָע אַהֲבַת כֶּסֶף אֲשֶׁר חָמְדוּ בְנֵי-אָדָם וְתָעוּ מִדֶּרֶךְ אֱמוּנָתָם וַיַּכְאִיבוּ נַפְשָׁם בְּמַכְאֹבִים רַבִּים:

10. Ki sho•resh kol - ra a•ha•vat ke•sef asher cham•doo v`ney - adam ve•ta•oo mi•de•rech emoo•na•tam va•yach•ee•voo naf•sham be•mach•o•vim ra•bim.

Rabbinic Jewish Commentary

The phrase is Jewish. So idolatry is said to be עיקר כל עונות, "the root of all iniquities" (q); see Heb_12:15.

The apostle seem to allude to the Hebrew word בצע, used for a covetous man, which signifies one that pierces, cuts, and wounds, as such an one does both himself and others.

(q) R. David Kimchi in Isa. xxvii. 9.

---

11. But thou, O man of God, flee these things; and follow after righteousness, godliness, faith, love, patience, meekness.

Greek/Transliteration
11. Σὺ δέ, ὦ ἄνθρωπε τοῦ θεοῦ, ταῦτα φεῦγε· δίωκε δὲ δικαιοσύνην, εὐσέβειαν, πίστιν, ἀγάπην, ὑπομονήν, πρᾳότητα.

11. Su de, o anthrope tou theou, tauta pheuge. dioke de dikaiosunein, eusebeyan, pistin, agapein, 'upomonein, praoteita.

Hebrew/Transliteration
יא. וְאַתָּה אִישׁ אֱלֹהִים בְּרַח-לְךָ מֵאֵלֶּה כִּי אִם-צֶדֶק תִּרְדּוֹף יִרְאַת אֱלֹהִים אֱמוּנָה אַהֲבָה עֹצֶר-רוּחַ וַעֲנָוָה:

11. Ve•a•ta eesh Elohim be•rach - le•cha me•e•le ki eem - tze•dek tir•dof yir•at Elohim e•moo•na a•ha•va o•tzer - roo•ach va•a•na•va.

Rabbinic Jewish Commentary
But thou, O man of God; The phrase is taken out of the Old Testament, where the prophets, Elijah and Elisha, are so called, 2Ki_1:9,

flee these things; the Arabic version reads "these abominations".

---

12. Fight the good fight of faith, lay hold on eternal life, whereunto thou art also called, and hast professed a good profession before many witnesses.

Greek/Transliteration
12. Ἀγωνίζου τὸν καλὸν ἀγῶνα τῆς πίστεως, ἐπιλαβοῦ τῆς αἰωνίου ζωῆς, εἰς ἣν ἐκλήθης, καὶ ὡμολόγησας τὴν καλὴν ὁμολογίαν ἐνώπιον πολλῶν μαρτύρων.

12. Agonizou ton kalon agona teis pisteos, epilabou teis aioniou zoeis, eis 'ein ekleitheis, kai 'omologeisas tein kalein 'omologian enopion pollon marturon.

Hebrew/Transliteration
יב. הִלָּחֵם מִלְחֶמֶת צֶדֶק לֶאֱמוּנָתֵנוּ וְהַחֲזֵק בְּנַחֲלַת חַיֵּי עוֹלָם אֲשֶׁר נוֹעַדְתָּ לָהּ וַאֲשֶׁר עֵדוּת טוֹבָה עָנִיתָ לְעֵינֵי עֵדִים רַבִּים:

12. Hi•la•chem mil•che•met tze•dek le•e•moo•na•te•noo ve•ha•cha•zek be•na•cha•lat cha•yey o•lam asher no•a•de•ta la va•a•sher e•doot to•va ani•ta le•ei•ney e•dim ra•bim.

Rabbinic Jewish Commentary

This fight is called "the fight of faith"; partly in opposition to the Torah, and to מלחמתה של תורה, "the fight", or "war of the Torah" the Jews (r) so much talk of; and in which the false teachers, in the apostle's time, were so much engaged, and against whom the apostles set themselves.

whereunto thou art also called; The word "also" is left out in the Alexandrian copy, and in the Vulgate Latin, and in all the Oriental versions.

(r) Zohar in Numb. fol. 99. 4. T. Hieros. Taanith, fol. 69. 2. & Bab. Chagiga, fol. 14. 1. Megilia, fol. 15. 2. & Sanhedrin, fol. 93. 2. & 111. 2. Midrash Ruth, fol. 31. 4. Echa Rabbati, fol. 53. 2. Caphtor, fol. 93. 2. & Seder Olam Rabba, c. 25. & Jarchi in Cant. iii. 8.

---

13. I give thee charge in the sight of God, who quickeneth all things, and before Christ Jesus, who before Pontius Pilate witnessed a good confession;

Greek/Transliteration

13. Παραγγέλλω σοι ἐνώπιον τοῦ θεοῦ τοῦ ζωοποιοῦντος τὰ πάντα, καὶ χριστοῦ Ἰησοῦ τοῦ μαρτυρήσαντος ἐπὶ Ποντίου Πιλάτου τὴν καλὴν ὁμολογίαν,

13. Parangello soi enopion tou theou tou zoopoiountos ta panta, kai christou Yeisou tou martureisantos epi Pontiou Pilatou tein kalein 'omologian,

Hebrew/Transliteration

יג. הִנְנִי פֹקֵד עָלֶיךָ הַיּוֹם נֶגֶד הָאֱלֹהִים הַמְחַיֶּה כֹל וְנֶגֶד יֵשׁוּעַ הַמָּשִׁיחַ אֲשֶׁר עָנָה הָעֵדוּת הַטּוֹבָה לְעֵינֵי פָּנְטִיּוֹס פִּילָטוֹס:

13. Hi•ne•ni fo•ked a•le•cha ha•yom ne•ged ha•Elohim ham•cha•ye chol ve•ne•ged Yeshua ha•Ma•shi•ach asher ana ha•e•doot ha•to•va le•ei•ney Fon•tiyos Pilatos.

---

14. That thou keep this commandment without spot, unrebukeable, until the appearing of our Lord Jesus Christ:

Greek/Transliteration

14. τηρῆσαί σε τὴν ἐντολὴν ἄσπιλον, ἀνεπίληπτον, μέχρι τῆς ἐπιφανείας τοῦ κυρίου ἡμῶν Ἰησοῦ χριστοῦ,

14. teireisai se tein entolein aspilon, anepileipton, mechri teis epiphaneias tou kuriou 'eimon Yeisou christou,

Hebrew/Transliteration

יד. כִּי-תִשְׁמֹר אֶת-הַמִּצְוָה הַזֹּאת בָּרָה וּתְמִימָה עַד-יוֹם הִתְגַּלּוֹת יֵשׁוּעַ הַמָּשִׁיחַ אֲדֹנֵינוּ:

14. Ki - tish•mor et - ha•mitz•va ha•zot ba•ra oot•mi•ma ad - yom hit•ga•lot Yeshua ha•Ma•shi•ach Ado•ney•noo.

15. Which in his times he shall shew, who is the blessed and only Potentate, the King of kings, and Lord of lords;

Greek/Transliteration
15. ἣν καιροῖς ἰδίοις δείξει ὁ μακάριος καὶ μόνος δυνάστης, ὁ βασιλεὺς τῶν βασιλευόντων, καὶ κύριος τῶν κυριευόντων,

15. 'ein kairois idiois deixei 'o makarios kai monos dunasteis, 'o basileus ton basileuonton, kai kurios ton kurieuonton,

Hebrew/Transliteration
טו. אֲשֶׁר בְּעִתּוֹ יַרְאֵנוּ הַמְבֹרָךְ הַמֹּשֵׁל הַיָּחִיד מֶלֶךְ הַמְּלָכִים וַאֲדֹנֵי הָאֲדֹנִים:

15. Asher be•ee•to yar•e•noo ham•vo•rach ha•Mo•shel ha•ya•chid Me•lech ha•m`la•chim va•Ado•ney ha•a•do•nim.

Rabbinic Jewish Commentary
who is the blessed; the Syriac version reads, "the blessed God".

These titles are used by the Jews, who style him, אדון כל האדונים מלך על כל המלכים, "Lord of all lords, King over all kings" (s). The same name is given to Yeshua Messiah, Rev_19:16 which shows him to be equal with the Father.

(s) Zohar in Numb. fol. 100. 2.

---

16. Who only hath immortality, dwelling in the light which no man can approach unto; whom no man hath seen, nor can see: to whom be honour and power everlasting. Amen.

Greek/Transliteration
16. ὁ μόνος ἔχων ἀθανασίαν, φῶς οἰκῶν ἀπρόσιτον, ὃν εἶδεν οὐδεὶς ἀνθρώπων, οὐδὲ ἰδεῖν δύναται· ᾧ τιμὴ καὶ κράτος αἰώνιον. Ἀμήν.

16. 'o monos echon athanasian, phos oikon aprositon, 'on eiden oudeis anthropon, oude idein dunatai. 'o timei kai kratos aionion. Amein.

Hebrew/Transliteration
טז. אֲשֶׁר עִמּוֹ לְבַדּוֹ מְקוֹר חַיִּים שֹׁכֵן אוֹר אֲשֶׁר אֵין לָגֶשֶׁת אֵלָיו לֹא רָאָה אֹתוֹ אָדָם וְלֹא יַעְצַר-כֹּחַ לִרְאוֹתוֹ: אֲשֶׁר לוֹ הַכָּבוֹד וְהַגְּבוּרָה לְעוֹלָם וָעֶד אָמֵן:

16. Asher ee•mo le•va•do me•kor cha•yim sho•chen or asher eyn la•ge•shet elav lo ra•ah o•to adam ve•lo ya•a•tzar - ko•ach lir•o•to asher lo ha•ka•vod ve•hag•voo•ra le•o•lam va•ed Amen.

---

17. Charge them that are rich in this world, that they be not highminded, nor trust in uncertain riches, but in the living God, who giveth us richly all things to enjoy;

Greek/Transliteration
17. Τοῖς πλουσίοις ἐν τῷ νῦν αἰῶνι παράγγελλε, μὴ ὑψηλοφρονεῖν, μηδὲ ἠλπικέναι ἐπὶ πλούτου ἀδηλότητι, ἀλλ᾽ ἐν τῷ θεῷ τῷ ζῶντι, τῷ παρέχοντι ἡμῖν πάντα πλουσίως εἰς ἀπόλαυσιν·

17. Tois plousiois en to nun aioni parangelle, mei 'upseilophronein, meide eilpikenai epi ploutou adeiloteiti, all en to theo to zonti, to parechonti 'eimin panta plousios eis apolausin.

Hebrew/Transliteration
יז. צַו עַל-עֲשִׁירֵי הָעוֹלָם הַזֶּה לְבִלְתִּי יָרוּם לְבָבָם וְלֹא-יִבְטְחוּ בָעֹשֶׁר אֲשֶׁר כְּנָפַיִם לוֹ כִּי אִם-בֵּאלֹהִים הַנֹּתֵן לָנוּ דַי וְהוֹתֵר לִשְׂבֹּעַ:

17. Tzav al - ashi•rey ha•o•lam ha•ze le•vil•ti ya•room le•va•vam ve•lo - yiv•te•choo va•o•sher asher k`na•fa•yim lo ki eem - be•Elohim ha•no•ten la•noo dai ve•ho•ter lis•bo•a.

Rabbinic Jewish Commentary
Charge them that are rich in this world,.... Or in the things of this world. The Arabic version reads, "in this present world".

that they be not high minded; the Ethiopic version reads, "that they be not lifted up in this world".

---

18. That they do good, that they be rich in good works, ready to distribute, willing to communicate;

Greek/Transliteration
18. ἀγαθοεργεῖν, πλουτεῖν ἐν ἔργοις καλοῖς, εὐμεταδότους εἶναι, κοινωνικούς,

18. agathoergein, ploutein en ergois kalois, eumetadotous einai, koinonikous,

Hebrew/Transliteration
יח. אַךְ יַעֲשׂוּ אֶת-הַטּוֹב וְיַעֲשִׁירוּ בְמַעֲשִׂים טוֹבִים לָתֵת וּלְחַלֵּק לַאֲשֶׁר אֵין נָכוֹן לוֹ:

18. Ach ya•a•soo et - ha•tov ve•ya•a•shi•roo ve•ma•a•sim to•vim la•tet ool•cha•lek la•a•sher eyn na•chon lo.

Rabbinic Jewish Commentary
The phrase seems to be Rabbinical. Frequent mention is made of עשיר בתורה, "rich in the Torah", and עשיר במצות, "rich in the commandments" (t); and it is said (u), no man is poor but he that is without the Torah, and good works, for the riches of a man are the Torah, and good works.

(t) Zohar in Numb. fol. 91. 3. Vajikra Rabba, sect. 34. fol. 173. 4. & Tzeror Hammaor, fol. 15. 2. (u) Raya Mehimna in Exod. fol 48. 3. Vid. T. Bab. Megilia, fol. 11. 1.

19. Laying up in store for themselves a good foundation against the time to come, that they may lay hold on eternal life.

Greek/Transliteration
19. ἀποθησαυρίζοντας ἑαυτοῖς θεμέλιον καλὸν εἰς τὸ μέλλον, ἵνα ἐπιλάβωνται τῆς αἰωνίου ζωῆς.

19. apotheisaurizontas 'eautois themelion kalon eis to mellon, 'ina epilabontai teis aioniou zoeis.

Hebrew/Transliteration
יט. וְלֶאֱצֹר לָהֶם אוֹצָר לִיסוֹד טוֹב לֶעָתִיד לָרֶשֶׁת אֶת-חַיֵּי הָאֱמֶת:

19. Ve•le•e•tzor la•hem o•tzar liy•sod tov le•a•tid la•re•shet et - cha•yey ha•e•met.

Rabbinic Jewish Commentary
So it is said of King Munbaz, when he dispersed his father's treasures to the poor, his brethren and friends came about him, complaining of it; to whom he said (w).

"My fathers treasured up below, I treasure up above. My fathers treasured "up for others", I treasure up לעצמי, "for myself"; my fathers treasured up for this world, I treasure up for the world to come."

(w) T. Bab. Bava Bathra, fol. 11. 1.

---

20. O Timothy, keep that which is committed to thy trust, avoiding profane and vain babblings, and oppositions of science falsely so called:

Greek/Transliteration
20. Ὦ Τιμόθεε, τὴν παραθήκην φύλαξον, ἐκτρεπόμενος τὰς βεβήλους κενοφωνίας καὶ ἀντιθέσεις τῆς ψευδωνύμου γνώσεως·

20. O Timothee, tein paratheikein phulaxon, ektrepomenos tas bebeilous kenophonias kai antitheseis teis pseudonumou gnoseos.

Hebrew/Transliteration
כ. אָנָּא טִימוֹתִיּוֹס שְׁמֹר אֶת-הַפִּקָּדוֹן אֲשֶׁר הָפְקַד אִתָּךְ וְהַרְחֵק נַפְשְׁךָ מִשִּׂיחוֹת חוּלִין רְעוּת רוּחַ וּמִן-הַבִּקֹּרֶת אֲשֶׁר יְכַנּוּ בְשִׂפַת שֶׁקֶר בְּשֵׁם נְתִיבוֹת הַחָכְמָה:

20. Ana Ti•mo•ti•yos sh`mor et - ha•pi•ka•don asher hoof•kad eet•cha ve•har•chek naf•she•cha mi•si•chot choo•lin r`oot roo•ach oo•min - ha•bi•ko•ret asher ye•cha•noo vis•fat she•ker be•shem n`ti•vot ha•choch•ma.

---

21. Which some professing have erred concerning the faith. Grace be with thee. Amen.

Greek/Transliteration
21. ἥν τινες ἐπαγγελλόμενοι περὶ τὴν πίστιν ἠστόχησαν. Ἡ χάρις μετὰ σοῦ. Ἀμήν.

21. 'ein tines epangellomenoi peri tein pistin eistocheisan. 'Ei charis meta sou. Amein.

Hebrew/Transliteration

כא. וַאֲשֶׁר מִן-הַהֹלְכִים בָּהֵן תָּעוּ מֵאֹרַח אֱמוּנָתָם הַחֶסֶד יְהִי עִמְּךָ אָמֵן:

21. Va•a•sher min - ha•hol•chim ba•hen ta•oo me•o•rach emoo•na•tam ha•che•sed ye•hee ee•mach Amen.

THE SECOND EPISTLE OF PAUL THE APOSTLE TO TIMOTHY

2 Timothy, Chapter 1

1. Paul, an apostle of Jesus Christ by the will of God, according to the promise of life which is in Christ Jesus,

Greek/Transliteration

1. Παῦλος, ἀπόστολος Ἰησοῦ χριστοῦ διὰ θελήματος θεοῦ, κατ' ἐπαγγελίαν ζωῆς τῆς ἐν χριστῷ Ἰησοῦ,

1. Paulos, apostolos Yeisou christou dya theleimatos theou, kat epangelian zoeis teis en Christo Yeisou,

Hebrew/Transliteration

א. פּוֹלוֹס שְׁלִיחַ יֵשׁוּעַ הַמָּשִׁיחַ בִּרְצוֹן אֱלֹהִים כַּאֲשֶׁר הִבְטִיחַ לָנוּ חַיִּים בְּיֵשׁוּעַ הַמָּשִׁיחַ:

1. Polos sh`li•ach Yeshua ha•Ma•shi•ach bir•tzon Elohim ka•a•sher hiv•ti•ach la•noo cha•yim bi•Yeshua ha•Ma•shi•ach.

---

2. To Timothy, my dearly beloved son: Grace, mercy, and peace, from God the Father and Christ Jesus our Lord.

Greek/Transliteration

2. Τιμοθέῳ ἀγαπητῷ τέκνῳ· χάρις, ἔλεος, εἰρήνη ἀπὸ θεοῦ πατρὸς καὶ χριστοῦ Ἰησοῦ τοῦ κυρίου ἡμῶν.

2. Timotheo agapeito tekno. charis, eleos, eireinei apo theou patros kai christou Yeisou tou kuriou 'eimon.

Hebrew/Transliteration

ב. אֶל-טִימוֹתִיּוֹס בֵּן יַקִּיר לִי חֶסֶד רַחֲמִים וְשָׁלוֹם לְךָ מֵאֵת אֱלֹהִים אָבִינוּ וּמֵאֵת יֵשׁוּעַ הַמָּשִׁיחַ אֲדֹנֵינוּ:

2. El - Ti•mo•ti•yos ben ya•kir li che•sed ra•cha•mim ve•sha•lom le•cha me•et Elohim Avi•noo oo•me•et Yeshua ha•Ma•shi•ach Ado•ney•noo.

---

3. I thank God, whom I serve from my forefathers with pure conscience, that without ceasing I have remembrance of thee in my prayers night and day;

Greek/Transliteration

3. Χάριν ἔχω τῷ θεῷ, ᾧ λατρεύω ἀπὸ προγόνων ἐν καθαρᾷ συνειδήσει, ὡς ἀδιάλειπτον ἔχω τὴν περὶ σοῦ μνείαν ἐν ταῖς δεήσεσίν μου νυκτὸς καὶ ἡμέρας,

3. Charin echo to theo, 'o latreuo apo progonon en kathara suneideisei, 'os adyaleipton echo tein peri sou mneian en tais deeisesin mou nuktos kai 'eimeras,

Hebrew/Transliteration

ג. בָּרוּךְ הוּא הָאֱלֹהִים אֲשֶׁר עֲבַדְתִּי אֹתוֹ בְּתָם-לְבָבִי מִימֵי אֲבוֹתַי כִּי-אֶזְכָּרְךָ תָמִיד בִּתְפִלָּתִי מִדֵּי אֶתְפַּלֵּל בַּלַּיְלָה וּבַיּוֹם:

3. Ba•rooch hoo ha•Elohim asher ava•d`ti o•to be•tom - le•va•vi mi•mey avo•tai ki - ez•kar•cha ta•mid bit•fi•la•ti mee•dey et•pa•lel ba•lai•la oo•va•yom.

---

4. Greatly desiring to see thee, being mindful of thy tears, that I may be filled with joy;

Greek/Transliteration
4. ἐπιποθῶν σε ἰδεῖν, μεμνημένος σου τῶν δακρύων, ἵνα χαρᾶς πληρωθῶ,

4. epipothon se idein, memneimenos sou ton dakruon, 'ina charas pleirotho,

Hebrew/Transliteration
ד. וְנַפְשִׁי כָלְתָה לִרְאוֹתֶךָ כִּי דִמְעוֹתֶיךָ עָלוּ לְזִכָּרוֹן לְפָנַי לִשְׂבֹּעַ שְׂמָחוֹת אֶת־פָּנֶיךָ:

4. Ve•naf•shi chal•ta lir•o•te•cha ki dim•o•te•cha a•loo le•zi•ka•ron le•fa•nai lis•bo•a s`ma•chot et - pa•ne•cha.

---

5. When I call to remembrance the unfeigned faith that is in thee, which dwelt first in thy grandmother Lois, and thy mother Eunice; and I am persuaded that in thee also.

Greek/Transliteration
5. ὑπόμνησιν λαμβάνων τῆς ἐν σοὶ ἀνυποκρίτου πίστεως, ἥτις ἐνῴκησεν πρῶτον ἐν τῇ μάμμῃ σου Λωΐδι καὶ τῇ μητρί σου Εὐνίκῃ, πέπεισμαι δὲ ὅτι καὶ ἐν σοί.

5. 'upomneisin lambanon teis en soi anupokritou pisteos, 'eitis enokeisen proton en tei mammie sou Loidi kai tei meitri sou Eunikei, pepeismai de 'oti kai en soi.

Hebrew/Transliteration
ה. וְהִגַּיְתִי בָּאֱמוּנָה הַצְּרוּפָה אֲשֶׁר הָיְתָה מִקֶּדֶם בְּלֵב לוֹאִיס אֵם אִמְּךָ וּבְלֵב אַבְנִיקָה אִמְּךָ וְיָדַעְתִּי מְאֹד כִּי הָאֱמוּנָה הַזֹּאת הִיא גַם-בְּלִבֶּךָ:

5. Ve•ha•gi•ti ba•e•moo•na hatz•roo•fa asher hai•ta mi•ke•dem be•lev Lo•ees em eem•cha oov•lev Av•ni•ka ee•me•cha ve•ya•da•a•ti me•od ki ha•e•moo•na ha•zot hee gam - be•li•be•cha.

Rabbinic Jewish Commentary
and thy mother Eunice: who was a Jewess, and a believer in Yeshua, Act_16:1 though her name is a Greek one, and so is her mother's name; hers signifies "good victory", and is the name of one of the Nereides, the daughters of Oceanus (a); and her mother's signifies "better", or "more excellent".

(a) Hesiod. Theogonia, Apollodorus de Deor. Orig. l. 1. p. 5. Vid. Theocrit. Idyll. 13.

---

6. Wherefore I put thee in remembrance that thou stir up the gift of God, which is in thee by the putting on of my hands.

Greek/Transliteration
6. Δι᾽ ἣν αἰτίαν ἀναμιμνήσκω σε ἀναζωπυρεῖν τὸ χάρισμα τοῦ θεοῦ, ὅ ἐστιν ἐν σοὶ διὰ τῆς ἐπιθέσεως τῶν χειρῶν μου.

6. Di 'ein aitian anamimneisko se anazopurein to charisma tou theou, 'o estin en soi dya teis epitheseos ton cheiron mou.

Hebrew/Transliteration
ו. וּבַעֲבוּר זֹאת בָּאתִי לְהַזְכִּירְךָ כִּי-תְעוֹרֵר מַתְּנַת הָאֱלֹהִים הַנְּתוּנָה לְךָ מֵעֵת אֲשֶׁר סָמַכְתִּי יָדַי עָלֶיךָ:

6. Oo•va•a•voor zot ba•ti le•haz•kir•cha ki - te•o•ret mat•nat ha•Elohim ha•ne•too•na le•cha me•et asher sa•mach•ti ya•dai a•le•cha.

---

7. For God hath not given us the spirit of fear; but of power, and of love, and of a sound mind.

Greek/Transliteration
7. Οὐ γὰρ ἔδωκεν ἡμῖν ὁ θεὸς πνεῦμα δειλίας, ἀλλὰ δυνάμεως καὶ ἀγάπης καὶ σωφρονισμοῦ.

7. Ou gar edoken 'eimin 'o theos pneuma deilias, alla dunameos kai agapeis kai sophronismou.

Hebrew/Transliteration
ז. כִּי לֹא נָתַן לָנוּ אֱלֹהִים רוּחַ פָּחַד כִּי אִם-רוּחַ גְּבוּרָה אַהֲבָה וּמוּסָר:

7. Ki lo na•tan la•noo Elohim roo•ach pa•chad ki eem - roo•ach g`voo•ra a•ha•va oo•moo•sar.

---

8. Be not thou therefore ashamed of the testimony of our Lord, nor of me his prisoner: but be thou partaker of the afflictions of the gospel according to the power of God;

Greek/Transliteration
8. Μὴ οὖν ἐπαισχυνθῇς τὸ μαρτύριον τοῦ κυρίου ἡμῶν, μηδὲ ἐμὲ τὸν δέσμιον αὐτοῦ· ἀλλὰ συγκακοπάθησον τῷ εὐαγγελίῳ κατὰ δύναμιν θεοῦ,

8. Mei oun epaischuntheis to marturion tou kuriou 'eimon, meide eme ton desmion autou. Alla sugkakopatheison to euangelio kata dunamin theou,

Hebrew/Transliteration
ח. וְלָכֵן אַל-תֵּבוֹשׁ מֵעֵדוּת אֲדֹנֵינוּ וְלֹא מִמֶּנִּי אֲסִירוֹ רַק נְשָׂא חֶבְלֵי הַבְּשׂוֹרָה כָּמוֹנִי בִּגְבוּרַת אֱלֹהִים:

8. Ve•la•chen al - te•vosh me•e•doot Ado•ney•noo ve•lo mi•me•ni asi•ro rak n`sa chev•ley ha•b`so•hra ka•mo•ni big•voo•rat Elohim.

9. Who hath saved us, and called us with an holy calling, not according to our works, but according to his own purpose and grace, which was given us in Christ Jesus before the world began,

Greek/Transliteration
9. τοῦ σώσαντος ἡμᾶς καὶ καλέσαντος κλήσει ἁγίᾳ, οὐ κατὰ τὰ ἔργα ἡμῶν, ἀλλὰ κατ᾽ ἰδίαν πρόθεσιν καὶ χάριν τὴν δοθεῖσαν ἡμῖν ἐν χριστῷ Ἰησοῦ πρὸ χρόνων αἰωνίων,

9. tou sosantos 'eimas kai kalesantos kleisei 'agia, ou kata ta erga 'eimon, alla kat idian prothesin kai charin tein dotheisan 'eimin en christo Yeisou pro chronon aionion,

Hebrew/Transliteration
ט. אֲשֶׁר הֵבִיא לָנוּ יֶשַׁע וַיִּקְרָא לָנוּ בִּדְבַר קָדְשׁוֹ לֹא כְמַעֲשֵׂינוּ כִּי אִם-כַּעֲצָתוֹ וּבְחַסְדּוֹ אֲשֶׁר חָלַק לָנוּ בְּיֵשׁוּעַ מְשִׁיחֵנוּ לִפְנֵי יְמוֹת עוֹלָם:

9. Asher he•vi la•noo ye•sha va•yik•ra la•noo bid•var kod•sho lo che•ma•a•sey•noo ki eem - ka•a•tza•to oov•chas•do asher cha•lak la•noo be•Yeshua Me•shi•che•noo lif•ney ye•mot o•lam.

Rabbinic Jewish Commentary
The Ethiopic version reads, "in Christ Jesus, who before the world *was*"; but without any foundation.

The Jews have a teaching regarding creation in the Talmud; seven things were created before the world; the Torah, repentance, the garden of Eden, Gehinnom, the throne of glory, the Temple and the name of the Messiah.
(Nedarim 39b. Pesachim 54a)

---

10. But is now made manifest by the appearing of our Saviour Jesus Christ, who hath abolished death, and hath brought life and immortality to light through the gospel:

Greek/Transliteration
10. φανερωθεῖσαν δὲ νῦν διὰ τῆς ἐπιφανείας τοῦ σωτῆρος ἡμῶν Ἰησοῦ χριστοῦ, καταργήσαντος μὲν τὸν θάνατον, φωτίσαντος δὲ ζωὴν καὶ ἀφθαρσίαν διὰ τοῦ εὐαγγελίου,

10. phanerotheisan de nun dya teis epiphaneias tou soteiros 'eimon Yeisou christou, katargeisantos men ton thanaton, photisantos de zoein kai aphtharsian dya tou euangeliou,

Hebrew/Transliteration
י. וְזֶה עַתָּה נִגְלָה לָאוֹר כַּאֲשֶׁר נִגְלָה מוֹשִׁיעֵנוּ יֵשׁוּעַ הַמָּשִׁיחַ אֲשֶׁר בִּבְשׂוֹרָתוֹ בִּלַּע אֶת-הַמָּוֶת וַיּוֹצֵא לָאוֹר חַיֵּי-עַד וּנְתִיב אַל-מָוֶת:

10. Ve•ze ata nig•la la•or ka•a•sher nig•la Mo•shi•e•noo Yeshua ha•Ma•shi•ach asher biv•sora•to bi•la et - ha•ma•vet va•yo•tze la•or cha•yey - ad oon•tiv al - ma•vet.

11. Whereunto I am appointed a preacher, and an apostle, and a teacher of the Gentiles.

Greek/Transliteration
11. εἰς ὃ ἐτέθην ἐγὼ κῆρυξ καὶ ἀπόστολος καὶ διδάσκαλος ἐθνῶν.

11. eis 'o etethein ego keirux kai apostolos kai didaskalos ethnon.

Hebrew/Transliteration
יא. הִיא הַבְּשׂוֹרָה אֲשֶׁר נִקְרֵאתִי לִהְיוֹת-לָהּ לְמַגִּיד וּלְשָׁלִיחַ וּלְמוֹרֶה הַגּוֹיִם:

11. Hee ha•b`so•hra asher nik•re•ti li•hee•yot - la le•ma•gid ool•sha•li•ach ool•mo•re ha•go•yim.

---

12. For the which cause I also suffer these things: nevertheless I am not ashamed: for I know whom I have believed, and am persuaded that he is able to keep that which I have committed unto him against that day.

Greek/Transliteration
12. Δι' ἣν αἰτίαν καὶ ταῦτα πάσχω, ἀλλ' οὐκ ἐπαισχύνομαι· οἶδα γὰρ ᾧ πεπίστευκα, καὶ πέπεισμαι ὅτι δυνατός ἐστιν τὴν παραθήκην μου φυλάξαι εἰς ἐκείνην τὴν ἡμέραν.

12. Di 'ein aitian kai tauta pascho, all ouk epaischunomai. oida gar 'o pepisteuka, kai pepeismai 'oti dunatos estin tein paratheikein mou phulaxai eis ekeinein tein 'eimeran.

Hebrew/Transliteration
יב. וּבַעֲבוּר זֹאת נָשָׂאתִי הַתְּלָאָה הַזֹּאת וְלֹא אֵבוֹשׁ כִּי-יָדַעְתִּי בְּמִי הֶאֱמַנְתִּי וּבוֹ בָטְחָה נַפְשִׁי כִּי-רַב כֹּחַ הוּא לִשְׁמֹר אֶת אֲשֶׁר הִפְקַדְתִּי בְיָדוֹ עַד-הַיּוֹם הַהוּא:

12. Oo•va•a•voor zot na•sa•ti hat•la•ah ha•zot ve•lo evosh ki - ya•da•a•ti be•mi he•e•man•ti oo•vo vat•cha naf•shi ki - rav ko•ach hoo lish•mor et asher hif•ka•de•ti ve•ya•do ad - ha•yom ha•hoo.

Rabbinic Jewish Commentary
Philo the Jew (b) speaks in like manner as the apostle here of παρακαταθηκη ψυχης, "the depositum of the soul": though he knew not where to commit it for safety, as the apostle did, and every true believer does.

(b) Quis rer. Divin. Haeres. p. 498, 499.

---

13. Hold fast the form of sound words, which thou hast heard of me, in faith and love which is in Christ Jesus.

Greek/Transliteration
13. Ὑποτύπωσιν ἔχε ὑγιαινόντων λόγων ὧν παρ' ἐμοῦ ἤκουσας, ἐν πίστει καὶ ἀγάπῃ τῇ ἐν χριστῷ Ἰησοῦ.

13. 'Upotuposin eche 'ugyainonton logon 'on par emou eikousas, en pistei kai agapei tei en christo Yeisou.

Hebrew/Transliteration
יג. אֶת-הַדְּבָרִים הַנֶּאֱמָנִים כְּצוּרָתָם וְתָכְנִיתָם תִּצְפֹּן אִתָּךְ כַּאֲשֶׁר שָׁמַעְתָּ מִפִּי בֶּאֱמוּנָה וּבְאַהֲבָה אֲשֶׁר בְּיֵשׁוּעַ הַמָּשִׁיחַ:

13. Et - ha•d`va•rim ha•ne•e•ma•nim ke•tzoo•ra•tam ve•toch•ni•tam titz•pon eet•cha ka•a•sher sha•ma•ata mi•pi ve•e•moo•na oov•a•ha•va asher be•Yeshua ha•Ma•shi•ach.

---

14. That good thing which was committed unto thee keep by the Holy Ghost which dwelleth in us.

Greek/Transliteration
14. Τὴν καλὴν παραθήκην φύλαξον διὰ πνεύματος ἁγίου τοῦ ἐνοικοῦντος ἐν ἡμῖν.

14. Tein kalein paratheikein phulaxon dya pneumatos 'agiou tou enoikountos en 'eimin.

Hebrew/Transliteration
:יד. וְאֶת-הַפִּקָּדוֹן הַטּוֹב אֲשֶׁר הָפְקַד אִתָּךְ שְׁמָר-לְךָ בְּרוּחַ הַקֹּדֶשׁ הַשֹּׁכֵן בָּנוּ

14. Ve•et - ha•pi•ka•don ha•tov asher hoof•kad eet•cha sh`mor - le•cha be•Roo•ach ha•Ko•desh ha•sho•chen ba•noo.

---

15. This thou knowest, that all they which are in Asia be turned away from me; of whom are Phygellus and Hermogenes.

Greek/Transliteration
15. Οἶδας τοῦτο, ὅτι ἀπεστράφησάν με πάντες οἱ ἐν τῇ Ἀσίᾳ, ὧν ἐστιν Φύγελος καὶ Ἑρμογένης.

15. Oidas touto, 'oti apestrapheisan me pantes 'oi en tei Asia, 'on estin Phugelos kai 'Ermogeneis.

Hebrew/Transliteration
:טו. הִנֵּה יָדַעְתָּ כִּי-עֲזָבוּנִי כֻלָּם אֲשֶׁר בְּאַסְיָא וּבְתוֹכָם פּוּגְלוֹס וְהַרְמוֹגְנִיס

15. Hee•ne ya•da•ata ki - aza•voo•ni choo•lam asher be•Asia oov•to•cham Poog•los ve•Har•mog•nis.

Rabbinic Jewish Commentary
The name of the first of these signifies a "fugitive", and such was he from the cause of Messiah Yeshua. Pliny (c) makes mention of a town in Asia, called Phygella, from the fugitives which built it; and the latter signifies born of Mercury; there was one of the name in Tertullian's time, against whom he wrote.

(c) Nat. Hist. l. 5. c. 29.

16. The Lord give mercy unto the house of Onesiphorus; for he oft refreshed me, and was not ashamed of my chain:

Greek/Transliteration

16. Δῴη ἔλεος ὁ κύριος τῷ Ὀνησιφόρου οἴκῳ· ὅτι πολλάκις με ἀνέψυξεν, καὶ τὴν ἅλυσίν μου οὐκ ἐπαισχύνθη,

16. Doei eleos 'o kurios to Oneisiphorou oiko. 'oti pollakis me anepsuxen, kai tein 'alusin mou ouk epaischunthei,

Hebrew/Transliteration

טז. יִגְמֹל הָאָדוֹן חֶסֶד עִם-בֵּית אֲנִיסִיפוֹרוֹס כִּי-הֵשִׁיב נַפְשִׁי פְּעָמִים רַבּוֹת וְלֹא-בוֹשׁ מִן-הַכֶּבֶל אֲשֶׁר נֶאֱסַרְתִּי בּוֹ:

16. Yig•mol ha•Adon che•sed eem - beit Oni•si•foros ki - he•shiv naf•shi pe•a•mim ra•bot ve•lo - vosh min - ha•ke•vel asher ne•e•sar•ti vo.

---

17. But, when he was in Rome, he sought me out very diligently, and found me.

Greek/Transliteration

17. ἀλλὰ γενόμενος ἐν Ῥώμῃ, σπουδαιότερον ἐζήτησέν με καὶ εὗρεν-

17. alla genomenos en 'Romei, spoudaioteron ezeiteisen me kai 'euren-

Hebrew/Transliteration

יז. וּבִהְיוֹתִי בְרוֹמִי שָׁקַד לְבַקְשֵׁנִי עַד כִּי-מָצָא אֹתִי:

17. Oo•vi•hi•yo•ti ve•Romi sha•kad le•vak•she•ni ad ki - ma•tza o•ti.

---

18. The Lord grant unto him that he may find mercy of the Lord in that day: and in how many things he ministered unto me at Ephesus, thou knowest very well.

Greek/Transliteration

18. δῴη αὐτῷ ὁ κύριος εὑρεῖν ἔλεος παρὰ κυρίου ἐν ἐκείνῃ τῇ ἡμέρᾳ- καὶ ὅσα ἐν Ἐφέσῳ διηκόνησεν, βέλτιον σὺ γινώσκεις.

18. doei auto 'o kurios 'eurein eleos para kuriou en ekeinei tei 'eimera- kai 'osa en Epheso dieikoneisen, beltion su ginoskeis.

Hebrew/Transliteration

יח. יִתֶּן-לוֹ הָאָדוֹן לִמְצֹא חֶסֶד מִלִּפְנֵי יְהוָֹה בַּיּוֹם הַהוּא וְכָל-אֲשֶׁר הֵיטִיב עִמָּדִי בְּאֶפְסוֹס נַפְשְׁךָ יֹדַעַת מְאֹד:

18. Yi•ten - lo ha•Adon lim•tzo che•sed mi•lif•ney Adonai ba•yom ha•hoo ve•chol – asher hey•tiv ee•ma•di be•Efsos naf•she•cha yo•da•at me•od.

2 Timothy, Chapter 2

1. Thou therefore, my son, be strong in the grace that is in Christ Jesus.

Greek/Transliteration
1. Σὺ οὖν, τέκνον μου, ἐνδυναμοῦ ἐν τῇ χάριτι τῇ ἐν χριστῷ Ἰησοῦ.

1. Su oun, teknon mou, endunamou en tei chariti tei en christo Yeisou.

Hebrew/Transliteration
א. וְאַתָּה בְּנִי חֲזַק בְּחֶסֶד יֵשׁוּעַ הַמָּשִׁיחַ:

1. Ve•a•ta b`ni cha•zak be•che•sed Yeshua ha•Ma•shi•ach.

Rabbinic Jewish Commentary
The phrase may stand opposed to תקיף באורייתא, or גבר, "one strong in the Torah", which is so often used by the Jews (d). Or rather by grace is meant the fulness of grace which is in Christ, for the supply of his people; for in that grace which is in him, and not in that which is in themselves, should their dependence be.

(d) Targum in Ruth ii. 1. & in Psal. lxxxii. 1. & cxii. 2. & in Eccl. x. 17. & in Cant. viii. 10, vid. T. Bab. Sota, fol. 14. 1. & Tzeror Hammor, fol. 9. 3.

---

2. And the things that thou hast heard of me among many witnesses, the same commit thou to faithful men, who shall be able to teach others also.

Greek/Transliteration
2. Καὶ ἃ ἤκουσας παρ' ἐμοῦ διὰ πολλῶν μαρτύρων, ταῦτα παράθου πιστοῖς ἀνθρώποις, οἵτινες ἱκανοὶ ἔσονται καὶ ἑτέρους διδάξαι.

2. Kai 'a eikousas par emou dya pollon marturon, tauta parathou pistois anthropois, 'oitines 'ikanoi esontai kai 'eterous didaxai.

Hebrew/Transliteration
ב. אֶת-אֲשֶׁר שָׁמַעְתָּ מִפִּי בִּפְנֵי עֵדִים רַבִּים הַשְׁמַע בְּאָזְנֵי אֲנָשִׁים נֶאֱמָנִים אֲשֶׁר יִכוֹנוּ לְלַמֵּד אֶת-הַדְּבָרִים הָאֵלֶּה גַּם-לְזוּלָתָם:

2. Et - asher sha•ma•ata mi•pi bif•ney e•dim ra•bim hash•ma ba•oz•ney a•na•shim ne•e•ma•nim asher yi•ko•noo le•la•med et - ha•d`va•rim ha•e•le gam - le•zoo•la•tam.

---

3. Thou therefore endure hardness, as a good soldier of Jesus Christ.

Greek/Transliteration
3. Σὺ οὖν κακοπάθησον ὡς καλὸς στρατιώτης Ἰησοῦ χριστοῦ.

3. Su oun kakopatheison 'os kalos stratioteis Yeisou christou.

Hebrew/Transliteration
ג. וּתְנָה שִׁכְמְךָ לִסְבֹּל עָמִּי כְּאִישׁ-חַיִל בְּצִבְא יֵשׁוּעַ הַמָּשִׁיחַ:

3. Oot•na shich•me•cha lis•bol ee•mi che•eesh - cha•yil bitz•va Yeshua ha•Ma•shi•ach.

---

4. No man that warreth entangleth himself with the affairs of this life; that he may please him who hath chosen him to be a soldier.

Greek/Transliteration
4. Οὐδεὶς στρατευόμενος ἐμπλέκεται ταῖς τοῦ βίου πραγματείαις, ἵνα τῷ στρατολογήσαντι ἀρέσῃ.

4. Oudeis strateuomenos empleketai tais tou biou pragmateiais, 'ina to stratologeisanti aresei.

Hebrew/Transliteration
ד. אִישׁ יֹצֵא לַצָּבָא לֹא-יִתְעָרֵב בְּעִנְיָנִים אֲחֵרִים וְיָפִיק רָצוֹן מִשַּׂר צְבָאוֹ:

4. Eesh yo•tze la•tza•va lo - yit•a•rev be•een•ya•nim a•che•rim ve•ya•fik ra•tzon mi•sar tze•va`o.

---

5. And if a man also strive for masteries, yet is he not crowned, except he strive lawfully.

Greek/Transliteration
5. Ἐὰν δὲ καὶ ἀθλῇ τις, οὐ στεφανοῦται ἐὰν μὴ νομίμως ἀθλήσῃ.

5. Ean de kai athlei tis, ou stephanoutai ean mei nomimos athleisei.

Hebrew/Transliteration
ה. וְאַף אִם-יִצְבֹּא צָבָא עוֹד לֹא יַשִּׂיג אֶת-הָעֲטָרָה עַד אֲשֶׁר יִצְבֹּא כַּמִּשְׁפָּט:

5. Ve•af eem - yitz•bo tza•va od lo ya•sig et - ha•a•ta•ra ad asher yitz•bo ka•mish•pat.

---

6. The husbandman that laboureth must be first partaker of the fruits.

Greek/Transliteration
6. Τὸν κοπιῶντα γεωργὸν δεῖ πρῶτον τῶν καρπῶν μεταλαμβάνειν.

6. Ton kopionta georgon dei proton ton karpon metalambanein.

Hebrew/Transliteration
ו. הָאִכָּר הָעֹבֵד אַדְמָתוֹ רִאשׁוֹן הוּא לֶאֱכֹל מִפְּרִי תְּבוּאָתוֹ:

6. Ha•ee•kar ha•o•ved ad•ma•to ri•shon hoo le•e•chol mip•ri t`voo•a•to.

7. Consider what I say; and the Lord give thee understanding in all things.

Greek/Transliteration
7. Νόει ἃ λέγω· δῴη γάρ σοι ὁ κύριος σύνεσιν ἐν πᾶσιν.

7. Noei 'a lego. doei gar soi 'o kurios sunesin en pasin.

Hebrew/Transliteration
:ז. בִּין בַּאֲשֶׁר-אֲנִי דֹבֵר וְהָאָדוֹן יִתֶּן-לְךָ חָכְמָה בַּכֹּל

7. Bin ba•a•sher - ani do•ver ve•ha•Adon yi•ten - le•cha choch•ma ba•kol.

---

8. Remember that Jesus Christ of the seed of David was raised from the dead according to my gospel:

Greek/Transliteration
8. Μνημόνευε Ἰησοῦν χριστὸν ἐγηγερμένον ἐκ νεκρῶν, ἐκ σπέρματος Δαυίδ, κατὰ τὸ εὐαγγέλιόν μου·

8. Mneimoneue Yeisoun christon egeigermenon ek nekron, ek spermatos Dauid, kata to euangelion mou.

Hebrew/Transliteration
:ח. זְכֹר אֶת-יֵשׁוּעַ הַמָּשִׁיחַ אֲשֶׁר קָם מִן-הַמֵּתִים וַאֲשֶׁר יָצָא מִזֶּרַע דָּוִד כִּדְבַר בְּשׂרָתִי

8. Ze•chor et - Yeshua ha•Ma•shi•ach asher kam min - ha•me•tim va•a•sher ya•tza mi•ze•ra David ki•d`var be•so•ra•ti.

---

9. Wherein I suffer trouble, as an evil doer, even unto bonds; but the word of God is not bound.

Greek/Transliteration
9. ἐν ᾧ κακοπαθῶ μέχρι δεσμῶν, ὡς κακοῦργος· ἀλλ' ὁ λόγος τοῦ θεοῦ οὐ δέδεται.

9. en 'o kakopatho mechri desmon, 'os kakourgos. all 'o logos tou theou ou dedetai.

Hebrew/Transliteration
:ט. אֲשֶׁר בַּעֲבוּרָהּ צָרוֹת עָבְרוּ עָלַי עַד אֲשֶׁר עֻנּוּ בַכֶּבֶל נַפְשִׁי כְּפֹעֵל אָוֶן אַךְ דְּבַר אֱלֹהִים לֹא יֵאָסֵר בַּכֶּבֶל

9. Asher ba•a•voo•ra tza•rot av•roo a•lai ad asher ee•noo va•ke•vel naf•shi ke•fo•el aven ach de•var Elohim lo ye•a•ser ba•ka•vel.

---

10. Therefore I endure all things for the elect's sakes, that they may also obtain the salvation which is in Christ Jesus with eternal glory.

Greek/Transliteration
10. Διὰ τοῦτο πάντα ὑπομένω διὰ τοὺς ἐκλεκτούς, ἵνα καὶ αὐτοὶ σωτηρίας τύχωσιν τῆς ἐν χριστῷ Ἰησοῦ, μετὰ δόξης αἰωνίου.

10. Dya touto panta 'upomeno dya tous eklektous, 'ina kai autoi soteirias tuchosin teis en Christo Yeisou, meta doxeis aioniou.

Hebrew/Transliteration
י׃. עַל-כֵּן אֶסְבֹּל כָּל-סֵבֶל לְמַעַן יַשִּׂיגוּ הַבְּחִירִים גַּם-הֵם תְּשׁוּעָתָם בְּיֵשׁוּעַ הַמָּשִׁיחַ וְתִפְאַרְתָּם תִּפְאֶרֶת עוֹלָמִים

10. Al - ken es•bol kol - se•vel le•ma•an ya•si•goo ha•b`chi•rim gam - hem te•shoo•a•tam be•Yeshua ha•Ma•shi•ach ve•tif•ar•tam tif•e•ret o•la•mim.

---

11. It is a faithful saying: For if we be dead with him, we shall also live with him:

Greek/Transliteration
11. Πιστὸς ὁ λόγος· εἰ γὰρ συναπεθάνομεν, καὶ συζήσομεν·

11. Pistos 'o logos. ei gar sunapethanomen, kai suzeisomen.

Hebrew/Transliteration
יא׃. אֱמֶת הַדָּבָר הַזֶּה אִם-נָמוּת עִמּוֹ גַּם-עִמּוֹ נִחְיֶה

11. Emet ha•da•var ha•ze eem - na•moot ee•mo gam - ee•mo nich•ye.

---

12. If we suffer, we shall also reign with him: if we deny him, he also will deny us:

Greek/Transliteration
12. εἰ ὑπομένομεν, καὶ συμβασιλεύσομεν· εἰ ἀρνούμεθα, κἀκεῖνος ἀρνήσεται ἡμᾶς·

12. ei 'upomenomen, kai sumbasileusomen. ei arnoumetha, kakeinos arneisetai 'eimas.

Hebrew/Transliteration
יב׃. אִם-נִסְבֹּל עִמּוֹ גַּם-עִמּוֹ נִמְלֹךְ אִם נְכַחֵשׁ-בּוֹ גַּם-הוּא יְכַחֶשׁ-בָּנוּ

12. Eem - nis•bol ee•mo gam - ee•mo nim•loch eem n`cha•chesh - bo gam - hoo ye•cha•chesh - ba•noo.

---

13. If we believe not, yet he abideth faithful: he cannot deny himself.

Greek/Transliteration
13. εἰ ἀπιστοῦμεν, ἐκεῖνος πιστὸς μένει· ἀρνήσασθαι ἑαυτὸν οὐ δύναται.

13. ei apistoumen, ekeinos pistos menei. arneisasthai 'eauton ou dunatai.

Hebrew/Transliteration
יג׃. אִם אֵין אֹמֶן בָּנוּ הוּא בֶּאֱמוּנָתוֹ יַעֲמֹד כִּי לְכַחֵשׁ בְּנַפְשׁוֹ לֹא יוּכָל

13. Eem eyn emoon ba•noo hoo ve•e•moo•na•to ya•a•mod ki le•cha•chesh be•naf•sho lo yoo•chal.

Rabbinic Jewish Commentary
The Syriac and Ethiopic versions read, "if we believe not him". This may be understood, either of such who are altogether destitute of faith, who do not believe in Christ at all.

---

14. Of these things put them in remembrance, charging them before the Lord that they strive not about words to no profit, but to the subverting of the hearers.

Greek/Transliteration
14. Ταῦτα ὑπομίμνησκε, διαμαρτυρόμενος ἐνώπιον τοῦ κυρίου μὴ λογομαχεῖν εἰς οὐδὲν χρήσιμον, ἐπὶ καταστροφῇ τῶν ἀκουόντων.

14. Tauta 'upomimneiske, dyamarturomenos enopion tou kuriou mei logomachein eis ouden chreisimon, epi katastrophei ton akouonton.

Hebrew/Transliteration
יד. אֶת-הַדְּבָרִים הָאֵלֶּה תַּזְכִּיר לִפְנֵיהֶם וְהָעֵד בָּם לִפְנֵי הָאָדוֹן לְבִלְתִּי יָבֹאוּ בְדִבְרֵי רִיבוֹת לְהוֹכַח מִלִּים אֲשֶׁר לֹא יוֹעִילוּ לִמְאוּמָה כִּי אִם-לִמְסֹד רוּחַ עֻוְעִים בְּלֵב שֹׁמְעֵיהֶם:

14. Et - ha•d`va•rim ha•e•le taz•kir lif•ney•hem ve•ha•ed bam lif•ney ha•Adon le•vil•ti ya•vo•oo ve•div•rey ri•vot le•ho•chach mi•lim asher lo yo•ee•loo lim•oo•ma ki eem - lim•soch roo•ach eev•eem be•lev shom•ey•hem.

---

15. Study to shew thyself approved unto God, a workman that needeth not to be ashamed, rightly dividing the word of truth.

Greek/Transliteration
15. Σπούδασον σεαυτὸν δόκιμον παραστῆσαι τῷ θεῷ, ἐργάτην ἀνεπαίσχυντον, ὀρθοτομοῦντα τὸν λόγον τῆς ἀληθείας.

15. Spoudason seauton dokimon parasteisai to theo, ergatein anepaischunton, orthotomounta ton logon teis aleitheias.

Hebrew/Transliteration
טו. בַּקֵּשׁ לִהְיוֹת טָהוֹר כְּכֶסֶף צָרוּף לִפְנֵי אֱלֹהִים כְּפֹעֵל אֲשֶׁר לֹא-יֵבוֹשׁ מִפָּעֳלוֹ וְכַיּוֹדֵעַ לְחַלֵּק דְּבַר-אֱמֶת דָּבָר דָּבוּר עַל-אָפְנָיו:

15. Ba•kesh li•hee•yot ta•hor ke•che•sef tza•roof lif•ney Elohim ke•fo•el asher lo - ye•vosh mi•po•o•lo ve•cha•yo•de•a le•cha•lek de•var - emet da•var da•voor al - of•nav.

Rabbinic Jewish Commentary
Study to show thyself approved unto God,.... The Alexandrian copy reads, "to Christ"; see Rom_16:10.

Some think that the allusion is to the verses of the Hebrew Bible, which are called פסוקים, "divisions", sections, or cuttings, from the word פסק, "to cut" or "divide", being cut or divided one from another; hence those that were employed in the law, and were conversant with the sacred writings, and exercised therein, were called פוסקים בתורת, "cutters", or "dividers of the Torah" (e); and so בעל פסוק is one that is well versed in the Bible, and knows every part of it, and readily uses it, in speaking or writing.

The apostle refers to a wrong way of dividing the Scriptures by the Jews, to which he opposes the right dividing of them. They had used not only to take away a letter out of one word, and add it to another, and so expound the text, but to remove words in it, and make that which went before to go behind, and that which was behind to go before; and this they call a sharp knife, which חותך ומפסיק הכתוב, "cuts and divides the Scriptures" (f): but this way, which his countrymen used, the apostle would not have Timothy, and other Gospel ministers, make use of; for this is not rightly to divide, but to mangle and tear in pieces the word of truth.

In short, one that divides the word of truth rightly, is, as the Vulgate Latin version renders it, one that "rightly handles"; or, as the Syriac version, that "rightly preaches the word of truth"; who gives the true sense of Scripture, does not pervert and wrest it, and take from it, or add to it; who points out the truth in it, and shows unto men the way of salvation, and plainly and faithfully preaches the Gospel contained in it, without keeping back anything that is profitable, but declares the whole counsel of God. This same Greek word is used by the Septuagint in Pro_3:6 where it answers to the Hebrew word ישר, which signifies to direct the way, and make it plain; and may here design a plain and open interpretation of the word of God: and to answer these several characters in the text should be the studious concern of every Gospel minister; and study is necessary thereunto; it requires great care that a man take heed to himself, and to his doctrine; and great industry, diligence, and application, and much reading, meditation, and prayer.

(e) Vid. Fuller Miscell. Saora, l. 3. c. 16. (f) Halichot Olim, port. 4. c. 3. p. 192.

16. But shun profane and vain babblings: for they will increase unto more ungodliness.

Greek/Transliteration
16. Τὰς δὲ βεβήλους κενοφωνίας περιΐστασο· ἐπὶ πλεῖον γὰρ προκόψουσιν ἀσεβείας,

16. Tas de bebeilous kenophonias peri'istaso. epi pleion gar prokopsousin asebeias,

Hebrew/Transliteration
טז. אַךְ הַרְחֵק נַפְשְׁךָ מִשִּׂיחוֹת חוּלִין וּרְעוּת רוּחַ אֲשֶׁר יִמְשְׁכוּ אֶת-בַּעֲלֵיהֶם לְהוֹסִיף רֶשַׁע לְמַכְבִּיר:

16. Ach har•chek naf•she•cha mi•si•chot choo•lin oor•oot roo•ach asher yim•she•choo et - ba•a•ley•hem le•ho•sif re•sha le•mach•bir.

17. And their word will eat as doth a canker: of whom is Hymenaeus and Philetus;

Greek/Transliteration
17. καὶ ὁ λόγος αὐτῶν ὡς γάγγραινα νομὴν ἕξει· ὧν ἐστιν Ὑμέναιος καὶ Φιλητός·

17. kai 'o logos auton 'os gangraina nomein 'exei. 'on estin 'Umenaios kai Phileitos.

Hebrew/Transliteration

יז. וּדְבַר פִּיהֶם כְּרָקָב יֹאכַל אֲשֶׁר מֵהֶם הוּמְנִיוֹס וּפִילֵיטוֹס:

17. Oo•d`var pi•hem ke•ra•kav yo•chal asher me•hem Hoom•niyos oo•Filitos.

Rabbinic Jewish Commentary

And their word will eat as doth a cancer,.... Or "gangrene", which gnaws and feeds upon the flesh, inflames and mortifies as it goes, and spreads swiftly, and endangers the whole body; and is therefore to be speedily taken notice of, and stopped. It is better rendered "gangrene", as in the marginal reading, than "cancer".

"The word "gangrene" is Greek (g), and is derived by some authors from the Paphlagonian "gangra", a goat; it being the character of a goat to browse the grass all around without shifting. It is more correct, perhaps, to derive it from the Greek word γραω, γραινω, "manduco", "consumo", I eat, I consume. The "gangrene" is a disease in the flesh of the part which it corrupts, consumes, and turns black, spreading and seizing itself of the adjoining parts, and is rarely cured without amputation. By the microscope, a gangrene has been discovered to contain an infinite number of little worms engendered in the morbid flesh; and which continually producing new broods, they swarm, and overrun the adjacent parts: if the gangrene proceed to an utter sphacelation (or mortification), and be seated in any of the limbs, or extreme parts, recourse must be had to the operation of amputation".

And so the errors and heresies of false teachers worm and spread, and feed upon the souls of men, and eat up the vitals of religion, or what seemed to be such, and even destroy the very form of godliness; and bring destruction and death, wherever they come.

Philetus is a Greek name as well as the other, though it is sometimes found in Roman inscriptions (h): it is very likely that these were both in Asia, and probably in Ephesus, or near to it, since the apostle mentions them by name to Timothy, that he might beware of them.

(g) See Chambers's Cyclopedia in the word "Gangrene". (h) Vid. Kirchman. de Funer. Roman. l. 3. c. 10. p. 390.

---

18. Who concerning the truth have erred, saying that the resurrection is past already; and overthrow the faith of some.

Greek/Transliteration

18. οἵτινες περὶ τὴν ἀλήθειαν ἠστόχησαν, λέγοντες τὴν ἀνάστασιν ἤδη γεγονέναι, καὶ ἀνατρέπουσιν τήν τινων πίστιν.

18. 'oitines peri tein aleitheyan eistocheisan, legontes tein anastasin eidei gegonenai, kai anatrepousin tein tinon pistin.

Hebrew/Transliteration

יח. וְהֵם סָרוּ מִדֶּרֶךְ אֱמֶת לֵאמֹר כִּי-תְחִיַּת הַמֵּתִים כְּבָר הָיְתָה מֵאָז וַיִּהְיוּ לֶאֱמוּנַת רַבִּים לְמוֹקֵשׁ:

18. Ve•hem sa•roo mi•de•rech emet le•mor ki - te•chi•at ha•me•tim k`var hai•ta me•az va•yi•hi•oo le•e•moo•nat ra•bim le•mo•kesh.

19. Nevertheless the foundation of God standeth sure, having this seal, The Lord knoweth them that are his. And, Let every one that nameth the name of Christ depart from iniquity.

Greek/Transliteration
19. Ὁ μέντοι στερεὸς θεμέλιος τοῦ θεοῦ ἕστηκεν, ἔχων τὴν σφραγῖδα ταύτην, Ἔγνω κύριος τοὺς ὄντας αὐτοῦ, καί, Ἀποστήτω ἀπὸ ἀδικίας πᾶς ὁ ὀνομάζων τὸ ὄνομα κυρίου.

19. 'O mentoi stereos themelios tou theou 'esteiken, echon tein sphragida tautein, Egno kurios tous ontas autou, kai, Aposteito apo adikias pas 'o onomazon to onoma kuriou.

Hebrew/Transliteration
יט. אַךְ יְסוֹד הָאֱלֹהִים יָקוּם לָנֶצַח וְזֶה הוּא חוֹתָמוֹ יוֹדֵעַ יְהֹוָה אֶת אֲשֶׁר-לוֹ וְגַם זֶה מִי אֲשֶׁר יִקְרָא בְשֵׁם הַמָּשִׁיחַ יֶחְדַּל מֵעֲשׂוֹת אָוֶן:

19. Ach ye•sod ha•Elohim ya•koom la•ne•tzach ve•ze hoo cho•ta•mo yo•dea Adonai et asher - lo ve•gam ze mee asher yik•ra ve•shem ha•Ma•shi•ach yech•dal me•a•sot aven.

Rabbinic Jewish Commentary
So, among the Jews, seals were used in buying and selling, that it might be known what was bought, and to confirm the purchase (i).

and let everyone that nameth the name of Christ; "or of the Lord", as the Alexandrian copy, and others, the Complutensian edition, the Vulgate Latin, Syriac, and Arabic versions read; that is, whoever either are called by the name of Christ, or Christians, or whoever call upon his name.

(i) Maimon. Hilchot Mechira, c. 7. sect. 6, 7, 8.

---

20. But in a great house there are not only vessels of gold and of silver, but also of wood and of earth; and some to honour, and some to dishonour.

Greek/Transliteration
20. Ἐν μεγάλῃ δὲ οἰκίᾳ οὐκ ἔστιν μόνον σκεύη χρυσᾶ καὶ ἀργυρᾶ, ἀλλὰ καὶ ξύλινα καὶ ὀστράκινα, καὶ ἃ μὲν εἰς τιμήν, ἃ δὲ εἰς ἀτιμίαν.

20. En megalei de oikia ouk estin monon skeuei chrusa kai argura, alla kai xulina kai ostrakina, kai 'a men eis timein, 'a de eis atimian.

Hebrew/Transliteration
כ. אוּלָם בְּבַיִת גָּדוֹל לֹא לְבַד כְּלֵי זָהָב וּכְלֵי כֶסֶף כִּי אִם-גַּם יִמָּצְאוּן שָׁם כְּלֵי עֵץ וּכְלֵי חֶרֶשׂ אֲשֶׁר יֵשׁ מֵהֶם לְכָבוֹד וְיֵשׁ מֵהֶם לְקָלוֹן:

20. Oo•lam be•va•yit ga•dol lo le•vad k`ley za•hav ooch•ley che•sef ki eem - gam yi•matz•oon sham k`ley etz ooch•ley cha•resh asher yesh me•hem le•cha•vod ve•yesh me•hem le•ka•lon.

21. If a man therefore purge himself from these, he shall be a vessel unto honour, sanctified, and meet for the master's use, and prepared unto every good work.

Greek/Transliteration
21. Ἐὰν οὖν τις ἐκκαθάρῃ ἑαυτὸν ἀπὸ τούτων, ἔσται σκεῦος εἰς τιμήν, ἡγιασμένον, καὶ εὔχρηστον τῷ δεσπότῃ, εἰς πᾶν ἔργον ἀγαθὸν ἡτοιμασμένον.

21. Ean oun tis ekkatharei 'eauton apo touton, estai skeuos eis timein, 'eigyasmenon, kai euchreiston to despotei, eis pan ergon agathon 'eitoimasmenon.

Hebrew/Transliteration
כא. וְאִישׁ כִּי-יִטַּהֵר נַפְשׁוֹ מֵהֶם וְהָיָה לִכְלִי כָבוֹד לִכְלִי קֹדֶשׁ וְלִכְלִי יְקָר בְּיַד בְּעָלָיו מוּכָן לְכָל-מַעֲשֶׂה טוֹב:

21. Ve•eesh ki - ye•ta•her naf•sho me•hem ve•ha•ya lich•li cha•vod lich•li ko•desh ve•lich•li ye•kar be•yad be•a•lav moo•chan le•chol - ma•a•se tov.

---

22. Flee also youthful lusts: but follow righteousness, faith, charity, peace, with them that call on the Lord out of a pure heart.

Greek/Transliteration
22. Τὰς δὲ νεωτερικὰς ἐπιθυμίας φεῦγε· δίωκε δὲ δικαιοσύνην, πίστιν, ἀγάπην, εἰρήνην, μετὰ τῶν ἐπικαλουμένων τὸν κύριον ἐκ καθαρᾶς καρδίας.

22. Tas de neoterikas epithumias pheuge. dioke de dikaiosunein, pistin, agapein, eireinein, meta ton epikaloumenon ton kurion ek katharas kardias.

Hebrew/Transliteration
כב. הַרְחֵק לִבְּךָ מִתַּאֲוֹת הַנְּעוּרִים אַךְ רְדֹף צֶדֶק אֱמוּנָה אַהֲבָה וְשָׁלוֹם עִם-כָּל-הַקֹּרְאִים בְּשֵׁם הָאָדוֹן מִלֵּב טָהוֹר:

22. Har•chek lib•cha mi•ta•a•vot ha•ne•oo•rim ach r`dof tze•dek e•moo•na a•ha•va ve•sha•lom eem - kol - ha•kor•eem be•shem ha•Adon mi•lev ta•hor.

---

23. But foolish and unlearned questions avoid, knowing that they do gender strifes.

Greek/Transliteration
23. Τὰς δὲ μωρὰς καὶ ἀπαιδεύτους ζητήσεις παραιτοῦ, εἰδὼς ὅτι γεννῶσιν μάχας.

23. Tas de moras kai apaideutous zeiteiseis paraitou, eidos 'oti gennosin machas.

Hebrew/Transliteration
כג. רַק מֶחְקְרֵי כֶסֶל וּרְעוּת רוּחַ חֲדַל לְךָ כִּי מִשָּׁרְשָׁם יִפְרֶה רִיב וּמָדוֹן:

23. Rak me•chik•rey che•sel oor•oot roo•ach cha•dal le•cha ki mi•shor•sham yif•re riv oo•ma•don.

24. And the servant of the Lord must not strive; but be gentle unto all men, apt to teach, patient,

Greek/Transliteration

24. Δοῦλον δὲ κυρίου οὐ δεῖ μάχεσθαι, ἀλλ᾽ ἤπιον εἶναι πρὸς πάντας, διδακτικόν, ἀνεξίκακον,

24. Doulon de kuriou ou dei machesthai, all eipion einai pros pantas, didaktikon, anexikakon,

Hebrew/Transliteration

כד: וְלֹא לְעֶבֶד הָאָדוֹן לָרִיב כִּי אִם-לִהְיוֹת נוֹחַ לַכֹּל וּמֵבִין לְלַמֵּד

24. Ve•lo le•e•ved ha•Adon la•riv ki eem - li•hee•yot no•ach la•kol oo•me•vin le•la•med.

---

25. In meekness instructing those that oppose themselves; if God peradventure will give them repentance to the acknowledging of the truth;

Greek/Transliteration

25. ἐν πραότητι παιδεύοντα τοὺς ἀντιδιατιθεμένους· μήποτε δῷ αὐτοῖς ὁ θεὸς μετάνοιαν εἰς ἐπίγνωσιν ἀληθείας,

25. en praoteiti paideuonta tous antidyatithemenous. meipote do autois 'o theos metanoyan eis epignosin aleitheias,

Hebrew/Transliteration

כה: וּבְעַנְוַת-חֵן יוֹרֶה אֶת-הַמַּמְרִים אוּלַי יִתֵּן אֱלֹהִים בִּלְבָבָם לָשׁוּב וּלְהַכִּיר אֶת-הָאֱמֶת

25. Oov•an•vat - chen yo•re et - ha•mam•rim oo•lai yi•ten Elohim bil•va•vam la•shoov ool•ha•kir et - ha•e•met.

---

26. And that they may recover themselves out of the snare of the devil, who are taken captive by him at his will.

Greek/Transliteration

26. καὶ ἀνανήψωσιν ἐκ τῆς τοῦ διαβόλου παγίδος, ἐζωγρημένοι ὑπ᾽ αὐτοῦ εἰς τὸ ἐκείνου θέλημα.

26. kai ananeipsosin ek teis tou dyabolou pagidos, ezogreimenoi 'up autou eis to ekeinou theleima.

Hebrew/Transliteration

כו: וּלְהִמָּלֵט מֵרֶשֶׁת הַשָּׂטָן אֲשֶׁר פָּרַשׂ לְרַגְלָם וַאֲשֶׁר נִשְׁבּוּ כִּרְצוֹנוֹ

26. Ool•hi•ma•let me•re•shet ha•Satan asher Pa•ras le•rag•lam va•a•sher nish•boo kir•tzo•no.

2 Timothy, Chapter 3

1. This know also, that in the last days perilous times shall come.

Greek/Transliteration
1. Τοῦτο δὲ γίνωσκε, ὅτι ἐν ἐσχάταις ἡμέραις ἐνστήσονται καιροὶ χαλεποί.

1. Touto de ginoske, 'oti en eschatais 'eimerais ensteisontai kairoi chalepoi.

Hebrew/Transliteration
א. וְעַתָּה דַע-לְךָ כִּי דֹרוֹת יִוָּלְדוּ בְּאַחֲרִית הַיָּמִים עַד-לְהַשְׁחִית:

1. Ve•a•ta da - le•cha ki do•rot yi•val•doo be•a•cha•rit ha•ya•mim ad - le•hash•chit.

---

2. For men shall be lovers of their own selves, covetous, boasters, proud, blasphemers, disobedient to parents, unthankful, unholy,

Greek/Transliteration
2. Ἔσονται γὰρ οἱ ἄνθρωποι φίλαυτοι, φιλάργυροι, ἀλαζόνες, ὑπερήφανοι, βλάσφημοι, γονεῦσιν ἀπειθεῖς, ἀχάριστοι, ἀνόσιοι,

2. Esontai gar 'oi anthropoi philautoi, philarguroi, alazones, 'upereiphanoi, blaspheimoi, goneusin apeitheis, acharistoi, anosioi,

Greek/Transliteration
ב. כִּי-יָקוּמוּ אֲנָשִׁים אֹהֲבֵי עַצְמָם רֹדְפֵי בֶצַע מַרְחִיבֵי פֶה וְעֵינַיִם רָמוֹת דֹּבְרֵי סָרָה מַמְרִים לְיֹלְדֵיהֶם חֶסֶד לֹא יַכִּירוּ וְכָל-קֹדֶשׁ יְחַלֵּלוּ:

2. Ki - ya•koo•moo a•na•shim o•ha•vey atz•mam rod•fey ve•tza mar•chi•vey fe ve•ey•na•yim ra•mot dov•rey sa•ra mam•rim le•yol•dey•hem che•sed lo ya•ki•roo ve•chol - ko•desh ye•cha•le•loon.

---

3. Without natural affection, trucebreakers, false accusers, incontinent, fierce, despisers of those that are good,

Greek/Transliteration
3. ἄστοργοι, ἄσπονδοι, διάβολοι, ἀκρατεῖς, ἀνήμεροι, ἀφιλάγαθοι,

3. astorgoi, aspondoi, dyaboloi, akrateis, aneimeroi, aphilagathoi,

Hebrew/Transliteration
ג. חַסְרֵי רַחֲמִים מְפִירֵי בְרִית וּמַלְשִׁינִים זוֹלְלִים אַכְזָרִים וְשֹׂנְאֵי כָל-טוֹב:

3. Chas•rey ra•cha•mim me•fi•rey ve•rit oom•lash•nim zo•le•lim ach•za•rim ve•son•ey chol - tov.

4. Traitors, heady, highminded, lovers of pleasures more than lovers of God;

Greek/Transliteration
4. προδόται, προπετεῖς, τετυφωμένοι, φιλήδονοι μᾶλλον ἢ φιλόθεοι,

4. prodotai, propeteis, tetuphomenoi, phileidonoi mallon ei philotheoi,

Hebrew/Transliteration
:ד. מֹסְרִים פֹּחֲזִים וְגֵדִים רֹדְפִים לְהִתְעַנֵּג בְּתַעֲנוּגִים מֵהִתְעַנֵּג בֵּאלֹהִים

4. Mos•rim po•cha•zim ve•ze•dim rod•fim le•hit•a•neg be•ta•a•noo•gim me•hit•a•neg be•Elohim.

---

5. Having a form of godliness, but denying the power thereof: from such turn away.

Greek/Transliteration
5. ἔχοντες μόρφωσιν εὐσεβείας, τὴν δὲ δύναμιν αὐτῆς ἠρνημένοι· καὶ τούτους ἀποτρέπου.

5. echontes morphosin eusebeias, tein de dunamin auteis eirneimenoi. kai toutous apotrepou.

Hebrew/Transliteration
:ה. וְהֵם פָּנִים לָהֶם כִּדְמוּת יִרְאַת שָׁמַיִם אַךְ מִכֹּחָהּ אֵין בְּקִרְבָּם וְעַל-כֵּן הַרְחֵק נַפְשְׁךָ מֵהֶם

5. Ve•hem pa•nim la•hem kid•moot yir•at sha•ma•yim ach mi•ko•cha eyn be•kir•bam ve•al - ken har•chek naf•she•cha me•hem.

---

6. For of this sort are they which creep into houses, and lead captive silly women laden with sins, led away with divers lusts,

Greek/Transliteration
6. Ἐκ τούτων γάρ εἰσιν οἱ ἐνδύνοντες εἰς τὰς οἰκίας, καὶ αἰχμαλωτεύοντες γυναικάρια σεσωρευμένα ἁμαρτίαις, ἀγόμενα ἐπιθυμίαις ποικίλαις,

6. Ek touton gar eisin 'oi endunontes eis tas oikias, kai aichmaloteuontes gunaikarya sesoreumena 'amartiais, agomena epithumiais poikilais,

Hebrew/Transliteration
ו. כִּי-מֵהֶם הֵם הַזֹּחֲלִים לָבוֹא אֶל-הַבָּתִּים לִנְהֹג כִּשְׁבָיוֹת חֶרֶב נָשִׁים סָרוֹת טַעַם מְלֵאוֹת עָוֹן וְנַפְשָׁן שׁוֹקֵקָה לְכָל-תְּשׁוּקָה:

6. Ki - me•hem hem ha•zo•cha•lim la•vo el - ha•ba•tim le•na•heg kish•voo•yot che•rev na•shim sa•rot ta•am me•le•ot a•von ve•naf•shan sho•ke•ka le•chol - t`shoo•ka.

Rabbinic Jewish Commentary
The Syriac version uses a word, from whence comes חולדא, "Chulda", which signifies "a weasel"; suggesting, that their entrance into houses was like to the way of that creature, which is sometimes covered, and sometimes open: there was also a gate of the temple,

which was called "Huldah"; whether there is any allusion in the word to that, may be inquired (k).

(k) Vid. L. Empercur in Misn. Middot, c. 1. sect. 3.

---

7. Ever learning, and never able to come to the knowledge of the truth.

Greek/Transliteration
7. πάντοτε μανθάνοντα, καὶ μηδέποτε εἰς ἐπίγνωσιν ἀληθείας ἐλθεῖν δυνάμενα.

7. pantote manthanonta, kai meidepote eis epignosin aleitheias elthein dunamena.

Hebrew/Transliteration
ז. הֵן הֵנָּה הַלֹּמְדוֹת תָּמִיד וְלָדַעַת אֶת-הָאֱמֶת אֵין לְאֵל יָדָן:

7. Hen he•na ha•lom•dot ta•mid ve•la•da•at et - ha•e•met eyn le•el ya•dan.

---

8. Now as Jannes and Jambres withstood Moses, so do these also resist the truth: men of corrupt minds, reprobate concerning the faith.

Greek/Transliteration
8. Ὃν τρόπον δὲ Ἰαννῆς καὶ Ἰαμβρῆς ἀντέστησαν Μωϋσῇ, οὕτως καὶ οὗτοι ἀνθίστανται τῇ ἀληθείᾳ, ἄνθρωποι κατεφθαρμένοι τὸν νοῦν, ἀδόκιμοι περὶ τὴν πίστιν.

8. 'On tropon de Yanneis kai Yambreis antesteisan Mousei, 'outos kai 'outoi anthistantai tei aleitheia, anthropoi katephtharmenoi ton noun, adokimoi peri tein pistin.

Hebrew/Transliteration
ח. כִּי-כְמוֹ יַנִּיס וְיַמְבְּרִיס הִתְיַצְּבוּ בִּפְנֵי מֹשֶׁה כֵּן גַּם-אֵלֶּה מִתְיַצְּבִים בִּפְנֵי הָאֱמֶת בָּנִים מַשְׁחִיתִים בְּדַעַת וּנְגְלוֹזִים בָּאֱמוּנָה:

8. Ki - che•mo Yanis ve•Yam•beris hit•yatz•voo bif•ney Moshe ken gam - ele mit•yatz•vim bif•ney ha•e•met ba•nim mash•chi•tim be•da•at oon•lo•zim ba•e•moo•na.

Rabbinic Jewish Commentary
Now as Jannes and Jambres withstood Moses,.... These were not Jews, who rose up and opposed Moses, as Dathan and Abiram did, as some have thought; but Egyptian magicians, the chief of those that Pharaoh sent for, when Moses and Aaron came before him, and wrought miracles; and who did in like manner by their enchantments, Exo_7:11 upon which place the Targum of Jonathan has these words:

"And Pharaoh called the wise men and the magicians; and Janis and Jambres, the magicians of the Egyptians, did so by the enchantments of their divinations."

Numenius; the philosopher, speaks of Jannes and Jambres as Egyptian scribes, and famous for their skill in the magic art; and who opposed themselves to Moses when the Jews were driven out of Egypt (l). Pliny also makes mention of Janme and Jotape as magicians; though he wrongly calls them Jews, and places Moses with them (m), as Jannes likewise is by

Apuleius (n). It is commonly said by the Jews (o), that these were the two sons of Balaam, and they are said to be the chief of the magicians of Egypt (p); the latter of these is called in the Vulgate Latin version Mambres; and in some Jewish writers his name is Mamre (q) by whom also the former is called Jochane or John; and indeed Joannes, Jannes, and John, are the same name; and R. Gedaliah (r) says, that their names in other languages are John and Ambrose, which is not unlikely. Mention is made of the sons of Jambri in the Apocrypha:

"But the children of Jambri came out of Medaba, and took John, and all that he had, and went their way with it." (1 Maccabees 9:36)

Whom Josephus (s) calls the sons of Amaraeus. These are said to be the persons that told Pharaoh, that a child should be born among the Israelites, by whom the whole land of Egypt should be destroyed, and which was the reason of Pharaoh's giving such a charge to the Hebrew midwives (t); also the making of the golden calf is ascribed to them (u); for, according to the Jews, they afterwards became proselytes; but these things are not to be depended on: however, certain it is, that they withstood Moses by their enchantments, and hardened Pharaoh's heart, so that, for a while, he would not let the children of Israel go.

(l) Apud Euseb. Praeparat. Evangel. l. 9. p. 411. (m) Nat. Hist. l. 30. c. 1. (n) Apolog. p. 248. (o) Targum Jon. in Numb. xxii. 22. & Zohar in Numb. fol. 78. 3. & Chronicon Mosis, fol. 6. 2. (p) Targum Jon. in Exod. i. 15. & vii. 11. & Zohar in Exod. fol. 75. 1. (q) T. Bab. Menachot, fol. 85. 1. Midrash Shemot Rabba, sect. 9. fol. 97. 3. & Aruch. in voce. (r) Shalsheleth Hakabala, fol. 7. 1. (s) Antiqu. l. 13. c. 1. sect. 2. (t) Targum Jon. in Exod. i. 15. (u) Zohar in Exod. fol. 75. 1. & in Numb. fol. 78. 3. Shalsheleth, ib.

---

9. But they shall proceed no further: for their folly shall be manifest unto all men, as theirs also was.

Greek/Transliteration

9. Ἀλλ' οὐ προκόψουσιν ἐπὶ πλεῖον· ἡ γὰρ ἄνοια αὐτῶν ἔκδηλος ἔσται πᾶσιν, ὡς καὶ ἡ ἐκείνων ἐγένετο.

9. All ou prokopsousin epi pleion. 'ei gar anoya auton ekdeilos estai pasin, 'os kai 'ei ekeinon egeneto.

Hebrew/Transliteration

ט. אַךְ חֶפְצָם לֹא יִצְלַח עוֹד בְּיָדָם כִּי תִגָּלֶה נִבְלָתָם לְעֵינֵי-כֹל כַּאֲשֶׁר קָרָה גַם-לָאֲנָשִׁים הָהֵם:

9. Ach chef•tzam lo yitz•lach od be•ya•dam ki ti•ga•le nav•loo•tam le•ei•ney - chol ka•a•sher ka•ra gam - la•a•na•shim ha•hem.

---

10. But thou hast fully known my doctrine, manner of life, purpose, faith, longsuffering, charity, patience,

Greek/Transliteration

10. Σὺ δὲ παρηκολούθηκάς μου τῇ διδασκαλίᾳ, τῇ ἀγωγῇ, τῇ προθέσει, τῇ πίστει, τῇ μακροθυμίᾳ, τῇ ἀγάπῃ, τῇ ὑπομονῇ,

10. Su de pareikoloutheikas mou tei didaskalia, tei agogei, tei prothesei, tei pistei, tei makrothumia, tei agapei, tei 'upomonei,

Hebrew/Transliteration
י. וְאַתָּה הָלַכְתָּ בְעִקְבוֹתַי בְּמַעְגְּלֵי תוֹרָתִי בַּהֲלִיכוֹת חַיַּי וּבִמְגַמַּת פָּנַי בֶּאֱמוּנָתִי בְּאֹרֶךְ רוּחִי בְּאַהֲבָתִי וּבְסַבְלוּת נַפְשִׁי:

10. Ve•a•ta ha•lach•ta ve•eek•vo•tai be•ma•ag•ley to•ra•ti ba•ha•li•chot cha•yai oo•vim•ga•mat pa•nai be•e•moo•na•ti be•o•rech roo•chi be•a•ha•va•ti oov•siv•loot naf•shi.

---

11. Persecutions, afflictions, which came unto me at Antioch, at Iconium, at Lystra; what persecutions I endured: but out of them all the Lord delivered me.

Greek/Transliteration
11. τοῖς διωγμοῖς, τοῖς παθήμασιν, οἷά μοι ἐγένετο ἐν Ἀντιοχείᾳ, ἐν Ἰκονίῳ, ἐν Λύστροις, οἵους διωγμοὺς ὑπήνεγκα· καὶ ἐκ πάντων με ἐρρύσατο ὁ κύριος.

11. tois diogmois, tois patheimasin, 'oia moi egeneto en Antiocheia, en Ykonio, en Lustrois, 'oious diogmous 'upeinegka. kai ek panton me errusato 'o kurios.

Hebrew/Transliteration
יא. וּבִרְדִיפוֹת וּבְצָרוֹת אֲשֶׁר יָדַעְתָּ כִּי אֲפָפוּנִי בְּאַנְטְיוֹכְיָא בְּאִיקוֹנְיָא וּבְלוּסְטְרָא כִּי-שָׁם נִרְדַּפְתִּי עַל-צַוָּארִי עַד אֲשֶׁר-הִצִּילַנִי הָאָדוֹן מִכָּל-רֹדְפָי:

11. Oo•vir•di•fot oov•tza•rot asher ya•da•ata ki afa•foo•ni be•An•te•yoch•ya be•Ee•konia oov•Loos•tera ki - sham nir•daf•ti al - tza•va•ri ad asher - hi•tzi•la•ni ha•Adon mi•kol - rod•fai.

---

12. Yea, and all that will live godly in Christ Jesus shall suffer persecution.

Greek/Transliteration
12. Καὶ πάντες δὲ οἱ θέλοντες εὐσεβῶς ζῆν ἐν χριστῷ Ἰησοῦ διωχθήσονται.

12. Kai pantes de 'oi thelontes eusebos zein en christo Yeisou diochtheisontai.

Hebrew/Transliteration
יב. כִּי הֲלֹא כֻלָּם הַחֲפֵצִים בְּחַיֵּי יִרְאַת שָׁמַיִם בְּיֵשׁוּעַ הַמָּשִׁיחַ נִרְדָּפִים הֵמָּה:

12. Ki ha•lo choo•lam ha•cha•fe•tzim be•cha•yey yir•at sha•ma•yim be•Yeshua ha•Ma•shi•ach nir•da•fim he•ma.

---

13. But evil men and seducers shall wax worse and worse, deceiving, and being deceived.

Greek/Transliteration
13. Πονηροὶ δὲ ἄνθρωποι καὶ γόητες προκόψουσιν ἐπὶ τὸ χεῖρον, πλανῶντες καὶ πλανώμενοι.

13. Poneiroi de anthropoi kai goeites prokopsousin epi to cheiron, planontes kai planomenoi.

Hebrew/Transliteration
יג: אַךְ אֲנָשִׁים רָעִים וְקֹסְמִים כֵּן יָרֵעוּ וְכֵן יַשְׁחִיתוּ מַתְעִים הֵם וְנִתְעִים.

13. Ach a•na•shim ra•eem ve•kos•mim ken ya•re•oo ve•chen yash•chi•too mat•eem hem ve•nit•eem.

---

14. But continue thou in the things which thou hast learned and hast been assured of, knowing of whom thou hast learned them;

Greek/Transliteration
14. Σὺ δὲ μένε ἐν οἷς ἔμαθες καὶ ἐπιστώθης, εἰδὼς παρὰ τίνος ἔμαθες,

14. Su de mene en 'ois emathes kai epistotheis, eidos para tinos emathes,

Hebrew/Transliteration
יד: אֲבָל אַתָּה שְׁמֹר אֶת-אֲשֶׁר לָמַדְתָּ וְהִשְׁכַּלְתָּ אֶל-נָכוֹן כִּי יָדַעְתָּ מִי-הוּא אֲשֶׁר מִפִּיו לָמַדְתָּ.

14. O•val ata sh`mor et - asher la•mad•ta ve•his•kal•ta el - na•chon ki ya•da•ata mee - hoo asher mi•piv la•mad•ta.

---

15. And that from a child thou hast known the holy scriptures, which are able to make thee wise unto salvation through faith which is in Christ Jesus.

Greek/Transliteration
15. καὶ ὅτι ἀπὸ βρέφους τὰ ἱερὰ γράμματα οἶδας, τὰ δυνάμενά σε σοφίσαι εἰς σωτηρίαν διὰ πίστεως τῆς ἐν χριστῷ Ἰησοῦ.

15. kai 'oti apo brephous ta 'iera grammata oidas, ta dunamena se sophisai eis soteirian dya pisteos teis en christo Yeisou.

Hebrew/Transliteration
טו: וְכִי-מִנְּעָרֶיךָ יָדַעְתָּ אֶת-כִּתְבֵי הַקֹּדֶשׁ אֲשֶׁר אַל-יָדָם תַּשְׂכִּיל לְהִוָּשַׁע בֶּאֱמוּנַת יֵשׁוּעַ הַמָּשִׁיחַ.

15. Ve•chi - min•oo•re•cha ya•da•ata et - kit•vey ha•ko•desh asher al - ya•dam tas•kil le•hi•va•sha be•e•moo•nat Yeshua ha•Ma•shi•ach.

Rabbinic Jewish Commentary
The Jews very early learned their children the holy Scripture. Philo the Jew says (w), εκ πρωτης ηλικιας "from their very infancy"; a phrase pretty much the same with this here used. It is a maxim with the Jews (x), that when a child was five years of age, it was proper to teach him the Scriptures. Timothy's mother being a Jewess, trained him up early in the knowledge of these writings, with which he became very conversant, and under divine influence and assistance, arrived to a large understanding of them.

(w) De Legat. ad Caium, p. 1022. (x) Pirke Abot, c. 5. sect. 21.

16. All scripture is given by inspiration of God, and is profitable for doctrine, for reproof, for correction, for instruction in righteousness:

Greek/Transliteration
16. Πᾶσα γραφὴ θεόπνευστος καὶ ὠφέλιμος πρὸς διδασκαλίαν, πρὸς ἔλεγχον, πρὸς ἐπανόρθωσιν, πρὸς παιδείαν τὴν ἐν δικαιοσύνῃ·

16. Pasa graphei theopneustos kai ophelimos pros didaskalian, pros elegchon, pros epanorthosin, pros paideian tein en dikaiosunei.

Hebrew/Transliteration
:טז. כָּל־כִּתְבֵי הַקֹּדֶשׁ עַל־פִּי רוּחַ אֱלֹהִים הֵמָּה וּנְכֹנִים לְהוֹרֹת וּלְהוֹכִיחַ לְהָשִׁיב נֶפֶשׁ וּלְיַשֵּׁר בְּמַעְגְּלֵי צֶדֶק

16. Kol - kit•vey ha•ko•desh al - pi roo•ach Elohim he•ma oo•n`cho•nim le•ho•rot ool•ho•chi•ach le•ha•shiv ne•fesh ool•ya•sher be•ma•ag•ley tze•dek.

Rabbinic Jewish Commentary
All Scripture is given by inspiration of God,.... That is, all holy Scripture; for of that only the apostle is speaking; and he means the whole of it, meaning the Hebrew Old Testament.

The Scriptures are the breath of God, the word of God and not men; they are "written by the Spirit", as the Syriac version renders it; or "by the Spirit of God", as the Ethiopic version.

---

17. That the man of God may be perfect, throughly furnished unto all good works.

Greek/Transliteration
17. ἵνα ἄρτιος ᾖ ὁ τοῦ θεοῦ ἄνθρωπος, πρὸς πᾶν ἔργον ἀγαθὸν ἐξηρτισμένος.

17. 'ina artios ei 'o tou theou anthropos, pros pan ergon agathon exeirtismenos.

Hebrew/Transliteration
:יז. וְעַל־פִּיהֶם שָׁלֵם יִהְיֶה אִישׁ הָאֱלֹהִים וְנָכוֹן לְכָל־מַעֲשֶׂה טוֹב

17. Ve•al - pi•hem sha•lem yi•hee•ye eesh ha•Elohim ve•na•chon le•chol - ma•a•se tov.

2 Timothy, Chapter 4

1. I charge thee therefore before God, and the Lord Jesus Christ, who shall judge the quick and the dead at his appearing and his kingdom;

Greek/Transliteration

1. Διαμαρτύρομαι οὖν ἐγὼ ἐνώπιον τοῦ θεοῦ, καὶ τοῦ κυρίου Ἰησοῦ χριστοῦ, τοῦ μέλλοντος κρίνειν ζῶντας καὶ νεκρούς, κατὰ τὴν ἐπιφάνειαν αὐτοῦ καὶ τὴν βασιλείαν αὐτοῦ,

1. Dyamarturomai oun ego enopion tou theou, kai tou kuriou Yeisou christou, tou mellontos krinein zontas kai nekrous, kata tein epiphaneyan autou kai tein basileian autou,

Hebrew/Transliteration

א. לָכֵן אֲנִי נֶגֶד פְּנֵי אֱלֹהִים וְנֶגֶד פְּנֵי יֵשׁוּעַ הַמָּשִׁיחַ אֲדוֹנֵינוּ אֲשֶׁר יִשְׁפֹּט אֶת-הַחַיִּים וְאֶת-הַמֵּתִים כַּאֲשֶׁר יִגָּלֶה בְּמַלְכוּתוֹ הִנְנִי מְצַוְּךָ הַיּוֹם לֵאמֹר:

1. La·chen ani ne·ged p`ney Elohim ve·ne·ged p`ney Yeshua ha•Ma•shi•ach Ado•ney•noo asher yish•pot et - ha•cha•yim ve•et - ha•me•tim ka•a•sher yi•ga•le ve•mal•choo•to hi•ne•ni me•tzav•cha ha•yom le•mor.

---

2. Preach the word; be instant in season, out of season; reprove, rebuke, exhort with all longsuffering and doctrine.

Greek/Transliteration

2. κήρυξον τὸν λόγον, ἐπίστηθι εὐκαίρως, ἀκαίρως, ἔλεγξον, ἐπιτίμησον, παρακάλεσον, ἐν πάσῃ μακροθυμίᾳ καὶ διδαχῇ.

2. keiruxon ton logon, episteithi eukairos, akairos, elegxon, epitimeison, parakaleson, en pasei makrothumia kai didachei.

Hebrew/Transliteration

ב. קְרָא אֶת-דְּבַר בְּשׂוֹרָתוֹ וְלֹא תֶחְדַּל מִקְּרֹא גַּם-בְּעִתּוֹ וְגַם בְּלֹא עִתּוֹ וּבְכָל-אֹרֶךְ רוּחֲךָ הוֹכֵחַ תּוֹכִיחַ וְתִגְעַר וְתַזְהֵר לְפִי כָל-דִּבְרֵי הַתּוֹרָה:

2. K`ra et - de·var be·so·ra·to ve·lo tech·dal mik·ro gam - be·ee·to ve·gam be·lo ee·to oov·chol - o·rech roo·cha·cha ho·che·ach to·chi·ach ve·tig·ar ve·taz·her le·fi chol - div·rey ha·torah.

---

3. For the time will come when they will not endure sound doctrine; but after their own lusts shall they heap to themselves teachers, having itching ears;

Greek/Transliteration

3. Ἔσται γὰρ καιρὸς ὅτε τῆς ὑγιαινούσης διδασκαλίας οὐκ ἀνέξονται, ἀλλὰ κατὰ τὰς ἐπιθυμίας τὰς ἰδίας ἑαυτοῖς ἐπισωρεύσουσιν διδασκάλους, κνηθόμενοι τὴν ἀκοήν·

3. Estai gar kairos 'ote teis 'ugyainouseis didaskalias ouk anexontai, alla kata tas epithumias tas idias 'eautois episoreusousin didaskalous, kneithomenoi tein akoein.

Hebrew/Transliteration
ג. כִּי־יָמִים יָבוֹאוּ אֲשֶׁר לֹא־יָכִילוּ בְנֵי־אָדָם תּוֹרַת חַיִּים כִּי אָזְנֵיהֶם הֵפוּ בְחֶרֶס וַהֲמוֹן מוֹרִים יִצְבְּרוּ לָהֶם בְּאַוָּתָם לְהִתְגָּרֶד־בָּם:

3. Ki - ya•mim ya•vo•oo asher lo - ya•chi•loo v`ney - adam to•rat cha•yim ki oz•ney•hem hoo•koo ve•cha•res va•ha•mon mo•rim yitz•be•roo la•hem be•a•va•tam le•hit•ga•red - bam.

---

4. And they shall turn away their ears from the truth, and shall be turned unto fables.

Greek/Transliteration
4. καὶ ἀπὸ μὲν τῆς ἀληθείας τὴν ἀκοὴν ἀποστρέψουσιν, ἐπὶ δὲ τοὺς μύθους ἐκτραπήσονται.

4. kai apo men teis aleitheias tein akoein apostrepsousin, epi de tous muthous ektrapeisontai.

Hebrew/Transliteration
ד. מִן־הָאֱמֶת יָסִירוּ אָזְנָם לִהְטוֹת אַחֲרֵי מִשְׁלֵי שָׁוְא:

4. Min - ha•e•met yasi•roo oz•nam le•ha•tot a•cha•rey mish•ley shav.

---

5. But watch thou in all things, endure afflictions, do the work of an evangelist, make full proof of thy ministry.

Greek/Transliteration
5. Σὺ δὲ νῆφε ἐν πᾶσιν, κακοπάθησον, ἔργον ποίησον εὐαγγελιστοῦ, τὴν διακονίαν σου πληροφόρησον.

5. Su de neiphe en pasin, kakopatheison, ergon poieison euangelistou, tein dyakonian sou pleirophoreison.

Hebrew/Transliteration
ה. אֲבָל אַתָּה עֲמֹד עַל־מִשְׁמַרְתֶּךָ הִתְעַנֵּה תַּחַת יְדֵי הָרָעָה עֲשֵׂה מְלֶאכֶת הַמְבַשֵּׂר וְכַלֵּה אֶת־עֲבֹדָתֶךָ:

5. Aval ata amod al - mish•mar•te•cha hit•a•ne ta•chat ye•dey ha•ra•ah ase me•le•chet ha•me•va•ser ve•cha•le et - avo•da•te•cha.

---

6. For I am now ready to be offered, and the time of my departure is at hand.

Greek/Transliteration
6. Ἐγὼ γὰρ ἤδη σπένδομαι, καὶ ὁ καιρὸς τῆς ἐμῆς ἀναλύσεως ἐφέστηκεν.

6. Ego gar eidei spendomai, kai 'o kairos teis emeis analuseos ephesteiken.

Hebrew/Transliteration
ו. וַאֲנִי נְכוֹנָה נַפְשִׁי לְהִשְׁתַּפֵּךְ עָלַי־זָבַח וְעֵת חֲלִיפָתִי בָּאָה:

6. Va•a•ni n`cho•na naf•shi le•hish•ta•pech aley - za•vach ve•et cha•li•fa•ti ba•ah.

---

7. I have fought a good fight, I have finished my course, I have kept the faith:

Greek/Transliteration
7. Τὸν ἀγῶνα τὸν καλὸν ἠγώνισμαι, τὸν δρόμον τετέλεκα, τὴν πίστιν τετήρηκα·

7. Ton agona ton kalon eigonismai, ton dromon teteleka, tein pistin teteireika.

Hebrew/Transliteration
ז. מִלְחֶמֶת צֶדֶק נִלְחַמְתִּי אֶת-מְרוּצָתִי הִשְׁלַמְתִּי וְאֶת-הָאֱמוּנָה נָצָרְתִּי:

7. Mil•che•met tze•dek nil•cham•ti et - me•roo•tza•ti hish•lam•tee ve•et - ha•e•moo•na na•tzar•ti.

Rabbinic Jewish Commentary
The Syriac and Ethiopic versions, which render it, "I have kept my faith"; or have been faithful to my trust, as a good steward of the mysteries of God; not concealing and keeping back any thing that was profitable, but declaring the whole counsel of God; and now what remained for him was the crown of righteousness; and this he says for the comfort and encouragement and imitation of Timothy and others. The phrase seems to be Jewish; it is said (y) by the Jews, that he that does not keep the feast of unleavened bread, is as he who does not נטיר מהימנותא, "keep the faith of the holy blessed God".

(y) Zohar in Exod. fol. 51. 2.

---

8. Henceforth there is laid up for me a crown of righteousness, which the Lord, the righteous judge, shall give me at that day: and not to me only, but unto all them also that love his appearing.

Greek/Transliteration
8. λοιπόν, ἀπόκειταί μοι ὁ τῆς δικαιοσύνης στέφανος, ὃν ἀποδώσει μοι ὁ κύριος ἐν ἐκείνῃ τῇ ἡμέρᾳ, ὁ δίκαιος κριτής· οὐ μόνον δὲ ἐμοί, ἀλλὰ καὶ πᾶσιν τοῖς ἠγαπηκόσιν τὴν ἐπιφάνειαν αὐτοῦ.

8. loipon, apokeitai moi 'o teis dikaiosuneis stephanos, 'on apodosei moi 'o kurios en ekeinei tei 'eimera, 'o dikaios kriteis. ou monon de emoi, alla kai pasin tois eigapeikosin tein epiphaneyan autou.

Hebrew/Transliteration
ח. וּלְמִן-הַיּוֹם הַזֶּה צָפוּן לִי כֶּתֶר הַצְּדָקָה אֲשֶׁר בַּיּוֹם הַהוּא יִתֶּן-לִי הָאָדוֹן שֹׁפֵט צֶדֶק וְלֹא-לִי לְבַדִּי כִּי אִם-גַּם לְכָל-הַחֲפֵצִים בְּהִתְגַּלּוֹתוֹ:

8. Ool•min - ha•yom ha•ze tza•foon li ke•ter ha•tz`da•ka asher ba•yom ha•hoo yi•ten – li ha•Adon sho•fet tze•dek ve•lo - li le•va•di ki eem - gam le•chol - ha•cha•fe•tzim be•hit•ga•lo•to.

Rabbinic Jewish Commentary

This seems to be a Jewish way of speaking. One of the Septuagint interpreters, whom Ptolomy king of Egypt sent for from Judea, to translate the Torah of Moses into Greek, in answer to a question put to him by the king, uses this phrase of στεφανος δικαιοσυνης, "a crown of righteousness"; and which he represents as the gift of God (z).

(z) Aristeae Hist. 72. Interpr. p. 91, Ed. Oxon.

---

9. Do thy diligence to come shortly unto me:

Greek/Transliteration
9. Σπούδασον ἐλθεῖν πρός με ταχέως·

9. Spoudason elthein pros me tacheos.

Hebrew/Transliteration
ט. חוּשָׁה וּבֹאָה אֵלַי עַד-מְהֵרָה:

9. Choo•sha oo•vo•ah e•lai ad - me•he•ra.

---

10. For Demas hath forsaken me, having loved this present world, and is departed unto Thessalonica; Crescens to Galatia, Titus unto Dalmatia.

Greek/Transliteration
10. Δημᾶς γάρ με ἐγκατέλιπεν, ἀγαπήσας τὸν νῦν αἰῶνα, καὶ ἐπορεύθη εἰς Θεσσαλονίκην· Κρήσκης εἰς Γαλατίαν, Τίτος εἰς Δαλματίαν.

10. Deimas gar me egkatelipen, agapeisas ton nun aiona, kai eporeuthei eis Thessalonikein. Kreiskeis eis Galatian, Titos eis Dalmatian.

Hebrew/Transliteration
י. דִּימָס עֲזָבַנִי כִּי אָהַב אֶת-הָעוֹלָם הַזֶּה וַיֵּלֶךְ-לוֹ לְתַסְלוֹנִיקִי קְרִיסְקִיס לְגָלַטְיָא וְטִיטוֹס לְדַלְמַטְיָא:

10. Dimas a•za•va•ni ki ahav et - ha•o•lam ha•ze va•ye•lech - lo le•Tas•loniki Kris•kis le•Ga•latya ve•Titos le•Dal•mat•ya.

Rabbinic Jewish Commentary

Epiphanius (a) places Demas among the heretics Ebion and Cerinthus, as if he was one of them.

Crescens to Galatia; he might not depart on the same account as Demas, but might be sent by the apostle to Galatia, to visit the churches there, to set things in order, and establish them in the faith, and bring an account of their state. Epiphanius (b), instead of Galatia, reads Gallia, or France; and so does Eusebius (c) and the Ethiopic version; and Jerom asserts, (d), that Crescens preached in France, and was there buried; though others say he was bishop of Chalcedon in Galatia, and put him among the seventy disciples. The Syriac version calls him "Crispus", and the Arabic version "Priscus".

Pliny says (e), that part of Pannonia, which lies to the Adriatic sea, was called Dalmatia; it had its name from Dalmius, a city in it. The Alexandrian copy reads "Dermatia". Here the apostle had doubtless been useful for the conversion of souls, and planting of churches, and therefore sent Titus thither, to assist them in their state and condition, and bring him an account of them. For in the "second" and "third" centuries we read of churches in Dalmatia; and likewise in the "fourth" century; for there were bishops from Dalmatia in the synod at Sardica; and in the "fifth" century, Glycerius was bishop of Salo, a city in this country; and in the "sixth" century, one Malchus was bishop of the Dalmatian church (f).

(a) Contra Haeres, Haeres. 51. (b) lbid. (c) Hist. Eccl l. 3. c. 4. (d) Catalog. Script. Eccles. sect. 13. p. 90. (e) Nat. Hist. l. 3. c. 25. (f) Hist. Eccl. Magdeburg, cent. 2. c. 2. p. 4. cent. 3. c. 2. p. 4. cent. 4. c. 2. p. 6. c. 9. p. 425. cent. 5. c. 2. p. 7. cent 6. c. 2. p. 8.

---

11. Only Luke is with me. Take Mark, and bring him with thee: for he is profitable to me for the ministry.

Greek/Transliteration
11. Λουκᾶς ἐστὶν μόνος μετ' ἐμοῦ. Μάρκον ἀναλαβὼν ἄγε μετὰ σεαυτοῦ· ἔστιν γάρ μοι εὔχρηστος εἰς διακονίαν.

11. Loukas estin monos met emou. Markon analabon age meta seautou. estin gar moi euchreistos eis dyakonian.

Hebrew/Transliteration
:יא. וְלוּקָס לְבַדּוֹ נִשְׁאָר עִמִּי קְחָה-נָא אֶת-מַרְקוֹס וַהֲבִיאֵהוּ עִמְּךָ לַעֲזָר-לִי בַּעֲבֹדָתִי

11. Ve•Lookas le•va•do nish•ar ee•mi ke•cha - na et - Markos va•ha•vi•e•hoo eem•cha la•a•zor - li ba•a•vo•da•ti.

---

12. And Tychicus have I sent to Ephesus.

Greek/Transliteration
12. Τυχικὸν δὲ ἀπέστειλα εἰς Ἔφεσον.

12. Tuchikon de apesteila eis Epheson.

Hebrew/Transliteration
:יב. אֶת-טוּכִיקוֹס שָׁלַחְתִּי לְאֶפְסוֹס

12. Et - Too•chi•kos sha•lach•ti le•Efsos.

---

13. The cloke that I left at Troas with Carpus, when thou comest, bring with thee, and the books, but especially the parchments.

Greek/Transliteration
13. Τὸν φελόνην ὃν ἀπέλιπον ἐν Τρῳάδι παρὰ Κάρπῳ, ἐρχόμενος φέρε, καὶ τὰ βιβλία, μάλιστα τὰς μεμβράνας.

13. Ton phelonein 'on apelipon en Troadi para Karpo, erchomenos phere, kai ta biblia, malista tas membranas.

Hebrew/Transliteration
יג. הָבֵא-נָא אִתְּךָ אֶת-מְעִילִי אֲשֶׁר עֲזַבְתִּי בִטְרוֹאַס תַּחַת יְדֵי קַרְפּוֹס וְגַם אֶת-הַסְּפָרִים אַךְ אֶת-הַקְּלָפִים בְּרֹאשָׁם:

13. Ha•ve - na eet•cha et - me•ee•li asher a•zav•ti vi•Tro•as ta•chat ye•dey Karpos ve•gam et - has•fa•rim ach et - hak•la•fim be•ro•sham.

Rabbinic Jewish Commentary
Jerom understands it of a book itself, of the Hebrew volume of the Pentateuch (g).

(g) Epist. ad Damas. qu. 2. p. 12. Tom. 3.

---

14. Alexander the coppersmith did me much evil: the Lord reward him according to his works:

Greek/Translitration
14. Ἀλέξανδρος ὁ χαλκεὺς πολλά μοι κακὰ ἐνεδείξατο· ἀποδῴη αὐτῷ ὁ κύριος κατὰ τὰ ἔργα αὐτοῦ·

14. Alexandros 'o chalkeus polla moi kaka enedeixato. apodoei auto 'o kurios kata ta erga autou.

Hebrew/Transliteration
יד. אֲלֶכְסַנְדְּרוֹס חָרַשׁ הַנְּחֹשֶׁת עָשָׂה לִי רָעוֹת רַבּוֹת יְשַׁלֶּם-לוֹ יְהוָֹה כְּמַעֲשֵׂהוּ:

14. Alex•san•dros cha•rash ha•ne•cho•shet asa li ra•ot ra•bot ye•sha•lem - lo Adonai ke•ma•a•se•hoo.

---

15. Of whom be thou ware also; for he hath greatly withstood our words.

Greek/Transliteration
15. ὃν καὶ σὺ φυλάσσου, λίαν γὰρ ἀνθέστηκεν τοῖς ἡμετέροις λόγοις.

15. 'on kai su phulassou, lian gar anthesteiken tois 'eimeterois logois.

Hebrew/Transliteration
טו. וְגַם-אַתָּה הִשָּׁתַמֵּר מִפָּנָיו כִּי הוּא הִתְיַצֵּב בְּפָנֵי לַמְרוֹת וּלְהָפֵר דְּבָרֵינוּ:

15. Ve•gam - ata hish•ta•mer mi•pa•nav ki hoo hit•ya•tzev be•fa•nai lam•rot ool•ha•fer de•va•rey•noo.

---

16. At my first answer no man stood with me, but all men forsook me: I pray God that it may not be laid to their charge.

Greek/Transliteration
16. Ἐν τῇ πρώτῃ μου ἀπολογίᾳ οὐδείς μοι συμπαρεγένετο, ἀλλὰ πάντες με ἐγκατέλιπον· μὴ αὐτοῖς λογισθείη.

16. En tei protei mou apologia oudeis moi sumparegeneto, alla pantes me egkatelipon mei autois logistheiei.

Hebrew/Transliteration
טז. כַּאֲשֶׁר בָּאתִי לְהִצְטַדֵּק בַּפַּעַם הָרִאשׁוֹנָה לֹא-עָמַד אִישׁ אִתִּי כִּי-כֻלָּם עֲזָבוּנִי אַל-יֵחָשֵׁב לָהֶם לְעָוֹן:

16. Ka•a•sher ba•ti le•hitz•ta•dek ba•pa•am ha•ri•sho•na lo - amad eesh ee•ti ki - choo•lam aza•voo•ni al - ye•cha•shev la•hem le•avon.

---

17. Notwithstanding the Lord stood with me, and strengthened me; that by me the preaching might be fully known, and that all the Gentiles might hear: and I was delivered out of the mouth of the lion.

Greek/Transliteration
17. Ὁ δὲ κύριός μοι παρέστη, καὶ ἐνεδυνάμωσέν με, ἵνα δι᾽ ἐμοῦ τὸ κήρυγμα πληροφορηθῇ, καὶ ἀκούσῃ πάντα τὰ ἔθνη· καὶ ἐρρύσθην ἐκ στόματος λέοντος.

17. 'O de kurios moi parestei, kai enedunamosen me, 'ina di emou to keirugma pleirophoreithei, kai akousei panta ta ethnei. kai errusthein ek stomatos leontos.

Hebrew/Transliteration
יז. אֲבָל הָאָדוֹן הָיָה בְעֶזְרִי וַיְחַזְּקֵנִי לְמַעַן תִּקָּרֵא הַבְּשֹׂרָה עַל-פִּי וְיִשְׁמְעוּ כָל-הַגּוֹיִם וְגַם-בְּעֶזְרָתוֹ מִפִּי אַרְיֵה נִצַּלְתִּי:

17. Aval ha•Adon ha•ya ve•ez•ri vay•chaz•ke•nee le•ma•an ti•ka•re ha•b`so•hra al - pi ve•yish•me•oo chol - ha•go•yim ve•gam - be•ez•ra•to mi•pi ar•ye ni•tzal•ti.

Rabbinic Jewish Commentary
Nero the Roman emperor, so called from his power and fierceness. So Tiberius is called by Marsyas, Agrippa's freeman, when he brought the news of his death to his master (g); and Ahasuerus by Esther (h); and Nero himself is called a civil beast by Apollonius Tyanaeus (i); though some think that not Nero, but Helius, whom he had appointed governor in his room, he being at this time in Greece, is here meant, before whom Paul was tried, and out of whose hands he was delivered.

(g) Joseph. Antiqu. l. 18. c. 7. sect. 10. (h) Apocryph.

"Give me eloquent speech in my mouth before the lion: turn his heart to hate him that fighteth against us, that there may be an end of him, and of all that are likeminded to him:" (Esther 14:13)

(i) Philostrat. Vit. Apollon. l. 4. c. 12.

18. And the Lord shall deliver me from every evil work, and will preserve me unto his heavenly kingdom: to whom be glory for ever and ever. Amen.

Greek/Transliteration
18. Καὶ ῥύσεταί με ὁ κύριος ἀπὸ παντὸς ἔργου πονηροῦ, καὶ σώσει εἰς τὴν βασιλείαν αὐτοῦ τὴν ἐπουράνιον· ᾧ ἡ δόξα εἰς τοὺς αἰῶνας τῶν αἰώνων. Ἀμήν.

18. Kai 'rusetai me 'o kurios apo pantos ergou poneirou, kai sosei eis tein basileian autou tein epouranion. 'o 'ei doxa eis tous aionas ton aionon. Amein.

Hebrew/Transliteration
יח. כֵּן יַצִּילֵנִי הָאָדוֹן מִכָּל-רָע וְיוֹשִׁיעֵנִי לָבוֹא אֶל-מַלְכוּת שָׁמַיִם וְלוֹ אָתֵן כָּבוֹד לְעוֹלָם וָעֶד אָמֵן:

18. Ken ya•tzi•le•ni ha•Adon mi•kol - ra ve•yo•shi•e•ni la•vo el - mal•choot sha•ma•yim ve•lo e•ten ka•vod le•o•lam va•ed Amen.

---

19. Salute Prisca and Aquila, and the household of Onesiphorus.

Greek/Transliteration
19. Ἄσπασαι Πρίσκαν καὶ Ἀκύλαν, καὶ τὸν Ὀνησιφόρου οἶκον.

19. Aspasai Priskan kai Akulan, kai ton Oneisiphorou oikon.

Hebrew/Transliteration
יט. שְׁאַל לִשְׁלוֹם פְּרִיסְקָה וַעֲקִילָס וּבֵית אֲנִיסִיפוֹרוֹס:

19. Sh`al lish•lom Pris•ka va•Akilas oo•veit Oni•si•foros.

---

20. Erastus abode at Corinth: but Trophimus have I left at Miletum sick.

Greek/Transliteration
20. Ἔραστος ἔμεινεν ἐν Κορίνθῳ· Τρόφιμον δὲ ἀπέλιπον ἐν Μιλήτῳ ἀσθενοῦντα.

20. Erastos emeinen en Korintho. Trophimon de apelipon en Mileito asthenounta.

Hebrew/Transliteration
כ. אֲרַסְטוֹס נִשְׁאַר בְּקוֹרִנְתּוֹס וְאֶת-טְרוֹפִימוֹס הִנַּחְתִּי בְּמִילְטוֹס כִּי חֹלֶה הוּא:

20. Aras•tos nish•ar be•Korintos ve•et - T`rofimos hi•nach•ti be•Mi•letos ki cho•le hoo.

---

21. Do thy diligence to come before winter. Eubulus greeteth thee, and Pudens, and Linus, and Claudia, and all the brethren.

Greek/Transliteration
21. Σπούδασον πρὸ χειμῶνος ἐλθεῖν. Ἀσπάζεταί σε Εὔβουλος, καὶ Πούδης, καὶ Λῖνος, καὶ Κλαυδία, καὶ οἱ ἀδελφοὶ πάντες.

21. Spoudason pro cheimonos elthein. Aspazetai se Euboulos, kai Poudeis, kai Linos, kai Klaudia, kai 'oi adelphoi pantes.

Hebrew/Transliteration
כא. מַהֵר נָבֹא אֵלַי לִפְנֵי יְמוֹת הַחֹרֶף אֶוְבוּלוֹס וּפוּדִיס וְלִינוֹס וּקְלוֹדְיָה וְכָל־אַחֵינוּ שֹׁאֲלִים לִשְׁלוֹמֶךָ:

21. Ma•her va•vo e•lai lif•ney ye•mot ha•cho•ref Ev•voo•los oo•Foodis ve•Linos oo•Klod•ya ve•chol - achey•noo sho•a•lim lish•lo•me•cha.

---

22. The Lord Jesus Christ be with thy spirit. Grace be with you. Amen.

Greek/Transliteration
22. Ὁ κύριος Ἰησοῦς χριστὸς μετὰ τοῦ πνεύματός σου. Ἡ χάρις μεθ' ὑμῶν. Ἀμήν.

22. 'O kurios Yeisous christos meta tou pneumatos sou. 'Ei charis meth 'umon. Amein.

Hebrew/Transliteration
כב. אֲדֹנֵינוּ יֵשׁוּעַ הַמָּשִׁיחַ עִם־רוּחֶךָ וְחַסְדּוֹ עִמָּכֶם אָמֵן:

22. Ado•ney•noo Yeshua ha•Ma•shi•ach eem - roo•che•cha ve•chas•do ee•ma•chem Amen.

---

^end^

THE EPISTLE OF PAUL TO TITUS

Titus, Chapter 1

1. Paul, a servant of God, and an apostle of Jesus Christ, according to the faith of God's elect, and the acknowledging of the truth which is after godliness;

Greek/Transliteration
1. Παῦλος, δοῦλος θεοῦ, ἀπόστολος δὲ Ἰησοῦ χριστοῦ, κατὰ πίστιν ἐκλεκτῶν θεοῦ καὶ ἐπίγνωσιν ἀληθείας τῆς κατ᾽ εὐσέβειαν,

1. Paulos, doulos theou, apostolos de Yeisou christou, kata pistin eklekton theou kai epignosin aleitheias teis kat eusebeyan,

Hebrew/Transliteration
א. פּוֹלוֹס עֶבֶד אֱלֹהִים וּשְׁלִיחַ יֵשׁוּעַ הַמָּשִׁיחַ כְּפִי אֱמוּנַת בְּחִירֵי אֱלֹהִים וּכְפִי-דַעַת הָאֱמֶת בְּיִרְאַת שָׁמַיִם:

1. Polos eved Elohim oosh•li•ach Yeshua ha•Ma•shi•ach ke•fi emoo•nat be•chi•rey Elohim ooch•fi - da•at ha•e•met be•yir•at sha•ma•yim.

---

2. In hope of eternal life, which God, that cannot lie, promised before the world began;

Greek/Transliteration
2. ἐπ᾽ ἐλπίδι ζωῆς αἰωνίου, ἣν ἐπηγγείλατο ὁ ἀψευδὴς θεὸς πρὸ χρόνων αἰωνίων,

2. ep elpidi zoeis aioniou, 'ein epeingeilato 'o apseudeis theos pro chronon aionion,

Hebrew/Transliteration
ב. בְּתִקְוַת חַיֵּי עוֹלָם אֲשֶׁר הִבְטִיחַ הָאֵל הַנֶּאֱמָן מֵרֹאשׁ מִקַּדְמֵי-אָרֶץ:

2. Be•tik•vat cha•yey o•lam asher hiv•ti•ach ha•El ha•ne•e•man me•rosh mi•kad•mey - a•retz.

---

3. But hath in due times manifested his word through preaching, which is committed unto me according to the commandment of God our Saviour;

Greek/Transliteration
3. ἐφανέρωσεν δὲ καιροῖς ἰδίοις τὸν λόγον αὐτοῦ ἐν κηρύγματι ὃ ἐπιστεύθην ἐγὼ κατ᾽ ἐπιταγὴν τοῦ σωτῆρος ἡμῶν θεοῦ,

3. ephanerosen de kairois idiois ton logon autou en keirugmati 'o episteuthein ego kat epitagein tou soteiros 'eimon theou,

Hebrew/Transliteration
ג. וְאֶת-דְּבָרוֹ גִלָּה בְעִתּוֹ עַל-פִּי קְרִיאַת הַבְּשׂוֹרָה הֲלֹא הִיא אֲשֶׁר מֻפְקְדָה בְיָדִי בִּפְקֻדַּת אֵל מוֹשִׁיעֵנוּ:

3. Ve•et - de•va•ro gila vei•to al - pi k`ri•at ha•be•so•ra ha•lo hee asher moof•ka•da ve•ya•di bif•koo•dat El Mo•shi•e•noo.

4. To Titus, mine own son after the common faith: Grace, mercy, and peace, from God the Father and the Lord Jesus Christ our Saviour.

Greek/Transliteration
4. Τίτῳ γνησίῳ τέκνῳ κατὰ κοινὴν πίστιν· χάρις, ἔλεος, εἰρήνη ἀπὸ θεοῦ πατρός, καὶ κυρίου Ἰησοῦ χριστοῦ τοῦ σωτῆρος ἡμῶν.

4. Tito gneisio tekno kata koinein pistin. charis, eleos, eireinei apo theou patros, kai kuriou Yeisou christou tou soteiros 'eimon.

Hebrew/Transliteration
ד. אֶל-טִיטוֹס בְּנִי כְּבֶן מֵחֲלָצַי בִּמְנַת חֵלֶק אֱמוּנָתֵנוּ חֶסֶד וְרַחֲמִים וְשָׁלוֹם לְךָ מֵאֵת הָאֱלֹהִים הָאָב וּמֵאֵת אֲדוֹנֵינוּ יֵשׁוּעַ הַמָּשִׁיחַ מוֹשִׁיעֵנוּ:

4. El - Titos b`ni ke•ven me•cha•la•tzai bim•nat che•lek emoo•na•te•noo che•sed ve•ra•cha•mim ve•sha•lom le•cha me•et ha•Elohim ha•Av oo•me•et Ado•ney•noo Yeshua ha•Ma•shi•ach Mo•shi•e•noo.

---

5. For this cause left I thee in Crete, that thou shouldest set in order the things that are wanting, and ordain elders in every city, as I had appointed thee:

Greek/Transliteration
5. Τούτου χάριν κατέλιπόν σε ἐν Κρήτῃ, ἵνα τὰ λείποντα ἐπιδιορθώσῃ, καὶ καταστήσῃς κατὰ πόλιν πρεσβυτέρους, ὡς ἐγώ σοι διεταξάμην·

5. Toutou charin katelipon se en Kreitei, 'ina ta leiponta epidiorthosei, kai katasteiseis kata polin presbuterous, 'os ego soi dietaxamein.

Hebrew/Transliteration
ה. בַּעֲבוּר זֹאת הִנַּחְתִּיךָ בִקְרֵיטִי לְמַלֹּאת כָּל-אֲשֶׁר יֶחְסַר שָׁם וּלְהָקִים זִקְנֵי הָעֵדָה בְּכָל-עִיר וָעִיר כַּאֲשֶׁר צִוִּיתִיךָ:

5. Ba•a•voor zot hi•nach•ti•cha bi•Krey•ti le•ma•lot kol - asher yech•sar sham ool•ha•kim zik•ney ha•e•da be•chol - eer va•eer ka•a•sher tzi•vi•ti•cha.

Rabbinic Jewish Commentary
and ordain elders in every city: for this island, though it was not above fifty miles in breadth, and two hundred and seventy in length, yet had an hundred cities in it (d); and it seems as if the Gospel had been preached in most, if not all of them, and churches were formed.

in the "second" century there were churches in this island, particularly at Gortyna, and other places, to whom Dionysius (e), bishop of Corinth, wrote letters, in which he greatly extols Philip their bishop; and in another letter of his to the Gnossians, or to the church at Gnossus, another city in Crete, he makes mention of Pinytus as their bishop, and whom he commends for his orthodox faith, great knowledge of divine things, and care of his flock; and both these lived in the times of the Emperors Antoninus Verus and Commodus (f); which churches, no doubt, continued in the "third" century, since in the "fourth" we read of bishops sent from Crete to the synod at Sardica: and in the "fifth" century, a bishop of Gortyna in Crete is reckoned among the bishops in the council of Chalcedon: and in the "sixth" century, Theodorus, bishop of the same place, subscribed in the fifth synod at Constantinople: and in the "seventh" century, Paul archbishop of Crete, Basil bishop of

Gortyna, with several other bishops of churches in the island, were present at the sixth synod at Constantinople: and in the "eighth" century, as appears from the acts of the Nicene synod, Helias was bishop of Crete, Anastasius bishop of Gnossus, a city in it, and Melito, Leontins, and Galatas, bishops of other places in the same island: and in the "ninth" century, a bishop of Gortyna, in defence of the cause of Christ, became a martyr (g); so far churches, and bishops, bearing the Christian name, are to be traced in this island.

(d) Plin. l. 4. c. 12. Mela, l. 2. c. 14. Solin, c. 16. (e) Apud Euseb. Eccl. Hist. l. 3. c. 24. (f) Sophronius in Hieron. Catalog. Script. Eccl. c. 38. 40. (g) Hist. Eccl. Magdeburg. cent. 4. c. 2. p. 5. c. 9. p. 425. cent. 5. c. 2. p. 6. cent. 6. c. 2. p. 6. cent. 7. c. 2. p. 4. c. 10. p. 255. cent. 8. c. 2. p. 6. cent. 9. c. 2. p. 4.

---

6. If any be blameless, the husband of one wife, having faithful children not accused of riot or unruly.

Greek/Transliteration
6. εἴ τίς ἐστιν ἀνέγκλητος, μιᾶς γυναικὸς ἀνήρ, τέκνα ἔχων πιστά, μὴ ἐν κατηγορίᾳ ἀσωτίας ἢ ἀνυπότακτα.

6. ei tis estin anegkleitos, myas gunaikos aneir, tekna echon pista, mei en kateigoria asotias ei anupotakta.

Hebrew/Transliteration
ו. כִּי-יִהְיֶה אִישׁ נָקִי וְאֵין-בּוֹ שֶׁמֶץ דָּבָר בַּעַל-אִשָּׁה אַחַת וּבָנָיו מַאֲמִינִים וְאֵין דִּבָתָם רָעָה כִּי בְנֵי בְלִיַּעַל הֵם אוֹ בְנֵי-מֶרִי:

6. Ki - yi•hee•ye eesh na•ki ve•eyn - bo she•metz da•var ba•al - ee•sha a•chat oo•va•nav ma•a•mi•nim ve•eyn di•ba•tam ra•ah ki v`ney ve•li•ya•al hem oh v`ney - me•ri.

---

7. For a bishop must be blameless, as the steward of God; not selfwilled, not soon angry, not given to wine, no striker, not given to filthy lucre;

Greek/Transliteration
7. Δεῖ γὰρ τὸν ἐπίσκοπον ἀνέγκλητον εἶναι, ὡς θεοῦ οἰκονόμον· μὴ αὐθάδη, μὴ ὀργίλον, μὴ πάροινον, μὴ πλήκτην, μὴ αἰσχροκερδῆ,

7. Dei gar ton episkopon anegkleiton einai, 'os theou oikonomon. mei authadei, mei orgilon, mei paroinon, mei pleiktein, mei aischrokerdei,

Hebrew/Transliteration
ז. כִּי עַל-רֹאשׁ הָעֵדָה לִהְיוֹת נָקִי מִכָּל-שֶׁמֶץ דָּבָר כְּבֶן-מֶשֶׁק בֵּית-אֱלֹהִים לֹא עֹשֶׂה כִרְצוֹן עַצְמוֹ לֹא אִישׁ חֵמָה לֹא סֹבֵא יַיִן לֹא בַּעַל מַהֲלֻמּוֹת וַאֲשֶׁר לֹא נָשָׂא לְבֶצַע נִבְזֶה נַפְשׁוֹ:

7. Ki al - rosh ha•e•da li•hee•yot na•ki mi•kol - she•metz da•var ke•ven - me•shek beit - Elohim lo o•se chir•tzon atz•mo lo eesh che•ma lo so•ve ya•yin lo va•al ma•ha•loo•mot va•a•sher lo na•sa le•ve•tza niv•ze naf•sho.

Rabbinic Jewish Commentary
It is a saying of R. Hillell (h), that

"Neither one that is ashamed (to ask questions) learns well, nor one that is "angry" teaches well"

And the Jews say (i), that

"The Torah is not rightly explained but by one that is not angry."

Hence, that direction (k),

"For ever let a man be meek as Hillell, and not angry as Shammai;"

Who were two of their principal Rabbis, the heads of their schools, in the times of Yeshua: a man that rules his own spirit, and has the command of his temper and passions, is fit to govern in the assembly of God.

(h) Pirke Abot, c. 2. sect. 5. (i) Buxtorf. Lex. Talmud. col. 2026. (k) T. Bab. Sabbat, fol. 30. 2.

---

8. But a lover of hospitality, a lover of good men, sober, just, holy, temperate;

Greek/Transliteration
8. ἀλλὰ φιλόξενον, φιλάγαθον, σώφρονα, δίκαιον, ὅσιον, ἐγκρατῆ,

8. alla philoxenon, philagathon, sophrona, dikaion, 'osion, egkratei,

Hebrew/Transliteration
ח: כִּי אִם-פֹּתֵחַ דְּלָתָיו לָאֹרֵחַ וְאֹהֵב כָּל-טוֹב הַשָּׂם עֵינוֹ עַל-דְּרָכָיו צַדִּיק וְקָדוֹשׁ וְכֹבֵשׁ אֶת-יִצְרוֹ.

8. Ki eem - po•teach de•la•tav la•o•re•ach ve•o•hev kol - toov ha•sam ey•no al - de•ra•chav tza•dik ve•ka•dosh ve•cho•vesh et - yitz•ro.

Rabbinic Jewish Commentary
a lover of good men, or "of good"; the Syriac version renders it, "of good things".

---

9. Holding fast the faithful word as he hath been taught, that he may be able by sound doctrine both to exhort and to convince the gainsayers.

Greek/Transliteration
9. ἀντεχόμενον τοῦ κατὰ τὴν διδαχὴν πιστοῦ λόγου, ἵνα δυνατὸς ᾖ καὶ παρακαλεῖν ἐν τῇ διδασκαλίᾳ τῇ ὑγιαινούσῃ, καὶ τοὺς ἀντιλέγοντας ἐλέγχειν.

9. antechomenon tou kata tein didachein pistou logou, 'ina dunatos ei kai parakalein en tei didaskalia tei 'ugyainousei, kai tous antilegontas elegchein.

Hebrew/Transliteration
ט: וּמַחֲזִיק בִּדְבַר אֱמֶת לְפִי הַתּוֹרָה וּבְכֵן יָדָיו רַב-לוֹ בְּתוֹרַת חַיִּים גַּם-לְהַזְהִיר וְגַם לְהוֹכִיחַ אֶת-הַקָּמִים עָלֵינוּ.

9. Oo•ma•cha•zik bid•var emet le•fi ha•Torah oov•chen ya•dav rav - lo be•to•rat cha•yim gam - le•haz•hir ve•gam le•ho•chi•ach et - ha•ka•mim aley•noo.

---

10. For there are many unruly and vain talkers and deceivers, specially they of the circumcision:

Greek/Transliteration

10. Εἰσὶν γὰρ πολλοὶ καὶ ἀνυπότακτοι, ματαιολόγοι καὶ φρεναπάται, μάλιστα οἱ ἐκ περιτομῆς,

10. Eisin gar polloi kai anupotaktoi, mataiologoi kai phrenapatai, malista 'oi ek peritomeis,

Hebrew/Transliteration

י. כִּי-רַבִּים הֵם הַמֹּאֲנִים לִשְׁמֹעַ וְהֶטֶף יַטִּיפוּן מַשָּׂאוֹת שָׁוְא וּמַדּוּחִים וְעַל-יֶתֶר מִבְּנֵי הַנִּמּוֹלִים:

10. Ki - ra•bim hem ha•me•a•nim lish•mo•a ve•ha•tef ya•ti•foon mas•ot shav oo•ma•doo•chim ve•al - ye•ter mi•b`ney ha•ni•mo•lim.

---

11. Whose mouths must be stopped, who subvert whole houses, teaching things which they ought not, for filthy lucre's sake.

Greek/Transliteration

11. οὓς δεῖ ἐπιστομίζειν· οἵτινες ὅλους οἴκους ἀνατρέπουσιν, διδάσκοντες ἃ μὴ δεῖ, αἰσχροῦ κέρδους χάριν.

11. 'ous dei epistomizein. 'oitines 'olous oikous anatrepousin, didaskontes 'a mei dei, aischrou kerdous charin.

Hebrew/Transliteration

יא. אֲשֶׁר הִסָּכֵר יִסָּכֵר פִּיהֶם כִּי הֵם הַהֹפְכִים בָּתִּים שְׁלֵמִים וּדְבָרִים יְלַמְּדוּן אֲשֶׁר לֹא כַדָּת עֵקֶב בֶּצַע נִבְזֶה:

11. Asher hi•sa•cher yi•sa•cher pi•hem ki hem ha•hof•chim ba•tim sh`le•mim ood•va•rim ye•lam•doon asher lo cha•dat e•kev be•tza niv•ze.

---

12. One of themselves, even a prophet of their own, said, The Cretians are always liars, evil beasts, slow bellies.

Greek/Transliteration

12. Εἶπέν τις ἐξ αὐτῶν, ἴδιος αὐτῶν προφήτης, Κρῆτες ἀεὶ ψεῦσται, κακὰ θηρία, γαστέρες ἀργαί.

12. Eipen tis ex auton, idios auton propheiteis, Kreites aei pseustai, kaka theiria, gasteres argai.

Hebrew/Transliteration

יב. וּכְבָר אָמַר אֶחָד מֵהֶם וְהוּא נָבִיא מִקִּרְבָּם הַקְּרֵטִים אַנְשֵׁי כָזָב הֵם מֵעוֹלָם דְּמִינָם כְּחַיְתוֹ יַעַר וּבִטְנָם בֶּטֶן עֲצֵלוּת:

12. Ooch•var amar e•chad me•hem ve•hoo na•vi mi•kir•bam ha•K`re•tim an•shey cha•zav hem me•o•lam dim•yo•nam ke•chay•to ya•ar oo•vit•nam be•ten atz•loot.

Rabbinic Jewish Commentary

This was Epimenides, in whose poems stand the words here cited; the apostle rightly calls him "one of themselves", since he was a Cretian by birth, of the city of Gnossus; it is reported of him, that being sent by his father to his sheep in the field, he by the way, at noon, turned aside into a cave, and slept fifty seven years (m) and he is very properly called a "prophet" of their own; for in Crete Jupiter had his prophets (n), and he might be one of them: the priests among the Heathens were called prophets; so Baal's priests are called the prophets of Baal, and the prophets of the groves, 1Ki_18:19. Besides, Epimenides was thought to be inspired by the gods: he is called by Apuleius (o), a famous fortune teller; and is said by Laertius (p) to be very skilful in divination, and to have foretold many things which came to pass; and by the Grecians were supposed to be very dear to the gods; so Balaam, the soothsayer and diviner, is called a prophet, 2Pe_2:16. Add to this, that the passage next cited stands in a poem of this writer, entitled, "Concerning Oracles"; and it is easy to observe, that poets in common were usually called "vates", or prophets; so that the apostle speaks here with great propriety.

said, the Cretians are always liars: living is a sin common to human nature, and appears in men as early, or earlier than any other; and all men are guilty of it, at one time or another; but all are not habitually liars, as it seems these Cretians were: lying was a governing vice among them; they were not only guilty of it in some particular instances, but always; not only for saying that Jupiter's sepulchre was with them, when it was the sepulchre of Minos his son, which they had fraudulently obliterated; and for which (q) Callimachus charges them with lying, and uses these very words of Epimenides; though he assigns a different reason from that now given, which is, that Jupiter died not, but always exists, and therefore his sepulchre could not be with them: but this single instance was not sufficient to fasten such a character upon them; it was a sin they were addicted to: some countries are distinguished by their vices; some for pride; some for levity, vanity, and inconstancy; some for boasting and bragging some for covetousness; some for idleness; some for effeminacy; some for hypocrisy and deceit; and others, as the Cretians, it seems, for lying; this was their national sin (r); and this is said by others, as well as Epimenides. Crete is, by Ovid (s), called "mendax Creta", lying Crete. Hence, with the Grecians, to "cretize", is proverbially used for to lie; this is a sin, than which nothing makes a man more like the devil, or more infamous among men, or more abominable to God. The Ethiopic version, instead of Cretes, or Cretians, reads "hypocrites".

evil beasts: slow bellies; by evil beasts are meant beasts of prey, savage and mischievous ones; see Gen_37:20 and are so called, to distinguish them from other beasts, as sheep, and the like, which are not so; and perhaps Crete might abound with such evil beasts; for the Cretians are said (t) to excel in hunting; and to these they themselves are compared, by one of their own prophets, for their cruelty, and savage disposition: so cruel persecutors are compared to beasts, 1Co_15:30 and the false teachers, the apostle has respect to in citing this passage, were cruel, if not to the bodies, yet to the souls of men, whom they poisoned and destroyed. And the Cretians are called, by the poet, slow bellies partly for their intemperance, their gluttony and drunkenness: which suited with the false teachers, whose god was their belly, and which they served, and not the Lord Jesus; and partly for their sloth and idleness, eating the bread of others without working.

(m) Laert. l. 1. Vita Epimenidis. (n) Alex. ab Alex. Genial. Dier, l. 4. c. 17. (o) Florida, sect. 15. (p) Ib. (q) Hymn. l. in Jovem, v. 8. (r) Alex. ab Alex. l. 4. c. 13. (s) De Arte Amandi, l. 1. (t) Alex. ab Alex. ib.

13. This witness is true. Wherefore rebuke them sharply, that they may be sound in the faith;

Greek/Transliteration
13. Ἡ μαρτυρία αὕτη ἐστὶν ἀληθής. Δι᾽ ἣν αἰτίαν ἔλεγχε αὐτοὺς ἀποτόμως, ἵνα ὑγιαίνωσιν ἐν τῇ πίστει,

13. 'Ei marturia 'autei estin aleitheis. Di 'ein aitian elegche autous apotomos, 'ina 'ugyainosin en tei pistei,

Hebrew/Transliteration
:יג. הָעֵדוּת הַזֹּאת עֵדוּת אֱמֶת וְעַל-כֵּן הוֹכֵחַ תּוֹכִיחַ אֹתָם תּוֹכֵחָה נִמְרָצָה לְמַעַן יַחֲלִיפוּ כֹחַ בָּאֱמוּנָה

13. Ha•e•doot ha•zot e•doot emet ve•al - ken ho•che•ach to•chi•ach o•tam to•che•cha nim•ra•tza le•ma•an ya•cha•li•foo cho•ach ba•e•moo•na.

---

14. Not giving heed to Jewish fables, and commandments of men, that turn from the truth.

Greek/Transliteration
14. μὴ προσέχοντες Ἰουδαϊκοῖς μύθοις, καὶ ἐντολαῖς ἀνθρώπων ἀποστρεφομένων τὴν ἀλήθειαν.

14. mei prosechontes Youdaikois muthois, kai entolais anthropon apostrephomenon tein aleitheyan.

Hebrew/Transliteration
:יד. וְלֹא יָשִׂימוּ עוֹד לֵב אֶל-אַגָּדוֹת הַיְּהוּדִים וְאֶל-מִצְוֹת אֲנָשִׁים אֲשֶׁר יַסְתִּירוּ פָנִים מִן-הָאֱמֶת

14. Ve•lo ya•si•moo od lev el - aga•dot ha•Ye•hoo•dim ve•el - mitz•vot a•na•shim asher yas•ti•roo fa•nim min - ha•e•met.

---

15. Unto the pure all things are pure: but unto them that are defiled and unbelieving is nothing pure; but even their mind and conscience is defiled.

Greek/Transliteration
15. Πάντα μὲν καθαρὰ τοῖς καθαροῖς· τοῖς δὲ μεμιασμένοις καὶ ἀπίστοις οὐδὲν καθαρόν· ἀλλὰ μεμίανται αὐτῶν καὶ ὁ νοῦς καὶ ἡ συνείδησις.

15. Panta men kathara tois katharois. tois de memyasmenois kai apistois ouden katharon; alla memiantai auton kai 'o nous kai 'ei suneideisis.

Hebrew/Transliteration
:טו. הַכֹּל טָהוֹר לַטְּהוֹרִים אַךְ לַטְּמֵאִים וְלִבְנֵי בְלִי-אֱמוּנָה אֵין טָהוֹר מְאוּמָה כִּי גַם-לִבָּם וְדַעְתָּם טְמֵאָתָם בָּם

15. Ha•kol ta•hor la•t`ho•rim ach lit•me•eem ve•liv•ney v•li - e•moo•na eyn ta•hor me•oo•ma ki gam - li•bam ve•da•a•tam tim•a•tam bam.

Rabbinic Jewish Commentary

There were some things among the Jews, which were prohibited to them that were defiled, and were free to them that were pure: thus, for instance (u),

"The flesh of the most holy things, and the flesh of those which are lightly holy, boiled with flesh of delight, (or common flesh,) are forbidden לטמאים, "to the defiled", but are free לטהורים, "to the pure"."

Which one of their commentators (w) thus explains;

"The flesh of the most holy things is forbidden to strangers, though pure; the flesh of things lightly holy is free to strangers that are pure, but forbidden to them that are defiled."

Whether there may be any allusion to this, may be considered: however, the reason the apostle gives why nothing is pure to the impure, is, because of the pollution of the superior powers and faculties of their soul.

(u) Minn. Orla, c. 2. sect. 17. (w) Bartenora, in Misn. Orla, c. 2. sect. 17.

---

16. They profess that they know God; but in works they deny him, being abominable, and disobedient, and unto every good work reprobate.

Greek/Transliteration
16. Θεὸν ὁμολογοῦσιν εἰδέναι, τοῖς δὲ ἔργοις ἀρνοῦνται, βδελυκτοὶ ὄντες καὶ ἀπειθεῖς καὶ πρὸς πᾶν ἔργον ἀγαθὸν ἀδόκιμοι.

16. Theon 'omologousin eidenai, tois de ergois arnountai, bdeluktoi ontes kai apeitheis kai pros pan ergon agathon adokimoi.

Hebrew/Transliteration
-טז. בְּפִיהֶם יַגִּידוּ כִּי-דַעַת אֱלֹהִים אִתָּם וּבְמַעֲשֵׂיהֶם יְכַזְּבוּ-לוֹ כִּי נִתְעָבִים הֵם וְלֹא אֵמֻן בָּם וְלֹא-יִצְלְחוּ לְכָל מַעֲשֶׂה טוֹב:

16. Be•fi•hem ya•gi•doo ki - da•at Elohim ee•tam oov•ma•a•sey•hem ye•chaz•voo - lo ki nit•a•vim hem ve•lo emoon bam ve•lo - yitz•le•choo le•chol - ma•a•se tov.

Rabbinic Jewish Commentary
but in works they deny him. The Syriac, Arabic, and Ethiopic versions read, "in their own works".

And unto every good work reprobate: or "unaccustomed", unused to them, as the Arabic version renders it; or rather "without judgment", and understanding, concerning them; there was no good in them, nor was it in them to do good; to do good they had no knowledge, nor any inclination.

Titus, Chapter 2

1. But speak thou the things which become sound doctrine:

Greek/Transliteration
1. Σὺ δὲ λάλει ἃ πρέπει τῇ ὑγιαινούσῃ διδασκαλίᾳ·

1. Su de lalei 'a prepei tei 'ugyainousei didaskalia.

Hebrew/Transliteration
א. וְאַתָּה תְּדַבֵּר דְּבָרֶיךָ כְּדָת תּוֹרַת חַיִּים:

1. Ve•a•ta te•da•ber d`va•re•cha ke•dat to•rat cha•yim.

---

2. That the aged men be sober, grave, temperate, sound in faith, in charity, in patience.

Greek/Transliteration
2. πρεσβύτας νηφαλέους εἶναι, σεμνούς, σώφρονας, ὑγιαίνοντας τῇ πίστει, τῇ ἀγάπῃ, τῇ ὑπομονῇ·

2. presbutas neiphaleous einai, semnous, sophronas, 'ugyainontas tei pistei, tei agapei, tei 'upomonei.

Hebrew/Transliteration
ב. דַּבֵּר אֶל-הַזְּקֵנִים כִּי יִפְקְחוּ עַיִן עַל-דַּרְכֵיהֶם לִהְיוֹת כְּבוּדִים מְאֻשָּׁרִים וּשְׁלֵמִים בֶּאֱמוּנָה בְּאַהֲבָה וּבְסַבְלָנוּת:

2. Da•ber el - haz`ke•nim ki yif•ke•choo a•yin al - dar•chey•hem li•hee•yot k`voo•dim me•oo•sha•rim oosh•le•mim ba•e•moo•na be•a•ha•va oo•va•sav•la•noot.

---

3. The aged women likewise, that they be in behaviour as becometh holiness, not false accusers, not given to much wine, teachers of good things;

Greek/Transliteration
3. πρεσβύτιδας ὡσαύτως ἐν καταστήματι ἱεροπρεπεῖς, μὴ διαβόλους, μὴ οἴνῳ πολλῷ δεδουλωμένας, καλοδιδασκάλους,

3. presbutidas 'osautos en katasteimati 'ieroprepeis, mei dyabolous, mei oino pollo dedoulomenas, kalodidaskalous,

Hebrew/Transliteration
ג. וְכֵן גַּם-אֶל-הַזְּקֵנוֹת לְפַלֵּס הֲלִיכוֹתֵיהֶן כְּמִשְׁפָּט לַהֲלִיכוֹת נָשִׁים בַּקֹּדֶשׁ לֹא לְהַלְשִׁין בִּלְשׁוֹנָן וְלֹא לִמְשׁוֹךְ בַּיַּיִן אֶת-בְּשָׂרָן כִּי אִם-לְהוֹרוֹת אֹרַח טוֹב:

3. Ve•chen gam - el - haz`ke•not le•fa•les ha•li•cho•tey•hen ke•mish•pat la•ha•li•chot na•shim ba•ko•desh lo le•hal•shin bil•sho•nan ve•lo lim•shoch ba•ya•yin et - be•sa•ran ki eem - le•ho•rot o•rach tov.

4. That they may teach the young women to be sober, to love their husbands, to love their children,

Greek/Transliteration
4. ἵνα σωφρονίζωσιν τὰς νέας φιλάνδρους εἶναι, φιλοτέκνους,

4. 'ina sophronizosin tas neas philandrous einai, philoteknous,

Hebrew/Transliteration
ד. לְאַשֵּׁר אֶת-הַנָּשִׁים הַצְעִירוֹת לְאַהֲבָה אֶת-בַּעֲלֵיהֶן וְאֶת-בְּנֵיהֶן:

4. Le•a•sher et - ha•na•shim hatz•ee•rot le•a•ha•va et - ba•a•ley•hen ve•et - be•ney•hen.

---

5. To be discreet, chaste, keepers at home, good, obedient to their own husbands, that the word of God be not blasphemed.

Greek/Transliteration
5. σώφρονας, ἁγνάς, οἰκουρούς, ἀγαθάς, ὑποτασσομένας τοῖς ἰδίοις ἀνδράσιν, ἵνα μὴ ὁ λόγος τοῦ θεοῦ βλασφημῆται·

5. sophronas, 'agnas, oikourous, agathas, 'upotassomenas tois idiois andrasin, 'ina mei 'o logos tou theou blaspheimeitai.

Hebrew/Transliteration
ה. לְהִצָּנֵעַ לֶכֶת לִזְכוֹת אֶת-אָרְחָן וְלַעֲשׂוֹת מְלַאכְתָּן בְּבֵיתָן וְלִהְיוֹת טוֹבוֹת וְנִכְנָעוֹת תַּחַת יְדֵי בַעֲלֵיהֶן לְבִלְתִּי יִנָּתֵן דְּבַר הָאֱלֹהִים לְגִדּוּפִים:

5. Le•hatz•na le•chet le•za•kot et - or•chan ve•la•a•sot me•lach•tan be•vey•tan ool•hi•yot to•vot ve•nich•na•ot ta•chat ye•dey va•a•ley•hen le•vil•ti yi•na•ten de•var ha•Elohim le•gi•doo•fim.

Rabbinic Jewish Commentary
This is said in opposition to what women are prone unto. It is reckoned among the properties of women, by the Jews, that they are יוצאניות, "gadders abroad" (x): they have some rules about women's keeping at home; they say (y),

"A woman may go to her father's house to visit him, and to the house of mourning, and to the house of feasting, to return a kindness to her friends, or to her near relations--but it is a reproach to a woman to go out daily; now she is without, now she is in the streets; and a husband ought to restrain his wife from it, and not suffer her to go abroad but about once a month, or twice a month, upon necessity; for there is nothing more beautiful for a woman, than to abide in the corner of her house; for so it is written, Psa_45:13 "the king's daughter is all glorious within".

And this they say (z) is what is meant by the woman's being an helpmeet for man, that while he is abroad about his business, she is יושבת בבית, "sitting at home", and keeping his house; and this they observe is the glory and honour of the woman. The passage in Isa_44:13 concerning an image being made "after the figure of a man, according to the beauty of a man, that it may remain in the house" is by the Targum thus paraphrased:

"According to the likeness of a man, according to the praise of a woman, to abide in the house."

Upon which Kimchi, has this note.

"It is the glory of a woman to continue at home, and not go abroad."

The tortoise, which carries its house upon its back, and very rarely shows its head, or looks out of it, was, with the ancients, an emblem of a good housewife. These also should be instructed to be "good" or "kind" to their servants, and beneficent to the poor, and to strangers, towards whom, very often, women are apt to be strait handed, and not so generous and liberal as they should be.

(x) Bereshit Rabba, sect. 45. fol. 40. 3. (y) Maimon. Hilchot Ishot, c. 13. sect. 11. (z) Tzeror Hammor, fol. 5. 4.

---

6. Young men likewise exhort to be sober minded.

Greek/Transliteration
6. τοὺς νεωτέρους ὡσαύτως παρακάλει σωφρονεῖν·

6. tous neoterous 'osautos parakalei sophronein.

Hebrew/Transliteration
ו. וְגַם עַל-הָאֲנָשִׁים הַצְּעִירִים תְּצַוֶּה לֵאמֹר כִּי יְיַשְׁרוּן אָרְחוֹתָם:

6. Ve•gam al - ha•a•na•shim hatz•ee•rim te•tza•ve le•mor ki ye•yash•roon or•cho•tam.

---

7. In all things shewing thyself a pattern of good works: in doctrine shewing uncorruptness, gravity, sincerity,

Greek/Transliteration
7. περὶ πάντα σεαυτὸν παρεχόμενος τύπον καλῶν ἔργων, ἐν τῇ διδασκαλίᾳ ἀδιαφθορίαν, σεμνότητα, ἀφθαρσίαν,

7. peri panta seauton parechomenos tupon kalon ergon, en tei didaskalia adyaphthorian, semnoteita, aphtharsian,

Hebrew/Transliteration
ז. וְאַתָּה בְּנַפְשְׁךָ הֱיֵה תָמִיד לְמוֹפֵת לָהֶם בְּמַעֲשֶׂיךָ הַטּוֹבִים וּבַאֲמָרִים נְכֹחִים וִיקָרִים אֲשֶׁר אֵין בָּהֶם נִפְתָּל וְעִקֵּשׁ:

7. Ve•a•ta be•naf•she•cha he•ye ta•mid le•mo•fet la•hem be•ma•a•se•cha ha•to•vim oo•va•a•ma•rim n`cho•chim viy•ka•rim asher eyn ba•hem nif•tal vei•kesh.

8. Sound speech, that cannot be condemned; that he that is of the contrary part may be ashamed, having no evil thing to say of you.

Greek/Transliteration
8. λόγον ὑγιῆ, ἀκατάγνωστον, ἵνα ὁ ἐξ ἐναντίας ἐντραπῇ, μηδὲν ἔχων περὶ ἡμῶν λέγειν φαῦλον.

8. logon 'ugiei, akatagnoston, 'ina 'o ex enantias entrapei, meiden echon peri 'eimon legein phaulon.

Hebrew/Transliteration
ח. וּבְלָקַח טוֹב אֲשֶׁר מִשְׁחָת אֵין-בּוֹ עַד אֲשֶׁר צָרֶיךָ יִלְבְּשׁוּ-בֹשֶׁת וְלֹא יִמְצְאוּ לְדַבֵּר עָלֵינוּ סָרָה:

8. Oov•le•kach tov asher mosh•chat eyn - bo ad asher tza•re•cha yil•be•shoo - vo•shet ve•lo yim•tze•oo le•da•ber aley•noo sa•ra.

---

9. Exhort servants to be obedient unto their own masters, and to please them well in all things; not answering again;

Greek/Transliteration
9. Δούλους ἰδίοις δεσπόταις ὑποτάσσεσθαι, ἐν πᾶσιν εὐαρέστους εἶναι, μὴ ἀντιλέγοντας,

9. Doulous idiois despotais 'upotassesthai, en pasin euarestous einai, mei antilegontas,

Hebrew/Transliteration
ט. וְעַל-הָעֲבָדִים תְּצַוֶּה כִּי-יִכָּנְעוּ תַּחַת יְדֵי אֲדֹנֵיהֶם וְלִהְיוֹת לָהֶם לְרָצוֹן תָּמִיד וְלֹא לְהָשִׁיב דָּבָר לַמְרוֹת עֵינֵיהֶם:

9. Ve•al - ha•a•va•dim te•tza•ve ki - yi•kan•oo ta•chat ye•dey ado•ney•hem ve•li•hi•yot la•hem le•ra•tzon ta•mid ve•lo le•ha•shiv da•var lam•rot ey•ne•hem.

---

10. Not purloining, but shewing all good fidelity; that they may adorn the doctrine of God our Saviour in all things.

Greek/Transliteration
10. μὴ νοσφιζομένους, ἀλλὰ πίστιν πᾶσαν ἐνδεικνυμένους ἀγαθήν, ἵνα τὴν διδασκαλίαν τοῦ σωτῆρος ἡμῶν θεοῦ κοσμῶσιν ἐν πᾶσιν.

10. mei nosphizomenous, alla pistin pasan endeiknumenous agathein, 'ina tein didaskalian tou soteiros 'eimon theou kosmosin en pasin.

Hebrew/Transliteration
י. וְלֹא לִגְנֹב כִּי אִם-לְהֵרָאוֹת בְּמַעֲשֵׂיהֶם כִּי רוּחָם נֶאֱמָנָה וּבְזֹאת יְפָאֲרוּ בַכֹּל אֶת-תּוֹרַת אֱלֹהֵינוּ הַמּוֹשִׁיעַ לָנוּ:

10. Ve•lo lig•nov ki eem - le•har•ot be•ma•a•sey•hem ki roo•cham ne•e•ma•na oov•zot ye•fa•a•roo va•kol et - to•rat Elohey•noo ha•Mo•shia la•noo.

11. For the grace of God that bringeth salvation hath appeared to all men,

Greek/Transliteration
11. Ἐπεφάνη γὰρ ἡ χάρις τοῦ θεοῦ ἡ σωτήριος πᾶσιν ἀνθρώποις,

11. Epephanei gar 'ei charis tou theou 'ei soteirios pasin anthropois,

Hebrew/Transliteration
יא. כִּי חֶסֶד אֱלֹהִים זָרַח כַּשַּׁחַר לְיֵשַׁע בְּנֵי הָאָדָם כֻּלָּם:

11. Ki che•sed Elohim za•rach ka•sha•char le•ye•sha b`ney ha•a•dam koo•lam.

Rabbinic Jewish Commentary
Some read this clause thus, "that bringeth salvation to all men"; to which agrees the Syriac version, which renders it, מחית כל, "that quickeneth" or "saveth all"; and so the Arabic version.

---

12. Teaching us that, denying ungodliness and worldly lusts, we should live soberly, righteously, and godly, in this present world;

Greek/Transliteration
12. παιδεύουσα ἡμᾶς ἵνα, ἀρνησάμενοι τὴν ἀσέβειαν καὶ τὰς κοσμικὰς ἐπιθυμίας, σωφρόνως καὶ δικαίως καὶ εὐσεβῶς ζήσωμεν ἐν τῷ νῦν αἰῶνι,

12. paideuousa 'eimas 'ina, arneisamenoi tein asebeyan kai tas kosmikas epithumias, sophronos kai dikaios kai eusebos zeisomen en to nun aioni,

Hebrew/Transliteration
יב. וּלְהוֹרֹת לָנוּ לְהִבָּדֵל מִכָּל-רָע וּמִתַּאֲוֹת חַיֵּי בְשָׂרִים וְלָגוּר בָּאָרֶץ הַלֵּזוּ בְּהַשְׂכֵּל וּבְמֵישָׁרִים וּבְיִרְאַת שָׁמָיִם:

12. Ool•ho•rot la•noo le•hi•ba•del mi•kol - ra oo•mi•ta•a•vot cha•yey ve•sa•rim ve•la•goor ba•a•retz ha•le•zoo be•has•kel oov•mey•sha•rim oov•yir•at sha•ma•yim.

---

13. Looking for that blessed hope, and the glorious appearing of the great God and our Saviour Jesus Christ;

Greek/Transliteration
13. προσδεχόμενοι τὴν μακαρίαν ἐλπίδα καὶ ἐπιφάνειαν τῆς δόξης τοῦ μεγάλου θεοῦ καὶ σωτῆρος ἡμῶν Ἰησοῦ χριστοῦ,

13. prosdechomenoi tein makarian elpida kai epiphaneyan teis doxeis tou megalou theou kai soteiros 'eimon Yeisou christou,

Hebrew/Transliteration
יג. וְעֵינֵינוּ נְשׂוּאוֹת אֶל-הַתִּקְוָה הַטּוֹבָה לְעֵת יִגָּלֶה כְבוֹד הָאֱלֹהִים הַגָּדוֹל וְיֵשׁוּעַ הַמָּשִׁיחַ מוֹשִׁיעֵינוּ:

13. Ve•ey•ney•noo n`soo•ot el - ha•tik•va ha•to•va le•et yi•ga•le che•vod ha•Elohim ha•ga•dol ve•Yeshua ha•Ma•shi•ach Mo•shi•ey•noo.

Rabbinic Jewish Commentary
and the glorious appearing of the great God, and our Saviour Jesus Christ; not two divine persons, only one, are here intended; for the word: rendered "appearing", is never used of God the Father, only of the second person; and the propositive article is not set before the word "Saviour", as it would, if two distinct persons were designed; and the copulative "and" is exegetical, and should be rendered thus, "and the glorious appearing of our great God and Saviour, Jesus Christ".

---

14. Who gave himself for us, that he might redeem us from all iniquity, and purify unto himself a peculiar people, zealous of good works.

Greek/Transliteration
14. ὃς ἔδωκεν ἑαυτὸν ὑπὲρ ἡμῶν, ἵνα λυτρώσηται ἡμᾶς ἀπὸ πάσης ἀνομίας, καὶ καθαρίσῃ ἑαυτῷ λαὸν περιούσιον, ζηλωτὴν καλῶν ἔργων.

14. 'os edoken 'eauton 'uper 'eimon, 'ina lutroseitai 'eimas apo paseis anomias, kai katharisei 'eauto laon periousion, zeilotein kalon ergon.

Hebrew/Transliteration
יד. אֲשֶׁר נָתַן אֶת-נַפְשׁוֹ בַּעֲדֵנוּ לְהַצִּיל אֹתָנוּ מִכָּל-עָוֹן וּלְטַהֵר אֶת-נַפְשֵׁנוּ לִהְיוֹת לוֹ לְעַם סְגֻלָּה מְלֵאֵי קִנְאָה לְמַעֲשִׂים טוֹבִים:

14. Asher na•tan et - naf•sho ba•a•de•noo le•ha•tzil o•ta•noo mi•kol - a•von ool•ta•her et - naf•she•noo li•hee•yot lo le•am se•goo•la me•le•ey kin•ah le•ma•a•sim to•vim.

---

15. These things speak, and exhort, and rebuke with all authority. Let no man despise thee.

Greek/Transliteration
15. Ταῦτα λάλει, καὶ παρακάλει, καὶ ἔλεγχε μετὰ πάσης ἐπιταγῆς. Μηδείς σου περιφρονείτω.

15. Tauta lalei, kai parakalei, kai elegche meta paseis epitageis. Meideis sou periphroneito.

Hebrew/Transliteration
טו. כַּדְּבָרִים הָאֵלֶּה תְּדַבֵּר וְתַזְהִיר בְּכָל-תֹּקֶף וְאִישׁ אַל-יָבוּז לָךְ:

15. Ka•d'va•rim ha•e•le te•da•ber ve•taz•hir be•chol - to•kef ve•eesh al - ya•vooz lach.

Titus, Chapter 3

1. Put them in mind to be subject to principalities and powers, to obey magistrates, to be ready to every good work,

Greek/Transliteration
1. Ὑπομίμνησκε αὐτοὺς ἀρχαῖς καὶ ἐξουσίαις ὑποτάσσεσθαι, πειθαρχεῖν, πρὸς πᾶν ἔργον ἀγαθὸν ἑτοίμους εἶναι,

1. 'Upomimneiske autous archais kai exousiais 'upotassesthai, peitharchein, pros pan ergon agathon 'etoimous einai,

Hebrew/Transliteration
א. צַו עֲלֵיהֶם לִזְכֹּר לִהְיוֹת נִכְנָעִים תַּחַת יְדֵי מֹשְׁלֵיהֶם וְשָׂרֵיהֶם לִשְׁמֹעַ בְּקוֹלָם וְלִהְיוֹת נְכוֹנִים לְכָל־פֹּעַל טוֹב:

1. Tzav aley•hem liz•kor li•hee•yot nich•na•eem ta•chat ye•dey mosh•ley•hem ve•sa•rey•hem lish•mo•a be•ko•lam ve•li•hi•yot n`cho•nim le•chol - po•al tov.

---

2. To speak evil of no man, to be no brawlers, but gentle, shewing all meekness unto all men.

Greek/Transliteration
2. μηδένα βλασφημεῖν, ἀμάχους εἶναι, ἐπιεικεῖς, πᾶσαν ἐνδεικνυμένους πραότητα πρὸς πάντας ἀνθρώπους.

2. meidena blaspheimein, amachous einai, epieikeis, pasan endeiknumenous praoteita pros pantas anthropous.

Hebrew/Transliteration
ב. לֹא לְגַדֵּף אִישׁ לֹא לְחָרְחָר מָדוֹן כִּי אִם־לְהִתְהַלֵּךְ בְּנַחַת וּבַעֲנָוָה לְעֵינֵי כָל־אָדָם:

2. Lo le•ga•def eesh lo le•char•cher ma•don ki eem - le•hit•ha•lech be•na•chat oo•va•ana•va le•ei•ney chol - adam.

---

3. For we ourselves also were sometimes foolish, disobedient, deceived, serving divers lusts and pleasures, living in malice and envy, hateful, and hating one another.

Greek/Transliteration
3. Ἦμεν γάρ ποτε καὶ ἡμεῖς ἀνόητοι, ἀπειθεῖς, πλανώμενοι, δουλεύοντες ἐπιθυμίαις καὶ ἡδοναῖς ποικίλαις, ἐν κακίᾳ καὶ φθόνῳ διάγοντες, στυγητοί, μισοῦντες ἀλλήλους.

3. Eimen gar pote kai 'eimeis anoeitoi, apeitheis, planomenoi, douleuontes epithumiais kai 'eidonais poikilais, en kakia kai phthono dyagontes, stugeitoi, misountes alleilous.

Hebrew/Transliteration
ג. כִּי לְפָנִים הָיִינוּ גַם־אֲנַחְנוּ בִּבְלִי־לֵב לָדַעַת בִּבְלִי־אֹזֶן לְהַקְשִׁיב וְתֹעֵי רוּחַ עֹבְדִים לְכָל־תַּאֲוָה וְחֶמְדָּה וּמִתְגַּדְּלִים בְּמַשְׂטֵמָה וּבְקִנְאָה שְׂנוּאִים וְשֹׂנְאִים אִישׁ לְרֵעֵהוּ:

3. Ki le•fa•nim ha•yi•noo gam - a•nach•noo biv•li - lev la•da•at biv•li - o•zen le•hak•shiv ve•to•ey roo•ach a•va•dim le•chol - ta•a•va ve•chem•da oom•goo•da•lim be•mas•te•ma oov•kin•ah s`noo•eem ve•son•eem eesh le•re•e•hoo.

---

4. But after that the kindness and love of God our Saviour toward man appeared,

Greek/Transliteration
4. Ὅτε δὲ ἡ χρηστότης καὶ ἡ φιλανθρωπία ἐπεφάνη τοῦ σωτῆρος ἡμῶν θεοῦ,

4. 'Ote de 'ei chreistoteis kai 'ei philanthropia epephanei tou soteiros 'eimon theou,

Hebrew/Transliteration
ד. אַךְ כַּאֲשֶׁר נִגְלוּ חַסְדֵי אֵל מוֹשִׁיעֵנוּ וְרַחֲמָיו לִבְנֵי אָדָם:

4. Ach ka•a•sher nig•loo chas•dey El Mo•shi•e•noo ve•ra•cha•mav liv•ney adam.

---

5. Not by works of righteousness which we have done, but according to his mercy he saved us, by the washing of regeneration, and renewing of the Holy Ghost;

Greek/Transliteration
5. οὐκ ἐξ ἔργων τῶν ἐν δικαιοσύνῃ ὧν ἐποιήσαμεν ἡμεῖς, ἀλλὰ κατὰ τὸν αὐτοῦ ἔλεον ἔσωσεν ἡμᾶς, διὰ λουτροῦ παλιγγενεσίας καὶ ἀνακαινώσεως πνεύματος ἁγίου,

5. ouk ex ergon ton en dikaiosunei 'on epoieisamen 'eimeis, alla kata ton autou eleon esosen 'eimas, dya loutrou palingenesias kai anakainoseos pneumatos 'agiou,

Hebrew/Transliteration
ה. הוֹשִׁיעָה לָנוּ יָדוֹ לֹא בְצִדְקָתֵנוּ אֲשֶׁר עָשִׂינוּ כִּי אִם-בְּחַסְדוֹ בּוֹלַדְנוּ מֵחָדָשׁ בְּמֵי הָרַחְצָה וַיְחַדְּשֵׁנוּ בְּרוּחַ קָדְשׁוֹ:

5. Ho•shi•ah la•noo ya•do lo ve•tzid•ka•te•noo asher asi•noo ki eem - be•chas•do no•lad•noo me•cha•dash be•mey ha•rach•tza vay•chad•she•noo be•Roo•ach Kod•sho.

Rabbinic Jewish Commentary
Now salvation, neither in whole, nor in part, is by these, either as causes; conditions, or means; See 2Ti_1:9; מעשים צדקה, "works of righteousness", is a Jewish phrase used for righteous or good works (z).

(z) Seder Tephillot, Ed. Amsterdam, fol. 46. 2.

---

6. Which he shed on us abundantly through Jesus Christ our Saviour;

Greek/Transliteration
6. οὗ ἐξέχεεν ἐφ᾽ ἡμᾶς πλουσίως, διὰ Ἰησοῦ χριστοῦ τοῦ σωτῆρος ἡμῶν,

6. 'ou execheen eph 'eimas plousios, dya Yeisou christou tou soteiros 'eimon,

Hebrew/Transliteration
ו. אֲשֶׁר שָׁפַךְ עָלֵינוּ שֶׁפַע רַב עַל־יְדֵי יֵשׁוּעַ הַמָּשִׁיחַ מוֹשִׁיעֵנוּ:

6. Asher sha•fach aley•noo she•fa rav al - ye•dey Yeshua ha•Ma•shi•ach Mo•shi•e•noo.

---

7. That being justified by his grace, we should be made heirs according to the hope of eternal life.

Greek/Transliteration
7. ἵνα δικαιωθέντες τῇ ἐκείνου χάριτι, κληρονόμοι γενώμεθα κατ᾽ ἐλπίδα ζωῆς αἰωνίου.

7. 'ina dikaiothentes tei ekeinou chariti, kleironomoi genometha kat elpida zoeis aioniou.

Hebrew/Transliteration
ז. לְמַעַן נִצְדַּק בְּחַסְדּוֹ וְנִירַשׁ לָנוּ חַיֵּי עוֹלָם כַּאֲשֶׁר קִוִּינוּ לוֹ:

7. Le•ma•an nitz•dak be•chas•do ve•ni•rash la•noo cha•yey o•lam ka•a•sher ki•vi•noo lo.

---

8. This is a faithful saying, and these things I will that thou affirm constantly, that they which have believed in God might be careful to maintain good works. These things are good and profitable unto men.

Greek/Transliteration
8. Πιστὸς ὁ λόγος, καὶ περὶ τούτων βούλομαί σε διαβεβαιοῦσθαι, ἵνα φροντίζωσιν καλῶν ἔργων προΐστασθαι οἱ πεπιστευκότες θεῷ. Ταῦτά ἐστιν τὰ καλὰ καὶ ὠφέλιμα τοῖς ἀνθρώποις·

8. Pistos 'o logos, kai peri touton boulomai se dyabebaiousthai, 'ina phrontizosin kalon ergon proistasthai 'oi pepisteukotes theo. Tauta estin ta kala kai ophelima tois anthropois.

Hebrew/Transliteration
ח. נֶאֱמָנִים אִמְרֵי־פִי וְזֶה הוּא חֶפְצִי כִּי־תְלַמֵּד הַדְּבָרִים הָאֵלֶּה בְּכָל־תֹּקֶף לְמַעַן יִתְאַמְּצוּ הַמַּאֲמִינִים בֵּאלֹהִים לִשְׁמֹר לַעֲשׂוֹת מַעֲשִׂים טוֹבִים אֵלֶּה הֵם הַדְּבָרִים הַטּוֹבִים לְהוֹעִיל לִבְנֵי אָדָם:

8. Ne•e•ma•nim eem•rey - fi ve•ze hoo chef•tzi ki - te•la•med ha•d`va•rim ha•e•le be•chol - to•kef le•ma•an yit•am•tzoo ha•ma•a•mi•nim be•Elohim lish•mor la•a•sot ma•a•sim to•vim ele hem ha•d`va•rim ha•to•vim le•ho•eel liv•ney adam.

---

9. But avoid foolish questions, and genealogies, and contentions, and strivings about the law; for they are unprofitable and vain.

Greek/Transliteration
9. μωρὰς δὲ ζητήσεις καὶ γενεαλογίας καὶ ἔρεις καὶ μάχας νομικὰς περιΐστασο· εἰσὶν γὰρ ἀνωφελεῖς καὶ μάταιοι.

9. moras de zeiteiseis kai genealogias kai ereis kai machas nomikas peri'istaso. eisin gar anopheleis kai mataioi.

Hebrew/Transliteration

ט. אַךְ חֲדַל לְךָ מִשְׁאֵלוֹת כֶּסֶל וְתוֹלְדֹת הַדּוֹרוֹת וּמִמְּרִיבוֹת וּמַחֲלֹקוֹת בְּדִבְרֵי הַתּוֹרָה אֲשֶׁר לֹא יוֹעִילוּ כִּי תֹהוּ הֵנָּה:

9. Ach cha•dal le•cha mish•e•lot ke•sel ve•tol•dot ha•do•rot oo•mim•ri•vot oo•mach•lo•kot be•div•rey ha•Torah asher lo yo•ee•loo ki to•hoo he•na.

Rabbinic Jewish Commentary

and genealogies; of their elders, Rabbis and scribes, by whom their traditions are handed down from one to another, in fixing which they greatly laboured; see 1Ti_1:4 and contentions and strivings about the Torah; the rites and ceremonies of it, and about the sense of it, and its various precepts, as litigated in the schools of Hillell and Shammai, the one giving it one way, and the other another; and what one declared to be free according to the Torah, the other declared forbidden; which occasioned great contentions and quarrels between the followers of the one, and of the other, as both the Mishna and Talmud show: and agreeably to this sense, the Syriac version renders it, "the contentions and strifes of the scribes"; the Jewish Rabbis, who were some on the side of Hillell, and others on the side of Shammai; as well as went into parties and strifes among themselves, and oftentimes about mere trifles; things of no manner of importance.

---

10. A man that is an heretick after the first and second admonition reject;

Greek/Transliteration

10. Αἱρετικὸν ἄνθρωπον μετὰ μίαν καὶ δευτέραν νουθεσίαν παραιτοῦ,

10. 'Airetikon anthropon meta mian kai deuteran nouthesian paraitou,

Hebrew/Transliteration

י. אִישׁ-מַמְרֶה אַחֲרֵי אֲשֶׁר הוֹכַח בְּתוֹכַחְתָּה פַּעַם וּשְׁתַּיִם שְׂטֵה מֵעָלָיו:

10. Eesh - mam•re a•cha•rey asher hoo•chach be•to•che•cha pa•am oosh•ta•yim s`te me•a•lav.

Rabbinic Jewish Commentary

An admonition with the Jews did not continue less than seven days (a); some say (b) thirty; that is, there were so many days before it was out, or between one and another.

(a) T. Bab. Moed Katon, fol. 16. 1. (b) Bereshit Rabba, sect. 33. fol. 28. 3.

---

11. Knowing that he that is such is subverted, and sinneth, being condemned of himself.

Greek/Transliteration

11. εἰδὼς ὅτι ἐξέστραπται ὁ τοιοῦτος, καὶ ἁμαρτάνει, ὢν αὐτοκατάκριτος.

11. eidos 'oti exestraptai 'o toioutos, kai 'amartanei, on autokatakritos.

Hebrew/Transliteration
יא. כִּי-אִישׁ כָּזֶה הֲלֹא תֵדַע כִּי עִקֵּשׁ הוּא וְאָשֵׁם כִּי לִבּוֹ יַאֲשִׁימֶנּוּ:

11. Ki - eesh ka•ze ha•lo te•da ki ee•kesh hoo ve•a•shem ki li•bo ya•a•shi•me•noo.

---

12. When I shall send Artemas unto thee, or Tychicus, be diligent to come unto me to Nicopolis: for I have determined there to winter.

Greek/Transliteration
12. Ὅταν πέμψω Ἀρτεμᾶν πρός σε ἢ Τυχικόν, σπούδασον ἐλθεῖν πρός με εἰς Νικόπολιν· ἐκεῖ γὰρ κέκρικα παραχειμάσαι.

12. 'Otan pempso Arteman pros se ei Tuchikon, spoudason elthein pros me eis Nikopolin. Ekei gar kekrika paracheimasai.

Hebrew/Transliteration
יב. כַּאֲשֶׁר אֶשְׁלַח אֵלֶיךָ אֶת-אַרְטְמָס אוֹ אֶת-טוּכִיקוֹס תָּחִישׁ לָבוֹא אֵלַי לְנִיקָפּוֹלִיס כִּי-חָרַצְתִּי לְחֶרַף שָׁם הַחֹרֶף הַזֶּה:

12. Ka•a•sher esh•lach e•le•cha et - Ar•temas oh et - Too•chi•kos ta•chish la•vo e•lai le•Nika•polis ki - cha•ratz•ti le•che•raf sham ha•cho•ref ha•ze.

---

13. Bring Zenas the lawyer and Apollos on their journey diligently, that nothing be wanting unto them.

Greek/Transliteration
13. Ζηνᾶν τὸν νομικὸν καὶ Ἀπολλῶ σπουδαίως πρόπεμψον, ἵνα μηδὲν αὐτοῖς λείπῃ.

13. Zeinan ton nomikon kai Apollo spoudaios propempson, 'ina meiden autois leipei.

Hebrew/Transliteration
יג. וְזֵינָס הַסֹּפֵר וְאַפּוֹלוֹס כַּאֲשֶׁר יֵלְכוּן לְדַרְכָּם תֵּלֵךְ עִמָּם לְשַׁלְּחָם וּרְאֵה כִּי לֹא-יַחְסְרוּן מְאוּמָה:

13. Ve•Zeynas ha•so•fer ve•A•polos ka•a•sher yel•choon le•dar•kam te•lech ee•mam le•shal•cham oor•eh ki lo - yach•se•roon me•oo•ma.

Rabbinic Jewish Commentary
Bring Zenas the lawyer,.... Whether he was brought up to the civil law, either among the Greeks or Romans, is not certain; it may be he was a Jewish lawyer, or scribe, an interpreter of Moses's Torah among the Jews; for with them a lawyer and a scribe were one and the same, as appears from Mat_22:35 compared with Mar_12:28 and the Syriac version here calls him "a scribe", and the Ethiopic version "a scribe of the city".

and Apollos, on their journey diligently; who was a Jew born at Alexandria, an eloquent man, and mighty in the Scriptures; who had preached at Corinth, but was now at Crete; and whom the apostle, with Zenas, would have provided with everything necessary for their journey.

14. And let ours also learn to maintain good works for necessary uses, that they be not unfruitful.

Greek/Transliteration
14. Μανθανέτωσαν δὲ καὶ οἱ ἡμέτεροι καλῶν ἔργων προΐστασθαι εἰς τὰς ἀναγκαίας χρείας, ἵνα μὴ ὦσιν ἄκαρποι.

14. Manthanetosan de kai 'oi 'eimeteroi kalon ergon proistasthai eis tas anagkaias chreias, 'ina mei osin akarpoi.

Hebrew/Transliteration
יד. וְגַם-אַנְשֵׁי הָעֵדָה שֶׁלָּנוּ יִלְמְדוּן לִשְׁמֹר לַעֲשׂוֹת מַעֲשִׂים טוֹבִים לְמַלֹּאת מַחְסוֹר זוּלָתָם לְבִלְתִּי יִהְיוּ כְּלֹא עֹשִׂים פֶּרִי:

14. Ve•gam - an•shey ha•e•da she•la•noo yil•me•doon lish•mor la•a•sot ma•a•sim to•vim le•ma•lot mach•sor zoo•la•tam le•vil•ti yi•hee•yoo ke•lo o•sim p`ri.

Rabbinic Jewish Commentary
The Jews say, that he that does not teach his son a trade, it is all one as if he taught him to rob or steal; hence their Rabbis were brought up to trades.

The Jews say (c).

"There are four things which a man should constantly attend to with all his might, and they are these; the Torah, "good works", prayer, ודרך ארץ, and "the way of the earth", or "business"; if a tradesman, to his trade; if a merchant, to his merchandise; if a man of war to war."

(c) T. Bab. Beracot, fol. 32. 2. & Gloss. in. ib.

---

15. All that are with me salute thee. Greet them that love us in the faith. Grace be with you all. Amen.

Greek/Transliteration
15. Ἀσπάζονταί σε οἱ μετ᾽ ἐμοῦ πάντες. Ἄσπασαι τοὺς φιλοῦντας ἡμᾶς ἐν πίστει. Ἡ χάρις μετὰ πάντων ὑμῶν. Ἀμήν.

15. Aspazontai se 'oi met emou pantes. Aspasai tous philountas 'eimas en pistei. 'Ei charis meta panton 'umon. Amein.

Hebrew/Transliteration
טו. כָּל-הָאַחִים אֲשֶׁר עִמִּי שֹׁאֲלִים לִשְׁלוֹמֶךָ שְׁאַל לִשְׁלוֹם אֹהֲבֵי נַפְשֵׁנוּ בֶּאֱמוּנָה הַחֶסֶד עִם-כֻּלְּכֶם אָמֵן:

15. Kol - ha•a•chim asher ee•mi sho•a•lim lish•lo•me•cha sh`al lish•lom o•ha•vey naf•she•noo be•e•moo•na ha•che•sed eem - kool•chem Amen.

---

^end^

THE EPISTLE OF PAUL TO PHILEMON

Philemon, Chapter 1

1. Paul, a prisoner of Jesus Christ, and Timothy our brother, unto Philemon our dearly beloved, and fellowlabourer,

Greek/Transliteration
1. Παῦλος δέσμιος χριστοῦ Ἰησοῦ, καὶ Τιμόθεος ὁ ἀδελφός, Φιλήμονι τῷ ἀγαπητῷ καὶ συνεργῷ ἡμῶν,

1. Paulos desmios christou Yeisou, kai Timotheos 'o adelphos, Phileimoni to agapeito kai sunergo 'eimon,

Hebrew/Transliteration
:א. פּוֹלוֹס אָסִיר יֵשׁוּעַ הַמָּשִׁיחַ וְטִימוֹתִיוֹס אָחִי אֶל-פִּילֵימוֹן אוֹהֵב לָנוּ וְתֹמֵךְ בְּיָדֵינוּ

1. Polos asir Yeshua ha•Ma•shi•ach ve•Timotiyos achi el - Pi•ley•mon o•hev la•noo ve•to•mech be•ya•dey•noo.

Rabbinic Jewish Commentary
The name of Philemon is Greek; there was a Greek poet of this name, and a Greek historian that Pliny made use of in compiling his history: there is indeed mention made in the Jewish writings (a), of a Rabbi whose name was **פלימו**, "Philemo".

(a) T. Bab. Sota, fol. 4. 1. & Menachot, fol. 37. 1. & Juchasin, fol. 101. 1. 108. 1. & 159. 2.

---

2. And to our beloved Apphia, and Archippus our fellowsoldier, and to the church in thy house:

Greek/Transliteration
2. καὶ Ἀπφίᾳ τῇ ἀγαπητῇ, καὶ Ἀρχίππῳ τῷ συστρατιώτῃ ἡμῶν, καὶ τῇ κατ᾽ οἶκόν σου ἐκκλησίᾳ·

2. kai Apphia tei agapeitei, kai Archippo to sustratiotei 'eimon, kai tei kat oikon sou ekkleisia.

Hebrew/Transliteration
:ב. וְאֶל-אַפִּיָה אֲחֹתִי וְאֶל-אַרְכִפּוֹס גֶּבֶר עֲמִיתִי בְּמִלְחֲמֹתֵינוּ וְאֶל-הַקָּהָל אֲשֶׁר בְּבֵיתֶךָ

2. Ve•el - Apiya a•cho•ti ve•el - Ar•chipos gever ami•ti be•mil•cha•mo•tey•noo ve•el - ha•ka•hal asher be•vey•te•cha.

---

3. Grace to you, and peace, from God our Father and the Lord Jesus Christ.

Greek/Transliteration
3. χάρις ὑμῖν καὶ εἰρήνη ἀπὸ θεοῦ πατρὸς ἡμῶν καὶ κυρίου Ἰησοῦ χριστοῦ.

3. charis 'umin kai eireinei apo theou patros 'eimon kai kuriou Yeisou christou.

Hebrew/Transliteration
ג. חֶסֶד לָכֶם וְשָׁלוֹם מֵאֵת אֱלֹהִים אָבִינוּ וּמֵאֵת יֵשׁוּעַ הַמָּשִׁיחַ אֲדֹנֵינוּ:

3. Che•sed la•chem ve•sha•lom me•et Elohim Avi•noo oo•me•et Yeshua ha•Ma•shi•ach Ado•ney•noo.

---

4. I thank my God, making mention of thee always in my prayers,

Greek/Transliteration
4. Εὐχαριστῶ τῷ θεῷ μου, πάντοτε μνείαν σου ποιούμενος ἐπὶ τῶν προσευχῶν μου,

4. Eucharisto to theo mou, pantote mneian sou poioumenos epi ton proseuchon mou,

Hebrew/Transliteration
ד. אֲבָרְכָה אֶת-אֱלֹהַי וְאַזְכִּירְךָ תָמִיד בִּתְפִלָּתִי:

4. Avar•cha et - Elohai ve•az•kir•cha ta•mid bit•fi•la•ti.

---

5. Hearing of thy love and faith, which thou hast toward the Lord Jesus, and toward all saints;

Greek/Transliteration
5. ἀκούων σου τὴν ἀγάπην, καὶ τὴν πίστιν ἣν ἔχεις πρὸς τὸν κύριον Ἰησοῦν καὶ εἰς πάντας τοὺς ἁγίους,

5. akouon sou tein agapein, kai tein pistin 'ein echeis pros ton kurion Yeisoun kai eis pantas tous 'agious,

Hebrew/Transliteration
ה. לִשְׁמֵעַת הָאַהֲבָה וְהָאֱמוּנָה אֲשֶׁר תִּנְצֹר בְּנַפְשְׁךָ אֶל-יֵשׁוּעַ אֲדֹנֵינוּ וְאֶל-כָּל-קְדֹשָׁיו:

5. Lish•moo•at ha•a•ha•va ve•ha•e•moo•na asher tin•tzor be•naf•she•cha el - Yeshua Ado•ney•noo ve•el - kol - ke•do•shav.

---

6. That the communication of thy faith may become effectual by the acknowledging of every good thing which is in you in Christ Jesus.

Greek/Transliteration
6. ὅπως ἡ κοινωνία τῆς πίστεώς σου ἐνεργὴς γένηται ἐν ἐπιγνώσει παντὸς ἀγαθοῦ τοῦ ἐν ἡμῖν εἰς χριστὸν Ἰησοῦν.

6. 'opos 'ei koinonia teis pisteos sou energeis geneitai en epignosei pantos agathou tou en 'eimin eis christon Yeisoun.

Hebrew/Transliteration

:ו. וּתְפִלָּתִי כִּי אֱמוּנָתְךָ תּוֹסִיף אֹמֶץ בַּאֲגֻדָּתָהּ עַל-יְדֵי הַדַּעַת מַה-טּוֹב בָּכֶם לִפְנֵי הַמָּשִׁיחַ יֵשׁוּעַ

6. Oot•fi•la•ti ki emoo•nat•cha to•sif o•metz ba•a•goo•da•ta al - ye•dey ha•da•at ma – tov ba•chem lif•ney ha•Ma•shi•ach Yeshua.

---

7. For we have great joy and consolation in thy love, because the bowels of the saints are refreshed by thee, brother.

Greek/Transliteration

7. Χάριν γὰρ ἔχομεν πολλὴν καὶ παράκλησιν ἐπὶ τῇ ἀγάπῃ σου, ὅτι τὰ σπλάγχνα τῶν ἁγίων ἀναπέπαυται διὰ σοῦ, ἀδελφέ.

7. Charin gar echomen pollein kai parakleisin epi tei agapei sou, 'oti ta splagchna ton 'agion anapepautai dya sou, adelphe.

Hebrew/Transliteration

:ז. כִּי אַהֲבָתְךָ הָיְתָה לִי לְשָׂשׂוֹן רָב וְתַנְחוּמִים אַחֲרֵי אֲשֶׁר אַתָּה אָחִי הָיִיתָ לְמֵשִׁיב נֶפֶשׁ בְּקֶרֶב הַקְּדוֹשִׁים

7. Ki aha•vat•cha hai•ta li le•sa•son rav ve•tan•choo•mim a•cha•rey asher ata achi ha•yi•ta le•me•shiv ne•fesh be•ke•rev ha•k`do•shim.

---

8. Wherefore, though I might be much bold in Christ to enjoin thee that which is convenient,

Greek/Transliteration

8. Διὸ πολλὴν ἐν χριστῷ παρρησίαν ἔχων ἐπιτάσσειν σοι τὸ ἀνῆκον,

8. Dio pollein en christo parreisian echon epitassein soi to aneikon,

Hebrew/Transliteration

:ח. וְעַתָּה אַף כִּי רָחָב לִבִּי בַּמָּשִׁיחַ לְצַוּוֹת עָלֶיךָ אֶת-הַטּוֹב לָךְ

8. Ve•a•ta af ki ra•chav li•bi ba•Ma•shi•ach le•tza•vot a•le•cha et - ha•tov lach.

---

9. Yet for love's sake I rather beseech thee, being such an one as Paul the aged, and now also a prisoner of Jesus Christ.

Greek/Transliteration

9. διὰ τὴν ἀγάπην μᾶλλον παρακαλῶ, τοιοῦτος ὢν ὡς Παῦλος πρεσβύτης, νυνὶ δὲ καὶ δέσμιος Ἰησοῦ χριστοῦ.

9. dya tein agapein mallon parakalo, toioutos on 'os Paulos presbuteis, nuni de kai desmios Yeisou christou.

Hebrew/Transliteration

:ט. בְּכָל-זֹאת לְמַעַן אַהֲבָתֵנוּ אֲנִי פוֹלוֹס הַזָּקֵן וְאָסִיר יֵשׁוּעַ הַמָּשִׁיחַ כַּיּוֹם הִנְנִי לְהַפְגִּיעַ בָּךְ

9. Be•chol - zot le•ma•an aha•va•te•noo ani Polos ha•za•ken va•a•sir Yeshua ha•Ma•shi•ach ka•yom hi•ne•ni le•haf•gia bach.

Rabbinic Jewish Commentary
Being such an one as Paul the aged; or "the elder"; meaning either in office, which he might mention with this view, that his request might have the greater weight and influence; or else in years, and which he might observe partly to move compassion in Philemon, and that he might not grieve him in his old age, as he would, should he deny his request; and partly to suggest to him, that the advice he was about to give him, to receive his servant, did not come from a raw young man, but from one well stricken in years, with whom were wisdom and understanding; and therefore not to be treated with neglect or contempt: how old the apostle was at this time, is not certain; he could not be less than sixty years of age, or he would not have called himself an old man; for no man was so called by the Jews, but he that was at the age of sixty (b). Some editions of the Vulgate Latin version, as that of the London Polyglot Bible, read, "seeing thou art such an one as Paul the aged"; as if Philemon was an old man, as the apostle was, and therefore he would not lay his commands upon him, as an ancient man might upon a young man, but rather entreat him as equal to him in years.

(b) Pirke Abot, c. 5. sect. 1.

---

10. I beseech thee for my son Onesimus, whom I have begotten in my bonds:

Greek/Transliteration
10. Παρακαλῶ σε περὶ τοῦ ἐμοῦ τέκνου, ὃν ἐγέννησα ἐν τοῖς δεσμοῖς μου, Ὀνήσιμον,

10. Parakalo se peri tou emou teknou, 'on egenneisa en tois desmois mou, Oneisimon,

Hebrew/Transliteration
:י. כִּי אַפְגִּיעַ בְּעַד בְּנִי אֲשֶׁר בְּבֵית הָאֲסוּרִים הוֹלַדְתִּיהוּ הֲלֹא הוּא אֲנְסִימוֹס בְּנִי

10. Ki af•gia be•ad b`ni asher be•veit ha•a•soo•rim ho•lade•ti•hoo ha•lo hoo Oni•si•mos b`ni.

---

11. Which in time past was to thee unprofitable, but now profitable to thee and to me:

Greek/Transliteration
11. τόν ποτέ σοι ἄχρηστον, νυνὶ δὲ σοὶ καὶ ἐμοὶ εὔχρηστον, ὃν ἀνέπεμψα·

11. ton pote soi achreiston, nuni de soi kai emoi euchreiston, 'on anepempsa.

Hebrew/Transliteration
:יא. אֲשֶׁר לֹא לְיִתְרוֹן הָיָה לְךָ מִלְּפָנִים אֲבָל מֵעַתָּה גַם-לְךָ גַם-לִי הוּא לְיִתְרוֹן גָּדוֹל

11. Asher lo le•yit•ron ha•ya le•cha mil•fa•nim aval me•a•ta gam - le•cha gam - li hoo le•yit•ron ga•dol.

12. Whom I have sent again: thou therefore receive him, that is, mine own bowels:

Greek/Transliteration
12. σὺ δὲ αὐτόν, τοῦτ᾽ ἔστιν τὰ ἐμὰ σπλάγχνα, προσλαβοῦ·

12. su de auton, tout estin ta ema splagchna, proslabou.

Hebrew/Transliteration
יב. וַאֲנִי הִנְנִי מְשִׁיבוֹ אֵלֶיךָ כַּיּוֹם שָׂא נָא אֶת-פָּנָיו כִּי כְבֶן-מַחֲלָצַי הוּא:

12. Va•a•ni hi•ne•ni me•shi•vo e•le•cha ka•yom sa na et - pa•nav ki ke•ven - me•cha•la•tzai hoo.

---

13. Whom I would have retained with me, that in thy stead he might have ministered unto me in the bonds of the gospel:

Greek/Transliteration
13. ὃν ἐγὼ ἐβουλόμην πρὸς ἐμαυτὸν κατέχειν, ἵνα ὑπὲρ σοῦ διακονῇ μοι ἐν τοῖς δεσμοῖς τοῦ εὐαγγελίου·

13. 'on ego eboulomein pros emauton katechein, 'ina 'uper sou dyakonei moi en tois desmois tou euangeliou.

Hebrew/Transliteration
יג. אַף כִּי חָמַדְתִּי לְהַחֲזִק-בּוֹ כִּי יַעֲמֹד לְשָׁרֶתְנִי תַחְתֶּיךָ בְּעוֹד אֲנִי אָסוּר בְּכַבְלֵי הַבְּשׂוֹרָה:

13. Af ki chi•ma•de•ti le•ha•cha•zek - bo ki ya•a•mod le•shar•te•ni tach•te•cha be•od ani a•soor be•chav•ley ha•be•so•ra.

---

14. But without thy mind would I do nothing; that thy benefit should not be as it were of necessity, but willingly.

Greek/Transliteration
14. χωρὶς δὲ τῆς σῆς γνώμης οὐδὲν ἠθέλησα ποιῆσαι, ἵνα μὴ ὡς κατὰ ἀνάγκην τὸ ἀγαθόν σου ᾖ, ἀλλὰ κατὰ ἑκούσιον.

14. choris de teis seis gnomeis ouden eitheleisa poieisai, 'ina mei 'os kata anagkein to agathon sou ei, alla kata 'ekousion.

Hebrew/Transliteration
יד. אֲבָל לֹא חָפַצְתִּי לַעֲשׂוֹת דָּבָר בִּבְלִי דַעְתֶּךָ לְמַעַן יִהְיֶה גְּמוּל טוּבְךָ לֹא כְמוֹ בְאֹנֶס כִּי אִם-בִּנְדָבָה:

14. Aval lo cha•fatz•ti la•a•sot da•var biv•li da•a•techa le•ma•an yi•hee•ye g`mool toov•cha lo che•mo ve•o•nes ki eem - bin•da•va.

15. For perhaps he therefore departed for a season, that thou shouldest receive him for ever;

Greek/Transliteration
15. Τάχα γὰρ διὰ τοῦτο ἐχωρίσθη πρὸς ὥραν, ἵνα αἰώνιον αὐτὸν ἀπέχῃς·

15. Tacha gar dya touto echoristhei pros 'oran, 'ina aionion auton apecheis.

Hebrew/Transliteration
טו. וְאוּלַי בַּעֲבוּר זֹאת נִפְרַד מִמְּךָ לִזְמַן קָצוּב לְמַעַן יִהְיֶה לְפָנֶיךָ לְעוֹלָם וָעֶד:

15. Ve•oo•lai ba•a•voor zot nif•rad mim•cha liz•man ka•tzoov le•ma•an yi•hee•ye le•fa•ne•cha le•o•lam va•ed.

---

16. Not now as a servant, but above a servant, a brother beloved, specially to me, but how much more unto thee, both in the flesh, and in the Lord?

Greek/Transliteration
16. οὐκέτι ὡς δοῦλον, ἀλλ᾽ ὑπὲρ δοῦλον, ἀδελφὸν ἀγαπητόν, μάλιστα ἐμοί, πόσῳ δὲ μᾶλλον σοὶ καὶ ἐν σαρκὶ καὶ ἐν κυρίῳ.

16. ouketi 'os doulon, all 'uper doulon, adelphon agapeiton, malista emoi, poso de mallon soi kai en sarki kai en kurio.

Hebrew/Transliteration
טז. וְלֹא עוֹד כְּעֶבֶד כִּי אִם-רַב מֵעֶבֶד כְּאָח יַקִּיר כִּי יַקִּיר הוּא לִי עַד-מְאֹד וּמַה-גַּם כִּי כֵן יְהִי לְךָ גַּם-נֶגֶד פְּנֵי אֲנָשִׁים וְגַם נֶגֶד פְּנֵי אֲדֹנֵינוּ:

16. Ve•lo od ke•e•ved ki eem - rav me•e•ved ke•ach ya•kir ki ya•kir hoo li ad - me•od oo•ma - gam ki chen ye•hee le•cha gam - ne•ged p`ney a•na•shim ve•gam ne•ged p`ney Ado•ney•noo?

---

17. If thou count me therefore a partner, receive him as myself.

Greek/Transliteration
17. Εἰ οὖν με ἔχεις κοινωνόν, προσλαβοῦ αὐτὸν ὡς ἐμέ.

17. Ei oun me echeis koinonon, proslabou auton 'os eme.

Hebrew/Transliteration
יז. וְעַל-כֵּן אִם לְחָבֵר לְךָ תַּחְשְׁבֵנִי קַבֶּל-נָא פָּנָיו כְּפָנָי:

17. Ve•al - ken eem le•cha•ver le•cha tach•she•ve•ni ka•bel - na pa•nav ke•fa•nai.

Rabbinic Jewish Commentary
A companion and friend, who reckon each other's affairs and interest their own: the word answers to **חבר,** a word often used in Talmudic writings, for an associate of the Rabbis or wise men.

18. If he hath wronged thee, or oweth thee ought, put that on mine account;

Greek/Transliteration
18. Εἰ δέ τι ἠδίκησέν σε ἢ ὀφείλει, τοῦτο ἐμοὶ ἐλλόγει·

18. Ei de ti eidikeisen se ei opheilei, touto emoi ellogei.

Hebrew/Transliteration
יח. וְאִם עָשַׁק אֹתְךָ אוֹ אֲשָׁמוֹ בְראֹשׁוֹ מִיָּדִי תִדְרְשֶׁנּוּ:

18. Ve•eem a•shak ot•cha oh a•sha•mo ve•ro•sho mi•ya•di tid•re•she•noo.

---

19. I Paul have written it with mine own hand, I will repay it: albeit I do not say to thee how thou owest unto me even thine own self besides.

Greek/Transliteration
19. ἐγὼ Παῦλος ἔγραψα τῇ ἐμῇ χειρί, ἐγὼ ἀποτίσω· ἵνα μὴ λέγω σοι ὅτι καὶ σεαυτόν μοι προσοφείλεις.

19. ego Paulos egrapsa tei emei cheiri, ego apotiso. 'ina mei lego soi 'oti kai seauton moi prosopheileis.

Hebrew/Transliteration
יט. אֲנִי פוֹלוֹס כָּתַבְתִּי זֶה בְּיָדִי אֲנִי אֲשַׁלֵּם וְלֹא אֹמַר אֵלֶיךָ כִּי חוֹב עָלֶיךָ לְשַׁלֶּם-לִי גַם-בְּעַד נַפְשֶׁךָ:

19. Ani Folos ka•tav•ti ze be•ya•di ani a•sha•lem ve•lo o•mar e•le•cha ki chov a•le•cha le•sha•lem - li gam - be•ad naf•she•cha.

---

20. Yea, brother, let me have joy of thee in the Lord: refresh my bowels in the Lord.

Greek/Transliteration
20. Ναί, ἀδελφέ, ἐγώ σου ὀναίμην ἐν κυρίῳ· ἀνάπαυσόν μου τὰ σπλάγχνα ἐν κυρίῳ.

20. Nai, adelphe, ego sou onaimein en kurio. anapauson mou ta splagchna en kurio.

Hebrew/Transliteration
כ. אָנָּא אָחִי אֶמְצָא בְךָ רְוָחָה זוּ בַּאֲדֹנֵינוּ הָשִׁיבָה-נָּא לִבִּי וְכִלְיוֹתַי בַּמָּשִׁיחַ:

20. Ana achi em•tza be•cha r`va•cha zoo ba•Ado•ne•noo ha•shi•va - na li•bi ve•chil•yo•tai ba•Ma•shi•ach.

Rabbinic Jewish Commentary
refresh my bowels in the Lord; or "in Christ"; as the Alexandrian copy, the Syriac and Ethiopic versions, read; and by his "bowels", he either means Onesimus, as in Phm_1:12 who, in a spiritual sense, came forth out of his bowels; or else himself, his soul, his spirit, his inward parts; and so the Ethiopic version renders it, "refresh my soul"; and the sense is, that he desired in the Lord, and for his sake, that he would receive Onesimus again, which would give him an inward pleasure, and refresh his spirit; and indeed he intimates, that nothing could be more cheering and reviving to him.

21. Having confidence in thy obedience I wrote unto thee, knowing that thou wilt also do more than I say.

Greek/Transliteration
21. Πεποιθὼς τῇ ὑπακοῇ σου ἔγραψά σοι, εἰδὼς ὅτι καὶ ὑπὲρ ὃ λέγω ποιήσεις.

21. Pepoithos tei 'upakoei sou egrapsa soi, eidos 'oti kai 'uper 'o lego poieiseis.

Hebrew/Transliteration
כא. בְּךָ בָטַחְתִּי כִּי תַעֲנֶה וָאֶכְתֹּב אֵלֶיךָ וְגַם יָדַעְתִּי כִּי-תוֹסִף לַעֲשׂוֹת מֵאֲשֶׁר אָמָרְתִּי:

21. Be•cha va•tach•ti ki ta•a•ne va•ech•tov e•le•cha ve•gam ya•da•a•ti ki - to•sif la•a•sot me•a•sher amar•ti.

---

22. But withal prepare me also a lodging: for I trust that through your prayers I shall be given unto you.

Greek/Transliteration
22. Ἅμα δὲ καὶ ἑτοίμαζέ μοι ξενίαν· ἐλπίζω γὰρ ὅτι διὰ τῶν προσευχῶν ὑμῶν χαρισθήσομαι ὑμῖν.

22. 'Ama de kai 'etoimaze moi xenian. elpizo gar 'oti dya ton proseuchon 'umon charistheisomai 'umin.

Hebrew/Transliteration
כב. נוֹסָף עַל-זֶה תָּכֶן-לִי בֵּית מָלוֹן כִּי הִנְנִי מְיַחֵל לְהִנָּתֵן לָכֶם כְּפִי תְפִלַּתְכֶם:

22. No•saf al - ze ta•chen - li beit ma•lon ki hi•ne•ni me•ya•chel le•hi•na•ten la•chem ke•fi t`fi•lat•chem.

---

23. There salute thee Epaphras, my fellowprisoner in Christ Jesus;

Greek/Transliteration
23. Ἀσπάζονταί σε Ἐπαφρᾶς ὁ συναιχμάλωτός μου ἐν χριστῷ Ἰησοῦ,

23. Aspazontai se Epaphras 'o sunaichmalotos mou en christo Yeisou,

Hebrew/Transliteration
כג. אֵלֶּה שֹׁאֲלִים לִשְׁלוֹמְךָ אֶפַּפְרָס אֲשֶׁר הוּא עָצוּר אִתִּי בְּיֵשׁוּעַ הַמָּשִׁיחַ:

23. Ele sho•a•lim lish•lo•me•cha Epaf•ras asher hoo atzoor ee•ti be•Yeshua ha•Ma•shi•ach.

Rabbinic Jewish Commentary
For by this time Nero began to persecute the Christians, which he did in the better and more moderate part of his reign; for among several things for which he is commended by the historian (b), this is one,

""Afficti suppliciis Christiani, genus hominum superstitionis novae ac maleficae"; the Christians were punished, a sort of men of a new and bad religion:

And Epaphras being at Rome, when this persecution broke out, was taken up and put in prison, as were also Aristarchus, Col_4:10 and Timothy, Heb_13:23.

(b) Suetonius in Vita Neronis, c. 16.

---

24. Marcus, Aristarchus, Demas, Lucas, my fellowlabourers.

Greek/Transliteration
24. Μᾶρκος, Ἀρίσταρχος, Δημᾶς, Λουκᾶς, οἱ συνεργοί μου.

24. Markos, Aristarchos, Deimas, Loukas, 'oi sunergoi mou.

Hebrew/Transliteration
:כד. וּמַרְקוֹס וַאֲרִסְטַרְכוֹס וְדִימָס וְלוּקָס הַתֹּמְכִים בְּיָדִי

24. Oo•Markos va•Aristar•chos ve•Di•mas ve•Lookas ha•tom•chim be•ya•di.

---

25. The grace of our Lord Jesus Christ be with your spirit. Amen.

Greek/Transliteration
25. Ἡ χάρις τοῦ κυρίου ἡμῶν Ἰησοῦ χριστοῦ μετὰ τοῦ πνεύματος ὑμῶν. Ἀμήν.

25. 'Ei charis tou kuriou 'eimon Yeisou christou meta tou pneumatos 'umon. Amein.

Hebrew/Transliteration
:כה. חֶסֶד יֵשׁוּעַ הַמָּשִׁיחַ אֲדֹנֵינוּ עִם-רוּחֲכֶם אָמֵן

25. Che•sed Yeshua ha•Ma•shi•ach Ado•ney•noo eem - roo•cha•chem Amen.

---

^end^

JEWISH INTERTESTAMENTAL AND EARLY RABBINIC LITERATURE: BIBLIOGRAPHY

Berenbaum, Michael and Fred Skolnik. *Encyclopaedia Judaica.* 2d ed.; 22 vols.; Detroit: Macmillan Reference USA and Keter, 2007. Also available electronically from Gale Virtual Reference Library. A fine substantial update of the original and still useful 16 volume *Encyclopaedia Judaica* (Jerusalem: Keter, 1972), which originally received several annual yearbooks and two update volumes (1982, 1994) and was issued on CD-ROM in 1997. Both editions were preceded by an incomplete 10-volume German set entitled *Encyclopaedia Judaica: das Judentum in Geschichte und Gegenwart* (Berlin: Eschkol, 1928–34), which only covered articles beginning with the letters A–L but often contained longer treatments than the 1972 version. [*EncJud*]

Collins, John J. and Daniel C. Harlow, eds. *The Eerdmans Dictionary of Early Judaism.* Grand Rapids/Cambridge: Eerdmans, 2010. Brief survey articles introduce "Early Judaism" (pp. 1–290) followed by dictionary entries on more specific matters (pp. 291–1360). Quite helpful. [*EDEJ*]

Evans, Craig A. and Stanley E. Porter, eds. *Dictionary of New Testament Background.* Downers Grove/Leicester: InterVarsity, 2000. Helpful articles with good bibliography. [*DNTB*]

Freedman, David Noel, ed. *The Anchor Bible Dictionary.* 6 vols. New York: Doubleday, 1992. Includes useful introductory articles on much intertestamental literature. Also on CD-ROM. [*ABD*]

Neusner, Jacob and Alan J. Avery-Peck, eds. *Encyclopaedia of Midrash: Biblical Interpretation in Formative Judaism.* 2 vols. Leiden: Brill, 2005.

Neusner, Jacob, Alan J. Avery-Peck, and William Scott Green, eds. *The Encyclopedia of Judaism.* 5 vols. New York: Continuum/Leiden: Brill, 1999–2003. 3 initial volumes plus 2 supplement volumes. Some articles with bibliography.

Neusner, Jacob and William Scott Green, eds. *Dictionary of Judaism in the Biblical Period: 450 B.C.E. to 600 C.E.* 2 vols. New York: Macmillan, 1996; repr. Peabody, MA: Hendrickson, 1999. Relatively short articles with no bibliography.

Singer, Isidore et al., eds. *The Jewish Encyclopedia.* 12 vols. New York/London:

---

* David Chapman is associate professor of New Testament and Archaeology at Covenant Theological Seminary, 12330 Conway Road, St. Louis, MO 63141. Andreas Köstenberger is research professor of New Testament and Biblical Theology at Southeastern Baptist Theological Seminary, 120 S. Wingate St., Wake Forest, NC 27587.

1 *JETS* 43 (2000): 577–618. Appreciation is again expressed to friends at Tyndale House and to the university and seminary libraries in Cambridge, Tübingen, and St. Louis.

Funk & Wagnalls, 1901–1906. Older than *EncJud* but often has fuller articles. Available online at http://www.jewishencyclopedia.com and scanned images at http://archive.org. [*JE*]

Werblowsky, R. J. Zwi and Geoffrey Wigoder, eds. *The Oxford Dictionary of the Jewish Religion.* Oxford: OUP, 1997. Competent (but very concise) articles with limited bibliography. [*ODJR*]

1.2 Works Containing Surveys of Jewish Literature

Davies, W. D., Louis Finkelstein, John Sturdy, William Horbury, and Steven T. Katz, eds. *Cambridge History of Judaism.* 4 vols. Cambridge: CUP, 1984–2006. [*CHJ*]

Evans, Craig A. *Ancient Texts for New Testament Studies: A Guide to the Background Literature.* Peabody, MA: Hendrickson, 2005. Update of his *Noncanonical Writings and New Testament Interpretation* (1992).

Grabbe, Lester L. *A History of the Jews and Judaism in the Second Temple Period.* 4 vols. London/New York: T & T Clark, 2004–. Emphasis on discussing sources, with a tendency toward some skepticism and late dating.

Haase, Wolfgang, ed. *Aufstieg und Niedergang der Römischen Welt* II.19.1–2, II.20.1–2, and II.21.1–2. Berlin: de Gruyter, 1979–1987. [*ANRW*]

Helyer, Larry R. *Exploring Jewish Literature of the Second Temple Period: A Guide for New Testament Students.* Downers Grove: InterVarsity, 2002.

Kraft, Robert A. and George W. E. Nickelsburg, eds. *Early Judaism and Its Modern Interpreters.* Philadelphia: Fortress/Atlanta: Scholars, 1986.

McNamara, Martin. *Intertestamental Literature.* Wilmington, DE: Michael Glazier, 1983.

Mulder, Martin Jan, ed. *Mikra: Text, Translation, Reading and Interpretation of the Hebrew Bible in Ancient Judaism and Early Christianity.* CRINT 2.1. Assen/Maastricht: Van Gorcum, 1988; Philadelphia: Fortress, 1988. Very helpful, especially on LXX, Targums, and other versions of the OT. [*Mikra*]

Neusner, Jacob, ed. *Judaism in Late Antiquity, Vol. 1: The Literary and Archaeological Sources.* Handbuch der Orientalistik 1.16; Leiden: Brill, 1995. [*JLA*]

Nickelsburg, George W. E. *Jewish Literature Between the Bible and the Mishnah.* 2d ed. Philadelphia: Fortress, 2005. Principally discusses DSS, Apocrypha, and Pseudepigrapha. With CD-ROM of entire book, plus images and a study guide. [Nickelsburg, *Jewish Literature*]

Sæbø, Magne, ed. *Hebrew Bible, Old Testament: The History of its Interpretation: Vol. 1 From the beginnings to the Middle Ages (until 1300).* Part 1: Antiquity. Göttingen: Vandenhoeck & Ruprecht, 1996.

Schürer, Emil. *The History of the Jewish People in the Age of Jesus Christ (175 B.C.– A.D. 135).* Ed. Geza Vermes et al. Rev. English ed. 3 vols. in 4. Edinburgh: T & T Clark, 1973–1987. For decades the standard work in the field (not to be confused with Hendrickson's reprinted translation of the original German edition, which is now out of date). [*HJPAJC*]

Stemberger, Günter. *Introduction to the Talmud and Midrash.* Fine work; see full bibliography under Rabbinic Literature. [Stemberger, *Introduction*]

Stone, Michael E., ed. *Jewish Writings of the Second Temple Period.* CRINT 2.2. Assen: Van Gorcum; Philadelphia: Fortress, 1984.

See further CRINT volumes under Rabbinic Literature below. [*JWSTP*]
VanderKam, James C. *An Introduction to Early Judaism.* Grand Rapids: Eerdmans, 2001. Esp. pp. 53–173. 1.3 Sourcebooks
Barrett, C. K. *The New Testament Background: Writings from Ancient Greece and the Roman Empire that Illuminate Christian Origins.* San Francisco: Harper, 1987. A more recent edition (with different subtitle) of this classic sourcebook. Chilton, Bruce D., gen. ed. *A Comparative Handbook to the Gospel of Mark: Comparisons with Pseudepigrapha, the Qumran Scrolls, and Rabbinic Literature.* The New Testament Gospels in their Judaic Contexts 1. Leiden: Brill, 2009.
After each pericope in Mark, an extensive array of comparable Jewish sources are quoted and followed by a very brief commentary on those sources. De Lange, Nicholas. *Apocrypha: Jewish Literature of the Hellenistic Age.* New York: Viking, 1978. Excerpts Apocrypha and Pseudepigrapha writings in thematic categories.
Elwell, Walter A. and Robert W. Yarbrough, eds. *Readings from the First-Century World: Primary Sources for New Testament Study.* Encountering Biblical Studies. Grand Rapids: Baker, 1998. Intended for college students. First part topical, second part quotes illuminating Jewish and Graeco-Roman sources in NT canonical order.
Feldman, Louis H. and Meyer Reinhold. *Jewish Life and Thought among Greeks and Romans: Primary Readings.* Minneapolis: Augsburg Fortress, 1996; Edinburgh: T & T Clark, 1996. A fine collection covering a broad array of key topics.
Fitzmyer, Joseph A. and Daniel J. Harrington. *A Manual of Palestinian Aramaic Texts (second century B.C.–second century A.D.).* BibOr 34. Rome: Biblical Institute Press, 1978. Highly significant collection of texts with translations and introduction (includes many Qumran documents).
Ginzberg, Louis. *The Legends of the Jews.* 7 vols. Jewish Publication Society of America, 1909–1938; repr. Baltimore: Johns Hopkins, 1998. Puts in narrative form the various rabbinic and apocryphal stories about OT heroes. Vols. 5–6 notes; vol. 7 index. Currently available online at several sites, though often without the vital endnotes and index volumes (see http://archive.org).
Hayward, C. T. R. *The Jewish Temple: A non-biblical sourcebook.* London/New York: Routledge, 1996.
Instone-Brewer, David. *Traditions of the Rabbis from the Era of the New Testament.* Grand Rapid: Eerdmans, 2004–. Following the order of Mishnah, excerpts selections from the Mishnah and the Tosefta that likely predate the year 70; provides text, translation, and brief commentary. [*TRENT*]
Nadich, Judah. *The Legends of the Rabbis.* 2 vols. London: Jason Aronson, 1994. Puts in narrative form the various rabbinic stories about early rabbis (Neusner's *Rabbinic Traditions about the Pharisees* is to be preferred for academic use).
Neusner, Jacob. *The Rabbinic Traditions about the Pharisees before 70.* 3 vols. Leiden: Brill, 1971. An enormously helpful source book with commentary

and summary analysis (reprints from University of South Florida and Wipf & Stock).

Runesson, Anders, Donald D. Binder, and Birger Olsson. *The Ancient Synagogue from its Origin to 200 C.E.: A Source Book.* Leiden: Brill, 2008; paperback Brill, 2010. Ancient literary sources, inscriptions and archaeological remains for both the land of Israel and the diaspora. Also includes a chapter on Jewish temples outside Jerusalem (e.g. Leontopolis).

Schiffman, Lawrence H. *Texts and Traditions: A Source Reader for the Study of Second Temple and Rabbinic Judaism.* Hoboken: Ktav, 1998. Complements his history of early Judaism.

Williams, Margaret H, ed. *The Jews among the Greeks and Romans: A Diasporan Sourcebook.* Baltimore: Johns Hopkins, 1998; London: Duckworth, 1998.

1.4 Bibliography

Anderson, Norman Elliott. *Tools for Bibliographical and Backgrounds Research on the New Testament.* 2d ed. South Hamilton, MA: Gordon-Conwell Theological Seminary, 1987.

Delling, Gerhard. *Bibliographie zur Jüdisch-Hellenistischen und Intertestamentarischen Literatur 1900–1965.* TU 106. Berlin: Akademie, 1969.

Noll, Stephen F. *The Intertestamental Period: A Study Guide.* Inter-Varsity Christian Fellowship of the United States of America, 1985.

1.5 General Computer Programs and English-based Websites
(current at time of writing)

Dinur Center for Research in Jewish History of the Hebrew University in Jerusalem (useful web links under "Second Temple and Talmudic Era"): http://jewishhistory.huji.ac.il/links/texts.htm.

Early Jewish Writings by Peter Kirby (links to older translations and introductions to Apocrypha, Pseudepigrapha, Philo and Josephus; currently many broken links but still useful): http://www.earlyjewishwritings.com.

4 Enoch: The Online Encyclopedia of Second Temple Judaism and Christian Origins by the Enoch Seminar (edited wiki that is still in process): http://www.4enoch.org.

HebrewBooks.org (classical Hebrew books for free download; website in Hebrew): http://www.hebrewbooks.org.

Internet Sacred Text Archive (older English translations of Jewish literature; primarily rabbinic works): http://www.sacred-texts.com/jud/index.htm.

The Judaic Classics Deluxe Edition: CD-ROM from Davka Software available for Windows or Mac (see below under Rabbinic Literature).

New Testament Gateway (Judaica page): http://www.ntgateway.com/tools-andresources/judaica.

Paleojudaica by James R. Davila: http://paleojudaica.blogspot.com.

Princeton University Library Jewish Studies Resources: http://www.princeton.edu/~pressman/jewsub.htm.

Resource Pages for Biblical Studies by Torrey Seland: http://torreys.org/bible.

Second Temple Synagogues by Donald Binder (includes links to introductions, texts, and photos of early Jewish literature): http://www.pohick.org/sts.

Thesaurus Linguae Graecae (searchable database of ancient Greek literature available on CD-ROM or via internet subscription; includes Philo, Josephus, Greek Apocrypha and Pseudepigrapha). Website at http://www.tlg.uci.edu.

Tyndale House (helpful links for Biblical Studies): http://www.tyndale.

cam.ac.uk/index.php?page=weblinks.
Virtual Religion Index: http://virtualreligion.net/vri/judaic.html (note links to Biblical Studies and to Jewish Studies).

2. Old Testament Versions 2.1 Greek Versions 2.1.1 Septuagint

The term "Septuagint" is properly attributed only to the Old Greek Pentateuch (translated c. 3d cent. BC), but common parlance labels the whole Old Greek OT and Apocrypha as Septuagint (LXX). It represents the earliest extant Jewish Greek translation of the OT. However, since the major LXX manuscripts are Christian, the possibility exists of Christian tampering with the text at some junctures. While earlier studies frequently focused on the LXX as a textual witness to its Hebrew *Vorlage*, a significant trend now also views its renderings of the OT as representing traditional Jewish interpretation. The individual biblical books vary in their translation style, indicating a plurality of translators and dates of translation.

Some biblical books differ significantly from the MT (e.g. Jeremiah, Samuel), and others exist in double recensions (e.g. Judges, Esther, Tobit, Daniel). The LXX also provides a major witness to all the Apocrypha except 4 Ezra [= 2 Esdras] (including also 3–4 Maccabees and Odes, which are not in the traditional English Apocrypha). *Bibliographies*: Dogniez, Cécile. *Bibliography of the Septuagint (1970–1993)*. VTSup 60. Leiden:

Brill, 1995. Brock, Sebastian P., Charles T. Fritsch, and Sidney Jellicoe. *A Classified Bibliography of the Septuagint.* ALGHJ 6. Leiden: Brill, 1973.

See also: bibliographic updates in *The Bulletin of the International Organization for Septuagint and Cognate Studies* (webpage at http://ccat.sas.upenn.edu/ioscs); also note the Septuagint Online webpage at http://www.kalvesmaki.com/LXX and the bibliography to the Septuaginta Deutsch at http://www.septuagintaforschung.de/files/WUNT-219-Bibilographie.pdf. *Critical and Diplomatic Texts*:

Septuaginta: Vetus Testamentum Graecum Auctoritate Academiae Scientiarum Gottingensis editum. 16 vols. Göttingen: Vandenhoeck & Ruprecht, 1931–. The standard scholarly critical edition, but incomplete. Known as the "Göttingen edition." Some volumes are divided into separate "parts."

Barthélemy, Dominique. *Les Devanciers D'Aquila: Première Publication Intégrale du Texte des Fragments du Dodécaprophéton.* VTSup 10. Leiden: Brill, 1963.

Greek Minor Prophets scroll from Naal ever (8HevXIIgr). Also see DJD 8, and Lifshitz in *IEJ* 12 (1962) 201–207 and in *Yedio☐ t* 26 (1962) 183–90.

Brooke, Alan England, Norman McLean, and Henry St. John Thackeray, eds. *The Old Testament in Greek.* London: Cambridge University Press, 1906–1940. Text of Codex Vaticanus with extensive apparatus. Since the Göttingen edition is incomplete, this still provides the best critical apparatus for the Former Prophets and Chronicles. Available online at http://archive.org. *Handbook Text*:

Rahlfs, Alfred and Robert Hanhart, eds. *Septuaginta.* Rev. ed. 2 vols. in 1. Stuttgart: Deutsche Bibelgesellschaft, 2006. An eclectic text, but without adequate critical apparatus to evaluate editorial decisions (with a "moderate revision" from Rahlfs's 1935 edition). Rahlfs's original text is frequently found in Bible software (e.g. Accordance, BibleWorks, etc.) and online. *Text and Translation*: Brenton, Lancelot C. L. *The Septuagint with Apocrypha: Greek and English.* London: Samuel Bagster & Sons, 1851; repr. Peabody, MA: Hendrickson, 1992. Now dated in comparison to the NETS translation (see below), but has the advantage of a facing Greek text. Digitized pages available free online at http://www.archive.org and at http://www.ccel.org/ccel/brenton/lxx.html and English text of Brenton at http://www.ecclesia.org/truth/septuagint-hyperlinked.html.

Translation:
Pietersma, Albert and Benjamin G. Wright, eds. *A New English Translation of the Septuagint.* Oxford/New York: Oxford University Press, 2007. Fine translation by a team of Septuagint scholars. Abbreviated NETS. Available for some Bible software, and free online access at http://ccat.sas.upenn.edu/nets/edition.

Concordance:
Hatch, Edwin and Henry A. Redpath. *A Concordance to the Septuagint and the Other Greek Versions of the Old Testament.* 3 vols. Oxford: Clarendon, 1897–1906. Available online at http://archive.org. "Second edition" (Grand Rapids: Baker, 1998) contains a Hebrew-Greek reverse index by Muraoka.

A number of volumes have been released in the Computer Bible Series (series editors J. Arthur Baird, David Noel Freedman, and Watson E. Mills) published by Biblical Research Associates or by Edwin Mellen Press. These have been produced by J. David Thompson and are entitled similar to *A Critical Concordance to the Septuagint Genesis* or to *A Critical Concordance to the Apocrypha: 1 Maccabees.* Each provides book-by-book concordances of the LXX with a number of statistical aides.

Many computer programs also contain tagged Septuagint texts (e.g. BibleWorks, Accordance).

Lexicons:
Chamberlain, Gary Alan. *The Greek of the Septuagint: A Supplemental Lexicon.* Peabody, MA: Hendrickson, 2011. Includes all words not in BDAG, and otherwise only supplements BDAG on words when Septuagintal Greek meanings differ from standard NT definitions (thus this book by itself does not include all LXX vocabulary).

Lust, Johan, Erik Eynikel, and Katrin Hauspie. *A Greek-English Lexicon of the Septuagint.* Rev. ed. Stuttgart: Deutsche Bibelgesellschaft, 2003. First edition issued in two volumes (1992, 1996). Helpful glosses of all LXX vocabulary.

Muraoka, T. *A Greek-English Lexicon of the Septuagint.* Louvain: Peeters, 2009. Now complete, whereas previous iterations just focused on the Twelve Prophets (1993) or the Twelve Prophets and the Pentateuch (2002). A fine work by a careful lexicographer; should be consulted regularly.

Muraoka, T. *A Greek-Hebrew-Aramaic Two-way Index to the Septuagint.* Louvain: Peeters, 2010. Allows one to see what Greek words are used to translate.

the Hebrew/Aramaic OT, and vice versa. Previous parts of this tool were published in his earlier LXX lexicons (1993 and 2002) and in the Baker edition of Hatch's LXX concordance; but with the publication of his 2009 lexicon, this is now a stand-alone document.

Rehkopf, Friedrich. *Septuaginta-Vokabular.* Göttingen: Vandenhoeck & Ruprecht, 1989. Provides a single German gloss for each Greek word. For each entry he lists some LXX texts and compares with word count usage in the NT.

Taylor, Bernard A. *Analytical Lexicon to the Septuagint: Expanded edition.* Peabody, MA: Hendrickson; Stuttgart: Deutsche Bibelgesellschaft, 2009. Revision of his 1994 Zondervan edition, listing every word form found in Rahlfs's edition and employing glosses from the Lust/Eynikel/Hauspie lexicon; especially helpful for difficult parsings.

Grammars:

Conybeare, F. C. and St. George Stock. *Grammar of Septuagint Greek.* Boston: Ginn & Co., 1905; repr. Peabody, MA: Hendrickson, 1995. Introductory, but with section on syntax not in Thackeray (or in the German grammar by Helbing). Available online at http://archive.org and at http://www.ccel.org/c/conybeare/greekgrammar.

Thackeray, Henry St. John. *A Grammar of the Old Testament in Greek*, Vol. 1: Introduction, Orthography and Accidence. Cambridge: CUP, 1909; repr. Hildesheim: Olms, 1987. Available online at http://archive.org.

Introductions:

Dines, Jennifer M. *The Septuagint.* Understanding the Bible and its World. London: T & T Clark, 2004. Good short survey, especially helpful for first exposure to LXX studies.

Fernández Marcos, Natalio. *The Septuagint in Context: Introduction to the Greek Versions of the Bible.* Trans. Wilfred G. E. Watson from 2d Spanish ed. Atlanta: Society of Biblical Literature, 2009. Useful introduction from standpoint of Spanish scholarship (previous English edition published by Leiden: Brill, 2000).

Harl, Marguerite, Gilles Dorival, and Olivier Munnich. *La Bible Grecque des Septante: Du judaïsme hellénistique au christianisme ancient.* Initiations au christianisme ancien; Paris: Cerf, 1988. Introduction by important French scholars.

Jellicoe, Sidney. *The Septuagint and Modern Study.* Oxford: Clarendon, 1968; repr. Winona Lake: Eisenbrauns, 1993. Assumes the earlier *Introduction* by Swete.

Jobes, Karen H. and Moisés Silva. *Invitation to the Septuagint.* Grand Rapids: Baker, 2000. Fine volume providing overall orientation to Septuagint study.

Siegert, Folker. *Zwischen Hebräischer Bibel und Altem Testament: Eine Einführung in die Septuaginta.* Münsteraner Judaistische Studien 9. Münster: LIT, 2001. Additional volume provides index and "Wirkungsgeschichte" of the LXX in antiquity (see *Register zur "Einführung in die Septuaginta"*; Münster:

LIT, 2003).

Swete, Henry Barclay. *An Introduction to the Old Testament in Greek.* Rev. Richard Rusden Ottley. Cambridge: CUP, 1914; repr. Peabody, MA: Hendrickson, 1989. Classic textbook available online at http://archive.org and at http://www.ccel.org/s/ swete/greekot.

Also see *HJPAJC* 3.1:474–493; *Mikra* 161–88; *CHJ* 2:534–562; *ABD* 5:1093–1104. *Commentaries:*

Harl, Marguerite, et al. *La Bible d'Alexandrie.* 17+ vols. Paris: Cerf, 1986–. Focuses on how the LXX would have been read by Greek speakers in Jewish and Christian antiquity.

Septuagint Commentary Series. Leiden: Brill, 2005–. Edited by S. E. Porter, R. Hess, and J. Jarick.

Wevers, John William. *Notes on the Greek Text of Genesis.* SBLSCS 35. Atlanta: Scholars, 1993. Discusses textual and philological issues. Wevers has produced similar volumes for the rest of the Pentateuch.

The International Organization for Septuagint and Cognate Studies (IOSCS) announced plans in 2005 to publish the SBL Commentary on the Septuagint (though no volumes have appeared at time of writing).

2.1.2 Aquila, Symmachus, Theodotion

Known primarily from the fragmentary sources of Origen's Hexapla, "the Three" represent Jewish Greek translations from the early Common Era (though there are some early traditions that Symmachus and even Theodotion were Ebionite Christians). Extensive Syro-Hexaplaric fragments and remnants of the Three exist in other languages (notably Armenian). Bibliographies, concordances, and introductions on the Three are also listed in works on the LXX above (see also *HJPAJC* 3.1:493–504).

Text: Field, Fridericus. *Origenis Hexaplorum quae supersunt.* 2 vols. Oxford: Clarendon, 1875. Available online at http://archive.org. Other fragments have surfaced since Field, thus see the bibliographies and introductions noted under LXX. Also note that Göttingen LXX volumes list Hexaplaric traditions in the bottom apparatus. An English translation of Field's own Latin prolegomena to this work has been produced by Gérard J. Norton (Paris: Gabalda, 2005). The "Hexapla Institute" has announced plans to publish a new critical edition of Hexapla fragments (see http://www.hexapla.org).

Concordance:

Reider, Joseph and Nigel Turner. *An Index to Aquila.* VTSup 12. Leiden: Brill, 1966. Use in addition to the listing in Hatch and Redpath, Vol. 3 (see under LXX).

Commentary:

Salvesen, Alison. *Symmachus in the Pentateuch.* JSS Monograph 15. Manchester: University of Manchester, 1991.

2.2 Targumim

Aramaic translations and paraphrases of the OT are known from as early as the Qumran community. The targumim appear to originate from liturgical use in the synagogue, when a *meturgeman* would compose an (occasionally paraphrastic or expansive) Aramaic rendering of the biblical text to be read in the service.

Such targumim can testify to how the biblical text was interpreted in Judaism. "Official" targumim on the Pentateuch (*Tg. Onqelos*) and the Prophets (*Tg. Jonathan*) ha been passed down from Babylonian rabbinic circles, while parallel traditions are also known from Palestine. There are additional targumic traditions for each of the non-Aramaic books of the Writings. Besides MSS and printed editions devoted to targumim, the official targumim are printed with the MT in Rabbinic Bibles alongside traditional rabbinic commentaries. Targumic texts also occur in Polyglot editions (e.g. those printed in Antwerp, Paris, and London [=Walton's]) in parallel with the MT and other translations. The issues of dating and transmission history of the various targumim are often quite complex.

2.2.1 General Bibliography *Bibliography:*

Grossfeld, Bernard. *A Bibliography of Targum Literature.* Vols. 1 and 2: Bibliographica Judaica 3 and 8. New York: Ktav, 1972, 1977. Vol. 3: New York: Sepher-Hermon, 1990.

Forestell, J. T. *Targumic Traditions and the New Testament: An Annotated Bibliography with a New Testament Index.* SBL Aramaic Studies 4. Chico, CA: Scholars, 1979.

Nickels, Peter. *Targum and New Testament: A Bibliography together with a New Testament Index.* Scripta Pontificii Instituti Biblici 117. Rome: Pontifical Biblical Institute, 1967. Updated in Forestell.

Ongoing listing of publications in the *Newsletter for Targumic and Cognate Studies* (now with its own website, including some targum translations at http://targum.info). Note also the bibliographic articles by Díez Macho in Vols. 4 and 5 of *Neophyti 1* (listed below).

Critical Texts:

Sperber, Alexander. *The Bible in Aramaic: Based on Old Manuscripts and Printed Texts.* 4 vols. in 5. Leiden: Brill, 1959–1973. Vol. 4b presents a series of helpful studies on the preceding volumes. Major critical text of *Targums Onqelos* and *Jonathan*; less reliable on the Writings.

Translations:

McNamara, Martin, gen. ed. *The Aramaic Bible.* 22 vols. Edinburgh: T & T Clark, 1987–2007. Standard contemporary translation series, with typically good introductions and notes. *Also see*: Etheridge under Pentateuch. Some translations are also being made available online (see http://targum.info/targumic-texts). Eldon Clem is producing English translations for Accordance Bible Software of Targums Onkelos, Jonathan, Neofiti, and Pseudo-Jonathan; see http://www.accordancebible.com and note the review in *Aramaic Studies* 5 (2007) 151–58.

Concordances:

Searchable morphologically tagged Aramaic texts are currently available for Accordance, BibleWorks, and Logos software packages. These are based on texts from the Comprehensive Aramaic Lexicon Project (sometimes drawing on older editions, such as those by Lagarde).

Lexicons:

Cook, Edward M. *A Glossary of Targum Onkelos: According to Alexander Sperber's Edition.* Studies in the Aramaic Interpretation of Scripture. Leiden: Brill,

2008.
Dalman, Gustav. *Aramäisch-neuhebräisches Wörterbuch zu Targum, Talmud, und Midrasch.* Göttingen, 1938. Available online at http://archive.org.
Jastrow, Marcus. *A Dictionary of the Targumim, the Talmud Babli and Yerushalmi, and the Midrashic Literature.* 2 vols. New York: Pardes, 1950; singlevolume repr. New York: Judaica, 1971 and Peabody, MA: Hendrickson, 2005. Convenient resource for translating all targumic and early rabbinic literature. Available online at http://www.tyndalearchive.com/tabs/jastrow.
Levy, J. *Chaldäisches Wörterbuch über die Targumim und einen grossen Theil des rabbinischen Schriftthums.* 2 vols. Leipzig: Baumgärtner, 1867–1868; repr. Köln: Joseph Melzer, 1959. Available online at http://archive.org.
Sokoloff, Michael. *A Dictionary of Jewish Babylonian Aramaic of the Talmudic and Geonic Periods.* Dictionaries of Talmud, Midrash and Targum 3. Ramat-Gan, Israel: Bar Ilan University Press; Baltimore: Johns Hopkins, 2002. Sokoloff's dictionaries generally employ better informed lexicography than Jastrow.
Sokoloff, Michael. *A Dictionary of Jewish Palestinian Aramaic of the Byzantine Period.* 2d ed. Dictionaries of Talmud, Midrash and Targum 2; Ramat-Gan, Israel: Bar Ilan University Press; Baltimore: Johns Hopkins, 2002. Also contains a marvelous set of indexes to the passages cited.
Also see: Comprehensive Aramaic Lexicon Project of Hebrew Union College at http://cal1.cn.huc.edu. This website includes a searchable database of Aramaic lexical information and of Aramaic texts through the 13th century. It also houses a bibliographic database, and lists "Addenda et Corrigenda" to the two Sokoloff dictionaries above.

Grammars:

Dalman, Gustaf. *Grammatik des Jüdisch-Palästinischen Aramäisch: Nach den Idiomen des Palästinischen Talmud des Onkelostargum und Prophetentargum und der Jerusalemischen Targume.* 2d ed. Leipzig: Hinrichs, 1905; repr. Darmstadt: Wissenschaftliche Buchgesellschaft, 1960. Available online at http://archive.org.
Fassberg, Steven E. *A Grammar of the Palestinian Targum Fragments from the Cairo Genizah.* HSS 38. Atlanta: Scholars, 1991. Focuses primarily on phonology and morphology.
Golomb, David M. *A Grammar of Targum Neofiti.* HSM 34. Chico, CA: Scholars, 1985. Attends primarily to morphology, but contains a final chapter reviewing matters of verbal and nominal syntax.
Kuty, Renaud J. *Studies in the Syntax of Targum Jonathan to Samuel.* Ancient Near Eastern Studies Supplements 30. Leuven: Peeters, 2010. Whereas other studies focus on morphology, this highlights key syntactical matters.
Stevenson, William B. *Grammar of Palestinian Jewish Aramaic.* 2d ed. Oxford: Clarendon, 1962. Beginning grammar (though without exercises) introducing the language of both Palestinian and Babylonian post-biblical Jewish Aramaic. Includes syntactical notes missing in Dalman. Secondedition reprint of 1924 with a new "Appendix on Numerals" by J. A. Emerton.

Some beginning grammars of Biblical Aramaic also touch on Targumic Aramaic (and other works of rabbinic origin); e.g. F. E. Greenspahn, *An Introduction to Aramaic.* 2d ed. Atlanta: SBL, 2003. Also see Y. Frank, *Grammar for Gemara* (below under Babylonian Talmud).

Introductions:

Bowker, John. *The Targums and Rabbinic Literature.* Cambridge: CUP, 1969. An introduction to the targumim in relation to other rabbinic literature. Also contains a translation of a substantial portion of *Tg. Ps.-J.* to Genesis.

Díez Macho, Alejandro. *El Targum: Introducción a las traducciones aramaicas de la Biblia.* Textos y Estudios 21. Madrid: Consejo Superior de Investigaciones Científicas, 1982. The classic introduction by the foremost member of the "Spanish school."

Flesher, Paul V. M., and Bruce Chilton. *The Targums: A Critical Introduction.* Studies in the Aramaic Interpretation of Scripture 12; Leiden: Brill, 2011; Waco, TX: Baylor University Press, 2011. Significant recent introduction that covers a wide array of academic topics.

Gleßmer, Uwe. *Einleitung in die Targume zum Pentateuch.* TSAJ 48. Tübingen: J. C. B. Mohr [Paul Siebeck], 1995.

Grelot, Pierre. *What Are the Targums? Selected Texts.* Trans. Salvator Attanasio; Old Testament Studies 7; Collegeville, MN: Liturgical, 1992. Selections of expansive targumic passages with introduction. Caution is required since Grelot combines different targumic traditions.

Le Déaut, Roger. *Introduction à la Littérature Targumique.* Rome: Institut Biblique Pontifical, 1966. "Premiere partie" and thus incomplete, but quite helpful.

Also see his brief article in *CHJ* 2:563–90; and his more substantial treatment of "Targum" in L. Pirot and A. Robert, *Supplément au Dictionnaire de la Bible.* Paris: Letouzey, 2005, 13:1*–344*.

Levine, Etan. *The Aramaic Version of the Bible: Contents and Context.* BZAW 174. Berlin: de Gruyter, 1988. Addresses the targumim as a whole, focusing on targumic themes.

McNamara, Martin. *Targum and Testament Revisited: Aramaic Paraphrases of the Hebrew Bible.* 2d ed. Grand Rapids: Eerdmans, 2010. Also contains a helpful appendix that introduces all extant targums.

See also: the useful articles by P. S. Alexander in *Mikra* 217–53 and in *ABD* 6:320–331; also note *HJPAJC* 1:99–114; *CHJ* 2:563–590.

2.2.2 Targumim on the Pentateuch Divided into the following categories:
(1) Official Targum of Babylonia = Onqelos (text in Sperber above).
(2) "Palestinian Targumim" (editions noted below)
  (a) Neofiti 1
  (b) Pseudo-Jonathan
  (c) Fragment Targum
  (d) Cairo Genizah Fragments
  (e) Toseftot
  (f) Festival Collections
  (g) Targumic Poems

For texts and bibliography on the last three categories see: Sperber, *Bible in Aramaic* 1:354–57 (above); *Mikra* 251; and Klein, *Genizah Manuscripts* Vol. 1: xxviii– xxxix (below).

Texts:

Diez Macho, Alexander, L. Diez Merino, E. Martinez Borobio, and Teresa Martinez Saiz, eds. *Biblia Polyglotta Matritensia IV: Targum Palaestinense in Pentateuchum.* 5 vols. Madrid: Consejo Superior de Investigaciones Científicas, 1977–88. Contains Palestinian Targumim in parallel columns (Neofiti, Pseudo-Jonathan, Fragment Targum, Cairo Genizah fragments) along with a Spanish translation of Pseudo-Jonathan. Very helpful.

Díez Macho, Alejandro, ed. *Neophyti 1: Targum Palestinense MS de la Biblioteca Vaticana.* 6 vols. Textos y Estudios 7–11 and 20; Madrid-Barcelona: Consejo Superior de Investigaciones Científicas, 1968–1979. Text of *Tg. Neof.* with facing Spanish translation and appended French and English translations. Each volume is prefaced with extensive introductory essays by Díez Macho. Volumes 2–5 also include verse-by-verse listings of (mostly rabbinic, but also pseudepigraphic and Christian) parallels to the interpretive elements in *Tg. Ps.-J.* and *Tg. Neof.* Volume 6 contains addenda, corrigenda, and indexes. A photocopy edition of the manuscript also exists (Jerusalem: Makor, 1970).

Ginsburger, M. *Pseudo-Jonathan (Thargum Jonathan ben Usiël zum Pentateuch). Nach der Londoner Handschrift (Brit. Mus. add. 27031).* Berlin: S. Calvary, 1903; repr. New York: Hildesheim, 1971. Editor's name can also be spelled Ginsberger in catalogs. There is another edition of this manuscript by D. Rieder (Jerusalem, 1974), reprinted with Modern Hebrew translation in 2 vols. in 1984–85. Also note the edition by Clarke (below under Concordances).

Klein, Michael L. *Genizah Manuscripts of Palestinian Targum to the Pentateuch.* 2 vols. Cincinnati: Hebrew Union College, 1986. Vol. 1 contains introduction, text, and translation of Genizah MSS of Pentateuchal targumim, also of festival collections, toseftot and targumic poems (additionally listing helpful bibliography for locating other toseftot, festival collections and targumic poems). Vol. 2 includes notes, glossary of vocabulary, and plates.

Klein, Michael L. *The Fragment-Targums of the Pentateuch: According to their Extant Sources.* 2 vols. AnBib 76. Rome: Biblical Institute Press, 1980. Vol. 1 introduction, text and indexes; Vol. 2 translation. Strongly preferred over Ginsburger's 1899 edition.

For Onqelos see Sperber (§2.2.1 above). Note also Masorah in Michael L. Klein, *The Masorah to Targum Onqelos: as preserved in MSS Vatican Ebreo 448, Rome Angelica Or. 7, Fragments from the Cairo Genizah and in Earlier Editions by A. Berliner and S. Landauer.* Targum Studies 1. Academic Studies in the History of Judaism; Binghamton, NY: Global Publications, SUNY Binghamton, 2000.

Translation:
Etheridge, J. W. *The Targums of Onkelos and Jonathan ben Uzziel on the Pentateuch with the Fragments of the Jerusalem Targum.* 1862; repr. New York: Ktav, 1968. Available online at http://targum.info/targumic-texts/pentateuchal-targumim and at http://archive.org. Also available for BibleWorks and Logos software. The McNamara *Aramaic Bible* series above is now generally preferred.

Le Déaut, Roger, with collaboration by Jacques Robert. *Targum du Pentateuque.* 5 vols. SC; Paris: Cerf, 1978–1981. French translation of Targum Neofiti and Targum Pseudo-Jonathan in parallel pages, with brief translational notes. The fifth volume serves as a topical index.

Also see: The *Aramaic Bible* series (above under 2.2.1 Targumim General Bibliography).

Concordances:
Brederek, Emil. *Konkordanz zum Targum Onkelos.* BZAW 9. Giessen: Alfred Töpelmann, 1906. Available online at http://archive.org.

Clarke, E. G., W. E. Aufrecht, J. C. Hurd, and F. Spitzer. *Targum Pseudo-Jonathan of the Pentateuch: Text and Concordance.* Hoboken: Ktav, 1984. Contains the same manuscript as Ginsberger and Rieder with KWIC concordance; on the concordance see M. Bernstein's cautious review in *JQR* 79 (1988) 227–30.

Kassovsky,. 5 vols. in 1. Jerusalem: Kiriath Moshe, 1933–40. For Onqelos.

Kaufman, Stephen A., Michael Sokoloff, and with the assistance of Edward M. Cook. *A Key-Word-in-Context Concordance to Targum Neofiti.* Publications of the Comprehensive Aramaic Lexicon Project 2. Baltimore: John Hopkins University Press, 1993. Also presents English glosses of the Aramaic words.

Note also some rabbinic search software contain searchable targumic texts (see under Rabbinic Literature).

Commentaries:
Aberbach, Moses and Bernard Grossfeld. *Targum Onkelos to Genesis: A Critical Analysis together with an English Translation of the Text.* New York: Ktav, 1982. Text of A. Berliner with English translation and comments (based on Sperber's edition).

Drazin, Israel. *Targum Onkelos to Exodus: An English Translation of the Text With Analysis and Commentary.* New York: Ktav, 1990. Text of A. Berliner with English translation and comments (based on Sperber's edition). Drazin has produced similar commentaries for *Tg. Onq.* to Leviticus (1994), Numbers (1998), and Deuteronomy (1982). Drazin emphasizes the literal translational elements of the Targum rather than seeing it as a full rabbinic interpretation. Note the cautious reviews by Emerton in *VT* 43 (1993) 280–81 and by Levine in *CBQ* 57 (1995) 766–67.

Grossfeld, Bernard. *Targum Neofiti 1: An Exegetical Commentary to Genesis, Including Full Rabbinic Parallels.* New York: Sepher-Hermon, 2000. Includes transcription of text and commentary with emphasis on rabbinic texts that parallel the Targum. 2.2.3 Targumim on the Prophets

Targum Jonathan forms the "official" targum to the Former and Latter

Prophets (text in Sperber, *Bible in Aramaic*, Vols. 2 and 3). There are also Palestinian Toseftot (marginal comments of other targumic traditions alongside Targum Jonathan in the MSS). On the Toseftot: see pp. vi–xlii of De Lagarde, *Prophetae Chaldaice* (below); see also Sperber, *Bible in Aramaic*, descriptions on pp. ix–x of Vol. 2 and p. xi of Vol. 3; further bibliography in *Mikra* 252.

Translation (with notes) in McNamara, *The Aramaic Bible* (see above).

Text:

De Lagarde, Paul. *Prophetae Chaldaice.* Leipzig: Teubner, 1872. Standard edition before Sperber (on which see §2.2.1 above). Available online at http://archive.org.

Stenning, J. F. *The Targum of Isaiah.* Oxford: Clarendon, 1949. A pointed critical text of Targum Jonathan to Isaiah with translation; Palestinian Toseftot to the Targum on pp. 224–28.

Concordances:

Moor, Johannes C. de, et al., eds. *A Bilingual Concordance to the Targum of the Prophets.* 21 vols. Leiden: Brill, 1995–2005. A concordance of the individual books of *Tg. Jon.* to the Former and Latter Prophets. Also lists Hebrew equivalents to the Aramaic vocabulary (providing English glosses to both the Aramaic and Hebrew terms).

Van Zijl, J. B. *A Concordance to the Targum of Isaiah: Based on the Brit. Mus. Or. MS. 2211.* SBLAS 3. Missoula, MT: Scholars, 1979.

Commentaries:

Levine, Etan. *The Aramaic Version of Jonah.* New York: Sepher-Hermon, 1975. Introduction, text, translation, and commentary of *Tg. Jon.* to Jonah.

Smelik, Willem F. *The Targum of Judges.* OTS 36. Leiden: Brill, 1995. Extensive introduction and commentary.

Van Staalduine-Sulman, Eveline. *The Targum of Samuel.* Studies in the Aramaic Interpretation of Scripture 1. Leiden: Brill, 2002. Commentary, translation, and study.

2.2.4 Targumim on the Writings

No known rabbinic targumic traditions exist for Daniel or for Ezra-Nehemiah (note these books already employ Aramaic). The study of the targumim to the Writings necessitates caution since frequently several targumic recensions exist for any one OT book (for overview see *ABD* 6:320–331). Note that Targum Job is different than the Qumran Job Targum (=11QtgJob =11Q10; see DJD 23 and further bibliography below under "Dead Sea Scrolls"). Two targumic traditions to Esther are recognized (Targum Rishon and Targum Sheni = *Tg. Esth I and II*). A so-called "Third Targum to Esther" exists in the Antwerp Polyglot, but it is disputed whether this Third Targum is essentially a condensation of Targum Rishon, the predecessor of Rishon, or properly a targum at all.

General Texts:

Sperber, Alexander. *The Bible in Aramaic: Based on Old Manuscripts and Printed Texts.* Vol. 4a. Leiden: Brill, 1968. Contains *Tg. Chron* (MS Berlin 125) and *Tg. Ruth* as in the De Lagarde edition, and includes from Brit. Mus. Or. 2375: *Tg. Cant, Tg. Lam, Tg. Eccl, and Tg. Esth* (mixed text type of Esther, due to the manuscript used).

De Lagarde, Paul. *Hagiographa Chaldaice.* Leipzig: Teubner, 1873. Text of Targumim to the Writings, including those not in Sperber (Psalms, Job, Proverbs, and both Esther Rishon and Esther Sheni). Available online at http://books.google.com.

Individual Texts:

Díez Merino, Luis. *Targum de Salmos: Edición Príncipe del Ms. Villa-Amil n. 5 de Alfonso de Zamora.* Bibliotheca Hispana Biblica 6. Madrid: Consejo Superior de Investigaciones Científicas, 1982. Introduction, text, Latin translation (by Alfonso de Zamora) and studies on this manuscript of *Tg. Psalms.*

Stec, David M. *The Text of the Targum of Job: An Introduction and Critical Edition.* AGJU 20. Leiden: Brill, 1994. A fine edition.

Díez Merino, Luis. *Targum de Job: Edición Principe del Ms. Villa-Amil n° 5 de Alfonso de Zamora.* Bibliotheca Hispana Biblica 8. Madrid: Consejo Superior de Investigaciones Científicas, 1984.

Díez Merino, Luis. *Targum de Proverbios. Edición Principe del Ms. Villa-Amil n° 5 de Alfonso de Zamora.* Madrid: Consejo Superior de Investigaciones Científicas, 1984. The next major edition of *Tg. Proverbs* since De Lagarde, *Hagiographa Chaldaice* (above).

Levine, Etan. *The Aramaic Version of Ruth.* AnBib 58. Rome: Biblical Institute Press, 1973. Introduction, text, translation, and commentary.

Jerusalmi, Isaac. *The Song of Songs in the Targumic Tradition: Vocalized Aramaic Text with Facing English Translation and Ladino Versions.* Cincinnati: Ladino, 1993.

Alonso Fontela, Carlos. *El Targum al Cantar de los Cantares (Edición Critica).* Collección Tesis Doctorales. Madrid: Editorial de la Universidad Complutense de Madrid, 1987.

Melamed, R. H. *The Targum to Canticles according to Six Yemenite MSS.* PhiladelJEWISH phia: Dropsie College, 1921. Covers the Yemenite recension, which differs from the Western texts at points. Reprinted from a series of articles in *JQR* n.s. 10–12 (1919–1921). Available online at http://archive.org.

Díez Merino, Luis. *Targum de Qohelet: Edición Principe del Ms. Villa-Amil n° 5 de Alfonso de Zamora.* Bibliotheca Hispana Biblica 13. Madrid: Consejo Superior de Investigaciones Científicas, 1987. An important edition of a manuscript otherwise unavailable.

Levine, Etan. *The Aramaic Version of Qohelet.* New York: Sepher-Hermon, 1978. Photocopy of MS Urb. 1 with translation and "conceptual analysis."

Levy, A. *Das Targum zu Qohelet nach sudarabischen Handschriften herausgegeben.* Breslau, 1905. Critical edition of *Tg. Eccl.*

Brady, Christian M. M. *The Rabbinic Targum of Lamentations: Vindicating God.* Studies in the Aramaic Interpretation of Scripture 3. Leiden: Brill, 2003. Study of this targum that includes a transcription of Codex Urbinas Hebr. 1 and translation.

Heide, Albert van der. *The Yemenite Tradition of the Targum of Lamentations: Critical Text and Analysis of the Variant Readings.* Leiden: Brill, 1981. The Yemenite tradition is significantly different from the Western text tradition.

Levine, Etan. *The Aramaic Version of Lamentations.* New York: Hermon, 1976. Introduction, text, translation, and commentary.

Ego, Beate. *Targum Scheni zu Ester: Übersetzung, Kommentar und theologische Deutung.* TSAJ 54. Tübingen: Mohr Siebeck, 1996.

Grossfeld, Bernard. *The Targum Sheni to the Book of Esther: A Critical Edition based on MS. Sassoon 282 with Critical Apparatus.* New York: Sepher-Hermon, 1994. Includes a full-length concordance and a photocopy of this manuscript.

Grossfeld, Bernard. *The First Targum to Esther: According to the MS Paris Hebrew 110 of the Bibliotheque Nationale.* New York: Sepher-Hermon, 1983. Critical text, translation, and commentary with introduction to Targum Rishon to Esther. Includes plates.

Le Déaut, R., and J. Robert. *Targum des Chroniques (Cod. Vat. Urb. Ebr. 1).* 2 vols. AnBib 51. Rome: Biblical Institute Press, 1971. Vol. 1 introduction and (French) translation; Vol. 2 text, indexes, and a glossary of vocabulary in Aramaic, French, and English.

Concordance:

Grossfeld, Bernard. *Concordance of the First Targum to the Book of Esther.* SBLAS 5. Chico, CA: Scholars, 1984. For the Second Targum (Targum Sheni) see the KWIC concordance in Grossfeld's edition noted above.

2.3 Other (Latin and Syriac)

Whereas the Vulgate is clearly Christian (translated by Jerome), the lineage of the Old Latin is more obscure. A frequent dependence on the LXX, and occasional portions that agree with Jewish tradition over the LXX, make it possible that the Old Latin contains some certifiable Jewish passages. The Peshi☐ta, though ultimately a Christian Bible, may originally have been allied with Jewish tradition, especially 252. when it agrees with the targumim. For sake of space, standard Latin and Syriac grammars and lexicons are not listed below. Other early translations that appear largely dependent on the Septuagint, such as Bohairic Coptic or Christian Palestinian Aramaic, are not represented below. For introductions see *Mikra* 255–97, 299–313; *ABD* 6:794–803.

Old Latin Texts: Vetus Latina: Die Reste der altlateinischen Bibel. Freiburg: Herder, 1951–. Critical edition currently covering Genesis, Canticles, Wisdom, Ecclesiasticus, and Isaiah from the OT and Apocrypha. Projected 26 volumes (with multiple parts).

Sabatier, Petri, ed. *Bibliorum Sacrorum Latinae Versiones Antiquae.* 3 vols. Rheims: Reginald Florentain, 1743–1749. Vulgate and Old Latin in parallel columns. Some volumes available on http://archive.org.

Peshi☐ta Bibliography:

Dirksen, P. B. *An Annotated Bibliography of the Peshita of the Old Testament.* Monographs of the Peshita Institute 5. Leiden: Brill, 1989.

Syriac Peshita Text:

Vetus Testamentum Syriace Iuxta Simplicem Syrorum Versionem [= *The Old Testament in Syriac According to the Peshita Version*]. Leiden: Brill, 1973–. In four parts, with multiple fascicles.

Peshita Translation:
Lamsa, George M. *The Holy Bible from Ancient Eastern Manuscripts: Containing the Old and New Testaments, translated from the Peshitta, the authorized Bible of the church of the East.* Philadelphia: Holman, 1957; repr. San Francisco: Harper & Row, 1985. Not fully reliable. Available online a http://www.aramaicpeshitta.com/OTtools/LamsaOT.htm.
Gorgias Press has inaugurated its Surath Ktobh series (overseen by George A. Kiraz, projected to be 30 volumes), featuring facing pages of the Peshi︐ta (without textual apparatus) and a literal English translation.
Peshita Concordances:
Borbone, P. G. and K. D. Jenner, eds. *The Old Testament in Syriac According to the Peshitta Version: Part 5 Concordance.* Vetus Testamentum Syriace. Leiden: Brill, 1997–. Strothmann, Werner, Kurt Johannes, and Manfred Zumpe. *Konkordanz zur Syrischen Bibel: Die Propheten.* 4 vols. GOF Reihe 1, Syriaca 25. Wiesbaden:
Otto Harrassowitz, 1984. They also produced a four volume 1986 concordance for *Der Pentateuch* (GOF Reihe 1, Syriaca 26).
Peshi︐ta texts are increasingly coming available for Bible software (e.g. Accordance and BibleWorks).
Peshita Introduction:
Weitzman, M. P. *The Syriac Version of the Old Testament: An Introduction.* University of Cambridge Oriental Publications 56. Cambridge: CUP, 1999.
See also: Pp. 1057–59 in *EDEJ*. 3. Apocrypha
Various Christian OT manuscripts (Greek, Latin, Syriac, etc.) contain books not found in the Masoretic tradition. Translations may be found in some English Bibles (e.g. RSV, NRSV, NEB, REB) of the Greek (LXX) apocrypha as well as Latin "2 Esdras." Other translations may be found in the editions edited by Charles, by Charlesworth (for 4 Ezra), and by Kümmel listed under General Pseudepigrapha
Bibliography below (cf. esp. Charlesworth, *OTP* 2:609–24 for apocryphal Psalms). English "2 Esdras" is listed in the Vulgate as 4 Ezra and should not be confused with LXX 2 Esdras (which is the Greek version of OT Ezra and Nehemiah). Most modern scholars believe 4 Ezra is a compilation, often designating (the probably Christian) chapters 1–2 and chapters 15–16 as 5 Ezra and 6 Ezra respectively. Thus the name "4 Ezra" in much modern scholarship has been reserved for Vulgate 4 Ezra 3–14.
The above listed LXX editions and concordances serve for the Greek Apocrypha. Greek fragments of 4 Ezra have been discovered (see Denis, *Fragmenta pseudepigraphorum* below under Pseudepigrapha). Latin versions of these books as well as the whole of 4 Ezra are also known in the Old Latin (see above) and Vulgate (for concordances to Latin 4 Ezra, see Denis or Lechner-Schmidt under General Pseudepigrapha Bibliography below). For Syriac editions, see the Peshita bibliography above. Many books of the Apocrypha are thought to stem from Semitic originals. Prior to the DSS, fragments in Hebrew were known of Ben Sira (= Sirach = Ecclesiasticus). Hebrew and Aramaic texts have been found in the DSS for Tobit (4Q196–200 in DJD XIX), Sirach (2Q18 in DJD III; 11QPsa [=11Q5] xxi–xxii in DJD IV; some Masada texts) and some of the apocryphal Psalms (11QPsa in DJD IV; for 4Q380–381 see Schuller, *Non-Canonical Psalms*

from Qumran below under "Dead Sea Scrolls"); for a list see Peter W. Flint "Appendix II," in Flint & Vanderkam, eds., *The Dead Sea Scrolls After Fifty Years*, pp. 666–68 (see "Introductions" under Dead Sea Scrolls below).
Other Bibliography:
Reiterer, Friedrich Vinzenz, ed. *Bibliographie zu Ben Sira.* BZAW 266. Berlin: de Gruyter, 1998. Not well indexed or annotated.
See also: Bibelwissenschaft by Franz Böhmisch (http://www.animabit.de/bibel/sir.htm). *Other Texts (Ordered by apocryphal book):*
Beentjes, Pancratius C. *The Book of Ben Sira in Hebrew: A Text Edition of all Extant Hebrew Manuscripts and a Synopsis.* VTSup 68. Leiden: Brill, 1997. Paperback repr. Society of Biblical Literature (2006).

The Book of Ben Sira: Text, Concordance and an Analysis of the Vocabulary. The Historical Dictionary of the Hebrew Language. Jerusalem: Academy of the Hebrew Language and Shrine of the Book, 1973. Synoptic edition of Hebrew MSS with concordance.

Yadin, Yigael. *The Ben Sira Scroll from Masada.* Jerusalem: Israel Exploration Society, 1965. Repr. from *Eretz-Israel* vol. 8.

Schechter, S. and C. Taylor. *The Wisdom of Ben Sira: Portions of the Book of Ecclesiasticus from Hebrew Manuscripts in the Cairo Genizah Collection Presented to the University of Cambridge by the Editors.* Cambridge: CUP, 1899.

Klijn, Albertus Frederik J. *Die Esra-Apokalypse (IV. Esra): Nach dem lateinischen Text unter Benutzung der anderen Versionen übersetzt.* GCS. Berlin: de Gruyter, 1992.

Stone, Michael E. *The Armenian Version of IV Ezra.* University of Pennsylvania Armenian Texts and Studies. Missoula, MT: Scholars Press, 1979.

Sievers, Joseph. *Synopsis of the Greek Sources for the Hasmonean Period: 1–2 Maccabees and Josephus War 1 and Antiquities 12–14.* Rome: Editrice Pontificio Istituto Biblico, 2001. Useful for comparative and historical studies. Texts are only presented in Greek.

Weeks, S. D. E., S. J. Gathercole, L. T. Stuckenbruck. *The Book of Tobit: Texts from the Principal Ancient and Medieval Traditions. With Synopsis, Concordances, and Annotated Texts in Aramaic, Hebrew, Greek, Latin, and Syriac.* Fontes et subsidia ad Bibliam pertinentes 3. Berlin: de Gruyter, 2004.

Wagner, Christian J. *Polyglotte Tobit-Synopse: Griechisch, Lateinisch, Syrisch, Hebräisch, Aramäisch: mit einem Index zu den Tobit-Fragmenten vom Toten Meer.* Mitteilungen des Septuaginta-Unternehmens 28. Göttingen: Vandenhoeck & Ruprecht, 2003. Greek, Latin, and Syriac in parallel columns, with separate section on Hebrew and Aramaic fragments.

See also: Berger synopsis of 4 Ezra with 2 Baruch (below under Pseudepigrapha: 2 Baruch). *Other Concordances:*
Barthélemy, D. and O. Rickenbacher. *Konkordanz zum hebräischen Sirach mit syrisch-hebräischem Index.* Göttingen: Vandenhoeck & Ruprecht, 1973. Also see concordance in *The Book of Ben Sira* (above).

Muraoka, T. *A Greek-Hebrew/Aramaic Index to I Esdras.* SBLSCS 11. Chico, CA: Scholars Press, 1984.

Strothmann, Werner, ed. *Wörterverzeichnis der apokryphen-deuterokanonischen Schriften des Alten Testaments in der Peshitta.* Göttinger Orientforschungen Reihe 1, Syriaca 27. Wiesbaden: Otto Harrassowitz, 1988. Also provides a Latin gloss for each Syriac word.

Winter, Michael M. *A Concordance to the Peshi☐ta Version of Ben Sira.* Monographs of the Peshitta Institute 2. Leiden: Brill, 1976.

Lexicon:

For Greek see above under Septuagint and below under General Pseudepigrapha Bibliography. For Hebrew text of Ben Sira see Clines, ed., *Dictionary of Classical Hebrew* (below under Dead Sea Scrolls).

Introductions:

Brockington, L. H. *A Critical Introduction to the Apocrypha.* London: Gerald Duckworth, 1961.

DeSilva, David A. *Introducing the Apocrypha: Message, Context, and Significance.* Grand Rapids: Baker, 2002.

Harrington, Daniel J. *Invitation to the Apocrypha.* Grand Rapids: Eerdmans, 1999.

Kaiser, Otto. *The Old Testament Apocrypha: An Introduction.* Peabody, MA: Hendrickson, 2004. Translation of his 2000 German edition.

Longenecker, Bruce W. *2 Esdras.* Guides to the Apocrypha and Pseudepigrapha; Sheffield: Sheffield Academic Press, 1995. Other helpful introductions have also appeared in this series, including Bartlett on *1 Maccabees*, DeSilva on *4 Maccabees*, Coggins on *Sirach*, Grabbe on *Wisdom of Solomon*, Otzen on *Tobit and Judith*.

Metzger, Bruce M. *An Introduction to the Apocrypha.* Oxford: OUP, 1957.

Oesterley, W. O. E. *An Introduction to the Books of the Apocrypha.* New York: Macmillan, 1935.

Torrey, Charles Cutler. *The Apocryphal Literature: A Brief Introduction.* New Haven: Yale University Press, 1945. Also introduces many books of the Pseudepigrapha.

See also: Nickelsburg, *Jewish Literature*; *JWSTP*; *HJPAJC* Vol. 3; *CHJ* 2:409–503; *ABD* 1:292–94 and s.v. by book; *EDEJ* 143–62 and s.v. by book.

Commentaries:

Abel, P. F.-M. *Les Livres des Maccabées.* Études Bibliques. Paris: J. Gabalda, 1949.

Larcher, C. *Le Livre de la Sagesse ou La Sagesse de Salomon.* Études Bibliques n.s. 1; 3 vols. Paris: J. Gabalda, 1983–1985.

Scarpat, Giuseppe. *Libro della Sapienza: Testo, traduzione, introduzione e comment.* 3 vols. Biblica Testi e studi 1, 3, 6. Brescia: Paideia, 1989–1999.

Talshir, Zipora. *I Esdras: A Text Critical Commentary.* SBLSCS 50. Atlanta: Society of Biblical Literature, 2001.

Commentaries exist on each book in some biblical commentary series. In English note especially Septuagint Commentary Series (Brill), Commentaries on Early Jewish Literature series (de Gruyter), Anchor Bible series (Doubleday), Jewish Apocryphal Literature series from Dropsie University (Harper), and Stone on *Fourth Ezra* in the Hermeneia series (Fortress). Shorter but still helpful are the volumes in the Cambridge Bible Commentary series (CUP) and the OT Message series (Michael Glazier). Also see the UBS Handbook Series (United Bible Societies) for translation comments. In German note the Herders Theologischer Kommentar zum Alten Testament series (Herder), Das Alte Testament Deutsch: Apokryphen, Neuer Stuttgarter Kommentar Altes Testament (Katholisches Bibelwerk), and Die Neue Echter Bibel (Echter). Some one-volume commentaries also include the Apocrypha; e.g. *Eerdmans Commentary on the Bible* (Eerdmans, 2003).

4. Pseudepigrapha (Jewish)

The term "pseudepigrapha" properly refers to literature written under an assumed name (generally of some famous OT person). However, "the Pseudepigrapha" has become almost a catch-all category for intertestamental works which do not fit elsewhere. The translation volume edited by Charlesworth, while focusing on works of primarily Jewish origin, also includes some Christian works. Below are listed the most important pseudepigraphal works for the study of Judaism. Since some Christian pseudepigrapha may include original Jewish material, a few of these are also noted. For bibliography of other Christian pseudepigrapha and some lesser known works see Haelewyck, *Clavis Apocryphorum* (noted below).

Pseudo-Philo and named Jewish authors are listed later in this bibliography.

4.1 General Pseudepigrapha Bibliography *Bibliography:*

Orlov, Andrei A. *Selected Studies in the Slavonic Pseudepigrapha.* SVTP 23. Leiden/ Boston: Brill, 2009. Note the "Selected Bibliography on the Transmission of the Jewish Pseudepigrapha in the Slavic Milieux" on pp. 201–434.

DiTommaso, Lorenzo. *A Bibliography of Pseudepigrapha Research 1850–1999.* JSPSup 39. Sheffield: Sheffield Academic Press, 2001. 1067 very helpful pages.

Lehnardt, Andreas. *Bibliographie zu den jüdischen Schriften aus hellenistisch-römischer Zeit.* JSHRZ VI/2. Gütersloh: Gütersloher Verlagshaus, 1999. Very useful.

Haelewyck, J.-C. *Clavis Apocryphorum Veteris Testamenti.* CChr. Turnhout: Brepols, 1998. Valuable list of texts, translations, and concordances for each pseudepigraphal book.

Charlesworth, James H. *The Pseudepigrapha and Modern Research with a Supplement.* New ed. SBLSCS. Chico, CA: Scholars, 1981. Dated, but also contains competent brief introductions.

See also: Arbeitshilfen für das Studium der Pseudepigraphen (http://www.unileipzig. de/~nt/asp/index.htm).

Texts (general):

Stone, Michael E. *Armenian Apocrypha Relating to Adam and Eve.* SVTP 14. Leiden: Brill, 1996. Not all of this material is early. Also see W. Lowndes Lipscomb, *The Armenian Apocryphal Adam Literature.* University of Pennsylvania Armenian Texts and Studies 8. Scholars Press, 1990.

Stone, Michael E. *Armenian Apocrypha Relating to the Patriarchs and Prophets.*

Jerusalem: Israel Academy of Sciences and Humanities, 1982.
Denis, Albert-Marie. *Fragmenta pseudepigraphorum quae supersunt graeca.*
PVTG 3.
Leiden: Brill, 1970. The standard edition of Greek fragments. Bound
with Black's edition of Greek 1 Enoch.
See also: Online Critical Pseudepigrapha (http://ocp.tyndale.ca), which provides
introductions (with bibliography on modern editions of texts) and
original language texts for many works.
Translations:
Charles, R. H., ed. *The Apocrypha and Pseudepigrapha of the Old Testament in English.* 2 vols. Oxford: Clarendon, 1913. Still quite useful, though supplanted
by Charlesworth and Sparks. Available online at http://archive.org
or at http://www.ccel.org/c/charles/otpseudepig.
Charlesworth, James H., ed. *The Old Testament Pseudepigrapha.* 2 vols. New
York: Doubleday, 1983–1985; paperback repr. Peabody, MA: Hendrickson,
2009. The current most common English translation; includes
helpful introductions and notes (see also Scripture Index listed below).
Many contributions are excellent, but some have been critiqued for poor
textual basis or for inadequacies in the notes and introductions; cf. the
detailed reviews by S. P. Brock in *JJS* 35 (1984) 200–209 and *JJS* 38
(1987) 107–14. [=*OTP*] Kümmel, Werner Georg, et al., gen. eds. *Jüdische
Schriften aus hellenistischrömischer Zeit.* Gütersloh: G. Mohn/Gütersloher
Verlagshaus, 1973– 2005. A highly respected multi-volume German translation
series with fine introductions and commentary. [= JSHRZ]
Lichtenberger, Hermann and Gerbern S. Oegema, gen. eds.
Jüdische Schriften aus hellenistisch-römischer Zeit Neue Folge. Gütersloh:
Gütersloher Verlagshaus, 2005–. Multi-volume continuation of *JSHRZ.*
[=*JSHRZNF*]
Sparks, H. F. D., ed. *The Apocryphal Old Testament.* Oxford: Clarendon, 1984. A
useful one-volume edition with succinct introductions of a subset of
works also found in Charlesworth's *OTP*; for comparison with *OTP* see
review by G. W. E. Nickelsburg in *CBQ* 50 (1988) 288–91 and those by
M. E. Stone and R. A. Kraft in *Religious Studies Review* 14 (1988) 111–17.
[= AOT]
Further important translations appear in Spanish (Alejandro Díez Macho, et
al., eds., *Apocrifos del Antiguo Testamento.* 5 vols. Madrid: Ediciones Cristiandad,
1982–1987) and in Italian (Paulo Sacchi, et al., eds., *Apocrifi
Dell'Antico Testamento.* 5 vols. Turin: Unione Tipografico-Editrice Torinese/
Brescia: Paideia, 1981–1997).
A new two-volume collection of lesser known pseudepigrapha is due out
soon, published by Eerdmans and edited by Richard Bauckham and
James R. Davila under the auspices of the More Old Testament Pseudepigrapha
Project (see http://www.st-andrews.ac.uk/divinity/rt
moreoldtestamentpseudepigrapha).
Also see: Translations of varying qualities available online at http://sacredtexts.
com/chr/apo/index.htm and at http://www.piney.com/ ApocalypticIndex.
html and at http://jewishchristianlit.com/Texts.

Concordances:
Bauer, Johannes B. *Clavis Apocryphorum supplementum: complectens voces versionis Germanicae Libri Henoch Slavici, Libri Jubilaeorum, Odarum Salomonis.* Grazer theologische Studien 4. Graz: Institut für Ökumenische Theologie und Patrologie an der Universität Graz, 1980. Not a concordance to the original languages but to German translations. For his book-by-book concordance of Greek pseudepigrapha, see below under "Lexicon."

Denis, Albert-Marie. *Concordance grecque des Pseudépigraphes d'Ancien Testament:*
Concordance, Corpus des textes, Indices. Louvain-la-Neuve: Institut Orientaliste, 1987. Very useful. Denis produced an earlier concordance of the Greek version of Baruch (Leuven: Peeters, 1970).

Denis, Albert-Marie. *Concordance latine des Pseudépigraphes d'Ancien Testament:*
Concordance, Corpus des textes, Indices. Turnhout: Brepols, 1993. A fine work. Denis released an earlier concordance of the Latin version of Jubilees (Université catholique de Louvain, 1973; repr. Turnhout: Brepols, 2002).

Lechner-Schmidt, Wilfried. *Wortindex der lateinisch erhaltenen Pseudepigraphen zum Alten Testament.* TANZ 3. Tübingen: Francke, 1990. Also contains some texts.

See also: the *Thesaurus Linguae Graecae* database for searchable Greek texts, as well as tagged Greek modules available for Accordance, BibleWorks, and Logos software. *Scripture Index:*

Delamarter, Steve. *A Scripure Index to Charlesworth's The Old Testament Pseudepigrapha.*
London/New York: Sheffield Academic Press, 2002. Indexes all references to OT and NT books in the introductions, notes and margins of *OTP*; necessarily dependent on the work of the original translators (which varies "in terms of quantity and focus" from book to book).

Lexicon:
Wahl, Christian Abraham. *Clavis Librorum Veteris Testamenti Apocryphorum Philologica.*
Leipzig: Johannes Ambrosius Barth, 1853; repr. Graz: Akademische Druck, 1972. Repr. contains Wahl's lexicon of the Greek Apocrypha and Pseudepigrapha, and J. B. Bauer's book-by-book concordance of the Greek Pseudepigrapha.

Introductions:
De Jonge, M., ed. *Outside the Old Testament.* Cambridge: CUP, 1985. Selected Jewish Pseudepigrapha excerpts with commentary.

Denis, Albert-Marie, et al. *Introduction à la littérature religieuse judéo-hellénistique.* 2 vols. Turnhout: Brepols, 2000. Also note his previous *Introduction aux Pseudépigraphes grecs d'Ancien Testament.* SVTP 1. Leiden: Brill, 1970.

Díez Macho, Alejandro. *Apocrifos del Antiguo Testamento.* Vol. 1: Introduccion General a Los Apocrifos del Antiguo Testamento. Madrid: Ediciones Cristiandad, 1984.

Turdeanu, Emile. *Apocryphes slaves et roumains de l'Ancien Testament.* SVTP 5. Leiden: Brill, 1981.
See also: Nickelsburg, *Jewish Literature*; Helyer, *Exploring Jewish Literature*; *JWSTP*; *HJPAJC* Vol. 3; *CHJ* 2:409–503; *EDEJ* 143–62 and s.v. by book. Older introduction by Torrey (see under Apocrypha). Individual introductions are appearing in the "Guides to the Apocrypha and Pseudepigrapha" series from Sheffield Academic Press (some are noted below).

4.2 Special Pseudepigrapha Bibliography (alphabetical by book)

This list contains the best-known books with likely Jewish lineage in collections of "Old Testament Pseudepigrapha." The principal languages of extant MSS for each book are noted below. Dates largely concur with those in Charlesworth *OTP*. If the texts available are clearly Christian (with an assumed Jewish substratum), this is indicated. Not included are some highly fragmented texts and those unlikely to be of Jewish provenance. Pseudo-Philo and other individual writers are found later in this bibliography. Consult also the General Pseudepigrapha Bibliography above (especially Lehnardt's *Bibliographie* and the introductions and translations in *OTP* and *JSHRZ*). More detailed bibliography of texts (including fragments and later versions) in Haelewyck, *Clavis Apocryphorum* and DiTommaso, *Bibliography*.

AHIQAR (Aramaic; 7th–6th cent. BC).
In the Elephantine papyri, with later recensions in many languages; thought to be related to the (Greek) Life of Aesop and so listed in Denis, *Fragmenta pseudepigraphorum* (see above).

Text and Translation:
Porten, Bezalel, and Ada Yardeni. *Textbook of Aramaic Documents from Ancient Egypt.* Vol. 3: Literature, Accounts, Lists. Winona Lake: Eisenbrauns, 1986–1993, 23–53.
Cowley, A. *Aramaic Papyri of the Fifth Century B.C.* Oxford: Clarendon, 1923, 204–48. Widely known edition with translation and extensive notes. Available online at http://archive.org.
Conybeare, F. C., J. Rendel Harris, and Agnes Smith Lewis. *The Story of A□i□ar from the Syriac, Arabic, Armenian, Ethiopic, Greek and Slavonic Versions.* London:
C. J. Clay & Sons, 1898. Extensive introduction with translations of versions listed in the title plus texts of Greek (Life of Aesop), Armenian, Syriac, and Arabic. Available online at http://archive.org.

Commentary:
Lindenberger, James M. *The Aramaic Proverbs of Ahiqar.* JHNES. Baltimore: Johns Hopkins University Press, 1983.

Grammar:
Muraoka, Takamitsu and Bezalel Porten. *A Grammar of Egyptian Aramaic.* 2d rev. ed. Leiden: Brill, 2003.

Concordance:
Porten, Bezalel and Jerome A. Lund. *Aramaic Documents from Egypt: A Key-Word-in-Context Concordance.* Winona Lake: Eisenbrauns, 2002.

APOCALYPSE OF ABRAHAM (Old Slavonic; 1st–2d cent. AD)

Text, Translation, and Commentary:
Rubinkiewicz, Ryszard. *L'Apocalypse d'Abraham en vieux slave: Introduction, texte critique, traduction et commentaire.* Lublin: Société des Lettres et des Sciences de l'Université Catholique de Lublin, 1987. Apparently edited without reference to the Philonenko edition.
Philonenko-Sayar, Belkis and Marc Philonenko. "L'Apocalypse d'Abraham: Introduction, texte slave, traduction et notes." *Sem* 31 (1981) 1–119.
APOCALYPSE OF ADAM (Coptic; 1st–4th cent. AD)
Found among Nag Hammadi gnostic texts, yet considered to be Jewish in origin. Consult Nag Hammadi scholarship for further translations (e.g. J. M. Robinson, ed., *Nag Hammadi Library in English*) and concordances (e.g. Folker Siegert, *Nag-Hammadi-Register*). Another possible Jewish gnostic text is *Poimandres* in the *Corpus Hermeticum* (see further *JWSTP* 443–81).
Text and Translation:
Parrott, Douglas M., ed. *Nag Hammadi Codices V,2–5 and VI with Papyrus Berolinensis 8502, 1 and 4.* NHS 11. Leiden: Brill, 1979, 151–95. Text edited by G. W. MacRae.
Text, Translation, and Commentary:
Morard, Françoise. *L'Apocalypse d'Adam (NH V, 5).* Bibliothèque copte de Nag Hammadi: Section textes 15. Québec: Les Presses de l'Université Laval, 1985.
APOCALYPSE OF ELIJAH (Coptic, Greek; 1st–4th cent. AD)
Christian text with likely Jewish substratum.
Text and Translation:
Pietersma, Albert, Susan Turner Comstock, and Harold W. Attridge. *The Apocalypse of Elijah based on P. Chester Beatty 2018.* SBLTT 19. Chico, CA, Scholars, 1981. Coptic text and translation, includes appendix on Greek fragment. Also in Denis, *Fragmenta pseudepigraphorum* (above). *See also* material in *HJPAJC* 3.2:799–803.
APOCALYPSE OF MOSES (*see* Life of Adam and Eve)
APOCALYPSE OF SEDRACH (*see note below* under 4 Ezra)
APOCALYPSE OF ZEPHANIAH (Coptic and Greek fragments; 1st cent. BC–1st cent. AD) Christian with possible Jewish substratum.
Text and Discussion:
Steindorff, Georg. *Die Apokalypse des Elias, eine unbekannte Apokalypse und Bruchstücke der Sophonias Apokalypse.* TU 17.3. Leipzig: Hinrichs, 1899. Available online at http://archive.org. Also see Denis, *Fragmenta pseudepigraphorum*.
APOCRYPHON OF EZEKIEL (Greek and Hebrew fragments; 1st cent. BC–1st cent. AD)
Probable Jewish work with possible Christian influence in extant fragments.
Text, Translation and Discussion:
Stone, Michael E., Benjamin G. Wright, and David Satran, eds. *The Apocryphal Ezekiel.* SBLEJL 18. Atlanta: Society of Biblical Literature, 2000. Includes the five fragments previously published by Mueller plus other possible contenders. Also studies later Christian traditions about Ezekiel.

Mueller, James R. *The Five Fragments of the Apocryphon of Ezekiel: A Critical Study.* Journal for the Study of the Pseudepigrapha Supplement Series 5. Sheffield: Sheffield Academic Press, 1994. Also see Denis, *Fragmenta pseudepigraphorum.*

(PSEUDO-) ARISTEAS, [LETTER OF] (Greek; 2nd cent. BC, possibly later)

Critical Text, Translation, Notes, and Concordance:
Pelletier, André. *Lettre D'Aristée à Philocrate: Introduction, texte critique, traduction et notes, index complet des mots grecs.* SC 89. Paris: Cerf, 1962. Best current critical text. A text can also be found appended to Swete's *Introduction to the Old Testament in Greek.*

Critical Text:
Wendland, Paul. *Aristeae ad Philocratem Epistula cum Ceteris de Origine Versionis LXX Interpretum Testimoniis.* Leipzig: Teubner, 1900. Available online at http://archive.org.

Text and Notes:
Hadas, Moses. *Aristeas to Philocrates (Letter of Aristeas).* New York: Harper & Brothers, 1951. Includes text, lengthy introduction, and brief notes.

Meecham, Henry G. *The Letter of Aristeas: A Linguistic Study with Special Reference to the Greek Bible.* Manchester: Manchester University Press, 1935. Notes focus on use of Greek language.

Online see http://www.voskrese.info/spl/miller-arist.pdf (Greek text and translation) and http://www.ccel.org/c/charles/otpseudepig/aristeas.htm (Charles, ed., translation).

Introduction:
See Jellicoe, *Septuagint and Modern Study* 29–58 (under Septuagint); Bartlett, *Jews in the Hellenistic World* 11–34 (under Josephus).

ASCENSION OF ISAIAH
(Ethiopic, Latin, Greek fragments, etc.; 2d cent. BC–4th cent. AD)
Christian with a probable Jewish section known as "Martyrdom of Isaiah" in 1:1–3:12 [omit 1:2b–6a] and 5:1b–14.

Texts:
Bettiolo, Paolo, et al. *Ascensio Isaiae: Textus.* CChr.SA 7. Turnhout: Brepols, 1995. Contains Ethiopic, Greek, Coptic, Latin, and Slavonic texts (with Italian translation). Earlier edition of Ethiopic and Latin texts by Dillmann (*Ascencio Isaiae: Aethiopice et Latine*, Leipzig: Brockhaus, 1877) available free at http://books.google.com. Greek text also in Denis, *Fragmenta pseudepigraphorum.*

Translation and Commentary:
Charles, R. H. *The Ascension of Isaiah.* London: Adam & Charles Black, 1900. Also includes Ethiopic, Latin, and Slavonic (transcribed) texts in parallel columns. Available online at http://archive.org.

Tisserant, Eugène. *Ascension d'Isaie.* Paris: Letouzey et Ané, 1909. Available online at http://archive.org.

Introduction:
Knight, Jonathan. *The Ascension of Isaiah.* Sheffield: Sheffield Academic Press, 1995.

Commentary:
Norelli, Enrico. *Ascensio Isaiae: Commentarius.* CChr.SA 8. Turnhout: Brepols,

1995. In Italian. Assumption (Testament) of Moses (Latin; 1st cent. AD)
Text, Translation, and Commentary:
Tromp, Johannes. *The Assumption of Moses: A Critical Edition with Commentary.* SVTP 10. Leiden: Brill, 1993. Supplants R. H. Charles, *Assumption of Moses.* London: Black, 1897. Abraham Schalit also began a commentary on chapter one before his death which was later published as *Untersuchungen zur Assumptio Moses* (Leiden: Brill, 1989). 2 BARUCH (=Syriac Apocalypse of Baruch; also Greek fragments and Arabic version; 2nd cent. AD)
Text:
Gurtner, Daniel M. *Second Baruch: A Critical Edition of the Syriac Text With Greek and Latin Fragments, English Translation, Introduction, and Concordances.* Jewish and Christian Texts in Contexts and Related Studies 5. London: T & T Clark, 2009.
Leemhuis, F., A. F. J. Klijn, and G. J. H. Van Gelder. *The Arabic Text of the Apocalypse of Baruch: Edited and Translated with a Parallel Translation of the Syriac Text.* Leiden: Brill, 1986.
Dedering, S., ed. *Apocalypse of Baruch.* Vetus Testamentum Syriace IV, 3. Leiden: Brill, 1973. For the final *Epistle* the Leiden edition remains forthcoming, use M. Kmoskó, *Epistola Baruch filii Neriae*, in R. Graffin, *Patrologia Syriaca* 1,2 (Paris: Firmin-Didot, 1907) col. 1208–1237. For Greek fragments see Denis, *Fragmenta pseudepigraphorum* in general bibliography.
Translation and Commentary:
Bogaert, Pierre. *Apocalypse de Baruch: Introduction, traduction du syriaque et commentaire.* 2 vols. SC 144–45. Paris: Cerf, 1969.
Also see: Berger, Klaus, Gabriele Fassbeck, and Heiner Reinhard. *Synopse des Vierten Buches Esra und der Syrischen Baruch-Apokalypse.* TANZ 8. Tübingen: Francke, 1992. Based on German translation.
3 BARUCH (= Greek Apocalypse of Baruch; Slavonic version in two recensions; 1st–3rd cent. AD) Christian with Jewish substratum.
Text:
Picard, J.-C. *Apocalypsis Baruchi Graece.* PVTG 2. Leiden: Brill, 1967.
Commentary:
Kulik, Alexander. *3 Baruch: Greek-Slavonic Apocalypse of Baruch.* CEJL. Berlin: de Gruyter, 2010. 4 BARUCH (*see* Paraleipomena Jeremiou)
1 ENOCH (Ethiopic Enoch; also in Greek, Aramaic fragments, and other versional fragments; 2d cent. BC–1st cent. AD)
Texts (and Translations):
Knibb, Michael A., in consultation with Edward Ullendorff. *The Ethiopic Book of Enoch: A New Edition in the Light of the Aramaic Dead Sea Fragments.* 2 vols. Oxford: Clarendon, 1978. Vol. 1: Text and Apparatus; Vol. 2: Introduction, Translation, and Commentary. Supplants previous editions by R. H. Charles (1906) and A. Dillmann (1851).
Milik, J. T. and Matthew Black. *The Books of Enoch: Aramaic Fragments of Qumrân Cave 4.* Oxford: Clarendon, 1976. Texts, translations, plates, and extensive comments.
Black, M. *Apocalypsis Henochi Graece.* PVTG 3. Leiden: Brill, 1970. Edition of Greek text; bound with Denis, *Fragmenta pseudepigraphorum*. For addenda and corrigenda see Black and Vanderkam, *The Book of Enoch or 1 Enoch* (below).

Commentaries:
Black, Matthew, in consultation with James C. Vanderkam. *The Book of Enoch or 1 Enoch: A New English Edition with Commentary and Textual Notes.* SVTP 7. Leiden: Brill, 1985. Extensive commentary, consciously revising Charles's 1912 commentary. With Otto Neugebauer on chaps. 72–82.

Charles, R. H. *The Book of Enoch or 1 Enoch.* Oxford: Clarendon, 1912. Translation with extensive commentary. The author prefers this (what amounts to a 2d edition) over his earlier *The Book of Enoch* (1893). Available online at http://archive.org.

Nickelsburg, George W. E. *1 Enoch 1: A Commentary on the Book of 1 Enoch, Chapters 1–36; 81–108.* Hermeneia; Minneapolis: Fortress, 2001.

Nickelsburg, George W. E. and James C. Vanderkam. *1 Enoch 2: A Commentary on the Book of 1 Enoch, Chapters 37–82.* Hermeneia. Minneapolis: Fortress, 2012. Nickelsburg and Vanderkam have also produced *1 Enoch: A New Translation.* Philadelphia: Fortress, 2004.

Stuckenbruck, Loren T. *1 Enoch 91–108.* CEJL. Berlin: de Gruyter, 2007.

Tiller, Patrick A. *A Commentary on the Animal Apocalypse of I Enoch.* SBL Early Judaism and Its Literature 4. Atlanta: Scholars, 1993.

Earlier important commentaries by A. Dillmann (Vogel, 1853) and François Martin (Letouzey, 1906). Short commentary article by Daniel C. Olson in J. D. G. Dunn, gen. ed., *Eerdmans Commentary to the Bible.* Grand Rapids: Eerdmans, 2003.

2 ENOCH (Slavonic Enoch, in two recensions; 1st cent. AD)

Text and Translation:
Vaillant, A. *Le Livre des secrets d'Hénoch.* Paris: Institut d'Etudes Slaves, 1952.

Translation and Commentary:
Morfill, W. R. and R. H. Charles. *The Book of the Secrets of Enoch.* Oxford: Clarendon, 1896.

Concordance to German Translation:
See above Bauer, *Clavis Apocryphorum Supplementum.*

3 ENOCH (Hebrew Enoch; 5th – 6th cent. AD): *See below* under Hekhalot literature.

4 EZRA (*see above* under Apocrypha)

Several Christian pseudepigraphic works also draw on Ezra as a central figure and may be indebted to Jewish sources (e.g. Greek Apocalypse of Ezra, Vision of Ezra, and Apocalypse of Sedrach); *see* Charlesworth *OTP* 1:561–613; text of some in Otto Wahl, ed. *Apocalypsis Esdrae—Apocalypsis Sedrach—Visio beati Esdrae.* PVTG 4. Leiden: Brill, 1977.

HISTORY OF JOSEPH (*see* Charlesworth, ed., *OTP* 2:467–75)

HISTORY OF THE RECHABITES (Greek, Syriac, and many versions; 1st–4th cent. AD) Substantially Christian, possible Jewish substratum.

Text and Translation:
Charlesworth, James H. *The History of the Rechabites. Volume I: The Greek Recension.* SBLTT 17. Chico, CA: Scholars, 1982. Critical Greek text; an edition of the Syriac text is still desired. Brief commentary by Chris H. Knights in *JSJ* 28 (1997) 413–36. JANNES AND JAMBRES (Greek and Latin fragments)

Text, Translation, and Commentary:
Pietersma, Albert. *The Apocryphon of Jannes and Jambres the Magicians.* Religions in the Graeco-Roman World 119. Leiden: Brill, 1994. Includes facsimile plates. JOSEPH AND ASENETH (Greek and Latin versions in two recensions, also Armenian, and other versions; 1st cent. BC–2d cent. AD)

Text and Translation:
Burchard, Christoph. *A Minor Edition of the Armenian Version of Joseph and Aseneth.* Hebrew University Armenian Studies 10. Leuven: Peeters, 2010. Diplomatic text supplemented with 12 other important manuscripts.
Fink, Uta Barbara. *Joseph und Aseneth: Revision des griechischen Textes und Edition der zweiten lateinischen Übersetzung.* Fontes et subsidia ad Bibliam pertinentes 5. Berlin/New York: de Gruyter, 2008. Important revision of Burchard's provisional Greek text of the long recension (though without a full textual apparatus), with a synoptic edition of Latin "L2" manuscripts. Includes study of manuscript stemma. See review in *BBR* 20 (2010) 110–12. Burchard, Christoph with Carsten Burfeind and Uta Barbara Fink. *Joseph und Aseneth: Kritisch Herausgegeben.* PVTG 5. Leiden/Boston: Brill, 2003. Critical edition focusing on the longer Greek recension (which Burchard believes is earlier than the short recension). While the apparatus is excellent, the text itself remains the same as Burchard's "provisional" Greek text. Burchard himself translated this longer recension into English in Charlesworth, *OTP*. Philonenko, Marc. *Joseph et Aséneth: Introduction, texte critique, traduction et notes.* SPB 13. Leiden: Brill, 1968. Standard edition of the shorter Greek reJEWISH cension plus word index. ET of this shorter recension in H. F. D. Sparks, *Apocryphal Old Testament.*

Introduction:
Humphrey, Edith M. *Joseph and Aseneth.* Guides to the Apocrypha and Pseudepigrapha 8. Sheffield: Sheffield Academic Press, 2000.

Other:
Burchard, Christoph. *Gesammelte Studien zu Joseph und Aseneth.* SVTP 13. Leiden: Brill, 1996. Collection of significant articles on the text, importance, and state of study (including bibliography). Includes a reprint of Burchard's Vorläufiger Text ("provisional text") of the long recension (pp. 161–209).
Reinmuth, Eckart, ed. *Joseph und Aseneth: Eingeleitet, ediert, übersetzt und mit interpretierenden Essays.* Scripta Antiquitatis Posterioris ad Ethicam Religionemque pertinentia 15. Tübingen: Mohr-Siebeck, 2009).
Note also "The Aseneth Home Page" at http://markgoodacre.org/aseneth/index.htm.

JUBILEES (Hebrew fragments; Ethiopic Versions; Latin, Greek, and Syriac fragments; 2d cent. BC)

Hebrew Texts:
For extensive Qumran cave 4 fragments (4Q216–228) see DJD 13; other fragments in DJD 1, 3, and 7. Also cf. *RevQ* 12.4 [= 48] (1987) 529–36; *RevQ* 14.1 [= 53] (1989) 129–30. For possible Masada fragments see *Er-Isr* 20 (1989) 278–86.

Texts:
Vanderkam, James C., ed. *The Book of Jubilees: A Critical Text.* CSCO 510. Leuven: Peeters, 1989. A critical text of the Ethiopic, supplanting the older edition by R. H. Charles (Oxford, 1895); also with Greek, Syriac, Latin, and some Hebrew fragments (though not the bulk of 4Q216–228). Not all Greek and Syriac fragments are included (cf. Denis, *Fragmenta pseudepigraphorum* above).

Translation and Textual Notes:
Vanderkam, James C. *The Book of Jubilees.* CSCO 511. Leuven: Peeters, 1989. Translates his critical text (including the fragments), with extensive notes on text and translation.

Translation and Commentary:
Charles, R. H. *The Book of Jubilees or The Little Genesis.* London: Adam & Charles Black, 1902. Available online at http://archive.org.

Concordance to German Translation:
See above Bauer, *Clavis Apocryphorum Supplementum.*

Introduction:
Vanderkam, James C. *The Book of Jubilees.* Guides to Apocrypha and Pseudepigrapha. Sheffield: Sheffield Academic Press, 2001.

LADDER OF JACOB (Slavonic)

Only known from Slavonic Christian excerpts, H. G. Lunt (in *OTP* 2:401–411) suggests a possible 1st-cent. date and potential Jewish Greek substratum. Cf. *HJPAJC* 3.2:805.

LIFE OF ADAM AND EVE

The subject of Adam and Eve appears in different manuscript traditions: Greek (= Apocalypse of Moses; also Armenian and other versions; 1st cent. AD), Latin, two Slavonic recensions, the Armenian "Penitence of Adam," and other recensions.

Textual Synopsis:
Anderson, Gary A., and Michael E. Stone, eds. *A Synopsis of the Books of Adam and Eve.* 2d rev. ed. SBL Early Judaism and Its Literature 5. Atlanta: Scholars, 1999. Armenian, Georgian, Greek, Latin, and Slavonic texts. Also see their website with translations (http://jefferson.village.virginia.edu/anderson, which links to http://www2.iath.virginia.edu/anderson).

Text:
Tromp, Johannes. *The Life of Adam and Eve in Greek: A Critical Edition.* PVTG 6. Leiden: Brill, 2005.

Stone, Michael E. *Texts and Concordances of the Armenian Adam Literature.* Volume 1. SBLEJL 12. Atlanta: Scholars Press, 1996. Volume 1 includes the Penitence of Adam, the Book of Adam, and Genesis 1–4 in Armenian (with concordances to each and a non-critical text of each). Volume 2 has been published as *A Concordance of the Armenian Apocryphal Adam Books* (Leuven: Peeters, 2001). For a critical edition of the Armenian texts see above works by Stone and by Lipscomb under General Pseudepigrapha Bibliography; also M. E. Stone, *The Penitence of Adam.* 2 vols.

CSCO 429–430. Leuven: Peeters, 1981.
Text, Translation, and Commentary:
Dochhorn, Jan. *Die Apokalypse des Mose: Text, Übersetzung, Kommentar.* TSAJ 106. Tübingen: Mohr-Siebeck, 2005.
Bertrand, Daniel A. *La vie grecque d'Adam et Eve: Introduction, texte, traduction et commentaire.* Recherches intertestamentaires 1. Paris: Maisonneuve, 1987.
Introductions:
De Jonge, Marinus and Johannes Tromp. *The Life of Adam and Eve and Related Literature.* Guides to the Apocrypha and Pseudepigrapha 4. Sheffield: Sheffield Academic Press, 1997.
Stone, Michael E. *A History of the Literature of Adam and Eve.* SBL Early Judaism and Its Literature 3. Atlanta: Scholars, 1992.
LIVES OF THE PROPHETS (Greek, Latin, Syriac, Armenian, Ethiopic, and other versions; 1st cent. AD). Christian with Jewish substratum.
Text, Translation, and Commentary:
Schwemer, Anna Maria. *Studien zu den frühjüdischen Prophetenlegenden* Vitae Prophetarum*: Einleitung, Übersetzung und Kommentar.* 2 vols. TSAJ 49–50; Tübingen: Mohr-Siebeck, 1995–1996. Based on the Greek text, which is edited in a synoptic edition at the end of Vol. 2 (this edition has also been published separately as *Synopse zu den Vitae Prophetarum*). Previous edition by C. C. Torrey (SBLMS 1; Philadelphia: Scholars Press, 1946). For other versions see listing in Schwemer's Vol. 1, pp. 18–22 (cf. Haelewyck, *Clavis Apocryphorum* 167–73).
3–4 Maccabees (Greek, Syriac, and other versions)
3 Maccabees (1st cent. BC) is edited in the Göttingen LXX, and 4 Maccabees (1st cent. AD) is found in Rahlfs's LXX; both appear in the LXX concordances; translations in *OTP* 2:509–64. See also LXX bibliography above.
Introduction:
DeSilva, David A. *4 Maccabees.* Guides to the Apocrypha and Pseudepigrapha 7. Sheffield: Sheffield Academic Press, 1998.
Commentaries:
Commentaries can be found in the Jewish Apocryphal Literature series (Dropsie/Harper) by Hadas, and in the Septuagint Commentary Series (Brill) on 3 Maccabees (by N. Clayton Croy) and 4 Maccabees (by David A. deSilva).
MARTYRDOM OF ISAIAH (*see* Ascension of Isaiah)
(PSEUDO-) MENANDER (Syriac; 3d cent. AD)
Traditionally included with Jewish corpus, though actual provenance is unsure. See discussion and translation in *OTP* 2:583–606; also *HJPAJC* 3.1:692–94.
ODES (*see* Septuagint)
ODES OF SOLOMON (Syriac, also portions in Greek and Coptic; 1st–2d cent. AD) Christian, though some propose a Jewish origin.
Texts, Translations, Concordance, and Bibliography:
Lattke, Michael. *Die Oden Salomos in ihrer Bedeutung für Neues Testament und Gnosis.* 4 vols. OBO 25. Fribourg Suisse: Editions Universitaires/Göttingen: Vandenhoeck & Ruprecht, 1979–1986. Band I contains texts (with a separate part Ia printing a Syriac facsimile with plates). Band II includes a concordance of each language. Band III is an extensive annotated bibliography

of studies on Odes (from 1799 to 1984). Band IV is a collection of articles by Lattke (note he extends his bibliography list to 1997 on pp. 233–51).

Text and Translation:

Charlesworth, James Hamilton. *The Odes of Solomon: The Syriac Texts.* SBLTT 13. Missoula, MT: Scholars Press, 1977. Corrected repr. of 1973 OUP edition. See also facsimile edition *Papyri and Leather Manuscripts of the Odes of Solomon* (Duke University, 1981). Charlesworth also released a translation under the title *The Earliest Christian Hymnbook* (Eugene, OR: Cascade, 2009).

Also see the Rendell Harris items listed under the Psalms of Solomon. An older text with German translation by Walter Bauer. *Die Oden Salomos.* Berlin: de Gruyter, 1933.

Translation and Commentary:

Lattke, Michael. *Odes of Solomon.* Trans. Marianne Ehrhardt. Hermeneia. Minneapolis: Fortress, 2009. Translates his 3 volume German commentary originally in NTOA 41. Göttingen: Vandenhoeck & Ruprecht, 1999–2005. Lattke produced a German translation with shorter notes for Fontes Christiani. FC 19. Freiburg: Herder, 1995.

Pierre, Marie-Joseph, with the collaboration of Jean-Marie Martin. *Les Odes de Salomon.* Apocryphes 4. Turnhout: Brepols, 1994.

Concordance to German Translation:

See above Bauer, *Clavis Apocryphorum Supplementum.*

PARALEIPOMENA JEREMIOU (also called 4 Baruch; Greek in two recensions, Ethiopic and other versions; 1st–3d cent. AD)

Text, Translation and Commentary:

Herzer, Jens. *4 Baruch (Paraleipomena Jeremiou).* SBLWAW 22. Atlanta: Society of Biblical Literature, 2005. Fine critical text.

Riaud, Jean. *Les Paralipomènes du Prophète Jérémie: Présentation, texte original, traduction et commentaries.* Université Catholique de l'Ouest, 1994.

Text and Translation:

Kraft, Robert A. and Ann-Elizabeth Purintun. *Paraleipomena Jeremiou.* SBLTT 1. Missoula, MT: Society of Biblical Literature, 1972.

PRAYER OF JACOB and PRAYER OF JOSEPH (*see* Charlesworth, ed., *OTP* 2:699–723; cf. *HJPAJC* 3.2:798–99)

PRAYER OF MANASSEH (*see* Septuagint; also in Charlesworth, ed., *OTP* 2:625–37)

PSALMS OF SOLOMON (Greek and Syriac; 1st cent. BC)

Greek Text:

Wright, Robert B. *The Psalms of Solomon: A Critical Edition of the Greek Text.* Jewish and Christian Texts in Contexts and Related Studies 1. London: T & T Clark, 2007. Wright also offers a CD-ROM with color images of extant Greek and Syriac manuscripts (see p. 224).

Gebhardt, Oscar von. *Die Psalmen Salomos.* TU 13/2. Leipzig: Hinrichs, 1895. Earlier critical text of Greek that only collates 8 of the 12 available MSS. Available online at http://archive.org. A handy Greek text can be found in Rahlfs's LXX edition (based on Gebhardt).

Syriac Critical Text:
See above "Syriac Peshita Text" (Vol. IV, 6).
Greek and Syriac texts:
Trafton, Joseph L. *The Syriac Version of the Psalms of Solomon: A Critical Evaluation.*
SBLSCS 11. Atlanta: Scholars, 1985. Comes with a separate fascicle of facing Greek and Syriac texts (with apparatus). See review in *JSS* 32 (1987) 204–207.
Translation:
Also translated in the NETS LXX translation (see above under Septuagint and http://ccat.sas.upenn.edu/nets/edition/31-pssal-nets.pdf).
Commentaries:
Atkinson, Kenneth. *An Intertextual Study of the Psalms of Solomon.* Studies in the Bible and Early Christianity 49. Lewiston, NY: Edwin Mellen, 2001. Includes Greek text, translation, parallel passages in other Jewish literature (esp. OT and Apocrypha), and commentary.
Rendell Harris, J. and A. Mingana. *The Odes and Psalms of Solomon Re-edited.* 2 vols. Manchester: John Rylands University Library, 1916–1920. Also note Rendell Harris's earlier *The Odes and Psalms of Solomon: Now First Published from the Syriac Version.* Cambridge: CUP, 1909. Both are available online at http://archive.org.
Ryle, Herbert Edward, and Montague Rhodes James. *Psalms of the Pharisees Commonly Called The Psalms of Solomon.* Cambridge: CUP, 1891. Classic edition with text, translation, introduction, and extensive notes. The Pharisaic identification is not accepted by all. Available at http://archive.org.
Viteau, J. *Les Psaumes de Salomon: Introduction, texte grec et traduction.* Paris: Letouzey et Ané, 1911. With extensive notes. Available online at http://archive.org.
SENTENCES OF (PSEUDO-) PHOCYLIDES (Greek; 1st cent. BC–1st cent. AD) Wisdom poetry of Jewish origin, but with muted OT references and written under a pagan Greek pseudonym.
Text:
Young, D. *Theognis, Ps-Pythagoras, Ps-Phocylides, Chares, Anonymi Aulodia, fragmentum teleiambicum.* 2 vols.; Leipzig, 1961, 1971. Volume 2 includes the critical text of Ps.-Phocylides.
Text, Translation, and Commentary:
Horst, P. W. van der. *The Sentences of Pseudo-Phocylides: With Introduction and Commentary.* SVTP 4. Leiden: Brill, 1978. Also includes a concordance.
Wilson, Walter T. *The Sentences of Pseudo-Phocylides.* CEJL. Berlin: de Gruyter, 2005. SIBYLLINE ORACLES (Greek with Latin fragments; 2d cent. BC–7th cent. AD) Large portions of Books 3 and 5 are considered Jewish; book 4 may have been ultimately redacted by a Jewish editor, and books 11–14 may have a later Jewish origin (this is disputed).
Greek Text:
Geffcken, Johannes. *Die Oracula Sibyllina.* GCS. Leipzig: Hinrichs, 1902. Available online at http://archive.org.

Introductions and Studies on Jewish Sections:
Buitenwerf, Rieuwerd. *Book III of the Sibylline Oracles and its Social Setting: with an Introduction, Translation, and Commentary.* SVTP 17. Leiden: Brill, 2003.
Collins, John J. *The Sibylline Oracles of Egyptian Judaism.* SBLDS 13. Missoula, MT: Society of Biblical Literature, 1974.
Nikiprowetzky, Valentin. *La troisième Sibylle.* Ecole pratique des hautes Etudes Sorbonne; Etudes juives 9; Paris: Mouton, 1970. Includes text, translation, notes, and extensive introduction.
Parke, H. W. *Sibyls and Sibylline Prophecy in Classical Antiquity.* Ed. B. C. McGing. London/New York: Routledge, 1988.
See also: Bartlett, *Jews in the Hellenistic World* 35–55 (under Josephus); older translation of Books 3–5 by H. N. Bate (SPCK, 1918).

TESTAMENT OF ABRAHAM (Greek, also Coptic and other versions; 1st–2nd cent. AD) Exists in both a long and short recension, with likely common ancestry.
Critical Text:
Roddy, Nicolae. *The Romanian Version of the Testament of Abraham: Text, Translation, and Cultural Context.* SBLEJL 19. Atlanta: SBL, 2001.
Schmidt, Francis. *Le Testament grec d'Abraham: Introduction, édition critique des deux recensions grecques, traduction.* TSAJ 11. Tübingen: Mohr-Siebeck, 1986.
Text and Translation:
Stone, Michael E. *The Testament of Abraham: The Greek Recensions.* SBLTT 2. Missoula, MT: Society of Biblical Literature, 1972. Based on M. R. James's (1892) edition of Greek texts. An older translation by G. H. Box (London: SPCK, 1927) exists of both recensions along with Gaselee's translation of the Testaments of Isaac and Jacob.
Commentary:
Allison, Dale C. Jr. *Testament of Abraham.* CEJL. Berlin: de Gruyter, 2003.
Delcor, Mathias. *Le Testament d' Abraham: Introduction, Traduction du texte grec, et Commentaire de la recension grecque longue.* SVTP 2. Leiden: Brill, 1973.
Bibliography:
Nickelsburg, George W. E. Jr. "Review of the Literature." In *Studies on the Testament of Abraham*, ed. George W. E. Nickelsburg Jr. SBLSCS 6. Missoula, MT: Scholars Press, 1976, 9–22. The same volume also contains translations of the Church Slavonic and Coptic versions.

TESTAMENT OF ADAM (Several recensions in Syriac, Greek, Armenian, and other versions; 2d–5th cent. AD). Christian, with possible Jewish substratum.
Texts and Translations:
Robinson, Stephen Edward. *The Testament of Adam: An Examination of the Syriac and Greek Traditions.* SBLDS 52. Chico, CA: Scholars, 1982. For Armenian editions, see Stone volumes in General bibliography of Pseudepigrapha.
See further Haelewyck, *Clavis Apocryphorum* 8–12.

TESTAMENT OF ISAAC and TESTAMENT OF JACOB (both Coptic, Arabic, Ethiopic; 2d–3d cent. AD). Christian, with some possible Jewish elements; see both Delcor and Box under *Testament of Abraham*, and note *OTP* 1:903–18; *JTS* n.s. 8 (1957) 225–39.

TESTAMENT OF JOB (Greek, also Coptic and Slavonic; 1st cent. BC–1st cent. AD)

Bibliography:

Spittler, Russell P. "The Testament of Job: a history of research and interpretation." In *Studies on the Testament of Job*, ed. Michael A. Knibb and Pieter W. Van Der Horst. SNTSMS 66. Cambridge: CUP, 1989, 7–32. The same volume also has an edition of the Coptic text.

Text:

Brock, S. P., ed. *Testamentum Iobi*. PVTG 2. Leiden: Brill, 1967.

Text and Translation:

Kraft, Robert A., et al., eds. *The Testament of Job: According to the SV Text*. SBLTT 5. Missoula, MT: SBL, 1974.

TESTAMENT OF MOSES (*see* Assumption of Moses)

TESTAMENT OF SOLOMON (Greek; 1st–3d cent. AD) Christian, with possible Jewish substratum.

Text:

McCown, Chester Charlton. *The Testament of Solomon*. Leipzig: Hinrichs, 1922. Available online at http://archive.org. For translation and introduction see *OTP* 1:935–87.

Commentary:

Busch, Peter. *Das Testament Salomos: Die älteste christliche Dämonologie, kommentiert und in deutscher Erstübersetzung*. TU 153. Berlin/New York: de Gruyter, 2006.

TESTAMENTS OF THE TWELVE PATRIARCHS (Aramaic and Hebrew fragments; two Greek recensions; Syriac, Armenian, and other versions; 2d cent. BC with later interpolations [disputed]). Christian, with Jewish substratum. Cf. with 1Q21 (in DJD 1), 3Q7 (in DJD 3), 4Q213–215 (in DJD 22); 4Q484, and 4Q537–541.

Bibliography:

Slingerland, H. Dixon. *The Testaments of the Twelve Patriarchs: A Critical History of Research*. SBLMS 21. Missoula, MT: Scholars Press, 1977.

Text:

Stone, Michael E. *An Editio Minor of the Armenian Version of the Testaments of the Twelve Patriarchs*. Hebrew University Armenian Studies 11. Leuven: Peeters, 2012.

Text (based on 11 selected extant MSS), translation and commentary.

De Jonge, M., et al. *The Testaments of the Twelve Patriarchs: A Critical Edition of the Greek Text*. PVTG I,2. Leiden: Brill, 1978. Updates Charles's 1908 edition and De Jonge's own shorter Brill edition of a single Cambridge UL manuscript from 1964 (entitled *Testamenta XII Patriarcharum*). Includes word index and partial listing of Armenian variants (note bibliography on p. 193).

Stone, Michael E. *The Armenian Version of the Testament of Joseph: Introduction, Critical Edition, and Translation.* SBLTT 6. Missoula, MT: Scholars Press, 1975.

Stone, Michael E. *The Testament of Levi: A First Study of the Armenian MSS of the Testaments of the XII Patriarchs in the Convent of St. James, Jerusalem: with Text, Critical Apparatus, Notes and Translation.* Jerusalem: St. James, 1969.

Charles, Robert Henry. *The Greek Versions of the Testaments of the Twelve Patriarchs: Edited from nine MSS together with the Variants of the Armenian and Slavonic versions and some Hebrew Fragments.* Oxford: Clarendon, 1908; repr. Darmstadt: Wissenschaftliche Buchgesellschaft, 1966. Available online at http://archive.org. Versional materials are unfortunately only in retroverted Greek. Aramaic fragments from Cairo Genizah.

Commentary:

Charles, R. H. *The Testaments of the Twelve Patriarchs: Translated from the Editor's Greek Text and Edited, with Introduction, Notes, and Indices.* London: Adam & Charles Black, 1908. Available online at http://archive.org.

Hollander, H. W., and M. de Jonge. *The Testaments of the Twelve Patriarchs: A Commentary.* SVTP 8. Leiden: Brill, 1985.

Introduction:

Kugler, Robert A. *The Testaments of the Twelve Patriarchs.* Guides to Apocrypha and Pseudepigrapha. Sheffield: Sheffield Academic Press, 2001.

TREATISE OF SHEM (Syriac; 1st cent. BC [disputed])

Text and Translation:

Charlesworth, James H. "Die 'Schrift des Sem': Einführung, Text und Übersetzung," in *ANRW* II.20.2. Berlin: de Gruyter, 1987, 951–87.

END

www.ingramcontent.com/pod-product-compliance
Lightning Source LLC
Chambersburg PA
CBHW060939230426
43665CB00015B/1996